LIBERALISM VERSUS CONSERVATISM

The Continuing Debate in American Government

VAN NOSTRAND POLITICAL SCIENCE SERIES

Editor

FRANKLIN L. BURDETTE
University of Maryland

WILLIAM G. ANDREWS—*European Political Institutions,* 2nd Ed.

WILLIAM G. ANDREWS—*Soviet Political Institutions*

BENJAMIN BAKER—*Urban Government*

HARWOOD L. CHILDS—*Public Opinion*

R. G. DIXON, JR., and ELMER PLISCHKE—*American Government: Basic Documents and Materials*

WILLIAM GOODMAN—*The Two-Party System in the United States,* 3rd Ed.

GUY B. HATHORN, HOWARD R. PENNIMAN, and MARK F. FERBER—*Government and Politics in the United States,* 2nd Ed.

SAMUEL HENDEL—*The Soviet Crucible: The Soviet System in Theory and Practice,* 2nd Ed.

DARNELL JACOBS and HAROLD ZINK—*Modern Governments,* 3rd Ed.

WILLMOORE KENDALL and GEORGE W. CAREY—*Liberalism versus Conservatism: The Continuing Debate in American Government*

P. M. A. LINEBARGER, C. DJANG, and A. W. BURKS—*Far Eastern Governments and Politics: China and Japan,* 2nd Ed.

RUSSELL W. MADDOX, JR.—*Issues in State and Local Government: Selected Readings*

RUSSELL W. MADDOX, JR., and ROBERT F. FUQUAY—*State and Local Government,* 2nd Ed.

MARTIN C. NEEDLER—*Political Systems of Latin America*

ELMER PLISCHKE—*Conduct of American Diplomacy,* 2nd Ed.

ELMER PLISCHKE—*International Relations: Basic Documents,* 2nd Ed.

H. B. SHARABI—*Governments and Politics of the Middle East in the Twentieth Century*

HAROLD and MARGARET SPROUT—*Foundations of International Politics*

WILLIS G. SWARTZ—*American Governmental Problems,* 2nd Ed.

LIBERALISM VERSUS CONSERVATISM

The Continuing Debate in American Government

Edited by

WILLMOORE KENDALL

University of Dallas

and

GEORGE W. CAREY

Georgetown University

D. VAN NOSTRAND COMPANY, INC.

Princeton, New Jersey

Toronto   New York   London

D. VAN NOSTRAND COMPANY, INC.
120 Alexander St., Princeton, New Jersey (*Principal office*)
24 West 40 Street, New York 18, New York

D. VAN NOSTRAND COMPANY, LTD.
358, Kensington High Street, London, W.14, England

D. VAN NOSTRAND COMPANY (Canada), LTD.
25 Hollinger Road, Toronto 16, Canada

Published simultaneously in Canada by
D. VAN NOSTRAND COMPANY (Canada), LTD.

PRINTED IN THE UNITED STATES OF AMERICA

Dedicated to the memory of
that most precocious of infants
"Publius" (b. 1787, d. 1789)
from whom we learned to love and value
the discussion process in America.

Preface

THIS volume of readings is intended not to replace but to supplement the textbooks normally used in introductory courses in American government. It "takes up" at a point where the textbooks "leave off." Well before reaching this point, our basic political institutions have been described and analyzed, and the student has become familiarized with what the American political system *is* and how it works. Beyond this point lies the realm of controversy. Here, for various reasons, the rules are quite different. Objectivity, in the strict sense of the term, goes by the board, and the political scientist feels (at last!) to speak of what our political system *ought* to be and how it *ought* to work.

Prior to the point in question, the political scientist is expected to hold himself aloof from what we fashionably call his "values," his own beliefs, loyalties, and commitments. He is expected to handle his materials in such a fashion that nobody can accuse him of tendentiousness, of card-stacking, of in any way attempting to "influence" the student to his value judgments. But beyond this point, once in the realm of controversy, the political scientist can shed the mantle of impartiality and take sides, get himself an axe to grind. He can remind himself that besides being a scientist concerned with documentable truths he is also a citizen concerned with the destiny of the Republic, and seek to win the student over to his point of view.

The readings in this book, then, address themselves to areas of controversy in contemporary American political discussion.

It is not the intention of this book to win over any student to any side in "the continuing debate in American government," the controversy between Liberalism and Conservatism. Rather we seek to let political scientists on each of the opposing sides present their views, grind their axes, attempt their own influencing, and give the student the advantage of assaying the merits of their arguments. (Right here it would seem appropriate to provide a definition of the terms "Liberalism" and "Conservatism." The rub is, as we point out in our Introduction to Chapter II, there is *no* precise definition of the terms. For the sake of convenience, however, we suggest that the student seize upon the *one* yardstick we suggest there, i.e. the yardstick of *equality*. All Liberal thinking—we repeat ALL—is directed in one degree or another in the last analysis toward the goal of universal equality, or what in an earlier age was called "leveling." Conversely ALL Conservative arguments are in some way opposed to the leveling process.)

The selection of readings was governed by the following limitation and principles: They are primarily concerned with the questions of how we Americans should govern ourselves and what we should do about the political institutions and practices that, today and every day, we "inherit" from the past. Should we try to hand them to the future pretty much unchanged, or should we deliberately try to "reform" them in one respect or another before tomorrow dawns? We have excluded all "policy" issues, that is, issues we still have to face no matter how we decide to govern ourselves, problems such as what to do about the Soviet Union, medical care for the aged, the tax system, government aid to education. This is not to suggest that questions of policy do not fall within the Liberal-Conservative controversy, or that they are not political, but they take a different twist and precipitate a different kind of controversy. We have, as far as possible, therefore, sought to keep such questions out of our book.

The distinction we have just drawn, however, is not always sharp and neat. Take for example the question, always present in any democracy, "Who shall be entitled to vote in the elections?". At first glance this appears to be a policy question. But on second glance we see that any change we may make in our suffrage arrangements may alter the political system under which we live, and therefore this query takes on the nature of a "How-shall-we-govern-ourselves" question. It would be incorrect to call it a border-line question. Rather, it is two questions at the same time, each needing to be discussed in its own context. In America, then, issues concerning the political system do not always come to us in the pure form we might wish, and for this reason we shall occasionally be caught departing from our general practice of confining ourselves only to issues concerning the political system itself.

We have also excluded from our selection of materials all issues that are no longer the topic of current debate, that are no longer in the process of being decided. There seem to be fashions in political issues, hardly less than in women's clothes. One of the present authors can remember a time when popular political debate seethed over something called "municipal ownership of public utilities," and political scientists argued such topics as "initiative and referendum," the allegedly tyrannical domination of municipal corporations by state legislatures, "proportional representation," and other issues which now have passed into such complete obscurity that we can hardly understand how they once stirred such a fuss. For our readings we have tried to select issues which will be of lasting value, although fully aware of the vagaries besetting such choice.

It now remains to mention a principle of selection which has *not* governed the selection of materials for this volume—namely, that of selection with an eye to more or less even balance, quantitatively speaking, between Conservative and Liberal writings. There exists a comparative dearth of apposite Conservative writings. Not, we hasten to add, that the finished volume is a further instance of notable (to use a term currently fashionable) "imbalance to the Left." For most of the topics we have been able to present a more or less equal amount of writings favorable to the traditional political system and those hostile to it. But we have accomplished that result by doing two things that sharply modify the principle of selection we should have preferred to rely on. First, we have hauled in on the Conservative side of the balance writers who are known, in general, as Liberals, but who happen to come up more Conservative than Liberal on this or that particular issue. Second, we relied more heavily than we would have liked on two Conservative writers, Burnham and Kendall. We did these two things because we had to. The Conservative selections included in the book represent pretty much the sum total of what we were able to turn up. The Liberal selections, by contrast, were chosen (on grounds of quality primarily) out of a veritable mountain of such items.

For this reason, we ourselves have tried to round out the Conservative position in our commentaries by drawing not upon what Conservatives have actually written but upon what over the years we have seen them do or heard them say. Some readers may therefore find our chapter introductions more or less tilted to the Right. To them we give our assurances that we would not have wished it so.

We have tried to keep our own preferences, despite this tax on our objectivity, out of it, and to render an unbiased report as to the progress of the struggle and as to what, actually, it is all about. It is not for us to say whether we have succeeded in being objective. We wish to note, however, we have not begrudged either space or the aura of famous names to the protagonist we are most likely to be suspected of not favoring.

We owe very special thanks to Miss Nellie Cooper, Mrs. Yvona Kendall Mason, Mr. Robert Harley, Mr. Edward Raffetto and the editorial staff of D. Van Nostrand. Without their willing help our task would have been immensely more difficult. We would also like to express our appreciation to five of our students, John Bernbach, Ira Bitz, Alfred J. Callahan, Joseph Patrick Dailey, and Charles McGettigan for their invaluable help during the final stages of preparation. Needless to say, we are indebted to the authors and publishers for their permission to reprint the materials contained in this volume.

W. K.
G. W. C.

Contents

CHAPTER III: WHAT TO DO ABOUT CONGRESS?

CHAPTER IV: WHAT TO DO ABOUT THE PRESIDENCY?

CHAPTER V: WHAT TO DO ABOUT THE COURT?

CHAPTER VI: WHAT TO DO ABOUT THE PARTIES?

General Introduction:
The Continuing Debate

MANY contemporary controversies are, in large measure, a continuation of the debates which began (as we know from James Madison's *Notes*) at the Philadelphia Constitutional Convention. The debates in that convention, for the most part, revolved around the structure, composition, and powers of the Congress, Presidency, and the Supreme Court. More: those debates proceeded, in the main, by canvassing various alternatives as to what each of the three great departments or branches of government might be, by then eliminating alternatives, and finally, by "marrying," in each case, the survivor among the alternatives. This was sometimes done on grounds of putative principle or "philosophy," sometimes (as John Roche shows us in his brilliant article) on those "keep-everybody-happy" grounds on which democratic statesmen and politicians are said to base their actions. Yet, the proponents of the alternatives that were eliminated (though most of them did sign the resulting draft and supported, no doubt loyally, the new plan of government) did not thereby necessarily cease to represent the tendencies they had expressed in the debates. The alternatives they had represented continued to be alternatives—to which, out of subsequent disillusionment or discontent with the Philadelphia "solutions," the American people might subsequently return. Consequently, the "stuff" for a continuing debate about the basic institutions of the new plan was already *there,* as a *given,* even as the proposed constitution was being signed. And it is a rare reformist proposal about these institutions that does not catch up, in one way or another, an alternative canvassed by, or at least a tendency that made itself felt in, the Philadelphia Convention.

Two major aspects of our contemporary debates are somewhat novel. The first of these is the Conservative argument as to the "success" of the Philadelphia plan in providing for the welfare and happiness of the American people, and the preservation of their "rights." And, second, the liberal arguments that are based on "equality," on the demand that our political arrangements should give to each of the citizens an equal capacity to affect public policy, and that our public policy should endeavor to make ever more equal.

The present phase of the great debate, what in this volume is called the "Liberal attack" on the inherited political system of the United States, began, roughly speaking, about fifty years ago with the publication of J. Allen Smith's *The Spirit of American Government.* It began at a moment when the overwhelming majority of writers on such topics were, certainly, Conservative. Moreover, the attack, it seems safe to say, had not cast before it much in the way of shadows: Smith appeared as out of nowhere, and the attack he launched was wholly unexpected. The conservatives, therefore, were in a two-fold sense far from ready for it. First not having expected the particular *kind* of attack they found themselves called on to meet, they were ill-prepared not only to cope with it, argument by argument, indictment by indictment, but also even to understand it (one might say that the initial reaction to Smith, whose book, incidentally, seems to have "rated" only a single review in the learned periodicals, was pretty much along "Who-ever-heard-of-such-a-thing?" lines—and, demonstrably, still ran along those lines as recently as the late '30's). Second, a similar but not the same point, the Smith attack found the Conservative custodians of our political lore unready not only for that kind of attack, but for any attack at all—so accustomed were they to *taking for granted,* assuming as things not requiring proof, the beneficent and even inspired character of the political system handed down to them from the past. Nor is that all. At the risk of appearing excessively harsh on them, we may note that the very fate had overtaken those custodians of our political lore that the late J. S. Mill had prophesied, perhaps even predicted, for all defenders of an orthodoxy not under constant challenge, namely, that of forgetting the arguments in favor of it and, what is of course much, much worse, ceasing to understand the orthodoxy itself.

That this "Liberal attack" has "succeeded" in the intellectual circles in America, among political scientists especially, is beyond dispute. Still, there is continuing debate in our society. This book will have served its purpose if it gives the student a better understanding of the nature of this continuing debate in American politics.

Chapter I

THE STATUS OF THE FRAMERS

Introduction

At first blush some readers may be curious that we treat the "status" of the Founding Fathers (by which we mean the state of opinion or judgment regarding them and their handiwork) as a topic of dispute between conservatives and liberals *in pari materia* with Congress, the Presidency, and the Supreme Court—that is, as an "issue" that divides conservatives from liberals. "Surely," a reader will object, "that is going a bit far! Everybody thinks well of the Founding Fathers. And even were that not true I don't quite see how the status of the Framers could be a *political* issue in the usual sense of that term, between anybody and anybody, much less between conservatives in particular and liberals in particular." For any such objector we have ready two decisive answers. First, upon a moment's reflection, anyone will see that the point we are making is not so surprising after all. Since the Founding Fathers actually founded the political system under which we live and since conservatives actually defend that system against proposals predicated upon principles different from those on which it rests, it is precisely the wisdom, the virtue (if we may use a phrase that the Framers were themselves fond of), the statesmanship of the Founding Fathers that come into question. If the Framers built —that is, "founded"—well, so well that that which they founded can be successfully defended against the proposals of the most able and energetic of contemporary and recent would-be new founders, then this conclusion is inescapable: the Founding Fathers must indeed have been wise, dedicated to the public good, and statesman-like. The conservatives, one might say, as defenders of the going system, are "stuck" with the Framers, and so with the necessity of combating any criticism that might tend to undermine their reputation for wisdom, virtue, and statesmanship. And the idea "proves out," so to speak, if we reflect on the liberals with their vocation to refashion the institutions the Founding Fathers founded. To criticize the institutions unfavorably is, by implication, to criticize the founders of those institutions. Such criticism places a question-mark beside their wisdom, their statesmanship perhaps (insofar as their "principles" or their fidelity to their professed principles are challenged), even their virtue. As the conservatives are stuck

3

with the Framers, so the liberals are stuck at least with the temptation to "run them down," to patronize them, to rub from their reputations any aura that might dispose their descendants to treat their handiwork as beyond criticism. Nor must the suggestion that the Framers were wise merely in their generation, merely for their time, be accepted as evidence of devotion to the Framers. It is, on the face of it, patronizing, or if not that, then question-begging.

The other answer is, to use a phrase made famous of late by Walter Cronkite, the television news commentator: "That's how it is," on the day these lines are written—and how it has been ever since the publication of J. Allen Smith's *Spirit of American Government*. The attack on the institutions devised by the Framers is always very difficult to pry loose from an attack on the Framers themselves. To be sure, not all literature that tends to lower the present reputation of the Framers is an attack on their institutions. Charles A. Beard's *Economic Interpretation of the Constitution,* which was an attempt to show that the Framers were *inter alia* a bunch of "smart cookies" who in writing the Constitution were also shoring up their own economic interests, was *not* an attack on the institutions. Beard, as his *The Republic* makes very clear, was on the showing of this book a conservative about our basic institutions and, in any case, seems to have had no particular objection to "smart cookies." But the influence of his book, which has fed the attack on the Framers over the decades since it was written, has undoubtedly strengthened and intensified the attack on the institutions. As for Smith, he, as the student will see in the excerpt from his book that we reproduce below, was *savage* in his moral judgment of the Founding Fathers—how savage, it is difficult for a man to realize who has not dipped into the literature of the period, and developed a "feel" for the *reverence* with which it treated the members of the Philadelphia Convention. Smith was also supremely confident—his confidence cries up at one out of every page of his book—of his own moral superiority to the Framers, and thus, for all that such a word would not have come naturally to his pen, of his own virtue, that is, rightness. His book is, accordingly, redolent of a certain kind of priggishness, which may or may not have continued to preside over the "attack" literature that he launched.

This book will have served one of its major purposes if it sensitizes the student to the continuing, though often veiled, debate about such questions as: What kind of men were they? Did they, or did they not, entertain so "black" a view of "human nature" as to set them apart from ourselves and our contemporaries, who are of course more "scientific" about such matters? Were they, or were they not, "for" democracy? *If* they were "for" democracy, were they "for" it out of some imperfect understanding—in sharp contrast, of course, to our own deepened and more generous understanding—of democracy? Were they—we have already made passing reference to such a question—so completely sons of their age—that is, of the now-remote 18th century —that, even *conceding* them wisdom and virtue and statesmanship, their thinking could not possibly be valid for *our* age?

1. The Constitution: A Reactionary Document*

JAMES ALLEN SMITH

THE sweeping changes made in our form of government after the Declaration of Independence were clearly revolutionary in character. The English system of checks and balances was discarded for the more democratic one under which all the important powers of government were vested in the legislature. This new scheme of government was not, however, truly representative of the political thought of the colonies. The conservative classes who in ordinary times are a powerful factor in the politics of every community had, by reason of their Loyalist views, no voice in this political reorganization; and these, as we have seen, not only on account of their wealth and intelligence, but on the basis of their numerical strength as well, were entitled to considerable influence.

With the return of peace these classes which so largely represented the wealth and culture of the colonies, regained in a measure the influence which they had lost. This tended strongly to bring about a conservative reaction. There was besides another large class which supported the Revolutionary movement without being in sympathy with its democratic tendencies. This also used its influence to undo the work of the Revolutionary radicals. Moreover, many of those who had espoused democratic doctrines during the Revolution became conservatives after the war was over.[1] These classes were naturally opposed to the new political doctrines which the Revolutionary movement had incorporated in the American government. The "hard times" and general discontent which followed the war also contributed to the reactionary movement; since many were led to believe that evils which were the natural result of other causes were due to an excess of democracy. Consequently we find the democratic tendency which manifested itself with the outbreak of the Revolution giving place a few years later to the political reaction which found expression in our present Constitution.

* Reprinted with permission of publisher from *The Spirit of American Government* by James Allen Smith. Copyright 1907 by the Macmillan Company. Renewed 1935 by James Allen Smith.

[1] "Who would have thought, ten years ago, that the very men who risked their lives and fortunes in support of republican principles, would now treat them as the fictions of fancy?" M. Smith in the New York Convention held to ratify the Constitution, *Elliot's Debates, Second Edition,* Vol. II, p. 250.

"The United States are the offspring of a long-past age. A hundred years, it is true, have scarcely passed since the eighteenth century came to its end, but no hundred years in the history of the world has ever before hurried it along so far over new paths and into unknown fields. The French Revolution and the First Empire were the bridge between two periods that nothing less than the remaking of European society, the recasting of European politics, could have brought so near.

"But back to this eighteenth century must we go to learn the forces, the national ideas, the political theories, under the domination of which the Constitution of the United States was framed and adopted." [2]

It is the general belief, nevertheless, that the Constitution of the United States is the very embodiment of democratic philosophy. The people take it for granted that the framers of that document were imbued with the spirit of political equality and sought to establish a government by the people themselves. Widely as this view is entertained, it is, however, at variance with the facts.

"Scarcely any of these men [the framers of the Constitution] entertained," says Fiske, "what we should now call extreme democratic views. Scarcely any, perhaps, had that intense faith in the ultimate good sense of the people which was the most powerful characteristic of Jefferson." [3]

Democracy—government by the people, or directly responsible to them— was not the object which the framers of the American Constitution had in view, but the very thing which they wished to avoid. In the convention which drafted that instrument it was recognized that democratic ideas had made sufficient progress among the masses to put an insurmountable obstacle in the way of any plan of gov-

ernment which did not confer at least the form of political power upon the people. Accordingly the efforts of the Constitutional Convention were directed to the task of devising a system of government which was just popular enough not to excite general opposition and which at the same time gave to the people as little as possible of the substance of political power.

It is somewhat strange that the American people know so little of the fundamental nature of their system of government. Their acquaintance with it extends only to its outward form and rarely includes a knowledge of the political philosophy upon which it rests. The sources of information upon which the average man relies do not furnish the data for a correct understanding of the Constitution. The ordinary textbooks and popular works upon this subject leave the reader with an entirely erroneous impression. Even the writings of our constitutional lawyers deal with the outward form rather than the spirit of our government. The vital question—the extent to which, under our constitutional arrangements, the people were expected to, and as a matter of fact do, control legislation and public policy, is either not referred to, or else discussed in a superficial and unsatisfactory manner. That this feature of our Constitution should receive more attention than it does is evident when we reflect that a government works well in practice in proportion as its underlying philosophy and constitutional forms are comprehended by those who wield political power.

"It has been common," says a late Justice of the United States Supreme Court, "to designate our form of government as a democracy, but in the true sense in which that term is properly used, as defining a government in which all its acts are performed by the people, it is about as far from it as any other of which we are aware." [4]

In the United States at the present

[2] Simeon E. Baldwin, *Modern Political Institutions*, pp. 83 and 84.

[3] Fiske, *Critical Period of American History*, p. 226.

[4] S. F. Miller, *Lectures on the Constitution of the United States*, pp. 84-85.

time we are trying to make an undemocratic Constitution the vehicle of democratic rule. Our Constitution embodies the political philosophy of the eighteenth century, not that of to-day. It was framed for one purpose while we are trying to use it for another. Is free government, then, being tried here under the conditions most favorable to its success? This question we can answer only when we have considered our Constitution as a means to the attainment of democratic rule.

It is difficult to understand how anyone who has read the proceedings of the Federal Convention can believe that it was the intention of that body to establish a democratic government. The evidence is overwhelming that the men who sat in that convention had no faith in the wisdom or political capacity of the people. Their aim and purpose was not to secure a larger measure of democracy, but to eliminate as far as possible the direct influence of the people on legislation and public policy. That body, it is true, contained many illustrious men who were actuated by a desire to further what they conceived to be the welfare of the country. They represented, however, the wealthy and conservative classes, and had for the most part but little sympathy with the popular theory of government.

"Hardly one among them but had sat in some famous assembly, had signed some famous document, had filled some high place, or had made himself conspicuous for learning, for scholarship, or for signal services rendered in the cause of liberty. One had framed the Albany plan of union; some had been members of the Stamp Act Congress of 1765; some had signed the Declaration of Rights in 1774; the names of others appear at the foot of the Declaration of Independence and at the foot of the Articles of Confederation; two had been presidents of Congress; seven had been, or were then, governors of states; twenty-eight had been members of Congress; one had commanded the armies of the United States; another had been Superintendent of Finance; a third had repeatedly been sent on important missions to England, and had long been Minister to France.

"Nor were the future careers of many of them to be less interesting than their past. Washington and Madison became Presidents of the United States; Elbridge Gerry became Vice-President; Charles Cotesworth Pinckney and Rufus King became candidates for the Presidency, and Jared Ingersoll, Rufus King, and John Langdon candidates for the Vice-Presidency; Hamilton became Secretary of the Treasury; Madison, Secretary of State; Randolph, Attorney-General and Secretary of State, and James McHenry, a Secretary of War; Ellsworth and Rutledge became Chief-Justices; Wilson and John Blair rose to the Supreme bench; Gouverneur Morris, and Ellsworth, and Charles C. Pinckney, and Gerry, and William Davie became Ministers abroad." [5]

The long list of distinguished men who took part in the deliberations of that body is noteworthy, however, for the absence of such names as Samuel Adams, Thomas Jefferson, Thomas Paine, Patrick Henry and other democratic leaders of that time. The Federal Convention assembled in Philadelphia only eleven years after the Declaration of Independence was signed, yet only six of the fifty-six men who signed that document were among its members.[6] Conservatism and thorough distrust of popular government characterized throughout the proceedings of that convention. Democracy, Elbridge Gerry thought, was the worst of all political evils.[7] Edmund Randolph observed

[5] McMaster, *With the Fathers*, pp. 112-113.
[6] "They [the framers of the Constitution] represented the conservative intelligence of the country; from this class there is hardly a name, except that of Jay, which could be suggested to complete the list." Article by Alexander Johnston on the Convention of 1787 in *Lalor's Cyclopaedia of Pol. Science, Pol. Econ. and U.S. Hist.*
[7] *Elliot's Debates*, Vol. V, p. 557.

that in tracing the political evils of this country to their origin, "every man [in the Convention] had found it in the turbulence and follies of democracy."[8] These views appear to reflect the general opinion of that body. Still they realized that it was not the part of wisdom to give public expression to this contempt for democracy. The doors were closed to the public and the utmost secrecy maintained with regard to the proceedings. Members were not allowed to communicate with any one outside of that body concerning the matters therein discussed, nor were they permitted, except by a vote of the Convention, to copy anything from the journals.[9]

It must be borne in mind that the Convention was called for the purpose of proposing amendments to the Articles of Confederation. The delegates were not authorized to frame a new constitution. Their appointment contemplated changes which were to perfect the Articles of Confederation with-

out destroying the general form of government which they established. The resolution of Congress of February 21, 1787, which authorized the Federal Convention, limited its business to "the sole and express purpose of revising the Articles of Confederation," and the states of New York, Massachusetts, and Connecticut copied this in the instructions to their delegates.[10] The aim of the Convention, however, from the very start was not amendment, but a complete rejection of the system itself, which was regarded as incurably defective.

This view was well expressed by James Wilson in his speech made in favor of the ratification of the Constitution before the Pennsylvania convention.

"The business, we are told, which was entrusted to the late Convention," he said, "was merely to amend the present Articles of Confederation. This observation has been frequently made, and has often brought to my mind a story that is related of Mr. Pope, who, it is well known, was not a little deformed. It was customary with him to use this phrase, 'God mend me!' when any little accident happened. One evening a link-boy was lighting him along, and, coming to a gutter, the boy jumped nimbly over it. Mr. Pope called to him to turn, adding, 'God mend me!' The arch rogue, turning to light him, looked at him, and repeated, 'God mend you! He would sooner make half-a-dozen new ones.' This would apply to the present Confederation; for it would be easier to make another than to amend this."[11]

The popular notion that this Convention in framing the Constitution was actuated solely by a desire to impart more vigor and efficiency to the general government is but a part of the truth. The Convention desired to establish not only a strong and vigorous central government, but one which would at the same time possess great

---

[8] *Ibid.*, p. 138.

[9] "By another [rule] the doors were to be shut, and the whole proceedings were to be kept secret; and so far did this rule extend, that we were thereby prevented from corresponding with gentlemen in the different states upon the subjects under our discussion. . . . So *extremely solicitous* were they that their proceedings should not transpire, that the members were prohibited even from taking copies of resolutions, on which the Convention were deliberating, or extracts of any kind from the Journals without formally moving for and obtaining permission, by a vote of the Convention for that purpose." Luther Martin's Address to the Maryland House of Delegates. *Ibid.*, Vol. I, p. 345.

"The doors were locked, and an injunction of strict secrecy was put upon everyone. The results of their work were known in the following September, when the draft of the Federal Constitution was published. But just what was said and done in this secret conclave was not revealed until fifty years had passed, and the aged James Madison, the last survivor of those who sat there, had been gathered to his fathers." Fiske, *The Critical Period of American History*, p. 229. McMaster, *With the Fathers*, p. 112.

[10] *Elliot's Debates*, Vol. I, pp. 119-127.

[11] *Elliot's Debates*, Vol. II, p. 470.

stability or freedom from change. This last reason is seldom mentioned in our constitutional literature, yet it had a most important bearing on the work of the Convention. This desired stability the government under the Confederation did not possess, since it was, in the opinion of the members of the Convention, dangerously responsive to public opinion; hence their desire to supplant it with an elaborate system of constitutional checks. The adoption of this system was the triumph of a skillfully directed reactionary movement.

Of course the spirit and intention of the Convention must be gathered not from the statements and arguments addressed to the general public in favor of the ratification of the Constitution, but from what occurred in the Convention itself. The discussions which took place in that body indicate the real motives and purposes of those who framed the Constitution. These were carefully withheld from the people and it was not until long afterward that they were accessible to students of the American Constitution. The preamble began with, "We, the people," but it was the almost unanimous sentiment of the Convention that the less the people had to do with the government the better. Hamilton wanted to give the rich and well born "a distinct, permanent share in the government." [12] Madison thought the government ought "to protect the minority of the opulent against the majority." [13] The prevalence of such views in this Convention reminds one of Adam Smith's statement, made a few years before in his "Wealth of Nations," that "civil government, so far as it is instituted for the interests of the well-to-do certainly the security of property, is in reality instituted for the defence of the rich against the poor, or of those who have some property against those who have none at all." [14] The solicitude shown by the members of this convention for tends to justify Adam Smith's observation.

The framers of the Constitution realized, however, that it would not do to carry this system of checks upon the people too far. It was necessary that the government should retain something of the *form* of democracy, if it was to command the respect and confidence of the people. For this reason Gerry thought that "the people should appoint one branch of the government in order to inspire them with the necessary confidence." [15] Madison also saw that the necessary sympathy between the people and their rulers and officers must be maintained and that "the policy of refining popular appointments by successive filtrations" might be pushed too far.[16] These discussions, which took place behind closed doors and under pledge of secrecy, may be taken as fairly representing what the framers of our Constitution really thought of popular government. Their public utterances, on the other hand, influenced as they necessarily were, by considerations of public policy, are of little value. From all the evidence which we have, the conclusion is irresistible that they sought to establish a form of government which would effectually curb and restrain democracy. They engrafted upon the Constitution just so much of the features of popular government as was, in their opinion, necessary to ensure its adoption.

[12] *Elliot's Debates,* Vol. I, p. 422.
[13] *Ibid.,* p. 450.

[14] Book 5, Ch. I, Part II.
[15] *Elliot's Debates,* Vol. V, p. 160.
[16] *Ibid.,* p. 137.

2. Democracy and *The Federalist:* A Reconsideration of the Framers' Intent*

MARTIN DIAMOND

IT has been a common teaching among modern historians of the guiding ideas in the foundation of our government that the Constitution of the United States embodied a reaction against the democratic principles espoused in the Declaration of Independence. This view has largely been accepted by political scientists and has therefore had important consequences for the way American political development has been studied. I shall present here a contrary view of the political theory of the Framers and examine some of its consequences.

What is the relevance of the political thought of the Founding Fathers to an understanding of contemporary problems of liberty and justice? Four possible ways of looking at the Founding Fathers immediately suggest themselves. First, it may be that they possessed wisdom, a set of political principles still inherently adequate, and needing only to be supplemented by skill in their proper contemporary application. Second, it may be that, while the Founding Fathers' principles are still sound, they are applicable only to a part of our problems, but not to that part which is peculiarly modern; and thus new principles are needed to be joined together with the old ones. Third, it may be that the Founding Fathers have simply become; they dealt with bygone problems and their principles were relevant only to those old problems. Fourth, they may have been wrong or radically inadequate even for their own time.

* *The American Political Science Review* (March, 1959), pp. 52-68. Reprinted by permission.

Each of these four possible conclusions requires the same foundation: an understanding of the political thought of the Founding Fathers. To decide whether to apply their wisdom, or to add to their wisdom, or to reject it as irrelevant or as unwise, it is absolutely necessary to understand what they said, why they said it, and what they meant by it. At the same time, however, to understand their claim to wisdom is to evaluate it: to know wherein they were wise and wherein they were not, or wherein (and why) their wisdom is unavailing for our problems. Moreover, even if it turns out that our modern problems require wholly new principles for their solution, an excellent way to discover those new principles would be to see what it is about modernity that has outmoded the principles of the Founding Fathers. For example, it is possible that modern developments are themselves partly the outcome of the particular attempt to solve the problem of freedom and justice upon which this country was founded. That is, our modern difficulties may testify to fundamental errors in the thought of the Founding Fathers; and, in the process of discerning those errors, we may discover what better principles would be.

The solution of our contemporary problems requires very great wisdom indeed. And in that fact lies the greatest justification for studying anew the political thought of the Founding Fathers. For that thought remains the finest American thought on political matters. In studying them we may raise ourselves to their level. In achieving their level we may free ourselves from limitations that, ironically, they tend to impose upon us, *i.e.*, insofar as we tend to be creatures of the society they founded. And in so freeing ourselves we may be enabled, if it is necessary, to go beyond their wisdom. The Founding Fathers still loom so large in our life that the contemporary political problem of liberty and justice for Americans could be stated as the need to choose whether to apply their wisdom, amend their wisdom, or reject it. Only an understanding of them will tell us how to choose.

For the reflections on the Fathers which follow, I employ chiefly *The Federalist* as the clue to the political theory upon which rested the founding of the American Republic. That this would be inadequate for a systematic study of the Founding Fathers goes without saying. But it is the one book, "to which," as Jefferson wrote in 1825, "appeal is habitually made by all, and rarely declined or denied by any as evidence of the general opinion of those who framed and of those who accepted the Constitution of the United States, on questions as to its genuine meaning." As such it is the indispensable starting point for systematic study.

I

Our major political problems today are problems of democracy; and, as much as anything else, the *Federalist* papers are a teaching about democracy. The conclusion of one of the most important of these papers states what is also the most important theme in the entire work: the necessity for "a republican remedy for the diseases most incident to republican government." [1] The theme is clearly repeated in a passage where Thomas Jefferson is praised for displaying equally "a fervent attachment to republican government and an enlightened view of the dangerous propensities against which it ought to

be guarded." [2] *The Federalist,* thus, stresses its commitment to republican or popular government, but, of course, insists that this must be an enlightened commitment.

But *The Federalist* and the Founding Fathers generally have not been taken at their word. Predominantly, they are understood as being only quasi- or even anti-democrats. Modern American historical writing, at least until very recently, has generally seen the Constitution as some sort of apostasy from, or reaction to, the radically democratic implications of the Declaration of Independence—a reaction that was undone by the great "democratic breakthroughs" of Jeffersonianism, Jacksonianism, etc. This view, I believe, involves a false understanding of the crucial political issues involved in the founding of the American Republic. Further, it is based implicitly upon a questionable modern approach to democracy and has tended to have the effect, moreover, of relegating the political teaching of the Founding Fathers to the pre-democratic past and thus of making it of no vital concern to moderns. The Founding Fathers themselves repeatedly stressed that their Constitution was wholly consistent with the true principles of republican or popular government. The prevailing modern opinion, in varying degrees and in different ways, rejects that claim. It thus becomes important to understand what was the relation of the Founding Fathers to popular government or democracy.

I have deliberately used interchangeably their terms, "popular government" and "democracy." The Founding Fathers, of course, did not use the terms entirely synonymously and the idea that they were less than "democrats" has been fortified by the fact that they sometimes defined "democracy" invidiously in comparison with "republic." But this fact does not really justify the opinion. For their basic view was that

[1] *Federalist*, No. 10, p. 62. All references are to the Modern Library edition, ed. E. M. Earle.

[2] *The Federalist*, No. 49, p. 327.

popular government was the genus, and democracy and republic were two species of that genus of government. What distinguished popular government from other genera of government was that in it, political authority is "derived from the great body of the society, not from . . . [any] favoured class of it." [3] With respect to this decisive question, of where political authority is lodged, democracy and republic—as *The Federalist* uses the terms—differ not in the least. Republics, equally with democracies, may claim to be wholly a form of popular government. This is neither to deny the difference between the two, nor to depreciate the importance *The Federalist* attached to the difference; but in *The Federalist's* view, the difference does not relate to the essential principle of popular government. Democracy means in *The Federalist* that form of popular government where the citizens "assemble and administer the government in person." [4] Republics differ in that the people rule through representatives and, of course, in the consequences of that difference. The crucial point is that republics and democracies are equally forms

of popular government, but that the one form is vastly preferable to the other because of the substantive consequences of the difference in form. Those historians who consider the Founding Fathers as less than "democrats," miss or reject the Founders' central contention that, while being perfectly faithful to the *principle* of popular government, they had solved the *problem* of popular government.

In what way is the Constitution ordinarily thought to be less democratic than the Declaration? The argument is usually that the former is characterized by fear of the people, by preoccupation with minority interests and rights, and by measures therefore taken against the power of majorities. The Declaration, it is true, does not display these features, but this is no proof of a fundamental difference of principle between the two. Is it not obviously possible that the difference is due only to a difference in the tasks to which the two documents were addressed? And is it not further possible that the democratic principles of the Declaration are not only compatible with the prophylactic measures of the Constitution, but actually imply them?

The Declaration of Independence formulates two criteria for judging whether any government is good, or indeed legitimate. Good government must rest, procedurally, upon the consent of the governed. Good government, substantively, must do only certain things, *e.g.,* secure certain rights. This may be stated another way by borrowing a phrase from Locke, appropriate enough when discussing the Declaration. That "the people shall be judge" is of the essence of democracy, is its peculiar form or method of proceeding. That the people shall judge rightly is the substantive problem of democracy. But whether the procedure will bring about the substance is problematic. Between the Declaration's two criteria, then, a tension exists: consent can be given or obtained for governmental actions which are not right—at least as the

[3] *Federalist*, No. 39, p. 244. Here Madison speaks explicitly of the republican form of government. But see on the same page how Madison compares the republican form with "every *other popular* government." Regarding the crucial question of the lodgment of political authority, Madison speaks of republic, democracy and popular government interchangeably. Consider that, in the very paper where he distinguishes so precisely between democracies and republics regarding direct versus representative rule, Madison defines his general aim both as a search for "a republican remedy" for republican diseases *and* a remedy that will "preserve the spirit and the form of *popular* government." (p. 58.) Interestingly, on June 6 at the Federal Convention, Madison's phrasing for a similar problem was the search for "the only defense against the inconveniences of democracy consistent with the *democratic* form of government." Madison, *Writings*, ed. G. Hunt, Vol. 3 (G. P. Putnam's Sons, New York, 1902), p. 103. Italics supplied throughout.

[4] *Federalist*, No. 10, p. 58.

men of 1776 saw the right. (To give an obvious example from their point of view: the people may freely but wrongly vote away the protection due to property.) Thus the Declaration clearly contained, although it did not resolve, a fundamental problem. Solving the problem was not its task; that was the task for the framers of the Constitution. But the man who wrote the Declaration of Independence and the leading men who supported it were perfectly aware of the difficulty, and of the necessity for a "republican remedy."

What the text of the Declaration, taken alone, tells of its meaning may easily be substantiated by the testimony of its author and supporters. Consider only that Jefferson, with no known change of heart at all, said of *The Federalist* that it was "the best commentary on the principles of government which was ever written." [5] Jefferson, it must be remembered, came firmly to recommend the adoption of the Constitution, his criticisms of it having come down only to a proposal for rotation in the Presidency and for the subsequent adoption of a bill of rights. I do not, of course, deny the peculiar character of "Jeffersonianism" nor the importance to many things of its proper understanding. I only state here that it is certain that Jefferson, unlike later historians, did not view the Constitution as a retrogression from democracy. Or further, consider that John Adams, now celebrated as America's great conservative, was so enthusiastic about Jefferson's draft of the Declaration as to wish on his own account that hardly a word be changed. And this same Adams, also without any change of heart and without complaint, accepted the Constitution as embodying many of his own views on government.

The idea that the Constitution was a falling back from the fuller democracy of the Declaration thus rests in part upon a false reading of the Dec-

[5] *The Works of Thomas Jefferson*, ed. Paul L. Ford (The Federal Edition), Vol. 5 (G. P. Putnam's Sons, New York, 1904), p. 434.

laration as free from the concerns regarding democracy that the framers of the Constitution felt. Perhaps only those would so read it who take for granted a perfect, self-subsisting harmony between consent (equality) and the proper aim of government (justice), or between consent and individual rights (liberty). This assumption was utterly foreign to the leading men of the Declaration.

II

The Declaration has wrongly been converted into, as it were, a super-democratic document; has the Constitution wrongly been converted in the modern view into an insufficiently democratic document? The only basis for depreciating the democratic character of the Constitution lies in its framers' apprehensive diagnosis of the "diseases," "defects" or "evil propensities" of democracy, and in their remedies. But if what the Founders considered to be defects *are* genuine defects, and if the remedies, without violating the principles of popular government, *are* genuine remedies, then it would be unreasonable to call the Founders anti- or quasi-democrats. Rather, they would be the wise partisans of democracy; a man is not a better democrat but only a foolish democrat if he ignores real defects inherent in popular government. Thus, the question becomes: are there natural defects to democracy and, if there are, what are the best remedies?

In part, the Founding Fathers answered this question by employing a traditional mode of political analysis. They believed there were several basic possible regimes, each having several possible forms. Of these possible regimes they believed the best, or at least the best for America, to be popular government, but only if purged of its defects. At any rate, an unpurged popular government they believed to be indefensible. They believed there were several forms of popular government, crucial among these direct democracy and republican—or representative—government (the latter perhaps divisible into two distinct forms, large and small republics). Their constitution and their defense of it constitute an argument for that form of popular government (large republic) in which the "evil propensities" would be weakest or most susceptible of remedy.

The whole of the thought of the Founding Fathers is intelligible and, especially, the evaluation of their claim to be wise partisans of popular government is possible, only if the words *"disease," "defect,"* and *"evil propensity"* are allowed their full force. Unlike modern "value-free" social scientists, the Founding Fathers believed that true knowledge of the good and bad in human conduct was possible, and that they themselves possessed sufficient knowledge to discern the really grave defects of popular government and their proper remedies. The modern relativistic or positivistic theories, implicitly employed by most commentators on the Founding Fathers, deny the possibility of such true knowledge and therefore deny that the Founding Fathers *could* have been actuated by knowledge of the good rather than by passion or interest. (I deliberately employ the language of *Federalist* No. 10. Madison defined faction, in part, as a group "united and actuated by . . . passion, or . . . interest." That is, factions are groups *not*—as presumably the authors of *The Federalist* were—actuated by reason.) How this modern view of the value problem supports the conception of the Constitution as less democratic than the Declaration is clear. The Founding Fathers did in fact seek to prejudice the outcome of democracy; they sought to alter, by certain restraints, the likelihood that the majority would decide certain political issues in bad ways. These restraints the Founders justified as mitigating the natural defects of democracy. But, say the moderns, there are no "bad" political decisions, wrong-in-themselves, from reaching which the majority ought to be restrained. Therefore, ul-

timately, nothing other than the specific interests of the Founders can explain their zeal in restraining democracy. And inasmuch as the restraints were typically placed on the many in the interest of the propertied, the departure of the Constitution is "anti-democratic" or "thermidorean." In short, according to this view, there cannot be what the Founders claimed to possess, "an *enlightened* view of the dangerous propensities against which [popular government] . . . ought to be guarded," the substantive goodness or badness of such propensities being a matter of opinion or taste on which reason can shed no light.

What are some of the arrangements which have been considered signs of "undemocratic" features of the Constitution? The process by which the Constitution may be amended is often cited in evidence. Everyone is familiar with the arithmetic which shows that a remarkably small minority could prevent passage of a constitutional amendment supported by an overwhelming majority of the people. That is, bare majorities in the thirteen least populous states could prevent passage of an amendment desired by overwhelming majorities in the thirty-six most populous states. But let us, for a reason to be made clear in a moment, turn that arithmetic around. Bare majorities in the thirty-seven least populous states can pass amendments against the opposition of overwhelming majorities in the twelve most populous states. And this would mean in actual votes today (and would have meant for the thirteen original states) constitutional amendment by a minority against the opposition of a majority of citizens. My point is simply that, while the amending procedure does involve qualified majorities, the qualification is not of the kind that requires an especially large numerical majority for action.

I suggest that the real aim and practical effect of the complicated amending procedure was not at all to give power to minorities, but to ensure that

will serve, is that it will strengthen the American people against the dangers of "foreign war" and secure them from the dangers of "domestic convulsion." These functions of government are the most frequently discussed and the most vehemently emphasized in the whole work. To a very great extent, then, *The Federalist* determines the role of government with reference only, or primarily, to the extremes of external and internal danger. It is to avoid the pre-civil forms of these dangers that men form government and it is the civil solution of these dangers which, almost exclusively, determines the legitimate objects of government. But again, *The Federalist* repeatedly emphasizes that a "novel" solution is at hand. The means now exist—and America is uniquely in a position to employ them—for a republican solution which avoids the extremes of tyranny and anarchy. But notice that, on this view, liberalism and republicanism are not the means by which men may ascend to a nobler life; rather they are simply instrumentalities which solve Hobbesean problems in a more moderate manner. It is tempting to suggest that if America is a "Lockean" nation, as is so often asserted, it is true in the very precise sense that Locke's "comfortable preservation" displaces the harshness of the Hobbesean view, while not repudiating that view in general.

To be sure, *The Federalist* does make other explicit statements regarding the ends of government. For example: "Justice is the end of government. It is the end of civil society." [16] But this statement, to the best of my knowledge, is made only once in the entire work; and the context suggests that "justice" means simply "civil rights" which in turn seems to refer primarily to the protection of economic interests. That justice has here this relatively narrow meaning, as compared with traditional philosophical and theological usage, is made more probable when we take ac-

count of the crucial statement in *Federalist* No. 10. There the "first object of government" is the protection of the diverse human faculties from which arise the "rights of property" and the unequal distribution of property. The importance of this statement of the function of government is underscored when it is recalled how large a proportion of *The Federalist* deals with the improvements in "commerce" made possible by the new Constitution. For example, in a list of the four "principal objects of federal legislation," [17] three (foreign trade, interstate trade, and taxes) deal explicitly with commerce. The fourth, the militia, also deals with commerce insofar as it largely has to do with the prevention of "domestic convulsion" brought on by economic matters.

The very great emphasis of *The Federalist* on commerce, and on the role of government in nurturing it, may not be at all incompatible with the theme of "happiness" which is the most frequently occurring definition of the "object of government." The most definite statement is the following:

A good government implies two things: first, fidelity to the object of government, which is the happiness of the people, secondly, a knowledge of the means by which that object can be best obtained.[18]

The Federalist is not very explicit in defining happiness. But there are firm indications that what it had in mind has little in common with traditional philosophical or theological understandings of the term. At one place, *The Federalist* indicates that happiness requires that government "provide for the security, advance the prosperity, [and] support the reputation of the commonwealth." [19] In another, happiness seems to require "our safety, our tranquility, our dignity, our reputa-

[16] *Federalist*, No. 51, p. 340.

[17] *Federalist*, No. 53, p. 350-51.
[18] *Federalist*, No. 62, p. 404.
[19] *Federalist*, No. 30, p. 186.

tion." [20] Part of what these words mean is made clear by the fact that they summarize a lengthy indictment of the Articles of Confederation, the particulars of which deal in nearly every case with commercial shortcomings. Happiness, "a knowledge of the means" to which *The Federalist* openly claims to possess, seems to consist primarily in physical preservation from external and internal danger *and* in the comforts afforded by a commercial society; which comforts are at once the dividends of security and the means to a republican rather than repressive security.

What is striking is the apparent exclusion from the functions of government of a wide range of non-economic tasks traditionally considered the decisive business of government. It is tempting to speculate that this reduction in the tasks of government has something to do with *The Federalist's* defense of popular government. The traditional criticism of popular government was that it gave over the art of government into the hands of the many, which is to say the unwise. It would be a formidable reply to reduce the complexity of the governmental art to dimensions more commensurate with the capacity of the many. I use two statements by Madison, years apart, to illustrate the possibility that he may have had something like this in mind. "There can be no doubt that there are subjects to which the capacities of the bulk of mankind are unequal." [21] But on the other hand, "the confidence of the [Republican party] in the capacity of mankind for self-government" [22] is what distinguished it from the Federalist party which distrusted that capacity.

The confidence in mankind's capacities would seem to require having removed from government the subjects to which those capacities are unequal.

IV

So far as concerns those ends of government on which *The Federalist* is almost wholly silent, it is reasonable to infer that what the Founders made no provision for they did not rank highly among the legitimate objects of government. Other political theories had ranked highly, as objects of government, the nurturing of a particular religion, education, military courage, civic-spiritedness, moderation, individual excellence in the virtues, etc. On all of these *The Federalist* is either silent, or has in mind only pallid versions of the originals, or even seems to speak with contempt. The Founders apparently did not consider it necessary to make special provision for excellence. Did they assume these virtues would flourish without governmental or other explicit provision? Did they consciously sacrifice some of them to other necessities of a stable popular regime—as it were, as the price of their solution to the problem of democracy? Or were these virtues less necessary to a country when it had been properly founded on the basis of the new "science of politics"? In what follows I suggest some possible answers to these questions.

The Founding Fathers are often criticized for an excessive attention to, and reliance upon, mechanical institutional arrangements and for an insufficient attention to "sociological" factors. While a moderate version of this criticism may finally be just, it is nonetheless clear that *The Federalist* pays considerable and shrewd attention to such factors. For example, in *Federalist* No. 51, equal attention is given to the institutional and non-institutional strengths of the new Constitution. One of these latter is the solution to the "problems of faction." It will be convenient to examine *Federalist* No. 10

[20] *Federalist*, No. 15, p. 88.
[21] Letter to Edmund Randolph, January 10, 1788.
[22] Letter to William Eustis, May 22, 1823. The letters to Randolph and Eustis were brought to my attention by Ralph Ketcham's article, "Notes on James Madison's Sources for the Tenth Federalist Paper," *Midwest Journal of Political Science*, Vol. 1 (May, 1957).

where the argument about faction is more fully developed than in No. 51. A close examination of that solution reveals something about *The Federalist's* view of the virtues necessary to the good life.

The problem dealt with in the tenth essay is how "to break and control the violence of faction." "The friend of popular governments never finds himself so much alarmed for their character and fate, as when he contemplates their propensity to this dangerous vice." Faction is, thus, *the* problem of popular government. Now it must be made clear that Madison, the author of this essay, was not here really concerned with the problem of faction generally. He devotes only two sentences in the whole essay to the dangers of *minority* factions. The real problem in a popular government, then, is *majority* faction, or, more precisely, *the* majority faction, *i.e.*, the great mass of the little propertied and unpropertied. This is the only faction that can "execute and mask its violence under the forms of the Constitution." That is, in the American republic the many have the legal power to rule and thus from them can come the greatest harm. Madison interprets that harm fairly narrowly; at least, his overwhelming emphasis is on the classic economic struggle between the rich and the poor which made of ancient democracies "spectacles of turbulence and contention." *The* problem for the friend of popular government is how to avoid the "domestic convulsion" which results when the rich and the poor, the few and the many, as is their wont, are at each others' throats. Always before in popular governments the many, armed with political power, invariably precipitated such convulsions. But the friend of popular government must find only "a republican remedy" for this disease which is "most incident to republican government." "To secure the public good and private rights against the danger of . . . [majority] faction, and at the same time to preserve the spirit and the form of pop-

ular government, is then the great object to which our inquiries are directed."

Without wrenching Madison's meaning too greatly, the problem may be put crudely this way: Madison gave a beforehand answer to Marx. The whole of the Marxian scheme depends upon the many—having been proletarianized—causing precisely such domestic convulsion and usurpation of property as Madison wished to avoid. Madison believed that in America the many could be diverted from that probable course. How will the many, *the* majority, be prevented from using for the evil purpose of usurping property the legal power which is theirs in a popular regime? "Evidently by one of two [means] only. Either the existence of the same passion or interest in a majority at the same time must be prevented, or the majority, having such co-existent passion or interest, must be rendered, by their number and local situation, unable to concert and carry into effect schemes of oppression." But "we well know that neither moral nor religious motives can be relied on" to do these things. The "circumstance principally" which will solve the problem is the "greater number of citizens and extent of territory which may be brought within the compass" of large republican governments rather than of small direct democracies.

Rather than mutilate Madison, let me complete his thought by quoting the rest of his argument before commenting on it:

The smaller the society, the fewer probably will be the distinct parties and interests, the more frequently will a majority be found of the same party; and the smaller the number of individuals composing a majority, and the smaller the compass within which they are placed, the more easily will they concert and execute their plans of oppression. Extend the sphere and you take in a greater variety of parties and interests; you make it less probable that at majority of the whole will have a common motive to invade the rights of other citizens; or if such a common motive exists, it will be more difficult for all who feel it to discover their own strength, and to act in unison with each other.

I want to deal only with what is implied or required by the first of the two means, *i.e.,* preventing the majority from having the same "passion or interest" at the same time. I would argue that this is the more important of the two remedial means afforded by a large republic. If the majority comes to have the same passion or interest and holds to it intensely for a period of only four to six years, it seems certain that it would triumph over the "extent of territory," over the barriers of federalism, and separation of powers, and all the checks and balances of the Constitution. I do not wish to depreciate the importance of those barriers; I believe they have enormous efficacy in stemming the tide Madison feared. But I would argue that their efficacy depends upon a prior weakening of the force applied against them, upon the majority having been fragmented or deflected from its "schemes of oppression." An inflamed Marxian proletariat would not indefinitely be deterred by institutional checks or extent of territory. The crucial point then, as I see it, is the means by which a majority bent upon oppression is prevented from ever forming or becoming firm.

Madison's whole scheme essentially comes down to this. The struggle of classes is to be replaced by a struggle of interests. The class struggle is domestic convulsion; the struggle of interests is a safe, even energizing, struggle which is compatible with, or even promotes, the safety and stability of society. But how can this be accomplished? What will prevent the many from thinking of their interest as that of the Many opposed to the Few? Madison, as I see it, implies that nothing can prevent it in a small democratic society where the many are divided into only a few trades and callings: these divisions are insufficient to prevent them from conceiving their lot in common and uniting for oppression. But in a large republic, numerous and powerful divisions will arise among the many to prevent that happening. A host of interests grows up "of necessity in civilized nations, and divide[s] them into different classes, actuated by different sentiments and views." "Civilized nations" clearly means here large, commercial societies. In a large commercial society the interest of the many can be fragmented into many narrower, more limited interests. The mass will not unite as a mass to make extreme demands upon the few, the struggle over which will destroy society; the mass will fragment into relatively small groups, seeking small immediate advantages for their narrow and particular interests.

If the Madisonian solution is essentially as I have described it, it becomes clear that certain things are required for the solution to operate. I only mention several of them. First, the country in which this is to take place will have to be profoundly democratic. That is, all men must be free—and even encouraged—to seek their immediate profit and to associate with others in the process. There must be no rigid class barriers which bar men from the pursuit of immediate interest. Indeed, it is especially the lowly, from whom the most is to be feared, who must feel most sanguine about the prospects of achieving limited and immediate benefits. Second, the gains must be real; that is, the fragmented interests must from time to time achieve real gains, else the scheme would cease to beguile or mollify. But I do not want to develop these themes here. Rather, I want to emphasize only one crucial aspect of Madison's design: that is, the question of the apparently narrow ends of society envisaged by the Founding Fathers. Madison's plan, as I have described it, most assuredly does not rest on the "moral and religious motives" whose efficacy he deprecated. Indeed there is not even the suggestion that the pursuit of interest should be an especially enlightened pursuit. Rather, the problem posed by the dangerous passions and interests of the many is solved primarily by a reliance upon passion and interest themselves. As Tocqueville pointed out, Americans employ the principle of "self-interest rightly understood."

> The principle of self-interest rightly understood is not a lofty one, but it is clear and sure. It does not aim at mighty objects, but it attains . . . all those at which it aims. By its admirable conformity to human weaknesses it easily obtains great dominion; nor is that dominion precarious, since the principle checks one personal interest by another, and uses, to direct the passions, the very same instrument that excites them.[23]

Madison's solution to his problem worked astonishingly well. The danger he wished to avert has been averted and largely for the reasons he gave. But it is possible to question now whether he did not take too narrow a view of what the dangers were. Living today as beneficiaries of his system, we may yet wonder whether he failed to contemplate other equally grave problems of democracy, or whether his remedy for the one disease has not had some unfortunate collateral consequences. The Madisonian solution involved a fundamental reliance on ceaseless striving after immediate interest (perhaps now immediate gratification). Tocqueville appreciated that this "permanent agitation . . . is characteristic of a peaceful democracy,"[24] one might even say, the price of its peace. And Tocqueville was aware of how great might be the price. "In the midst of this universal tumult, this incessant

conflict of jarring interests, this continual striving of men after fortune, where is that calm to be found which is necessary for the deeper combinations of the intellect?"[25]

V

There is, I think, in *The Federalist* a profound distinction made between the qualities necessary for Founders and the qualities necessary for the men who come after. It is a distinction that bears on the question of the Founding Fathers' view of what is required for the good life and on their defense of popular government. Founding requires "an exemption from the pestilential influence of party animosities";[26] but the subsequent governing of America will depend on precisely those party animosities, moderated in the way I have described. Or again, founding requires that "reason" and not the "passions," "sit in judgment."[27] But, as I have argued, the society once founded will subsequently depend precisely upon the passions, only moderated in their consequences by having been guided into proper channels. The reason of the Founders constructs the system within which the passions of the men who come after may be relied upon.

Founders need a knowledge of the newly improved "science of politics" and a knowledge of the great political alternatives in order to construct a durable regime; while the men who come after need be only legislators who are but interested "advocates and parties to the causes they determine."[28] *The Federalist* speaks, as has often been observed, with harsh realism about the shortcomings of human nature, but, as has not so often been observed, none of its strictures can characterize the Founders; they must be free of these shortcomings in order to have had

---

[23] *Democracy in America*, ed. Phillips Bradley (Knopf, New York, 1951), Vol. 2, pp. 122-23.
[24] *Ibid.*, p. 42.

[25] *Idem.*
[26] *Federalist*, No. 37, p. 232.
[27] *Federalist*, No. 49, p. 331.
[28] *Federalist*, No. 10, p. 56.

disinterested and true knowledge of political things. While "a nation of philosophers is as little to be expected as the philosophical race of kings wished for by Plato," [29] it is tempting to speculate that *The Federalist* contemplates a kind of philosopher-founder the posthumous duration of whose rule depends upon "that veneration which time bestows on everything," [30] and in particular on a regime well-founded. But once founded, it is a system that has no necessary place and makes no provision for men of the founding kind.

It is clear that not all now regarded as Founding Fathers were thought by the authors of *The Federalist* to belong in that august company. Noting that "it is not a little remarkable" that all previous foundings of regimes were "performed by some individual citizen of pre-eminent wisdom and approved integity," [31] *The Federalist* comments on the difficulty that must have been experienced when it was attempted to found a regime by the action of an assembly of men. I think it can be shown that *The Federalist* views that assembly, the Federal Convention, as having been subject to all the weaknesses of multitudes of men. The real founders, then, were very few in number, men learned in the new science of politics who seized upon a uniquely propitious moment when their plans were consented to first by a body of respectable men and subsequently, by equally great good fortune, by the body of citizens. As it were, America provided a rare moment when "the prejudices of the community" [32] were on the side of wisdom. Not unnaturally, then, *The Federalist* is extremely reluctant to countenance any re-opening of fundamental questions or delay in ratifying the Constitution.

This circumstance—wisdom meeting with consent—is so rare that "it is impossible for the man of pious reflection not to perceive in it a finger of that Almighty hand." [33] But once consent has been given to the new wisdom, when the government has been properly founded, it will be a durable regime whose perpetuation requires nothing like the wisdom and virtue necessary for its creation. The Founding Fathers' belief that they had created a system of institutions and an arrangement of the passions and interests, that would be durable and self-perpetuating, helps explain their failure to make provision for men of their own kind to come after them. Apparently, it was thought that such men would not be needed.

But does not the intensity and kind of our modern problems seem to require of us a greater degree of reflection and public-spiritedness than the Founders thought sufficient for the men who came after them? One good way to begin that reflection would be to return to their level of thoughtfulness about fundamental political alternatives, so that we may judge for ourselves wisely regarding the profound issues that face us. I know of no better beginning for that thoughtfulness than a full and serious contemplation of the political theory that informed the origin of the Republic, of the thought and intention of those few men who fully grasped what the "assembly of demi-gods" was doing.

[29] *Federalist*, No. 49, p. 329.
[30] *Ibid.*, p. 328.
[31] *Federalist*, No. 38, p. 233.
[32] *Federalist*, No. 49, p. 329.

[33] *Federalist*, No. 38, p. 231.

3. The Founding Fathers: An Age of Realism*

RICHARD HOFSTADTER

WHEREVER *the real power in a government lies, there is the danger of oppression. In our Government the real power lies in the majority of the community. . . .* JAMES MADISON

POWER *naturally grows . . . because human passions are insatiable. But that power alone can grow which already is too great; that which is unchecked; that which has no equal power to control it.* JOHN ADAMS.

LONG ago Horace White observed that the Constitution of the United States "is based upon the philosophy of Hobbes and the religion of Calvin. It assumes that the natural state of mankind is a state of war, and that the carnal mind is at enmity with God." Of course the Constitution was founded more upon experience than any such abstract theory; but it was also an event in the intellectual history of Western civilization. The men who drew up the Constitution in Philadelphia during the summer of 1787 had a vivid Calvinistic sense of human evil and damnation and believed with Hobbes that men are selfish and contentious. They were men of affairs, merchants, lawyers, planter-businessmen, speculators, investors. Having seen human nature on display in the market place, the courtroom, the legislative chamber, and in every secret path and alleyway where wealth and power are courted, they felt they knew it in all its frailty. To them a human being was an atom of self-interest. They did not believe in man, but they did believe in the power of a good political constitution to control him.

This may be an abstract notion to ascribe to practical men, but it follows the language that the Fathers themselves used. General Knox, for example, wrote in disgust to Washington after the Shays Rebellion that Americans were, after all, "men—actual men possessing all the turbulent passions belonging to that animal." Throughout the secret discussions at the Constitutional Convention it was clear that this distrust of man was first and foremost a distrust of the common man and democratic rule. As the Revolution took away the restraining hand of the British government, old colonial grievances of farmers, debtors, and squatters against merchants, investors, and large landholders had flared up anew; the lower orders took advantage of new democratic constitutions in several states, and the possessing classes were frightened. The members of the Constitutional Convention were concerned to create a government that could not only regulate commerce and pay its debts but also prevent currency inflation and stay laws, and check such uprisings as the Shays Rebellion.

Cribbing and confining the popular spirit that had been at large since 1776 were essential to the purposes of the new Constitution. Edmund Randolph, saying to the Convention that the evils from which the country suffered originated in "the turbulence and follies of democracy," and that the great danger

* Chapter 1, *The American Political Tradition* (New York: Vintage Books, 1956). Reprinted by permission of Alfred A. Knopf, Inc. Copyright 1948 by Alfred A. Knopf, Inc.

lay in "the democratic parts of our constitutions"; Elbridge Gerry, speaking of democracy as "the worst of all political evils"; Roger Sherman, hoping that "the people . . . have as little to do as may be about the government"; William Livingston, saying that "the people have ever been and ever will be unfit to retain the exercise of power in their own hands"; George Washington, the presiding officer, urging the delegates not to produce a document of which they themselves could not approve simply in order to "please the people"; Hamilton, charging that the "turbulent and changing" masses "seldom judge or determine right" and advising a permanent governmental body to "check the imprudence of democracy"; the wealthy young planter Charles Pinckney, proposing that no one be president who was not worth at least one hundred thousand dollars— all these were quite representative of the spirit in which the problems of government were treated.

Democratic ideas are most likely to take root among discontented and oppressed classes, rising middle classes, or perhaps some sections of an old, alienated, and partially disinherited aristocracy, but they do not appeal to a privileged class that is still amplifying its privileges. With a half-dozen exceptions at the most, the men of the Philadelphia Convention were sons of men who had considerable position and wealth, and as a group they had advanced well beyond their fathers. Only one of them, William Few of Georgia, could be said in any sense to represent the yeoman farmer class which constituted the overwhelming majority of the free population. In the late eighteenth century "the better kind of people" found themselves set off from the mass by a hundred visible, tangible, and audible distinctions of dress, speech, manners, and education. There was a continuous lineage of upper-class contempt, from pre-Revolutionary Tories like Peggy Hutchinson, the Governor's daughter, who wrote one day: "The dirty mob

was all about me as I drove into town," to a Federalist like Hamilton, who candidly disdained the people. Mass unrest was often received in the spirit of young Gouverneur Morris: "The mob begin to think and reason. Poor reptiles! . . . They bask in the sun, and ere noon they will bite, depend upon it. The gentry begin to fear this." Nowhere in America or Europe—not even among the great liberated thinkers of the Enlightenment—did democratic ideas appear respectable to the cultivated classes. Whether the Fathers looked to the cynically illuminated intellectuals of contemporary Europe or to their own Christian heritage of the idea of original sin, they found quick confirmation of the notion that man is an unregenerate rebel who has to be controlled.

And yet there was another side to the picture. The Fathers were intellectual heirs of seventeenth-century English republicanism with its opposition to arbitrary rule and faith in popular sovereignty. If they feared the advance of democracy, they also had misgivings about turning to the extreme right. Having recently experienced a bitter revolutionary struggle with an external power beyond their control, they were in no mood to follow Hobbes to his conclusion that any kind of government must be accepted in order to avert the anarchy and terror of a state of nature. They were uneasily aware that both military dictatorship and a return to monarchy were being seriously discussed in some quarters—the former chiefly among unpaid and discontented army officers, the latter in rich and fashionable Northern circles. John Jay, familiar with sentiment among New York's mercantile aristocracy, wrote to Washington, June 27, 1786, that he feared that "the better kind of people (by which I mean the people who are orderly and industrious, who are content with their situations, and not uneasy in their circumstances) will be led, by the insecurity of property, the loss of confidence in their rulers, and the want of public faith and rectitude, to consider the charms of liberty as imaginary and delusive." Such men, he thought, might be prepared for "almost any change that may promise them quiet and security." Washington, who had already repudiated a suggestion that he become a military dictator, agreed, remarking that "we are apt to run from one extreme to the other."

Unwilling to turn their backs upon republicanism, the Fathers also wished to avoid violating the prejudices of the people. "Notwithstanding the oppression and injustice experienced among us from democracy," said George Mason, "the genius of the people is in favor of it, and the genius of the people must be consulted." Mason admitted "that we had been too democratic," but feared that "we should incautiously run into the opposite extreme." James Madison, who has quite rightfully been called the philosopher of the Constitution, told the delegates: "It seems indispensable that the mass of citizens should not be without a voice in making the laws which they are to obey, and in choosing the magistrates who are to administer them." James Wilson, the outstanding jurist of the age, later appointed to the Supreme Court by Washington, said again and again that the ultimate power of government must of necessity reside in the people. This the Fathers commonly accepted, for if government did not proceed from the people, from what other source could it legitimately come? To adopt any other premise not only would be inconsistent with everything they had said against British rule in the past but would open the gates to an extreme concentration of power in the future. Hamilton saw the sharp distinction in the Convention when he said that "the members most tenacious of republicanism were as loud as any in declaiming the vices of democracy." There was no better expression of the dilemma of a man who has no faith in the people but insists that government be based upon them than that of Jeremy Belknap, a New England clergyman, who wrote to a friend: "Let it stand as a principle that government originates from the people; but let the people be taught . . . that they are not able to govern themselves."

II

If the masses were turbulent and unregenerate, and yet if government must be founded upon their suffrage and consent, what could a Constitutionmaker do? One thing that the Fathers did not propose to do, because they thought it impossible, was to change the nature of man to conform with a more ideal system. They were inordinately confident that they knew what man always had been and what he always would be. The eighteenth-century mind had great faith in universals. Its method, as Carl Becker has said, was "to go up and down the field of history looking for man in general, the universal man, stripped of the accidents of time and place." Madison declared that the causes of political differences and of the formation of factions were "sown in the nature of man" and could never be eradicated. "It is universally acknowledged," David Hume had written, "that there is a great uniformity among the actions of men, in all nations and ages, and that human nature remains still the same, in its principles and operations. The same motives always produce the same actions. The same events always follow from the same causes."

Since man was an unchangeable creature of self-interest, it would not do to leave anything to his capacity for restraint. It was too much to expect that vice could be checked by virtue; the Fathers relied instead upon checking vice with vice. Madison once objected during the Convention that Gouverneur Morris was "forever inculcating the utter political depravity of men and the necessity of opposing one vice and interest to another vice and interest." And yet Madison himself in the *Federalist* number 51 later set forth an excellent statement of the same thesis:[1]

> Ambition must be made to counter-act ambition. . . . It may be a re-flection on human nature that such devices should be necessary to con-trol the abuses of government. But what is government itself, but the greatest of all reflections on human nature? If men were angels, no government would be necessary. . . . In framing a government which is to be administered by men over men, the great difficulty lies in this: you must first enable the government to control the governed; and in the next place oblige it to control itself.

Political economists of the laissez-faire school were saying that private vices could be public benefits, that an economically beneficent result would be providentially or "naturally" achieved if self-interest were left free from state interference and allowed to pursue its ends. But the Fathers were not so optimistic about politics. If, in a state that lacked constitutional balance, one class or one interest gained control, they believed, it would surely plunder all other interests. The Fathers, of course, were especially fearful that the poor would plunder the rich, but most of them would probably have admitted that the rich, unrestrained, would also plunder the poor. Even Gouverneur Morris, who stood as close to the ex-treme aristocratic position as candor and intelligence would allow, told the Convention: "Wealth tends to corrupt the mind and to nourish its love of power, and to stimulate it to oppression. History proves this to be the spirit of the opulent."

What the Fathers wanted was known

as "balanced government," an idea at least as old as Aristotle and Polybius. This ancient conception had won new sanction in the eighteenth century, which was dominated intellectually by the scientific work of Newton, and in which mechanical metaphors sprang as naturally to men's minds as did biologi-cal metaphors in the Darwinian atmos-phere of the late nineteenth century. Men had found a rational order in the universe and they hoped that it could be transferred to politics, or, as John Adams put it, that governments could be "erected on the simple principles of nature." Madison spoke in the most precise Newtonian language when he said that such a "natural" government must be so constructed "that its several constituent parts may, by their mutual relations, be the means of keeping each other in their proper places." A properly designed state, the Fathers believed, would check interest with interest, class with class, faction with faction, and one branch of government with another in a harmonious system of mutual frustra-tion.

In practical form, therefore, the quest of the Fathers reduced primarily to a search for constitutional devices that would force various interests to check and control one another. Among those who favored the federal Constitution three such devices were distinguished.

The first of these was the advantage of a federated government in maintain-ing order against popular uprisings or majority rule. In a single state a faction might arise and take complete control by force; but if the states were bound in a federation, the central government could step in and prevent it. Hamilton quoted Montesquieu: "Should a popu-lar insurrection happen in one of the confederate states, the others are able to quell it." Further, as Madison argued in the *Federalist* number 10, a majority would be the most dangerous of all factions that might arise, for the major-ity would be the most capable of gain-ing complete ascendancy. If the political society were very extensive, however,

---

[1] Cf. the words of Hamilton to the New York ratifying convention: "Men will pursue their interests. It is as easy to change human nature as to oppose the strong current of self-ish passions. A wise legislator will gently divert the channel, and direct it, if possible, to the public good."

and embraced a large number and variety of local interest, the citizens who shared a common majority interest "must be rendered by their number and local situation, unable to concert and carry into effect their schemes of oppression." The chief propertied interests would then be safer from "a rage for paper money, for an abolition of debts, for an equal division of property, or for any other improper or wicked project."

The second advantage of good constitutional government resided in the mechanism of representation itself. In a small direct democracy the unstable passions of the people would dominate lawmaking; but a representative government, as Madison said, would "refine and enlarge the public views by passing them through the medium of a chosen body of citizens." Representatives chosen by the people were wiser and more deliberate than the people themselves in mass assemblage. Hamilton frankly anticipated a kind of syndical paternalism in which the wealthy and dominant members of every trade or industry would represent the others in politics. Merchants, for example, were "the natural representatives" of their employees and of the mechanics and artisans they dealt with. Hamilton expected that Congress, "with too few exceptions to have any influence on the spirit of the government, will be composed of landholders, merchants, and men of the learned professions."

The third advantage of the government the Fathers were designing was pointed out most elaborately by John Adams in the first volume of his *Defence of the Constitutions of Government of the United States of America,* which reached Philadelphia while the Convention was in session and was cited with approval by several delegates.[2] Adams believed that the aristoc-

racy and the democracy must be made to neutralize each other. Each element should be given its own house of the legislature, and over both houses there should be set a capable, strong, and impartial executive armed with the veto power. This split assembly would contain within itself an organic check and would be capable of self-control under the governance of the executive. The whole system was to be capped by an independent judiciary. The inevitable tendency of the rich and the poor to plunder each other would be kept in hand.

III

It is ironical that the Constitution, which Americans venerate so deeply, is based upon a political theory that at one crucial point stands in direct antithesis to the main stream of American democratic faith. Modern American folklore assumes that democracy and liberty are all but identical, and when democratic writers take the trouble to make the distinction, they usually assume that democracy is necessary to liberty. But the Founding Fathers thought that the liberty with which they were most concerned was menaced by democracy. In their minds liberty was linked not to democracy but to property.

What did the Fathers mean by liberty? What did Jay mean when he spoke of "the charms of liberty"? Or Madison when he declared that to destroy liberty in order to destroy factions would be a remedy worse than the disease? Certainly the men who met at Philadelphia were not interested in extending liberty to those classes in America, the Negro slaves and the indentured servants, who were most in need of it, for slavery was recognized in the organic structure of the Constitution and indentured servitude was

---

[2] "Mr. Adams' book," wrote Benjamin Rush, often in the company of the delegates, "has diffused such excellent principles among us that there is little doubt of our adopting a vigorous and compounded Federal Legislature.

Our illustrious Minister in this gift to his country has done us more service than if he had obtained alliances for us with all the nations of Europe."

no concern of the Convention. Nor was the regard of the delegates for civil liberties any too tender. It was the opponents of the Constitution who were most active in demanding such vital liberties as freedom of religion, freedom of speech and press, jury trial, due process, and protection from "unreasonable searches and seizures." These guarantees had to be incorporated in the first ten amendments because the Convention neglected to put them in the original document. Turning to economic issues, it was not freedom of trade in the modern sense that the Fathers were striving for. Although they did not believe in impeding trade unnecessarily, they felt that failure to regulate it was one of the central weaknesses of the Articles of Confederation, and they stood closer to the mercantilists than to Adam Smith. Again, liberty to them did not mean free access to the nation's unappropriated wealth. At least fourteen of them were land speculators. They did not believe in the right of the squatter to occupy unused land, but rather in the right of the absentee owner or speculator to pre-empt it.

The liberties that the constitutionalists hoped to gain were chiefly negative. They wanted freedom from fiscal uncertainty and irregularities in the currency, from trade wars among the states, from economic discrimination by more powerful foreign governments, from attacks on the creditor class or on property, from popular insurrection. They aimed to create a government that would act as an honest broker among a variety of propertied interests, giving them all protection from their common enemies and preventing any one of them from becoming too powerful. The Convention was a fraternity of types of absentee ownership. All property should be permitted to have its proportionate voice in government. Individual property interests might have to be sacrificed at times, but only for the community of propertied interests. Freedom for property would result in liberty for men—perhaps not for all

men, but at least for all worthy men.[3] Because men have different faculties and abilities, the Fathers believed, they acquire different amounts of property. To protect property is only to protect men in the exercise of their natural faculties. Among the many liberties, therefore, freedom to hold and dispose property is paramount. Democracy, unchecked rule by the masses, is sure to bring arbitrary redistribution of property, destroying the very essence of liberty.

The Fathers' conception of democracy, shaped by their practical experience with the aggressive dirt farmers in the American states and the urban mobs of the Revolutionary period, was supplemented by their reading in history and political science. Fear of what Madison called "the superior force of an interested and overbearing majority" was the dominant emotion aroused by their study of historical examples. The chief examples of republics were among the city-states of antiquity, medieval Europe, and early modern times. Now, the history of these republics—a history, as Hamilton said, "of perpetual vibration between the extremes of tyranny and anarchy"—was alarming. Further, most of the men who had overthrown the liberties of republics had "begun

---

[3] The Fathers probably would have accepted the argument of the Declaration of Independence that "all men are created equal," but only as a legal, not as a political or psychological proposition. Jefferson himself believed in the existence of "natural aristocrats," but he thought they were likely to appear in any class of society. However, for those who interpreted the natural-rights philosophy more conservatively than he, the idea that all men are equal did not mean that uneducated dirt farmers or grimy-handed ship-calkers were in any sense the equals of the Schuylers, Washingtons, or Pinckneys. It meant only that British colonials had as much natural right to self-government as Britons at home, that the average American was the legal peer of the average Briton. Among the signers of the Constitution, it is worth noting, there were only six men who had also signed the Declaration of Independence.

their career by paying an obsequious court to the people; commencing demagogues and ending tyrants."

All the constitutional devices that the Fathers praised in their writings were attempts to guarantee the future of the United States against the "turbulent" political cycles of previous republics. By "democracy," they meant a system of government which directly expressed the will of the majority of the people, usually through such an assemblage of the people as was possible in the small area of the city-state.

A cardinal tenet in the faith of the men who made the Constitution was the belief that democracy can never be more than a transitional stage in government, that it always evolves into either a tyranny (the rule of the rich demagogue who has patronized the mob) or an aristocracy (the original leaders of the democratic elements). "Remember," wrote the dogmatic John Adams in one of his letters to John Taylor of Caroline, "democracy never lasts long. It soon wastes, exhausts, and murders itself. There never was a democracy yet that did not commit suicide." [4] Again:

If you give more than a share in the sovereignty to the democrats, that is, if you give them the command or preponderance in the . . . legislature, they will vote all property out of the hands of you aristocrats, and if they let you escape with your lives, it will be more humanity, consideration, and generosity than any triumphant democracy ever displayed since the creation. And what will follow? The aristocracy among the democrats will take your places, and treat their fellows as severely and sternly as you have treated them.

Government, thought the Fathers, is based on property. Men who have no property lack the necessary stake in an orderly society to make stable or reliable citizens. Dread of the propertyless masses of the towns was all but universal. George Washington, Gouverneur Morris, John Dickinson, and James Madison spoke of their anxieties about the urban working class that might arise some time in the future—"men without property and principle," as Dickinson described them—and even the democratic Jefferson shared this prejudice. Madison, stating the problem, came close to anticipating the modern threats to conservative republicanism from both communism and fascism:

In future times, a great majority of the people will not only be without landed but any other sort of property. These will either combine, under the influence of their common situation—in which case the rights of property and the public liberty will not be secure in their hands— or, what is more probable, they will become the tools of opulence and ambition, in which case there will be equal danger on another side.

What encouraged the Fathers about their own era, however, was the broad dispersion of landed property. The small land-owning farmers had been troublesome in recent years, but there was a general conviction that under a properly made Constitution a *modus vivendi* could be worked out with them. The possession of moderate plots of property presumably gave them a sufficient stake in society to be safe and responsible citizens under the restraints of balanced government. Influence in government would be proportionate to property: merchants and great landholders would be dominant, but small property-owners would have an independent and far from negligible voice. It was "politic as well as just,"

---

[4] Taylor labored to confute Adams, but in 1814, after many discouraging years in American politics, he conceded a great part of Adams's case: "All parties, however loyal to principles at first, degenerate into aristocracies of interest at last; and unless a nation is capable of discerning the point where integrity ends and fraud begins, popular parties are among the surest modes of introducing an aristocracy."

said Madison, "that the interests and rights of every class should be duly represented and understood in the public councils," and John Adams declared that there could be "no free government without a democratical branch in the constitution."

The farming element already satisfied the property requirements for suffrage in most of the states, and the Fathers generally had no quarrel with their enfranchisement. But when they spoke of the necessity of founding government upon the consent of "the people," it was only these small property-holders that they had in mind. For example, the famous Virginia Bill of Rights, written by George Mason, explicitly defined those eligible for suffrage as all men "having sufficient evidence of permanent common interest with and attachment to the community"—which meant, in brief, sufficient property.

However, the original intention of the Fathers to admit the yeoman into an important but sharply limited partnership in affairs of state could not be perfectly realized. At the time the Constitution was made, Southern planters and Northern merchants were setting their differences aside in order to meet common dangers—from radicals within and more powerful nations without. After the Constitution was adopted, conflict between the ruling classes broke out anew, especially after powerful planters were offended by the favoritism of Hamilton's policies to Northern commercial interests. The planters turned to the farmers to form an agrarian alliance, and for more than half a century this powerful coalition embraced the bulk of the articulate interests of the country. As time went on, therefore, the main stream of American political conviction deviated more and more from the antidemocratic position of the Constitution-makers. Yet, curiously, their general satisfaction with the Constitution together with their growing nationalism made Americans deeply reverent of the founding generation, with the result that as it grew stronger, this deviation was increasingly overlooked.

*   *   *

There is common agreement among modern critics that the debates over the Constitution were carried on at an intellectual level that is rare in politics, and that the Constitution itself is one of the world's masterpieces of practical statecraft. On other grounds there has been controversy. At the very beginning contemporary opponents of the Constitution foresaw an apocalyptic destruction of local government and popular institutions, while conservative Europeans of the old regime thought the young American Republic was a dangerous leftist experiment. Modern critical scholarship, which reached a high point in Charles A. Beard's *An Economic Interpretation of the Constitution of the United States,* started a new turn in the debate. The antagonism, long latent, between the philosophy of the Constitution and the philosophy of American democracy again came into the open. Professor Beard's work appeared in 1913 at the peak of the Progressive era, when the muckraking fever was still high; some readers tended to conclude from his findings that the Fathers were selfish reactionaries who do not deserve their high place in American esteem. Still more recently, other writers, inverting this logic, have used Beard's facts to praise the Fathers for their opposition to "democracy" and as an argument for returning again to the idea of a "republic."

In fact, the Fathers' image of themselves as moderate republicans standing between political extremes was quite accurate. They were impelled by class motives more than pietistic writers like to admit, but they were also controlled, as Professor Beard himself has recently emphasized, by a statesmanlike sense of moderation and unscrupulously republican philosophy. Any attempt, however, to tear their ideas out of the eighteenth-century context is sure to make them seem starkly reactionary. Consider, for example, the favorite maxim of John Jay: "The people who own the country ought to govern it." To the Fathers this was simply a swift axiomatic statement of the stake-in-society theory of political rights, a moderate conservative position under eighteenth-century conditions of property distribution in America. Under modern property relations this maxim demands a drastic restriction of the base of political power. A large portion of the modern middle class—and it is the strength of this class upon which balanced government depends—is propertyless; and the urban proletariat, which the Fathers so greatly feared, is almost one half the population. Further, the separation of ownership from control that has come with the corporation deprives Jay's maxim of twentieth-century meaning even for many propertied people. The six hundred thousand stockholders of the American Telephone & Telegraph Company not only do not acquire political power by virtue of their stock-ownership, but they do not even acquire economic power: they cannot control their own company.

From a humanistic standpoint there is a serious dilemma in the philosophy of the Fathers, which derives from their conception of man. They thought man was a creature of rapacious self-interest, and yet they wanted him to be free—free, in essence, to contend, to engage in an umpired strife, to use property to get property. They accepted the mercantile image of life as an eternal battleground, and assumed the Hobbesian war of each against all; they did not propose to put an end to this war, but merely to stabilize it and make it less murderous. They had no hope and they offered none for any ultimate organic change in the way men conduct themselves. The result was while they thought self-interest the most dangerous and unbrookable quality of man, they necessarily underwrote it in trying to control it. They succeeded in both respects: under the competitive capitalism of the nineteenth century America continued to be an arena for various grasping and contending interests, and the federal government continued to provide a stable and acceptable medium within which they could contend; further, it usually showed the wholesome bias on behalf of property which the Fathers expected. But no man who is as well abreast of modern science as the Fathers were of eighteenth-century science believes any longer in unchanging human nature. Modern humanistic thinkers who seek for a means by which society may transcend eternal conflict and rigid adherence to property rights as its integrating principles can expect no answer in the philosophy of balanced government as it was set down by the Constitution-makers of 1787.

4. The Founding Fathers: A Reform Caucus in Action*

JOHN P. ROCHE

OVER the last century and a half, the work of the Constitutional Conven-

* The American Political Science Review (March, 1962), pp. 799-816. Reprinted by permission.

tion and the motives of the Founding Fathers have been analyzed under a number of different ideological auspices. To one generation of historians, the hand of God was moving in the assembly; under a later dispensation, the dialectic (at various levels of philosophical sophistication) replaced the Deity: "relationships of production" moved into the niche previously reserved for Love of Country. Thus in counterpoint to the Zeitgeist, the Framers have undergone miraculous metamorphoses: at one time acclaimed as liberals and bold social engineers, today they appear in the guise of sound Burkean conservatives, men who in our time would subscribe to *Fortune,* look to Walter Lippmann for political theory, and chuckle patronizingly at the antics of Barry Goldwater. The implicit assumption is that if James Madison were among us, he would be President of the Ford Foundation, while Alexander Hamilton would chair the Committee for Economic Development.

The "Fathers" have thus been admitted to our best circles; the revolutionary ferocity which confiscated all Tory property in reach and populated New Brunswick with outlaws has been converted by the "Miltown School" of American historians into a benign dedication to "consensus" and "prescriptive rights." The Daughters of the American Revolution have, through the ministrations of Professors Boorstin, Hartz, and Rossiter, at last found ancestors worthy of their descendants. It is not my purpose here to argue that the "Fathers" were, in fact, radical revolutionaries; that proposition has been brilliantly demonstrated by Robert R. Palmer in his *Age of the Democratic Revolution.* My concern is with the further position that not only were they revolutionaries, but also they were democrats. Indeed, in my view, there is one fundamental truth about the Founding Fathers that *every* generation of Zeitgeisters has done its best to obscure: they were first and foremost superb democratic politicians. I suspect that in a contemporary setting, James Madison would be Speaker of the House of Representatives and Hamilton would be the *eminence grise* dominating (*pace* Theodore Sorenson

or Sherman Adams) the Executive Office of the President. They were, with their colleagues, *political men*— not metaphysicians, disembodied conservatives or Agents of History—and as recent research into the nature of American politics in the 1780s confirms,[1] they were committed (perhaps willy-nilly) to working within the democratic framework, within a universe of public approval. Charles Beard *and* the filiopietists to the contrary notwithstanding, the Philadelphia Convention was not a College of Cardinals or a council of Platonic guardians working within a manipulative, pre-democratic framework; it was a *nationalist* reform caucus which had to operate with great delicacy and skill in a political cosmos full of enemies to achieve the one definitive goal—popular approbation.

Perhaps the time has come, to borrow Walton Hamilton's fine phrase, to raise the Framers from immortality to mortality, to give them credit for their magnificent demonstration of the art of democratic politics. The point must be reemphasized; they *made* history and did it within the limits of consensus. There was nothing inevitable about the future in 1787; the *Zeitgeist,* that fine Hegelian technique of begging causal questions, could only be discerned in retrospect. What they did was to hammer out a pragmatic compromise which would both bolster the "National interest" and be acceptable

---

[1] The view that the right to vote in the states was severely circumscribed by property qualifications has been thoroughly discredited in recent years. See Chilton Williamson, *American Suffrage from Property to Democracy, 1760-1860* (Princeton, 1960). The contemporary position is that John Dickinson actually knew what he was talking about when he argued that there would be little opposition to vesting the right of suffrage in freeholders since "The great mass of our Citizens is composed at this time of freeholders, and will be pleased with it." Max Farrand, *Records of the Federal Convention,* Vol. 2, p. 202 (New Haven, 1911). (Henceforth cited as *Farrand.*)

to the people. What inspiration they got came from their collective experience as professional politicians in a democratic society. As John Dickinson put it to his fellow delegates on August 13, "Experience must be our guide. Reason may mislead us."

In this context, let us examine the problems they confronted and the solutions they evolved. The Convention has been described picturesquely as a counter-revolutionary junta and the Constitution as a *coup d'etat*,[2] but this has been accomplished by withdrawing the whole history of the movement for constitutional reform from its true context. No doubt the goals of the constitutional elite were "subversive" to the existing political order, but it is overlooked that their subversion could only have succeeded if the people of the United States endorsed it by regularized procedures. Indubitably they were "plotting" to establish a much stronger central government than existed under the Articles, but only in the sense in which one could argue equally well that John F. Kennedy was, from 1956 to 1960, "plotting" to become President. In short, on the fundamental *procedural* level, the Constitutionalists had to work according to the prevailing rules of the game. Whether they liked it or not is a topic for spiritualists—and is irrelevant: one may be quite certain that had Washington agreed to play the De Gaulle (as the Cincinnati once urged), Hamilton would willingly have held his horse, but such fertile speculation in no way alters the actual context in which events took place.

I

When the Constitutionalists went forth to subvert the Confederation, they utilized the mechanisms of political legitimacy. And the roadblocks which confronted them were formidable. At the same time, they were endowed with certain potent political assets. The history of the United States from 1786 to 1790 was largely one of a masterful employment of political expertise by the Constitutionalists as against bumbling, erratic behavior by the opponents of reform. Effectively, the Constitutionalists had to induce the states, by democratic techniques of coercion, to emasculate themselves. To be specific, if New York had refused to join the new Union, the project was doomed; yet before New York was safely in, the reluctant state legislature had *sua sponte* to take the following steps: (1) agree to send delegates to the Philadelphia Convention; (2) provide maintenance for these delegates (these were distinct stages: New Hampshire was early in naming delegates, but did not provide for their maintenance until July); (3) set up the special *ad hoc* convention to decide on ratification; and (4) concede to the decision of the *ad hoc* convention that New York should participate. New York admittedly was a tricky state, with a strong interest in a *status quo* which permitted her to exploit New Jersey and Connecticut, but the same legal hurdles existed in every state. And at the risk of becoming boring, it must be reiterated that the *only* weapon in the Constitutionalist arsenal was an effective mobilization of public opinion.

The group which undertook this struggle was an interesting amalgam of a few dedicated nationalists with the self-interested spokesmen of various parochial bailiwicks. The Georgians, for example, wanted a strong central authority to provide military protection

---

[2] The classic statement of the *coup d'etat* theory is, of course, Charles A. Beard, *An Economic Interpretation of the Constitution of the United States* (New York, 1913), and this theme was echoed by Vernon L. Parrington, Merrill Jensen and others in "populist" historiographical tradition. For a sharp critique of this thesis see Robert E. Brown, *Charles Beard and the Constitution* (Princeton, 1956). See also Forrest McDonald, *We the People* (Chicago, 1958); the trailblazing work in this genre was Douglas Adair, "The Tenth Federalist Revisited," *William and Mary Quarterly,* Third Series, Vol. VIII (1951), pp. 48-67.

for their huge, underpopulated state against the Creek Confederacy; Jerseymen and Connecticuters wanted to escape from economic bondage to New York; the Virginians hoped to establish a system which would give that great state its rightful place in the councils of the republic. The dominant figures in the politics of these states therefore cooperated in the call for the Convention.[3] In other states, the thrust towards national reform was taken up by opposition groups who added the "national interest" to their weapons system; in Pennsylvania, for instance, the group fighting to revise the Constitution of 1776 came out foursquare behind the Constitutionalists, and in New York, Hamilton and the Schuyler *ambiance* took the same tack against George Clinton. There was, of course, a large element of personality in the affair: there is reason to suspect that Patrick Henry's opposition to the Convention and the Constitution was founded on his conviction that Jefferson was behind both, and a close study of local politics elsewhere would surely reveal that others supported the Constitution for the simple (and politically quite sufficient) reason that the "wrong" people were against it.

To say this is not to suggest that the Constitution rested on a foundation of impure or base motives. It is rather to argue that in politics there are no immaculate conceptions, and that in the drive for a stronger general government, motives of all sorts played a part. Few men in the history of mankind have espoused a view of the "common good" or "public interest" that militated against their private status; even Plato with all his reverence for disembodied reason managed to put philosophers on

top of the pile. Thus it is not surprising that a number of diversified private interests joined to push the nationalist public interest; what would have been surprising was the absence of such a pragmatic united front. And the fact remains that, however motivated, these men did demonstrate a willingness to compromise their parochial interests in behalf of an ideal which took shape before their eyes and under their ministrations.

As Stanley Elkins and Eric McKitrick have suggested in a perceptive essay,[4] what distinguished the leaders of the Constitutionalist caucus from their enemies was a "Continental" approach to political, economic and military issues. To the extent that they shared an institutional base of operations, it was the Continental Congress (thirty-nine of the delegates to the Federal Convention had served in Congress), and this was hardly a locale which inspired respect for the state governments. Robert de Jouvenal observed French politics half a century ago and noted that a revolutionary Deputy had more in common with a non-revolutionary Deputy than he had with a revolutionary non-Deputy;[5] similarly one can surmise that membership in the Congress under the Articles of Confederation worked to establish a continental frame of reference, that a Congressman from Pennsylvania and one from South Carolina would share a universe of discourse which provided them with a conceptual common denominator *vis à vis* their respective state legislatures. This was particularly true with respect to external affairs: the average state legislator was probably about as concerned with foreign policy then as he is today, but Congressmen were constantly forced to take the broad view of American prestige, were compelled to listen to the re-

---

[3] A basic volume, which, like other works by Warren, provides evidence with which one can evaluate the author's own opinions, is Charles Warren, *The Making of the Constitution* (Boston, 1928). The best brief summary of the forces behind the movement for centralization is Chapter 1 of *Warren* (as it will be cited hereafter).

[4] Stanley Elkins and Eric McKitrick, "The Founding Fathers: Young Men of the Revolution," *Political Science Quarterly*, Vol. 76, p. 181 (1961).

[5] In *La Republique des Camarades* (Paris, 1914).

ports of Secretary John Jay and to the dispatches and pleas from their frustrated envoys in Britain, France and Spain. From considerations such as these, a "Continental" ideology developed which seems to have demanded a revision of our domestic institutions primarily on the ground that only by invigorating our general government could we assume our rightful place in the international arena. Indeed, an argument with great force—particularly since Washington was its incarnation —urged that our very survival in the Hobbesian jungle of world politics depended upon a reordering and strengthening of our national sovereignty.

Note that I am not endorsing the "Critical Period" thesis; on the contrary, Merrill Jensen seems to me quite sound in his view that for most Americans, engaged as they were in self-sustaining agriculture, the "Critical Period" was not particularly critical. In fact, the great achievement of the Constitutionalists was their ultimate success in convincing the elected representatives of a majority of the white male population that change was imperative. A small group of political leaders with a Continental vision and essentially a consciousness of the United States' *international* impotence, provided the matrix of the movement. To their standard other leaders rallied with their own parallel ambitions. Their great assets were (1) the presence in their caucus of the one authentic American "father figure," George Washington, whose prestige was enormous; (2) the energy and talent of their leadership (in which one must include the towering intellectuals of the time, John Adams and Thomas Jefferson, despite their absence abroad), and their communications "network," which was far superior to anything on the opposition side; (3) the preemptive skill which made "their" issue The Issue and kept the locally oriented opposition permanently on the defensive; and (4) the subjective consideration that these men were spokesmen of a new and com-

pelling credo: *American* nationalism, that ill-defined but nonetheless potent sense of collective purpose that emerged from the American Revolution.

Despite great institutional handicaps, the Constitutionalists managed in the mid-1780s to mount an offensive which gained momentum as years went by. Their greatest problem was lethargy, and paradoxically, the number of barriers in their path may have proved an advantage in the long run. Beginning with the initial battle to get the Constitutional Convention called and delegates appointed, they could never relax, never let up the pressure. In practical terms, this meant that the local "organizations" created by the Constitutionalists were perpetually in movement building up their cadres for the next fight. (The word organization has to be used with great caution: a political organization in the United States—as in contemporary England—generally consisted of a magnate and his following, or a coalition of magnates. This did not necessarily mean that it was "undemocratic" or "aristocratic," in the Aristotelian sense of the word: while a few magnates such as the Livingstons could draft their followings, most exercised their leadership without coercion on the basis of popular endorsement. The absence of organized opposition did not imply the impossibility of competition any more than low public participation in elections necessarily indicated an undemocratic suffrage.)

The Constitutionalists got the jump on the "opposition" (a collective noun: opposition*s* would be more correct) at the outset with the demand for a Convention. Their opponents were caught in an old political trap: they were not being asked to approve any specific program of reform, but only to endorse a meeting to discuss and recommend needed reforms. If they took a hard line at the first stage, they were put in the position of glorifying the *status quo* and of denying the need for *any* changes. Moreover, the Constitutionalists could go to the people with a persuasive argument for "fair play"— "How can you condemn reform before you know precisely what is involved?" Since the state legislatures obviously would have the final say on any proposals that might emerge from the Convention, the Constitutionalists were merely reasonable men asking for a chance. Besides, since they did not make any concrete proposals at that stage, they were in a position to capitalize on every sort of generalized discontent with the Confederation.

Perhaps because of their poor intelligence system, perhaps because of overconfidence generated by the failure of all previous efforts to alter the Articles, the opposition awoke too late to the dangers that confronted them in 1787. Not only did the Constitutionalists manage to get every state but Rhode Island (where politics was enlivened by a party system reminiscent of the "Blues" and the "Greens" in the Byzantine Empire) to appoint delegates to Philadelphia, but when the results were in, it appeared that they dominated the delegations. Given the apathy of the opposition, this was a natural phenomenon: in the ideologically nonpolarized political atmosphere those who get appointed to a special committee are likely to be the men who supported the movement for its creation. Even George Clinton, who seems to have been the first opposition leader to awake to the possibility of trouble, could not prevent the New York legislature from appointing Alexander Hamilton—though he did have the foresight to send two of his henchmen to dominate the delegation. Incidentally, much has been made of the fact that the delegates to Philadelphia were not elected by the people; some have adduced this fact as evidence of the "undemocratic" character of the gathering. But put in the context of the time, this argument is wholly specious: the central government under the Articles was considered a creature of the component states and in all the states but Rhode Island, Connecticut and New Hampshire, members of the national Congress were chosen by the state legislatures. This was not a consequence of elitism or fear of the mob; it was a logical extension of states'-rights doctrine to guarantee that the national institution did not end-run the state legislatures and make direct contact with the people.

II

With delegations safely named, the focus shifted to Philadelphia. While waiting for a quorum to assemble, James Madison got busy and drafted the so-called Randolph or Virginia Plan with the aid of the Virginia delegation. This was a political master-stroke. Its consequence was that once business got underway, the framework of discussion was established on Madison's terms. There was no interminable argument over agenda; instead the delegates took the Virginia Resolutions—"just for purposes of discussion"—as their point of departure. And along with Madison's proposals, many of which were buried in the course of the summer, went his major premise: a new start on a Constitution rather than piecemeal amendment. This was not necessarily revolutionary—a little exegesis could demonstrate that a new Constitution might be formulated as "amendments" to the Articles of Confederation—but Madison's proposal that this "lump sum" amendment go into effect after approval by nine states (the Articles required unanimous state approval for any amendment) was thoroughly subversive.

Standard treatments of the Convention divide the delegates into "nationalists" and "states'-righters" with various improvised shadings ("moderate nationalists," etc.), but these are *a posteriori* categories which obfuscate more than they clarify. What is striking to one who analyzes the Convention as a case-study in democratic politics is the lack of clear-cut ideological divisions in the Convention. Indeed, I submit that the evidence—Madison's *Notes*, the correspondence of the delegates, and debates on ratification—indicates that this was a remarkably homogeneous body on the ideological level. Yates and Lansing, Clinton's two chaperones for Hamilton, left in disgust on July 10. (Is there anything more tedious than sitting through endless disputes on matters one deems fundamentally misconceived? It takes an iron will to spend a hot summer as an ideological *agent provocateur*.) Luther Martin, Maryland's bibulous narcissist, left on September 4 in a huff when he discovered that others did not share his self-esteem; others went home for personal reasons. But the hard core of delegates accepted a grinding regimen throughout the attrition of a Philadelphia summer precisely because they shared the Constitutionalist goal.

Basic differences of opinion emerged, of course, but these were not ideological; they were *structural*. If the so-called "states'-rights" group had not accepted the fundamental purposes of the Convention, they could simply have pulled out and by doing so have aborted the whole enterprise. Instead of bolting, they returned day after day to argue and to compromise. An interesting symbol of this basic homogeneity was the initial agreement on secrecy: these professional politicians did not want to become prisoners of publicity; they wanted to retain that freedom of maneuver which is only possible when men are not forced to take public stands in the preliminary stages of negotiation. There was no legal means of binding the tongues of the delegates: at any stage in the game a delegate with basic principled objections to the emerging project could have taken the stump (as Luther Martin did after his exit) and denounced the convention to the skies. Yet Madison did not even inform Thomas Jefferson in Paris of the course of the deliberations and available correspondence indicates that the delegates generally observed the injunction. Secrecy is certainly uncharacteristic of any assembly marked by strong ideo-

logical polarization. This was noted at the time: the *New York Daily Advertiser,* August 14, 1787, commented that the ". . . profound secrecy hitherto observed by the Convention [we consider] a happy omen, as it demonstrates that the spirit of party on any great and essential point cannot have arisen to any height." [6]

Commentators on the Constitution who have read *The Federalist* in lieu of reading the actual debates have credited the Fathers with the invention of a sublime concept called "Federalism." Unfortunately *The Federalist* is probative evidence for only one proposition: that Hamilton and Madison were inspired propagandists with a genius for retrospective symmetry. Federalism, as the theory is generally defined, was an improvisation which was later promoted into a political theory. Experts on "federalism" should take to heart the advice of David Hume, who warned in his *Of the Rise and Progress of the Arts and Sciences* that ". . . there is no subject in which we must proceed with more caution than in [history], lest we assign causes which never existed and reduce what is merely contingent to stable and universal principles." In any event, the final balance in the Constitution between the states and the nation must have come as a great disappointment to Madison, while Hamilton's unitary views are too well known to need elucidation.

It is indeed astonishing how those who have glibly designated James Madison the "father" of Federalism have overlooked the solid body of fact which indicates that he shared Hamilton's quest for a unitary central government. To be specific, they have avoided examining the clear import of the Madison-Virginia Plan, and have disregarded Madison's dogged inch-by-inch retreat from the bastions of centralization. The Virginia Plan envisioned a unitary national government effectively freed from and dominant over the states. The

---

[6] Cited in *Warren*, p. 138.

lower house of the national legislature was to be elected directly by the people of the states with membership proportional to population. The upper house was to be selected by the lower and the two chambers would elect the executive and choose the judges. The national government would be thus cut completely loose from the states.

The structure of the general government was freed from state control in a truly radical fashion, but the scope of the authority of the national sovereign as Madison initially formulated it was breathtaking—it was a formulation worthy of the Sage of Malmesbury himself. The national legislature was to be empowered to disallow the acts of state legislatures,[7] and the central government was vested, in addition to the powers of the nation under the Articles of Confederation, with plenary authority wherever ". . . the separate States are incompetent or in which the harmony of the United States may be interrupted by the exercise of individual legislation."[8] Finally, just to lock the door against state intrusion, the national Congress was to be given the power to use military force on recalcitrant states.[9] This was Madison's "model" of an ideal national government, though it later received little publicity in *The Federalist*.

The interesting thing was the reaction of the Convention to this militant program for a strong autonomous central government. Some delegates were startled, some obviously leery of so comprehensive a project of reform, but nobody set off any fireworks and nobody walked out. Moreover, in the two weeks that followed, the Virginia Plan received substantial endorsement *en principe;* the initial temper of the gathering can be deduced from the approval "without debate or dissent," on May 31, of the Sixth Resolution which granted Congress the authority to dis-

allow state legislation ". . . contravening *in its opinion* the Articles of Union." Indeed, an amendment was included to bar states from contravening national treaties.[10]

The Virginia Plan may therefore be considered, in ideological terms, as the delegates' Utopia, but as the discussions continued and became more specific, many of those present began to have second thoughts. After all, they were not residents of Utopia or guardians in Plato's Republic who could simply impose a philosophical ideal on subordinate strata of the population. They were practical politicians in a democratic society, and no matter what their private dreams might be, they had to take home an acceptable package and defend it—and their own political futures— against predictable attack. On June 14 the breaking point between dream and reality took place. Apparently realizing that under the Virginia Plan, Massachusetts, Virginia and Pennsylvania could virtually dominate the national government—and probably appreciating that to sell this program to "the folks back home" would be impossible—the delegates from the small states dug in their heels and demanded time for a consideration of alternatives. One gets a graphic sense of the inner politics from John Dickinson's reproach to Madison: "You see the consequences of pushing things too far. Some of the members from the small States wish for two branches in the General Legislature and are friends to a good National Government; but we would sooner submit to a foreign power than . . . be deprived of an equality of suffrage in both branches of the Legislature, and thereby be thrown under the domination of the large States." [11]

The bare outline of the *Journal* entry for Tuesday, June 14, is suggestive to anyone with extensive experience in

---

[7] Resolution 6 gave the National Legislature this power subject to review by the Council of Revision proposed in Resolution 8.

[8] Resolution 6.

[9] *Ibid.*

[10] *Farrand*, I, 54. (Italics added.)

[11] *Ibid.*, p. 242. Delaware's delegates had been instructed by their general assembly to maintain in any new system the voting equality of the states. *Farrand*, III, 574.

deliberative bodies. "It was moved by Mr. Patterson [*sic*, Paterson's name was one of those consistently misspelled by Madison and everybody else] seconded by Mr. Randolph that the further consideration of the report from the Committee of the whole House [endorsing the Virginia Plan] be postponed til tomorrow, and before the question for postponement was taken. It was moved by Mr. Randolph seconded by Mr. Patterson that the House adjourn." [12] The House adjourned by obvious prearrangement of the two principals: since the preceding Saturday when Brearley and Paterson of New Jersey had announced their fundamental discontent with the representational features of the Virginia Plan, the informal pressure had certainly been building up to slow down the steamroller. Doubtless there were extended arguments at the Indian Queen between Madison and Paterson, the latter insisting that events were moving rapidly towards a probably disastrous conclusion, towards a political suicide pact. Now the process of accommodation was put into action smoothly—and wisely, given the character and strength of the doubters. Madison had the votes, but this was one of those situations where the enforcement of mechanical majoritarianism could easily have destroyed the objectives of the majority: the Constitutionalists were in quest of a qualitative as well as a quantitative consensus. This was hardly from deference to local Quaker custom; it was a political imperative if they were to attain ratification.

III

According to the standard script, at this point the "states'-rights" group intervened in force behind the New Jersey Plan, which has been characteristically portrayed as a reversion to the *status quo* under the Articles of Confederation with but minor modifications. A careful examination of the evidence indicates that only in a marginal sense is this an accurate description. It is true that the New Jersey Plan put the states back into the institutional picture, but one could argue that to do so was a recognition of political reality rather than an affirmation of states'-rights. A serious case can be made that the advocates of the New Jersey Plan, far from being ideological addicts of states'-rights, intended to substitute for the Virginia Plan a system which would both retain strong national power and have a chance of adoption in the states. The leading spokesman for the project asserted quite clearly that his views were based more on counsels of expediency than on principle; said Paterson on June 16: "I came here not to speak my own sentiments, but the sentiments of those who sent me. Our object is not such a Governmt. as may be best in itself, but such a one as our Constituents have authorized us to prepare, and as they will approve." [13] This is Madison's version; in Yates' transcription, there is a crucial sentence following the remarks above: "I believe that a little practical virtue is to be preferred to the finest theoretical principles, which cannot be carried into effect." [14] In his preliminary speech on June 9, Paterson had stated ". . . to the public mind we must accommodate ourselves," [15] and in his notes for this and his later effort as well, the emphasis is the same. The *structure* of government under the Articles should be retained:

2. Because it accords with the Sentiments of the People

    [Proof:] 1. Coms. [Commissions from state legislatures defining the jurisdiction of the delegates]

          2. News-papers — Political Barometer. Jersey never would have sent

---

[12] *Ibid.*, p. 240.

[13] *Ibid.*, p. 250.
[14] *Ibid.*, p. 258.
[15] *Ibid.*, p. 178.

Delegates under the first [Virginia] Plan—

Not here to sport Opinions of my own. Wt. [What] can be done. A little practicable Virtue preferrable to Theory.[16]

This was a defense of political acumen, not of states'-rights. In fact, Paterson's notes of his speech can easily be construed as an argument for attaining the substantive objectives of the Virginia Plan by a sound political route, *i.e.,* pouring the new wine in the old bottles. With a shrewd eye, Paterson queried:

Will the Operation and Force of the [central] Govt. depend upon the mode of Representn.—No—it will depend upon the Quantum of Power lodged in the leg. ex. and judy. Departments—Give [the existing] Congress the same Powers that you intend to give the two Branches, [under the Virginia Plan] and I apprehend they will act with as much Propriety and more Energy . . .[17]

In other words, the advocates of the New Jersey Plan concentrated their fire on what they held to be the *political liabilities* of the Virginia Plan—which were matters of institutional structure —rather than on the proposed scope of national authority. Indeed, the Supremacy Clause of the Constitution first saw the light of day in Paterson's Sixth Resolution; the New Jersey Plan contemplated the use of military force to secure compliance with national law; and finally Paterson made clear his view that under either the Virginia or the New Jersey systems, the general government would ". . . act on individuals and not on states." [18] From the states'-

rights viewpoint, this was heresy: the fundament of that doctrine was the proposition that any central government had as its constituents the states, not the people, and could only reach the people through the agency of the state government.

Paterson then reopened the agenda of the Convention, but he did so within a distinctly nationalist framework. Paterson's position was one of favoring a strong central government in principle, but opposing one which in fact *put the big states in the saddle.* (The Virginia Plan, for all its abstract merits, did very well by Virginia.) As evidence for this speculation, there is a curious and intriguing proposal among Paterson's preliminary drafts of the New Jersey Plan:

Whereas it is necessary in Order to form the People of the U.S. of America in to a Nation, that the States should be consolidated, by which means all the Citizens thereof will become equally intitled to and will equally participate in the same Privileges and Rights . . . it is therefore resolved, that all the Lands contained within the Limits of each state individually, and of the U.S. generally be considered as constituting one Body or Mass, and be divided into thirteen or more integral parts.

Resolved, That such Divisions or integral Parts shall be styled Districts.[19]

This makes it sound as though Paterson was prepared to accept a strong unified central government along the lines of the Virginia Plan if the existing states were eliminated. He may have gotten the idea from his New Jersey colleague Judge David Brearley, who on June 9 had commented that the only remedy to the dilemma over representation was ". . . that a map of the U.S. be spread out, that all the existing boundaries be erased, and that a new partition of the whole be made into 13

---

[16] *Ibid.,* p. 274.

[17] *Ibid.,* pp. 275-76.

[18] "But it is said that this national government is to act on individuals and not on states; and cannot a federal government be so framed as to operate in the same way? It surely may." *Ibid.,* pp. 182-83; also *ibid.* at p. 276.

[19] *Farrand,* III, 613.

equal parts." [20] According to Yates, Brearley added at this point, ". . . then a government on the present [Virginia Plan] system will be just." [21]

This proposition was never pushed— it was patently unrealistic—but one can appreciate its purpose: it would have separated the men from the boys in the large-state delegations. How attached would the Virginians have been to their reform principles if Virginia were to disappear as a component geographical unit (the largest) for representational purposes? Up to this point, the Virginians had been in the happy position of supporting high ideals with that inner confidence born of knowledge that the "public interest" they endorsed would nourish their private interest. Worse, they had shown little willingness to compromise. Now the delegates from the small states announced that they were unprepared to be offered up as sacrificial victims to a "national interest" which reflected Virginia's parochial ambition. Caustic Charles Pinckney was not far off when he remarked sardonically that ". . . the whole [conflict] comes to this": "Give N. Jersey an equal vote, and she will dismiss her scruples, and concur in the Natil. system." [22] What he rather unfairly did not add was that the Jersey delegates were not free agents who could adhere to their private convictions; they had to take back, sponsor and risk their reputations on the reforms approved by the Convention—and in New Jersey, not in Virginia.

Paterson spoke on Saturday, and one can surmise that over the weekend there was a good deal of consultation, argument, and caucusing among the delegates. One member at least prepared a full length address: on Monday Alexander Hamilton, previously mute, rose and delivered a six-hour oration. It was a remarkably apolitical speech; the gist of his position was that *both* the

Virginia and New Jersey Plans were inadequately centralist, and he detailed a reform program which was reminiscent of the Protectorate under the Cromwellian *Instrument of Government* of 1653. It has been suggested that Hamilton did this in the best political tradition to emphasize the moderate character of the Virginia Plan, to give the cautious delegates something *really* to worry about; but this interpretation seems somehow too clever. Particularly since the sentiments Hamilton expressed happened to be completely consistent with those he privately—and sometimes publicly—expressed throughout his life. He wanted, to take a striking phrase from a letter to George Washington, a "strong well mounted government" [23] in essence, the Hamilton Plan contemplated an elected life monarch, virtually free of public control, on the Hobbesian ground that only in this fashion could strength and stability be achieved. The other alternatives, he argued, would put policymaking at the mercy of the passions of the mob; only if the sovereign was beyond the reach of selfish influence would it be possible to have government in the interests of the whole community.

From all accounts, this was a masterful and compelling speech, but (aside from furnishing John Lansing and Luther Martin with ammunition for later use against the Constitution) it made little impact. Hamilton was simply transmitting on a different wave-length from the rest of the delegates; the latter adjourned after his great effort, admired his rhetoric, and then returned to business. It was rather as if they had taken a day off to attend the opera. Hamilton, never a particularly patient man or much of a negotiator, stayed for another ten days and then left, in considerable disgust, for New York. Although he came back to Philadelphia sporadically and attended the last two

---

[20] *Farrand*, I, 177.
[21] *Ibid.*, p. 182.
[22] *Ibid.*, p. 255.

[23] Hamilton to Washington, July 3, 1787, *Farrand*, III, 53.

weeks of the Convention, Hamilton played no part in the laborious task of hammering out the Constitution. His day came later when he led the New York Constitutionalists into the savage imbroglio over ratification—an arena in which his unmatched talent for dirty political infighting may well have won the day. For instance, in the New York Ratifying Convention, Lansing threw back into Hamilton's teeth the sentiments the latter had expressed in his June 18 [1788] oration in the Convention. However, having since retreated to the fine defensive positions immortalized in *The Federalist,* the Colonel flatly denied that he had ever been an enemy of the states, or had believed that conflict between states and nation was inexorable! As Madison's authoritative *Notes* did not appear until 1840, and there had been no press coverage, there was no way to verify his assertions, so in the words of the reporter, ". . . a warm personal altercation between [Lansing and Hamilton] engrossed the remainder of the day [June 28, 1788]." [24]

IV

On Tuesday morning, June 19, the vacation was over. James Madison led off with a long, carefully reasoned speech analyzing the New Jersey Plan which, while intellectually vigorous in its criticisms, was quite conciliatory in mood. "The great difficulty," he observed, "lies in the affair of Representation; and if this could be adjusted, all others would be surmountable." [25] (As events were to demonstrate, this diagnosis was correct.) When he finished, a vote was taken on whether to continue with the Virginia Plan as the nucleus for a new constitution: seven states voted "Yes"; New York, New Jersey, and Delaware voted "No"; and Maryland, whose position often depended on which delegates happened to be on the floor, divided. Paterson, it

seems, lost decisively; yet in a fundamental sense he and his allies had achieved their purpose: from that day onward, it could never be forgotten that the state governments loomed ominously in the background and that no verbal incantations could exorcise their power. Moreover, nobody bolted the convention: Paterson and his colleagues took their defeat in stride and set to work to modify the Virginia Plan, particularly with respect to its provisions on representation in the national legislature. Indeed, they won an immediate rhetorical bonus; when Oliver Ellsworth of Connecticut rose to move that the word "national" be expunged from the Third Virginia Resolution ("Resolved that a *national* Government ought to be established consisting of a *supreme* Legislative, Executive and Judiciary" [26]), Randolph agreed and the motion passed unanimously. The process of compromise had begun.

For the next two weeks, the delegates circled around the problem of legislative representation. The Connecticut delegation appears to have evolved a possible compromise quite early in the debates, but the Virginians and particularly Madison (unaware that he would later be acclaimed as the prophet of "federalism") fought obdurately against providing for equal representation of states in the second chamber. There was a good deal of acrimony and at one point Benjamin Franklin— of all people—proposed the institution of a daily prayer; practical politicians in the gathering, however, were meditating more on the merits of a good committee than on the utility of Divine intervention. On July 2, the ice began to break when through a number of fortuitous events[27]—and one that seems

[26] This formulation was voted into the Randolph Plan on May 30, 1787, by a vote of six states to none, with one divided. *Farrand,* I, 30.

[27] According to Luther Martin, he was alone on the floor and cast Maryland's vote for equality of representation. Shortly thereafter, Jenifer came on the floor and "Mr. King,

[24] *Farrand,* III, 338.
[25] *Farrand,* I, 321.

deliberate[28]—the majority against equality of representation was converted into a dead tie. The Convention had reached the stage where it was "ripe" for a solution (presumably all the therapeutic speeches had been made), and the South Carolinians proposed a committee. Madison and James Wilson wanted none of it, but with only Pennsylvania dissenting, the body voted to establish a working party on the problem of representation.

The members of this committee, one from each state, were elected by the delegates—and a very interesting committee it was. Despite the fact that the Virginia Plan had held majority support up to that date, neither Madison nor Randolph was selected (Mason was the Virginian) and Baldwin of Georgia, whose shift in position had resulted in the tie, was chosen. From the composition, it was clear that this was not to be a "fighting" committee: the emphasis in membership was on what might be described as "second-level political entrepreneurs." On the basis of the discussions up to that time, only Luther Martin of Maryland could be described as a "bitter-ender." Admittedly, some divination enters into this sort of analysis, but one does get a sense of the mood of the delegates from

these choices—including the interesting selection of Benjamin Franklin, despite his age and intellectual wobbliness, over the brilliant and incisive Wilson or the sharp, polemical Gouverneur Morris, to represent Pennsylvania. His passion for conciliation was more valuable at this juncture than Wilson's logical genius, or Morris' acerbic wit.

There is a common rumor that the Framers divided their time between philosophical discussions of government and reading the classics in political theory. Perhaps this is as good a time as any to note that their concerns were highly practical, that they spent little time canvassing abstractions. A number of them had some acquaintance with the history of political theory (probably gained from reading John Adams' monumental compilation *A Defense of the Constitutions of Government,* the first volume of which appeared in 1786), and it was a poor rhetorician indeed who could not cite Locke, Montesquieu, or Harrington *in support* of a desired goal. Yet up to this point in the deliberations, no one had expounded a defense of states'-rights or the "separation of powers" on anything resembling a theoretical basis. It should be reiterated that the Madison model had no room either for the states or for the "separation of powers": effectively *all* governmental power was vested in the national legislature. The merits of Montesquieu did not turn up until *The Federalist*; and although a perverse argument could be made that Madison's ideal was truly in the tradition of John Locke's *Second Treatise of Government,* the Locke whom the American rebels treated as an honorary president was a pluralistic defender of vested rights, not of parliamentary supremacy.

It would be tedious to continue a blow-by-blow analysis of the work of the delegates; the critical fight was over representation of the states and once the Connecticut Compromise was adopted on July 17, the Convention was over the hump. Madison, James Wilson, and Gouverneur Morris of New

---

from Massachusetts, valuing himself on Mr. Jenifer to divide the State of Maryland on this question . . . requested of the President that the question might be put again; however, the motion was too extraordinary in its nature to meet with success." Cited from "The Genuine Information, . . ." *Farrand,* III, 188.

[28] Namely Baldwin's vote *for* equality of representation which divided Georgia—with Few absent and Pierce in New York fighting a duel, Houston voted against equality and Baldwin shifted to tie the state. Baldwin was originally from Connecticut and attended and tutored at Yale, facts which have led to much speculation about the pressures the Connecticut delegation may have brought on him to save the day (Georgia was the last state to vote) and open the way to compromise. To employ a good Russian phrase, it was certainly not an accident that Baldwin voted the way he did. See *Warren,* p. 262.

York (who was there representing Pennsylvania!) fought the compromise all the way in a last-ditch effort to get a unitary state with parliamentary supremacy. But their allies deserted them and they demonstrated after their defeat the essentially opportunist character of their objections—using "opportunist" here in a non-pejorative sense, to indicate a willingness to swallow their objections and get on with the business. Moreover, once the compromise had carried (by five states to four, with one state divided), its advocates threw themselves vigorously into the job of strengthening the general government's substantive powers—as might have been predicted, indeed, from Paterson's early statements. It nourishes an increased respect for Madison's devotion to the art of politics, to realize that this dogged fighter could sit down six months later and prepare essays for *The Federalist* in contradiction to his basic convictions about the true course the Convention should have taken.

V

Two tricky issues will serve to illustrate the later process of accommodation. The first was the institutional position of the Executive. Madison argued for an executive chosen by the National Legislature and on May 29 this had been adopted with a provision that after his seven-year term was concluded, the chief magistrate should not be eligible for reelection. In late July this was reopened and for a week the matter was argued from several different points of view. A good deal of desultory speechmaking ensued, but the gist of the problem was the opposition from two sources to election by the legislature. One group felt that the states should have a hand in the process; another small but influential circle urged direct election by the people. There were a number of proposals: election by the the people, election by state governors, by electors chosen by state legislatures,

by the National Legislature (James Wilson, perhaps ironically, proposed at one point that an Electoral College be chosen by lot from the National Legislature!), and there was some resemblance to three-dimensional chess in the dispute because of the presence of two other variables, length of tenure and reeligibility. Finally, after opening, reopening, and re-reopening the debate, the thorny problem was consigned to a committee for resolution.

The Brearley Committee on Postponed Matters was a superb aggregation of talent and its compromise on the Executive was a masterpiece of political improvisation. (The Electoral College, its creation, however, had little in its favor as an *institution*—as the delegates well appreciated.) The point of departure for all discussion about the presidency in the Convention was that in immediate terms, the problem was non-existent; in other words, everybody present knew that under any system devised, George Washington would be President. Thus they were dealing in the future tense and to a body of working politicians the merits of the Brearley proposal were obvious: everybody got a piece of cake. (Or to put it more academically, each viewpoint could leave the Convention and argue to its constituents that it had *really* won the day.) First, the state legislatures had the right to determine the mode of selection of the electors; second, the small states received a bonus in the Electoral College in the form of a guaranteed minimum of three votes while the big states got acceptance of the principle of proportional power; third, if the state legislatures agreed (as six did in the first presidential election), the people could be involved directly in the choice of electors; and finally, if no candidate received a majority in the College, the right of decision passed to the National Legislature with each state exercising equal strength. (In the Brearley recommendation, the election went to the Senate, but a motion from the floor substituted the House; this was accepted on the ground that the Senate already had enough authority over the executive in its treaty and appointment powers.)

This compromise was almost too good to be true, and the Framers snapped it up with little debate or controversy. No one seemed to think well of the College as an *institution;* indeed, what evidence there is suggests that there was an assumption that once Washington had finished his tenure as President, the electors would cease to produce majorities and the chief executive would usually be chosen in the House. George Mason observed casually that the selection would be made in the House nineteen times in twenty and no one seriously disputed this point. The vital aspect of the Electoral College was that it got the Convention over the hurdle and protected everybody's interests. The future was left to cope with the problem of what to do with this Rube Goldberg mechanism.

In short, the Framers did not in their wisdom endow the United States with a College of Cardinals—the Electoral College was neither an exercise in applied Platonism nor an experiment in indirect government based on elitist distrust of the masses. It was merely a jerry-rigged improvisation which has subsequently been endowed with a high theoretical content. When an elector from Oklahoma in 1960 refused to cast his vote for Nixon (naming Byrd and Goldwater instead) on the ground that the Founding Fathers intended him to exercise his great independent wisdom, he was indulging in historical fantasy. If one were to indulge in counter-fantasy, he would be tempted to suggest that the Fathers would be startled to find the College still in operation—and perhaps even dismayed at their descendants' lack of judgment or inventiveness.

The second issue on which some substantial practical bargaining took place was slavery. The morality of slavery was, by design, not at issue; but in its other concrete aspects, slavery colored the arguments over taxation, commerce, and representation. The "Three-Fifths Compromise," that three-fifths of the slaves would be counted both for representation and for purposes of direct taxation (which was drawn from the past—it was a formula of Madison's utilized by Congress in 1783 to establish the basis of state contributions to the Confederation treasury) had allayed some Northern fears about Southern over-representation (no one then foresaw the trivial role that direct taxation would play in later federal financial policy), but doubts still remained. The Southerners, on the other hand, were afraid that Congressional control over commerce would lead to the exclusion of slaves or to their excessive taxation as imports. Moreover, the Southerners were disturbed over "navigation acts," *i.e.,* tariffs, or special legislation providing, for example, that exports be carried only in American ships; as a section depending upon exports, they wanted protection from the potential voracity of their commercial brethren of the Eastern states. To achieve this end, Mason and others urged that the Constitution include a proviso that navigation and commercial laws should require a two-thirds vote in Congress.

These problems came to a head in late August and, as usual, were handed to a committee in the hope that, in Gouverneur Morris' words, ". . . these things may form a bargain among the Northern and Southern states." [29] The Committee reported its measures of reconciliation on August 25, and on August 29 the package was wrapped up and delivered. What occurred can best be described in George Mason's dour version (he anticipated Calhoun in his conviction that permitting navigation acts to pass by majority vote would put the South in economic bondage to the North—it was mainly on this ground that he refused to sign the Constitution):

[29] *Farrand,* II, 374. Randolph echoed his sentiment in different words.

The Constitution as agreed to till a fortnight before the Convention rose was such a one as he would have set his hand and heart to. . . . [Until that time] The 3 New England States were constantly with us in all questions . . . so that it was these three States with the 5 Southern ones against Pennsylvania, Jersey and Delaware. With respect to the importation of slaves, [decision-making] was left to Congress. This disturbed the two Southernmost States who knew that Congress would immediately suppress the importation of slaves. Those two States therefore struck up a bargain with the three New England States. If they would join to admit slaves for some years, the two Southern-most States would join in changing the clause which required the $\frac{2}{3}$ of the Legislature in any vote [on navigation acts]. It was done.[30]

On the floor of the Convention there was a virtual love-feast on this happy occasion. Charles Pinckney of South Carolina attempted to overturn the committee's decision, when the compromise was reported to the Convention, by insisting that the South needed protection from the imperialism of the Northern states. But his Southern colleagues were not prepared to rock the boat and General C. C. Pinckney arose to spread oil on the suddenly ruffled waters; he admitted that:

It was in the true interest of the [Southern] States to have no regulation of commerce; but considering the loss brought on the commerce of the Eastern States by the Revolution, their liberal conduct towards the views of South Carolina [on the regulation of the slave trade] and the interests the weak Southn. States had in being united with the strong Eastern states, he thought it proper that no fetters should be imposed on

the power of making commercial regulations; *and that his constituents, though prejudiced against the Eastern States, would be reconciled to this liberality.* He had himself prejudices agst the Eastern States before he came here, but would acknowledge that he had found them as liberal and candid as any men whatever. (Italics added)[31]

Pierce Butler took the same tack, essentially arguing that he was not too happy about the possible consequences, but that a deal was a deal. Many Southern leaders were later—in the wake of the "Tariff of Abominations"—to rue this day of reconciliation; Calhoun's *Disquisition on Government* was little more than an extension of the argument in the Convention against permitting a congressional majority to enact navigation acts.

VI

Drawing on their vast collective political experience, utilizing every weapon in the politician's arsenal, looking constantly over their shoulders at their constituents, the delegates put together a Constitution. It was a makeshift affair; some sticky issues (for example, the qualification of voters) they ducked entirely; others they mastered with that ancient instrument of political sagacity, studied ambiguity (for example, citizenship), and some they just overlooked. In this last category, I suspect, fell the matter of the power of the federal courts to determine the constitutionality of acts of Congress. When the judicial article was formulated (Article III of the Constitution), deliberations were still in the stage where the legislature was endowed with broad power under the Randolph formulation, authority which by its own terms was scarcely amenable to judicial review. In essence, courts could hardly determine when ". . . the separate States are incompetent or . . . the harmony of the United States may be inter-

[30] Mason to Jefferson, cited in *Warren*, p. 584.

[31] August 29, 1787, *Farrand*, II, 449-50.

rupted"; the National Legislature, as critics pointed out, was free to define its own jurisdiction. Later the definition of legislative authority was changed into the form we know, a series of stipulated powers, *but the delegates never seriously reexamined the jurisdiction of the judiciary under this new limited formulation.*[32] All arguments on the intention of the Framers in this matter are thus deductive and *a posteriori,* though some obviously make more sense than others.[33]

The Framers were busy and distinguished men, anxious to get back to their families, their positions, and their constituents, not members of the French Academy devoting a lifetime to a dictionary. They were trying to do an important job, and do it in such a fashion that their handiwork would be acceptable to very diverse constituencies. No one was rhapsodic about the final document, but it was a beginning, a

[32] The Committee on Detail altered the general grant of legislative power envisioned by the Virginia Plan into a series of specific grants; these were examined closely between August 16 and August 23. One day only was devoted to the Judicial Article, August 27, and since no one raised the question of judicial review of *Federal* statutes, no light was cast on the matter. A number of random comments on the power of the judiciary were scattered throughout the discussions, but there was another variable which deprives them of much probative value: the proposed Council of Revision which would have joined the Executive with the judges in *legislative* review. Madison and Wilson, for example, favored this technique—which had nothing in common with what we think of as judicial review except that judges were involved in the task.

[33] For what it may be worth, I think that judicial review of congressional acts was logically on all fours with review of state enactments and that it was certainly consistent with the view that the Constitution could not be amended by the Congress and President, or by a two-thirds vote of Congress (overriding a veto), without the agreement of three-quarters of the states. *External* evidence from that time supports this view, see Charles Warren, *Congress, the Constitution, and the Supreme Court* (Boston, 1925), pp. 41-128, but the debates *in* the Convention prove nothing.

move in the right direction, and one they had reason to believe the people would endorse. In addition, since they had modified the impossible amendment provisions of the Articles (the requirement of unanimity which could always be frustrated by "Rogues Island") to one demanding approval by only three-quarters of the states, they seemed confident that gaps in the fabric which experience would reveal could be rewoven without undue difficulty.

So with a neat phrase introduced by Benjamin Franklin (but devised by Gouverneur Morris) which made their decision sound unanimous, and an inspired benediction by the Old Doctor urging doubters to doubt their own infallibility, the Constitution was accepted and signed. Curiously, Edmund Randolph, who had played so vital a role throughout, refused to sign, as did his fellow Virginian George Mason and Elbridge Gerry of Massachusetts. Randolph's behavior was eccentric, to say the least—his excuses for refusing his signature have a factitious ring even at this late date; the best explanation seems to be that he was afraid that the Constitution would prove to be a liability in Virginia politics, where Patrick Henry was burning up the countryside with impassioned denunciations. Presumably, Randolph wanted to check the temper of the populace before he risked his reputation, and perhaps his job, in a fight with both Henry and Richard Henry Lee. Events lend some justification to this speculation: after much temporizing and use of the conditional subjunctive tense, Randolph endorsed ratification in Virginia and ended up getting the best of both worlds.

Madison, despite his reservations about the Constitution, was the campaign manager in ratification. His first task was to get the Congress in New York to light its own funeral pyre by approving the "amendments" to the Articles and sending them on to the state legislatures. Above all, momentum had to be maintained. The anti-

Constitutionalists, now thoroughly alarmed and no novices in politics, realized that their best tactic was attrition rather than direct opposition. Thus they settled on a position expressing qualified approval but calling for a second Convention to remedy various defects (the one with the most demagogic appeal was the lack of a Bill of Rights). Madison knew that to accede to this demand would be equivalent to losing the battle, nor would he agree to conditional approval (despite wavering even by Hamilton). This was an all-or-nothing proposition: national salvation or national impotence with no intermediate positions possible. Unable to get congressional approval, he settled for second best: a unanimous resolution of Congress transmitting the Constitution to the states for whatever action they saw fit to take. The opponents then moved from New York and the Congress, where they had attempted to attach amendments and conditions, to the states for the final battle.

At first the campaign for ratification went beautifully: within eight months after the delegates set their names to the document, eight states had ratified. Only in Massachusetts had the result been close (187-168). Theoretically, a ratification by one more state convention would set the new government in motion, but in fact until Virginia and New York acceded to the new Union, the latter was a fiction. New Hampshire was the next to ratify; Rhode Island was involved in its characteristic political convulsions (the Legislature there sent the Constitution out to the towns for decision by popular vote and it got lost among a series of local issues); North Carolina's convention did not meet until July and then postponed a final decision. This is hardly the place for an extensive analysis of the conventions of New York and Virginia. Suffice it to say that the Constitutionalists clearly outmaneuvered their opponents, forced them into impossible political positions, and won both states narrowly. The Virginia

Convention could serve as a classic study in effective floor management: Patrick Henry had to be contained, and a reading of the debates discloses a standard two-stage technique. Henry would give a four- or five-hour speech denouncing some section of the Constitution on every conceivable ground (the federal district, he averred at one point, would become a haven for convicts escaping from state authority!);[34] when Henry subsided, "Mr. Lee of Westmoreland" would rise and literally poleaxe him with sardonic invective (when Henry complained about the militia power, "Lighthorse Harry" really punched below the belt: observing that while the former Governor had been sitting in Richmond during the Revolution, *he* had been out in the trenches with the troops and thus felt better qualified to discuss military affairs). Then the gentlemanly Constitutionalists (Madison, Pendleton and Marshall) would pick up the matters at issue and examine them in the light of reason.

Indeed, modern Americans who tend to think of James Madison as a rather desiccated character should spend some time with this transcript. Probably Madison put on his most spectacular demonstration of nimble rhetoric in what might be called "The Battle of the Absent Authorities." Patrick Henry in the course of one of his harangues alleged that Jefferson was known to be opposed to Virginia's approving the Constitution. This was clever: Henry hated Jefferson, but was prepared to use any weapon that came to hand. Madison's riposte was superb: First, he said that with all due respect to the great reputation of Jefferson, he was not in the country and therefore could not formulate an adequate judgment; second, no one should utilize the reputation of an outsider—the Virginia Convention was there to think for itself; third, if there were to be recourse to

[34] See *Elliot's Debates on the Federal Constitution* (Washington, 1836), Vol. 3, pp. 436-438.

outsiders, the opinions of George Washington should certainly be taken into consideration; and finally, he knew from privileged personal communications from Jefferson that in fact the latter *strongly favored* the Constitution.[35] To devise an assault route into this rhetorical fortress was literally impossible.

VII

The fight was over; all that remained now was to establish the new frame of government in the spirit of its framers. And who were better qualified for this task than the Framers themselves? Thus victory for the Constitution meant simultaneous victory for the Constitutionalists; the anti-Constitutionalists either capitulated or vanished into limbo—soon Patrick Henry would be offered a seat on the Supreme Court and Luther Martin would be known as the Federalist "bull-dog." And irony of ironies, Alexander Hamilton and James Madison would shortly accumulate a reputation as the formulators of what is often alleged to be our political theory, the concept of "federalism." Also, on the other side of the ledger, the arguments would soon appear over what the Framers "really meant"; while these disputes have assumed the proportions of a big scholarly business in the last century, they began almost before the ink on the Constitution was dry. One of the best early ones featured Hamilton versus Madison on the scope of presidential power, and other Framers characteristically assumed positions in this and other disputes on the basis of their political convictions.

Probably our greatest difficulty is that we know so much more about what the Framers *should have meant* than they themselves did. We are intimately acquainted with the problems that their Constitution should have been designed to master; in short, we have read the mystery story backwards. If we are to get the right "feel" for their time and their circumstances, we

[35] *Ibid.*, p. 329.

must in Maitland's phrase, ". . . think ourselves back into a twilight." Obviously, no one can pretend completely to escape from the solipsistic web of his own environment, but if the effort is made, it is possible to appreciate the past roughly on its own terms. The first step in this process is to abandon the academic premise that because we can ask a question, there must be an answer.

Thus we can ask what the Framers meant when they gave Congress the power to regulate interstate and foreign commerce, and we emerge, reluctantly perhaps, with the reply that (Professor Crosskey to the contrary notwithstanding)[36] they may not have known what

[36] Crosskey in his sprawling *Politics and the Constitution* (Chicago, 1953), 2 vols., has developed with almost unbelievable zeal and intricacy the thesis that the Constitution *was* designed to establish a centralized unitary state, but that the political leadership of the Republic in its formative years betrayed this ideal and sold the pass to states'-rights. While he has unearthed some interesting newspaper articles and other material, it is impossible for me to accept his central proposition. Madison and the other delegates, with the exceptions discussed in the text *supra*, did *want* to diminish the power of the states and create a vigorous national government. But they were not fools, and were, I submit, under no illusions when they departed from Philadelphia that this end had been accomplished. The crux of my argument is that *political realities* forced them to water down their objectives and they settled, like the good politicians they were, for half a loaf. The basic difficulty with Crosskey's thesis is that he knows *too* much—he assumes that the Framers had a perfectly clear idea of the road they were taking; with a semantic machete he cuts blandly through all the confusion on the floor of the meeting to the *real* meanings. Thus, despite all his ornate research apparatus, there is a fundamentally nonempirical quality about Crosskey's work: at crucial points in the argument he falls back on a type of divination which can only be described as Kabbalistic. He may be right, for example, in stating (without any proof) that Richard Henry Lee did *not* write the "Letters from a Federal Farmer," but in this country spectral evidence has not been admissible since the Seventeenth Century.

they meant, that there may not have been any semantic consensus. The Convention was not a seminar in analytic philosophy or linguistic analysis. Commerce was *commerce*—and if different interpretations of the word arose, later generations could worry about the problem of definition. The delegates were in a hurry to get a new government established; when definitional arguments arose, they characteristically took refuge in ambiguity. If different men voted for the same proposition for varying reasons, that was politics (and still is); if later generations were unsettled by this lack of precision, that would be their problem.

There was a good deal of definitional pluralism with respect to the problems the delegates did discuss, but when we move to the question of extrapolated intentions, we enter the realm of spiritualism. When men in our time, for instance, launch into elaborate talmudic exegesis to demonstrate that federal aid to parochial schools is (or is not) in accord with the intentions of the men who established the Republic and endorsed the Bill of Rights, they are engaging in historical Extra-Sensory Perception. (If one were to join this E. S. P. contingent for a minute, he might suggest that the hard-boiled politicians who wrote the Constitution and Bill of Rights would chuckle scornfully at such an invocation of authority: obviously a politician would chart his course on the intentions of the living, not of the dead, and count the number of Catholics in his constituency.)

The Constitution, then, was not an apotheosis of "constitutionalism," a triumph of architectonic genius; it was a patch-work sewn together under the pressure of both time and events by a group of extremely talented democratic politicians. They refused to attempt the establishment of a strong, centralized sovereignty on the principle of legislative supremacy for the excellent reason that the people would not accept it. They risked their political fortunes by opposing the established doctrines

of state sovereignty because they were convinced that the existing system was leading to national impotence and probably foreign domination. For two years, they worked to get a convention established. For over three months, in what must have seemed to the faithful participants an endless process of give-and-take, they reasoned, cajoled, threatened, and bargained amongst themselves. The result was a Constitution which the people, in fact, by democratic processes, did accept, and a new and far better national government was established.

Beginning with the inspired propaganda of Hamilton, Madison and Jay, the ideological build-up got under way. *The Federalist* had little impact on the ratification of the Constitution, except perhaps in New York, but this volume had enormous influence on the image of the Constitution in the minds of future generations, particularly on historians and political scientists who have an innate fondness for theoretical symmetry. Yet, while the shades of Locke and Montesquieu *may* have been hovering in the background, and the delegates *may* have been unconscious instruments of a transcendent *telos,* the careful observer of the day-to-day work of the Convention finds no over-arching principles. The "separation of powers" to him seems to be a by-product of suspicion, and "federalism" he views as a *pis aller,* as the farthest point the delegates felt they could go in the destruction of state power without themselves inviting repudiation.

To conclude, the Constitution was neither a victory for abstract theory nor a great practical success. Well over half a million men had to die on the battlefields of the Civil War before certain constitutional principles could be defined—a baleful consideration which is somehow overlooked in our customary tributes to the farsighted genius of the Framers and to the supposed American talent for "constitutionalism." The Constitution was, however, a vivid demonstration of effective democratic political action, and of the forging of a national elite which literally persuaded its countrymen to hoist themselves by their own boot straps. American pro-consuls would be wise not to translate the Constitution into Japanese, or Swahili, or treat it as a work of semi-Divine origin; but when students of comparative politics examine the process of nation-building in countries newly freed from colonial rule, they may find the American experience instructive as a classic example of the potentialities of a democratic elite.

5. The Constitution: An Economic Document*

CHARLES A. BEARD

At the close of this long and arid survey—partaking of the nature of catalogue—it seems worth while to bring together the important conclusions for political science which the data presented appear to warrant.

The movement for the Constitution of the United States was originated and carried through principally by four groups of personalty interests which had been adversely affected under the Articles of Confederation: money, public securities, manufactures, and trade and shipping.

The first firm steps toward the formation of the Constitution were taken by a small and active group of men immediately interested through their personal possessions in the outcome of their labors.

No popular vote was taken directly or indirectly on the proposition to call the Convention which drafted the Constitution.

A large propertyless mass was, under the prevailing suffrage qualifications, excluded at the outset from participation (through representatives) in the work of framing the Constitution.

* An Economic Interpretation of the Constitution (New York: The Macmillan Co., 1961), pp. 324-325. Reprinted by permission of The Macmillan Company. Copyright 1913 by The Macmillan Company. Renewed 1941 by Charles A. Beard.

The members of the Philadelphia Convention which drafted the Constitution were, with a few exceptions, immediately, directly, and personally interested in, and derived economic advantages from, the establishment of the new system.

The Constitution was essentially an economic document based upon the concept that the fundamental private rights of property are anterior to government and morally beyond the reach of popular majorities.

The major portion of the members of the Convention are on record as recognizing the claim of property to a special and defensive position in the Constitution.

In the ratification of the Constitution, about three-fourths of the adult males failed to vote on the question, having abstained from the elections at which delegates to the state conventions were chosen, either on account of their indifference or their disfranchisement by property qualifications.

The Constitution was ratified by a vote of probably not more than one-sixth of the adult males.

It is questionable whether a majority of the voters participating in the elections for the state conventions in New York, Massachusetts, New Hampshire, Virginia, and South Carolina, actually approved the ratification of the Constitution.

The leaders who supported the Constitution in the ratifying conventions represented the same economic groups as the members of the Philadelphia Convention; and in a large number of instances they were also directly and personally interested in the outcome of their efforts.

In the ratification, it became manifest that the line of cleavage for and against the Constitution was between substantial personalty interests on the one hand and the small farming and debtor interests on the other.

The Constitution was not created by "the whole people" as the jurists have said; neither was it created by "the states" as Southern nullifiers long contended; but it was the work of a consolidated group whose interests knew no state boundaries and were truly national in their scope.

6. The Constitution: A Democratic Document*

ROBERT E. BROWN

At the end of Chapter XI Beard summarized his findings in fourteen paragraphs under the heading of "Conclusions" (pp. 324-25). Actually, these fourteen conclusions merely add up to the two halves of the Beard thesis. One half, that the Constitution originated with and was carried through by personalty interests—money, public securities, manufactures, and commerce—is to be found in paragraphs two, three, six, seven, eight, twelve, thirteen, and fourteen. The other half—that the Constitution was put over undemocratically in an undemocratic society—is expressed in paragraphs four, five, nine, ten, eleven, and fourteen. The lumping of these conclusions under two general headings makes it easier for the reader to see the broad outlines of the Beard thesis.

Before we examine these two major divisions of the thesis, however, some comment is relevant on the implications contained in the first paragraph.

* Charles Beard and the Constitution (Princeton: Princeton University Press, 1956), pp. 194-200. Reprinted by permission of the Princeton University Press. Copyright 1956 by the Princeton University Press.

In it Beard characterized his book as a long and arid survey, something in the nature of a catalogue. Whether this characterization was designed to give his book the appearance of a coldly objective study based on the facts we do not know. If so, nothing could be further from reality. As reviewers pointed out in 1913, and as subsequent developments have demonstrated, the book is anything but an arid catalogue of facts. Its pages are replete with interpretation, sometimes stated, sometimes implied. Our task has been to examine Beard's evidence to see whether it justifies the interpretation which Beard gave it. We have tried to discover whether he used the historical method properly in arriving at his thesis.

If historical method means the gathering of data from primary sources, the critical evaluation of the evidence thus gathered, and the drawing of conclusions consistent with this evidence, then we must conclude that Beard has done great violation to such method in this book. He admitted that the evidence had not been collected which, given the proper use of historical method, should have precluded the writing of the book.

Yet he nevertheless proceeded on the assumption that a valid interpretation could be built on secondary writings whose authors had likewise failed to collect the evidence. If we accept Beard's own maxim, "no evidence, no history," and his own admission that the data had never been collected, the answer to whether he used historical method properly is self-evident.

Neither was Beard critical of the evidence which he did use. He was accused in 1913, and one might still suspect him, of using only that evidence which appeared to support his thesis. The amount of realty in the country compared with the personalty, the vote in New York, and the omission of the part of *The Federalist* No. 10 which did not fit his thesis are only a few examples of the uncritical use of evidence to be found in the book. Sometimes he accepted secondary accounts at face value without checking them with the sources; at other times he allowed unfounded rumors and traditions to color his work.

Finally, the conclusions which he drew were not justified even by the kind of evidence which he used. If we accepted his evidence strictly at face value, it would still not add up to the fact that the Constitution was put over undemocratically in an undemocratic society by personalty. The citing of property qualifications does not prove that a mass of men were disfranchised. And if we accept his figures on property holdings, either we do not know what most of the delegates had in realty and personalty, or we know that realty outnumbered personalty three to one (eighteen to six). Simply showing that a man held public securities is not sufficient to prove that he acted only in terms of his public securities. If we ignore Beard's own generalizations and accept only his evidence, we would have to conclude that most of the property in the country in 1787 was real estate, that real property was widely distributed in rural areas, which included most of the country, and that

even the men who were directly concerned with the Constitution, and especially Washington, were large holders of realty.

Perhaps we can never be completely objective in history, but certainly we can be more objective than Beard was in this book. Naturally the historian must always be aware of the biases, the subjectivity, the pitfalls that confront him, but this does not mean that he should not make an effort to overcome these obstacles. Whether Beard had his thesis before he had his evidence, as some have said, is a question that each reader must answer for himself. Certain it is that the evidence does not justify the thesis.

So instead of the Beard interpretation that the Constitution was put over undemocratically in an undemocratic society by personal property, the following fourteen paragraphs are offered as a possible interpretation of the Constitution and as suggestions for future research on that document.

1. The movement for the Constitution was originated and carried through by men who had long been important in both economic and political affairs in their respective states. Some of them owned personalty, more of them owned realty, and if their property was adversely affected by conditions under the Articles of Confederation, so also was the property of the bulk of the people in the country, middle-class farmers as well as town artisans.

2. The movement for the Constitution, like most important movements, was undoubtedly started by a small group of men. They were probably interested personally in the outcome of their labors, but the benefits which they expected were not confined to personal property or, for that matter, strictly to things economic. And if their own interests would be enhanced by a new government, similar interests of other men, whether agricultural or commercial, would also be enhanced.

3. Naturally there was no popular vote on the calling of the convention

which drafted the Constitution. Election of delegates by state legislatures was the constitutional method under the Articles of Confederation, and had been the method long established in this country. Delegates to the Albany Congress, the Stamp Act Congress, the First Continental Congress, the Second Continental Congress, and subsequent congresses under the Articles were all elected by state legislatures, not by the people. Even the Articles of Confederation had been sanctioned by state legislatures, not by popular vote. This is not to say that the Constitutional Convention should not have been elected directly by the people, but only that such a procedure would have been unusual at the time. Some of the opponents of the Constitution later stressed, without avail, the fact that the Convention had not been directly elected. But at the time the Convention met, the people in general seemed to be about as much concerned over the fact that they had not elected the delegates as the people of this country are now concerned over the fact that they do not elect our delegates to the United Nations.

4. Present evidence seems to indicate that there were no "propertyless masses" who were excluded from the suffrage at the time. Most men were middle-class farmers who owned realty and were qualified voters, and, as the men in the Convention said, mechanics had always voted in the cities. Until credible evidence proves otherwise, we can assume that state legislatures were fairly representative at the time. We cannot condone the fact that a few men were probably disfranchised by prevailing property qualifications, but it makes a great deal of difference to an interpretation of the Constitution whether the disfranchised comprised ninety-five per cent of the adult men or only five per cent. Figures which give percentages of voters in terms of the entire population are misleading, since less than twenty per cent of the people were adult men. And finally, the voting qualifications favored realty, not personalty.

5. If the members of the Convention were directly interested in the outcome of their work and expected to derive benefits from the establishment of the new system, so also did most of the people of the country. We have many statements to the effect that the people in general expected substantial benefits from the labors of the Convention.

6. The Constitution was not just an economic document, although economic factors were undoubtedly important. Since most of the people were middle-class and had private property, practically everybody was interested in the protection of property. A constitution which did not protect property would have been rejected without any question, for the American people had fought the Revolution for the preservation of life, liberty, and property. Many people believed that the Constitution did not go far enough to protect property, and they wrote these views into the amendments to the Constitution. But property was not the only concern of those who wrote and ratified the Constitution, and we would be doing a grave injustice to the political sagacity of the Founding Fathers if we assumed that property or personal gain was their only motive.

7. Naturally the delegates recognized that the protection of property was important under government, but they also recognized that personal rights were equally important. In fact, persons and property were usually bracketed together as the chief objects of government protection.

8. If three-fourths of the adult males failed to vote on the election of delegates to ratifying conventions, this fact signified indifference, not disfranchisement. We must not confuse those who could *not* vote with those who *could* vote but failed to exercise their right. Many men at the time bewailed the fact that only a small portion of the voters ever exercised their prerogative. But this in itself should stand as evi-

dence that the conflict over the Constitution was not very bitter, for if these people had felt strongly one way or the other, more of them would have voted.

Even if we deny the evidence which I have presented and insist that American society was undemocratic in 1787, we must still accept the fact that the men who wrote the Constitution believed that they were writing it for a democratic society. They did not hide behind an iron curtain of secrecy and devise the kind of conservative government that they wanted without regard to the views and interests of "the people." More than anything else, they were aware that "the people" would have to ratify what they proposed, and that therefore any government which would be acceptable to the people must of necessity incorporate much of what was customary at the time. The men at Philadelphia were practical politicians, not political theorists. They recognized the multitude of different ideas and interests that had to be reconciled and compromised before a constitution would be acceptable. They were far too practical, and represented far too many clashing interests themselves, to fashion a government weighted in favor of personalty or to believe that the people would adopt such a government.

9. If the Constitution was ratified by a vote of only one-sixth of the adult men, that again demonstrates indifference and not disfranchisement. Of the one-fourth of the adult males who voted, nearly two-thirds favored the Constitution. Present evidence does not permit us to say what the popular vote was except as it was measured by the votes of the ratifying conventions.

10. Until we know what the popular vote was, we cannot say that it is questionable whether a majority of the voters in several states favored the Constitution. Too many delegates were sent uninstructed. Neither can we count the towns which did not send delegates on the side of those opposed to the Constitution. Both items would signify indifference rather than sharp conflict over ratification.

11. The ratifying conventions were elected for the specific purpose of adopting or rejecting the Constitution. The people in general had anywhere from several weeks to several months to decide the question. If they did not like the new government, or if they did not know whether they liked it, they could have voted *no* and there would have been no Constitution. Naturally the leaders in the ratifying conventions represented the same interests as the members of the Constitutional Convention—mainly realty and some personalty. But they also represented their constituents in these same interests, especially realty.

12. If the conflict over ratification had been between substantial personalty interests on the one hand and small farmers and debtors on the other, there would not have been a constitution. The small farmers comprised such an overwhelming percentage of the voters that they could have rejected the new government without any trouble. Farmers and debtors are not synonymous terms and should not be confused as such. A town-by-town or county-by-county record of the vote would show clearly how the farmers voted.

13. The Constitution was created about as much by the whole people as any government could be which embraced a large area and depended on representation rather than on direct participation. It was also created in part by the states, for as the *Records* show, there was strong state sentiment at the time which had to be appeased by compromise. And it was created by compromising a whole host of interests throughout the country, without which compromises it could never have been adopted.

14. If the intellectual historians are correct, we cannot explain the Constitution without considering the psychological factors also. Men are motivated by what they believe as well as by what they have. Sometimes their actions can

be explained on the basis of what they hope to have or hope that their children will have. Madison understood this fact when he said that the universal hope of acquiring property tended to dispose people to look favorably upon property. It is even possible that some men support a given economic system when they themselves have nothing to gain by it. So we would want to know what the people in 1787 thought of their class status. Did workers and small farmers believe that they were lower-class, or did they, as many workers do now, consider themselves middle-class? Were the common people trying to eliminate the Washingtons, Adamses, Hamiltons, and Pinckneys, or were they trying to join them?

As did Beard's fourteen conclusions, these fourteen suggestions really add up to two major propositions: the Constitution was adopted in a society which was fundamentally democratic, not undemocratic; and it was adopted by a people who were primarily middle-class property owners, especially farmers who owned realty, not just by the owners of personalty. At present these points seem to be justified by the evidence, but if better evidence in the future disproves or modifies them, we must accept that evidence and change our interpretation accordingly.

After this critical analysis, we should at least not begin future research on this period of American history with the illusion that the Beard thesis of the Constitution is valid. If historians insist on accepting the Beard thesis in spite of this analysis, however, they must do so with the full knowledge that their acceptance is founded on "an act of faith," not an analysis of historical method, and that they are indulging in a "noble dream," not history.

Chapter II

THE BASIC CLASH:
LIBERALISM VS. CONSERVATISM

Introduction

THE two most frequently used labels in contemporary American political debates are "liberal" and "conservative." When these labels are used in ordinary discourse, the clear implication is that they characterize institutions or individuals who hold divergent opinions on substantive issues of public policy. When we say, for example, that former Senator Goldwater is a conservative and Vice-President Humphrey is a liberal, we are, at a minimum, saying that there is a wide difference in the views of these two men on important, or basic, political questions. By the same token, when we label *National Review* as a conservative journal of opinion and *The New Republic* and *Nation* as liberal, we are saying that there is a marked difference in the stands taken by these journals on many, if not most, issues of public policy.

This much seems clear enough: We assert merely that, as the two terms are commonly used, they signify a difference of viewpoint. The "hard" questions are: What is the basis for the differences we discern between liberals and conservatives? What is it that really divides liberals from conservatives? Put still another way, What are the characteristics and beliefs common to those whom, on the one hand, we call liberals, and, on the other, conservatives? While we readily grasp that liberals and conservatives differ and that they are, in fact, engaged in "warfare" of sorts in contemporary America, it is not so easy to say why the "war" is taking place.

There are great difficulties that stand in the way of our answering these questions quickly or easily. But let us work our way into the matter by briefly examining a few of the answers that have been most frequently advanced.

1. There are those who hold that the major distinguishing difference between liberals and conservatives is party affiliation, i.e., that liberals are for the most part Democrats, and conservatives Republicans. Yet a moment's reflection will reveal the questionability of this view of the matter. Democratic senators Byrd, Lausche, Russell, and Eastland, to mention just a few, are commonly labeled conservatives; on the other hand, Republican Senators Javits, Case, and Kuchel can vie with the Senators Kennedy in their public devotion to liberalism. We can

also note that the so-called "conservative coalition," which often votes against, and defeats, some of the President's legislative program, contains a high percentage of Democrats.

2. The commonest explanation of the liberal-conservative split runs in terms of their respective attitudes toward "change." Clinton Rossiter, for example, notes several important connotations of the word "conservatism," and speaks finally of four types of conservative: "temperamental," "possessive," "practical," and "philosophical." The "temperamental conservative" is opposed to "any substantial change in his manner of life, work, and enjoyment"; the "possessive conservative" resists change because he has "something substantial" such as "status, power, reputation," which he wants to defend "against the erosion of change"; the "practical conservative" is one who feels that his society is "worth defending against reform and revolution"; and finally, the "philosophical conservative" is one who "subscribes consciously to principles designed to justify the established order and guard against careless tinkering and determined reform."

Thus Rossiter tells us that the difference between liberals and conservatives is, for one reason or another, resistant to change. The liberal, by contrast, takes "a balanced view of social progress" and is "optimistic, rather than pessimistic, about the possibilities of reform." [1]

There are, however, serious difficulties here. If, for example, we look to the contemporary American political scene and, in particular, to those who claim and are generally acknowledged to be conservatives and liberals, we can readily see that the issue of change is not in itself sufficient to explain why the battle between them is taking place. The objection to Rossiter's explanation can be easily seen in the following terms: suppose there were 100 Barry Goldwaters in the Senate, 435 in the House, nine on the Supreme Court, and one in the White House. Would we, under these circumstances, see much in the way of changes? If we are to take former Senator Goldwater at his word, there would be substantial and drastic alterations in the status quo, and they would be made rather rapidly. We could expect them in any number of areas: federal-state relations, welfare spending, farm policies, taxation policy, and, among others, labor policy. Again, even a cursory reading of *National Review* would serve to confirm the belief that it is not simply change that is the issue at stake in the liberal-conservative controversies. Here, too, we would find pleas for changing the face of contemporary reality by adopting radically new policies.

---

[1] For Clinton Rossiter's statement see Chapter One of his *Conservatism in America* (New York: Vintage Books, 1962).

In fact, it is safe to say that among those who call themselves conservatives and are acknowledged in most quarters to be genuine conservatives, there is a high degree of discontent with "things as they are."

It might be objected that the changes sought by modern American conservatives are "reactionary" in nature: that is, the changes sought would take us back in time to conditions as they existed before, say, the "revolution" of Roosevelt's New Deal. To some extent, the objection is valid; but there is a wide range of issues, associated with the internal and external menace of communism, on which the conservatives find themselves in substantial disagreement with the liberals but on which the conservative position can hardly be called "reactionary" in any normal sense of this word. With respect to these issues, the conservative would be *more* inclined than the liberal to push for an extremely stringent internal security program for government employees, although the "tradition" he extols made no room for any such measures, *more* inclined to act "tough" toward the Russians, though only the day before yesterday, so to speak, he was an isolationist; and *less* inclined to believe that the foreign aid program, surely a part now of the *status quo,* should be continued as a means of combating communism. Here, then, are three conservative positions, all of them involving sharp changes in existing policy but not "reactionary" in the sense that they constitute an attempt to retreat into the past.

3. Still others suggest that the issue that separates liberals from conservatives is the Communist threat itself, and the question of how best to meet it. The liberals, on this showing, are those who favor a "containment" policy and, along with it, coexistence and compromise. The conservatives, by contrast, are said to advocate a "hard line" policy: liberation rather than containment, use of military force rather than negotiation. Thus, for some, the basic difference between liberals and conservatives is simply that between the "soft" line (liberals) and the "hard" line (conservatives).

Again, however, if we were to apply this formulation of the liberal-conservative "battle" to the "real world," we would end up with some bizarre findings. Senator Douglas, an acknowledged and even outstanding liberal by almost anyone's standard, would have to be numbered among the conservatives. Similarly, Senator Dodd, whose voting record on domestic issues rates well-nigh 100% with the liberal Americans for Democratic Action, would, because of his outspoken "hard"-line anti-communism have to be ranked very high among conservatives.

We are not denying that the Communist issue is *one* issue that serves to divide liberals-in-general from conservatives-in-general. But, clearly, it is not *the* issue.

4. Another school of thought holds that conservatives believe in "minimal" government, particularly in the economic sphere.[2] The conservatives, this school holds, are those who advocate a free enterprise system—free, that is, from governmental control and regulation. Or again, to go a little further, the conservatives are those who believe in "rugged individualism"—in allowing the capable, strong, and industrious to seek their economic fulfillment without state interference, even should that prove a little hard on the feckless, the weak, and the lazy. Pictured at the other extreme from this position are the liberals, who want relatively stringent control over the economy, and welfare measures to help the less fortunate and underprivileged.

Two observations should be made about this view of the matter: (a) it can, at best, only be a partial explanation for the differences between liberals and conservatives, for, as we shall see shortly, liberals and conservatives divide over numerous issues that are not economic in character at all. A complete explanation of the conflicts between liberals and conservatives would of necessity have, then, to be broader in scope than the one we have in hand. (b) The straight "free enterprise" or "free market" position is not, in fact, shared by any means by all conservatives; for some, at least, it is too "doctrinaire." For some conservatives, indeed, it is the quest for social justice that is paramount, and while they no doubt place great value on the preservation and advancement of the free enterprise system, their overriding concern is to adjust and control the economic system so as to give every member of the community his fair (though not equal) "shake." In any case, many acknowledged conservatives shy away from a position which, *tout court,* would minimize governmental control over the economic activities of the society.

5. Another formulation runs in the following terms: The conservatives "strive to conserve" that which is the "Christian understanding of the nature and destiny of man." In this vein, a leading conservative figure writes: "The conservative believes ours is a God-centered universe; that man's purpose is to shape his life to the pattern of order proceeding from the Divine Center of life."[3]

This school, in short, stresses the alleged *religious* foundations of conservatism. While it cannot be denied that contemporary conserva-

[2] Ayn Rand and her followers are the chief contemporary exponents of this school of thought.
[3] See the symposium, "Do-It-Yourself Conservatism," *National Review,* Vol. XII, January 30, 1962, pp. 57-59.

tism does include many persons who would acquiesce in this view, it is equally true that there are many liberals who believe in a "God-centered universe" and, conversely, that many individuals who feel "at home" among conservatives are either agnostics or atheists.

The foregoing points up some of the difficulties involved in identifying the basis of the disagreement between liberals and conservatives. That there are difficulties is acknowledged by Clinton Rossiter, who writes:

> One need not spend more than an hour with the literature of the revival to realize that few words are quite so variable in color and content. The failure of Americans to agree on the meaning of 'conservatism' has distorted opinion and cramped discussion of some of the most pressing issues of our time. Small wonder that several leading political theorists have proposed that *conservatism,* along with its partner-in-confusion *liberalism,* be sold for scrap.[4]

Nor are political theorists the only persons on the horizon who urge the abandonment of our two terms. Said former President Eisenhower not long ago in a television interview: "We should discard such shopworn terms as 'liberal' and 'conservative'. . . . I have never yet found anyone who could convincingly explain his own definition of these political classifications."

Our brief survey of current theses regarding the dividing-line between conservatives and liberals at least, however, enables us to identify certain requirements that an adequate explanation would have to meet. First, an adequate explanation must not be too narrow: that is, it must not focus on one single issue or set of issues as *the* bone of contention between liberals and conservatives. It must, that is to say, be capable of explaining the split in terms of a wide range of issues, both domestic and international. Second, in order to be relevant to contemporary American political debates, an adequate explanation must be concerned with actual issues—issues that do, in fact and visibly, divide liberals and conservatives *at present.* Third, a satisfactory formulation cannot be so arbitrary as to exclude, from either "side," persons who are notoriously in the "thick" of the liberal-conservative political battle. We shall surely misunderstand the nature of the ongoing set-to between liberals and conservatives in contemporary America if our attempt to formulate it is cast in terms of a struggle so remote from the politics we know as that between those who believe in a "God-centered universe" and those who do not.

[4] Rossiter, *op. cit.,* p. 5.

In order to grasp the reasons for the dividing-line between liberals and conservatives, it will perhaps be useful to take a sampling of the issues that have produced actual conflict, actual exchanges of blows, between them and see whether we can decide what principles or beliefs seem to have been at stake. Among such issues, both past and present, we could safely list, on the domestic side, at least the following: medicare, federal aid to education, immigration policy, public housing, public versus private power, social security, unemployment compensation, and a wide variety of social welfare proposals, many of them involving grant-in-aid programs to the states.

There is, on each of these issues, a relatively distinct liberal and conservative position. The liberal certainly favors federal aid to education, public power, steep progressive taxation, medical care for the aged, unemployment compensation, and, in general, those measures we can fairly label "welfarist" in tendency. The conservative, on the other hand, certainly resists the expansion of existing social welfare programs and vigorously opposes the launching of new ones. He can be counted on, for example, to fight against proposals to extend social security to groups not now covered by it, to seek to reduce the financial burden placed upon upper-income groups through progressive taxation, and to resist any further growth of public power.

The inescapable question remains, Why? Why do the liberals take their stand on one side with reference to these issues, and the conservatives on the other? The answer, we hold, is to be found by seeking out the common denominator of the liberal positions, i.e., the principles or beliefs common to all of them. And that common denominator, we hold, emerges clearly when we recognize that each of the liberal positions we have noted tends in the direction of *equality*. For example, the intended effect of any large scale federal-aid program is to reduce differences in quality between schools in different parts of the country. The "gap" or inequality that exists, say, between the suburban high schools of Chicago, San Francisco, or New York and those of rural Alabama, Mississippi, or Georgia will—certainly according to the supporters of federal aid—be narrowed by the projected massive grants to the states. Or take progressive taxation. It has long been recognized that one of the most effective ways of redistributing wealth with an end to producing a substantial degree of economic equality among citizens is through a progressive taxation plan, which takes a substantial proportion of the income of higher economic groups. Similarly with programs such as medical care for the aged, social security, public housing, unemployment compensation—all of them tend to close an allegedly unjustified gap, to lessen the degree of allegedly fortuitous inequality, between those groups that are "covered" by these programs and those that clearly do not need to be covered by them. The net effect of these programs, then, would be to produce a greater equality of conditions (medical service, housing, income, etc.) among our citizens.

There is another, though corollary, principle that separates liberals from conservatives. Given the liberal objective, namely, the reduction of inequalities among the citizens in the areas mentioned above, the liberals logically seek to accomplish this objective through that agency of government that exercises the most sweeping jurisdiction, i.e., the national government. To do otherwise, that is, to seek to accomplish liberal purposes through the state and local governments would not only be very costly (so, at least, the liberals contend) but also would probably run us up against a refusal, on the part of at least some states or localities, to move in the desired directions at all. The result of working through states and/or localities would probably be a "patch work" pattern, with, on the one extreme, some localities adopting the liberal measures in question completely, to, at the other extreme, those who would say "Nothing doing!" And that pattern would still involve conditions of egregious inequality among the citizens: for example, older residents of Oklahoma might be living without the benefits of a medicare program, while those in New York would be fully covered. Consequently, alike for the sake of economy and for that of uniform achievement of liberal goals ("if a thing is worth doing, it is worth doing *thoroughly*"), the liberal tends to pin his hopes on the national government.

By contrast the conservative, for a variety of reasons, would prefer to see many of these programs handled at the local or state level.[5] He argues that turning to the federal government in these and related areas means "big government," that the local community best knows its own needs, and that the programs actually required (as, he thinks, many liberal programs are not) will be devised and administered at their best at the local level, or even through voluntary (that is, non-governmental) effort. For reasons that will have become apparent even in this brief discussion, the conservative also knows that he can best resist liberal programs, and their extension, through the diffusion of decision-making authority.

The liberal goal in America is, then, to effectuate greater and greater

---

[5] For an exposition of this view see Senator Barry Goldwater's *Conscience of a Conservative* (Shepardsville, Kentucky: Victor Publishing Co., March 1960).

equality among the citizens, principally through the agencies of the national government. And the question logically arises at this point, What degree of equality do the liberals actually want? How far are they prepared to go with their "egalitarian" measures? It would seem that the liberal does stop well short of advocating absolue equality, or identity of condition, among the citizens; yet, it is difficult to find out exactly where, short of complete equality, his stopping point is going to be. We frequently hear that he will wish to go no further once we have a "basic" or "minimal" standard of living for all citizens. Clearly, however, this form of words raises about as many questions as it answers as to what the correct "basic" standard would be, since "our" views change from one generation and even from one place to another. There is, then, so far as one can learn, no reasonably definite stopping point for liberal egalitarianism, and for the moment all one can say is: the liberals do back policies that serve to advance the goal of equality. More: the liberal strives mightily to "push" such issues into our political debates.

The current agitation about the racial problem illustrates vividly the liberals' preoccupation with greater equality. They have sought legislation requiring fair employment practices, ending discrimination against Negroes in both private and public housing, and, perhaps most importantly in terms of contemporary debate, requiring integration of the public schools. The conservatives are, for the most part, resisters; even when they do not openly oppose the liberal programs in question they "drag their feet" though the grounds or basis they allege for doing so vary from case to case. Sometimes the conservatives, short of openly challenging liberal goals—integration and Negro voting rights are examples here—insist that the problem or problems be handled at the state or local level; the "ends" question (integration, enfranchisement of Negroes) should, they insist, be subordinated to the preservation and cultivation of local community responsibility. Thus William Buckley longs for the day "when the Negroes have finally realized their long dream of attaining to the status of the white man. . . ." [6] But he is careful to add:

> A conservative is seldom disposed to use the federal government as the sword of social justice, for the sword is generally two-edged ('The Government can only do something for the people in proportion as it can do something to the people,' Jefferson said). If it is doubtful just what enduring benefits the Southern Negro would

[6] *Rumbles Left and Right* (New York: G. P. Putnam's Sons, 1963), p. 127.

receive from the intervention of government on the scale needed to, say, integrate the schools in South Carolina, it is less doubtful what the consequences of interposition would be to the ideal of local government and the sense of community, ideals which I am not ready to abandon, not even to kill Jim Crow.[7]

The liberal goal of greater equality is not, we must now notice, confined to the field of "social welfare"—that is, to equality as regards the material conditions in which people live. On the question of how political decisions are made, an equally urgent question, the liberal seems to have a strong commitment to such principles as one-man-one-vote and majority rule. In appraising our governmental institutions and practices, therefore, the liberal is quick to point out any and all departures from these interrelated principles. His motto has been and still is "every man's preference is to have an equal impact on public policy." He has long protested against the "malapportionment" of state legislatures; the latter, in his view, has permitted a minority of rural folk to control state policies. He, over the years, denounced the "gerrymandering" of congressional districts as no less objectionable than the exclusion of certain groups from the suffrage. Finally, he has taken vigorous exception to the seniority rule and the filibuster; these, he claims, frequently permit a mere, even an insignificant, minority to control Congress. Moreover, the liberal believes that the majority ought to be able to rule *directly*, that is, without any intermediate institutions to translate or "refine" its "will." Thus he tends to favor steps that would transform the American political system into a *plebiscitary* system, under which the "will" of the majority would make itself felt immediately, that is, without delay, directly, that is, without its being sifted through representatives, and faithfully, that is, without distortion. Not surprisingly, therefore, he has always favored the initiative, which allows for popular initiation of legislation; the referendum, by which the people can accept or reject laws passed by the legislature; and the recall, which allows for the removal of elected officials whose voting or performance deviates markedly from what the majority, in the interelection period, may decide it wants.

The equality goal and its implementation, then, do explain satisfactorily the differences between liberals and the conservatives on a wide range of *domestic issues*. The question arises, however, whether it can also explain their differences on foreign policy, especially on the issue: how best to combat the internal and external threat of com-

[7] *Ibid.*, p. 128.

munism. We believe the explanation we have offered to be equally satisfactory here, though with this warning: certain considerations, which we are about to review, must be constantly kept in mind through any discussion of the point now before us (i.e., how equality relates to the entire communist problem), namely: Both liberals and conservatives are anti-communist. Both groups deplore the slave-labor camps, the numberless atrocities committed in the name of Soviet power, and the U.S.S.R.'s aggressive actions on the international scene. The liberal-conservative clash in this area, though substantial, has to do almost entirely with the question of how to combat communism most effectively. James Burnham, on the conservative side, urges upon us a policy of "liberation," which might well involve the use of military force in the achievement of our goals. Arthur Schlesinger, Jr., in reviewing Burnham's book, *Containment or Liberation?*, argues that Burnham's proposals would probably lead us into war with the Soviet Union. Schlesinger goes on to argue that the choice available to us is that "between the attempt to save the captive peoples by peaceful pressures—a policy to which the country has been committed since 1945—and the certainty of destroying them and perhaps the rest of us, through war." [8] We see vividly that the difference of opinion, which we believe to divide the two camps as well as the two writers we cite, is for the most part one about *means*.[9] The conservative demands a policy based upon greater use of might and force, while the liberal advocates "peaceful pressures." So much for our preliminary considerations.

With those considerations before us, the relation between the conservative "tough line" on communism on the one hand, and the equality issue on the other, is easy to grasp. The communist movement, at least in theory, represents for the conservative the worst of all possible worlds. The movement, for him, embodies the equality principle worked out in its most extreme form in the most minute details, and in a single theoretical package. The conservative thinks that we are really up against the grave possibility that, with the backing of Soviet military power, communist doctrinaires may, within the foreseeable future, achieve domination of the world, and use that domination precisely for the purpose of destroying those *inequalities,* inherited mostly from the past, that the conservative deems to be the essence of a decent society—hence the "tougher" conservative response to the communist threat, both internally and externally.

[8] "Middle-aged Man with a Horn," *New Republic,* Vol. 9, March 16, 1953, p. 17.
[9] It should be emphasized again that this is a crucial point.

The absence of a similarly "tough" response from the liberals toward communism is not a matter for wonder, according at least to some conservatives. The liberals, they say, possess no corpus of theoretical goals that conflict basically with those of the communists.[10] Moreover, the conservatives add, there are yet other considerations that stay the hands of the liberals, particularly with respect to internal communism. The liberals, more than the conservatives, are committed to premises that dispose them to the view that all opinions, like all men, and to some extent for the same reasons, ought to be treated *equally* (the equality principle again), and that such equal treatment necessarily involves toleration. In accordance with John Stuart Mill's philosophy, they are more apt than conservatives to believe that to silence an expression of opinion, or to persecute the minority that holds the opinion, involves an assumption of infallibility on the part of the silencer; that, further, such silencing obstructs the realization of truth, which is the product of a free "give and take" of ideas; and that, finally, one act of suppression leads to another and so on to "total" thought-control.

Conservatives and liberals, of course, divide over foreign policy matters other than the communist problem. Not unexpectedly, in those areas where inequality exists among nations, the liberal backs such measures as seem likely to reduce it. The conservative fights such programs, usually on the grounds that the existent inequalities are due to the lack of initiative and industry of the peoples designated for such aid.

In a more subtle way, the "equality principle" underlies yet other liberal-conservative differences. The conservative certainly tends to be more nationalistic than the liberal, which is to say, he does not hesitate to put the United States and its interests first in all foreign-policy equations. Reinhold Niebuhr has gone so far as to suggest: "In terms of international policy, confusion would be avoided if the word 'conservative' were confined to the pure nationalist." [11] And so, while the idea of a world government notoriously tickles the fancy of many liberals, it is repugnant to most conservatives. They believe it would involve the subordination of America's national interest to an international organization that must, of necessity, be constituted on a basis of equal-

[10] Likewise, the liberal reaction to Hitler was stronger than the conservative reaction because Hitler did provide the stimulus that always triggers the liberal conscience, namely, the blanket defense of a gross form of inequality. While conservatives also deplored Hitler and the atrocities committed by his regime, their opposition was by no means so sharp or militant as that of the liberals. In many ways, the conservatives assume a posture toward the present communist threat like that of the liberals toward Hitler and Nazism in 1940-41.

[11] "Liberalism: Illusions and Realities," *New Republic*, Vol. 133, July 4, 1955, p. 11.

ity between states. It is for this reason, probably, that the conservative is less than enthusiastic about the United Nations because, among other things, one of its main organs, the General Assembly, *is* based on equality between states, and seems to him to act usually (as he would expect) in a manner contrary to American national interests.

In this connection, the liberal is inclined to show great concern for the "uncommitted" nations of the world. In particular he tends, much more than the conservative, to cultivate the "good will" of the newly emergent nations, and is ready, not to say eager, to accord them a status of equality in the family of nation states. The conservative, by contrast, is more apt to "scoff" at the pretensions of these newly emergent states and, because he does have a hierarchical view of the nation-state system, to think of them as belonging at the "bottom" of the hierarchy. By the same token, the conservative is less concerned than the liberal as how those states may react to American policies.

The reader may well be asking himself at this point, Who is winning this "battle" between liberals and conservatives? The general opinion seems to be that the liberals are winning. Norman Thomas, six-time Socialist party candidate for the Presidency, frequently boasts that the platforms of the two major parties have, over the years, incorporated most of the measures that he originally advocated. And, since the Roosevelt revolution of the early and mid-30's, the liberals do indeed seem to have chalked up some impressive "victories": a public housing program, social security, more public power, urban renewal, at least some integration of the public schools, and finally more extensive grant-in-aid programs to the states.

But the liberal "victories," as Willmoore Kendall has suggested, could be "optical illusions." First, there is a sense in which liberal victories have been "paper victories"—that is, have been adopted, but by no means on the scale the liberals would have wished. It is true, for example, that we have a public housing program, but the liberals themselves have been most unhappy about the limited nature of the program; certainly they would prefer a more substantial and comprehensive national program. To take another area, public power, Kendall writes:

Everyone familiar with the politics of the [1930's] knows that the TVA enthusiasts intended TVA to be the first of a *series* of 'authorities,' which would have the effect of shifting the entire American economy away from 'capitalism' and 'free private enterprise.' That was what the liberals wanted, and that was what the conservatives, if they meant business, had to prevent; that was what was 'most important,' against the background of which the creation and main-tenance of a single TVA (one, moreover, that men could support out of no animus whatever against private enterprise) was at most 'unimportant;' and, once we put the question, 'Who won?' in *those* terms, and remind ourselves where the White House and the bureaucracy stood, we are obliged to give an answer quite different from that which we are in the habit of giving: The Executive got its TVA in particular, but Congress put a stop to TVA's in general (nor is there any issue so dead in America today as that of socialism).[12]

We must note in this connection that the liberals are, for the most part, on the "offensive" and the conservatives on the "defensive," and that we are in the habit, rightly or wrongly, of thinking of the "offensive team" as winning—particularly if it is now, or just has been, making some gains. In the championship match between liberals and conservatives, however, that approach to the matter may well be erroneous. The liberals have the football, to be sure, and are advancing at, say, a rate of three yards per down. But in order to tell how "good" this rate of advance is we would have to know, at least, on what yard-line the ball rests—and, also, how the clock reads. Certainly, three yards per down would represent a substantial rate of advance inside their opponents' ten-yard line, and would soon result in a touchdown. But if the ball is on the liberals' ten-yard line, this rate of advance will not suffice even for a first down—providing they are prudent enough to kick on "fourth and one." And if it is late in the game, and the liberals are showing signs of fatigue, that also would have to be taken into account.

In short: a correct estimate as to who is winning would have to take cognizance of the extent to which the conservatives have thwarted liberal goals within existing programs (public power, social security, public housing, taxation policy, etc.). And, beyond that, another very difficult calculation must be made, namely that concerning the extent to which the strength of the conservative opposition modifies or "tones down" liberal offensive thrusts. As a subsequent document will seek to show, for example, it seems safe to presume that the President and his advisers (generally responsive as they are to liberal interests) will not ask of Congress (which tends to be conservative) all they want, all they would like to ask for, since they know in advance that if they

[12] "The Two Majorities," *Midwest Journal of Political Science,* Vol. IV (November 1960), pp. 326-27.

did they would be roundly rebuffed. So too, in terms of the broader fight, one must constantly keep this factor in mind in trying to determine who is winning at any given moment. And still another factor is highly relevant here. Not all "liberal thrusts" are to be considered of equal importance. Some obviously are regarded by both liberals and conservatives as far more "important" than others. One must always weigh the liberal proposals and determine whether those deemed "highly important" achieve some degree of success or whether, at the other extreme, the successes are limited to those of minor importance —leaving the goal of equality as far off as ever.

Despite all these difficulties, there is one thing that seems certain: there will always be liberals and conservatives. No society can be free of inequalities of one sort or another; and so long as this remains true there will always be those "attacking" and those "defending" existing inequalities. Hence, we repeat, the liberals and conservatives, like the biblical poor, "we have always with us."

*   *   *

This chapter covers only a few areas of liberal-conservative conflict. The reader should keep in mind the following materials and ask himself whether the distinction we have drawn between liberalism and conservatism helps him to understand why the following writers take the positions they do.

A. Have We Gone Welfarist, And If Not, Should We?

7. The Welfare State*

BARRY GOLDWATER

Washington—The President estimated that the expenditures of the Department of Health, Education and Welfare in the fiscal year 1961 (including Social Security payments) would exceed $15,000,000,000. Thus the current results of New Deal legislation are Federal disbursements for human welfare in this country second only to national defense.

The *New York Times*, January 18, 1960, p. 1.

FOR many years it appeared that the principal domestic threat to our freedom was contained in the doctrines of Karl Marx. The collectivists—non-Communists as well as Communists—had adopted the Marxist objective of "socializing the means of production." And so it seemed that if collectivization were imposed, it would take the form of a State owned and operated economy. I doubt whether this is the main threat any longer.

The collectivists have found, both in this country and in other industrialized nations of the West, that free enterprise has removed the economic and social conditions that might have made a class struggle possible. Mammoth productivity, wide distribution of wealth, high standards of living, the trade union movement—these and other factors have eliminated whatever incentive there might have been for the "proletariat" to rise up, peaceably or

otherwise, and assume direct ownership of productive property. Significantly, the bankruptcy of doctrinaire Marxism has been expressly acknowledged by the Socialist Party of West Germany, and by the dominant faction of the Socialist Party of Great Britain. In this country the abandonment of the Marxist approach (outside the Communist Party, of course) is attested to by the negligible strength of the Socialist Party, and more tellingly perhaps, by the content of left wing literature and by the programs of left wing political organizations such as the Americans For Democratic Action.

The currently favored instrument of collectivization is the Welfare State. The collectivists have not abandoned their ultimate goal—to subordinate the individual to the State—but their strategy has changed. They have learned that Socialism can be achieved through Welfarism quite as well as through Nationalization. They understand that private property can be confiscated as effectively by taxation as by expropriating it. They understand that the individual can be put at the mercy of the

* Chapter 8, *Conscience of a Conservative* (Shepardsville, Kentucky: Victor Publishing Co., 1960), pp. 68-75. Reprinted by permission of the author and Victor Publishing Co. Copyright 1960 by Victor Publishing Co.

State—not only by making the State his employer—but by divesting him of the means to provide for his personal needs and by giving the State the responsibility of caring for those needs from cradle to grave. Moreover, they have discovered—and here is the critical point—that *Welfarism is much more compatible with the political processes of a democratic society.* Nationalization ran into popular opposition, but the collectivists feel sure the Welfare State can be erected by the simple expedient of buying votes with promises of "free" federal benefits—"free" housing, "free" school aid, "free" hospitalization, "free" retirement pay and so on . . . The correctness of this estimate can be seen from the portion of the federal budget that is now allocated to welfare, an amount second only to the cost of national defense.[1]

I do not welcome this shift of strategy. Socialism-through-Welfarism poses a far greater danger to freedom than Socialism-through-Nationalization precisely because it *is* more difficult to combat. The evils of Nationalization are self-evident and immediate. Those of Welfarism are veiled and tend to be postponed. People can understand the consequences of turning over ownership of the steel industry, say, to the State; and they can be counted on to oppose such a proposal. But let the government increase its contribution to the "Public Assistance" program and we will, at most, grumble about excessive government spending. The effect of Welfarism on freedom will be felt later on—after its beneficiaries have become its victims, after dependence on government has turned into bondage and it is too late to unlock the jail.

But a far more important factor is

[1] The total figure is substantially higher than the $15,000,000,000 noted above if we take into account welfare expenditures outside the Department of Health, Education and Welfare—for federal housing projects, for example.

Welfarism's strong emotional appeal to many voters, and the consequent temptations it presents the average politician. It is hard, as we have seen, to make out a case for State ownership. It is very different with the rhetoric of humanitarianism. How easy it is to reach the voters with earnest importunities for helping the needy. And how difficult for Conservatives to resist these demands without appearing to be callous and contemptuous of the plight of less fortunate citizens. Here, perhaps, is the best illustration of the failure of the Conservative demonstration.

I know, for I have heard the questions often. Have you no sense of social obligation? the Liberals ask. Have you no concern for people who are out of work? for sick people who lack medical care? for children in overcrowded schools? Are you unmoved by the problems of the aged and disabled? Are you *against* human welfare?

The answer to all of these questions is, of course, no. But a simple "no" is not enough. I feel certain that Conservatism is through unless Conservatives can demonstrate and communicate the difference between being concerned with these problems and believing that the federal government is the proper agent for their solution.

The long range political consequences of Welfarism are plain enough: as we have seen, the State that is able to deal with its citizens as wards and dependents has gathered unto itself unlimited political and economic power and is thus able to rule as absolutely as any oriental despot.

Let us, however, weigh the consequences of Welfarism on the individual citizen.

Consider, first, the effect of Welfarism on the donors of government welfare—not only those who pay for it but also the voters and their elected representatives who decide that the benefits shall be conferred. Does some credit redound on them for trying to care for the needs of their fellow citizens? Are they to be commended and rewarded, at some moment in eternity, for their "charity"? I think not. Suppose I should vote for a measure providing for free medical care: I am unaware of any moral virtue that is attached to my decision to confiscate the earnings of X and give them to Y.

Suppose, however, that X approves of the program—that he has voted for welfarist politicians with the idea of helping his fellow man. Surely the wholesomeness of his act is diluted by the fact that he is voting not only to have his own money taken but also that of his fellow citizens who may have different ideas about their social obligations. Why does not such a man, instead, contribute what he regards as his just share of human welfare to a private charity?

Consider the consequences to the recipient of welfarism. For one thing, he mortgages himself to the federal government. In return for benefits—which, in the majority of cases, he pays for—he concedes to the government the ultimate in political power —the power to grant or withhold from him the necessities of life as the government sees fit. Even more important, however, is the effect on him—the elimination of any feeling of responsibility for his own welfare and that of his family and neighbors. A man may not immediately, or ever, comprehend the harm thus done to his character. Indeed, this is one of the great evils of Welfarism—that it transforms the individual from a dignified, industrious, self-reliant *spiritual* being into a dependent animal creature without his knowing it. There is no avoiding this damage to character under the Welfare State. Welfare programs cannot help but promote the idea that the government *owes* the benefits it confers on the individual,

and that the individual is entitled, by right, to receive them. Such programs are sold to the country precisely on the argument that government has an *obligation* to care for the needs of its citizens. Is it possible that the message will reach those who vote for the benefits, but not those who receive them? How different it is with private charity where both the giver and the receiver understand that charity is the product of the humanitarian impulses of the giver, not the due of the receiver.

Let us, then, not blunt the noble impulses of mankind by reducing charity to a mechanical operation of the federal government. Let us, by all means, encourage those who are fortunate and able to care for the needs of those who are unfortunate and disabled. But let us do this in a way that is conducive to the spiritual as well as the material well-being of our citizens—and in a way that will preserve their freedom. Let welfare be a private concern. Let it be promoted by individuals and families, by churches, private hospitals, religious service organizations, community charities and other institutions that have been established for this purpose. If the objection is raised that private institutions lack sufficient funds, let us remember that every penny the federal government does *not* appropriate for welfare is potentially available for private use—and without the overhead charge for processing the money through the federal bureaucracy. Indeed, high taxes, for which government Welfarism is so largely responsible, is the biggest obstacle to fund raising by private charities.

Finally, if we deem public intervention necessary, let the job be done by local and state authorities that are incapable of accumulating the vast political power that is so inimical to our liberties.

The Welfare State is *not* inevitable,

as its proponents are so fond of telling us. There is nothing inherent in an industrialized economy, or in democratic processes of government that *must* produce de Tocqueville's "guardian society." Our future, like our past, will be what we make it. And we can shatter the collectivists' designs on individual freedom if we will impress upon the men who conduct our affairs this one truth: that the material and spiritual sides of man are intertwined; that it is impossible for the State to assume responsibility for one without intruding on the essential nature of the other; that if we take from a man the personal responsibility for caring for his material needs, we take from him also the will and the opportunity to be free.

8. Our Invisible Poor*

DWIGHT MACDONALD

[*This is a portion of Dwight Macdonald's review and discussion of recent works dealing with the poverty problem (principally, Michael Harrington's* The Other Poverty in the United States; *Gabriel Kolko,* Wealth and Power In America; Income and Welfare in the United States *authorized by four members of the Survey Research Center of the Institute for Social Research at the University of Michigan; and a pamphlet entitled* "Poverty and Deprivation" *issued by the Conference on Economic Progress.*]

THE main reason the American poor have become invisible is that since 1936 their numbers have been reduced by two-thirds. Astounding as it may seem, the fact is that President Roosevelt's "one-third of a nation" was a considerable understatement; over two-thirds of us then lived below the poverty line,

But today the poor are a minority, and minorities can be ignored if they are so heterogeneous that they cannot be organized. When the poor were a majority, they simply could not be overlooked. Poverty is also hard to see today because the middle class ($6,000 to $14,999) has vastly increased—from 13 per cent of all families in 1936 to a near-majority (47 per cent) today. That mass poverty can persist despite this rise to affluence is hard to believe, or see, especially if one is among those who have risen.

Two tables in "Poverty and Deprivation" summarize what has been happening in the last thirty years. They cover only multiple-person families; all figures are converted to 1960 dollars; and the income is before taxes. I have omitted, for clarity, all fractions.

The first table is the percentage of families with a given income:

	1935-6	1947	1953	1960
Under $ 4,000	68%	37%	28%	23%
$4,000 to $ 5,999	17	29	28	23
$6,000 to $ 7,499	6	12	17	16
$7,500 to $14,999	7	17	23	31
Over $15,000	2	4	5	7

as is shown by the tables that follow.

The New Yorker (January 19, 1963), pp. 82 ff. Reprinted by permission of the author.

The second table is the share each group had in the family income of the nation:

	1935-6	1947	1953	1960
Under $ 4,000	35%	16%	11%	7%
$4,000 to $ 5,999	21	24	21	15
$6,000 to $ 7,499	10	14	17	14
$7,500 to $14,999	16	28	33	40
Over $15,000	18	18	19	24

Several interesting conclusions can be drawn from these tables:

(1) The New Deal didn't do anything about poverty: The under-$4,000 families in 1936 were 68 per cent of the total population, which was slightly *more* than the 1929 figure of 65 per cent.

(2) The war economy (hot and cold) did do something about poverty: Between 1936 and 1960 the proportion of all families who were poor was reduced from 68 per cent to 23 per cent.

(3) If the percentage of under-$4,000 families decreased by two-thirds between 1936 and 1960, their share of the national income dropped a great deal more—from 35 per cent to 7 per cent.

(4) The well-to-do ($7,500 to $14,999) have enormously increased, from 7 per cent of all families in 1936 to 31 per cent today. The rich ($15,000 and over) have also multiplied—from 2 to 7 per cent. But it should be noted that the very rich, according to another new study, "The Share of Top Wealth-Holders in National Wealth, 1922-1956," by Robert J. Lampman (Princeton), have experienced a decline. He finds that the top 1 per cent of wealth-holders owned 38 per cent of the national wealth in 1929 and own only 28 per cent today. (Though let's not get sentimental over that "only.") Thus, *pace* Dr. Kolko, there has in fact been a redistribution of wealth—in favor of the well-to-do and the rich at the expense of the poor and the very rich.

(5) The reduction of poverty has slowed down. In the six years 1947-53, the number of poor families declined 9 per cent, but in the following seven years only 5 per cent. The economic stasis that set in with Eisenhower and that still persists under Kennedy was responsible. (This stagnation, however, did not affect the over-$7,500 families, who increased from 28 per cent to 38 per cent between 1953 and 1960.) In the New York *Times Magazine* for last November 11th, Herman P. Miller, of the Bureau of the Census, wrote, "During the forties, the lower-paid occupations made the greatest relative gains in average income. Laborers and service workers . . . had increases of about 180% . . . and professional and managerial workers, the highest paid workers of all, had the lowest relative gains—96%." But in the last decade the trend has been reversed; laborers and service workers have gained 39% while professional-managerial workers have gained 68%. This is because in the wartime forties the unskilled were in great demand, while now they are being replaced by machines. Automation is today the same kind of menace to the unskilled—that is, the poor—that the enclosure movement was to the British agricultural population centuries ago. "The facts show that our 'social revolution' ended nearly twenty years ago," Mr. Miller concludes, "yet important segments of the American public, many of them highly placed Government officials and prominent educators, think and act as though it were a continuing process."

"A reduction of about 19% [in the under-$6,000 families] in more than thirty years, or at a rate of about 0.7% per year, is no ground for complacency," the authors of "Poverty and Deprivation" justly observe. There is even less ground for complacency in the recent figures on *extreme* poverty. The authors estimate the number of families in 1929 with incomes of under $2,000 (in current dollars) at 7,500,000. By

1947 there were less than 4,000,000, not because of any philanthropic effort by their more prosperous fellow-citizens but entirely because of those first glorious years of a war economy. Six years later, in 1953, when the economy had begun to slow down, there were still 3,300,000 of these families with incomes of less than $2,000, and seven years later, in 1960, "there had been no further reduction." Thus in the last fifteen years the bottom dogs have remained on the bottom, sharing hardly at all in the advances that the income groups above them have made in an ascending scale that is exquisitely adjusted, by the automatic workings of capitalism, so that it is inversely proportionate to need.

There are, finally, the bottommest bottom dogs; i.e., *families* with incomes of *under $1,000*. I apologize for the italics, but some facts insist on them. According to "Poverty and Deprivation," the numbers of these families "appear to have risen slightly" of late (1953-60), from 800,000 to about 1,000,000. It is only fair, and patriotic, to add that according to the Commerce Department study, about 10,000,000 of our families and unattached individuals now enjoy incomes of $10,000 a year and up. So while some 3,500,000 Americans are in under-$1,000 families, ten times as many are in over-$10,000 families. Not bad at all—in a way.

The post-1940 decrease in poverty was not due to the policies or actions of those who are not poor, those in positions of power and responsibility. The war economy needed workers, wages went up, and the poor became less poor. When economic stasis set in, the rate of decrease in poverty slowed down proportionately, and it is still slow. Kennedy's efforts to "get the country moving again" have been unsuccessful, possibly because he has, despite the suggestions of many of his economic advisers, not yet advocated the one big step that might push the economy off dead center: a massive increase in government spending. This would be politically courageous, perhaps even dangerous, because of the superstitious fear of "deficit spending" and an "unbalanced" federal budget. American folklore insists that a government's budget must be arranged like a private family's. Walter Lippmann wrote, after the collapse of the stock market last spring:

> There is mounting evidence that those economists were right who told the Administration last winter that it was making the mistake of trying to balance the budget too soon. It will be said that the budget is not balanced: it shows a deficit in fiscal 1962 of $7 billion. . . . But . . . the budget that matters is the Department of Commerce's income and product accounts budget. Nobody looks at it except the economists [but] while the Administrative budget is necessary for administration and is like a man's checkbook, the income budget tells the real story. . . .
>
> [It] shows that at the end of 1962 the outgo and ingo accounts will be virtually in balance, with a deficit of only about half a billion dollars. Thus, in reality, the Kennedy administration is no longer stimulating the economy, and the economy is stagnating for lack of stimulation. We have one of the lowest rates of growth among the advanced industrial nations of the world.

One shouldn't be hard on the President. Franklin Roosevelt, a more daring and experimental politician, at least in his domestic policy, listened to the American disciples of J. M. Keynes in the early New Deal years and unbalanced his budgets, with splendid results. But by 1936 he had lost his nerve. He cut back government spending and there ensued the 1937 recession, from which the economy recovered only when war orders began to make up for the deficiency in domestic buying power. "Poverty and Deprivation" estimates that between 1953 and 1961 the annual growth rate of our economy was "only 2.5 per cent per annum contrasted with an estimated 4.2 per cent required to maintain utilization of manpower and other productive resources." The poor, who always experience the worst the first, understand quite personally the meaning of that dry statistic, as they understand Kipling's "The toad beneath the harrow knows/Exactly where each toothpoint goes." They are also most intimately acquainted with another set of statistics: the steady postwar rise in the unemployment rate, from 3.1 per cent in 1949 to 4.3 per cent in 1954 to 5.1 per cent in 1958 to over 7 per cent in 1961. (The Tory Government is worried because British unemployment is now at its highest point for the last three years. This point is 2.1 per cent, which is less than our lowest rate in the last fifteen years.)

Some of the post-1940 gains of the poor have been their own doing. "Moonlighting"—or holding two or more jobs at once—was practiced by about 3 per cent of the employed in 1950; today this percentage has almost doubled. Far more important is what might be called "wife-flitting": Between 1940 and 1957, the percentage of wives with jobs outside the home doubled, from 15 per cent to 30 per cent. The head of the United States Children's Bureau, Mrs. Katherine B. Oettinger, announced last summer, not at all triumphantly, that there are now two-thirds more working mothers than there were ten years ago and that these mothers have about 15,000,000 children under eighteen—of whom 4,000,000 are under six. This kind of economic enterprise ought to impress Senator Goldwater and the ideologues of the *National Review,* whose reaction to the poor, when they think about such an uninspiring subject, is "Why don't they *do* something about it?" The poor have done something about it and the family pay check is bigger and the statistics on poverty look better. But the effects on family life and on those 4,000,000 pre-school children is something else. Mrs. Oettinger quoted a roadside sign, "IRONING, DAY CARE AND WORMS FOR FISHING BAIT," and mentioned a baby-sitter who pacified her charge with sleeping pills and another who met the problem of a cold apartment by putting the baby in the oven. "The situation has become a 'national disgrace,' with many unfortunate conditions that do not come to public attention until a crisis arises," the *Times* summed up her conclusion. This crisis has finally penetrated to public attention. The President recently signed a law that might be called Daycare. It provides $5,000,-000 for such facilities this fiscal year, which works out to $1.25 for each of the 4,000,000 under-six children with working mothers. Next year, the program will provide all of $2.50 per child. This is a free, democratic society's notion of an adequate response. Almost a century ago, Bismarck instituted in Germany state-financed social benefits far beyond anything we have yet ventured. Granted that he did it merely to take the play away from the Social Democratic Party founded by Marx and Engels. Still, one imagines that Count Bismarck must be amused—in the circle of Hell reserved for reactionaries—by that $2.50 a child.

It's not that Public Opinion doesn't become Aroused every now and then. But the arousement never leads to much. It was aroused twenty-four years ago when John Steinbeck published "The Grapes of Wrath," but Mr. Harrington reports that things in the Imperial Valley are still much the same: low wages, bad housing, no effective union. Public Opinion is too public—that is, too general; of its very nature, it can have no sustained interest in California agriculture. The only groups with such a continuing interest are the workers and the farmers who hire them. Once Public Opinion ceased to be Aroused, the battle was again between the two antagonists with a real, personal stake in the outcome, and there was no question about which was stronger. So with the rural poor in general. In the late fifties, the average annual wage for white male American farm workers was slightly over $1,000; women, children, Negroes, and Mexicans got less. One recalls Edward R. Murrow's celebrated television program about these people, "Harvest of Shame." Once more everybody was shocked, but the harvest is still shameful. One also recalls that Mr. Murrow, after President Kennedy had appointed him head of the United States Information Agency, tried to persuade the B.B.C. not to show "Harvest of Shame." His argument was that it would give an undesirable "image" of America to foreign audiences.

There is a monotony about the injustices suffered by the poor that perhaps accounts for the lack of interest the rest of society shows in them. Everything seems to go wrong with them. They never win. It's just boring.

Public housing turns out not to be for them. The 1949 Housing Act authorized 810,000 new units of low-cost housing in the following four years. Twelve years later, in 1961, the A.F.L.-C.I.O. proposed 400,000 units to complete the lagging 1949 program. The Kennedy administration ventured to recommend 100,000 to Congress. Thus, instead of 810,000 low-cost units by 1953, the poor will get, if they are lucky, 500,000 by 1963. And they are more likely to be injured than helped by slum clearance, since the new projects usually have higher rents than the displaced slum-dwellers can afford. (There has been no dearth of government-financed *middle*-income housing since 1949.) These refugees from the bulldozers for the most part simply emigrate to

other slums. They also become invisible; Mr. Harrington notes that half of them are recorded as "address unknown." Several years ago, Charles Abrams, who was New York State Rent Administrator under Harriman and who is now president of the National Committee Against Discrimination in Housing, summed up what he had learned in two decades in public housing: "Once social reforms have won tonal appeal in the public mind, their slogans and goal-symbols may degenerate into tools of the dominant class for beleaguering the minority and often for defeating the very aims which the original sponsors had intended for their reforms." Mr. Abrams was probably thinking, in part, of the Title I adventures of Robert Moses in dealing with New York housing. There is a Moses or two in every American city, determined to lead us away from the promised land.

And this is not the end of tribulation. The poor, who can least afford to lose pay because of ill health, lose the most. A National Health Survey, made a few years ago, found that workers earning under $2,000 a year had twice as many "restricted-activity days" as those earning over $4,000.

The poor are even fatter than the rich. (The cartoonists will have to revise their clichés.) "Obesity is seven times more frequent among women of the lowest socio-economic level than it is among those of the highest level," state Drs. Moore, Stunkard, and Srole in a recent issue of the *Journal of the American Medical Association*. (The proportion is almost the same for men.) They also found that overweight associated with poverty is related to mental disease. Fatness used to be a sign of wealth, as it still is in some parts of Africa, but in more advanced societies it is now a stigma of poverty, since it means too many cheap carbohydrates and too little exercise—which has changed from a necessity for the poor into a luxury for the rich, as may be confirmed by a glance at the models in any fashion magazine.

Although they are the most in need of hospital insurance, the poor have the least, since they can't afford the premiums; only 40 per cent of poor families have it, as against 63 per cent of all families. (It should be noted, however, that the poor who are war veterans can get free treatment, at government expense, in Veterans Administration Hospitals.)

The poor actually pay more taxes, in proportion to their income, than the rich. A recent study by the Tax Foundation estimates that 28 per cent of incomes under $2,000 goes for taxes, as against 24 per cent of the incomes of families earning five to seven times as much. Sales and other excise taxes are largely responsible for this curious statistic. It is true that such taxes fall impartially on all, like the blessed rain from heaven, but it is a form of egalitarianism that perhaps only Senator Goldwater can fully appreciate.

The final irony is that the Welfare State, which Roosevelt erected and which Eisenhower, no matter how strongly he felt about it, didn't attempt to pull down, is not for the poor, either. Agricultural workers are not covered by Social Security, nor are many of the desperately poor among the aged, such as "unrelated individuals" with incomes of less than $1,000, of whom only 37 per cent are covered, which is just half the percentage of coverage among the aged in general. Of the Welfare State, Mr. Harrington says, "Its creation had been stimulated by mass impoverishment and misery, yet it helped the poor least of all. Laws like unemployment compensation, the Wagner Act, the various farm programs, all these were designed for the middle third in the cities, for the organized workers, and for the . . . big market farmers. . . . [It] benefits those least who need help most." The industrial workers, led by John L. Lewis, mo-

bilized enough political force to put through Section 7 (a) of the National Industrial Recovery Act, which, with the Wagner Act, made the C.I.O. possible. The big farmers put enough pressure on Henry Wallace, Roosevelt's first Secretary of Agriculture—who talked a good fight for liberal principles but was a Hamlet when it came to action—to establish the two basic propositions of Welfare State agriculture: subsidies that now cost $3 billion a year and that chiefly benefit the big farmers; and the exclusion of sharecroppers, tenant farmers, and migratory workers from the protection of minimum-wage and Social Security laws.

No doubt the Kennedy administration would like to do more for the poor than it has, but it is hampered by the cabal of Republicans and Southern Democrats in Congress. The 1961 revision of the Fair Labor Standards Act, which raised the national minimum wage to the not exorbitant figure of $1.15 an hour, was a slight improvement over the previous act. For instance, it increased coverage of retail-trade workers from 3 per cent to 33 per cent. (But one-fourth of the retail workers still excluded earn less than $1 an hour.) There was also a considerable amount of shadowboxing involved: Of the 3,600,000 workers newly covered, only 663,000 were making less than $1 an hour. And there was the exclusion of a particularly ill-paid group of workers. Nobody had anything against the laundry workers *personally*. It was just that they were weak, unorganized, and politically expendable. To appease the conservatives in Congress, whose votes were needed to get the revision through, they were therefore expended. The result is that of the 500,000 workers in the laundry, dry-cleaning, and dyeing industries, just 17,000 are now protected by the Fair Labor Standards Act.

In short, one reaches the unstartling conclusion that rewards in class societies, including Communist ones, are according to power rather than need. A recent illustration is the campaign of an obscure organization called Veterans of World War I of the U.S.A. to get a bill through Congress for pensions of about $25 a week. It was formed by older men who think other veterans' organizations (such as the American Legion, which claims 2,500,000 members to their 200,000) are dominated by the relatively young. It asks for pensions for veterans of the First World War with incomes of under $2,400 (if single) or $3,600 (if married)—that is, only for *poor* veterans. The editorials have been violent: "STOP THIS VETERANS' GRAB," implored the *Herald Tribune*; "WORLD WAR I PENSION GRAB," echoed the *Saturday Evening Post*. Their objection was, in part, that many of the beneficiaries would not be bonafide poor, since pensions, annuities, and Social Security benefits were excluded from the maximum income needed to qualify. Considering that the average Social Security payment is about $1,000 a year, this would not put any potential beneficiary into the rich or even the comfortably-off class, even if one assumes another $1,000, which is surely too high, from annuities and pensions. It's all very confusing. The one clear aspect is that the minuscule Veterans of World War I of the U.S.A. came very near to bringing it off. Although their bill was opposed by both the White House and by the chairman of the House Committee on Veterans' Affairs, two hundred and one members of the House signed a petition to bring the measure to a vote, only eighteen less than needed "to accomplish this unusual parliamentary strategy," as the *Times* put it. These congressmen were motivated by politics rather than charity, one may assume. Many were up for reëlection last November, and the two hundred thousand Veterans of World War I had two advantages over the fifty million poor: They were

organized, and they had a patriotic appeal only a wink away from the demagogic. Their "unusual parliamentary strategy" failed by eighteen votes in the Congress. But there will be another Congress.

It seems likely that mass poverty will continue in this country for a long time. The more it is reduced, the harder it is to keep on reducing it. The poor, having dwindled from two-thirds of the population in 1936 to one-quarter today, no longer are a significant political force, as is shown by the Senate's rejection of Medicare and by the Democrats' dropping it as an issue in the elections last year. Also, as poverty decreases, those left behind tend more and more to be the ones who have for so long accepted poverty as their destiny that they need outside help to climb out of it. This new minority mass poverty, so much more isolated and hopeless than the old majority poverty, shows signs of becoming chronic. "The permanence of low incomes is inferred from a variety of findings," write the authors of the Michigan survey. "In many poor families the head has never earned enough to cover the family's present needs." They give a vignette of what the statistics mean in human terms:

For most families, however, the problem of chronic poverty is serious. One such family is headed by a thirty-two-year-old man who is employed as a dishwasher. Though he works steadily and more than full time, he earned slightly over $2,000 in 1959. His wife earned $300 more, but their combined incomes are not enough to support themselves and their three children. Although the head of the family is only thirty-two, he feels that he has no chance of advancement partly because he finished only seven grades of school. . . . The possibility of such families leaving the ranks of the poor is not high.

Children born into poor families today have less chance of "improving themselves" than the children of the pre-1940 poor. Rags to riches is now more likely to be rags to rags. "Indeed," the Michigan surveyors conclude, "it appears that a number of the heads of poor families have moved into less skilled jobs than their fathers had." Over a third of the children of the poor, according to the survey, don't go beyond the eighth grade and "will probably perpetuate the poverty of their parents." There are a great many of these children. In an important study of poverty, made for a Congressional committee in 1959, Dr. Robert J. Lampman estimated that eleven million of the poor were under eighteen. "A considerable number of younger persons are starting life in a condition of 'inherited poverty,' " he observed. To which Mr. Harrington adds, "The character of poverty has changed, and it has become more deadly for the young. It is no longer associated with immigrant groups with high aspirations; it is now identified with those whose social existence makes it more and more difficult to break out into the larger society." Even when children from poor families show intellectual promise, there is nothing in the values of their friends or families to encourage them to make use of it. Dr. Kolko, citing impressive sources, states that of the top 16 per cent of high-school students—those scoring 120 and over in I.Q. tests—only half go on to college. The explanation for this amazing—and alarming—situation is as much cultural as economic. The children of the poor now tend to lack what the sociologists call "motivation." At least one foundation is working on the problem of why so many bright children from poor families don't ever try to go beyond high school.

Mr. Raymond M. Hilliard, at present director of the Cook County (i.e., Chicago) Department of Public Aid and formerly Commissioner of Welfare for New York City, recently directed a "representative-sample" investigation, which showed that more than half of the 225,000 able-bodied Cook County residents who were on relief were "functionally illiterate." One reason Cook County has to spend $16,500,000 a month on relief is "the lack of basic educational skills of relief recipients which are essential to compete in our modern society." An interesting footnote, apropos of recent happenings at "Ole Miss," is that the illiteracy rate of the relief recipients who were educated in Chicago is 33 per cent, while among those who were educated in Mississippi and later moved to Chicago it is 77 per cent.

The problem of educating the poor has changed since 1900. Then it was the language and cultural difficulties of immigrants from foreign countries; now it is the subtler but more intractable problems of internal migration from backward regions, mostly in the South. The old immigrants wanted to Better Themselves and to Get Ahead. The new migrants are less ambitious, and they come into a less ambitious atmosphere. "When they arrive in the city," wrote Christopher Jencks in an excellent two-part survey, "Slums and Schools," in the *New Republic* last fall, "they join others equally unprepared for urban life in the slums—a milieu which is in many ways utterly dissociated from the rest of America. Often this milieu is self-perpetuating. I have been unable to find any statistics on how many of these migrants' children and grandchildren have become middle-class, but it is probably not too inaccurate to estimate that about 30,000,000 people live in urban slums, and that about half are second-generation residents." The immigrants of 1890-1910 also arrived in a milieu that was "in many ways utterly dissociated from the rest of America," yet they had a vision—a rather materialistic one, but still a vision—of what life in America could be if they worked hard enough; and they did work, and they did aspire to something more than they had; and they did get out of the slums. The disturbing thing about the poor today is that so many of them seem to lack any such vision. Mr. Jencks remarks:

> While the economy is changing in a way which makes the eventual liquidation of the slums at least conceivable, young people are not seizing the opportunities this change presents. Too many are dropping out of school before graduation (more than half in many slums); too few are going to college. . . . As a result there are serious shortages of teachers, nurses, doctors, technicians, and scientifically trained executives, but 4,500,000 unemployables.

"Poverty is the parent of revolution and crime," Aristotle wrote. This is now a half truth—the last half. Our poor are alienated; they don't consider themselves part of society. But precisely because they don't they are not politically dangerous. It is people with "a stake in the country" who make revolutions. The best—though by no means the only—reason for worrying about the Other America is that its existence should make us feel uncomfortable.

The federal government is the only purposeful force—I assume wars are not purposeful—that can reduce the numbers of the poor and make their lives more bearable. The authors of "Poverty and Deprivation" take a dim view of the Kennedy administration's efforts to date:

> The Federal Budget is the most important single instrument available to us as a free people to induce satisfactory economic performance, and to reduce poverty and deprivation. . . .
>
> Projected Federal outlays in the fiscal 1963 Budget are too small. The items in this Budget covering programs directly related to human improvement and the reduction

of mass poverty and deprivation allocate far too small a portion of our total national production to these great purposes.

The effect of government policy on poverty has two quite distinct aspects. One is the indirect effect of the stimulation of the economy by federal spending. Such stimulation—though by wartime demands rather than government policy—has in the past produced a prosperity that did cut down American poverty by almost two-thirds. But I am inclined to agree with Dr. Galbraith that it would not have a comparable effect on present-day poverty:

> It is assumed that with increasing output poverty must disappear [he writes]. Increased output eliminated the general poverty of all who worked. Accordingly it must, sooner or later, eliminate the special poverty that still remains. . . . Yet just as the arithmetic of modern politics makes it tempting to overlook the very poor, so the supposition that increasing output will remedy their case has made it easy to do so too.

He underestimates the massiveness of American poverty, but he is right when he says there is now a hard core of the specially disadvantaged—because of age, race, environment, physical or mental defects, etc.—that would not be significantly reduced by general prosperity. (Although I think the majority of our present poor *would* benefit, if only by a reduction in the present high rate of unemployment.)

To do something about this hard core, a second line of government policy would be required; namely, direct intervention to help the poor. We have had this since the New Deal, but it has always been grudging and miserly, and we have never accepted the principle that every citizen should be provided, at state expense, with a reasonable minimum standard of living regardless of any other considerations. It should not depend on earnings, as does Social Security, which continues the inequalities and inequities and so tends to keep the poor forever poor. Nor should it exclude millions of our poorest citizens because they lack the political pressure to force their way into the Welfare State. The governmental obligation to provide, out of taxes, such a minimum living standard for all who need it should be taken as much for granted as free public schools have always been in our history.

It may be objected that the economy cannot bear the cost, and certainly costs must be calculated. But the point is not the calculation but the principle. Statistics—and especially statistical forecasts—can be pushed one way or the other. Who can determine in advance to what extent the extra expense of giving our 40,000,000 poor enough income to rise above the poverty line would be offset by the lift to the economy from their increased purchasing power? We really don't know. Nor did we know what the budgetary effects would be when we established the principle of free public education. The rationale then was that all citizens should have an equal chance of competing for a better status. The rationale now is different: that every citizen has a right to become or remain part of our society because if this right is denied, as it is in the case of at least one-fourth of our citizens, it impoverishes us all. Since 1932, "the government"—local, state, and federal—has recognized a responsibility to provide its citizens with a subsistence living. Apples will never again be sold on the street by jobless accountants, it seems safe to

predict, nor will any serious political leader even again suggest that share-the-work and local charity can solve the problem of unemployment. "Nobody starves" in this country any more, but, like every social statistic, this is a tricky business. Nobody starves, but who can measure the starvation, not to be calculated by daily intake of proteins and calories, that reduces life for many of our poor to a long vestibule to death? Nobody starves, but every fourth citizen rubs along on a standard of living that is below what Mr. Harrington defines as "the minimal levels of health, housing, food, and education that our present stage of scientific knowledge specifies as necessary for life as it is now lived in the United States." Nobody starves, but a fourth of us are excluded from the common social existence. Not to be able to afford a movie or a glas of beer is a kind of starvation—if everybody else can.

The problem is obvious: the persistence of mass poverty in a prosperous country. The solution is also obvious: to provide, out of taxes, the kind of subsidies that have always been given to the public schools (not to mention the police and fire departments and the post office)—subsidies that would raise incomes above the poverty level, so that every citizen could feel he is indeed such. *"Civis Romanus sum!"* cried St. Paul when he was threatened with flogging—and he was not flogged. Until our poor can be proud to say *"Civis Americanus sum!,"* until the act of justice that would make this possible has been performed by the three-quarters of Americans who are not poor—until then the shame of the Other America will continue.

B. Should the Rich Be "Soaked"?

9. The Gentle Art of Tax Avoidance*

JOHN L. HESS

[*While there has been substantial revision of our tax laws in recent years, Hess's position here is indicative of the liberals' attitude toward the practices associated with our taxation policies.*]

"I DON'T feel as though the government is entitled to anything," said the $25,-000-a-year call girl on the Ed Murrow broadcast, "because these men are all legitimate businessmen. They deduct you at the end of the year."

The young lady was of course in error about her tax liability. The government has no scruples against getting its share of *any* earned income, including the wages of sin. To be sure, the Supreme Court has ruled that an embezzler is not required to pay a tax on his take because the money isn't really his after all. But an extortionist, it held later, may not make the same defense, nor may a taker of bribes. They've got to pay because, in a manner of speaking, they earned the money. The *payer* of a bribe, on the other hand, may not deduct it lawfully as a business expense. But the *Wall Street Journal* has advised in its tax column that corporations can get around that in foreign operations by setting up subsidiaries to handle the payoffs. Recently, moreover, the deduction of kickbacks has been allowed in certain fields where

* *The Reporter* (April 16, 1959), pp. 12-17. Reprinted by permission of the author and *The Reporter*. Copyright 1959 by the Reporter Magazine Co.

they are regarded as normal business practice. For the distinction between normal and abnormal practices, see your tax lawyer.

The quirks of tax morality would be more amusing but for the fact that taxes of all sorts now take roughly a quarter of the gross national product and are a palpable burden to every citizen. Even so, many state and local governments, not to mention the Federal government itself, are floundering in budgetary crises. The taxpayer can afford to pay more, one may argue; indeed he must if the nation is to meet its pressing needs. And yet last November he rejected one-third of the borrowings proposed for local school construction and other projects, and much of the remainder barely squeezed through. The breadwinner-taxpayer-voter is obviously dragging his feet. Of course people have been trying to get out of paying taxes ever since there were any, but something more than a simple reluctance to part with cash is involved in the present difficulties. Resentment at the inequities of the tax burden and contempt for the hypocrisy of the tax laws have become a serious national issue.

Evasion and Avoidance

That call girl who was unwilling to report her income has at least one thing in common with millions of other citizens who are rewarded for their services on an individual basis rather than by salary: the government cannot tax her earnings at the source. The National Bureau of Economic Research has estimated conservatively that 30 per cent of the income of private entrepreneurs—doctors, gamblers, lawyers, call girls, butchers, con men, farmers, and free-lance writers—is not reported to Uncle Sam. The same applies to 61 per cent of interest paid on savings and 13 per cent of dividends. But not more than 5 per cent of salaries go unreported. Over the years, there have been proposals that income taxes be deducted from interest and dividends at the source, as they are on wages. But the suggestions have never gotten anywhere.

A certified public accountant helping a newspaperman friend prepare his tax return not long ago shook his head pityingly and said, "You chumps on salaries pay *all* the taxes." He did not mean to imply that the very rich lie in reporting their incomes; their returns are scrutinized too closely for that. But while, in the curious semantics of the tax specialist, the rich do not often *evade* taxes, they are able to *avoid* them to a degree only dimly realized by the general public. (Tax evasion, according to the latest practitioners' guide, is doing something that, if you get caught, will mean a fine or jail. Tax avoidance at worst comes to an honest disagreement with the Revenue Commissioner; if you lose, you just pay up what you owe, plus interest.)

In 1929, taxpayers with reported incomes above $100,000 paid two-thirds of total Federal income-tax revenues; in 1956, they paid roughly one-twentieth. For persons earning less than $10,000 the change has been just the reverse: in 1929, they paid less than one-twentieth of the income-tax revenues; in 1956 they paid two-thirds. Nearly five-sixths of the income tax now is levied upon the lowest, or 20 per cent, bracket.

It should be emphasized that this extraordinary shift in the tax burden reflects the enormous rise in government spending and in the numbers and prosperity of people within the below-$10,000 group. But in some measure it also reflects the increasing ability of the upper brackets to *avoid* taxes, coupled with the inability of the salary earners to *evade* them since the enactment in 1943 of the law establishing the withholding of 18 per cent of taxable income from wages.

.   .   .   .   .

The Swindle Sheet

Probably no aspect of our tax mores has received more attention in recent years than the expense account. In the *Yale Law Journal* last July, V. Henry Rothschild and Rudolf Sobernheim wrote that expense-account spending might be conservatively estimated at $5 billion a year, resulting in a tax loss to the Treasury of from $1 to $2 billion. Regarding the "loose use" of this money, they commented: "The Treasury is keenly aware of the problem, but its efforts at regulation have met with stubborn resistance, both from the luxury services sustained by the expense account and from the individuals who find the account essential to their accustomed standard of living." Last year the Treasury went so far as to order taxpayers to account for expenses in detail, but it beat an ignominious retreat under a storm of protest.

While the expense account gives many a salesman and junior executive a taste of the high life, it should not be concluded that it has an equalitarian effect. "A physician undoubtedly would be questioned if he chartered a plane for his trip to the A.M.A. convention and used a $300-a-day executive suite at a luxury hotel," *U.S. News & World Report* has observed. "But the tax agents usually don't bat an eye when a big executive spends on that scale."

Speaking of conventions, it is a poor trade group these days that does not charter a cruise ship to the Caribbean for its annual business meeting. The

J. I. Case Company last winter flew all of its dealers and their wives to the Bahamas to look at its tractors, made in Milwaukee. A doctor with any ingenuity now arranges his European vacation to coincide with a medical meeting.

Many companies award mass vacation trips to their dealers as "prizes" (cash rebates would be taxable), although more than one dealer has said he would rather take the cash and pay the tax. One, quoted in the *Wall Street Journal,* grumbled, "Who wants to spend his vacation with a lot of appliance dealers?"

Given the choice between a ten-dollar lunch and a ten-dollar bill, many salesmen would take the money and eat at the Automat—indeed, there is some suspicion that some do just that. But legally the expense account does not permit such freedom. It has been observed that it gives the beneficiary a split-level existence: filet mignon on business and hamburger at home. Like other elements of the tax structure, it distorts the way of life of even those who get away with the most.

In one respect, at least, the expense account appears to have elevated our moral standards: a British observer has noted that a businessman used to take his secretary on a trip and say she was his wife; now, he takes his wife and says she is his secretary.

*   *   *

To its defenders, the expense account is a useful way of giving executives a standard of living they otherwise could not achieve under our tax structure. The difficulty here is that the tax benefits are limited rather capriciously to top executives, salesmen, entrepreneurs, and staff members of the advertising, TV, and public-relations fields. The great majority of citizens, who never see the inside of a posh club or sit down front at a hit musical, may feel that they are being discriminated against.

In any case, the thing is clearly getting out of hand when a court will rule, as in one case celebrated among tax practitioners, that the head of a dairy company and his wife might deduct the $17,000 cost of a safari to Africa because of the publicity value to the business. The *Yale Law Journal* article cited above recommended that misuse of the business-expense deduction be made subject to a cash penalty. But this would hardly stem the tide without a redefinition of "misuse."

A straightforward, drastic attack on the disease would be to bar *all* deductions for entertainment. It also would rule out club dues, town apartments, yachts, hunting lodges, executive dining rooms, and the private use of company cars, with or without chauffeurs. It would limit expenses on the road to a fixed per diem scale, such as some old-fashioned companies still impose on their lower employees. Any luxuries whatever would be considered compensation, and taxable. The increase in revenues would then be applied to reducing tax rates.

The suggestion is offered here without optimism. For one thing, its enactment into law would hit all congressmen in the pocketbook. For another, it would get the hotel, resort, and entertainment industries up in arms, as did even the Treasury's feeble effort at a checkup last year. (Is it really necessary for the U.S. Treasury to subsidize the Stork Club?) Further, it would seem to threaten the standard of living of hundreds of thousands of businessmen, executives, and salesmen. Doubtless if they had to spend their own money they would not make quite the same splash. But they might drink less and actually live better with lower tax rates and more control over their own money. And outlawing swindle sheets might do wonders for their immortal souls.

Bread upon the Waters

The erosion of public morality by the tax system is perhaps nowhere more apparent than in the area of charity. Jesus said, "It is more blessed to give than to receive"; nowadays hardly any appeal for a worthy cause fails to add, "and it is tax-deductible, too." More and more, wealthy people are learning that it often actually pays to give.

Let us take a gentleman in the 60 per cent tax bracket, who five years ago picked up a nice little painting in Paris for $10,000. Today it is worth $20,000. If he were to die owning it, his estate would have to pay an inheritance tax. So he *gives* the painting to a museum, and deducts the full $20,000 value from his current income. Or he can give the picture in annual installments, according to his tax needs. (A Solomon must have thought that one up.) Or he may deduct one-third of a painting's value by arranging to let a museum have it for four months of the year, thus perhaps saving storage and insurance costs while he is away during the summer, and keep it right up on his own wall the rest of the year. Who said you can't eat your cake and have it too?

Similarly, one may give stocks or bonds to a charitable organization or school, deducting a substantial amount from present income but retaining the interest or dividends on the securities for life—and for the lifetime of an heir as well. The Research Institute of America, commending this device to upper-bracket clients, remarks that in this way they may not only increase their after-tax income but also "obtain the immediate personal satisfaction and community respect that comes with a present rather than a post-mortem gift."

A number of colleges and church groups have banded together to promote a give-us-the-securities-you-keep-the-income campaign. There is a kind of admirable farsightedness and selflessness about this business of raiding the Treasury today for benefits that only future generations will be able to enjoy. It compensates a little for the national debt that we are leaving to those generations.

Whatever it signifies about human nature, the tax code clearly has been a windfall for philanthropy. According to a study published last month, donations to colleges alone soared from $50 million in the 1943-1944 school year to $411 million in 1957-1958. Foundations have proliferated like rabbits, and for many of them the chief preoccupation has been how to get rid of money. Organizations have sprung up to combat various diseases (and in at least one case, two organizations are bitterly contesting the same disease and each other). Museums large and small, all over the country, have been enjoying a stream of gifts of works they could never before even dream of owning.

In donating contemporary art, the philanthropist may easily contrive to clear more money than the artist. Recently, the revenue men have been ungraciously demanding evidence of a market value for the gift, but appraisals are still bound to be on the generous side. A whisper is heard of one big taxpayer who made a package deal in a casual conversation over a dinner table. He bought $30,000 worth of art, which was donated to a string of small museums at a valuation upward of $70,000, which he deducted from income at a substantial profit. He never saw the pictures, but he may drop in on one or another museum some time with a friend to admire his gift and the plaque acknowledging it. No museum has ever listed the Treasury as a co-donor.

On the contrary, many institutions have lost all inhibitions about raiding the government till. A number of charities, for example, employ a direct tax appeal to collect used clothing, cars, furniture, and junk of all kinds, which they sell, well aware that the deduction for tax purposes is far greater than the money they actually receive. One New York clothing chain, noted for its sincere-type advertising, invites taxpayers to turn in their old dinner jackets. The store provides without charge a signed appraisal for tax purposes, gives the clothing to charity, and stands quietly available if the taxpayer wants to buy new evening clothes.

The director of a great missionary organization, which ships a great deal of used clothing overseas (though presumably not dinner jackets), was asked the other day how tax avoidance squared with religion. "We are quite sensitive to the problem," he replied. "We live with it every day. And at the end of the year, we get that flood of contributions with carefully worded letters," the accountants having told their clients how much to give to the Lord. He had no proposal for a solution.

A national spokesman for a leading Protestant denomination defended the deduction as a perfectly legitimate decision of society to divert up to 30 per cent of income to charity, education, and religion, thus preserving privately directed social activities in the era of the welfare state. (To be sure, those who do not choose to give must assume part of the tax burden of those who do give.) But he was concerned about quite another aspect—the exemption of churches themselves from income, property, and business taxes on nonreligious ventures. A worldly member of his board of trustees, being apprised of this exemption recently, said, "Why, if I had known that a few years ago, we would own the oil industry now." But the churchman did not want to own the oil industry. Rich men die and leave much of their wealth to churches, he pointed out, "but churches never die—ultimately, they could own everything." Before that happened, he could foresee state intervention.

Everybody's Doing It

The social acceptability of raiding the Treasury is demonstrated by a common gimmick in the field of so-called municipal bonds. The billions of interest paid each year by state and local governments are exempt from income tax for the bondholder. This generous (not to say incomprehensible) treatment is accorded by the Federal government to make it easier and cheaper for the localities to borrow. In gratitude, they frequently conspire with the bond marketers to do the Treasury out of even more tax income.

Thus, a part of the bond issue will carry an abnormally high interest rate, which is offset by a price above the face value of the bond. Now the bond house, or a favored customer who buys such a bond, will report a deductible loss when it comes due, since the face value is less than the price paid for it. Actually, the holder will have received an exorbitant interest payment, entirely exempt from the Federal income tax. The loss is quite fictitious but entirely legal.

The Treasury tried to narrow this loophole by denying the "loss" to dealers who held the bonds themselves for more than a month. But how could it stop a dealer from selling a packet of bonds to another dealer, who might sell him a similar packet?

It would obviously be cheaper as well as more honest for Congress to subsidize directly any activity it wants to help, but it has always found it easier to grant tax exemptions. Exemptions are noticed chiefly by those who take advantage of them; subsidies show up in appropriations. The budget debate rages about deficit spending, never about deficit taxation. Has anybody asked why income-tax revenues have failed to grow as fast as income?

The answer is that every time Congress is persuaded to block one unintended loophole, it opens three or four more in order to "eliminate inequities"—or give someone a tax break. Last year, for example, Congress spurned all efforts to lower taxes as an anti-recession measure. Yet Congress also voted a special and rapid depreciation provision for "small business" that removed huge amounts of income from the tax rolls, eased the deduction of present losses from past years' profits, increased the tax-exempt reserves that corporations may set aside from earnings, made easier the formation of "collapsible" corporations—a form of alchemy that turns income into capital gains—and approved the formation of new private investment companies that will get *both* government subsidies and tax exemptions. And that was a relatively inactive year in the matter of exemptions.

One might suppose that tax practitioners would be the last to object to a system of such wild complexity that the courts themselves are perpetually engaged in wrangles over what it means and a deduction is frequently legal in one judicial district and outlawed in others. But J. S. Seidman, delivering a committee report of the American Institute of C.P.A.s back in 1956, denounced all one thousand pages of the Federal tax code as a crazy quilt of exceptions, exemptions, deductions, and special provisions, many so abstruse that the legislators who adopt them seldom know what they're about.

If one hundred "special provisions" in the code were eliminated, Seidman figured, tax rates could be cut by one-third. The brackets then would run from 13 to 61 per cent, instead of from 20 to 91 per cent.

One thing virtually all the special provisions have in common is that however reasonable or meritorious they may seem, they help the upper-bracket taxpayer most and do little or nothing for the low-income group. Take the case of the joint return: a man earning a net taxable income of $4,000 saves $40, while one earning $200,000 saves $22,180. And then there is the exemption for interest paid on debt. Here the tax code appears to be saying that only fools pay cash. It favors the mortgagee as against the tenant or the man so old-fashioned as to own his home outright. And people in the upper brackets have found it profitable to borrow money to buy insurance and annuities, the tax deductions on the interest paying much of the cost of the premiums. In effect, Uncle Sam pays their insurance bills.

Pity the Poor Wildcatter

The most nortorious of the loopholes deliberately created by Congress is the oil-depletion allowance. All business is, of course, permitted to deduct from income the depreciation, or using up, of its assets; in the mineral field this is called depletion. The allowance varies among minerals (even oyster shells are now eligible), but an oil producer may subtract 27.5 per cent of his gross income. A well may easily repay its investment within a couple of years, but the allowance goes on as long as it yields oil, which may be for a generation or two. An indication of the sums involved was contained in the report by the Venezuelan government that its oil industry, largely U.S.-owned, cleared a net income after taxes of $829,500,000 in 1957, a return of 32.5 per cent on its investment in a single year.

Practically nobody, even in the financial journals, defends the 27.5 per cent depletion rate—except, of course, the oil men themselves. Like so many other advocates of more or less noble causes, they raise the banner of national defense. Only a generous incentive, they argue, will keep the thousands of independent little wildcatters drilling and thus maintain the nation's oil industry in a posture of readiness. Yet of the $2 billion of depletion claimed in 1953, J. S. Seidman reported, companies with more than $100 million of assets accounted for 63 per cent. Companies with less than $100,000 accounted for 4 per cent.

Over the years, many a congressman seeking to strengthen the government revenues has wistfully eyed the depletion loss. But with both houses firmly guided by Texans, the fund raisers have been obliged to look elsewhere. On this rock have foundered all proposals for tax relief for lower incomes. The *Wall Street Journal* once reported that Speaker Sam Rayburn had been asked how he reconciled his opposition to a tax cut with the Democratic Party platform, which had promised to raise the personal exemption from $600 to $800. Mr Rayburn frowned, then chuckled and replied: "I didn't write all that platform myself."

Congress has given to all business a little of the same treatment it has accorded the oil industry by speeding up the period of depreciation. Here as in so many cases, the taxpayer and tax collector play a game of let's pretend. They pretend that a plant, machine, or apartment house wears out in, say, five or eight or twenty years, when actually it has a useful life of fifteen, twenty, or fifty years. Each year the owner deducts the fictitious rate of depreciation from income. In theory this merely postpones taxes, since when the item is fully depreciated the deductions halt. But meanwhile the government loses the use of the tax money, and must borrow it elsewhere. During and after the Korean War, the privilege of unusually rapid write-offs was extended to roughly $35 billion of investments, some of them connected with defense only by the exercise of a supple imagination. It is estimated that the Treasury lost $3 to $5 billion on this program just in the interest it paid on the money it had to borrow.

But that is by no means the whole story. Once an investment is fully depreciated, it may be sold—frequently, in these inflationary times, at a higher price than was originally paid for it. The original owner then pays, at maximum, a 25 per cent capital-gains tax on the profit. The second owner begins to depreciate his purchase all over again—at a higher cost basis. The miracle of the loaves and fishes has been brought up to date.

Years ago some clever chap figured out another amiable fiction that has bled the Treasury out of billions. His client, let us assume, sold turpentine from a large storage tank, which he replenished from time to time. Prices had been rising for years and seemed destined to rise indefinitely. The tax adviser thought it would be helpful, "taxwise," if every time his client sold turpentine the very last batch he had bought—and therefore the costliest—happened to come out of the spigot. The profit on the sale thus would be smaller.

This, said a professor later in the *Journal of Accountancy,* is "an assault on common sense." Physically, it couldn't be done. But in tax accounting, it was done. "My client has some of the oldest turpentine in Georgia," an accountant once told me.

This method of inventory accounting is called LIFO (last in, first out), to distinguish it from FIFO (first in, first out). One oil company told its stockholders that it saved $12 million the year it switched from FIFO to LIFO.

It was a great day in retailing when department stores won the right to apply LIFO to their inventories—preposterous as it may be to assume that stores are keeping goods for years when actually they try to turn over their stocks a dozen times a year. R. H. Macy & Co. even tried to apply LIFO *retroactively,* and persuaded one court to go along, but lost on an appeal by the government. Had it won, it is estimated that the department-store industry would have collected a billion dollars in tax refunds.

There is a theoretical drawback to LIFO. If a decline in prices were to set in, LIFO would increase taxable profits rather than decrease them. But in that event, there might not be any profits to pay taxes on anyway, and furthermore, there is little doubt that the Treasury or Congress would permit the taxpayer to switch back to FIFO.

Now You See It . . .

Where taxes are concerned, said Judge Learned Hand in a famous opinion, if it is legal it is not immoral. In fact, the aim of most avoidance devices and tax-relief measures is to conceal the honest origin of funds—i.e., to pretend that the taxpayer did not get the money for services rendered. Thus the film star forms a corporation and pretends to be a speculator rather than an actor. An honest profit, like an honest wage, is penalized under the law; hence it must be postponed, renamed, turned into a capital gain, or made to vanish entirely. These goals may be achieved in a number of ways, of which the following are no more than a small sampling:

¶ A company or individual may set up a corporation in a tax-free haven abroad, which may keep its profits from exports and other foreign operations intact until the firm is liquidated and the profits brought home as capital gains. A *Wall Street Journal* reporter recently encountered subsidiaries of many such taxpayers as U.S. Steel and Bethlehem in the sunny Bahamas. Most of them were close-mouthed about what they were doing there.

¶ Within certain limits one can also organize a separate corporation for each aspect of a business operation, each corporation paying the reduced rate on the first $25,000 of income. Some of the profits may be carried over as reserves until liquidation, when they become capital gains.

¶ One may give stock to members of one's family, and set up multiple trusts to get out of the high brackets, both in this life and in the hereafter. Through various means, a business may be made to support one's poor relations without the money ever passing through the donor's hands and thus being taxed.

¶ As Sylvia Porter advised recently in the New York *Post*: "Make sure to investigate the possibility of organizing a corporation which elects NOT to be taxed as a corporation—the so-called pseudo-corporation.'" Among the many incentives, she points out, is that an owner can become his own employee and set up various fringe benefits, such as pension plans, tax free.

*   *   *

One penalty of doing business under a tax system based on legal fictions is that it becomes difficult to tell what is truth. One company may be reporting a loss and actually be thriving. Another may be reporting a profit but wasting away its assets. Only the expert knows. Keeping two sets of books is no longer evidence of fraud. Some railroads legally keep at least three: one for the icc and rate proceedings, one for the tax collector, and one for the board of directors to know what's really going on.

What this does to statistics may be imagined. How can one tell whether to buy or sell a stock, whether the money supply should be tightened or eased, whether prices and wages are too low or too high, what the outlook is for sales and for plant investment—in short, what our private and public economic policies should be—if we keep changing the rules to permit the concealment of income from the tax collector? Economic data have far too wide a margin of error to begin with; using them now is like piloting a ship into port at night while somebody keeps shifting the beacons. . . .

10. Is Progressive Taxation Just? *

FRIEDRICH A. HAYEK

As is true of many similar measures, progressive taxation has assumed its present importance as a result of having been smuggled in under false pretenses. When at the time of the French Revolution and again during the socialist agitation preceding the revolutions of 1848 it was frankly advocated as a means of redistributing incomes, it was decisively rejected. "One ought to execute the author and not the project," was the liberal Turgot's indignant response to some early proposals of this sort. When in the 1830's they came to be more widely advocated, J. R. McCulloch expressed the chief objection in the often quoted statement: "The moment you abandon the cardinal principle of exacting from all individuals the *same proportion of their income* or *of their property,* you are at sea without rudder or compass, and there is no amount of injustice and folly you may not commit." In 1848 Karl Marx and Friedrich Engels frankly proposed "a heavy progressive or graduated income tax" as one of the measures by which, *after* the first stage of the revolution, "the proletariat will use its political supremacy to wrest, by degrees, all capital from the bourgeois, to centralize all instruments of production in the hands of the state." And these measures they described as "means of despotic inroads on the right of property, and on the condition of bourgeois production . . . measures . . . which appear economically insufficient and untenable but which, in the course of the movement outstrip themselves, necessitate further inroads upon the old

* *The Constitution of Liberty* (Chicago: University of Chicago Press, 1960), pp. 308-315. Reprinted by permission of the University of Chicago Press. Copyright 1960 by University of Chicago Press.

social order and are unavoidable as a means of entirely revolutionizing the mode of production." But the general attitude was still well summed up in A. Thiers's statement that "proportionality is a principle, but progression is simply hateful arbitrariness," or John Stuart Mill's description of progression as "a mild form of robbery."

But after this first onslaught had been repelled, the agitation for progressive taxation reappeared in a new form. The social reformers, while generally disavowing any desire to alter the distribution of incomes, began to contend that the total tax burden, assumed to be determined by other considerations, should be distributed according to "ability to pay" in order to secure "equality of sacrifice" and that this would be best achieved by taxing incomes at progressive rates. Of the numerous arguments advanced in support of this, which still survive in the textbooks on public finance, one which looked most scientific carried the day in the end. It requires brief consideration because some still believe that it provides a kind of scientific justification of progressive taxation. Its basic conception is that of the decreasing marginal utility of successive acts of consumption. In spite of, or perhaps because of, its abstract character, it has had great influence in making scientifically respectable what before had been admittedly based on arbitrary postulates.

Modern developments within the field of utility analysis itself have, however, completely destroyed the foundations of this argument. It has lost its validity partly because the belief in the possibility of comparing the utilities to different persons has been generally abandoned and partly because it is more than doubtful whether the conception of decreasing marginal utility can legitimately be applied at all to income as a whole, i.e., whether it has meaning if we count as income all the advantages a person derives from the use of his resources. From the now generally accepted view that utility is a purely relative concept (i.e., that we can only say that a thing has greater, equal, or less utility compared with another and that it is meaningless to speak of the degree of utility of a thing by itself), it follows that we can speak of utility (and of decreasing utility) of income only if we express utility of income in terms of some other desired good, such as leisure (or the avoidance of effort). But if we were to follow up the implications of the contention that the utility of income in terms of effort is decreasing, we would arrive at curious conclusions. It would, in effect, mean that, as a person's income grows, the incentive in terms of additional income which would be required to induce the same marginal effort would increase. This might lead us to argue for regressive taxation, but certainly not for progressive. It is, however, scarcely worthwhile to follow this line of thought further. There can now be little doubt that the use of utility analysis in the theory of taxation was all a regrettable mistake (in which some of the most distinguished economists of the time shared) and that the sooner we can rid ourselves of the confusion it has caused, the better.

Those who advocated progressive taxation during the latter part of the nineteenth century generally stressed that their aim was only to achieve equality of sacrifice and not a redistribution of income; also they generally held that this aim could justify only a "moderate" degree of progression and that its "excessive" use (as in fifteenth-century Florence, where rates had been pushed up to 50 per cent) was, of course, to be condemned. Though all attempts to supply an objective standard for an appropriate rate of progression failed and though no answer was offered when it was objected that, once the principle was accepted, there would be no assignable limit beyond which progression might not be carried with equal justification, the discussion moved entirely in a context of contemplated rates which made any effect on the distribution of income appear negligible. The suggestion that rates would not stay within these limits was treated as a malicious distortion of the argument, betraying a reprehensible lack of confidence in the wisdom of democratic government.

It was in Germany, then the leader in "social reform," that the advocates of progressive taxation first overcame the resistance and its modern evolution began. In 1891, Prussia introduced a progressive income tax rising from 0.67 to 4 per cent. In vain did Rudolf von Geist, the venerable leader of the then recently consummated movement for the *Rechtsstaat,* protest in the Diet that this meant the abandonment of the fundamental principle of equality before the law, "of the most sacred principle of equality," which provided the only barrier against encroachment on property. The very smallness of the burden involved in the new schemes made ineffective any attempt to oppose it as a matter of principle.

Though some other Continental countries soon followed Prussia, it took nearly twenty years for the movement to reach the great Anglo-Saxon powers. It was only in 1910 and 1913 that Great Britain and the United States adopted graduated income taxes rising to the then spectacular figures of 8¼ and 7 per cent, respectively. Yet within thirty years these figures had risen to 97½ and 91 per cent.

Thus in the space of a single generation what nearly all the supporters of progressive taxation had for half a century asserted could not happen came to pass. This change in the absolute rates, of course, completely changed the character of the problem, making it different not merely in degree but in kind. All attempt to justify these rates on the basis of capacity to pay was, in consequence, soon abandoned, and the supporters reverted to the original, but long avoided, justification of progression as a means of bringing about a more just distribution of income. It has come to be generally accepted once more that the only ground on which a progressive scale of over-all taxation can be defended is the desirability of changing the distribution of income and that this defense cannot be based on any scientific argument but must be recognized as a frankly political postulate, that is, as an attempt to impose upon society a pattern of distribution determined by majority decision.

An explanation of this development that is usually offered is that the great increase in public expenditure in the last forty years could not have been met without resort to steep progression, or at least that, without it, an intolerable burden would have had to be placed on the poor and that, once the necessity of relieving the poor was admitted, some degree of progression was inevitable. On examination, however, the explanation dissolves into pure myth. Not only is the revenue derived from the high rates levied on large incomes, particularly in the highest brackets, so small compared with the total revenue as to make hardly any difference to the burden borne by the rest; but for a long time after the introduction of progression it was not the poorest who benefited from it but entirely the better-off working class and the lower strata of the middle class who provided the largest number of voters. It would probably be true, on the other hand, to say that the illusion that by means of progressive taxation the burden can be shifted substantially onto the shoulders of the wealthy has been the chief reason why taxation has increased as fast as it has done and that, under the influence of this illusion, the masses have come to accept a much heavier load than they would have done otherwise. The only major

result of the policy has been the severe limitation of the incomes that could be earned by the most successful and thereby gratification of the envy of the less-well-off.

How small is the contribution of progressive tax rates (particularly of the high punitive rates levied on the largest incomes) to total revenue may be illustrated by a few figures for the United States and for Great Britain. Concerning the former it has been stated (in 1956) that "the entire progressive superstructure produces only about 17 per cent of the total revenue derived from the individual income tax"—or about 8½ per cent of all federal revenue—and that, of this, "half is taken from taxable income brackets up through $16,000-$18,000, where the tax rate reaches 50 per cent [while] the other half comes from the higher brackets and rates." As for Great Britain, which has an even steeper scale of progression and a greater proportional tax burden, it has been pointed out that "*all* surtax (on both earned and unearned incomes) only brings in about 2½ per cent of all public revenue, and that if we collared every £1 of income over £2.000 p.a. [$5.600], we would only net an extra 1½ per cent of revenue. . . . Indeed the massive contribution to income tax and sur-tax comes from incomes between £750 p.a. and £3.000 p.a. [$2.100-$8.400]—i.e. just those which begin with foremen and end with managers, or begin with public servants just taking responsibility and end with those at the head of our civil and other services."

Generally speaking and in terms of the progressive character of the two tax systems as a whole, it would seem that the contribution made by progression in the two countries is between 2½ and 8½ per cent of total revenue, or between ½ and 2 per cent of gross national income. These figures clearly do not suggest that progression is the only method by which the revenue required can be obtained. It seems at least probable (though nobody can speak on this with certainty) that under progressive taxation the gain to revenue is less than the reduction of real income which it causes.

If the belief that the high rates levied on the rich make an indispensable contribution to total revenue is thus illusory, the claim that progression has served mainly to relieve the poorest classes is belied by what happened in the democracies during the greater part of the period since progression was introduced. Independent studies in the United States, Great Britain, France, and Prussia agree that, as a rule, it was those of modest income who provided the largest number of voters that were let off most lightly, while not only those who had more income but also those who had less carried a much heavier proportional burden of total taxation. The best illustration of this situation, which appears to have been fairly general until the last war, is provided by the results of a detailed study of conditions in Britain, where in 1936-37 the total burden of taxation on fully earned income of families with two children was 18 per cent for those with an annual income of £100 per annum, which then gradually fell to a minimum of 11 per cent at £350 and then rose again, to reach 19 per cent only at £1,000. What these figures (and the similar data for other countries) clearly show is not only that, once the principle of proportional taxation is abandoned, it is not necessarily those in greatest need but more likely the classes with the greatest voting strength that will profit, but also that all that was obtained by progression could undoubtedly have been obtained by taxing the masses with modest incomes as heavily as the poorest groups.

It is true, of course, that developments since the last war in Britain, and probably elsewhere, have so increased the progressive character of the income tax as to make the burden of taxation progressive throughout and that, through redistributive expenditure on subsidies and services, the income of the very lowest classes has been increased (so far as these things can be meaningfully measured: what can be shown is always only the cost and not the value of the services rendered) by as much as 22 per cent. But the latter development is little dependent on the present high rates of progression but is financed mainly by the contributions of the middle and upper ranges of the middle class.

* * *

The real reason why all the assurances that progression would remain moderate have proved false and why its development has gone far beyond the most pessimistic prognostications of its opponents is that all arguments in support of progression can be used to justify any degree of progression. Its advocates may realize that beyond a certain point the adverse effects on the efficiency of the economic system may become so serious as to make it inexpedient to push it any further. But the argument based on the presumed justice of progression provides for no limitation, as has often been admitted by its supporters, before all incomes above a certain figure are confiscated and those below left untaxed. Unlike proportionality, progression provides no principle which tells us what the relative burden of different persons ought to be. It is no more than a rejection of proportionality in favor of a discrimination against the wealthy without any criterion for limiting the extent of this discrimination. Because "there is no ideal rate of progression that can be demonstrated by formula," it is only the newness of the principle that has prevented its being carried at once to punitive rates. But there is no reason why "a little more than before" should not always be represented as just and reasonable.

It is no slur on democracy, no ignoble distrust of its wisdom, to maintain that, once it embarks upon such a policy, it is bound to go much further than originally intended. This is not to say that "free and representative institutions are a failure" or that it must lead to "a complete distrust in democratic government," but that democracy has yet to learn that, in order to be just, it must be guided in its action by general principles. What is true of individual action is equally true of collective action, except that a majority is perhaps even less likely to consider explicitly the long-term significance of its decision and therefore is even more in need of guidance by principles. Where, as in the case of progression, the so-called principle adopted is no more than an open invitation to discrimination and, what is worse, an invitation to the majority to discriminate against a minority, the pretended principle of justice must become the pretext for pure arbitrariness.

What is required here is a rule which, while still leaving open the possibility of a majority's taxing itself to assist a minority, does not sanction a majority's imposing upon a minority whatever burden it regards as right. That a majority, merely because it is a majority, should be entitled to apply to a minority a rule which does not apply to itself is an infringement of a principle much more fundamental than democracy itself, a principle on which the justification of democracy rests. We have seen before (in chaps. x and xiv) that if the classifications of persons which the law must employ are to result neither in privilege nor in discrimination, they must rest on distinctions which those inside the group singled out, as well as those outside it, will recognize as relevant.

It is the great merit of proportional taxation that it provides a rule which is likely to be agreed upon by those who will pay absolutely more and those who will pay absolutely less and which, once accepted, raises no problem of a separate rule applying only to a minority. Even if progressive taxation does not name the individuals to be taxed

at a higher rate, it discriminates by introducing a distinction which aims at shifting the burden from those who determine the rates onto others. In no sense can a progressive scale of taxation be regarded as a general rule applicable equally to all—in no sense can it be said that a tax of 20 per cent on one person's income and a tax of 75 per cent on the larger income of another person are equal. Progression provides no criterion whatever of what is and what is not to be regarded as just. It indicates no halting point for its application, and the "good judgment" of the people on which its defenders are usually driven to rely as the only safeguard is nothing more than the current state of opinion shaped by past policy.

That the rates of progression have, in fact, risen as fast as they have done is, however, also due to a special cause which has been operating during the last forty years, namely, inflation. It is now well understood that a rise in aggregate money incomes tends to lift everybody into a higher tax bracket, even though their real income has remained the same. As a result, members of the majorities have found themselves again and again unexpectedly the victims of the discriminatory rates for which they had voted in the belief that they would not be affected.

This effect of progressive taxation is often represented as a merit, because it tends to make inflation (and deflation) in some measure self-correcting. If a budget deficit is the source of inflation, revenue will rise proportionately more than incomes and may thus close the gap; and if a budget surplus has produced deflation, the resulting fall of incomes will soon bring an even greater reduction in revenue and wipe out the surplus. It is very doubtful, however, whether, with the prevailing bias in favor of inflation, this is really an advantage. Even without this effect, budgetary needs have in the past been the main source of recurrent inflations;

and it has been only the knowledge that an inflation, once started, is difficult to stop that in some measure has acted as a deterrent. With a tax system under which inflation produces a more than proportional increase in revenue through a disguised increase in taxes which requires no vote of the legislature, this device may become almost irresistibly tempting.

C. Minimum Risk or Maximum Risk?

11. The Sense of Despair*

DAVID RIESMAN

OUR two-party system has among its great risks the fact that, when a bipartisan consensus develops, the view of a majority may attain a virtual unanimity in Congress and in our public policy. Now this has taken place in a society where differences of social class, of region and of ethnic origin are becoming attenuated—even those most devoted to the dogma of states' rights have never in my experience shown the slightest concern with the growing *federal* power to exterminate the planet. (Many who object violently to the fluoridation of local water supplies now urge the resumption of hydrogen bomb tests.) When the mass media were less massive, there was a large isolationist belt in the country, in the Midwest and in the working class, but today there is hardly an American who hasn't heard of Castro and who isn't apt to say to an interviewer that he's "tired" of being pushed around by the Communists.

In fact, a more accurate statement would be to say that he was simply tired, tired of thinking, tired of complexity, tired of trying to grasp a world that has poured in on him all too soon. Merge the quick impatience of the educated with the slow impatience of what Veblen called the "underlying population" and a sense of despair is

* *New Republic* (October 2, 1961), pp. 15-18. Reprinted by permission of the *New Republic*.

apt to be the result, whether in the South before the firing on Fort Sumter or in the whole country at present before the closing off of East Berlin from West Berlin. While despair may drive some people into apathy, it tends to drive many Americans to what soldiers in the war termed "flight forward," when out of near paralyzing fear soldiers rush at the enemy "to get it over with."

President Eisenhower had a gift for doing nothing benignly that for a long time moderated this spirit, only to have it break out more fiercely in the last years of his monarchial reign and to become perhaps the chief issue on which President Kennedy sought to take power away from the Republicans. Indeed President Kennedy set the tone of the campaign so that it was fought by both candidates in terms of proposing more strenuous, more effective, and in Kennedy's case more purposive and self-sacrificing responses to the Communist bloc.

Convinced by his own rhetoric, and encouraged by his own abilities and those of his new team, President Kennedy seems to have taken office with the illusion of having more freedom of action at home and abroad than he had. In fact, his room for maneuver had already been curbed by the history of American-Soviet relations in the postwar years and by the fact that the latent pool of ethnocentric patriotism and hostility to most foreigners endemic to this country had been turned increasingly against the Communists through the ability of right-wing propagandists to profit from Communist aggressions and successes. The more liberal and internationalist forces, very much on the defensive, managed to put Adlai Stevenson and a few other spokesmen into visible posts, but as opinion in the country hardened over Cuba and Berlin, the minority constituencies of these men were further narrowed by the militant and military mobilization that the President has tried to manage, but which, in my judgment, may end by managing him.

To understand what is occurring we must remind ourselves that the history of United States-Soviet relations has been marked on our side by wildly erratic swings of trust and mistrust, fear and condescension. I refer here to the attitudes of the educated, for the uneducated have always—even during World War II—mistrusted the Russians if they thought about them at all. The elites concerned with international affairs underestimated Soviet industrial and hence military accomplishments in the 1920's and 1930's, and hence were overimpressed by Russian successes during the Second World War, failing to notice that Stalin's planes were caught on the ground on a June Sunday (despite years of apparent fear of a Hitler attack, and ample warnings from the British, the Americans, his own military attaché in Berlin, and even from German dissidents), and that, before holding the line at Stalingrad, Stalin's leadership managed to lose a third of his country and most of his armies.

There then followed a period when Stalin was "Uncle Joe," when his American supporters had considerable influence, and when insufficient thought was given to and precautions taken against revived Soviet military and ideological power. The Red (though not Soviet) assault in Greece, the blockade of Berlin, the coup in

Prague, the attack in Korea, and the revelation of domestic Communist conspiracies led in another wild swing to our totalist outlook on the Cold War: we hastily concluded it was impossible to arrive at agreements with the USSR; and anyway, they would be broken, or regarded as a step in the calculated campaign of world dominion. We were entirely unprepared to seize the opportunity for serious negotiation that the death of Stalin provided, prior to the East German riots that so frightened proponents of a policy of liberalization within the USSR.

While we had repeatedly insisted that we should negotiate only from a position of strength, and that we did not bow to threats, the fact is that we have not taught the Russians any consistent way of dealing with us: when they are quiet, we tend to interpret this as weakness on their part, based on the success of our earlier policies, while when they are belligerent we tend to respond by an amalgamation of bluster, conciliation and counterthreats.

At the Geneva Foreign Ministers' Conference of May-July, 1959, the Soviets demanded cessation of aggressive propaganda beamed East from West Berlin, and troop reductions in Berlin. Secretary Herter agreed in principle on both points, while there was no agreement on the details. Gromyko, however, refused to guarantee the Western access to Berlin, helping perhaps in this way to give grounds to the current anxieties that this access is what Khrushchev is really out to destroy. Very possibly Khrushchev had instructed Gromyko to leave these concessions to be made by him at the hoped-for meeting with President Eisenhower; and after the Conference adjourned Khrushchev's visit to Washington followed, an important sign of recognition for himself personally as well as for his country. A joint communiqué after Camp David (September 27, 1959) referred to the reopening of negotiations on Berlin, whose situation Eisenhower spoke of as "abnormal," and Khrushchev on returning had his visit described in the Soviet press as a great success.

At that time, buoyed by his friendship with the President, Khrushchev would probably have been satisfied by the limited concessions on Berlin discussed at Geneva and in addition some tacit recognition for East Germany; such a compromise might then have seemed a sufficient support against neo-Stalinist and Chinese critics, who in and out of season accuse him of being taken in by the wily imperialists who can only understand the language of force. When Khrushchev's visit to this country was not quickly followed up by a return visit of our President, the West German leaders and their American supporters had ample opportunity to make short work of the "era of good feelings." Secretary Herter's speech in Chicago of March, 1960, was followed by Under-Secretary Dillon's blunt attack on April 20 against Khrushchev's "peaceful coexistence" platform. While the Russians (and even Ulbricht in a speech the same day as Dillon's) talked hopefully about an *interim* solution on Berlin, Dillon—while nominally adhering to the Administration program for such a solution—accused the Soviets of poisonous propaganda, attacked their imperialist ambitions, emphasized our need for strong arms and allies, and declared that we would not accept the Russian "distorted picture of the German problem as a factual premise upon which to negotiate." Since the Russians think America is run by a power elite, they have little sense of the depth of popular anti-Communist feeling and of the impact this feeling has in politics and in the mass media. Were they to assume from Dillon's speech a renewed move by "Wall Street" to intensify the Cold War? Yuri Zhukov was sent to Washington to find out, and on the basis of his report Khrushchev reacted to the altered American climate with an aggressive speech in Baku, although as yet he avoided attacking the President and took no aggressive action.

We had insisted throughout—as we insist now—that we do not negotiate under pressure of deadlines; Khrushchev had yielded by not mentioning any time limit; yet the Camp David spirit had proved, as Khrushchev no doubt had been warned by his critics, insufficient to contain the President's chief deputies in foreign affairs. The forthcoming Summit thereupon appeared as if it would intensify Khrushchev's political embarrassment; but the affair might have gone forward anyway, though it seems unlikely, had the Dillon speech not been followed by the U-2 incident which not only (as Leo Szilard has pointed out) made clear our awareness of where Soviet bases lay hidden and thus jeopardized the precarious balance of terror, but also led our President to accept personal responsibility in the face of Khrushchev's last-minute efforts to leave him an opening. Apart from the President's natural inclination toward candor, this action betokened the Administration's increasingly unmitigated concern with images, how men and issues can be made to look, as against the more difficult and dangerous task of educating our people as to how things are.

At the present time, at any rate, having repressed whatever twinges of shame and guilt some Americans felt about the U-2, all that most people remember is that Khrushchev reacted with brutal rage at Paris—forgetting that (having let himself go and shown his own partisans and rivals that he could not be permanently gulled) he then two days later in Berlin made a relatively mild speech, containing no new time limits concerning that city.

Since May, 1960, Khrushchev has felt he had to wait for the election. His Ambassador in this country had made clear that he was impatient for a meeting with Kennedy; very likely he feared, as after Camp David, that something would occur to disrupt the possibility of negotiations with the new incumbent over Berlin and over Central Europe generally. Something of course did happen: Cuba. While this was not the doing of the Soviet Union (which at various times has tried to restrain Castro), the public took it in a paranoid way, as if every revolution and anything that goes wrong with us were part of some huge plot. The public cannot experience a riot in Japan or a man in space without anxious scrutiny of the Cold War box score and a cumulative, frustrating feeling of impending defeat.

Of course, on a rational level it is true that the United States no longer has its unequivocal way in the United Nations and in the world. It is also true that in Latin America, Africa, and Asia, the old colonial ways are eroding; but this is not necessarily a boon to the Communists or a blow to this country —on the contrary, if we stand for freedom and justice we should welcome these changes. But it is a blow if the colonial powers are permitted to blackmail us repeatedly by threatening to desert the flimsy structure of NATO, an organization brought into being to do a necessary but no longer needed job, now going ahead with a life of its own and leading us at times against our will. America is still immensely rich and strong—so much so that we set the models by which the Russians and a number of other countries judge themselves, judge their developments and progress, and indeed the very idea of development and progress.

American Self-Doubts

Thus, it would seem that the realistic changes in the world balance of power are insufficient to explain the degree of defeatism in this country. Mussolini was admired because he made the trains run on time. Americans don't consciously admire the Russians and the Chinese because they make people run on time (or so they say). But I think this is a latent attraction of an authoritarian system, a system that has or appears to have an unequivocal national purpose. Business-

men who go to the Soviet Union are impressed in spite of themselves. Having thought the Russians barbarians, they are astonished by Soviet industrial know-how. And while it is true that machines and organizations sometimes break down, this can be excused in a newly-developing country, especially since it isn't due to strongly unionized workers lying down on their featherbeds; labor discipline in the USSR would gladden the heart of Weirton steel! Every time a train or plane is late in this country; every time sloppy work is done or people goof off, every time orders are sabotaged and not obeyed; every time one feels guilty about one's indolence or that of one's children or that of "the masses"; every time the President urges government departments to release people for the long Fourth of July weekend—on all such occasions, which go against the grain of our traditional American morality, many people must have a feeling of sin or guilt which is intensified by the contrast with the energetic, hardworking and dynamic Communists. And while the elite has long had these feelings, symbolized by the misgivings about the affluence that became endemic in recent years, the public at large has only begun to feel this way with Sputnik; and the "failure" in Cuba—so much less a failure than a victory would have been—has greatly intensified these feelings.

Whether President Kennedy came away from the Vienna meeting convinced that Khrushchev wanted, as the headlines say, to "grab Berlin" is not clear; it is likely that he realized that one doesn't give six months' notice if one wants to make a grab, and Khrushchev has made amply clear that what worries him is his deliquescent East German satellite and West German rearmament and not West Berlin *per se,* which simply gives him the leverage for pressure on us. At any rate, President Kennedy decided that *he* would "grab Berlin," that is, Berlin as a symbol, to assist the shift away from reliance on massive retaliation by building up conventional forces, to get his foreign aid program through Congress, and to satisfy a partly phantom, partly real public opinion that insists that something—no matter what—be done. Undoubtedly also he wanted to make amply clear to Khrushchev and to our allies American willingness to defend exposed positions, so that the very fact that West Berlin presents a militarily hopeless problem in terms of conventional warfare *behind the Iron Curtain* may make it seem a terrain attractive for nuclear brinkmanship.

In spite of the fact that there are many ways in which a compromise could be reached over Berlin that would both satisfy Khrushchev's own need for Eastern Zone stability and the West's needs for reassured access to West Berlin, it is hard for me to imagine a way in which this game of brinkmanship can be won by President Kennedy. If the crisis is resolved in a way that can be interpreted as satisfactory, the right-wing will almost certainly insist that this is the result of his show of "strength": mobilization and bellicosity, rather than diplomacy and flexibility, will be credited with the results. The doctrine of brinkmanship will continue to tempt the clever or the demagogic, increasing the fears of the Communist bloc and of our less foolhardy allies, until that day of judgment when both armed camps, dug in deep psychologically and geologically, have run out of all possible compromises and have convinced themselves that the other side has lost the will to fight. On the other hand, if the right-wing can charge the President with making too many concessions, and any may seem too many, the country may become still more alarmed and defeatist than it already is; and President Kennedy will also be wholly dug in as the captive of his aroused followers.

What Might Be Done?

Yet even as things are, there are things the President could do to regain some freedom of action. He could make his own aims less unclear to this country, to our allies, and to our potential foes, if the moves he makes toward mobilization could be coupled with measures demonstrating that our build-up of conventional forces is in the pursuance of the long-run aim of scaling down the nuclear threat. For instance, the President might announce that all nuclear weapons on the continent were being withdrawn from field stations and placed in reserve depots inaccessible to local troops or otherwise hobbled (perhaps placed in Spain and England). The United States might announce that military planes were being kept a stated distance away from the Soviet borders, or that Russian observers were invited to visit bases in West Germany to satisfy themselves that no attack was in preparation and that the forces were only in reserve in case access to Berlin was stopped. Now that the Russians have disrupted the test ban negotiations it is all the more important to emphasize that disarmament still remains our goal and to seek for new areas in which we can work toward world stability. For what is perfectly clear is that the policy of meeting provocation with provocation and tit for tat has been a dismal failure since Vienna.

The sense of despair in the West that is the source of some of the feeling that we must make a "Custer's last stand" on Berlin is an outlook beyond military remedy. It can only be combated by evidence that the West is flexible as well as firm, creative as well as courageous. As President Kennedy periodically realizes, it is necessary to mobilize, not more National Guard units, but more experimentalism and imagination in dealing with problems at home and abroad—as illustrated by what could be done to invigorate the commercial and cultural life of West Berlin, or of other, still more significant "showcases of democracy," such as India. In the present crisis there is a possibility that, by negotiations with the Russians, both sides could emerge with a positive achievement: the United States with new and clearer guarantees for West Berlin's freedom and access to the city; Khrushchev with a peace treaty with East Germany and a greater security for his satellite regimes in the area that has become his *cordon sanitaire,* as well as improved relations with the West; both sides with a lessened danger of war.

With the world as it is, we could be grateful for that. But over that horizon lies the possibility that the Russians would preoccupy us less, and our own needs and values would preoccupy us more; that we could shed our new form of the white man's burden: the image of ourselves as either omnipotent or nothing; and that we could persuade both ourselves and the Russians—and even, some day, the Chinese—that we live in a pluralistic world of give and take and that, all things considered, we have not fared so badly in that world. The dangers of Soviet misinterpretation of our intentions can be coped with by untiring patience, insistent search for points of common interest, and systematic efforts to look at matters as the other side (for whatever reasons) sees them, and with an eye single to the question, not of scoring this or that point in the Cold War, but of beginning to create an international order appropriate to the nuclear age.

12. Doctrine and Policy in Communist Imperialism: The Problem of Security and Risk*

JOHN COURTNEY MURRAY

As one observes the courses of American action in the world today, the doubt arises whether we at all "hold these truths" or any truths as determinative of our purposes and directive of our policies. This doubt has more than once arisen in the preceding pages. It has also been a stimulus in the recent efforts to define our National Purpose, or at least to launch a public debate about the National Purpose. A new situation seems to have come to pass. History attests that the Founding Fathers—practical men, all of them—were well aware of the uses of doctrine. Today there is evidence that we have no use for doctrine—or perhaps even no doctrines to use.

* Chapter 10, *We Hold These Truths* (New York: Sheed and Ward, 1960), pp. 221-247. Reprinted by permission of Sheed and Ward, Inc. Copyright 1960 by Sheed and Ward, Inc.

If now there is a vacuum where once there was substance, the fact is serious. It is particularly serious in view of our present confrontation with the Soviet Union. Coexistence with the Communist empire is the present fact. There are those who wish to transform the fact into a policy by adding various adjectives to the word "coexistence." There is talk, for instance, of "peaceful" coexistence, or of "competitive" coexistence. But, before coexistence, however qualified adjectivally, can become a policy, it is necessary to know just what kind of an empire we are coexisting with. This is the first difficulty. Academic and public opinion in the matter is divided. There is little common agreement, of a firmly articulated kind, with regard to the aims and motivations and scope of Communist imperialism in its action on the world scene. One could distinguish at least four or five different schools of thought. Their major differences derive from their variant estimates of the role of doctrine or ideology in Soviet behavior. There are even those who refuse to admit that ideology plays any significant role. The Soviet doctrine, they say, is pretty much the same as our doctrine —namely, that doctrine has no uses.

There are also those who are content to cite as the single characteristic of the Soviet empire that it is intent on "world domination"; and they let it go at that. But one cannot let it go at that. The intellectual tyranny of phrases, to which we have long been accustomed in domestic politics, has invaded the field of foreign policy in consequence of the impact of democracy on the conduct of war and on the making of peace. The trouble is that the stock phrases tend to become simply incantations. They are invoked as curses on the enemy or as cries of alarm to sustain a mood of fear and opposition. So it is with the phrase "world domination." It has ceased to yield any clear demonstrable meaning. It has even acquired false connotations, as if the primary Soviet aim were domination by military conquest. In consequence some would wish to discard the phrase altogether, as unreal and unhelpful. But this would be a mistake of method that would lead to substantial error in viewing the structure of the problem that confronts America today. The phrase has meaning, but it needs to be analyzed in the light of the four unique aspects of the Soviet empire.

A Fourfold Uniqueness

First, Russia is unique as a state or a power. For the first time in history it has brought under a single supreme government the 210,000,000 people scattered over the 8,600,000 square miles of the Euro-Asiatic plain, the great landmass that stretches from the River Elbe to the Pacific Ocean. This gigantic power is a police state of new proportions and unique efficiency. Within it there is no such thing as the "rule of law"; there is only the thing called "Soviet legality." Power is used according to certain forms; but there is no concern for justice and no sense of human rights. The Soviet Union has not adopted the Western concept of law nor has it evolved a comparable concept of its own. Its theory of government is purely and simply despotism. In this respect Sir Winston Churchill was right in viewing the Russians (as Sir Isaiah Berlin reports) as a "formless, quasi-Asiatic mass beyond the walls of European civilization." These walls, that contain the Western realization of civility, were erected by men who understood the Western heritage of law—Roman, Greek, Germanic, Christian. The Soviet Union has no such understanding of law.

Moreover, through a novel set of institutions the Soviet Union has succeeded in centralizing all governmental power to a degree never before achieved. The ultimate organ of control is the Communist party, a small group of men who think and act under an all-embracing discipline that has likewise never before been achieved. Under its historically new system—a totally socialized economy—the Soviet Union has become an industrial and technological power whose single rival is the United States. In rising to this status of power it has chosen to emphasize industries and technologies that are related to war. This state is consequently a military power of the first order. It has no rival in ground forces; its air power is adequate to all the new exigencies of war; and for the first time in history the state that controls the Heartland of the World Island has become a sea power of a special kind, an underwater power. Finally, its nuclear and missile capabilities are at least equal to those of the United States, for all practical purposes and many impractical ones.

Second, Russia is unique as an empire, as a manner and method of rule, as an *imperium*. It is organized and guided in accordance with a revolutionary doctrine. For the first time in history this doctrine has consciously erected an atheistic materialism into a political and legal principle that furnishes the substance of the state and determines its procedures. Soviet doctrine is exclusive and universal in its claim to furnish, not only an account of nature and history, but also a technique of historical change. It is therefore inherently aggressive in its intent; and it considers itself destined to sole survival as an organizing force in the world of politics. The Communist doctrine of the World Revolution has indeed undergone a century of change, since the days of Marx and Engels. Substantially, however, the change has been simply development. The basic inspiration has been steady and the continuity has been organic. As Prof. Alfred G. Meyer has pointed out in his book on Leninism, "Stalinism can and must be defined as a pattern of thought and action that flows directly from Leninism." [1] Prof. Bertram D. Wolfe has documented the same thesis in *Khrushchev and Stalin's Ghost*.[2] This thesis is in possession. And there is no convincing evidence that Mr. Khrushchev represents apostasy or even heresy.

Third, Russia is unique as an imperialism. The Soviet Union is essentially an empire, not a country. Nearly half her subjects should be considered "colonial peoples." Many of the "sister republics" are no more part of Russia than India was of Great Britain. As Mr. Edward Crankshaw has reminded us, "Even if Moscow retreated to the frontiers of the Soviet Union tomorrow, Russia would still be the greatest imperial power in the world." [3] But Mr. Crankshaw's other proposition,

that "Russian imperialism is at a dead end," is by no means true. It may indeed be difficult to describe the Soviet imperial design, but this is only because it is difficult to define Soviet imperialism. It is a new historical force, not to be likened to prior mysticisms of power. It is not at all based on the concept of a master-race, or on the aggrandizement of the sacred "nation," or on the fulfillment of a noble idea, such as the rule of law to be brought to the "lesser breeds." The newness of the imperialism has almost masked the fact that it is an imperialism.

It has exhibited a new mastery of older imperialistic techniques—military conquest, the enduring threat of force, political puppetry, centralized administration of minorities, economic exploitation of "colonial" regions. It has expanded the old concept of the "ally" into the new concept of the "satellite." But perhaps its newness is chiefly revealed in the creation of the historically unique imperialistic device known as "Soviet patriotism." This is not a thing of blood and soil but of mind and spirit. It is not born of the past, its deeds and sufferings, borne in common; it looks more to the future, to the deeds yet to be done and to the sufferings still to be borne. It is a "patriotism of a higher order," and of a more universal bearing, than any of the classic feelings for *das Vaterland, la patrie,* my country. It is a loyalty to the Socialist Revolution; it is also a loyalty to the homeland of the Revolution, Russia. Its roots are many—in ideology, in economic facts, and in the love of power; in a whole cluster of human resentments and idealisms; and in the endless capacities of the human spirit for ignorance, illusion, and self-deception. This higher patriotism claims priority over all mere national loyalties. It assures to the Soviet Union a form of imperialistic penetration into other states, namely, the Fifth Column, that no government in history has hitherto commanded. Soviet imperialism, unlike former imperialisms, can be content

---

[1] *Leninism.* Cambridge: Harvard University Press, 1957.

[2] New York: Praeger, 1956.

[3] *Russia Without Stalin: The Emerging Pattern.* New York: Viking, 1956.

with the creation of chaos and disorder; within any given segment of time it need not seek to impose a dominion, an order. The Soviet Union may indeed lack a finished imperial design; in any case, the concept of design is too rational for a force that owes little to reason. But it has something better for its purposes, which are inherently dark. It has a revolutionary vision.

If there must be a single phrase to sum up the intentions of Soviet imperialism, it would be far better to speak of "world revolution" than of "world domination." The word "revolution" has a definite meaning that signifies a definite possibility. The world as we know it can be radically changed; it is, in fact, changing daily before our eyes. Moreover, it is possible to know the directions of change that are implicit in the Communist world revolution, as it is guided by Communist doctrine. On the other hand, "world domination" defines not a process but a term. The term may be a Communist dream. It may even be admitted that this term is an historical possibility, if one admits that anything is possible in history. However, what we are called upon to cope with is an actuality, a process that is really going on, an intention that is presently operative—the imperialism of the World Revolution.

Finally, the Soviet Union is unique as the legatee of a longer history. It is the inheritor both of Tsarist imperialism and of mystical panslavist messianism. It carries on, at the same time that it fundamentally transforms, the myth of Holy Russia, the "spiritual people," the "godbearing children of the East," whose messianic destiny is to rescue humanity from the "Promethean West." Communism, whether in theory or in practice, is not a legacy of Western history, nor is it a "Christian heresy" (the pernicious fallacy popularized by Prof. Toynbee). Essentially, it came out of the East, as a conscious apostasy from the West. It may indeed be said that Jacobinism was its forerunner; but Jacobinism was itself an apostasy from the liberal tradition of the West, as well as from Christianity, by its cardinal tenet (roundly condemned by Pope Leo XIII) that there are no bounds to the juridical omnipotence of government, since the power of the state is not under the law, much less under God. In any case, Communism has assumed the task to which Jacobinism failed—that of putting an end to the history of the West. Communism has undertaken to inaugurate a new history, the so-called Third Epoch, that will abolish and supplant what are called the two Western epochs, feudalism and capitalism.

The Primacy of Communist Dogma

My proposition is that each of these four unique aspects of the Soviet Empire has consequences for American policy. No structure of policy will be intelligent or successful that does not reckon with all of them. Indeed, all our past mistakes of policy have resulted from the American disposition to ignore, or to misunderstand, one or the other of these four unique aspects of Russia.

It would be a lengthy task, although not a difficult one, to demonstrate this proposition with a fair measure of certitude. However, I shall make only two major points.

First, if the Soviet Union be regarded simply in the first of its unique aspects, as a state or power, under precision from its other aspects, there need be no serious conflict between it and the United States. By itself, the fact that a single government rules the Euro-Asiatic plain and possesses the technical competence to exploit its natural and human resources poses no serious threat to American interests. There is no reason why the Soviet Union, regarded simply as a state or power-complex, could not live in decently cooperative harmony with the other world-power, the United States. The American locus of power lies in another hemisphere. Our geopolitical position is secure; so too is theirs. Conflicts of interests and clashes of power would arise, but they could be composed peacefully. This point needs making in order to disallow the conception that the American-Soviet confrontation is purely a power-struggle between two colossi of power, whose sheer power is reciprocally a threat, one to the other. To see the problem thus, and to base American policy on anxious conjectures as to which power is "ahead" or "behind" in the accumulation of power, is to mistake the problem completely.

Second, the many-sided conflict known, not inappropriately, as the cold war is unintelligible (and therefore must seem unreal) except in the light of the second unique aspect of the Soviet state. It is an *imperium,* a mode of rule, guided in its internal and external policy by a comprehensive systematic doctrine that contradicts at every important point the tradition of the West. Soviet theory and practice stand in organic interdependence. Only Soviet doctrine makes Soviet power a threat to the United States. Only Soviet doctrine explains the peculiar nature of Soviet imperialism and shows it to be unappeasable in its dynamism. Only Soviet doctrine illumines the intentions of the new messianism that has come out of the East, fitted with an armature of power, and organized implacably against the West.

Here, of course, in the concept of an empire controlled by a dogma, is the sticking-point for the pragmatic American mind. Two questions arise. First, is this concept of the Soviet Empire true? Second, if it is, can the pragmatic mind take in its truth and be guided accordingly in the fashioning of policy? For my part, the answer to the first question is unhesitatingly yes. I am less sure about the answer to the second question. The American mind is consciously pragmatist. When questions can no longer be postponed, they are approached with an empirical, experimentalist attitude that focuses on contingencies of fact. The search is for compromise, for the "deal" that will be acceptable to both parties in the dispute. The notion of being controlled by theory is alien to this mentality. The further notion of a great state submitting its purposes and action to the control of a dogmatic philosophy seems absurd. The pragmatist mind instinctively refuses to take in this notion or to study its implications.

When, therefore, this pragmatist mind reads Stalin's statement about Soviet doctrine, that "there can be no doubt that as long as we are faithful to this doctrine, as long as we possess this compass, we shall be successful in our work," it can only conclude that Stalin must have been somehow "insincere." There is the further consideration that Soviet doctrine is couched in a technical jargon that is not only alien but very boring. The practical man puts it all aside. His distrust of ideas has itself become an idea. What he wants is "the facts." And he rapidly overlooks the essential fact that the purposes and actions of the Soviet Empire are unintelligible without reference to the ideas on which its leaders act.

In his book, *The Illusion of the Epoch: Marxism-Leninism as a Philosophical Creed,*[4] Prof. H. B. Acton makes this concluding statement: "Marxism is a philosophical farrago." Other scholars, within the Academy and within the Church, after even more extensive studies have likewise stigmatized the Soviet dogma as scientific, historical, philosophical, and theological nonsense. But what matters for the statesman is not that the dogma is nonsense but that the Soviet leaders act on the dogma, nonsense though it be. The evidence for this fact may not be unambiguously demonstrable; no historical evidence ever is. But it amply suffices for a firm case that may be made the premise of sound policy. This is

[4] Boston: Beacon Press, 1957.

not the place to present all of the evidence. The record runs back to Lenin's signing of the Peace of Brest-Litovsk. But the segment of history immediately succeeding World War II deserves a brief mention.

In 1945, despite her war losses, Russia was on the crest of the wave. She had territorial defense in sufficient depth on all fronts. Fellow-traveling governments controlled the new states, including the crucial salient, Czechoslovakia. In the United States, Britain, and France a mood of general, if not unbroken, goodwill towards Russia prevailed to a degree that was almost pathological. Germany, the old enemy of Czarist regimes, was in ruins, impotent, under a military government imposed by the Allies. The Western nations were disarming at breakneck speed. If Russia's own security were the goal, it had been achieved. If the goal were the fulfillment of an old-fashioned Czarist imperial design, looking to the consolidation of power, it too was substantially complete. Or, if the goal was simply the extension of the new imperialism through international enlistments under the device of the "higher patriotism," looking to what Crankshaw calls the "inconsequent mischief-making of the Comintern," the way to it lay open, and eager wishful thinkers in all lands were busily engaged in enlarging the possibilities of mischief, under hardly any opposition or even serious suspicion.

In any case, one would have expected subtle tactics of restraint. Instead the "tough line" suddenly appeared— ruthless pressure for direct control of the satellites, intervention in Greece (and Persia), obstructive opposition to the Marshall Plan and the Austrian Treaty, the Berlin blockade, and the creation of the Cominform. In consequence, within three years the Kremlin had dissipated its major asset of international goodwill. It created for itself a peril that had not previously existed. A divided and disarmed West had begun to unite and arm itself against the menace now visible, though not yet understood.

Why did all this happen? The only satisfactory answer is that the Kremlin was guided by Communist doctrine. The capitalist powers were well disposed? They could not be; the doctrine holds that the capitalist "camp" is irreconcilably hostile. Constitutional socialist governments would protect the socialist homeland against capitalist aggression? No; the doctrine holds that Social Democracy is inherently untrustworthy and ought to be destroyed, because it only deceives the worker and confuses the issue by its pretension to be a Third Force. World peace is the common goal, through negotiations within the framework of the United Nations? Nonsense; the doctrine holds that the conflict between the two homeland "camps" and the two colonial "fronts" is unappeasable. It is the necessary means to the World Revolution. It will be resolved only by the World Revolution. And in its resolution the methods of force cannot be dispensed with. Finally, the doctrine held that at the end of the War the capitalist "camp" simply had to be in a state of "weakness"; its "internal contradictions" were actively at work, presaging its downfall. By the doctrine, therefore, it was the moment for the strategy of the Revolution, the strategy of forceful aggression.

All this may sound rather silly to the pragmatist. In a sense it all was rather silly. The point is that it all happened. And it only happened because Soviet doctrine decreed its happening.

Moreover, it will not do to say that this dictation of policy and events by doctrine will not happen again; that Stalin is dead; that Russia is "different"; that new men are in charge; that they are realists and opportunists, men rather like ourselves who take the pragmatic view. Russia is indeed somewhat different, but only within the limits of the doctrine. The men in charge are new, but only within the limits imposed by their thorough conditioning by the doctrine. The Soviet leadership is not subject to changes of heart. What is more important (and to the pragmatist, unintelligible), it does not even learn by experience. The doctrine is forever at hand to discount Soviet experience of how the capitalist world acts.

The doctrine casts up an image of the capitalist world that does not derive from experience and is not to be altered by experience. It is a "scientific" image, the product of a science, dialectical materialism, whose basic postulate is that determinism rules the world of human history as well as the world of nature. It is through the distorting one-way glass, as it were, of this deterministic theory of capitalism that the Soviet leaders view what we consider to be the contingencies of the historical world —only they are not seen as contingencies but as determined. So far from altering the scientific image, they are interpreted in such a way as either to confirm it or at least leave it intact. When, for instance, the capitalist world professes its desire to be friendly, just, peaceful, cooperative, etc., such professions cannot but be bogus. Historical determinism will not permit the capitalist world to be other than hostile, unjust, aggressive, and war-mongering. Mr. George F. Kennan has commented, in rather baffled, but still superior, fashion, on "the systematic Soviet distortion of the realities of our world and of the purposes to which we are dedicated" (in *Russia, the Atom and the West*[5]). Mr. Kennan too views reality through his special glass. Apparently it does not occur to him that Soviet analysts of "fact" really believe in the categories of Marxist-Leninist ideology as instruments of interpretation. Like a good American, he believes that if only the Soviet leaders could be brought to see "the facts," with complete "freedom of mind," all would be well.

It is, of course, not impossible that some basic change may take place in Soviet doctrine. But if it did the reper-

cussions would be felt all through the edifice of power erected on the doctrine; and if they were not checked, the edifice could not long survive. The basic Soviet structure is an indivisible and interlocking whole. It cannot permit itself to be tampered with at any point, save on peril of destruction. Still less can it contemplate changes in the dogmas that sustain the edifice of imperialistic power.

The official atheism is necessary in order that the individual may claim no moral rights against the state and no freedom except within the "collective" freedom of the state. This exploitation of the individual in the service of the state is necessary as the premise of forcing further the gigantic technological development. The cult of Soviet patriotism is necessary to preserve the solidarity of the colonial empire over the more than thirty-five national minorities within the Soviet Union, and over the ring of satellite states, as well as to retain that indispensable adjunct of Soviet imperialism, the motley Fifth Column. The maintenance of the police state makes it necessary that there should be "danger from without," from irreconcilable, hostile, aggressive capitalist imperialism. This danger is also necessary to explain to the puzzled inquirer why the state is not withering away. The rejection of the possibility of entirely peaceful evolution to world socialism and the belief in force as the indispensable agent of the Revolution are necessary to sustain the burden of militarization and armament. And the whole edifice rests squarely in the basic Marxist dogma—the conflict of two opposed worlds leading dialectically and deterministically to the World Revolution. Finally, the personal security of the Soviet rulers and the continuing privileges of the "new class" are dependent on the maintenance both of the empire and of the revolutionary doctrine that sustains it. Thus self-interest buttresses belief in the doctrine.

The conclusion is that the Soviet Empire not only has been, and is, an

[5] New York: Harper and Brothers, 1958.

empire controlled by doctrine, but must continue to be such, on peril of ceasing to be itself. Even to speculate about making a basic change in the established doctrine of the World Revolution would be to raise the specter of the disintegration of the empire. The specter, we may be sure, will be forbidden to rise.

Communist Dogma and American Policy

This fourfold view of the unique reality of the Soviet Empire is the only solid premise of American foreign policy in foreign affairs and military defense. It is a more intelligent premise than the concept of "world domination" in any of the current understandings or misunderstandings of that phrase. It is also a more comprehensive premise than any analysis of the relatively superficial "facts of power."

The major value of a full view of the unique character of the Soviet Union is that it creates a limited but useful set of expectations on which to base American policy. We need not be left to the resources of improvisation or even to the instinctive reactions of purely practical wisdom—the kind of wisdom that made us enter the Korean War but was never able to explain why we did enter it. The Soviet Empire is governed by the inner laws of its own nature; like any laws they create expectabilities. We may, for instance, expect Communist leadership to yield only to calculations of power and success; force and the prospect of success by its use are the determinants of Soviet action. This expectation would clarify the problem of negotiations. It would suggest that we put an end, as quietly as possible, to the Wilsonian era of diplomacy with its exaggerated trust in world assemblies and in spectacular international conferences. It would further suggest the advisability of direct negotiations with Russia. For instance, if and when any agreement on disarmament is reached, it will be reached directly between the Kremlin and the White House, without the confusing assistance of additional nations, allied or neutral.

Again, a true view of the Soviet Union, as a unique imperialism, would suggest that we cease to confuse foreign policy with diplomatic negotiations. To paraphrase a famous remark, foreign policy is when you know what you want. It supposes that you know the possibility of getting what you want, before you decide that you want it. Negotiation is simply the means of getting what you want. The Soviet Union understands this. For instance, it is a fixed Soviet foreign policy to gain public international recognition of the successes of the Communist revolution as they are racked up. This policy is pursued through "negotiations" at international conferences. These conferences negotiate nothing. Either they simply register the political and military results to date and thus fulfill Soviet policy (e.g., the 1954 Geneva "settlement" on Korea and Indo-China) or they run out in sheer futility after two million words (e.g., the prior Berlin Conference). It is time we, too, learned not to fix our policy by negotiations but to conduct negotiations in order to fulfill our policies. It is time, too, that we laid aside completely the concept of "sincerity" as a category of political morality even though it is so dear to a type of Eastern-seaboard political mind that believes in nothing else. To inquire into Soviet "sincerity" or to require "sincerity" of the Soviet Union is a complete waste of time.

The chiefly important expectability or "sincerity" is that the Soviet Union will always act on its own doctrine. As the situation dictates, it will employ either the strategy of the Revolution or the tactics of the protection of the homeland and of the Revolution's imperialist advances. In either case, since the doctrine is inherently aggressive, it permits no "disengagement." It continually probes for every vacuum of power and for every soft spot of purpose. This is why "disengagement" as an American policy could not be other than disastrous. It would surely heighten the danger of war, most probably by permitting the creation of situations that we could not possibly accept. Only the very opposite policy is safe—a policy of continuous engagement at every point, on all levels of action, by both tactical and strategic moves. At times this policy of continuous engagement might well be enforced simply by variants of the highly effective argumentative technique of the blank and silent stare. The Russians employed it well in the tent at Panmunjom. Turkey has always used it successfully; and West Berlin has learned its value. We still talk too much.

A policy of continuous engagement with the World Revolution does not mean solely a policy of hostility, contradiction, and opposition. Nor is it to be translated primarily into military terms. The engagement can be cooperative, positive, constructive in a number of ways. Here I shall mention only one, because it is so neglected.

Perhaps the most alarming pages in Wolfgang Leonhard's book, *Child of the Revolution,*[6] are those in which he reports the effect had on him by Western newspapers, broadcasts, etc. The effect was nil. In fact, practically everything he heard or read about the West only delayed his break with Stalinism. On the intellectual or doctrinal level the disengagement between West and East seems to be almost complete. Torrents of words are poured out Eastward, of course. But they do not even engage the attention of the East. "Why do they always go on about freedom?" asked one of Leonhard's companions, as he got up, bored to death, to turn off a Western broadcast. "In the first place there is no freedom in the West, and in the second place people in the West do not even know what freedom is."

[6] Chicago: Regnery, 1958

The young Communist's disgusted comment makes the necessary point. Do people of the West understand what freedom is? Can they intelligently dispute the Communist thesis, that freedom means insight into historical necessity—an insight that is based on scientific theory? (One recalls General Eisenhower and Marshal Zhukov baffling one another in Berlin over the notion of freedom.) Or is it rather the American disposition to dismiss the whole dispute as "impractical," and irrelevant to politics? Or do we think that this basic issue of theory would be settled by distributing (as has been seriously suggested) an avalanche of Sears-Roebuck catalogues in the Soviet Union?

It may be that the Illusion of our Epoch will not be overcome by argument. Certainly it cannot be overcome by force. Perhaps it will succumb only to the enemy of all illusions—time. The fact remains that Communist doctrine is an affront to the Western tradition of reason; and the manner of empire that it sustains is a further affront to the liberal tradition of politics and law that was born of the Western tradition of reason. The further fact is that the West was so late in feeling the affront and still seems largely impotent to deliver against it an effective doctrinal answer, in a moment when a doctrinal answer is of the highest practical importance, not only to the East that will hear it, but to the West that will utter it—immediately, to itself. It may, of course, be that the West has ceased to understand itself. Prof. Toynbee may, in fact, be right in saying that the West now identifies itself with technology, as its cult and its sole export. If this be true, this failure of understanding, leading to a denial, more or less explicit, of the Western tradition by the West itself, would be the fateful "internal contradiction" that might lead to downfall. Ironically, Marx never saw this form of "internal contradiction," though it is the greatest weakness in the "camp" that he opposed.

The Domestic Issue

This may be the place to comment on the basic fiasco of our engagement with Communism on the domestic scene. The subject is a bit complicated. It is, of course, not necessary to invoke Communist influence to explain the various stupidities of American wartime and postwar policies. Stupidity itself is sufficient explanation. The pattern of it was set by the American President who was "certain," he said in all good faith, "that Stalin is not an imperialist." The anti-Communist movement, centering on the issue of internal subversion, probably compounded the confusion by transforming issues of stupidity into issues of "disloyalty." The muzzy sentimentalism of the 1945 climate has indeed been altered. Reckon this, if you like, to the credit of those who raised the cry of subversion. Public opinion, in the sense of public passion (which it very largely is), has been transformed. Everybody now mortally hates and fears what is known, rather vaguely, as "the Communist menace." It was "brought home" to them amid great tumult and shouting (only in this way, it seems, can things be brought home to the American people). This was a good thing. At that, by a strange irony, those who were the loudest in bringing the menace home were or are the last ones on American earth whom one would want to see in charge of combating the menace abroad, in the field of foreign policy, where the massive menace lies. By a contrasting irony, many of those who took the sound view in matters of foreign policy were fuzzy on the issue of internal subversion.

In any case, whatever its effect on public emotion, the anti-Communist movement has been fairly spectacular in its failure to contribute to public understanding. The problem of understanding centers on three large issues. What *is* this "thing from the East"? What *is* the "Western thing" in the name of which we oppose it? What

were the corrosive forces that were able to create a yawning spiritual and intellectual vacuum within the West, but were not able to fill it, with the result that the "thing from the East" found some lodgment there? Thousands of questions and answers before Congressional committees and bushels of propaganda sheets from patriotic societies have contributed almost nothing to an answer to these questions. In their turn, the forces that opposed the anti-Communist movement have rivaled it in their failure to contribute to public understanding. In considerable part they failed even to speak of the real issues, being content to retire, embattled, behind a rather porous barricade —a concept of democracy as an ensemble of procedures, a legal system of civil rights. It was not strange that in the end the public, with some instinctive feeling that the quarrel wasn't getting anywhere, and had become trivial anyway, should have grown bored with it. Imposed on a prior fiasco of understanding, this was a most lamentable result. The three basic questions still stand.

Even yet the response to Communist imperialism is largely in emotional terms—fear and hatred (or, conversely, pathetic appeals to "understand the Russians") and bursts of brief excitement over every new Communist success, and, for the rest, a last-minute rush to the resources of pragmatism in all its forms (notably including military technology) to meet particular issues as they arise.

The Uses of Force

This brings up the question that looms so large—the question of armaments and war. The underlying issue is whether a full view of the unique reality of the Soviet empire furnishes any reliable expectations in this critical area. There are several.

Soviet doctrine as a whole dictates a policy of maximum security and minimum risk. Risks can and must be minimum because the dialectic of history decrees that the capitalist world, though still powerful, is decaying and must inevitably disintegrate from within, whereas the forces of socialism are in constant ascendancy and must inevitably triumph. Security must be maximal because at every point the gains made by political or military means must be consolidated as the base for further revolutionary advance. The Soviet Union cannot be provoked into taking risks that exceed the minimum; for it does not act under external provocation but under an internal dynamism. These conclusions, already implicit in the doctrine, are confirmed by all the evidence in the historical record.

We may expect that Soviet doctrine will continue to dictate the same policy of maximal security and minimal risk. This expectation furnishes a measure by which to decide the gravest and most pervasive problem of foreign and military policy, namely, how to balance the elements of security and of risk. We may safely invert the Soviet proportions. Our policy should envisage a minimum of security and a maximum of risk. Only by such a policy can we seize and retain the initiative in world affairs. And it is highly dangerous not to have the initiative. On the premise of this balance we did, in fact, enter the Korean war, which was right. But then we retreated from the premise to a policy of minimal risk, which was a mistake.

Moreover, it would be prudent even to create situations of risk for the Soviet Union—situations in which the risk would be too great for it to take. We may be sure that the Soviet leadership will not risk the debacle of the World Revolution through a major war for the sake of anything less than the soil of the homeland of the Revolution. We may expect that it will yield tactical ground, or refrain from going after tactical ground, if the risk of holding it or going after it becomes serious. But if there is no risk, or only a minimal risk, aggressive policies will be carried

through, as they were in Hungary, where nothing was done to create a risk.

At the same time, Soviet doctrine serves to warn us to be wary of the facile persuasion now being spread about that "Russia doesn't want war." There is no reason to believe that Communism has been converted to the faith of Social Democracy, which holds that the evolution to world socialism can be wholly peaceful. Any notion that the Soviet Union has tacitly entered some sort of Kellogg Pact is absurd. The use of force, as an instrument of national policy, is still an essential tenet in the Communist creed. By the whole force of Communist "insight into historical necessity" Russia still wants war —the kind of war, in the time and place, that would be necessary or useful to further the multiple ends of the World Revolution, not least perhaps by extending the colonial "liberation front."

Moreover, this same insight convinces the Soviet leadership that the capitalist world wants war. War, like imperialism and aggression in general, is inherent in capitalism. This is a matter of scientific doctrine; the Communist understands it to be so, and he cannot be persuaded otherwise. To admit that the capitalist world does not want war would be to go against the doctrine. It would also be to cancel the "danger from without" that helps to justify the police state and to explain why it cannot yet wither away. In the face of the standing Soviet conviction about the war-mongering capitalist world, it would be doubly absurd to believe that the Soviet Union does not want war.

It is all a matter of the measure of risk that war would entail and of the measure of its usefulness for the World Revolution.

Precisely here, however, the present Communist insight into historical necessity—in the case, the necessity of the use of force to further the Revolution—must be less naive than once it was. It was Lenin's emphatic doctrine that "frightful collisions" must take place between East and West before capitalism is overthrown and socialism installed. Lenin was thinking not only of major wars but of other revolutionary violences. But he did believe in the inevitability of major wars. Stalin too believed that war was inevitable and that it would inevitably advance the fortunes of the Revolution. But this simple faith can no longer stand. One cannot doubt that the Leninist-Stalinist doctrine has been subjected to revision in Communist high councils in the light of the realities of nuclear war. What usefulness would attach to this manner of "frightful collision"? What risks of it should be run?

The results of this revision of doctrine may have been hinted at by Khrushchev at the 20th Party Congress in 1956. He did not refer to the new instrument of frightfulness, the H-bomb. His utterance was cautious. The Communist will not renounce his essential weapon, the threat of force. Nor will he renounce force itself. But he will carefully calculate its uses and its usefulness for his own purposes and on his own premise of policy—maximum security and minimal risk. This manner of calculation is his specialty. Moreover, he will make the conclusions of this calculation serve as the premise of his armament policies. His industry and technology are, after all, largely geared to war—not to war in general but to war as a possibly useful instrument of the World Revolution. To the Communist war is not a game, or a galvanic reaction, or an exercise in righteous anger, or a romantic adventure, or a way to develop the national character, or a sin. It is strictly and coldly a means to an end. And the end is clearly defined.

*   *   *

What conclusions has the Communist come to, what policies has he consequently defined for himself (he always defines his own policies, in what concerns both ends and means), in this historical moment so different from Lenin's—in this our nuclear age? The answer to this question would presumably be an important premise of American policies with regard to war and the weapons of war. Some answers should be clear.

First, all-out nuclear war is not a means of furthering the World Revolution; its only outcome would be the end of the Revolution, in the end of the world; the risk of it therefore must be avoided in the conduct of political affairs. Second, an all-out surprise attack on the capitalist world, with nuclear weapons, would run a maximum risk of the retaliatory destruction of the Homeland and of the Revolution itself; it is therefore excluded as a strategy of conquest. Third, on the other hand, the capitalist world is intrinsically imperialistic, aggressive, and bent on military conquest, as its hostile "encirclement" of the Soviet Union shows. It is ready for all-out nuclear war; and, despite its professions, it might launch a surprise attack. Therefore the Soviet Union must be ready for both contingencies. Maximum security requires maximum armament, conventional and nuclear. Fourth, military force is still a factor in political affairs, through its use, and especially through the sheer threat of its use. The doctrine of the Revolution—the doctrine of "collisions" —still holds. It will come into play whenever the risks are sufficiently minimal, and the chances of success sufficiently solid. These conditions will be more readily verified when the use of force, including nuclear force, is on a small scale for settling (or aggravating) local disturbances. Therefore small-scale nuclear force must be available in quantity, together with conventional arms. But if the risk appears that the tactical action will be enlarged to the dimensions of strategic action, through the employment of strategic nuclear weapons, it must be broken off, lest the Homeland of the Revolution itself be endangered.

In sum, major nuclear "collisions" with the capitalist world are not inevitable; on the contrary, they must be avoided, since they cannot advance the Communist cause. World socialism can and must be achieved without major war, by peaceful means—political, diplomatic, economic, propagandistic (this, in effect, is what Khrushchev said in 1956). Adventurism is to be rejected, since it violates the policy of minimal risk. On the other hand, the threat of force is still a valid revolutionary weapon; so too is the use of force itself in determined circumstances. Finally, the Homeland is in "danger from without." Therefore the armament program must be pushed through the whole spectrum of nuclear weapons—large weapons as a deterrent for maximum security; small weapons for use with a minimum of risk.

If this diagnosis of Communist thinking is generally correct, it suggests several conclusions with regard to American thought.

First, the danger of an all-out sneak nuclear attack on the United States has been vastly exaggerated. We have maximal security against it in the Soviet policy of minimal risk as long as the massive deterrent is sustained. Second, the correlative danger of an all-out nuclear war has likewise been vastly exaggerated. Many tend to make maximal a risk that is only minimal. It could only happen as the result of enormous stupidity, basically attributable to a complete misunderstanding of Soviet doctrine. This stupidity is no more inevitable than war itself. Third, the danger of limited wars has been underestimated. This maximal risk has been made minimal. It seems to be the historical American delusion that no war is worth while unless it is unlimited, waged for "ultimate" causes. There is also the special delusion proper to the nuclear age, that any use of nuclear weapons, however low in the kiloton range, must inevitably lead to world catastrophe. Hence the false dilemma: either to begin with catastrophe

or to renounce all use of nuclear force.

Fourth, more generally, the whole concept of the cold war has been over-militarized and therefore superficialized. This overmilitarization, combined with the exaggerations noted above, has affected national policy adversely in many respects. Moreover, it has tended to obscure or even discredit the validity of the very concept of the cold war. This too is lamentable, because the concept is fully valid, if it is interpreted in the light of the full reality of the Soviet empire in its fourfold uniqueness. Unfortunately, it has become too easy to say that, since the Communist threat is not primarily military (which is true), it is no threat at all and we should make disengagement our policy (which is completely false). Unfortunately too, it has become too easy to say that, since the United States is sufficiently safe from foreign military aggression (which is true), the real threat is internal Communist subversion (which is false).

Finally, all the confusions in American thinking come to a focus in the opinion that the issue of American "survival" is squarely put to the Department of Defense, supported by the Atomic Energy Commission. This opinion is entirely disastrous. We may be quite sure that the Communist mind, with its realistic and strategic habits of thought, has carefully separated the problem of the "survival" of the Communist Revolution from the problem of war. The Communist leadership has no slightest intention of making "survival" the issue to be settled by force of arms. In fact, it is prepared to abandon resort to arms, as soon as the issue of "survival" is raised. Survival is the one thing it is not willing to risk. In contrast, America is not prepared to resort to arms until the issue of "survival" is raised. Survival is the only thing it is willing to risk. Not the least irony in the current situation is the fact that the West has surrendered to the East its own traditional doctrine, that "survival" is not, and should never be allowed to become, the issue at stake in war.

The major problem put to American policy at the moment is the problem that the Soviet Union has already solved in terms of policy, namely, how to be prepared to use force on all necessary or useful occasions, and at the same time to withdraw "survival" from the issues at stake in the use of force. "The children of this world are shrewder than the children of light in their dealings with their own kind" (Luke 16:9). The children of this world understand better the uses, and the uselessnesses, of this world's darkest thing, force. They are shrewd enough to know that the institutions of this world can be advanced by force, but that their survival should not be put to the test of force.

The irony in the Gospel saying seems to be magnificently fulfilled in the American nuclear armament program. It seems to have been conceived to insure "survival" but not to fight a legitimate war for limited and justifiable ends. Perhaps one should not blame the Department of Defense or the Atomic Energy Commission. They could not get their budgets through the Congress unless they "proved" that "survival" is the issue at stake. And the Congress could not levy taxes on the people unless it "proved" that the "survival" of the people is at stake. But this is moral absurdity, not least because it is military absurdity. We have got the problem of "survival" and the problem of war so mixed up that we may finally be incapable of solving either.

Nor will it do to say that we have been forced into this position by the Communist menace. It would be almost impossible to set limits to the danger of Communism as a spiritual menace. It has induced not simply a crisis in history but perhaps the crisis of history. Its dream of the Third Epoch that will cancel Western and Christian history and the major institutions of that history (notably the rule of law and the spiritual supremacy of the Church) has

gone too far toward realization over too wide a sweep of earth to be lightly dismissed as a mere dream. On the other hand, as a sheerly military menace Communism is strictly limited. It is limited in the first instance by its own doctrine. This doctrine has always assigned to military force a real role in the advancement of the World Revolution. Nevertheless, the role of force has always been ancillary, subordinate, supportive of political, economic, and ideological initiatives. Force is to be employed only when the historical moment is right and the military or political risk is minimal. Moreover, there is every reason to believe that in the nuclear age, in which all risks are enhanced most horribly, Communist doctrine has set a still more diminished value on the use of force. By a sort of perverse genius, proper to the children of darkness, it has at the same time set a higher value on the sheer threat of force.

The Soviet Union as a power-imperialism must be confronted by power, steadily and at every point. But when the question is military engagement it is quite false to say that the issue is "survival." And American persistence in thinking this could easily reduce American power to impotence. The real issue is to know how and why "survival" got to be thought of as the military issue, and then to withdraw it from the limited political and moral issues at stake in our military engagement with the Soviet Union. It is impossible to think of any other way in which our nuclear armament program can be reduced to rationality—to some sensible conformity to the canons of moral reason (which look to justice in war), and to a hardly less desirable conformity to the rules of military reason (which look to success in war).

The clue to the distortions in the present structure of American policy is deposited in a remark made by the Military Operations Subcommittee in its nineteenth report, submitted on February 20, 1958. It said: "Under present methods of operation we do not know what we are trying to accomplish through military aid." Military aid programs, it added, "are not clearly related to a strategy of defense . . . Logistical plans have not been revised to keep step with strategic concepts and strategic concepts lag behind war technology." The general sense of this judgment, made directly with regard to military aid programs, holds with greater force of our nuclear armament program and its newer adjuncts, rockets and missiles.

The general uneasiness among the public—here at home and abroad—derives from an instinctive sense that America does not know what it is trying to do. And the uneasiness is sharpened by the general knowledge of what we are in fact doing, and have in fact been doing since the Manhattan Project. We are engaged in the exploitation of technological possibilities simply because they are possibilities, in the absence of any clearly defined strategic purposes that would be consonant with the institution of war as a valid instrument for altering the political will of an enemy—in the case, the Communist enemy, whose political will, and whose doctrine on the limited use of force in support of his will, are by no means mysterious or unknowable. The general public senses that this situation is irrational and therefore immoral. And it focuses its deeper fear and its more diffused disapproval on the relatively minor question of nuclear tests.

It is doubtless true that military concepts have always lagged behind weapons technology. The lag was tolerable when the technology was limited. This is not so today. The resources of military technology are unlimited, and there is no principle in technology itself to call a halt to their exploitation. Weapons technology has already gone

so far that it has raised the issue of "survival" and thrust it into the problem of war, in defiance of every military rule and moral principle, and in defiance too of every sound calculation with regard to the enemy's will to power as supported by a will to war. It is bad enough when policy and armaments run in opposite directions; as Theodore Roosevelt said, we cannot be a nation "opulent, aggressive, and unarmed." But it is worse when policy runs after armaments, and armaments run after technology, and the pressures of budgetary considerations buttress the primacy of the technology of multimegaton weapons, because they are cheaper. An armaments race that may end in war is bad enough, since there is always an element of irrationality in war, even when it is a just war. But an armaments race that seems already to have ended in absurdity is vastly worse, because what is militarily absurd is irredeemably immoral.

It may well be that the pragmatist American mind will not hearken to discourse on the morality of war, especially since it bears beneath its pragmatism the American-Protestant taint of pacifism. However, it might listen to discourse on success in war—concretely, on the kind of success that is politically valuable in the kind of war that is possible or likely, in present circumstances, against a particular enemy, who has a fully constructed "compass" (as Stalin called it) whereby to set his intentions and to direct his action in history, and who, finally, has an articulated doctrine with regard to the limited uses of military force in support of his political will. The moralist, of course, will not object to such discourse on success in war. It forms, in fact, an essential part of his own moral discourse, as the following chapter will show.

Chapter III

WHAT TO DO ABOUT CONGRESS?

Introduction

"IN republican government," wrote Publius in *The Federalist,* "the legislative authority, necessarily, predominates."[1]

Even a cursory reading of the Constitution will reveal the predominant role accorded Congress by the Founding Fathers. Following their usual practice of "putting first things first" (a practice that even their severe critics have noted), the Framers dealt with the Congress in Article I (*not* in Article II, or III). They tell us, accordingly, how Congress is to be organized, and what powers it is to exercise, before the presidency and the judiciary (which, by clear implication, are lesser matters) are so much as mentioned. And there is other evidence, not inferential in character, concerning the place of Congress in the Framers' political philosophy—alike the place it was in fact to occupy in the new form of government, and the place that rightfully belonged to it. Congress was to have—because as they saw it, it should have—the biggest "say," and the last one, on all questions of "policy" it might wish to affect. Thus virtually all of the important powers vested in the national government by the Constitution prove, upon examination, to be *congressional* powers. Congress, according to Section VIII of Article I, "shall have the power . . . to lay and collect taxes . . . provide for the common defense and general welfare . . . to declare war . . . to raise and support armies . . . to regulate commerce with foreign nations and among the several States," and "to make all laws which shall be necessary and proper for carrying into execution the foregoing powers . . ." These powers, to be sure, are in the special sense of the American political system, "limited powers"—subject always to the grand limitation that Congress must employ its powers in a manner satisfactory to the tastes and tempers of the electorate or, failing that, be brought to heel at the next election; subject, too, to the long series of "restraints," calculated to prevent hasty, ill-considered or tyrannical enactments, that are built into the Constitution and explicated, at great lengths, in *The Federalist*. But the student who wishes to see this matter in perspective must not leap to the conclusion that these limita-

---

[1] *The Federalist,* Jacob E. Cooke (ed.) (New York: World Publishing Co., 1961), p. 350. All references to *The Federalist* are to this edition.

tions in any sense tend to undermine Congress' position of predominance over and against the two other branches of government. To a very
considerable extent, rather, the "built-in" guarantees against hasty Congressional action prove, on second glance, to be limitations not on
the power of Congress as such, but on what (let's call) "Congress itself
undecided." By this we mean on Congress divided as between Senate
and House, or on either or both houses attempting to act by "simple"
majority, or on Congress unprepared to make use, against either or
both of the other two branches, of the "weapons" with which it is
armed by the Constitution (the power to withhold funds, the impeachment power, and the like). And, while Congress is in a sense
indeed subject to restraint by the "people" (that is, the electorate), who
can indeed vote the members of a rumbustious Congress out of office,
the real restraint, as far as legislation is concerned, is imposed by the
subsequent *Congress*—and it turns out that Congress itself, as contrasted with its individual members, is restrained in the fullness of
time only by itself, and is therefore really not restrained at all. Put
otherwise: the decision as to whether Congress *has* acted rashly, un-
wisely, or unjustly is a *congressional* decision, even though taken at a
later session. No such statement can be made about its "rivals," the
President and the Supreme Court, which a Congress feeling its oats
can nearly always circumvent or bring to heel. True, on most matters,
most of the time, Congress is *not* so united within itself, or so determined, as to make full use of its powers. But that does not affect the
validity of the point we are making. We do not think of the powers
of the President as diminished constitutionally because the President
sometimes can't make up his mind ("half" of him wishing to do this,
the other "half" that, like Buridan's ass). His powers remain, though
temporarily unused. And so do those of Congress when, for whatever
reason, it fails to exert them. And to that we may add: one at least of
the reasons why Congress, normally, *is* a place of divided counsels
is that the other branches, only too aware of the extent of congressional
power when it is mobilized, are careful not to do the things that would
bring the members of Congress together for determined action.

Many contemporary appraisals of Congress stress the fact that Congress has "fallen" from the predominant position accorded it by the
Framers. The following are typical judgments: ". . . operating under
its ancient ritual, the streamlined age of the Giant Clipper, radar, and
the atomic bomb seemed to have passed it by." [2] "In vast areas of

[2] George B. Galloway, *Congress at the Crossroads* (New York: Thomas Y. Crowell Co.,
1946), p. 6.

defense, foreign, economic and scientific policy Congress in recent years has either deferred to the President, or has worked in close and patriotic understanding with him. This sharing of power—sometimes to the point of abdication—has been an inevitable result of the times in which we live."[3]

Indeed, in view of this widespread, though by no means unanimous, agreement concerning the "fall" or "decline" of Congress in recent decades, we might expect to find a spate of books and articles devoted to the problem of how Congress might recapture the functions and powers that allegedly have slipped from its hands, and begin once again to play the role prescribed for it by the Framers. But no such literature has sprung up; and even writers who are most "pro"-Congress, and so most cognizant of how a Congress-in-decline would endanger our system as conceived by the Framers, are far from advocating any reforms calculated to restore Congress (as on their showing it needs to be restored) to its traditional position. Even James Burnham's *Congress and the American Tradition,* probably the strongest "pro-Congress" statement to be found in contemporary literature, envisages no way to set matters right in this regard. Writes Burnham: "For Congress to survive politically means that it shall be prepared to say *Yes* or *No,* on its own finding and responsibility in answer to the questions of major policy; and this it cannot do unless the individual members of Congress have the courage to speak, to say *No* even against the tidal pressures from the executive, the bureaucracy, and the opinion-molders so often allied in our day with the executive and bureaucracy, even against the threat that the semi-Caesarean executive will rouse his masses for reprisal at the polls—or in the streets."[4] Perhaps we may descry here a summons to the Congressmen to mend their ways, and throw their weight around more than, in Burnham's view, they are in the habit of doing, and so a remedy "of sorts." But that is not the main thing to notice about Burnham's statement of the matter. For *if* what is meant by the "decline" of Congress is merely a change in attitude on the part of the men elected to Congress, so that things would be different if the electorate were to begin to send to Congress men of another stamp, then it would seem to follow that the powers of Congress as such have *not* declined. (Let any reader of Mr. Burnham's book, any reader with a talent for fanciful speculation, ask himself what would happen in Washington if Congress included 218

---

[3] Stephen K. Bailey, "Is Congress the Old Frontier?" in *Continuing Crisis in American Politics,* Marian D. Irish (ed.) (Englewood Cliffs, New Jersey: Prentice-Hall, 1963), p. 76.

[4] (Chicago: Henry Regnery, 1959), p. 350.

James Burnhams, with James Burnham's attitude toward the Presidency, toward bureaucrats, and toward the "masses" upon whom, in his view, the President and the bureaucrats rely for *their* power.) What is missing from the Burnham statement, in any case, is the recognition that the so-called "decline" cannot be *merely* a matter of the individual Congressmen having become excessively humble over the decades, and that the decline, which in some important sense *has* indeed occurred, has taken the form of institutional developments that lie outside Congress. What is missing also, therefore, is any suggestion of the program those 218 Burnhams would have to adopt in order to right the boat. For the *passive* or even *negative* role that Congress seems to have got in the habit of playing has as its counterpart a wide range of institutions and practices that embody an *active* and *affirmative* role for the President (and, recently at least, for the Supreme Court)—at the expense of one for Congress.

But to go back. We possess no literature setting forth a program for cutting the President down to "man-size" in favor of a revivified Congress determined to "accentuate the positive" (and "not mess around with Mr. In-Between"). If what Burnham calls the "traditional balance" between Congress and President is ever to be restored in full, it would be necessary for most Congressmen to change their attitude and begin to think of Congress as their predecessors used to think of it. But it would also, we are saying, be necessary for the Executive and Judiciary to change their *behavior*. And, to that end, change many existing patterns of executive and judicial practice—those patterns through which the Executive and Judiciary, but especially of course the Executive, have taken up the "slack" created by Congress' session-to-session failure to use the powers that are still vested in it. In the crucial sense therefore, the "decline" might be said to be illusory.

What, now, of the evidence with which contemporary writers support the statement that congressional power has drastically declined? Such evidence, as we have tacitly conceded in the foregoing paragraphs, certainly exists, and our intention here is by no means to brush it aside. The questions we are raising are, rather, these: Do the writers who bring the evidence forward tend to ignore important data that point in another direction? And, does the evidence, on balance, really justify the "decline" thesis? Or, if you like: Have the rumors regarding the eclipse of congressional power, like those of Mark Twain's death, been enormously exaggerated? Take, for instance, Burnham's contention that Congress has come to be like the Jennie of the well-known song, who in 27 languages couldn't say No—so that the President and the bureaucracy are forever getting their way. Even the most casual newspaper reader should realize that if that is true, the newspapers have somehow not found out about it. Do they not keep a running box-score on what each session of Congress does to the President's legislative proposals? And is not the conclusion always to the effect that Congress says No most of the time—that, indeed, what is wrong with Congress is precisely that it says No too often, too uncompromisingly, and almost as a matter of course?

The President and his administration, in point of fact, usually "strike out" and seldom, if ever, go as much as three for five on the "key" bills they sponsor. That is, indeed, exactly what is meant by the epithet a "do-nothing Congress." For a "do-nothing" Congress gets its reputation for being one precisely by saying No (Burnham's phrase) again and again and again, and No to just that branch of government that has allegedly acquired the power Congress has allegedly "lost." And that would seem to indicate—since there isn't much the President can "do" about a congressional No—that the power of Congress is still something to conjure with.

The point moreover emerges all the more clearly if we consider it in the context of the so-called "principle of anticipated reactions." That principle, briefly restated for our purposes, asserts that power and influence are not always exerted directly and visibly: the child who does not raid the cookie-jar because he knows Mummy will punish him if he does, feels Mummy's power—and without Mummy's raising a finger. So, too, the President who does not introduce a bill he would like, because he knows Congress will slap it down, is experiencing an exercise, though nothing is said about it in the newspapers, of the vast power the Framers vested in Congress. We are familiar enough with the way the anticipated reactions work on the other side of the street, and were not surprised when President Kennedy, during the debates with Richard Nixon, emphasized repeatedly the importance of a threatened Presidential veto in preventing Congress from so much as considering many measures favored by a majority of Congressmen. We know that Congress does not waste its precious time probing and debating measures on which the President will impose a veto that cannot be "overridden" by a two-thirds vote. But we must, if we are to think clearly in this area, recognize that the President also is controlled to a great extent by such considerations. His legislative program is usually in for "rough sledding" in any event. Why, therefore, should he propose measures that he knows have no chance of passing and might, moreover, serve to alienate those Congressmen whose support he needs for getting through less daring proposals?

A similar point can be made about what Burnham calls the "attack on Congress"—the attempt, a continuing one if Burnham is to be believed, to discredit Congress and its members, to hold them up to ridicule, even to vilify them. Burnham marshals impressive proof that such an attack, carried on by journalists, cartoonists, novelists, playwrights, and, not least of all, political scientists, has been sustained now for several decades, presumably not without some effect on public attitudes. Here again, however, we must not overlook the fact that what seems, from one point of view, evidence of a "decline" on the part of Congress becomes, from another point of view, proof that Congress is still "ridin' high." For if the attack continues, and continues *unabated,* it would appear to mean this: Those who sustain the attack recognize, by sustaining it, that the enemy flag is still there—so that, without venturing very far into the forbidden field of motivations, we may safely conclude that what is worrying the attackers is, precisely, that Congress is *not* in decline. The attackers, of course, are in general folk who dislike congressional opposition and resistance to the programs and policies of the Executive and bureaucracy, and would like, *coûte que coûte,* to put a stop to it. Indeed, as the student must learn to keep himself reminded, the history of American institutions has been to a very considerable extent one of "tensions" between the Executive and Legislative branches, tensions that are perhaps at their greatest "height" at the present day. Nor is the reason for this hard to put one's finger on. The President is more inclined to accept and promote liberal programs (civil rights, medical care for the aged, expanded social security, federal aid to education), whereas Congress tends to dislike these programs, and either refuses to approve them or enacts them on a much more limited scale than the President would like. As Clinton Rossiter puts it: "In domestic affairs, he [the President] tends to take the broad and progressive point of view; in world affairs, the adventurous and cooperative. In the former, Congress tends to be more parochial and desultory; in the latter, more cautious and nationalistic." [5] Supporters of such programs must, accordingly, "have at" Congress; but current teachings as to the low estate to which Congress has fallen will make sense only if and when the moment comes when the attackers no longer deem the attack necessary.

Let us look a little further into the matter of Executive-Congres-

[5] "President and Congress in the 1960's," in *Continuing Crisis in American Politics,* p. 105.

sional "conflict" and what causes it. The explanation most frequently offered runs something like this: The President, because of the mode of his election, represents *the whole people,* and is, in consequence, the only elected official of the United States who can claim truly a "national" "mandate." It is perhaps true, the explanation continues, that the President pays greater attention to urban interests and, in particular, to the aspirations and wants of the minorities in urban areas— because of their crucial importance when it comes to garnering those states with the largest electoral vote. Nevertheless the President retains, they insist, a stronger claim than any other of our institutions to represent the will of the majority of the nation—which, in the absence of unanimity, must be accepted as that of the entire people. Congress, by contrast, represents narrower local concerns. The Representatives, in order to gain re-election, must cater to the interests of their constituencies, each of which constitutes only a very small part of the whole nation or even a state. Similarly, Senators must be responsive to the interests of their particular states, and these often run counter to the interests of the nation as a whole. Critics of Congress are, moreover, quick to point out yet other reasons why Congress cannot, while the Executive can, speak for a majority of the people. House election districts are in many cases "gerrymandered" by "rurally dominated" state legislatures, so that in the House rural areas and so, specifically, rural interests, have more weight than their numbers warrant.[6] This, combined with the fact that in the Senate the smallest state (in terms of population) has the same number of Senators as the largest, makes for further "overrepresentation" of rural areas. Finally—so runs the argument—the internal organization of each house of Congress tends to favor certain areas and interests. Committee chairmen, selected by the seniority principle, must of necessity come from strong one-party areas; the Senate filibuster frequently enables a small recalcitrant minority to block legislation desired by a majority; and the Rules Committee in the House of Representatives, composed of only fifteen members, has and exercises the power to kill off much majority-supported legislation.

While this constitutes one explanation for the sources of tension between the Congress and the President and might lead the student to conclude that the President has an unchallenged claim to representation of the majority-will, we should note that there is controversy about this matter. Specifically, it can be argued that there are, in fact, two

---

[6] This is one reason why the critics of Congress rejoice at the recent Supreme Court decisions relating to apportionment at both the state and national levels. Let us be clear, however, about this; the reapportionment decisions have not, as yet, dealt with the problem of "gerrymandering" which remains the heart of the problem.

majorities: one which is expressed in the election of the President every four years and another which is expressed through Congress after a long process of deliberation, adjustment, and continued "give and take" between the congressional representatives and their constituents. According to this line of analysis, the "mandates" expressed by the people through, respectively, presidential and congressional elections, differ considerably from one another. The presidential candidates naturally make the broadest possible appeal to the electorate in an effort to gain votes and avoid alienation of any significant groups. They are, both of them, apt or even compelled to speak in terms of lofty and abstract principles, which become the stuff of which presidential mandates are made. Congressional campaigns, by contrast, are likely to be conducted in more meaningful and concrete terms, and to center upon issues and problems of immediate concern to the voters. Accordingly, on this showing, the fundamental reason for the tensions between the President and Congress relates almost exclusively to the difference between their respective modes of election, and not to those aspects of congressional organization and procedure which seem to deviate from the majority principle.

In reading the materials included in this section, the student should keep constantly in mind this controversy about the competing claims of Congress and the President as representatives of the majority-will. Even scholars thoroughly familiar with Congress, the congressional "experts," differ sharply about this. Some of them are convinced that Congress' rules, procedures, and organization serve only to thwart the will of the national majority. They think of it as a "cumbersome, overstaffed pair of assemblies that speak in a confusion of tongues." [7] Others, because they start out in their thinking from the fact of profound diversity in the United States, think Congress, as it is, is just what the doctor ordered to represent that diversity. They hold that "the political will of the people must . . . be projected through a multiplicity of representatives and of representative institutions, both formal and informal. Only in this way can the irreducible variety of people's interests, activities and aspirations find political expression." [8] As he reads the selections which follow, the student will find that each author's "position" about Congress is derivative for the most part from his views on this "representativeness" controversy. But the issue—let him be clear with himself about this—is, as we have been suggesting

---

[7] Clinton Rossiter, *The American Presidency* (New York: Harcourt, Brace and Company, 1956), p. 65.
[8] James Burnham, *op. cit.,* p. 321.

in the foregoing remarks, mainly an issue in political theory, and not to any great extent an issue as to the nature of Congress (men on both sides of the controversy offer basically the same "picture" of what Congress is, and how it works).

The political theory issue, for the rest, can be stated in various ways. As for instance, an issue between those who insist that where there is so much diversity as in America there can be *no* "will" of the people, and those who hold that there *must* be such a will and that the task at any given time is merely to discover it. Or as an issue between those to whom it is obvious that only a political entity that itself makes room for diversity (as Congress evidently does) can represent diversity, and those to whom it is equally obvious that our very diversity (which is only too likely, they think, to end us up acting at cross purposes and out of divided counsels) renders necessary the exercise of the greatest power by a political entity which is by definition at one with itself (which the presidency is indeed more likely to be than the Congress). Or, on another level, as an issue between those who believe that the way to handle diversity is to represent it and let it talk itself through to agreement (which, they contend, a legislative assembly is able to do), and those who think that a legislative assembly invariably degenerates into a "talk-shop," incapable of taking concerted action.

Congress: Intention and Reality

According to "Madisonian theory" (that being the currently fashionable designation for the political theory of *The Federalist*), the people's representatives in Congress would play a crucial role in advancing the public interest, above all by keeping "factions" from imposing, contrary to the aggregate and long-term interests of the community, their own will. They were, hopefully, to be a "chosen body of citizens, whose wisdom may best discern the true interest of their country, and whose patriotism and love of justice will be least likely to sacrifice it to temporary or partial considerations." [9]

Publius, writing in the most famous of the *Federalist* papers, argued concretely that the members of the representative assembly in America would be the more likely to fulfil this prescription because ours is an "extensive" not a small republic. The republic's very "extensiveness," that is to say, would create conditions in which the people "will be more likely to centre on men who possess the most attractive merit, and the most diffusive and established characters" [10]—conditions, he

[9] *The Federalist*, p. 62.
[10] *Ibid.*, p. 63.

went on, in which "enlightened views and virtuous sentiments [would] render [those men] superior to local prejudices, and to schemes of injustice . . ." [11]

Certain questions arise: What is the record in this regard, some 175 years later? Do the representatives of Congress possess the characteristics ascribed to them in the Madisonian "prophesy"? The Congressman's "image," as one finds in certain quarters today (in, for example, political cartoons) would, as we have noted above, suggest the contrary. He is, according to that image, either a jolly, plump old windbag, or a devious, sinister "operator" bent on achieving some ulterior objective. But it is a matter of considerable interest that no such image can be documented out of what we may fairly call "serious" writing about Congress. The generalization such writing would seem to support is rather, this: both houses are composed, for the most part, of able, dedicated, hardworking men who are well above the average in educational and professional attainments. A recent and exhaustive study of United States senators, for example, purports to show that Madison's expectations have, to an astonishing degree, paid off:

> The senators were selected, with only rare exceptions, from near the top of the society's class system. . . . A stratified society places different evaluation on various social positions, and the prestige of the office or position tends to be transferred to the person who fills it. Thus the bank president or lawyer is a 'better' man than the janitor or policeman. . . . Voters seem to prefer candidates who are not like themselves but are what they would like to be.[12]

Nor is the Madisonian "pay-off" confined to the rank-and-file members of the two houses; rather the leaders, whose impact on the deliberations and activities of both chambers is known to be considerable, get equally handsome treatment at the hands of the serious writers. Writes Ernest S. Griffith, one of the most penetrating observers of Congress, "Usually [the leader] is one who recognizes a measure of individuality, a zone of freedom as necessary to the rank and file of members. He is a man with a sense of national interest, often an overriding sense. He rarely behaves autocratically in little things, and only within limits in great things when the public interest dictates. He builds up a sizeable reserve of good will by assisting members when he can, and draws

[11] *Ibid.*, p. 64.

[12] Donald R. Matthews, *U.S. Senators and Their World* (Chapel Hill, University of North Carolina Press, 1960), pp. 44-45.

upon this reserve when the occasion warrants. He evokes admiration for his skill and sureness of touch, for his sense of fair play and his hard work." [13]

If such statements are indeed accurate (which is another question on which the student must, little by little, make up his mind), the American people have good reason to celebrate the fact. The Congressman's powers and responsibilities, for all the reasons we have noted in this section, are, for good or ill, enormous. Political scientists may argue as they will concerning the respective merits of congressional and presidential "mandates" and the alleged decline and obsolescence of Congress. But it remains true, and so worth insisting upon here this once more, that the Constitution vests in Congress really "ultimate" weapons that it can use against the other branches when and if, in its view, the situation warrants recourse to them.

True enough, there are obstacles that Congress might have to overcome in order to impose its will. The presidential veto, for example, has been used by modern presidents with increasing frequency to prevent bare congressional majorities from getting their way. But it is by no means clear that the President could, by wielding the veto, thwart even a persistent and intense bare majority in Congress for very long. Congress could, to go no further, make the President pay very dearly for his everybody-out-of-step-but-Johnnie stance—by bottling up his entire legislative program, withholding approval from his appointees, etc. (Nor is it any answer to this to say: It has never happened. What really has never happened is for a President to confront a "persistent and intense" congressional majority with sustained defiance.) Nor is that all: persistent congressional majorities do not develop in a vacuum. They are conditioned by deeply-held attitudes and beliefs on the part of the generality of the American people, and can, at the margin, count on wide popular support that no President can long ignore. Nor is even that all: a persistent and intense congressional majority has not one but two ways of bringing a rambunctious (from its point of view) president to heel. When and if it might fail to move the President himself by exerting pressure on him, it can "win" by attracting to itself enough senators and representatives to make a two-thirds majority, and so overturn the veto. (In any showdown between a President and a persistent and intense congressional majority, that is, the "last say" lies with the individual members of the congressional *minority,* and

---

[13] *Congress: Its Contemporary Role* (New York: New York University Press, 1961), Third Edition, p. 23.

the latter, at the margin, are perhaps more likely to come up heads, i.e. pro-Congress, than tails, i.e. pro-President.)

All that is, moreover, pretty much what we should expect, given the organization and structure of Congress—as described alike by friendly and hostile observers. Congress, as the hostile observers in particular never worry about pointing out, is so "set up" as to positively discourage the formation of "persistent and intense" majorities—so that, when such a majority does form, we may safely assume that it has done so in response to deeply-felt popular needs and wants. So, too, despite popular impressions to the contrary, with the Supreme Court as an effective barrier against congressional power: Robert Dahl writes (in a selection included in Chapter V):

> . . . the elaborate "democratic" rationalizations of the Court's de-
> fenders and the hostility of its "democratic" critics are largely ir-
> relevant, for lawmaking majorities generally have had their way.
> . . . Although the Court seems never to have succeeded in holding
> out indefinitely, in a very small number of important cases it has
> delayed the application of policy up to as much as twenty-five years.[14]

All this indicates that the political process in America works in such fashion that congressional majorities can and in fact do, when they choose to, play the decisive role. Nor, we repeat, given the formidable "weapons" with which, as a matter of strict constitutional law, Congress is armed, should we expect it to work otherwise. If, for example, the Supreme Court did not yield to persistent congressional majorities, Congress could, within its constitutional powers, take steps to overcome its resistance. It could increase or decrease the size of the Court, with the end in view of securing a Court majority favorable to its views. Similarly it could manipulate the "appellate jurisdiction" of the Court—for example, by removing the controversial legislation in question from the Court's purview. Congress did, in fact, use both of these powers during the Reconstruction Period (and the second of them once, during the New Deal), in order to prevent Court interference with its policies. It is hardly too much to say, indeed, that Congress emerges as the supreme constitutional arbiter *between* the other two branches. During the Roosevelt "Court packing" controversy in the 1930's, the Senate it was that made the "final" decision; by refusing to

---

[14] "Decision-making in a Democracy: The Supreme Court as a National Policy-Maker," 6 *Journal of Public Law* (1957), p. 291. Dahl's "lawmaking" majority includes "the president's formal approval."

enlarge the Court, it thwarted the entire Roosevelt strategy. (The dispute, we are assuming here, was essentially one between the President and the Court, with Congress, in this instance, siding with the Court.)

The ultimate congressional "weapon," of course, is the impeachment process (for all that it is infrequently mentioned in this connection), by which the President and the justices can be removed from office. Almost from the beginning of the republic, our constitutional morality has dictated (so, in general anyhow, we are told) that this power should not, or even cannot without violating the Constitution, be used for simply "political" or partisan reasons. But this question, since the power to impeach has rarely been invoked, is surrounded with obscurity. Most of the instances of impeachment, successful or unsuccessful, have indeed been of such character as to exclude anyone's saying, in retrospect, that Congress' purpose *was* "political" or partisan. But the most famous instance of unsuccessful impeachment proceedings, those against President Johnson nearly a century ago, was, in large part at least, "political" (in the sense that the charges would pretty certainly not have been brought but for the fact that a good many congressmen found President Johnson's policies unacceptable); and neither of the present writers has ever found it easy to follow the logic by which numerous textbook writers have arrived at the conclusion that the Johnson proceedings somehow "prove" or "show" that it would be improper for Congress to use its impeachment power as a means of imposing its own policy conceptions on the White House. That conclusion would be warranted only if it could be demonstrated: (a) that the senators who "saved" Johnson's political life (by one vote) were voting not on the merits but on the constitutional issue (if merely on the merits, the case would seem rather to *assert* Congress' power to use impeachment as a weapon against policies it deems objectionable). And (b) that a single precedent is enough to establish a rule. It would be difficult indeed to show that Johnson's saviors intended their action as a foreswearing of political impeachment. Nor is it less difficult to answer the question, "Who is to *keep* Congress from impeaching for a political purpose?", except with a flat "Nobody." Here, as in so many cases we have noted, Congress would appear to enjoy the well-nigh-supreme power to determine, unilaterally, the limits of its own power. (Let the student ask himself what *he* thinks would happen if a considerable majority of congressmen "intensely" believed, and kept on "intensely" believing for several weeks, that the President's foreign policy was sure to get the United States occupied by the U.S.S.R.—as Czechoslovakia was occupied by it!)

Congress: Liberalism and Conservatism

Congress has long been the object of liberal attack and of liberal reform proposals. Doubtless the basic reason for this (as we have already suggested) is that Congress for the most part resists, frequently with great success, executive-sponsored programs that would advance liberal goals. Even in those areas where initial Congressional resistance has been overcome, Congress frequently does not give these programs the financial support that the President and most liberals think necessary.

The liberal attributes Congress' failure to "go along" with his program to, almost exclusively, the departures from the majority-principle that are, admittedly, characteristic of congressional organization and procedures. He (the liberal) is deeply convinced that, if and when congressional procedures have at last been "democratized," Congress' anti-liberal stance will, for the most part anyway, quickly become a thing of the past. Now: The liberals have a wide range of reform proposals on which they rely for the long-postponed democratization, but the most comprehensive is that whose slogan is "disciplined and responsible parties"—under presidential direction, of course, and capable of transforming Congress, to all intents and purposes, into a mere ratifying body for executive-initiated programs. (For further elaboration of this point, the student should see our introduction to the chapter on political parties.) Lesser liberal reform proposals include elimination of the seniority principle in congressional committees and of the filibuster in the Senate, together with a diminution of the powers of the House Rules Committee and the powers of committee chairmen. Most conservatives, it hardly needs be said, oppose these "reforms."

The student, as he reads the articles that follow, should ask himself several questions: What value, if any, is to be attached to the slow processes of deliberation in Congress? Do we pay too high a price for the resulting delays? Is Congress more apt than the other branches of our government to act in a manner contrary to the long-term, aggregate interests of the United States? In what ways, if any, do the President and Congress differ in their representation of the American people? What are likely to be the consequences of the reforms intended to make Congress more "democratic," and so more subservient to the Presidential will?

A. The "Attack on Congress": Defense and Indictment

13. The Case Against Congress*

JAMES BURNHAM

ACCORDING to the most familiar set of charges, Congress is slow, inefficient, archaic, horse-and-buggy in its methods, "out of touch with the 20th century." By the 1950's, remarks Dr. Galloway, "Few any longer regard [Congress] as the keystone of the federal arch. With Congress overwhelmed by its great responsibilities, operating under its ancient ritual, the streamlined age of the Giant Clipper, radar, and the atomic bomb seemed to have passed it by." [1] "What the framers did not reckon with," Professor Rossiter feels, "was the astounding growth of the republic, which has turned Congress into a cumbersome, overstaffed pair of assemblies that speak in a confusion of tongues." [2]

The accuracy of this description seems to almost everyone, both friend and foe of Congress, to be self-evident, quite too obvious to require any proof

beyond the mere statement. Somehow the slowness and inefficiency of Congress just seems to leap to the eye. What could be slower reading than the *Congressional Record,* no skipping permitted? What could be a more inefficient way of getting business over and done with than entrusting it to two divided Houses, the infinitely complicated parliamentary rules, the long rigmarole of committee referrals and hearings and studies, the circumlocutions of debate, the amendments and joint conference committees? What, compared to the streamlined charts of a jet-age firm of management consultants, could be more outmoded than the congressional "table of organization"?

Yet when anything seems all that obvious we ought to suspect that some factor may have been dropped. A whale would look slow on the Santa Anita racetrack, but in his ocean he can beat any horse in the stable. An octopus would be clumsy at a computer console, but he does well enough on his rocks. It is necessary to check both the meaning and relevance of the terms we use. Congress is "slow" and "inefficient"? Compared to what? And if so, why not?

Cost for work done is considered one measure of efficiency. For the legislature of the richest nation of the world,

* Chapter 19, *Congress and the American Tradition* (Chicago: Henry Regnery and Co., 1959), pp. 262-270. Reprinted by permission of Henry Regnery and Co.

[1] George B. Galloway, *Congress at the Crossroads,* p. 8.

[2] Clinton Rossiter, *The American Presidency,* p. 65. "Overstaffed"—as applied to Congress' poor little supporting platoon alongside the multitudinous corps of the executive bureaucracy—is an adjective that Prof. Rossiter's unconscious must have slipped by his scholarly censor.

the congressional budget seems modest enough by today's standards: about a hundred million dollars annually for the whole legislative establishment—a fraction of one percent of the executive budget, and much less than the expenses of hundreds of private corporations. Members of Congress, most of whom work from twelve to sixteen hours daily, are paid the salary of junior executives in a small company, less than Cabinet members or Supreme Court Justices, less than a tenth that of the chief officers of a big corporation. The professional staff of Congress (legal, research, and administrative aides) is as competent as the average in comparable jobs, and turns out more work at lower pay.

Is Congress slower and less efficient than the bureaucracy? The comparison can be made only where the operations are more or less similar. With respect to these, no one who has much acquaintance with the ways of Washington will rule Congress too far behind in the race. Generally speaking, a citizen can get a letter or appointment or advice from a congressional office in much shorter time than from an executive bureau. A congressional committee and its staff can turn out a competent report on an urgent problem at least as quickly as an executive agency. Congress cannot, by the nature of the legislative procedure, take more than a year on military budget problems that may have been five years crawling through the Pentagon. . . .

Neither the Fathers nor the philosophers before and after them ever listed speed and efficiency among the virtues of a representative assembly. They wanted "energy and dispatch" in the executive, but "in the legislature," they believed, "promptitude of decision is oftener an evil than a benefit. The differences of opinion, and the jarrings of parties in that department of the government, though they may sometimes obstruct salutary plans, yet often promote deliberation and circumspection, and serve to check excesses in the majority." [3] White-haired, slow speaking Nestor, not the impulsive Achilles, the aged Priam and not passionate Troilus, are the archetypes of the legislator.

What is it that Congress is supposed to be so speedy about? Is the efficiency of Congress measured by the average number of laws it turns out, or dollars it appropriates, per hour? Naturally, a bureaucrat asking a doubled appropriation for his agency, a lobbyist needing an industry-favoring bill to get his contract renewed, a newspaper reader hopped up by sensational headlines and the cry of "crisis" that has become endemic to our era, get impatient with what from their standpoint is congressional slow-motion. And one very good reason why tradition has built up its elaborate procedures is to resist such impatient pressures until they can be sorted and weighed.

Many who complain about congressional slowness and inefficiency have not stopped to reflect that many of the ways in which Congressmen "waste their time" are apt methods for accomplishing the tasks of a representative legislature in a democratic republic: by the chats and correspondence with constituents, the encounters with the press, the lunches with experts from the bureaucracy and even the cocktails with the lobbyists, the informal hours with each other and the staff professionals, the lecture trips to cities and universities, the travel junkets at home and abroad, the members are not merely helping to get themselves re-elected (which is also part of a legislator's business in a democracy), but getting to know—or, better, to feel—the myriad problems and interests, the competing needs and desires, complaints and demands, that the legislature, if it performs its function, must try to weave into some sort of working resolution.

For an intellectual, the right or wrong of a bill on foreign aid or prices or housing or subversion is likely to be

[3] *Federalist*, No. 70.

the product of a few minutes of deduction from ideological premises. Every Congressman, after a few months' service, knows that it can seldom be that simple. The political equations are too complex; there are too many values and wants and problems simultaneously at issue; and in a democracy, laws and policies must meet the test—very subtle to determine in advance—of sufficient public acceptability, whatever else may be their merits. That perennial cartoon subject, the last-minute rush of laws at the end of the session, which an intellectual despises as a symptom of laziness and sloppy method, is only an appearance: the final votes are the Q.E.D. of theorems that have been developed step by step over the months preceding. And in the elaboration of that sort of political theorem the Congress of the United States is a mathematician of remarkable delicacy.

When the legislative function is limited, as it normally should be, to issues of principle and broad policy, there is seldom any real need for immediate action. Even when quick action might seem abstractly desirable, there are usually compensating advantages—through, for example, the achievement of a wider public consensus—from legislative delay. For the most part, the circumstances that call for quick action fall within the province of the executive, and the American Constitution is marvelously designed to permit executive firmness and speed—although in practice the executive has often failed to display either when they have been most in order. The speedy rendering of justice is, or should be, a duty of the executive and the courts, not of the legislature. It is for the executive to repel a sudden invasion, suppress domestic insurrection, or communicate to the legislature and the nation any sudden grave turn in international or domestic affairs. When a President has convincingly shown the existence of an emergency requiring congressional action, Congress has usually responded; but Congress, and much

of the nation besides, have grown a little skeptical of perpetual crises.

No convincing evidence has been offered to show that the United States Congress is slower or less efficient than other representative assemblies in other free nations. The workings of the congressional machinery, the moves and squabbles and countermoves, are more open to the public gaze than in the British sort of parliament, but this does not mean that in Britain and the Commonwealth there is no grinding of the hidden wheels. Dr. Ernest S. Griffith, the brilliant director of the Legislative Reference Service of the Library of Congress, who is as intimately acquainted with the operations of Congress as any man outside its own senior ranks, has stressed this point:

> The fact that Congress, as well as the American people, makes up its mind in public has much to do with the appearance of indecision. The reaching of decision is a process over which the British throw a veil of secrecy. There is little or no evidence in recent years to indicate that the United States is any less slow or more slow in arriving at an answer than is Britain.[4]

If we are looking for modern, streamlined speed and efficiency in assemblies, there is one and only one place to find it: in the operations of the assemblies —no longer either representative or legislative—of the authoritarian states: Hitler's Reichstag, the Kremlin's Supreme Soviet, Franco's Cortes, Mao's and Mussolini's and Trujillo's Chambers. No delays, no confusions, no upsets in running a resolution through the prescribed procedures. But even that speed is deceptive, if we look beyond the ritualistic ceremonies to the governing process as a whole:

> The revelations of the inefficiencies, lost motion, internal friction, and

[4] Ernest S. Griffith, "The Place of Congress in Foreign Relations" (*The Annals of the American Academy of Social and Political Science*, Sept. 1953).

other errors of the dictatorships of Italy, Germany, and Japan are now a matter of record, exposed so that he who wishes may read and ponder. They apparently are at least equal to the errors made by the democracies and may well exceed them by an appreciable margin. . . . Every report of any reality that comes out of the Soviet Union carries the same story of inefficiency and waste through terror, lack of incentive, cynicism, suspicion, and espionage. Yet, however inefficiently these dictatorships may in fact have administered their societies, it is important to remember that for many years they gave the appearance of effectiveness, both to their own people and to others. They could cover up their mistakes and liquidate their critics.[5]

It may be just as well to recall, now and then, that the American system of government has been more successful, in practice, than any other in history.

2

At the beginning of this century the muckrakers set a liberal precedent, more lately followed by historians, political scientists, popular journalists and President Truman, for the opinion that Congress is anti-democratic, reactionary, and servile to "the interests." Granted a suitable definition of terms, this charge—or let us say, this description —is true.

When Congress is called anti-democratic, the reference is partly to the fact that its structural forms and its procedures distort the purely quantitative, plebiscitary relations which, according to democratist ideology, are the ultimate sanction of sovereignty. Many of these distortions are obvious. It is a distortion, to begin with, to have a bicameral legislature with each chamber elected according to different rules. The

representation in the Senate, with two members from each state of whatever size, is grossly out of line with population mathematics. But election from local districts (instead of national slates) and the well-known "over-representation of the rural districts" keeps the House also much short of the democratist ideal.

Congress operates through its committees, and especially through the committee chairmen. From the standpoint of democratism, the seniority system of selecting chairmen is a scandal that provokes regular denunciation. Unquestionably, as a glance at any session's roster of committee chairmen proves, seniority upsets the plebiscitary relations in favor of age, of social stability in the constituencies, of southern and normally one-party states against more volatile regions, and of farming or small-town districts against the big cities.

In the House, the power of the Speaker, of the Rules Committee, and of the exceedingly complicated procedural rules can be used to steamroller the majority as well as minorities. In the Senate the right of almost unlimited debate permits and almost invites a minority thwarting of the chamber's majority. And for certain very important purposes—such as the confirmation of treaties, the over-riding of a veto, and the initiating of a constitutional amendment—a two-thirds vote is required instead of the simple majority that by the logic of democratism ought always to be binding.

Because of its many-layered, labyrinthine, non-democratic internal structure, Congress seldom gives direct or isomorphic expression to the raw popular will. As it passes through the congressional processes the popular will is filtered, sifted, blunted, organized and reorganized, fitted into a pattern that retains a still recognizable but only indirect connection with its source.

As a result of this non-democratic structure, the localizing principle of representation in Congress, and the

[5] Ernest S. Griffith, *Congress, Its Contemporary Role* (New York: New York University Press, 1956), pp. 190-1.

lively play of semi-autonomous forces in American life, individual members of Congress, informal groups of members, and in some respects Congress as a whole do often represent what are called "the interests": that is to say— if the term is to be assigned a definable meaning—the needs or wants of organized groups and institutions within the community. From the point of view of rigorous democratism, this is a grievous fault, because a government ought to represent or express only the "common," "national" or "general" interest.

Part Three will undertake a fuller analysis of the relation of Congress to "democracy" and "the interests." Let us here remark that, while it is true that Congress is in some degree non-democratic and representative of the interests, these are, of themselves, morally neutral facts. They are not "faults" or deficiencies of Congress, or charges against Congress, except within the framework of certain assumptions, values and principles: the assumptions, values and principles, namely, of what we defined in Part One as liberalism. And it is of course liberals—including some liberal members of Congress— who bring forward these two characteristics as items in their indictment of Congress as it presently functions.

It is also liberals who declare Congress to be "reactionary"—an epithet which they assume to be adverse. The goals of modern liberalism are, by definition, "progressive." Therefore, whatever goes counter to these goals, or slows their realization, is reactionary. Now it is a fact that Congress, though it has more or less drifted along toward the progressive liberal goals (welfare statism, egalitarianism, internationalism, and so on), has shown a good deal less than the bureaucracy's zest for the journey, and has been at times downright mulish. A fair number of individual Congressmen are in their own minds squarely opposed to the progressive goals; not a few others tend to stray out of line. The liberals have

never forgotten the dread example of the Senate murder of the League of Nations in 1919, which touched off a fourteen-year revival of congressional power and national reaction.

"In point of fact," as Professor Rossiter puts it, "the struggle over the powers of the Presidency as against Congress, fierce though it may seem, is only a secondary campaign in a political war over the future of America." And he adds, in a self-identification with history typical of the liberal syndrome: "The cause of the opponents of a strong Presidency . . . is ill-starred because they cannot win a war against American history. The strong Presidency is the product of events that cannot be undone and of forces that continue to roll. We have made our decisions for the New Economy and the New Internationalism." [6]

Although the total context is too different for an exact comparison, the political relations here are roughly the reverse of those that held during the nation's early years. Then it was, by and large, the conservatives who supported an executive sufficiently strong and independent to counterbalance what they feared would be the overly democratic forces working through Congress. It was the liberals of that era—"Left" Jeffersonians, who were not so much for States' Rights as for a social radicalism in the mode of the French Jacobins—who wanted congressional supremacy and a weak President.

But this comparison in reverse, though attractive as a historical exercise, cannot be pressed too far. Except for a few extremists in the early years, who were true Jacobins or Tory monarchists, the citizens in all factions entered under the new constitutional dispensation with a common belief in the

[6] Clinton Rossiter, *op. cit.*, pp. 150-1. Professor Rossiter is generally called, by himself as well as others, a "conservative"—specifically, a "new conservative." By our definitions, however, he is of course a liberal, though not of the extreme democratist variety.

principles of diffused sovereignty and of coordinate, counterbalancing governmental departments. No one then conceived that the legislature should be subordinate to the executive, and most assumed that the legislature would be the determining and predominate arm. The disputes were over questions of degree—just how far the executive

should have an independent role apart from his duties as administrator of the laws passed by Congress—and not, as today, of the political essence. Whether regarded as heresy or revelation, the idea of executive supremacy is, so far as American history goes, a product peculiarly of our time.

14. The Internal Organization of Congress*

ERNEST S. GRIFFITH

[*Although there have been some changes with respect to the Rules Committee of the House, namely expansion of its membership and the adoption of a "modified" "21 day rule," Griffith's comments here are still very pertinent.*]

ORGANIZATION and procedure have always been vital factors in the efficient operation of any legislative body. They are central in this day and age, for the business of legislatures has multiplied beyond all reckoning. The opportunities for service and betrayal of the public interest have correspondingly increased, with these formal matters at least influential in determining whether service or betrayal shall prevail. Books such as Galloway's *The Legislative Process,* Young's *This Is Congress* and *The American Congress,* Kefauver and Levin's *Twentieth Century Congress,* Burns's *Congress on Trial,* Bailey and Samuel's *Congress at Work,* Gross's *The Legislative Struggle,* or Riddick's *Congress: Organization and Procedure* contain such a wealth of illuminating detail on the internal organization of Congress that repetition is quite unwarranted. Therefore, at this point there are merely offered certain observations

that may be helpful in understanding the broad spirit and purpose of Congress in its corporate capacity rather than in its details.

There are certain determining factors that must preface any such overall understanding. There are 435 members of the House and 100 of the Senate. Allowing for a session of 32 weeks, 5 hours a day, 5 days a week, this gives a total of about 800 hours in which floor business must be transacted.[1] Obviously the House at least must organize so as to limit debate. On the whole, it has done this well. The Senate, on the other hand, emphasizing other values, prides itself on unlimited debate. The larger body in practice is the more expeditious.

Both houses are engaged in a constant and, to a considerable extent, a losing struggle against the avalanche of business which the complexities, crises, and political insistences of the present day have produced. The quantitative aspect of the problem is the less acute. More serious is the qualitative. The quantitative has found a measure of solution in the floor rules and in division of labor among committees. However, it is the qualitative aspect that even more strikingly finds expression

* Chapter 4, *Congress: Its Contemporary Role* (3rd ed.: New York, New York University Press, 1960), pp. 25-37. Reprinted by permission of New York University Press. Copyright 1960 by New York University Press.

[1] The first session of the Eighty-sixth Congress showed the Senate in session 1,009 hours and the House 527.

in the committee organization. The standing committee is the chief instrument with which Congress uses specialization to confront complexity.

It is interesting to note that the British House of Commons has faced a similar situation but has met the problem in a fundamentally different fashion. Its committees play a minor role, largely in examination of bills for soundness of detail. Legislation itself emanates from the "government"—in practice largely from the permanent officials of the civil service. These latter provide the element of specialization. Cabinet committees exist, but their role and influence are unclear.

Another generally operative factor in influencing Congressional procedure is the natural desire on the part of most members for re-election. So much of American politics is made up of the activities of the various groups—economic, racial, religious, and others—that re-election often seems like a game in which a member avoids offending and caters to the desires of the maximum number of such groups as are represented in a given constituency. This reflects itself in procedures as well. On the positive side, it appears in the introduction of many bills, in insertions in the *Congressional Record,* in speeches on (and off) the floor, in differential treatment of witnesses in committee hearings, and, of course, in numerous activities not directly related to either organization or procedure.

On the negative side, various devices are used to avoid offense. In a democratic, representative government in this day and age, it seems to be a practical necessity that ways and means be found whereby an elected representative, desirous of serving the broader public interest, can avoid taking positions publicly on issues strongly felt by minorities, if the positions thus urged are regarded by the representative as not in line with general welfare.

For many years the Rules Committee of the House has occasionally performed this particular role by refusing to allow a measure to reach the floor. This it did when it felt the measure was not in the public interest and—this is the important aspect—when it had reason to suppose that the majority of the House felt as the Committee did concerning the measure. Yet because of the terrific organized pressure behind such a measure—pressure perhaps of veterans' organizations, of labor, of the Negro, of the aged (it matters not which)—many members would be faced with the alternatives of political suicide or a vote against their convictions if the measure ever reached the floor, and under such circumstances the measure would probably pass. Thus the Rules Committee saved them from having to go on record. It should be borne in mind that a discharge petition with 218 signatures could have brought the measure to the floor at any time if the Rules Committee had misjudged the temper of the House. The Committee itself normally consisted of members from districts in which re-election was virtually assured.

Between January 1949 and January 1951 the House Rules Committee no longer had this power. It could delay a measure but it could not block. At any time after twenty-one days the chairman of a committee for whose bill the Rules Committee had failed to grant a rule might call it up for House consideration. Yet other committee chairmen seldom[2] had the temerity to challenge this Committee, for it still had the power to punish members though it could not permanently block consideration of bills. With the opening of the Eighty-second Congress in January 1951 the power of the Rules Committee was restored, and since then it has functioned at least occasionally in the fashion described.[3]

[2] Eight times in the Eighty-first Congress.

[3] This is not to say that in its built-in conservatism it has not from time to time thwarted the will of the majority; while fear of reprisals has kept that majority from producing the necessary number of signatures on a discharge petition.

Congress is an institution in which power and position are highly valued. Seniority is not only a rule governing committee chairmanships, it is also a spirit pervading the total behavior. This is especially true between new members and the older ones. The latter want the former to seek their advice and have their own ways of clipping the wings of upstarts. This does not mean that a first-termer is not listened to in committee or even on the floor if he is really master of his subject, has something to say, and is not merely seeking prominence. After one or two years, during which his colleagues have taken his measure, he may be entrusted with a subcommittee chairmanship dealing with some problem close to his heart or even with the chairmanship of a special committee. By these devices many of the admitted disadvantages connected with rigid adherence to the seniority rule are overcome and its good side preserved.

Of all the criticisms of Congress from outside its own membership, that of the seniority rule is perhaps the most universal in educated circles. The term "senility rule" is occasionally used, and those who know Congress intimately will find it not too difficult to think of appropriate examples. More fundamental are two other bases of criticism —the obstacle the rule presents to responsible party government, and its alleged overweighting in the direction of conservatism.

If one is an advocate of responsible and disciplined party government, the seniority rule is certainly an obstacle. It is not so much that the committee chairmen frequently and sharply diverge from "party line" votes. Goodwin has shown that such divergence, while present, is certainly not as great as is usually supposed.[4] What is more important is that the rule insures a

[4] See George Goodwin, Jr., "The Seniority System in Congress," *American Political Science Review,* June 1959, pp. 412-36 for this, and for many other interesting facts concerning the rule.

rival network of power and leadership. Moreover, it tends to overlap a third center of leadership, that of the subject matter specialist. It will appear later that the author does not believe in the desirability of strengthening a party-enforced majority rule as against rule by shifting majorities, inasmuch as these are determined by members' individual views on specific issues. The latter would seem more suited to contemporary needs.[5]

The overweighting in the direction of conservatism is a more serious charge. To put the matter in concrete terms, if the Democrats are in control, about 60% of the committee chairmen are from the South, which is in general its conservative sector. If the Republicans control, about 60% of the chairmen are from the Middle West, which is usually more conservative than this party's second center of strength on the Eastern seaboard. If leadership is, as it should be, a reflection of the general will of the majority of a legislative body, then such overweighting is a serious matter, unless adaptations to circumvent or modify it have been forthcoming. Perhaps the discrepancy is more serious in the Senate than in the House. The latter seems normally to have a conservative majority in any event. In the Senate one must look, if at all, to adaptations for remedy. Yet a conservative mood is more characteristic of the Senate than would ordinarily be inferred.

Health and age considerations should also be subject to remedy by adaptation, if criticism of the rule is to be blunted.

Have there been such adaptations? The answer is certainly "Yes," though in varying degree and not in every instance. If he will exercise it wisely, a chairman has great power. Chairmen usually call meetings apart from those which a committee may schedule at stated intervals. They usually name the staff and assign their duties. They have

[5] See chap. 16 for a fuller discussion of the issue.

priority in questioning witnesses and assume floor leadership on reported bills. They are members of conference committees. They ordinarily name the subcommittees and strongly influence the selection and priority of agendas. As presiding officers, they can rule as to quorums, points of order, and other matters. They have very considerable opportunity to penalize individual committee members if they wish to use it. In the great majority of instances, these powers are exercised after consultation with the membership, and the decisions are often submitted to vote. In such cases, no adaptation is necessary other than that which the chairman himself voluntarily exercises.

Such adaptation was forthcoming in the House Foreign Affairs Committee when health factors stood in the way of full activity on the part of Representatives Eaton and Chiperfield, its two Republican chairmen in the last two decades. Both of them delegated major responsibility to colleagues junior to themselves. Senator Green voluntarily relinquished the chairmanship of the Senate Foreign Relations Committee when he was over ninety. In most committees with heavy agendas, the subcommittee device is freely used, and this gives to a number of other members the chance to exercise substantial leadership.

Where the chairman is out of tune with the majority of his committee, or even the parent body, and is obdurate or autocratic in the use of his powers, a number of remedies are open. By law a majority of a committee can do almost anything within the function of the chairman, provided it can find a chance to vote on the issues. A revolt in the House Government Operations Committee in the Eighty-third Congress transferred most of the powers from its chairman to subcommittees. During Senator McKellar's old age, Senator Hayden unselfishly took over the burden of the work of the Senate Appropriations Committee, while allowing his colleague to retain the chair-

manship with its prerogatives. If the chairman—or the committee as a whole, for that matter—is out of harmony with the will of its parent body, other adaptations are available. A bill can be referred to a more friendly committee. A special committee can be set up, and the standing committee bypassed. The discharge rule can be invoked. To cite an extreme case, civil rights legislation bypassed altogether the Senate Judiciary Committee and its chairman, Senator Eastland, and was considered directly on the floor of the Senate.

Adaptations of the types suggested have gone far toward mitigating the evils and disadvantages of the seniority rule. It is at this point that another approach is relevant. Evils there are and evils there always will be, but what are the alternatives? The most usual proposals call for selection of chairmen either by the party machinery or by vote of the committee. In either instance the ever-present struggle for power is intensified. Basically, the members of Congress are overwhelmingly in favor of removing to the sphere of automatic operation a matter as controversial, as likely to produce personal animosities, as unpredictable in its results, as susceptible of clandestine or even sinister forces as the election of committee chairmen. When there is added to these negative arguments against alternatives the affirmative consideration of guaranteed long experience under seniority, Congress would far rather approach the problem by adaptations than by drastic change.

The only type of alternative which would bypass these dangers and at the same time might mitigate some of the evils of the seniority rule would appear to be to limit the term of the chairman to eight or ten years. At the expiration of this period he would be succeeded by the second in length of service. Such a proposal has never really been taken seriously outside of academic circles.

Centers of power are necessary in any body that would accomplish things, and the desideratum is that this power be responsibly exercised. When it becomes too concentrated or too arbitrary, as in the case of Speaker Joseph G. Cannon in 1910, there is revolt; but new centers necessarily arise. As of today, power is fairly well diffused, though in the House the Speaker and the Majority Leader, partly in their own right and partly because of their close relations and influence with the President if of his party, are the two most powerful single members. Party policy committees have developed in the Senate and on the Republican side in the House and wield some measure of power. Within his own bailiwick, a House committee chairman ordinarily can have his way in blocking legislation, and often in promoting it as well.

The House Rules Committee is obviously a powerful force. It may refuse to report out a bill unless discharged by a petition signed by a majority of the House or unless the bill is called under a special procedure on "Calendar Wednesday," if luck of location favors the bill. It may grant any one of several types of rule, certain of which are favorable and others unfavorable to the prospects of a given measure. It can make a favorable rule conditional upon an amendment which it favors. A rule, by the way, for those who are not familiar with the term in this connection, is the regulation stipulating the kind, the control, and the extent of floor debate on a given measure.[6] It may also cover matters such as the date or conditions of effectiveness, limitations on amendment, conditions governing points of order. The rule under which a bill is reported may be influential in or even determinative of the subsequent action. Thus a rule forbidding floor amendment, especially in tax bills, is a means of preventing raids by special interests.

These rules are near the heart of the way the House organizes the final legislative stages of a given measure. The Senate, incidentally, is much less formal or rigid. Its principal traffic manager is not its Rules and Administration Committee, but its Majority Leadership or Policy Committee.

One of the traditional functions attributed to Congress is the illumination of issues with the consequent education of the public. It is doubtful whether this objective has figured very much in any conscious fashion in the evolution of organization and procedure. Nevertheless, the accord given to the right of the minority to be heard, expressed in such a fashion as the equal division of time in floor debate; the value put upon dramatization in hearings, through the custom of securing "headliners" as witnesses; the emphasis on open hearings written into the Reorganization Act—all these are evidence that a consciousness of the values inherent in education of the electorate has not been without its influence.

Finally, no one can be intimately related to Congress for long without a genuine appreciation of the role played by a desire to promote and safeguard the general welfare as expressed in its organization and procedure.

A good organization and procedure should include the following:[7]

(1) Time for reflection. Except in crises, delay in passage should be such as to give the members opportunity to study measures, not so much for their major substantive content as for their probable public reception in detail. Committee scrutiny, bicameralism, the split session are devices thus used. In other words, the operability of a measure in terms of the cultural setting is the type of question on which a legislature is competent to pass; and delay should be sufficient to permit study with this objective in mind.

(2) Time and opportunity for pub-

---

[6] See J. A. Robinson, "The Role of the Rules Committee in Arranging the Program of the United States House of Representatives," *Western Political Quarterly,* September 1959, pp. 653-69.

[7] Ernest S. Griffith, *The Impasse of Democracy* (New York: Harrison-Hilton Books, 1939), pp. 144 ff.

lic reaction. This is closely related to (1). It argues for a procedure which assures public debate at two stages—the introduction of the measure and the time immediately prior to its final passage. Our bicameralism is an inferior substitute for a system of two debates with intervals in a single house. Various rules of procedure can assure two such public discussions. In England, the objective is attained by allowing debate on the general principles of a bill at the so-called "second reading," and then again when it has come out of committee just prior to final passage or rejection. If a nation's written or unwritten constitution provides for an economic advisory committee or other devices to obtain the reactions of interest groups, procedure might perhaps provide for remission to them.[8] In any event, the procedure should be such that the main issues are so clarified at the initial public debate as to permit public reaction. Hearings and petitions are the usual ways to render such reaction articulate.

(3) Full public debate to be confined to essentials. This is necessary if a legislative body is to perform its important function of educating the electorate. Debates on the budget, votes of no confidence, and other devices provide the opportunity for reviewing the success or failure of the general policy of the leadership in power at a given moment. Power given to the presiding officer to rule certain types of debate out of order in full session, as belonging rather in committees; time limits; and, most of all, a party procedural leadership and a sense of individual responsibility that will apportion most time to the essential issues—all these will go far toward promoting the type of discussion which will facilitate the education of the electorate. It is nothing

[8] On the other hand, it might be better to incorporate these advisory devices at the stage of administrative maturing rather than during legislative deliberation and amendment.

short of criminal that a filibuster should sometimes be necessary to direct attention to a vital issue.

(4) Proportionate consideration. This should apply as between measures and as between clauses within a specific measure. With rare exceptions the procedural leadership should ultimately determine what measures should be introduced, the amount of time which should be allocated to each bill and each clause, and the order of their consideration. These latter two provisos should be subject to overruling provisos indicated under (2) and (5). In most nations, the procedural leader will be the majority party leader or steering committee.

(5) Respect for opposition and minorities. Procedure should grant equal time in all discussions to the opposition. It should also allow the opposition equal time at the presentation of the budget; and by one device or another allow a certain number of days each session for criticism and discussion of general policy. These should be under the absolute control of the opposition as regards subject matter, but an equal amount of time should be allowed the incumbent leadership to defend itself.

(6) Opportunities for detailed amendment. For the most part, legislation will tend more and more to follow the French example and be couched in general terms. Yet this is always a relative matter, and procedure should always provide an opportunity for informed criticism on the basis of additional information, chiefly such information as would be comprised under the term "public reaction." Committee is obviously the place for this, for the entire house would not have the time for such detail. Whether the British system with its non-specialized committees or the more usual American system of specialized ones is adopted, the function is the same. The latter is more intelligent, the former less dispersive.

(7) Facility. Delays other than

those contemplated under (1) and (2) must not be allowed in this day and age. Restrictions on debate must bear some relationship to the amount of business to be transacted. In Chapters 16, 25, and 26 below, the possibilities of devolving a large number of decisions upon subordinate bodies will be considered; but in any event facility and absence of undue obstruction can only be obtained, I think, through vesting semi-autocratic powers either in leadership or in an impartial presiding officer, or in both, to control time and order of debate and voting. The safeguards proposed under (1), (2), (5), and (6) will mitigate the obvious dangers of this procedure.

(8) Clarity of ultimate phraseology. The drafting of the original bill should be by experts. After the amending stage is over, the bill should again be submitted to these draftsmen, for recommendations as to ultimate phraseology.

(9) No "riders" or irrelevancies. Procedural rules should be adopted making it illegal to include "riders" or clauses dealing with matters outside of the main subject of a bill. Such irrelevancies are unthinkable in most legislatures, and the time is long overdue for reform of the practice in the United States.

(10) All private or special legislation should be relegated to subordinate legislation in one of the departments.

We may add three other rules of procedure designed especially to facilitate the type of criticism of the administration which will render the latter more alert and responsive.

(11) Regular opportunity for questioning administrators. This can be done in committee or in regular session. It is not essential that it follow the ritual of the British Parliamentary system whereby the cabinet member is the one questioned. Under either the parliamentary or presidential system it should be part of the normal procedure to bring the key administrators onto the floor of the house or into committee, there to be questioned.

(12) Supervision of subordinate legislation. Where appropriate, procedure should provide for delegated legislation to "lie on the table" for a stated period. During this period either a member or a party or a certain number of members may, by simple request, force either its withdrawal or consideration by an appropriately constituted committee of the house itself. Inasmuch as this legislation is not of a uniform type, it would probably be unwise to stereotype its supervision in any one fashion. However, three or four more or less standardized rules for requiring and obtaining further consideration (should such be desired) would be sufficient.

(13) Use of *ad hoc* commissions. In the nature of the case, probably formal procedural rules cannot provide for such commissions. The rules can, however, somewhat regularize their use. For the most part, the traditions or mores of a legislative body should be such that fairly frequently major recommendations for change of policy or the unsatisfactory functioning of existing policy should be made the subject of inquiry by a commission constituted for the purpose. Customarily this device should also be used by the legislature to deal with questions affecting the vested interests of the civil service itself—salaries, personnel policies, overlapping, coordination, dispersive tendencies. A "Joint Standing Committee on the Public Service" might well be set up, whose business it would be to propose the formation of such *ad hoc* commissions. Important committee chairmen from the two houses might constitute its personnel.

Among these criteria, Congress is probably at its best as regards 1, 2, 5, 6,

8, 11; it is weakest as regards 3, 9, 10, 12.

Political parties are the basis for the organization of Congress. They play a much less important role in Congress' policies.[9] From an organizational standpoint, they determine the membership of the committees in each house, especially the number of positions allocated to the majority and minority respectively. In determining individual committee personnel, their influence is severely limited by the seniority convention and the tradition that a member once on a committee remains there, if he so wills. Modifications of this convention and tradition necessarily take place when a majority party becomes the minority and occasionally under other circumstances when deemed appropriate. Rarely is removal from a committee an instrument of party discipline, though transfer to a more desirable committee may be a party reward.

[9] Cf. chap. 16.

Organization and procedure are woven into a seamless fabric through all the aspects of Congressional activity. Some aspects are sharply criticized; others are highly praised. Neither praise nor blame is attempted here. Where organization is defective, adaptation and custom frequently come to the rescue. The use of the special committee and subcommittee to mitigate the handicaps of the seniority rule has already been mentioned. So with many another device. Things are not always what they seem. Nor are smoothness and speed of operation by any means the highest rung on the hierarchical ladder of values. Given things as they are—the nature of the electorate, the size of Congress, the complexity, number, and magnitude of the issues—Congressional organization and procedure do not come off badly, especially when it is borne in mind that failure to act may in some instances be a deliberately chosen wiser course, with procedural devices the instrument making such failure to act practicable.

15. The House of Representatives and Democracy*

WOODROW WILSON

[*Although Woodrow Wilson's Congressional Government was first published in 1885, his observations concerning the organization and procedure of the House of Representatives are still extremely relevant. His perspectives of Congress are shared by many contemporary political scientists.*]

THE leaders of the House are the chairmen of the principal Standing Com-

* Congressional Government (New York: Meridian Books, World Publishing Co., 1956), pp. 58-73. Reprinted by permission of World Publishing Co.

mittees. Indeed, to be exactly accurate, the House has as many leaders as there are subjects of legislation; for there are as many Standing Committees as there are leading classes of legislation, and in the consideration of every topic of business the House is guided by a special leader in the person of the chairman of the Standing Committee, charged with the superintendence of measures of the particular class to which that topic belongs. It is this multiplicity of leaders, this many-headed leadership, which makes the organization of the House too complex to afford uninformed people and unskilled observers any easy clue to its methods of rule. For the chairmen of the Standing Committees do not constitute a coöperative body like a ministry. They do not consult and concur in the adoption of homogeneous and mutually helpful measures; there is no thought of acting in concert. Each Committee goes its own way at its own pace. It is impossible to discover any unity or method in the disconnected and therefore unsystematic, confused, and desultory action of the House, or any common purpose in the measures which its Committees from time to time recommend.

And it is not only to the unanalytic thought of the common observer who looks at the House from the outside that its doings seem helter-skelter, and without comprehensible rule; it is not at once easy to understand them when they are scrutinized in their daily headway through open session by one who is inside the House. The newly-elected member, entering its doors for the first time, and with no more knowledge of its rules and customs than the more intelligent of his constituents possess, always experiences great difficulty in adjusting his preconceived ideas of congressional life to the strange and unlooked-for conditions by which he finds himself surrounded after he has been sworn in and has become a part of the great legislative machine. Indeed there are generally many things connected with his career in Washington to disgust and dispirit, if not to aggrieve, the new member. In the first place, his local reputation does not follow him to the federal capital. Possibly the members from his own State know him, and receive him into full fellowship; but no one else knows him, except as an adherent of this or that party, or as a newcomer from this or that State. He finds his station insignificant, and his identity indistinct. But this social humiliation which he experiences in circles in which to be a congressman does not of itself confer distinction, because it is only to be one among many, is probably not to

be compared with the chagrin and disappointment which come in company with the inevitable discovery that he is equally without weight or title to consideration in the House itself. No man, when chosen to the membership of a body possessing great powers and exalted prerogatives, likes to find his activity repressed, and himself suppressed, by imperative rules and precedents which seem to have been framed for the deliberate purpose of making usefulness unattainable by individual members. Yet such the new member finds the rules and precedents of the House to be. It matters not to him, because it is not apparent on the face of things, that those rules and precedents have grown, not out of set purpose to curtail the privileges of new members as such, but out of the plain necessities of business; it remains the fact that he suffers under their curb, and it is not until "custom hath made it in him a property of easiness" that he submits to them with anything like good grace.

Not all new members suffer alike, of course, under this trying discipline; because it is not every new member that comes to his seat with serious purposes of honest, earnest, and duteous work. There are numerous tricks and subterfuges, soon learned and easily used, by means of which the most idle and self-indulgent members may readily make such show of exemplary diligence as will quite satisfy, if it does not positively delight, constituents in Buncombe. But the number of congressmen who deliberately court uselessness and counterfeit well-doing is probably small. The great majority doubtless have a keen enough sense of their duty, and a sufficiently unhesitating desire to do it; and it may safely be taken for granted that the zeal of new members is generally hot and insistent. If it be not hot to begin with, it is like to become so by reason of friction with the rules, because such men must inevitably be chafed by the bonds of restraint drawn about them by the inexorable observances of the House.

Often the new member goes to Washington as the representative of a particular line of policy, having been elected, it may be, as an advocate of free trade, or as a champion of protection; and it is naturally his first care upon entering on his duties to seek immediate opportunity for the expression of his views and immediate means of giving them definite shape and thrusting them upon the attention of Congress. His disappointment is, therefore, very keen when he finds both opportunity and means denied him. He can introduce his bill; but that is all he can do, and he must do that at a particular time and in a particular manner. This he is likely to learn through rude experience, if he be not cautious to inquire beforehand the details of practice. He is likely to make a rash start, upon the supposition that Congress observes the ordinary rules of parliamentary practice to which he has become accustomed in the debating clubs familiar to his youth, and in the mass-meetings known to his later experience. His bill is doubtless ready for presentation early in the session, and some day, taking advantage of a pause in the proceedings, when there seems to be no business before the House, he rises to read it and move its adoption. But he finds getting the floor an arduous and precarious undertaking. There are certain to be others who want it as well as he; and his indignation is stirred by the fact that the Speaker does not so much as turn towards him, though he must have heard his call, but recognizes someone else readily and as a matter of course. If he be obstreperous and persistent in his cries of "Mr. Speaker," he may get that great functionary's attention for a moment,—only to be told, however, that he is out of order, and that his bill can be introduced at that stage only by unanimous consent: immediately there are mechanically-uttered but emphatic exclamations of objection, and he is forced to sit down confused and disgusted. He has, without knowing it, obtruded himself in the way of the "regular order of business," and been run over in consequence, without being quite clear as to how the accident occurred.

Moved by the pain and discomfiture of this first experience to respect, if not to fear, the rules, the new member casts about, by study or inquiry, to find out, if possible, the nature and occasion of his privileges. He learns that his only safe day is Monday. On that day the roll of the States is called, and members may introduce bills as their States are reached in the call. So on Monday he essays another bout with the rules, confident this time of being on their safe side,—but mayhap indiscreetly and unluckily over-confident. For if he supposes, as he naturally will, that after his bill has been sent up to be read by the clerk he may say a few words in its behalf, and in that belief sets out upon his long-considered remarks, he will be knocked down by the rules as surely as he was on the first occasion when he gained the floor for a brief moment. The rap of Mr. Speaker's gavel is sharp, immediate, and peremptory. He is curtly informed that no debate is in order; the bill can only be referred to the appropriate Committee.

This is, indeed, disheartening; it is his first lesson in committee government, and the master's rod smarts; but the sooner he learns the prerogatives and powers of the Standing Committees the sooner will he penetrate the mysteries of the rules and avoid the pain of further contact with their thorny side. The privileges of the Standing Committees are the beginning and the end of the rules. Both the House of Representatives and the Senate conduct their business by what may figuratively, but not inaccurately, be called an odd device of *disintegration*. The House virtually both deliberates and legislates in small sections. Time would fail it to discuss all the bills brought in, for they every session number thousands; and it is to be doubted whether, even if time allowed, the ordinary processes of debate and amend-

ment would suffice to sift the chaff
from the wheat in the bushels of bills
every week piled upon the clerk's desk.
Accordingly, no futile attempt is made
to do anything of the kind. The work is
parceled out, most of it to . . . Standing
Committees which constitute the regular organization of the House, some of
it to select committees appointed for
special and temporary purposes. . . .
Practically, no bill escapes commitment
—save, of course, bills introduced by
committees, and a few which may now
and then be crowded through under a
suspension of the rules, granted by a
two-thirds vote—though the exact disposition to be made of a bill is not always determined easily and as a matter
of course. . . . [because] it is not always evident to which Committee each
particular bill should go. Many bills
affect subjects which may be regarded
as lying as properly within the jurisdiction of one as of another of the
Committees; for no hard and fast lines
separate the various classes of business
which the Committees are commissioned to take in charge. Their jurisdictions overlap at many points, and it
must frequently happen that bills are
read which cover just this common
ground. Over the commitment of such
bills sharp and interesting skirmishes
often take place. There is active competition for them, the ordinary, quiet
routine of matter-of-course reference
being interrupted by rival motions
seeking to give very different directions to the disposition to be made of
them. . . .

The fate of bills committed is generally not uncertain. As a rule, a bill
committed is a bill doomed. When it
goes from the clerk's desk to a com-
mittee-room it crosses a parliamentary
bridge of sighs to dim dungeons of
silence whence it will never return.
The means and time of its death are
unknown, but its friends never see it
again. Of course no Standing Committee is privileged to take upon itself
the full powers of the House it represents, and formally and decisively re-

ject a bill referred to it; its disapproval,
if it disapproves, must be reported to
the House in the form of a recommendation that the bill "do not pass."
But it is easy, and therefore common,
to let the session pass without making
any report at all upon bills deemed
objectionable or unimportant, and to
substitute for reports upon them a few
bills of the Committee's own drafting;
so that thousands of bills expire with
the expiration of each Congress, not
having been rejected, but having been
simply neglected. There was not time
to report upon them.

Of course it goes without saying that
the practical effect of this Committee
organization of the House is to con-
sign to each of the Standing Committees the entire direction of legislation
upon those subjects which properly
come to its consideration. As to those
subjects it is entitled to the initiative,
and all legislative action with regard to
them is under its overruling guidance.
It gives shape and course to the determinations of the House. In one respect,
however, its initiative is limited. Even
a Standing Committee cannot report a
bill whose subject-matter has not been
referred to it by the House, "by the
rules or otherwise"; it cannot volunteer
advice on questions upon which its
advice has not been asked. But this is
not a serious, not even an operative,
limitation upon its functions of suggestion and leadership; for it is a very
simple matter to get referred to it any
subject it wishes to introduce to the
attention of the House. Its chairman,
or one of its leading members, frames
a bill covering the point upon which
the Committee wishes to suggest legislation; brings it in, in his capacity as a
private member. . . .

It is by this imperious authority of
the Standing Committees that the new
member is stayed and thwarted whenever he seeks to take an active part in
the business of the House. Turn which
way he may, some privilege of the
Committees stands in his path. The
rules are so framed as to put all busi-

ness under their management; and one of the discoveries which the new member is sure to make, albeit after many trying experiences and sobering adventures and as his first session draws towards its close, is, that under their sway freedom of debate finds no place of allowance, and that his long-delayed speech must remain unspoken. For even a long congressional session is too short to afford time for a full consideration of all the reports of the . . . Committees, and debate upon them must be rigidly cut short, if not altogether excluded, if any considerable part of the necessary business is to be gotten through with before adjournment. . . .

One very noteworthy result of this system is to shift the theatre of debate upon legislation from the floor of Congress to the privacy of the committee-rooms. Provincial gentlemen who read the Associated Press dispatches in their morning papers as they sit over their coffee at breakfast are doubtless often very sorely puzzled by certain of the items which sometimes appear in the brief telegraphic notes from Washington. What can they make of this for instance: "The House Committee on Commerce to-day heard arguments from the congressional delegation from" such and such States "in advocacy of appropriations for river and harbor improvements which the members desire incorporated in the River and Harbor Appropriations Bill"? They probably do not understand that it would have been useless for members not of the Committee on Commerce to wait for any opportunity to make their suggestions on the floor of Congress, where the measure to which they wish to make additions would be under the authoritative control of the Committee, and where, consequently, they could gain a hearing only by the courteous sufferance of the committee-man in charge of the report. Whatever is to be done must be done by or through the Committee.

It would seem, therefore, that practically Congress, or at any rate the House of Representatives, delegates not only its legislative but also its deliberative functions to its Standing Committees. The little public debate that arises under the stringent and urgent rules of the House is formal rather than effective, and it is the discussions which take place in the Committees that give form to legislation. Undoubtedly these siftings of legislative questions by the Committees are of great value in enabling the House to obtain "undarkened counsel" and intelligent suggestions from authoritative sources. All sober, purposeful, business-like talk upon questions of public policy, whether it take place in Congress or only before the Committees of Congress, is of great value; and the controversies which spring up in the committee-rooms, both amongst the committeemen themselves and between those who appear before the Committees as advocates of special measures, cannot but contribute to add clearness and definite consistency to the reports submitted to the House.

There are, however, several very obvious reasons why the most thorough canvass of business by the Committees, and the most exhaustive and discriminating discussion of all its details in their rooms, cannot take the place or fulfill the uses of amendment and debate by Congress in open session. In the first place, the proceedings of the Committees are private and their discussions unpublished. The chief, and unquestionably the most essential, object of all discussion of public business is the enlightenment of public opinion; and of course, since it cannot hear the debates of the Committees, the nation is not apt to be much instructed by them. Only the Committees are enlightened. . . .

. . . . . For the instruction and elevation of public opinion, in regard to national affairs, there is needed something more than special pleas for special privileges. There is needed public discussion of a peculiar sort: a discussion by the sovereign legislative body itself, a discussion in which every feature of each mooted point of policy shall be distinctly brought out, and every argument of significance pushed to the farthest point of insistence, by recognized leaders in that body; and, above all, a discussion upon which something—something of interest or importance, some pressing question of administration or of law, the fate of a party or the success of a conspicuous politician—evidently depends. It is only a discussion of this sort that the public will heed; no other sort will impress it. . . .

16. The Two Majorities*

WILLMOORE KENDALL

My point of departure: the tension between Executive and Legislature on the federal level of the American political system. My preliminary thesis: that the character and meaning of that tension, as also its role in the formation of American policy, has been too little examined during the period in which the tension has been at its highest; that the explanations of the tension that are, so to speak, "in the air," do not in fact explain it, but rather tend to lead us away from a correct explanation—and, by the same token, away from a correct understanding of our recent political history; that the entire matter, once we have the elements of a correct explanation in hand, opens up a rich field for investigation by our "behaviorists," hitherto unexplored because (in part at least) of the latter's lack of interest in what politics is really about.[1]

First, then, as to the character of the tension:

A. The tension between our "national" Executive and our "national" Legislature, though as suggested above it varies in "height" from time to time, and at one moment seemed to have disappeared altogether, has in recent decades been a characteristic feature of our politics.

B. The tension typically arises in the context of an attempt or expressed wish on the part of the Executive to "do" something that a majority of one or both houses is inclined to oppose. Typically, that is to say, we have an Executive *proposal*, which now successfully, now unsuccessfully, a large number of legislators seek to disallow, either as a whole or in part.[2]

C. The tension is peculiarly associated with certain readily identifiable

* *Midwest Journal of Political Science* (November, 1960), Vol. IV, pp. 317-345. Reprinted by permission of Wayne State University Press.

[1] This is almost, but not quite, the same point as that involved in the frequently-repeated charge that the behaviorists spend their time (and a great deal of money) studying the trivial and the obvious, a charge too often put forward by writers who are something less than ready with an answer to the question, "What *is* important?" My point is less that the reader of our behavioral literature finds himself asking, "So what?" (though indeed he does), than that he finds himself asking (to quote Professor Rogow), "What happened to the great issues?" The behaviorists go on and on as if the latter did not exist.

[2] A distinction that is indispensable for a clear grasp of the problem. We may call it the distinction between "whether to?" and "how much?" And failure to keep it in mind often results, as I shall argue below, in our seeing Executive "victories" where there are in fact Executive defeats.

areas of public policy; and in these areas it is both continuing and predictable.[3] Those that come most readily to mind (we shall ask later what they may have in common) are:

1. The Legislature tends to be "nervous" about "internal security." The Executive tends to become active on behalf of internal security only under insistent pressure from Congress; it (the bureaucracy probably more than the President and his official family) here tends to reflect what is regarded as enlightened opinion[4] in the universities and among the nation's intellectuals in general.

2. The Congress adheres unabashedly to the "pork barrel" practices for which it is so often denounced; it tends to equate the national interest, at least where domestic economic policies are concerned, with the totality of the interest of our four-hundred-odd congressional districts.[5] The Executive regards "pork barrel" measures as "selfish" and "particular," and does what it can, through pressure and maneuver, to

forestall them; it appeals frequently to a national interest that is allegedly different from and superior to the interests of the constituencies.

3. The Legislature tends to be "protectionist" as regards external trade policy. The Executive, again reflecting what is regarded as enlightened opinion among intellectuals, tends to favor ever greater steps in the direction of "free trade," and acceptance by the United States of a general responsibility for the good health of the world economy.

4. The Legislature (again a similar but not identical point) tends to "drag its feet" on foreign aid programs, unless these promise a demonstrably *military* "pay-off." The Executive seems to be deeply committed to the idea of foreign aid programs as the appropriate means for gaining American objectives that are not exclusively, or even primarily, military.[6]

5. The Congress (though we must speak with greater caution than has been necessary above because the relevant tension expresses itself in a different and less readily visible way) does not, by its actions at least, reflect what is regarded as enlightened opinion among intellectuals on the complex of issues related to the integration of the southern schools, withholding all action that might ease the Executive's path in the matter. The Executive stands ready to enforce the ruling in the Brown case, and seems unconcerned about the difficulty of pointing to any sort of popular mandate for it.

6. The Legislature insists upon perpetuating the general type of immigration policy we have had in recent decades. The Executive would apparently like to bring our immigration legislation under, so to speak, the all-men-are-created-equal clause of the Declaration of Independence.

7. The Legislature is, in general, jealous concerning the level of the national

---

[3] We shall have something to say below about what we might call the "latent but always-present tension" in certain other areas of public policy, where the Executive would like to do such and such, but because of Professor Friedrich's "law of anticipated reactions" does not dare even to formulate a "proposal." Much of what we hear about the so-called "decline" or "eclipse" or "fall" of Congress becomes less convincing when we take into account the matters in which Congress always gets it way because the Executive, much as it would *like* to do such and such, is not sufficiently romantic even to attempt it.

[4] No implication is intended, at this point, as to whether the opinion *is* enlightened, as that question is inappropriate to our immediate purposes.

[5] Cf., *The Federalist,* ed. Edward Mead Earle ("The Modern Library" [New York: Random House, n. d.]), No. 64: ". . . the government must be a weak one indeed if it should forget that the good of the whole can only be promoted by advancing the good of each of the parts or members which compose the whole." All subsequent citations to *The Federalist* are by number of the relevant paper.

[6] It perhaps gives to "military objectives" a wider and looser meaning than the congressmen are willing to accept.

debt, and thus about government spending; it clings, in principle at least, to traditional notions about sound government finance. The Executive, at least the vast majority of the permanent civil servants (who are, as is well known, in position to bring notable pressures to bear even upon a President who would like to side with Congress), appears to have moved to what we may call a Keynesian position about the national debt and year-to-year spending.

8. The Legislature tends to be "bullish" about the size of the United States Air Force and, in general, about military expenditure as opposed to expenditures for "welfare." The Executive, though no simple statement is in order about its policies, continuously resists congressional pressure on both points.

9. The Legislature tends to be "nationalistic," that is, to be oriented to the "conscience" of its constituents rather than the "conscience of mankind." The Executive tends to be "internationally minded," that is, to subordinate its policies in many areas to certain "principles" concerning the maintenance of a certain kind of international order.

10. The Legislature appears to have no quarrel with Right-wing dictatorships; it tends to favor policies with respect to them based rather upon expediency than upon commitment to democratic forms of government. The Executive, despite the tendentious charges we often hear to the contrary, is disposed to hold governments not based upon free elections at arm's length.

11. The Executive[7] tends to favor each and every component of the current program (the product of what is generally regarded as enlightened opinion among political scientists at our universities) for transforming the

[7] For the sake of simplicity of exposition, I here reverse the previous order, and speak first of the Executive.

American political system into a *plebiscitary* political system, capable of producing and carrying through *popular mandates*. These components, so well known as to require only the briefest mention, are: Remake our major political parties in such fashion that their programs, when laid before the American people in presidential elections, will present them with "genuine" "choices" concerning policy, and that candidates for office within each party will stand committed to their party's program. (The major public spokesmen for such a reform are the chairmen of the national committees, one of whom is of course the appointee of the President.) Get rid of the Senate filibuster, as also of the seniority principle in congressional committees (which do indeed make it possible for little bands of willful men to "frustrate" alleged majority mandates). Iron out inequalities of representation in Congress, since these, theoretically at least, are capable of substituting the will of a minority for that of the majority. (Although it is perhaps difficult to attribute any policy on the latter two components to the White House itself, anyone who has himself been a permanent civil servant knows that in the executive departments the animosity against the filibuster, the seniority principle, and the alleged "over-representation" of rural folk and white southerners is both intense and deeply-rooted.) Further assure equal representation, and thus genuine majority mandates, by enacting ever stronger "civil rights" legislation calculated to prevent the white southerners from disfranchising or intimidating potential Negro voters, and by putting the Justice Department permanently into the business of enforcing the "strengthened" civil rights. (The extreme "proposals" here do normally originate with senators and congressmen, but it will hardly be disputed that the White House is consistently on the side of the proponents, and consistently disappointed by Congress' final reply, from session to session, to the question "How much?") "Streamline" the executive branch of government, so as to transform it into a ready and homogeneous instrument that the President, backed up by his "disciplined" majority in Congress, can use effectively in carrying out his mandate, and so as to "concentrate" power and make it more "responsible" (by getting rid of the independent agencies, and eliminating the duplication and competition between agencies that perform the same or very similar tasks). Finally, glorify and enhance the office of President, and try to make of presidential elections the central ritual of American politics—so that, even if the desired reform of the party system cannot be achieved at once, a newly-elected President with a popular majority will be able to plead, against a recalcitrant Congress, that *his* mandate must prevail.

Congress seldom shows itself available to any such line of argument, and off-year congresses like to remind presidents, in the most forceful manner possible, that the system has rituals other than that of the presidential election. For the rest, it resists the entire program with cool determination. With respect to the party system, it is clearly wedded to our traditional system of decentralized parties of a non-"ideological" and non-programmatic character. With respect to mandates, it clearly continues to regard the American system as that which, as I contend below, its Framers intended it to be—that is, one in which the final decisions upon at least the important determinations of policy are hammered out, in accordance with "the republican principle," in a deliberative assembly made up of uninstructed representatives, chosen by their neighbors because they are the "virtuous" men; thus as a system which has no place for mandates. As for the filibuster and the committee chairmen, it clearly regards as their peculiar virtue that which the Executive and its

aggrandizers within the bureaucracy and out among the nation's intellectuals regard as their peculiar vice, namely, that they *are* capable of frustrating an alleged majority mandate. With respect to "streamlining" the executive branch of government, it appears to yield to proposals in this sense only when it has convinced *itself* that further resistance is an invasion of presidential prerogatives rooted in the same constitution from which it derives its own; it clearly clings to the traditional view, again that of the Framers themselves, that power should *not* be concentrated, but rather (since a most efficient Executive might well come to be the most efficient against the liberties of the people) shared out in such fashion that ambition may counter ambition. With respect to civil liberties, it clearly cherishes the notion that the Tenth Amendment has not been repealed, and that, accordingly, there is room in the American system for differences in civil liberties from state to state and even, within a state, for differences in civil liberties from differently situated person to differently situated person. With respect to the aggrandizement of the office of president and the glorification of presidential elections, it again takes its stand with the tradition and the Framers: there is no room in the American system for a presidential office so aggrandized as to be able itself to determine how much farther the aggrandizement shall go; the ultimate decisions on that point must be made not by the President but by *itself*, in the course of the continuing dialectic between its members and their constituents; plebiscitary presidential elections cannot become the central ritual of our system without destroying the system.

II

What general statements—of a sort that might throw light on their meaning in the American political system—

may we venture to make about these areas of tension? [8]

At least, I believe, these:

A. They all involve matters of policy which, by comparison with those involved in areas where tension is *not* evident and predictable, bear very nearly indeed upon the central destiny of the United States—on the kind of society it is going to become ("open" or relatively "closed," egalitarian and redistributive or shot through and through with great differences in reward and privilege, a "welfare state" society or a "capitalist" society); on the form of government the United States is to have (much the same as that intended by the Framers, or one tailored to the specifications of democratic ideology); or on our relatedness to the outside world on points that, we are often told, nearly affect the central destiny of mankind itself. They are all areas, therefore, in which we should *expect* disagreement and thus tension in a heterogeneous society like ours (though by no means necessarily, I hasten to add, tension between its Legislature and its Executive—not, at least,

[8] I do not forget that the areas of tension are also areas of tension *within* both houses of Congress, where the Executive always, when the big issues are "up," has considerable support, and sometimes "wins" (or at least seems to). It would be interesting, though not relevant to the purposes of the present paper, to study the incidence of the tensions within Congress (as revealed, e.g., in voting, about which we have a rich and growing literature), particularly with a view to discovering whether there is a discernible "trend" in this regard. As also whether there is any relation, of the kind my analysis below would lead us to expect, between the character of an M. C.'s constituency and the "side" he takes in these matters. One imagines that the tensions are also repeated within the bosom of the Executive. But we must not get in the habit of permitting our sophistication about such matters to obscure for us the fact that "Congress" acts finally as *an* institution, whose "behavior" as an institution can and for some purposes must be observed without regard to its internal divisions.

for any reason that leaps readily to the eye).

B. They are areas in which the Executive (as I have already intimated) is able, with good show of reason, to put itself forward on any particular issue as the spokesman for either *lofty and enlightened principle* or still undiffused professional *expertise,* or both. The Executive tends, that is to say, to have the nation's ministers and publicists with it on "peace," the nation's professors and moralizers with it on desegregation, the nation's economists with it on fiscal policy and redistribution, the nation's political scientists with it on political reform and civil rights, etc. To put it otherwise, Congress at least *appears,* in all the areas in question, to be holding out for either the repudiation or evasion of the moral imperatives that the nation's proper teachers urge upon us, or the assertion of an invincibly ignorant "layman's" opinion on topics that are demonstrably "professional" or "expert" in character, or both. The Executive is *for* world government, *for* the outlawing of war, *for* unselfishness in our relations with the outside world, *for* the brotherhood of man, *for* majority-rule, *for* progress, *for* generosity toward the weak and lowly, *for* freedom of thought and speech, *for* equality, *for* the spreading of the benefits of modern civilization to "underdeveloped" lands, *for* science and the "scientific outlook," *for* civil rights; apparently it is its being *for* these things that somehow runs it afoul of Congress in the areas in question; and it is difficult to avoid the impression that Congress is somehow *against* these things, and against them because wedded to bigotry, to selfishness both at home and abroad, to oppression, to the use of force, to minority rule, to outmoded notions in science. Because the Executive so clearly represents high principle and knowledge, the conclusion is well nigh irresistible that Congress represents low principle (or, *qui est pire,* no principle at all), reaction, and unintelligence, and does so in full knowledge that the President (both he and his opponent having, in the latest election, asserted the same high principles and the same generally enlightened outlook)[9] has not merely a majority mandate but a virtually unanimous mandate to go ahead and act upon high principle.

C. They are areas that, for the most part, do not lend themselves to what is fashionably called "polyarchical bargaining." For example, the internal security policies that Congress has in recent years imposed upon the Executive have been in no sense the result of protracted negotiations among groups, conducted with an eye to leaving no group too unhappy; so, too, with the policy that it imposes (by inaction) with regard to the desegregation of the southern schools, and that which it imposes (by action) concerning immigration and the armed forces. To put it otherwise, the policy problems involved are by their very nature problems about which everybody can't have a little bit of his way, because either we move in *this* direction (which some of us want to do) or in *that* direction (which others of us want to do); and the line Congress takes with respect to them seems to be determined much as, before Bentley and Herring and Truman and Latham and Dahl, we fondly supposed all policy lines to be determined—that is, by the *judgment* of individuals obliged to choose between more or less clearly understood *alternatives,* and obliged ultimately to choose in terms of such notions as they may have of justice and the public weal.

D. They are areas—though we come now to a more delicate kind of point —in which, little as we may like to think so and however infrequently we may admit it to ourselves, Congress pretty consistently gets its way; indeed the widespread impression to the con-

trary seems to me the strangest optical illusion of our politics, and worth dwelling upon for a moment: the question actually at issue becomes, quite simply, whether in recent decades (since, say, 1933) the "liberals"—for, as intimated repeatedly above, the tension between Executive and Legislature is normally a liberal-conservative tension—have or have not been "winning"; and I contend that the reason both liberals and conservatives tend (as they do) to answer that question in the affirmative is that we are all in the habit of leaving out of account two dimensions of the problem that are indispensable to clear thinking about it, and that we may express as follows:

First, we cannot answer the question without somehow "ranking" political issues in order of "importance" —without, for example, distinguishing at least between those issues that are "most important," those that are "important" but not most important, those that are "relatively unimportant," and those that are "not important at all"— meaning here by "important" and "unimportant" merely that which the liberals and conservatives themselves deem important or unimportant. In the context of such a ranking we readily see that "winning" in our politics is a matter of getting your way on the matters that are most important to you, not getting defeated too often on those that are merely important to you, and taking your big defeats on those are relatively unimportant to you or not important at all. Take for instance that liberal "victory" of the period in question that comes most readily to mind: the creation and maintenance of the Tennessee Valley Authority. Everyone familiar with the politics of the period knows that the TVA enthusiasts intended TVA to be the first of a *series* of "authorities," which would have the effect of shifting the entire American economy away from "capitalism" and "free private enterprise." That was what the liberals wanted, and that was what the conservatives, if they meant business, had to prevent; that was what was "most important," against the background of which the creation and maintenance of a single TVA (one, moreover, that men could support out of no animus whatever against private enterprise) was at most "unimportant"; and, once we put the question, "Who won?" in *those* terms, and remind ourselves where the White House and the bureaucracy stood, we are obliged to give an answer quite different from that which we are in the habit of giving: The Executive got its TVA in particular, but Congress put a stop to TVA's in general (nor is there any issue so dead in America today as that of "socialism").

Secondly, there is the dimension we have mentioned briefly above, that of the things that the Executive would like to propose but has the good sense not to because of its certain foreknowledge of the impossibility of getting the proposals through Congress, it being here that Congress *most* consistently gets its way, and without anyone's noticing it.[10] James Burnham is quite right in arguing that the capacity to say "No" to the Executive is the essence of congressional power;[11] but he exaggerates the infrequency with which Congress does say "No," partly by ignoring the "No's" that Congress does not have to say for the reason just given, and partly by failing to distin-

guish between the "No's" that are "most important" to the Congress itself and those that are not.

To summarize: The areas of tension are typically "most important" areas in which this or that application of high principle desired by the Executive gets short shrift from enough congressmen and senators to prevent it, or at least to prevent it on anything like the *scale* desired by the Executive. And in these areas the Congress normally "wins," "high principle" seemingly going by the board. Nor would it be easy to show—and this brings us to the nub of the matter—that the tensions are less acute, or produce a notably different result, during the two-year periods that *precede* presidential elections than during the two-year periods that *follow* them, which if it were true might enable us to argue that the tensions arise because of *shifts* of opinion in the electorate; or that they relate particularly to the two-thirds of the senators who, after any biennial election, are "holdovers." And, that being the case, we are obliged, as I have already intimated, to confront an unexplained mystery of our politics, namely: the fact that *one and the same electorate maintains in Washington, year after year, a President devoted to high principle and enlightenment, and a Congress that gives short shrift to both;* that, even at one and the same election, they elect to the White House a man devoted to the application of high principle to most important problems of national policy, and to the Hill men who consistently frustrate him. More concretely: the voters give an apparent majority mandate to the president to apply principles "x, y, and z," and a simultaneous (demonstrable) majority-mandate[12] to the Congress to keep him from applying them. And the question arises, why, at the end of a newly-elected

---

[10] Let anyone who doubts the point (a) poll his liberal acquaintances on the question, is it proper for non-believers in America to be taxed for the support of churches and synagogues (which they certainly are so long as churches and synagogues are exempted from taxation)? and, (b) ask himself what would happen in Congress if the Treasury Department were to propose removal of the exemption. There is no greater symbol of Executive-Legislative tension than the fact that the sessions of both houses open with prayer, whereas we cannot imagine a prayer at the beginning of a meeting of, say, an interdepartmental committee of bureaucrats.

[11] Cf., James Burnham, *Congress and the American Tradition* (Chicago: Henry Regnery Co., 1959), p. 278.

[12] Unless we want to argue that Congress does *not* have a majority mandate. See below my reasons for thinking such a position untenable.

President's first two years, do the voters not "punish" the congressmen? Are the voters simply "irrational"? Our political science has, it seems to me, no adequate or convincing answer to these (and many kindred) questions.

III

What *is* "in the air" in American political science (to return now to the hint thrown out above) because of which my statement of the problem of executive-legislative tension sounds unfamiliar—not to say "against the grain"? Not, I think, any doctrines that clash head-on with such a statement on the ground that it appears to move in a direction that might be "pro-Congress"; that would be true only if contemporary American political science were "anti-Congress," which I, for one, do not believe to be the case[13] (besides which the statement is *not*, up to this point, "pro-Congress"). Not either, I think, any specific doctrine or doctrines concerning executive-legislative tensions as such; for though contemporary American political science is certainly not unaware of the tensions (it might, at most, be accused of sweeping them now and then under the rug, contrary to the rules of tidy housekeeping), it seems safe to say that there is no prevailing "theory" of the problem. The answer to our question lies rather, I believe, in this: there are *overtones* in the statement, perhaps even *implications,* that simply do not "fit in" with what we are accustomed, these days, to say or assume, and hear others say and assume, not about legislative-executive tensions, but about some very different matters, namely, elections, majority rule, and the comparative "representativeness," from the standpoint of "democratic theory," of the Executive and the Legislature. And perhaps the best way to bring the relevant issues out into the open is to fix attention on what we *are* accustomed to hear said and assumed about these matters.

I propose to use for this purpose Robert A. Dahl's celebrated Walgreen lectures,[14] which precisely because they are *not* "anti-Congress" (are, rather, the handiwork of one of our major and most dispassionate experts on Congress) have the more to teach us about the problem in hand. The lectures seem to me to show that we are accustomed now to assume (if not to say), and to hear it assumed, that when we speak of "democratic theory," of majority rule in the United States, we can for the most part simply ignore Congress and congressional elections. This is nowhere *asserted* in the *Preface,* but I submit to anyone familiar with it *both* that such a tacit premise is present throughout its argument, which goes on and on as if our presidential elections were not merely the *central* ritual of our politics but also the *sole* ritual, and that Dahl's procedure in the matter seems, in the present atmosphere, perfectly natural.

But let us think for a moment about that tacit premise, and the resultant tacit exclusion of executive-legislative tension as a problem for democratic theory (Dahl, I think I am safe in saying, nowhere in the *Preface* refers to it).[15] To put the premise a little differently: the majority-rule problem in America *is* the problem of the presidential elections; either the majority rules through the presidential elections (which Dahl thinks it does not), or it does not rule at all; a book about majority rule in America does not, in consequence, need to concern itself at any point with the possibility that fasci-

---

[13] There is, of course, an "anti-Congress" literature, but there is also an enormous literature that is friendly to Congress.

[14] Robert A. Dahl, *Preface to Democratic Theory* (Chicago: University of Chicago Press, 1956).

[15] The function of his Congress, in the *Preface* anyhow, is that of "legitimizing basic decisions by some process of *assent"* (italics added), and of registering pressures in the process he likes to call "polyarchical bargaining." See respectively pp. 136, 145.

nated the authors of *The Federalist*, namely, that of the "republican principle" as working precisely through the election of members to the two houses of Congress. And the *effect* of that premise, whether intended or not, is to deny legitimacy, from the standpoint of "democratic theory," alike to Congress as a formulator of policy, and to the elections that produce Congress as expressions of majority "preferences"; that is, to deny the relevance of those elections to the problem to which the authors of *The Federalist* regarded them as *most* relevant, i.e., the problem of majority rule in America.[16] Nor is the reason for the premise difficult to discover: for Dahl, and for the atmosphere of which his book may fairly be regarded as an accurate summary, Congress, especially the lower house, is a stronghold of entrenched minorities,[17] and in any case is, and was always intended to be, a *barrier* to majority rule, not an *instrument* of majority rule.[18] It is bicameral; its members are chosen in elections deliberately staggered to prevent waves of popular enthusiasm from transmitting themselves directly to its floors; it "overrepresents" rural and agricultural areas and interests; many of its members are elected in constituencies where civil liberties, in-

cluding even the liberty to vote, are poorly protected, so that the fortunate candidate can often speak only for a minority of his constituents; and as the decades have passed it has developed internal procedures—especially the filibuster and the seniority principle in the choice of committee chairman—that frequently operate to defeat the will of the majority even of its own members;[19] it reflects, in a word, the anti-democratic, anti-majority-rule bias of the Framers, who notoriously distrusted human nature (because of their commitment to certain psychological axioms).[20]

Now the doctrine just summarized is so deeply imbedded in our literature that it may seem an act of perversity to try, at this late a moment, to call it into question (as the overtones and implications of my discussion in I and II certainly do). The present writer is convinced, however, that a whole series of misunderstandings,[21] partly about the Framers and partly about majority rule, have crept into our thinking about the matter, and that these have disposed us to beg a number of questions that it is high time we reopened. The Framers, we are being told, distrusted the "people," cherished a profound animus against majority rule, and were careful to write "barriers" to majority rule into their constitution. But here, as it seems to me, the following peculiar thing has happened. Taught as we are by decades of political theory whose creators have been increasingly committed to the idea of majority mandates arising out of plebiscitary elections, we tend to forget that that alternative, not having been invented yet, was *not* in the mind of the Framers at all; which is to say, we end up accusing the Framers of trying to prevent something they had never

---

[16] Cf., *The Federalist*, No. 54: "Under the proposed Constitution, the federal acts . . . will depend merely on the majority of votes in the federal legislature. . . ." Cf., No. 21: "The natural cure for an ill-administration, in a popular or representative constitution, is a change of men"—through, of course, elections. Cf. also No. 44: If Congress were to ". . . misconstrue or enlarge any . . . power vested in them . . . in the last resort a remedy must be obtained from the people, who can, by the election [in elections where the candidate who gets the largest number of votes wins?] of more faithful representatives, annul the acts of the usurpers."

[17] Dahl, *op. cit.*, p. 142.

[18] *Ibid.*, p. 14. I am sure Professor Dahl will not object to my mentioning that the point about civil liberties, although not present in his book, he has pressed upon me in private conversation.

[19] *Ibid.*, p. 15.

[20] *Ibid.*, p. 8.

[21] To which I must plead myself guilty of having contributed, particularly in my *John Locke and the Doctrine of Majority-Rule* (Urbana: University of Illinois Press, 1941).

even heard of,[22] and so cut ourselves off from the possibility of understanding their intention. Above all we forget that what the Framers (let us follow the fashion and accept *The Federalist* as a good enough place to go to find out what they thought) were above all concerned to prevent was the *states'* going their separate ways, their becoming an "infinity of little, jealous, clashing, tumultuous commonwealths,"[23] so that there would *be* no union in which the question of majority rule could arise. The "majority rule" they feared was the unlimited majority rule within the several states that would, they thought, result from disintegration of the union; and we are misreading most of the relevant passages if we read them in any other sense. We take an even greater liberty, moreover, when we sire off on the Framers the (largely uncriticized) premise that the proper remedy for the evils of some form of majority rule is as a matter of course non-majoritarian. No one knew better than they that the claim of the majority to have its way in a "republican" (or "free") government cannot be successfully denied;[24] indeed what

most amazes one upon rereading *The Federalist,* in the context of the literature with which we have been deluged since J. Allen Smith, is precisely the degree of their *commitment* to the majority principle,[25] and their respect and affection for the "people" whose political problem they were attempting to "solve." [26] Their concern, throughout, is that of *achieving* popular control over government, not that of *preventing* it.[27] That they thought to do by leaving the "people" of the new nation organized in a particular way,[28] that is, in constituencies which would return senators and congressmen, and by inculcating in that people a constitutional morality that would make of

[22] This is not to deny that the "barriers" do, as it turns out, operate to prevent a plebiscitary system. My point is they were not, and could not, have been intended to, but also that a plebiscitary system is not the only possible majority-rule system.

[23] *The Federalist,* No. 9.

[24] Cf., *ibid.,* No. 58: ". . . the fundamental principle of free government would be reversed. It would no longer be the majority that would rule. . . ." Cf., No. 22, with its reference to the fundamental maxim of republican government as being: that the "sense of the majority shall prevail." Cf., *ibid.*: ". . . two thirds of the people of America could not long be persuaded . . . to submit their interests to the management and disposal of one third." Compare Dahl, *op. cit.,* pp. 34, 35, where after citing various strong pro-majority-rule statements, from political philosophers, he concludes that they are all "clearly at odds with the Madisonian view." Note that one of the statements, curiously, is from Jefferson, whom Dahl immediately describes as a "Madisonian."

[25] See preceding note. The point has been obscured by our habit of reading the numerous passages that insist on ultimate control by the "people" on the assumption, impossible in my opinion to document, that the authors of *The Federalist* thought they had discovered some way to have matters decided by the people in elections, *without* having them decided by a majority of the people. See following note.

[26] Cf., *ibid.,* No. 14: "I submit to you, my fellow-citizens, these considerations, in full confidence that the good sense which has so often marked your decisions will allow them due weight and effect. . . . Hearken not to the unnatural voice which tells you that the people of America . . . can no longer continue the mutual guardians of their mutual happiness. . . . Is it not the glory of the people of America [that they have heeded] . . . the suggestions of their own good sense, the knowledge of their own situation, and the lessons of their own experience?" Such passages abound in *The Federalist.*

[27] Cf., *ibid.,* No. 40: ". . . the Constitution . . . ought . . . to be embraced, if it be calculated to accomplish the views and happiness of the people of America." Cf., No. 46: ". . . the ultimate authority . . . resides in the people alone. . . ."

[28] Cf., *ibid.,* No. 39: "Were the people regarded . . . as forming one nation, the will of the *majority of the whole people* . . . would bind the majority . . . and the will of the majority must be determined either by a comparison of the individual votes, or by considering the will of the majority of the States. . . . Neither of these rules has been adopted." (Italics added.)

the relevant elections a quest for the "virtuous" men[29]—the latter to come to the capital, normally, without "instructions" (in the sense of that term —not the only possible sense—that we are most familiar with). These virtuous men were to *deliberate* about such problems as seemed to them to require attention and, off at the end, make decisions by majority vote; and, as *The Federalist* necessarily conceived it, the majority votes so arrived at would, because each of the virtuous men would have behind him a majority vote back in his constituency, represent a popular majority. (My guess, based on long meditation about the relevant passages, is that they hoped the deliberation would be of such character that the votes would seldom be "close," so that the popular majority represented would be overwhelming.) That, with one exception, is the only federal popular majority of which Madison and Hamilton were thinking—the exception being the popular majority bent on taking steps adverse to natural rights,[30] that is, to justice. What they seem to have been thinking of here, however, and took measures (though not drastic ones)[31] to prevent, was precisely *not,* I repeat, an electoral majority acting through a plebiscitarily-chosen president, but rather a demagogically-led movement that might sweep through the constituencies and bring pressure to bear upon the congressmen; nor must we permit our own emancipation, because of which we know that the difference between unjust steps and just ones is merely a matter of opinion, to

blind us to the implied distinction between a popular majority as such and a popular majority determined to commit an injustice. Madison and Hamilton not only thought they knew what they meant, but *did* know what they meant, when they used such language;[32] and we err greatly when we confuse their animus against the popular majority bent on injustice with an animus against the popular majority, the majority of the people, as such.

Ah, someone will object, but you have conceded that the measures they took operate equally against both; the Framers, that is to say, made it just as difficult for a popular majority as such, even a popular majority bent upon *just* measures, to capture the Congress, and use it for its purposes, as for an "unjust" majority. But here again we must hold things in their proper perspective—by keeping ourselves reminded that Madison did not think the measures we have in mind (staggered elections and bicameralism in particular) would constitute much of a barrier to either. As Dahl himself points out, Madison placed his sole reliance against the popular movement that snowballs through the constituencies in the hope that the constituencies would, because of the growth and development of the nation, become so numerous, so widely flung, and so diverse as to make it impossible to bring people together into the kind of popular movement he feared, which is one point. But there are several other dimensions to the thought implicit in *The Federalist* on this matter. There

---

[29] Cf., *ibid.,* No. 57. The chosen are to be those "whose merit may recommend [them] to . . . esteem and confidence. . . . Cf., No. 64, with its reference to assemblies made up of "the most enlightened and respectable citizens" who will elect people "distinguished by their abilities and virtue. . . ."

[30] *I.e.,* a majority "faction." See *ibid.,* No. 10, *passim.*

[31] Indeed, Madison clearly believed (*ibid.*) that nothing could be done *constitutionally* to block a majority "faction."

[32] That is, when they distinguished between just and unjust, and measures adverse to the rights of others and measures not adverse to them. Cf., *ibid.*: ". . . measures are too often decided, not according to the rules of justice and the rights of the minor party, but by the superior force of an interested and overbearing majority." Cf., Dahl, *op. cit.,* p. 29, where he illustrates the gulf between himself and the Madisonians by writing "good" and "bad," the implication being, I take it, that the distinction is operationally meaningless.

is, first, the constitutional morality suggested in the doctrine concerning the virtuous men; these being, by definition, men bent upon justice, constituency elections turning upon the identification of virtuous men would, on the face of them, constitute a major barrier to a popular movement bent upon injustice,[33] *but not to a widespread popular movement demanding something just.*[34] There is, second, the fact that the constitution, being a constitution that limits governmental power, might fairly be expected to bear more heavily upon the prospects of an unjust movement, which as Madison must have known is of the two the more likely to run afoul of the relevant limitations, than on a just one. And there is, thirdly, the fact that so long as the system works as Madison intended it to, bicameralism and staggered elections themselves might be expected to bear more heavily upon an unjust movement than upon a just one: they constitute a "barrier," as far as Congress is concerned, only to the extent that the hold-over senators and the congressmen from constituencies not yet captured by the spreading popular movement *resist* the relevant popular pressures—which they are most likely to do by *debate* in the course of deliberation, and can do most effectively precisely when they are able to wrap themselves in the mantle of justice (which by definition they cannot do if the popular movement is itself bent upon justice). In fine: once we grant the distinction between a popular majority in the constituencies bent upon injustice and a popular movement bent

upon something just, grant it with all the literalness with which it was intended, there remains no reason to attribute to Madison, or to the constitution he defended, any animus against popular majorities (as such) having their way. He simply wanted, I repeat, the majority to be articulated and counted in a certain way, and had confidence that so long as it was it would produce just results. And we must, if we are to bring the whole problem into proper focus, recognize that the Madisonian majority, articulated through and counted within the constituencies, is still present in the American political system; which is to say that we must learn to think in terms of what we may call *two* popular majorities, the congressional and the presidential, and that we must accept, as an unavoidable problem for American political theory, the problem of the respective merits of the two (and must not, like Professor Dahl, talk as if one of them did not exist). What is at stake when there is tension between Congress and President is *not* the majority principle (the "Rule," Dahl calls it), but rather the question of where and how we are to apply it.

IV

What we are always dealing with in the American system is, on the present showing, Two Majorities, two *numerical* majorities,[35] *each* of which can, by pointing to the Rule, claim what Dahl calls the "last say," and each of which merits the attention of that part of "democratic theory" that deals with the problem of majority rule. The moment this is conceded, moreover, the problem of executive-legislative tensions begins to appear in the light in which it is presented above.

As for the merits of the respective claims of the two majorities, I content

[33] Cf., *ibid.,* No. 51: ". . . a coalition of a majority . . . could seldom take place [except on] principles . . . of justice and the general good."

[34] Cf., *ibid.,* No. 57, where it is argued that a political constitution should aim at obtaining for "rulers men who possess most wisdom to discern, and most virtue to pursue, the common good of the society"—and taking the "most effectual precautions for keeping them virtuous. . . ."

[35] But cf., Burnham, *op. cit.,* p. 316 (and the preceding discussion) for a different view of the two majorities. Burnham, of course, follows Calhoun.

myself here with the following observations:

A. One of the two majorities, the presidential, has (as I have intimated) been *engrafted* on our political system: it was not intended by the Framers, not even present to their minds as something to be "frustrated" and have "barriers" put in its way. It is, in other words, insofar as we can satisfy ourselves that it exists *qua* majority and eventuates in "mandates," something new in our politics, something therefore whose appropriateness to the spirit and machinery of our system may fairly be regarded as still open to question. (I hope I shall not be understood to mean that its newness necessarily establishes a presumption against it.)

B. Professor Dahl, for all his fascination with presidential elections, is himself the author of the most brilliant demonstration we have (or could ask for) that nothing properly describable as a majority mandate, sanctioned by the Rule, emerges from a presidential election.[36] Indeed, one way of stating the question concerning the merits of the respective claims of the two majorities is, Is the congressional majority open to the same objections, from the standpoint of the Rule, that Dahl brings so tellingly against the presidential? If not, we should be obliged to view with suspicion Dahl's contention that, there *being* no majority in America, the majority cannot rule (so that we can stop worrying about majority tyranny).[37]

C. It is interesting to notice some of the claims that Madison (were we, like Professor Dahl, to go so to speak to his

assistance) might be imagined as making for *his* majority "mandate" that, as Dahl demonstrates, cannot be made for the side that gets the more votes in a presidential election:

1. It does not stand or fall with the possibility of proving that the voters who are its ultimate sanction voted for the same man because they endorse the same policies; the other, as Dahl admirably shows, does.[38] It is *heterogeneous* by definition, and is supposed to be, was intended to be, heterogeneous; it cannot, indeed, accomplish without being heterogeneous its intended purpose, which is the ultimate arriving at policy decisions through a process of deliberation among virtuous men representing potentially conflicting and in any case different "values" and interests.

2. It is at least potentially *continuous* in its relation to the voters, whereas, as Dahl shows, the presidential sanction is *discontinuous*[39] (his majority speaks, insofar as it speaks at all, then promptly disappears), and potentially therefore *simultaneous* with the policy decisions in which it eventuates. Indeed, the major difference between Madison and Dahl as theorists of majority-rule is precisely that Dahl clearly cannot, or at least does not, imagine a popular majority-rule system as working through any process other than that of elections, which, as he himself sees, are in the nature of the case discontinuous and prior to actual policy decisions. Madison, on the other hand, is not in the first place all that preoccupied with elections, and ends up describing a majority-rule process rich in possibilities (as we all know) for what we may, with Burnham, call a continuing dialectical relationship between the virtuous men and their constituents, though one which by no means necessarily takes the form of the member of Congress "keeping his ear to the ground" and seeking to carry

---

[36] Dahl, *op. cit.,* pp. 124-131.

[37] *Ibid.,* p. 25, and Chap. V, *passim.* It might be pointed out that Dahl has difficulty deciding just how to phrase the point; "rarely, if ever," does not say the same thing as "rarely," and "ruling on matters of specific policy" does not say the same thing as "ruling."

[38] *Ibid.,* pp. 127-129.

[39] *Ibid.,* p. 130.

out automatically the "will" of a majority of his constituents; he is himself a part *of* his constituency, potentially "representative" in the special sense of reacting to policy problems just as his constituents *would* were they present, and also informed (which, of course, they often are not); besides which the dialectic, as Madison could hardly have failed to realize, may take the form of actually *thinking* with them, whether by communication back and forth or in the course of visits back home.[40] Finally, as again Madison certainly knew, the member of Congress will, if normally ambitious, wish to be reelected, and will not willingly become a party to policy decisions that, when they come to the attention of his constituents, will seem to them foolish or outrageous; which means that he must ask himself continuously how at least his general course of behavior is *ultimately* going to go down at home.

3. In two senses, it does not need to be, and Madison did not expect it to be, "positive" in the way that a writer like Dahl assumes a mandate must be if it is to be really a mandate.[41] First, it is as likely to express itself in prohibitions and "vetoes" as in imperatives. And second, the popular command involved is basically, as Madison conceived it, a command to help produce *just* policy decisions in a certain manner, and normally does not presuppose a positive mandatory relation with respect to particular matters.

4. It is a mandate that emerges from a process that was always intended to emphasize specifically *moral* considerations, e.g., the kind of considerations involved in deciding who are the virtuous men. To put the point otherwise:

it is a process that was originally conceived in terms of a moral theory of politics, where the theorists of the presidential mandate tend, to say the least, to a certain relativism about morals (which is why they can end up insisting that this and this must be done because the majority demands it *tout court*). Its emphasis, therefore, is on the ability of the people, i.e., at least a majority of the people, to make sound judgments regarding the virtue of their neighbors, not on the ability of the people to deliberate on matters of policy. (Dahl leaves us in no doubt about its inability to do the latter.)

V

The above considerations seem to me not only to throw light on the respective claims of the Two Majorities, but also to show why (assuming that the older of the two continues to function much as Madison intended it to, which I do believe to be the case) we have no cause to be astonished at the fact of executive-legislative tension in our system: since there is no reason *a priori* to expect the virtuous men to be attracted as a matter of course to the proposals put forward by the Executive (with whatever claim to a "majority mandate" for them); at least, that is to say, we see how such tension *might* occur. But there are some further considerations that seem to me to show why it *must* occur, and at the same time to throw light on how each of us should go about making up his mind as to which of the two to support. These are:

A. The essentially *aristocratic* character of the electoral process that produces the older of the majorities as over against the essentially *democratic* character of the electoral process that produces the newer (despite the fact that the electors are in the two cases the same men and women). A moment's reflection will reveal at least one reason for that artistocratic character: al-

---

[40] The essence of *Federalist* thought here is that of a "deliberate sense of the community" (meaning by community, surely, not less than a majority?) formed as problems arise and get themselves discussed in the Congress and out over the nation, and by no means necessarily expressing itself always through elections.

[41] *Ibid.*, pp. 129, 131.

though the constituencies and states differ greatly in this regard, they all nevertheless approximate, in a way in which the national constituency cannot do, to *structured communities,* involving more or less endless series of face-to-face hierarchical relations among individuals—of superordination and subordination, of capacity to influence or subject to pressure and susceptibility to being influenced or subjected to pressure, of authority and obedience, of economic power and economic dependence, of prestige enjoyed and respect tendered, etc., that are patently relevant to the choice of a congressman or senator in a way that they are not relevant to the choice of a president. In the election of the member of Congress, a community faithful to the constitutional morality of *The Federalist* makes a decision about whom to send forward as its most virtuous man, a decision which is the more important, and which it accordingly takes the more seriously, because the community knows that it can have little effect on a presidential election (i.e., its most direct means of defending its own interests and "values" is by sending the right senator or representative to Washington, and sending the right one becomes therefore a matter of sending a man who will represent the hierarchical relations in which those interests and values are articulated). In the congressional election, therefore, the "heat" can and will go on, if there is a powerful community "value" or interest at stake in the choice among available candidates; so that although the voters vote as nominal "equals" (one man, one vote) they do so under pressures that are quite unlikely to be brought to bear on their "equal" voting for President (especially as the powerful and influential in the community are normally unable to estimate accurately, for reasons we shall notice below, the probable impact of the presidential candidates upon their interests and "values," whereas they *can* do so with the candidates for

the legislature). This state of affairs is reflected in the notorious fact that congressmen and senators, when they phone home to consult, are more likely, other things being equal, to phone bank presidents than plumbers, bishops than deacons, editors than rank-and-file newspaper readers, school superintendents than schoolmarms—and would be very foolish if they were not more likely to. And the unavoidable result is that the men chosen are likely to be far more "conservative," far more dedicated to the "status quo," than the candidate whom the same community on the same day helps elect President (or, to anticipate, than the candidate whom the same community on the same day helps defeat for President); and the chances of their disagreeing with that candidate a few months later on "most important" and "important" questions are, on the face of it, excellent. So that we have at least one built-in reason for *expecting* executive-legislative tension.

B. The difference in the discussion process as we see it go forward in the constituencies and the discussion process as we see it go forward in the national forum. This is partly a matter of the point just made (that the constituency is to a far greater extent a structured community), and partly a matter (not quite the same thing) of the sheer difference in *size* between the local constituency and the nation—or, as I should prefer to put it, of the kind of considerations that led that remarkable "empirical" political theorist, J.-J. Rousseau, to declare, at a crucial point in *Du contrat social,* that there is more wisdom in small bands of Swiss peasants gathered around oak trees to conduct their affairs than, so to speak, in all the governments of Europe. One of the questions that that sentence necessarily poses, when we examine it carefully, and that which leads on to what I believe to be a correct interpretation of it, is whether it intends a tribute (which the attribution of wisdom certainly was for Rousseau), (1) to the

Swiss, or (2) to peasants, or (3) to peasants who are also Swiss, or (4) to small groups of persons caught up in a certain kind of discussion situation. The context, I suggest, leaves no doubt that the correct answer here is (4): Rousseau certainly thought highly of the Swiss, but not so highly as to claim any sort of monopoly of wisdom for them; he also thought highly of peasants, because of their simplicity of life (if you like—which I don't—because of their closer approximation to the "noble savage"), but precisely *not* because of their native wisdom in the sense intended here, which evidently has to do with wise decisions concerning public affairs; by the same token, as we know from the *Julie,* he thought highly of Swiss peasants in particular, but not so highly as to permit himself the claim that the small bands, merely *because* made up of Swiss peasants, are the repositories of wisdom. The emphasis, in other words, is upon the "small bands," the fact that each embraces only a *small number* of individuals, and on the fact of that small number being gathered to dispatch the public business of a small community— the Swiss peasants and the oak tree being simply the symbol, the example, that comes most readily to Rousseau's mind. So we are led on to ask, what difference or differences does Rousseau think he sees between their "deliberation" and other kinds of deliberation? We can, I think, answer with some confidence. First, there is a presumption that each small band is talking about *something,* not *nothing.* Second, there is a presumption, because of each band's relatedness to the community whose affairs it is dispatching, that its members are reasonably well-informed about the *something* they are talking about—the implication being (it is caught up and developed in the *Government of Poland*) that, as a discussion group increases in number and a constituency in size, there is greater and greater danger that the persons concerned will find themselves talking

about *nothing,* not *something,* and will also find themselves talking about situations and problems that are too large, too complicated, for them to understand. Wise deliberation—the point recurs again and again in Rousseau's political writings—occurs only where people are discussing problems that they can, so to speak, "get outside of," and where the participants in the discussion are not so numerous as to give scope to the gifts of the orator and the rhetorician.

Now: evidently a congressional or senatorial constituency is *not* a small band gathered around an oak tree; but also nothing can be more certain than that the national constituency in America long ago became so large and complex that, even were there candidates who themselves understood it (which is doubtful), the audiences to which they must address themselves do not understand it, cannot even visualize it. Yet we have engrafted upon our constitution an additional electoral process that *forces* discussion of "national" problems in the national constituency; that obliges candidates to "go to the people" and court votes; and that, for the reason just mentioned, makes it necessary for them to avoid talking about something and leaves them no alternative but to talk about nothing —that is (for this is always the most convenient way of talking about nothing), to talk about high—or at least high-sounding—principle, without application to any concrete situation or problem. Add to this the fact that the candidates, hard put to it to produce in a few weeks enough speeches to see them through the campaign, must enlist the assistance of speech-writers, who come as a matter of course from the intellectual community we have frequently mentioned above, and things —*inter alia,* the sheer impossibility of saying, after a presidential election, what "issues" it has decided—begin to fall into place. There are no issues, because both candidates for the most part merely repeat, as they swing from whistle-stop to whistle-stop and television studio to television studio, the policy platitudes that constitute the table-talk in our faculty clubs: no one, not even the most skilled textual analyst, can tease out of the speeches any dependable clue as to what difference it will actually make which of the two is elected; it seems probable, indeed, that the candidates themselves, unless one of them be a White House incumbent, do not know what use they would make of the vast powers of the presidency. And the inevitable result, as intimated above, is that what you get out of the presidential election is what amounts to a *unanimous* mandate for the principles *both* candidates have been enunciating, which is to say: the presidential election not only permits the electorate, but virtually *obliges* it, to overestimate its dedication to the pleasant-sounding maxims that have been poured into its ears. Even did the electorate *not* deceive itself on this point, moreover, it has no way to arrest the process: it must vote for one of the two candidates, and tacitly commit itself, whether it likes it or not, to what they have been saying.

We now stand in the presence, I believe, of the decisive explanation of executive-legislative tension in the American political system, and the decisive clue to its meaning. Elections for congressmen, and up to now at least most elections for senator, do not and cannot follow the pattern just outlined. With rare exceptions, for one thing, the relevant campaigns are *not* running debates between the candidates, and thus do not offer them the temptation to raise each other's ante in the matter of principle. For another thing, principle is for the most part *not* what gets talked about, but rather realities, problems, the potential benefits and potential costs (and for whom?) of doing this rather than that, and in a context where the principles that are applied are those (very different we may be sure from those of the presidential candidates) upon which the constituents

are actually accustomed to act. The talk generated by the campaign, much of it at least, is in small groups made up of persons involved in the actual face-to-face situations we spoke of earlier, and is, therefore, *not* wholly dissimilar to that of those peasants under the oak tree. So that, insofar as the presidential election encourages the electorate to overestimate its dedication to moral principle, the congressional election encourages them, nay, obliges them, to take a more realistic view of themselves, and to send forth a candidate who will represent, and act in terms of, that more realistic view. By remaining pretty much what the Framers intended them to be, in other words, the congressional elections, in the context of the engrafted presidential election, provide a highly necessary corrective against the bias toward quixotism inherent in our presidential elections; they add the indispensable ingredient of Sancho Panzism, of *not liking* to be tossed up in a blanket even for high principle, and of *liking* to see a meal or two ahead even if the crusade for justice has to bide a little. And it is well they do; the alternative would be national policies based upon a wholly false picture of the sacrifices the electorate are prepared to make for the lofty objectives held up to them by presidential aspirants. And executive-legislative tension is the means by which the corrective works itself out.

If the foregoing analysis is correct, the tension between Executive and Legislative has a deeper meaning—one which, however, begins to emerge only when we challenge the notion that the "high principle" represented by the President and the bureaucracy is indeed high principle, and that the long run task is to somehow "educate" the congressmen, and out beyond the congressmen the electorate, to acceptance of it. That meaning has to do with the dangerous gap that yawns between high principle as it is understood in the intellectual community (which makes its influence felt through the President and the bureaucracy) and high principle as it is understood by the remainder of the population (which makes its influence felt through the Congress). To put it differently: the deeper meaning emerges when we abandon the fiction (which I have employed above for purposes of exposition) that we have on the one hand an Executive devoted to high principle, and a Legislature whose majority simply refuse to live up to it, and confront the possibility that what we have is in fact two *conceptions* of high principle about which reasonable men may legitimately differ. Whilst we maintain the fiction, the task we must perform is indeed that of "educating" the congressmen, and, off beyond them, the electorate, "up" to acceptance of high principle; once we abandon it, the task *might* become that of helping the congressmen to "educate" the intel-

lectual community "up" to acceptance of the principles that underlie congressional resistance to executive proposals. In the one case (whilst we maintain the fiction), discussion is unnecessary; in the other case (where we recognize that what we stand over against is two sharply differing conceptions of the destiny and perfection of America and of mankind, each of which conceivably has something to be said for it), discussion is indispensable; and in order to decide, as individuals, whom to support when executive-legislative tension arises, we must reopen (that is, cease to treat as closed), reopen in a context of mutual good faith and respect, the deepest issues between American conservatism and American liberalism. Reopen them, and, I repeat, discuss them; which we are much out of the habit of doing.

B. The "Attack on Congress": Bill of Particulars

17. Seniority, Sectionalism, and Senility*

ESTES KEFAUVER AND JACK LEVIN

[*The student should read the Goodwin article which follows this because, as Goodwin points out, there have been changes, largely of an informal nature, relative to the seniority principle. Yet, the Kefauver and Levin statement reflects the basic liberal attitude toward the rules and procedures of Congress.*]

MUCH of the progress that will be achieved by modernizing the committee structure of Congress might easily be lost if at the same time certain improvements are not made in the procedures and conduct of these congressional units. Foremost among present evils is the ancient and rigid seniority system that governs the selection of committee chairmen and determines rank in almost every other phase of group activity in the national legislature.

Under this system, the member of the party in power who has served the longest on any given committee is for practical purposes the *only* person eligible for the chairmanship of that committee, regardless of his qualifications, physical fitness, or any other factor that might be weighed, or any other method

* Chapter 10, *A Twentieth-Century Congress* (New York: Duell, Sloan and Pearce, 1947), pp. 133-142. Reprinted by permission of Duell, Sloan and Pearce. Copyright 1947 by Essential Books.

of trying to pick the best person for the post.

The minority party follows the same rule with slavish devotion. When there is a change in party control, the member who, while in the minority, had the greatest tenure, moves into the chairmanship. Thus at the beginning of the 8oth Congress Democratic chairmen had to abdicate in favor of Republican chairmen, who took over on the same seniority principle. True, there was the formality of an election when the 8oth Congress was organized. But it was only a formality. Any member who tried to buck the system on any such occasion would be howled down as an upstart or maverick and probably subjected to such political punishment as denial of patronage. It has happened.

This much can be said in favor of rule by seniority: the law of averages works in its favor. In many cases, because of knowledge and skill acquired during years of grappling with problems that regularly come before his committee, the man who is handed the chairmanship through seniority in most cases would be chosen for the post by any system of more democratic election that might be devised. But there is abundant evidence to prove that fitness and leadership are not based upon years in office alone. We will cite one or two examples that dramatize the inherent danger of the system, and that can be spelled out without reflecting in any way upon any present member of the Senate or House.

When a vacancy occurs and there happen to be two men on a committee who took their oath of office at the same time, the seniority system resorts to the alphabet to determine who shall be chairman. When Congressman Edward Taylor of Colorado died, there were two members who could claim the chairmanship of the important House Appropriations Committee: Representative Clifton A. Woodrum of Virginia and Representative Clarence Cannon of Missouri. Both had served with distinction. Mr. Cannon's skill in handling budget matters was exceptional. Mr. Woodrum had become one of the recognized leaders of the House whose advice carried weight on both sides of the aisle. Representative Cannon got the chairmanship because his name began with *C*, which ranks far ahead of *W* in the alphabet. The noted Scripps-Howard columnist, Thomas L. Stokes, Jr., made this comment in recalling the incident when, during the 79th Congress, Mr. Woodrum retired:

"This bit of monkey business shows how silly the seniority system is without going into the qualifications of the two men. *Neither the committee itself, nor the House, had anything to say about the chairmanship of this most important committee, nor do they for any others.*[1] A man moves up on the committee list through the years and automatically becomes chairman when he gets to the top, whatever his abilities. In this case of rival claims, the alphabet was invoked."

By the same method of alphabetical selection, former Representative Andrew J. May of Kentucky headed the House Military Affairs Committee in recent years because *M* comes before *T*. Representative Robert Ewing Thomason of Texas had exactly the same length of service, but there was no

opportunity to choose between the two. On the Senate side, few, if any, members had a record of more distinguished public service than the late Senator Carter Glass of Virginia. It is nevertheless true that he retained his important post as chairman of the Senate Appropriations Committee although physically unable even to attend a session of the Senate, or of his committee, for more than three years.

There was a potentially dangerous situation in the Senate at the outbreak of World War II, when former Senator Robert R. Reynolds of North Carolina headed the Military Affairs Committee. Senator Reynolds held widely voiced views that were directly opposed to the policy and course of action upon which the country and the Congress had agreed. But seniority had put him there and only death or retirement could take him away. The Senate was helpless to do anything about the situation. The senator in question retired, but not until the war was nearly over. This is too much of a chance to take with the prestige and efficiency of a branch of the government already in a dangerously low state. A hostile chairman has in times past, and may again at any unpredictable moment in the future, impede a very vital and constructive part of the congressional program. The Legislative Reorganization Act completely omits treatment of this paramount problem.

The present Senate offers a striking example of the penalties of seniority. There are several younger members who generally are acclaimed as possessing uncommon leadership and insight in fields which today loom as second to none in deciding the future course of the country. Typical of this group are Senators Wayne Morse of Oregon, J. William Fulbright of Arkansas, Henry Cabot Lodge, Jr., of Massachusetts, Brien McMahon of Connecticut, John Sparkman of Alabama, and Edward J. Thye of Minnesota. Unless tradition is violated and the averages upset, none of these senators is likely

[1] These, and all italics hereinafter, supplied by the authors.

to attain an important regular committee chairmanship until he begins his thirteenth year of consecutive service —that is to say, has been elected for a third six-year term. Senator McMahon upset precedent in the 79th Congress when he became head of the special committee to study atomic-energy control.

Another serious defect of the seniority system challenges the very character of truly representative government. Many men are returned by the voters time and time again on the record of their statesmanship and service to their respective states and districts. But no one will deny that others of lesser abilities have remained in office and advanced without undue effort or unusual ability to positions of power on Capitol Hill, because they happened to come from areas where the tradition for one particular party, plus the power of entrenched city, courthouse, and state machines, make a farce of the two-party system.

Once a member is "in," as a Democrat from the South or a Republican from the Middle West, it is relatively easy, by comparison with more politically sensitive sections of the country, to remain in office. In the South, the question of constitutional rights of a large minority and the operation of a poll tax have served to limit the electorate to in some cases as few as ten per cent of the potential voting population. Without reflecting personally on any individual, it seems pertinent to observe the House Rules Committee roster in the 79th Congress. This committee is the most powerful unit in either House or Senate, controlling the priority of all bills that are to be taken up in the lower chamber. Of the eight Democratic members, five were from the South, while all four Republican members were from the Middle West. The same disproportionate representation of particular sections of the United States ran through the entire list of committee chairmanships. The great Far West, which during the past war demonstrated its tremendous physical and economic importance to the nation, and which is increasing in population faster than any other section, was almost without a voice in the leadership of the national legislature. Likewise, as modern industrialization has made once rockribbed Republican New England a more closely matched political battleground, with resulting turnover in office, some important states in that area lacked proper apportionment of congressional positions of power and influence.

We offer a solution to this serious dilemma. At the beginning of each Congress, members of the majority party of each committee should elect chairmen by majority vote. Secret ballots should be used. If a chairman becomes incapacitated by reason of ill health or otherwise, a new leader for the committee should be chosen immediately in a similar manner. However, once a post is filled for a term, the chairman should not be removed except for physical incapacity or for conduct that would also disqualify him to remain a member of Congress. The minority party should follow the same procedure in allocating the posts of ranking members of the committee.

The Reorganization Act recognizes that the dictatorial powers of committee chairmen should be curbed. The act says it shall be the "duty" of the chairmen of committees to report bills promptly to the floor on any measure approved by the committee, and that "necessary steps" shall be taken to bring the bill to a vote. This adds little to the obligation a chairman of a committee has always had. We doubt if it will change the present procedure appreciably, for the reason that no easy method of enforcement is provided for in the act.

There have been cases where committee chairmen permitted overzealous investigators to violate fundamental civil rights in prosecuting investigations, and to make public reports in the name of the committee that blackened the reputations of innocent citizens who had no redress available. Members of committees in some instances have publicly denounced such actions, but, under the present system, are powerless to prevent their repetition. As a good example of this bad practice we cite the House Committee on Un-American Activities under the chairmanship of former Representative Martin Dies of Texas.

Even under the provisions of the Reorganization Act, a chairman can at many stages of the consideration of a bill in committee still exercise virtual veto powers, by "sitting on a bill" or "carrying it around in his pocket." Some years ago, when Representative Philip P. Campbell of Kansas headed the House Rules Committee, he was dubbed by his enemies the "Walking Pigeonhole," because of an alleged habit of stuffing important bills into his inside coat pocket and carrying them around until the session ended.

In the middle 'thirties a carefully considered retirement bill, aimed at making low-paid government jobs attractive to a better class of workers, passed the House. Senator William J. Bulow of South Dakota, chairman of the Senate Civil Service Committee, opposed it. All efforts to get this senator to call a committee meeting were futile. He sat on the bill for an entire session of Congress and delayed action on a measure which would have passed by an overwhelming vote both in the committee and on the floor. A chairman should be a servant, not the czar, of his committee, and these arbitrary and capricious powers must be effectively curbed by definite, effectuating provisions available to any member.

The Reorganization Act wisely provides for regular meetings of all committees, which are worked into a schedule that will permit members to attend sessions with the same regularity that businessmen show up at their favorite civic luncheon clubs. We would propose, as a fixed feature of these committee meetings, that an allocation of time be made for members to present their own bills. Upon unanimous report by the committee, we suggest that bills should be assigned automatically to the regular calendar of the Senate and House. Likewise, the request of one-third of the members should automatically discharge a bill from a committee and place it on the calendar. This would prevent a chairman from thwarting the will of his committee by delaying the reporting of a measure.

Under the general direction of the National Legislative Policy Committee, each staff would prepare for the committee's approval, early in each session, an agenda of the anticipated problems to be dealt with and time assigned to each major topic. Changes necessitated by new bills would be fitted into this program as the committee might decide. With such assignments, the chairman could hold his subcommittee chiefs to a definite schedule, and members could serve efficiently on several such groups.

There is growing dissatisfaction with the gradual increase of "star chamber" committee sessions. During the war many such closed meetings were deemed necessary as a security measure. In the public interest, the Reorganization Act provides that as a general rule all committee meetings shall be open to the public, aside from purely executive sessions. In addition, it should be mandatory that committees publish all votes on pending legislation and amendments considered, including adverse votes. A daily digest should be prepared by each committee staff for publication in the *Congressional Record,* and a monthly indexed summary should be furnished committee members. The status of pending programs would be included, as well as the roll calls referred to above. These things should be done by the staffs of the various committees rather than by the Joint Committee on Printing, as is provided in the Reorganization Act.

With the staffs taking over the routine, members will be relieved of many man-hours of work and will have more time for deliberation and discussion of policies, and to follow the work of other committees. They will also be able to take regular inspection trips to secure firsthand information on the work regularly coming under the jurisdiction of their committees. This will be criticized as more "congressional junkets," but it is well to recall that if President Truman, then senator, had not taken one such inspection trip on his own initiative, there would have been no Truman committee with its brilliant record of searching out wartime recklessness and exposing weak spots in America's war production.

The story of how the Truman committee was born shows exactly how much is left to chance. The Missourian was on the Senate Appropriations Committee and, because of his World War I experience, was particularly interested in the War Department budget. Frank McNaughton and Walter Hehmeyer in their excellent biography, *This Man Truman,* tell what happened:

"In mid-January of 1941, Truman began to receive disturbing reports on the conduct of the national defense program. . . . Letters from Missouri complained that money was being wasted in the construction work being done at Fort Leonard Wood. The Senator decided to see for himself. He loaded his suitcases into his car and drove from Washington straight and unannounced to the fort.

"He strolled quietly through the sprawling huts and skeleton framework of the great barracks. On every hand he saw evidence of waste and poor management. Then he drove back to Washington, visiting camp construction projects along the way. Everywhere the story was the same.

"Truman returned to Washington angry clear through. On February 10, 1941, he told the Senate about it. He insisted that to avoid a national scandal and to spur on the defense effort a special committee should be established that would hunt down waste and inefficiency and open up the bottlenecks.

On March 1, 1941, the Senate set up a committee of seven Senators and granted $15,000 to it. Truman was made chairman. . . .

"It is impossible to assess the accomplishments of the committee in terms of dollars and cents. Thoughtful persons have estimated that it saved between four and six billions of dollars and hundreds of thousands of lives. . . ."

Requiring members to make a complete report to their committee immediately upon their return from field trips, and having digests of these prepared by the staff and printed in the committee bulletins, would tighten up on the admitted possibility of abuse of congressional traveling.

We believe this modernized system should be all-inclusive and cover every aspect of committee work. There will be no need for additional units, special or select, as such committees are generally known. We do not set this down as iron-clad procedure. There probably will not be many occasions when a Congress is faced with such a revolutionary problem as the atom. When such cases do occur, the question of whether or not a separate group should be assigned to the job might be decided first by the National Legislative Policy Committee, subject to the approval of the Senate or House, whichever is involved. Any issue worthy of such unusual consideration should be studied jointly by both houses; this would be facilitated by the recommendations that we have made concerning parallel committees and joint action. The advisability of joint consideration in special cases is well illustrated by congressional handling of the domestic control of atomic energy. The special McMahon committee in the Senate gave the problem a thorough study, in contrast to that of the House Military Affairs Committee, which was comparatively superficial. Had a joint committee been established, both houses would have been equally well informed on the subject and the friction that resulted would have been avoided.

18. The Seniority System in Congress*

GEORGE GOODWIN, JR.

THE seniority system ordinarily rates no more than two or three pages in books devoted to Congress. There is likely to be a brief description and a weighing of the arguments, pro and con, followed generally by the conclusion that the system is a poor one; occasionally an author will defend it stoutly. Regardless of the conclusions, the analyses are rarely thorough. This article attempts to fill a gap in the literature on Congress by describing and analyzing various aspects of its seniority system.

It is well to remember at the outset that very few human institutions ignore seniority entirely. Champ Clark, in his autobiography, noted that it is observed in all the affairs of life:

> No sane man would for one moment think of making a graduate from West Point a full general, or one from Annapolis an admiral, or one from any university or college chief of a great newspaper, magazine or business house. A priest or a preacher who has just taken orders is not immediately made a bishop, archbishop or cardinal. In every walk of life "men must tarry at Jericho till their beards are grown."

Yet, as George Galloway states, "in no other place, perhaps, does seniority or length of service carry so much weight as it does in the Congress of the United States." It is more than a means of choosing committee chairmen; it is a means of assigning members to committees, of choosing subcommittee chairmen and conference committee members. It affects the deference shown legislators on the floor, the assignment

of office space, even invitations to dinners. In short, "it is a spirit pervading the total behavior of Congress." Its significance for constituencies was expressed by Senator Byrd, who, when he was persuaded to run again for his seat, explained that "seniority of service and committee rank have importance over and above the capabilities of the members." The system seems absolute in the assignment of office space, and nearly absolute in the choice of committee chairmen. Yet in other areas, it is often bypassed to a surprising degree. Our concern here is seniority as it relates to the standing committees of Congress.

I. Working Rules

As might be expected, seniority is not mentioned in the House or Senate rules, although it has drastically changed their effect. Senate Rule XXIV states simply, "in the appointment of standing committees, the Senate, unless otherwise ordered, shall proceed by ballot to appoint severally the chairmen of each committee, and then by one ballot, the other members necessary to complete the same." House Rule X reads, in part, "at the commencement of each Congress, the House shall elect as chairman of each standing committee one of the members thereof. . . . All vacancies in the standing committees of the House shall be filled by election by the House."

A distinction should be made between Congressional and committee seniority. Taking the former first, senators are ranked according to the length of uninterrupted service, dating in most cases from the opening day of the Congress to which they are elected. If they are elected or appointed to fill an unexpired term, different provisions prevail. The

* The American Political Science Review (June, 1959), pp. 412-436. Reprinted by permission.

appointee starts accumulating seniority on the date on which a governor certifies his appointment. If a special election has been held, however, seniority commences on the day on which the new senator takes the oath of office, if the Senate is in session; or if it is not in session, then on the day after the election. Those entering on the same day are listed alphabetically, with the same rank number. House procedure is similar, except that greater credit is given for non-consecutive service. Those with three non-consecutive terms are ranked above those with two consecutive terms, for example. Congressional seniority is followed on social occasions, in the allocation of office space, and in making assignments to committees.

Committee seniority is established by consecutive service on a given committee. If two or more members go on a committee at the same time, note is taken of previous political experience, preference being given to former senators, to former representatives and finally to former governors. If previous political experience is equal, they are likely to be ranked alphabetically; in the House they may draw lots.[1]

When the committee party ratio changes because of a change in the party ratio of the house, members of the minority party with the least seniority may thereby lose their committee assignments. Otherwise the right to remain on a committee and to move up the ladder is generally unquestioned.[2]

. . .

[1] So John M. Vorys of Ohio lost the draw to Robert B. Chiperfield of Illinois in 1939 when both were assigned as Republican freshmen to the House Foreign Affairs Committee. Twenty years later, when Vorys retired, though he had been for most of that period the Republican mainstay on the Committee, he was still only second ranking minority member—Chiperfield's district was as safe as his, and the seniority order once established was not disturbed.

[2] In 1964, however, Democratic Congressmen who supported Barry Goldwater's presidential candidacy were penalized, after a fashion.

If a ranking member leaves a vacancy because of transfer to another committee or retirement from Congress, all his fellow party members on the committee who were beneath him move up in rank. The career of Representative Sabath, to cite a case, gives a unique illustration of what can be accomplished by transfer, if it is combined with longevity. He entered Congress in 1907, transferred to the Rules Committee in 1929, after 22 years of service, became its chairman in 1939 after another ten years, and remained the ranking Democrat on the Committee for 13 more years.

A member who is defeated or who fails to run, and later returns to Congress again, loses his congressional and his committee seniority. He is likely, however, to receive more important committee assignments than the average freshman. Alben Barkley, for example, after a tour of duty as Vice-President, was reassigned to his former committees, Finance and Foreign Relations.

In short, to become a chairman, a legislator must remain continuously on a given committee longer than any other fellow party member, and be of the majority party. It is not uncommon to find men on a given committee of higher House and Senate rank than the committee chairman. This is partly a matter of luck and partly a feeling on the part of some that it is better to be second or third on an important committee than chairman of a minor one. In the 85th Congress, for example, fourteen Democratic senators who were not chairmen had seen greater service in the upper house than Senator Hennings, the Rules Committee chairman, and sixty-one Democratic representatives who were not chairmen had seen greater service in the lower house than Congressman Burleson, chairman of the Committee on House Administration. But other members will stay with an early assignment, preferring to be bigger fish in smaller ponds.

Although they have no power to determine who shall be committee

TABLE I. COMMITTEES-ON-COMMITTEES IN THE 85TH CONGRESS

No. of Members	Senate Democrats	Senate Republicans	House Democrats	House Republicans
	15	23	15	38
How Chosen	By Floor Leader (Johnson); called Steering Committee	By Conference Chairman (Saltonstall) with Conference approval	Democratic members of Ways & Means, *ex officiis*, who are chosen by Democratic Caucus	Each State Republican delegation chooses one member, with as many votes as state has Republican Congressmen
Chairman	Floor Leader (Johnson)	(Bricker), designated by Conference Chairman	Ranking Democrat on Ways & Means (Cooper, followed in '58 by Mills)	Floor Leader (Martin)

chairmen, party committees-on-committees in the House and Senate make important decisions on initial committee assignments and transfers from one committee to another. There is great variety in these committees, as can be seen from Table I, which describes the situation prevailing in the 85th Congress (1957-1958). House committee-on-committee members are chosen in a way that would seem to make them less subject to party leadership control than Senate members; however, there is no doubt that the House party leaders can influence the appointment of these members when they find it advisable.

In working out the "giant jig saw puzzle" of committee assignments certain limitations are generally observed by these committees-on-committees. They must, of course, be guided by the number of vacancies and by the number of applications for transfer. Care is taken to attain geographical distribution, if not balance.[3] Attention

is paid to group desires[4] and to the experience and training of individual legislators. And balance among the various factions of the party is sought. Beyond these more or less objective factors, being in the good graces of the party leader is certainly important in getting on a major committee. . . .

Party control, which is expected in the more tightly knit House, is also found, though perhaps to a lesser degree, among the Senate Democrats. The so-called "Johnson Rule," initiated in 1953 when he was Democratic majority leader, allows for departures from seniority in making appointments and, in so doing, leaves room for the application of less automatic criteria. According to the rule, no Senate Democrat is entitled to a second top committee assignment until every party member, no matter how junior, has one top position.

For all the committees-on-committees "it is handy to have the seniority system to pull them out of a dilemma"; but seniority has not been a controlling factor in the making of initial appoint-

[3] In the Senate, for example, there may not be two senators of the same party from the same state on any committee, a practice that is convenient on other grounds, since it eliminates what otherwise might be a source of intrastate jurisdictional disputes between the two senators.

[4] Farm state representatives dominate the agriculture committees, for example, and only lawyers are seated on the judiciary committees.

ments and transfers, except among the Senate Republicans. Until the 86th Congress this group, however, placed the utmost emphasis on making the appointment process entirely automatic. Seniority was carefully measured, previous government service weighed and, if all else failed, the alphabet was resorted to in order to solve the committee assignment problem on an impersonal basis. In 1959, the Senate Republicans moved far in the direction of the "Johnson Rule," after considerable discussion in the Policy Committee and the Committee on Committees.

In making initial appointments and transfers there is room for choice and for favoritism, but there is almost no room for this in choosing committee chairmen. Becoming a chairman is a matter of party luck and of individual endurance. Once a member becomes a committee chairman, nothing but a change of party control or removal from the Congress is at all likely to force a change.[5] Chairmen have great powers. They subdivide the work of the committees, arrange the agenda and the work schedule, control the staff, preside over committee meetings, manage floor debate, and dominate conference committee proceedings, to mention only their more obvious activities.

Seniority also plays a part in the appointment of conference committee members and subcommittee chairmen. It is difficult to generalize about the former, because there is great variety in practice: but if the legislation involved is important, the chairmen of the committees which handled the bill originally, the ranking minority members and other senior members, will in all likelihood make up the conference committee.

Subcommittee chairmen are generally the senior members of the majority party on a given committee. In the 85th Congress, for example, every senior member had his own subcommittee on 12 of the 34 committees (three had no standing subcommittees at all). On 19 committees, one or more of the senior members of the majority party was passed over in favor of a junior. In most cases a reason for this variance from seniority was obvious. The member, for example, may have been a party leader or the chairman of another committee. Yet in a number of instances there was no evident "automatic" reason for ignoring seniority. (One can guess at the reason why House Education and Labor Chairman Barden of North Carolina passed over Representative Adam Clayton Powell in favor of more junior members.)

II. Historical Development

Historians of the House and Senate are not entirely clear as to when the seniority system, as we now know it, developed. This is not surprising, since it is a custom enforced by opinion, rather than by written rules. Seniority undoubtedly evolved first in the Senate, for this body was reluctant to give its presiding officer, the Vice-President, the appointment power. He was thrust upon them by the Constitution, not chosen by the senators, and was not treated as a member of the Senate. Appointment power was vested in the President *pro tem* and in the majority leader, from time to time; but apparently the seniority system became firmly established with the development of standing rather than select committees, and with the crisis of the Mexican War. Since then, although there is no definitive listing, at least five departures from the seniority rule in choosing or displacing committee chairmen apparently have occurred in

[5] The voluntary abdication, early in 1959, of Senator Theodore F. Green of Rhode Island, then well into his nineties, as chairman of the Foreign Relations Committee, in order to make room for J. William Fulbright of Arkansas in that post, was a startling exception widely hailed as a tribute to Johnson's persuasive powers. Thomas S. Gordon of the House Foreign Affairs Committee relinquished his chairmanship during the 85th Congress on account of ill health.

the Senate. In 1859 Stephen A. Douglas was denied the chairmanship of the Committee on Territories; in 1871 Charles Sumner, the chairmanship of the Committee on Interstate Commerce; in 1913 Benjamin R. Tillman, the chairmanship of the Appropriations Committee; in 1924 Albert Cummins, the chairmanship of the Agriculture Committee; and in 1925 Edwin F. Ladd, the Committee on Public Lands.

In the House the power of making committee appointments evidently gravitated early to the Speaker, who, unlike the Vice-President, was a member and the choice of his peers. It remained there until the revolt against Speaker Cannon in 1910 and 1911, when the seniority system took full hold. Even prior to this, however, seniority was a factor to be taken carefully into consideration. In carrying out the complex task of making committee assignments, the Speaker inevitably sought to regularize his work. One study, for example, notes that seniority prevailed in four-fifths of Cannon's appointments during the 58th through the 61st Congresses. . . .

III. The Pros and Cons of Seniority

The debate over the seniority system generally centers on the choice of committee chairmen. The favorable arguments stress the harmony which results from the system, the emphasis which it places on experience, and the lack of any more suitable alternative. The unfavorable arguments stress the effect of the system on party responsibility and Presidential leadership, the lack of any dependable relation between seniority and qualified leadership, and the fact that the committee leaders in Congress are by no means representative of many of the dominant interests either in the party or in the nation.

The most telling argument of the proponents of seniority is that the system promotes legislative harmony. It prevents hurt feelings on the part of those passed over in the struggle for appointment, and incidentally, it keeps pressure groups out of this struggle. As a result, it helps to create a more cooperative atmosphere, both in the legislative body as a whole, and on the various committees. Committees can act as more of a unit, and in a more non-partisan manner. Roland Young makes this point in this fashion:

The adjustment of rival claims must precede the adjustment of major conflicts without being permitted to divert attention for long from the larger task at hand. Some harmony within the legislature—including agreement on the location of internal authority—must exist before the legislature can itself promote harmony between conflicting groups.

Senator Barkley spoke in similar terms, when he opposed the Morse-Lehman attempt to prevent Senator Eastland from becoming Judiciary Chairman in 1956:

The element of favoritism would come into play, and there would be log-rolling and electioneering for the votes of the committee members by those who wanted to be committee chairmen. . . . Jealousies, ambitions, and all the frailties of human nature would crop out in the electioneering methods of men who wanted to be chairmen of committees.

Another argument of the proponents is that the system produces experienced chairmen—experienced both in the subject matter of the committee on which they have served so long, and in legislative procedure. They may also be better acquainted with the officials at working levels in the executive branch with whom they have to deal than the more transient department heads, who come and go with changes of Presidents. Robert Luce suggests that "though not the only factor in deciding merit, experience is the most important factor."

Finally, the proponents argue that

the system is better than the alternatives, which range all the way from the even more arbitrary automatic proposal once made that the chairman be the member of the committee from the most Northern state, to one in which the President is responsible for the appointments. They take the essentially conservative position that there is no reason to change from a system that is working satisfactorily to a system about which the results are largely unknown. Some wonder if the system has not turned out to be a "rather handy scapegoat for Congressional inertia."

People on both sides of the fence tend to agree that when and if Americans turn toward party responsibility, "seniority will be an early casualty." The proponents of seniority, as one might expect, emphasize the harmonizing, rather than the issue-defining role of political parties, while the most outspoken critics of seniority favor responsible parties. They emphasize the diffusion of leadership among the 36 standing committees of Congress, and the fact that there is no adequate way of integrating their various programs. In fact, they hold, the people most likely to become chairmen, the people from one-party constituencies, are the ones most likely to be out of tune with the party's program:

A chairmanship, after all, is the position of a quarterback on a football team. It should not be given to someone who refuses to be part of the team or who might even carry the ball across the wrong goal line.

The system, the critics argue, is no guarantee that chairmen will be well qualified. A hardy constitution and the ability to get reelected in the home district do not necessarily fit a man to preside over committee meetings or to defend committee reports on the floor. If the system puts so much emphasis on experience, why, they ask, is a man who leaves to take an administrative post, but who returns later to Congress, given little or no credit for his previous

experience? There have been examples, also, of chairmen who were too senile to be effective. When Senator Capper became chairman of the Agriculture Committee he could neither make himself understood, nor understand others. "The seniority principle is followed mainly because the seniors are pleased with themselves and see no sufficient reason for consigning their powers to others."

Finally, the critics suggest that the system produces a large number of chairmen who are representative of only one element of the party, and that, generally, a minority element. They represent "stagnant" districts made safe by restrictions on voting, by a one-party monopoly, by the ascendency of a major interest group, or by an effective rural or urban political machine. Thus, the leaders of Congress, produced by the seniority system, are almost guaranteed to oppose the President, regardless of party, and a new non-constitutional dimension is added to our constitutional system of separation of powers. . . .

Voting records also lend themselves to analysis of the degree of support that party chairmen, or ranking minority members, have accorded their President. Figure 2 compares the support given the President by the chairmen or ranking committee members of his party, by all the members of his party and by his party leaders in the House and Senate. The chairmen's, or ranking members' score is not far below the average party member's score. It averages 4 per cent below in the House and 5 per cent in the Senate. The House chairmen's, or ranking members', score averages 24 per cent below that of the floor leader, while the gap in the Senate is 21 per cent.

In conclusion, a comparison should be made between the seniority system as it operates in the House and as it operates in the Senate, as well as a comparison of its operation under Democrats and Republicans. Turning first to its operation in the two houses, the analysis above shows some interesting similarities. The House and the Senate are about equally likely to get Southern committee chairmen, and voting participation in the states furnishing chairmen and ranking Republican committee members in the 1956 election showed a remarkably similar pattern. Further, there is a close similarity in the House and Senate party system patterns with 50 per cent of the Senate and 51 per cent of the House chairmen being chosen from two-party states.

However, House chairmen come from more urban states (46 per cent from the most urban quartile while only 11 per cent of the Senate chairmen came from these states) and from states with higher total personal incomes (with 53 per cent from the first quartile compared to 17 per cent for the Senate). It is tempting to hazard a guess, therefore, that House chairmen, with a generally more urban-industrial background, should tend to be more closely aligned with their party and with a President of their party. The statistics presented on the voting records of chairmen fail to show this conclusively, however.[6] House chairmen and ranking members voted on an average 2.8 per cent more with their President than did Senate chairmen (60.8 per cent compared to 58.0 per cent for the Senate), but Senate chairmen voted, on the average, .7 per cent more with their party than did House chairmen (79.2 per cent compared to 78.5 per cent). . . .

V. *Alternatives to the Present System*

Americans have shown great ingenuity in suggesting alternatives to the seniority system. Most possibilities were presented by those who testified in 1945 before the Joint Committee on the Or-

ganization of Congress, popularly known as the LaFollette-Monroney Committee.[7] The most drastic proposals would change the system of choosing chairmen, either by substituting some other automatic means of choice, or by giving the decision to a specific constituency such as the members of each committee, the full membership of the entire house, or to some party mechanism. A more moderate type of proposal would attempt to mitigate the effects of the seniority system while continuing to work within it, either by more careful initial recruitment of committee members or by limiting the power of committee chairmen.

One proposal for changing the system completely, that of rotation in office, would act as automatically as the present system. This could take the form of passing the chairmanship around among all majority members with six years or more service after a chairman has been in office for an equal length of time, or after he has reached the age of 65. It could also take the form of putting a limit on the length of time a legislator can spend on any committee.

Chairmen, it is often suggested, should not be chosen automatically, but rather by some constituency on the basis of certain rationally thought out criteria. Members of the various committees could be given the power to choose their own chairmen, or at least to override the seniority system when a majority (or two-thirds) of the committee so decides. Another possibility, of course, would be to have the chairmen chosen by the entire house, by secret ballot. Senator Morse argued for this when he objected to the choice of Senator Eastland as Judiciary Committee chairman in 1956. He reasoned that Senators have a right to sit in Congress, unchallenged, as agents of their states, but that Senators, themselves, should be able to choose their

---

[6] It must be remembered that much of the information concerning House Chairmen applies to the entire states from which they come, and not to the specific congressional districts which may be atypical of the states.

[7] Of a total of 16 people who spoke at the hearings on the seniority system, 14 were critical of its operation.

own agents, even if they are members of the minority party.

These alternatives may give a chance to choose chairmen on the basis of ability or devotion to the "public" interest or some other criterion, but they do not place any emphasis on party responsibility. Many feel that Congress would be greatly strengthened if its committee leaders were also acknowledged party leaders. To this end chairmanship appointments could be made by one of a number of party organs: the caucus, the committee on committees, the rules committee, the policy or steering committee, the floor leader or the presiding officer.

The second general approach to the problem is to attempt to lessen the effects of the system while continuing to work within it. One such proposal stresses recruitment of new members to important committees. Carefully selected committees on committees should give great attention, according to some proposals, to procuring geographical and political balance on each committee. Not only should each region be represented, but representation of consumer, agricultural, business and labor interests, should also be assured. Recent political trends would be more clearly felt if each committee had a number of first, second and third termers in proportion to the number of each group in the house. Some have further suggested that the controlling party should exaggerate its majority on each committee.

Another means of mitigating the effects of the system is to limit the powers of committee chairmen by stripping them of some of the perquisites which give them control over their members and by making it easier for committee majorities to override chairmen's decisions.

Aside from democratizing committee procedure, another means of limiting the power of chairmen would be to give non-committee members certain powers. One suggestion along these lines is the institution of a docket day, a day on which those who filed a bill may appear before the committee handling it and urge action. A further approach is to liberalize the discharge rule. A House discharge rule was adopted in 1910 as part of the anti-Cannon revolt. It has been modified three times and, at present, discharge is so difficult to achieve that the rule is largely ineffective.

Finally, some feel that, if there is no flexibility in the seniority system, certain flexibilities can be developed elsewhere in the legislative process when necessary. Now and then it may be possible to pack a committee in order to get a favorable result. Committee jurisdiction should not be so clearly defined that there is not some leeway to choose between committees (and committee chairmen) when bills are assigned. And occasionally, certain matters can be assigned to select committees, for the seniority custom does not operate here.

VI. The "Johnson Rule" and Other Ameliorations

At the present time the most fruitful area for change, in the eyes of the author, lies in the second type of proposal discussed above, that of ameliorating the effects of the system. Some quiet but important changes have taken place in the past few years in connection with the recruitment of new committee members and the lessening of the powers of committee chairmen.

Senate Democratic Floor Leader Lyndon Johnson has devised a formula which makes it possible for younger men to get on important committees. According to the formula, no member of the party, regardless of seniority, is to receive a second top committee seat until every Democratic Senator has been given at least one such assignment. This was cited by Senator Kennedy when he made his successful bid for membership on the Foreign Relations Committee, transferring from

Government Operations. The fact that he was chosen over Senator Kefauver, who had four more years of Senate seniority, caused the latter to comment, "I am interested to learn that the seniority system is a rule that may or may not be applied by the Senate leadership in deciding the rights of Senators."

Before the results of the Johnson rule can be tested, some attempt is necessary to determine what the top committees are. No complete agreement is in sight on a definitive list ranking committees in order of their importance. The man with a business background might well consider Banking and Cur-

TABLE VIII. PREFERENCE RANKING OF SENATE COMMITTEES*

Senate Committees	Senators Transferred				
	To (A)	From (B)	Net Shifts (A−B) (C)	No. Committee Members (D)	Net Transfers Per Unit of Membership (C÷D) (E)
Foreign Relations	17	1	+16	84	+.19
Finance	16	2	+14	84	+.17
Interstate Commerce	17	4	+13	84	+.15
Judiciary	16	3	+13	84	+.15
Appropriations	23	4	+19	132	+.14
Armed Services	12	3	+ 9	84	+.11
Agriculture	11	5	+ 6	84	+.57
Interior	5	5	0	84	0
Banking and Currency	5	9	− 4	84	−.05
Labor	3	7	− 4	78	−.05
Public Works	5	15	−10	76	−.13
Government Operations	5	20	−15	78	−.19
Rules	7	20	−13	66	−.20
Post Office	3	21	−18	76	−.23
District of Columbia	4	29	−25	66	−.38

* Information in this Table was gathered from appropriate volumes of the *Congressional Directory*. Column A gives the number of senators who transferred to each committee during the 81st through the 85th Congresses. (Initial 80th Congress appointments, when the new committee system went into effect, and freshmen appointments are excluded.) Column B lists the number of legislators who transferred off each committee during the same period. Column C gives the number who transferred onto the committee less the number who transferred off. Column D lists the total number on each committee for the entire period under study. (The entire membership of each committee was counted anew for each Congress, since the size of the various committees was changed at a number of different times.) Column E, which gives the net transfers per unit of membership, was arrived at by dividing column C by column D. A similar survey of freshmen assignments bears out this listing remarkably well, for the results are almost exactly the reverse of this listing.

rency a top committee, a man with union interests might feel the same way about Labor, and a Westerner similarly about the Interior committees. A practical approach to the problem, however, is to measure the desirability of the committees by finding the relation between the number of members who transfer to, and the number who transfer from, each committee. If these numbers are weighted according to the number of members on each committee, a fairly accurate indication of committee desirability can be reached. Table VIII presents this ranking for Senate committees. A preference ranking of House committees, following the same procedure, lists them in this order: Rules, Foreign Affairs, Ways and Means, Un-American Activities, Appropriations, Armed Services, Interstate Commerce, Judiciary, District of Columbia, Agriculture, Education and Labor, Banking and Currency, Interior, House Administration, Public Works, Government Operations, Merchant Marine, Post Office, Veterans Affairs. The high esteem for Foreign Affairs in the House is a recent phenomenon.

The Johnson rule has made a difference, as can be seen from Table IX,

All but two Democratic Senators in the 85th Congress had membership on at least one of the top eight committees as ranked in Table VIII, whereas nine Republican Senators had no important posts. As has been pointed out above, Senate Republicans moved to equalize committee assignments in the 86th Congress. As a result, only three (nine per cent) of the 34 Republican Senators received no important assignments.

In the House, where the average member has only one committee position, the Johnson rule could not apply. But both houses have taken some important steps to limit the powers of committee chairmen. Action along these lines became more practicable after the passage of the Legislative Reorganization Act of 1946. By decreasing the number of committees from 80 to 34, while expanding the jurisdiction of each committee, the reorganization made chairmen much more visible. It also increased the number of members on each committee, thus making a broader committee base possible.

The same act contained provisions designed to limit one-man rule and to make committee decisions subject to

TABLE IX. PERCENTAGE DISTRIBUTION OF TOP
SENATE COMMITTEE ASSIGNMENTS

	Democrats		Republicans	
	85th Cong.	82d Cong.	85th Cong.	82d Cong.
None	4	16	19	26
One	54	45	36	38
Two	42	39	45	36
	100	100	100	100

which lists the percentages of Democratic and Republican Senators who have important committee assignments in the 85th Congress and compares them with assignments in the 82d, before the Johnson rule went into effect.

majority will. Section 33 called on each committee to set regular meeting dates, to hold open hearings (except when marking up bills, or voting, or when a majority of the committee decides to go into executive session), to keep a complete record of all committee actions and to report out measures only after majority consideration. Once such action is taken, "it shall be the duty of the chairman of each such committee to report or cause to be reported promptly . . . and to take or cause to be taken necessary steps to bring the matter to a vote." While these provisions are evidently not always observed, they make it more possible for committee members to insist on democratic procedure when they desire it.

The Senate has not amended its rules to democratize committee procedure further, although an attempt to do so was made in the 84th Congress. The House of Representatives, which, because of its size, is more likely than the Senate to spell out its rules, has taken action, however. Paragraphs 24 and 5 of Rule XI incorporate portions of the Legislative Reorganization Act and go beyond it. For example, provision is made for the calling of special committee meetings over the objection of the chairman.

Further, an increasing number of committees are adopting procedural rules which help safeguard action. Eight of the 15 Senate committees and nine of the 19 House committees informed the author that they had some procedural regulations other than those of their respective houses or of the La-Follette-Monroney Act. Most frequently these rules spell out the rights of committee witnesses in considerable detail, but many give protection against arbitrary action by the chairman. Signs of democratization of committee procedure were noted by Arizona's Congressman Stewart Udall in an article in the *New York Times*. He cited as a model the rules and procedure of the House Committee on Interior and Insular Affairs. These rules limit the power of the chairman by providing that bills be automatically referred to the standing subcommittees, whose jurisdiction is clearly defined, and that

subcommittee chairmen be chosen on the basis of seniority.[8]

Udall cited the other committee of which he was a member, Education and Labor, as an example of an unreformed committee. Its rules were brief and to the point:

> Be it resolved by the Committee on Education and Labor of the House of Representatives for the 84th Congress that the Chairman of the Committee be authorized to appoint such subcommittees as he may see fit to carry out the prescribed duties of the Committee.

> Be it resolved . . . that it be the policy of the Committee to meet at the call of the Chair.

In 1957, after careful bipartisan groundwork by Representative Udall, rules essentially similar to those of the Interior Committee were adopted.

Udall suggests the following steps designed to democratize committee procedure, all of which have been adopted by one or more committees: (1) provision should be made for regular committee meetings and for special meetings when the majority so desires. (2) Subcommittees should be organized on a permanent basis, each with clear jurisdiction, and with members having some choice of subcommittee assignments, but with subcommittee chairmen chosen on the basis of seniority. (3) Executive sessions should be limited. (4) Finally, it should be made impossible to pigeonhole bills without at least the tacit consent of the entire committee.

The approach of this article has been tempered somewhat as a result of dis-

[8] It is interesting to note that some who are seeking to limit the effects of the seniority system by lessening the power of committee chairmen, are, paradoxically, most anxious to have subcommittee chairmen chosen on the basis of seniority, so as to lessen the rewards and punishments available to committee chairmen.

cussion with a number of Congressional staff people who have an intimate knowledge of legislative procedure. Most of them feel that traditional academic criticism of the seniority system is both unrealistic and unfair. All are convinced that the system will remain for the foreseeable future. The approach has been further tempered by respect for some of the conservative checks on majorities which are found in our government. The seniority system is among the more defensible of these Congressional checks. One can readily understand the reasons for its development, for it is common to most institutions. An acceptable alternative is extremely difficult to devise.[9]

The realistic approach for a reformer, therefore, seems to lie along the lines of improving the system as it now operates. Already significant strides have been made in that direction.

[9] In spite of the many criticisms of seniority voiced by those who testified before the La-Follette-Monroney Committee, no action was taken "because of lack of agreement within the Committee as to workable changes in existing practices." Joint Committee on the Organization of Congress, *The Organization of Congress,* Senate Report 1011, 79th Cong., 2d. sess. (1946), p. 35.

19. Some Queensberry Rules for Congressional Investigators*

JACOB K. JAVITS

[*This piece, written during the height of the McCarthy era, still reflects basic liberal attitudes toward the procedures to be followed in Congressional investigation.*]

THIRTY years ago Congress was considered to have done quite a lot of investigating if as many as twenty-five investigations were conducted in any one session. Last year there were 236 separate Congressional investigations, and this year the total will probably be even higher. The legislative work of Congress is often pushed onto the back pages by news from Representative Harold Velde's House Un-American Activities Committee, Senator William Jenner's Internal Security Committee, or Senator Joseph R. McCarthy's Permanent Subcommittee on Investigations

* *The Reporter* (September 1, 1953), pp. 23-25. Reprinted by permission of the author and *The Reporter.* Copyright 1953 by the Reporter Magazine Co.

of the Senate Committee on Government Operations.

It is too little known that as matters now stand there are no standard rules to govern the operations of these investigating committees. It is true that several of the committees have adopted their own rules. The House Committee on Un-American Activities adopted a set of rules as recently as July 15 to protect the rights of witnesses called before it; Senator McCarthy's subcommittee also has a set of rules and Representative Keating's Subcommittee of the House Judiciary investigating the Justice Department has a modern and complete set of rules that have earned it a high reputation for fairness. But it is largely a hit-or-miss matter, and there are no over-all standards to protect the reputations of witnesses who may be called.

There are, for instance, no rules of evidence like those in a court of law, and although some committees have adopted rules of their own, treatment of witnesses is generally dependent upon the attitude of the chairman and the members of the committee. Often Congressional investigation committees do not offer a witness the elementary protection that would be available to him in court—to have advance notice of the charge, to be represented by counsel, to be confronted by the witnesses against him and entitled to cross-examine them, to call witnesses in his own behalf, and to be presumed innocent until proven guilty. Unless the committee adopts its own rules, witnesses before Congressional committees have only the Constitutional right to refuse to answer on grounds of self-incrimination and to answer only questions having some ultimate purpose to further legislation—which is a pretty broad latitude.

There is solid and growing support for the effort to get the Senate and the House of Representatives to adopt rules of standard procedure that would bind all investigating committees. The effort is backed by a widespread desire to change the climate of these investigations to one that will be helpful to legislation and to avoid the use of investigations to attack social, economic, or political views so long as they are consistent with our Constitution.

As long ago as January, 1947, a report of the Senate Judiciary Committee, then headed by Senator Alexander Wiley of Wisconsin, stated that "much confusion and ill-feeling might well be avoided by the adoption in each house of the Congress of standard rules and procedures for the guidance of committees conducting investigations."

Suggestions for rules have been made recently by Senators Paul Douglas (D., Illinois) and Estes Kefauver (D., Tennessee) in the Senate, and in the House by Representative Martin Dies, who himself had a stormy career as chairman of the House Un-American Activities Committee from 1938 to 1945.

The suggestions for rules made by Senator Douglas include one that "witnesses reflecting adversely upon other persons should be called to testify only after they have been examined in executive session and their relative credibility established."

Interestingly enough, Representative Dies is in agreement with Senator Douglas on the need for private hearings before public ones. The rules already put out by Chairman Velde of the Un-American Activities Committee call for a registered-mail notice to people mentioned adversely in public hearings, but they get no advance notice.

'Wicked Tool'

In the set of rules contained in my bill HR 4123, under consideration by a subcommittee of the House Rules Committee, I was particularly concerned with the problem of preventing the release of information from a committee file by an employee or a member of the committee except with the vote of a majority of the committee. The wording is taken from the text of the policy statement on Congressional investigations of Communism in education adopted by the General Board of the National Council of the Churches of Christ in the U.S.A. and seeks to deal with the particular matter that Bishop G. Bromley Oxnam criticized during his appearance before the House Committee on Un-American Activities. In his extraordinary ten-hour hearing Bishop Oxnam asserted that although the committee files, which were made available to anyone who sought information about him, showed his connection with forty-odd allegedly "Communist-front" organizations, he had not joined some of the organizations at all and had quit others after learning of their leanings. He said that the practice of releasing such information created a "wicked tool" for the use of "irresponsible" persons.

J. Edgar Hoover, head of the FBI, also emphasized the need for remedial legislation before a Senate subcommittee in March, 1950:

"Should a given file be disclosed, the issue would be a far broader one than concerns the subject of the investigation. Names of persons who by force of circumstance entered into the investigation might well be innocent of any wrong. To publicize their names, without explanation of their associations, would be a grave injustice. Even though they were given an opportunity to later give their explanation, the fact remains that truth seldom, if ever, catches up with charges. I would not want to be a party to any action which would smear innocent individuals for the rest of their lives. We cannot disregard the fundamental principles of common decency and the application of basic American rights of fair play."

Another important point with which I was concerned is the fixing of responsibility in the body which has authorized the investigating committee—the Senate or the House of Representatives as the case may be—for what the committee does I have proposed that the Rules Committee of the House of Representatives shall have legislative oversight of the operations of all House investigating committees. As the Rules Committee is generally considered to be the instrument of the leadership of the House of Representatives, responsibility would be established at the highest echelon of authority. Representative Dies has come to somewhat the same conclusions on this point as I have, and he further suggests that members of Congress should be entitled to complain to the Rules Committee if investigating committees are charged with being unfair.

In the final analysis, of course, the public must be the judge of excesses charged against Congressional investigating committees. In that mysterious way in which American public opinion takes form, crystallizes, and then becomes irresistible, there is more and more agreement that hunting out subversives without destroying the individual rights and values we are seeking to protect can best be done through the reform of the procedures of Congressional committees.

To that end, I invite the readers of *The Reporter* to consider the following rules of procedure I have proposed. The text was largely the work of the Committee on the Bill of Rights of the Association of the Bar of the City of New York. The work of a similar committee of the New York County Lawyers Association was also very helpful.

RULES OF PROCEDURE

(1) No major investigation shall be initiated without approval of a majority of the committee. Preliminary inquiries may be initiated by the committee staff with the approval of the chairman of the committee.

(2) The subject of any investigation in connection with which witnesses are summoned shall be clearly stated before the commencement of any hearings, and the evidence sought to be elicited shall be relevant and germane to the subject as so stated.

(3) All witnesses at public or executive hearings who testify as to matters of fact shall be sworn.

(4) Executive hearings shall be held only with the approval of a majority of the members of the committee, present and voting. All other hearings shall be public.

(5) Attendance at executive sessions shall be limited to members of the committee and its staff and other persons whose presence is requested or consented to by the committee.

(6) All testimony taken in executive session shall be kept secret and shall not be released or used in public session without the approval of a majority of the committee.

(7) Any witness summoned at a public session and, unless the committee by a majority vote determines otherwise, any witness before an executive session, shall have the

right to be accompanied by counsel, who shall be permitted to advise the witness of his rights while on the witness stand.

(8) Every witness shall have an opportunity, at the conclusion of the examination by the committee, to supplement the testimony which he has given, by making a brief written or oral statement, which shall be made part of the record; but such testimony shall be confined to matters with regard to which he has previously been examined. In the event of dispute, a majority of the committee shall determine the relevancy of the material contained in such written or oral statement.

(9) An accurate stenographic record shall be kept of the testimony of each witness, whether in public or in executive session. In either case, the record of his testimony shall be made available for inspection by the witness or his counsel; and, if given in public session, he shall be furnished with a copy thereof at his expense if he so requests; and, if given in executive session, he shall be furnished upon request with a copy thereof, at his expense, in case his testimony is subsequently used or referred to in a public session.

(10) Any person who is identified by name in a public session before the committee and who has reasonable grounds to believe that testimony or other evidence given in such session, or comment made by any member of the committee or its counsel, tends to affect his reputation adversely, shall be afforded the following privileges:

(a) To file with the committee a sworn statement, of reasonable length, concerning such testimony, evidence, or comment, which shall be made a part of the record of such hearing.

(b) To appear personally before the committee and testify in his own behalf, unless the committee by a majority vote shall determine otherwise.

(c) Unless the committee by a majority vote shall determine otherwise, to have the committee secure the appearance of witnesses whose testimony adversely affected him, and to submit to the committee written questions to be propounded by the committee or its counsel to such witnesses. Such questions must be proper in form and material and relevant to the matters alleged to have adversely affected the person claiming this privilege. The committee reserves the right to determine the length of such questioning; and no photographs, moving pictures, television, or radio broadcasting of the proceedings shall be permitted while such person or such witness is testifying without the consent of such person or witness.

(d) To have the committee call a reasonable number of witnesses in his behalf, if the committee by a majority vote determines that the ends of justice require such action.

(11) Any witness desiring to make a prepared or written statement in executive or public sessions shall be required to file a copy of such statement with the counsel or chairman of the committee twenty-four hours in advance of the hearing at which the statement is to be presented.

(12) No report shall be made or released to the public without the approval of a majority of the committee.

(13) No summary of a committee report or statement of the contents of such report shall be released by any member of the committee or its staff prior to the issuance of the report of the committee.

(14) No committee shall circulate on its letterhead or over the signature of its members or its employees charges against individuals or organizations except as the committee by a majority vote shall so determine.

20. The Attack on Investigations*

JAMES BURNHAM

I

In the past, congressional investigations have been intermittently and sometimes sharply attacked. The 1923-24 investigations into the oil industry and the Departments of the Navy and Justice were condemned by Owen J. Roberts, speaking before the American Bankers Association, as mere "propaganda for nationalization." The *Wall Street Journal* dismissed them as a "political smokescreen." The *New York Times* declared that Congress was "investigation-mad," and was trying to introduce "government by clamor [and] hole in corner gossip." The *Times* (in February 1924) upheld Attorney General Daugherty as a sturdy patriot who was defending "decency [and] honor . . . , the honor which ought to prevail among gentlemen, if not among politicians." [1] In the same month the Communist *Daily Worker* created the label, "smelling committees."

A few years earlier Walter Lippmann, in his book, *Public Opinion,*[2] had described investigations as "that legalized atrocity . . . where Congressmen starved of their legitimate food for thought, go on a wild and feverish man-hunt, and do not stop at cannibalism." In 1925 the influential legal authority, J. H. Wigmore, characterized the investigators as "on the level of

professional searchers of the municipal dunghills." The investigators to whom Wigmore was thus referring (Senators Walsh, Wheeler, Borah and LaFollette) were also termed, in the contemporary press, "scandal-mongers," "mud-gunners," "assassins of character." Their inquiries were described as "lynching bees," "poisoned-tongued partisanship, pure malice, and twittering hysteria," and "in plain words, contemptible and disgusting."

A decade later the New Deal inquiries into investment, banking, utilities, and munitions were the targets for denunciations comparable in content though less colorful in rhetoric. Long before, congressional investigating methods had been eloquently criticized even from the floor of Congress itself. In 1860, during the course of the Senate inquiry into John Brown's raid on Harper's Ferry, Senator Charles Sumner defended a contumacious witness, Thaddeus Hyatt, who had been "incarcerated in the filthy jail" for having refused to answer the committee's questions:[3] "To aid a committee of this body merely in a legislative purpose, a citizen, guilty of no crime, charged with no offense, presumed to be innocent, honored and beloved in his neighborhood, may be seized, handcuffed, kidnapped, and dragged away from his home, hurried across State lines, brought here as a criminal, and then thrust into jail."

Senator John P. Hale of New Hampshire, agreeing with his colleague from Massachusetts, declared: "I ask . . . if

---

* Chapter 17, *Congress and the American Tradition* (Chicago: Henry Regnery and Co., 1959), pp. 236-252. Reprinted by permission of Henry Regnery and Co.

[1] Within six months Daugherty had resigned in disgrace, after the investigators had shown that during his two and a half years in Washington on a $15,000 salary, his personal holdings had shifted from a $19,000 debt to a $100,000 fortune.

[2] Published in 1922.

[3] Here and below, the quotations of the Harper's Ferry debate are taken from *Congressional Globe,* 36th Congress, 1st session, March 12, 1860, pp. 1100-09; and Part 4, June 15, 1860, pp. 3006-7.

there ever was a despotism on earth that could define its position more satisfactorily than that? . . . If Louis Napoleon has more than that I think he would be willing to give it up readily."

Sumner's rhetoric, in antiphony, swelled still higher: "For myself, sir, I confess a feeling of gratitude to the witness [Hyatt], who, knowing nothing which he desires to conceal, and chiefly anxious that the liberties of all might not suffer through him, feeble in body and broken in health, hardly able to endure the fatigue of appearing at your bar, now braves the prison which you menace, and thrusts his arm as a bolt to arrest an unauthorized and arbitrary proceeding."

Generally speaking, as these prominent instances suggest, it has been the gored ox that has bellowed. Whether well-grounded or not, vigorous congressional inquiries usually threaten institutionalized as well as individual interests. The spokesmen and friends of these interests, along with the individuals directly involved, fight back as best they are able. Usually the best defense, in a public polemic, is to drop the question of one's own private concern out of sight, and to counterattack either with *ad hominem* grapeshot or with seemingly general considerations of propriety, morals and political philosophy.

It was natural enough that the *Wall Street Journal,* the American Bankers Association, the *New York Times* (as edited in the 1920's) and the Hearst press (with large Hearst mining interests in the background) should look with initial disfavor on a probing of oil leases by a partisan and already suspect Public Lands Committee. The established banking and investment interests, the utility holding companies, and the great industrial corporations that had armed the nation for the first world war could not, even though cowed by the long depression, welcome the inquiries of the 1930's into their carefully unpublic ways. John Brown was a

martyred hero of the abolitionists, who had provoked and financed his raid on Harper's Ferry. The abolitionist Senators from New England could hardly have been expected to further an investigation, headed by a Senator from Virginia, which was likely to confirm the formal case against Brown and to uncover the links in the conspiracy. It was no doubt natural also that the committee chairman from Virginia, James M. Mason, and Senator Jefferson Davis from Mississippi made the replies that Senators Sumner and Hale might have formulated if the interests at stake had been reversed.

Jefferson Davis. How shallow the plea is, when a witness is brought here for great purposes, that he should say his conscience was too tender to tell the truth. What criminal, or what man who had been in a conspiracy, criminal in all its ends and aims, would not shelter himself, when commanded before a Committee to testify, if his tender conscience at the last hour, when steeped in crime and treason, might plead against the right of a Committee to know from him the truth? . . .

James Mason. The matter inquired into here . . . was matter affecting the very existence of this government —treasonable purposes; and if there is any citizen in the land who can give information on the subject he is bound by every obligation of honor, of duty, of loyalty to his country, voluntarily to come; not to seek to avoid this duty by evasion, or subterfuge, or pretense that his conscience will not allow him to give his testimony.

Hugo L. Black, writing in 1936 when he was an investigator and not a Supreme Court Justice, summed up the natural response: "The instant that a resolution [authorizing an investigation] is offered, or even rumored, the call to arms is sounded by the interest to be investigated." [4]

2

I do not mean to suggest that all of these past criticisms of inquiries have been subjectively biased or hypocritical. It may be presumed that Dean Wigmore was concerned primarily with the investigative procedures that are too coarse and unrestrained for so judicially oriented a mind as his was. Mr. Lippmann has been long and persistently critical of investigations differing widely in subject-matter and political direction. For that matter, most of the critics have doubtless been sincere enough when they voiced their criticisms.

At the same time we may note that until recent years, most of the attacks on the investigations, like the defending replies, seem to be part of the general political struggle in the nation over issues and problems that have successively arisen. The impetus of the attacks has been specific: against this particular inquiry or related set of inquiries. The legislative inquiry as an accredited institution of the American political system has not been in dispute. The critics did not question Congress' autonomous right to investigate, with adequate compulsory sanctions, in its own way and on its own sovereign authority. In the Senate debate over the Harper's Ferry inquiry, the critics made their appeal for gentler treatment of Hyatt to the Senate itself. They did not suggest that there was a relevant recourse to the courts or to the executive. Senator Hale, recognizing that he and Sumner would lose the vote in the Chamber and not questioning its power to act as it saw fit, directed his words to what was logically the only supreme tribunal of a sovereign legislature: "You may imprison him; you may lock him up; you may make his bars and his

bolts fast, and turn your key upon him; but I tell you that the great *habeas corpus* of freedom, the ballot, will reverse your judgment, and pronounce sentence of condemnation, not on him, but on you."

During the past decade the attack on the investigations has assumed a very different character. Although it has arisen primarily out of inquiries dealing with Communism and other forms of subversion, it is no longer specific or limited. In fact, it is no longer an attack on investigations, but on the investigatory power, and it has come in waves from all directions: from journalists, cartoonists, publicists and academicians; from the courts; from the executive; and even from within Congress itself

As pictured by the most influential liberal cartoonists, led by Herblock and Fitzgerald, the typical congressional investigator is either a gangster, a Star Chamber hanging-judge, or a rubber-truncheoned fascist. Thousands of editorials, articles, monographs, lectures and sermons have condemned the investigating committees, their methods, their results and their most prominent members. In 1955 two general books— Alan Barth's *Government by Investigation* and Telford Taylor's *Grand Inquest*—broadened the adverse critique that had been undertaken by such preliminary studies as Robert K. Carr's *The House Committee on Un-American Activities*. A number of organizations—among them Americans for Democratic Action, the American Civil Liberties Union and the Committee for an Effective Congress—have in these recent years made the defects of investigations and investigators a principal element of their public agitation. For several years prior to his death in 1957, the figure of Senator Joseph R. McCarthy of Wisconsin became the symbolic target for this massive campaign against the investigatory power—a campaign which began, however, before McCarthy's entry on the national stage, as it continues after his exit.

[4] Hugo L. Black, "Inside a Senate Investigation" (*Harper's*, February, 1936).

3

The opponents and critics of congressional investigations do not explicitly call for the abolition of the investigatory power; that is, they do not state that Congress should be altogether deprived of the right and power to make investigations. They argue, rather, that the investigations should be curbed, limited and controlled in such ways as to prevent violations of rights, demagogic exploitation, encroachments on the executive or judiciary, and other excesses. The restrictive proposals go along such lines as the following:

(A.) *Some topics should be outside the purview of investigations.* These prohibited subjects would include all private affairs, rather broadly defined.[5] It has also been urged that all the varied matters included under "espionage" and "subversion" should be put under the exclusive jurisdiction of the Federal Bureau of Investigation and other security agencies: that is, should be shifted wholly out of the legislative into the executive branch.

(B.) *Investigating committee proceedings should be governed by detailed rules for the protection of the rights and privileges of witnesses, similar to the rules governing judicial actions.* Witnesses should have right to counsel, to confront accusers, to cross-examine, to call rebuttal witnesses and submit rebuttal evidence, to obtain full transcripts, and so on.[6]

It should perhaps be added that many of the rules proposed by the critics—such as the requirement of a committee quorum for all hearings and for all decisions in preparation of hearings—are virtually impossible under the real conditions of congressional activity. Others, drawn from courtroom practice, are inappropriate to an investigation, which by the nature of the case, is partly a "fishing expedition" in which the issues are not known fully in advance—unlike a court action, where the issue is defined in the indictment. And it is seldom remarked that the loose investigatory procedures, though they undoubtedly sometimes violate what would generally be regarded as individual rights and are often disturbing to individual pleasure and convenience, at the same time frequently offer witnesses unusual liberties that they do not possess in the courtroom: to make long statements; to argue with interlocutors; to bring in hearsay, subjective motivation, mitigating circumstances; to delay and repeat; to become the accuser and to counterattack.

(C.) *The self-incrimination clause of the Fifth Amendment should have total application to inquiry proceedings.* That is, a witness, without any motivating explanation on his part or any objective indication that the refusal is well-grounded, should have the right to refuse to answer any question whatever on the ground that by answering it he risks possible incrimination. This blanket restraint on the investigatory function seems to be accepted at present by the courts and by Congress. It is further and persistently being proposed that the grounds for a refusal to testify should also include the First Amendment guarantees of freedom of belief and speech. Historically there is no foundation for applying these amendments to congressional inquiries. "These guarantees," observe Messrs. Kelly and Harbison, "were historically associated almost entirely with the business of the courts. And the substantive guarantees of the Bill of Rights—freedom of speech, press, and the like—appeared to apply to the content of congressional

---

[5] Thus extending a principle recognized by the Supreme Court in the Kilbourn case.

[6] Actually, many such procedural rules have in fact been adopted by the committees, either through customary practice or on formal action. The House Committee on Un-American Activities—to cite one of the most controversial instances—operates in accordance with a printed list of fourteen rules in addition to the governing rules of the House itself.

legislation, not to the mode of enacting it." [7]

(D.) *All phases of congressional investigations should be subject to review and adjudication by the courts.* For a hundred and fifty years the Supreme Court shied as far away as it could from intervention in the legislature's investigatory power, finally summing up its traditional recognition of legislative autonomy therein by its sweeping decision in McGrain *v.* Daugherty (1927). In the late 1940's, by refusing to review three lower court decisions that reasserted congressional autonomy in investigations,[8] the Court held fast to McGrain *v.* Daugherty against the rising liberal clamor. Then, in a series of decisions that began with Christoffel *v.* United States (1950) and reached a high point in Watkins *v.* United States (1957), the Supreme Court asserted what would be by implication its general right to define the rules, limits, methods, scope and sanctions of the investigatory power. On the meaning of the Watkins case, which reversed the decision of both the District Court and the Court of Appeals, dissenting Justice Tom C. Clark wrote that the Supreme Court was appointing itself "Grand Inquisitor and supervisor of congressional investigations."

(E.) *Congressional investigators who get out of bounds should be disciplined.* This proposal, a frequent exhortation of the critics of Congress, is difficult to apply, because of the explicit words of Article I, Section 6 of the Constitution: "[Senators and Representatives] shall in all Cases, except Treason, Felony and Breach of the Peace, be privileged from Arrest during their Attendance at the Session of their respective Houses, and in going to and returning from the same; and for any Speech or Debate in either House, they shall not be questioned in any other Place." Since these words seem to put members of Congress, so far as their official acts go, out of reach of the courts, traditional doctrine has left their due punishment to the ballot. As a disciplinary supplement, the new critics urge—though so far unsuccessfully—that too savage investigators might be tamed by being deprived of committee chairmanships, or even of membership on committees that conduct investigations.

The temporary focusing of the problem in Senator Joseph McCarthy provoked a novel, and momentous sanction. In 1954, through combined pressure from a liberal-led public opinion and the executive branch, Congress was induced to turn its investigatory power against itself; and then, by the Senate vote of an unprecedented censure against one of its own members, to make common cause with its critics.

In the winter of 1953-54 the Senate's Permanent Subcommittee on Investigations, under Senator McCarthy's chairmanship, was conducting a free-wheeling inquiry into various of the Army's affairs. This exploded into a volcanic scandal after a bitter clash between McCarthy and Major General Ralph Zwicker, who had been called as a witness in the case of a drafted dentist-officer, Irving Peress, who had been routinely promoted in rank after having refused, on the ground of the Fifth Amendment privilege, to declare whether he had been a communist.

By a sudden coup,[9] the subcommittee's inquiry into the Army was transformed into an investigation of the countercharges that the Army brought against McCarthy—that is, against a

---

[7] Alfred H. Harbison and Winfred A. Kelly, *The American Constitution,* p. 908.

[8] United States *v.* Bryan (1947), United States *v.* Josephson (1948), Barsky *v.* United States (1948). In the latter two decisions there had been a sharp division in the Court of Appeals.

[9] The full history of this coup has never been publicly disclosed. According to most accounts, it was the result of an informal bipartisan agreement among part of the White House staff, some Pentagon officials, and several Senators of both parties, prominently including Senators Stuart Symington (Dem.) and Charles E. Potter (Rep.).

member of the Senate, and by plain extension, against the Senate itself and its investigatory power. Under Senator Karl Mundt, who replaced McCarthy as chairman, televised hearings continued for months, solidifying emotions but not clarifying many facts. These hearings led to the appointment of a special committee under Senator Arthur Watkins to consider the complaints against McCarthy. The report of this special committee, though it was accepted only in part, prepared the way for the Senate's 67-22 vote of condemnation on December 2, 1954.

As the bitterness and crudities on both sides of the McCarthy controversy recede into the tranquillizing past, it takes its historical place, from a constitutional point of view, not as a great battle either of the war against communism (as Senator McCarthy's admirers saw it) or in the struggle for human rights (as it appeared in his enemy's eyes), but rather as a symptomatic episode in the erosion of congressional power. This was plainly recognized by relentless critics of Congress, such as General Telford Taylor, who, writing in early 1955, summed up his own analysis in the rhetoric of executive supremacy: "The essence of the constitutional crisis of 1954 . . . is *the effort of some legislators, notably Senator McCarthy, to destroy the President's effective control of the executive branch and bring it under their own domination*." [10] This corresponds exactly, when rhetorical translation is made, to Senator McCarthy's declaration in the midst of the Zwicker-Peress explosion that the basic question was "whether the Army as agent of the executive branch is supreme over the Congress . . . and the American people, and can enjoy special dictatorial immunity in covering up its own wrong-doings."

At the last moment, however, the Senate, diverting the battle into its purely personal channel, avoided formal surrender of any part of the battered investigatory power, and thus suspended the constitutional issue. "It is especially noteworthy," General Taylow comments sorrowfully, "that Senator McCarthy was not censured for his misuse of the Senate's investigatorial prerogatives, for his attack against the executive branch, or for his treatment of anyone other than his fellow-senators." [11]

*   *   *

We have seen that a true investigatory power cannot exist unless the investigator (individual or institution) is equipped with immunity, autonomy, and the power of compulsion. The public critique and the Supreme Court decisions since 1950, though not openly directed against the investigatory power itself, have attacked and much weakened these three conditions of its effective operation.

The power of compulsion is meaningless unless there is assured, speedy punishment for contumacious witnesses. Such punishment, under the now prevailing court rulings and congressional practice, is neither sure nor speedy. It can be postponed indefinitely when it is not avoided altogether, by legal technicalities, the plea of civil rights, or Congress' own unwillingness to pursue the matter vigorously. Thus, with very little personal hazard, witnesses may defeat the ends of a current inquiry: there will be a new Congress with new interests, before the question of punishment is decided one way or the other.

The investigator's immunity and autonomy do not mean that he can properly do anything that he wishes, but that the major decisions about what he can properly do will be his. More specifically applied to congressional investigation: that Congress shall itself decide when an investigation has a legislative purpose, what sort of evidence is relevant to that purpose and from whom, how evidence and information may be most fruitfully gathered.

[10] Telford Taylor, *Grand Inquest* (New York: Simon & Schuster, 1955), p. 122. The italics are in the original.

[11] *Ibid.*, p. 134.

Quite possibly this is too great a license to be granted without restriction to any single institution. That is not here at issue, but merely the historical observation that in recent years the investigatory power of Congress, at the same time that it has emerged as the first among the remaining congressional powers, has been shorn and blunted by a many-sided and continuing attack.

4

The public controversy over the investigatory power has often failed to distinguish between two types of inquiry that are profoundly different in their political meaning: investigations into the activities of private citizens, associations and institutions, on the one hand; and on the other, investigations of the administration of the government—that is, of the executive branch and the bureaucracy. A particular inquiry may bridge the two types (as in a study of the relation between a government regulatory agency and the industry it is supposed to regulate), but the functional distinction remains clear.

Most of the formal arguments that are advanced against investigations concern, primarily or exclusively, the first type. It is alleged that the civil rights or personal life of private citizens who appear as witnesses are violated, and that the protection of these private rights is a duty that takes precedence over the possible public gains from investigating this or that subject-matter. That is to say, the argument is cast in the form of: individual liberty *vs.* despotism.

For Americans, an argument in this form has roots in both tradition and rhetoric. It is persuasive to many citizens even apart from their opinion on the particular content of the investigations which provoke the controversy. And it is a fact that an unchecked investigatory power always threatens and sometimes subverts what Americans wish to regard as inviolable individual rights.

But inquiries into the doings of the executive and the bureaucracy are of a different order, in which private and individual rights are only coincidentally at stake. By making an artificial amalgam between the two types of investigation, we smear the second with the doubtful or negative feelings attached to the first. Objectively, the principal similarity between the two is the mere fact that both express the investigatory power of the legislature.

Traditionally it has never been questioned, either in doctrine or practice, that the legislature possesses the power, as it was put in early years, "to inquire into the honesty and efficiency of the executive branch." Under the American system it is this that is the heart of the investigatory power. It is conceivable that, without a major constitutional transformation, Congress could cede all investigations of the affairs of private citizens to the executive and judiciary. But if it lost the power to investigate the executive, Congress would retain only the name of legislature.

The late Senator George Norris, once the dean of liberals, accurately remarked during the controversies of 1924: "Whenever you take away from the legislative body of any country in the world the power of investigation, the power to look into the executive department of the government, you have taken a full step that will eventually lead into absolute monarchy[12] and destroy any government such as ours."

Woodrow Wilson's distaste for the practices of Congress did not lead him to obscure the basic relations:

Quite as important as legislation is vigilant oversight of administration. . . . An effective representative body [ought] to serve as [the nation's] eyes in superintending all matters of government. . . . There is some scandal and discomfort, but infinite

---

[12] In the traditional American vocabulary, "absolute monarchy" was the term often used to refer to "despotism."

advantage, in having every affair of administration subjected to the test of constant examination on the part of the assembly which represents the nation. . . . Congress is the only body which has the proper motive for inquiry. . . . It is the proper duty of a representative body to look diligently into every affair of government and to talk much about what it sees. It is meant to be the eyes and the voice and to embody the wisdom and will of its constituents. Unless Congress have and use every means of acquainting itself with the acts and the dispositions of the administrative agents of the government, the country must be helpless to learn how it is being served. . . . The only really self-governing people is that people which discusses and interrogates its administration.[13]

Professor McGeary has put the situation still more bluntly: "An administrator's knowledge that at some future time he and his activities might be subjects of congressional investigation has probably been the principal external deterrent to wrong-doing in the executive branch." [14]

Scholars who have taken refuge in the United States from totalitarian regimes have been still more deeply impressed with the crucial role of legislative investigations into the operations of the executive. Dr. Henry W. Ehrmann, a refugee from Nazism, concludes that a lack of this power was a prime factor both in the failure of German pre-Nazi parliamentarism and in the bureaucratic sclerosis of the French political system.[15] He recalls the judgment of Ger-

many's great sociologist, Max Weber: "In his criticism of the political situation in Imperial Germany, [Weber] attributed greater responsibility for the unsatisfactory results of constitutional life to the lack of parliamentary investigation than to any other single factor. The German parliament was condemned to dilettantism as well as ignorance."

Under Weber's influence, a right of parliamentary inquiry was introduced into the Weimar Constitution, but, as in the case of the inquiry function in France, there was no real power of compulsion to back it up. In both countries it could therefore have only minor political significance. "The unsatisfactory results in both France and Germany can easily be explained by the insufficient powers obtained by the parliamentary committees."

It is against this background that we may evaluate the progressive undermining of the investigatory power during the past decade by the executive as well as by liberal publicists and the courts. The executive under Presidents Franklin Roosevelt, Truman and Eisenhower has challenged the investigatory power in the most direct of ways: with respect to an ever expanding mass of data, it has simply refused to supply information to the investigating committees.

These refusals have been formally motivated by: the doctrine of "the separation of powers"; the need for secrecy; various laws, and in particular a "housekeeping act" of 1789 originally passed to authorize executive departments to set up files and records; an alleged traditional practice within the American system. These considerations were systematically stated in a memorandum submitted in May, 1954 by Attorney General Herbert Brownell to President Eisenhower, and countered by a Staff Study of the House Committee on Government Operations, dated May 3, 1956.

The executive's argument from tradition is undoubtedly specious. It is true that a number of Presidents, beginning

---

[13] Woodrow Wilson, *Congressional Government*, pp. 277-303 *passim*.

[14] N. Nelson McGeary, "Historical Development," a contribution to the symposium on congressional investigations in *University of Chicago Law Review*, Vol. 18, No. 3, Spring 1951; p. 430.

[15] Henry W. Ehrmann, "The Duty of Disclosure in Parliamentary Investigation: A Comparative Study" (*Univ. of Chicago Law Review*, Vol. 2, No. 2, Feb. 1944), pp. 117-53.

with the first, have denied the universal right of Congress to call for testimony and documents from the executive branch. Among them have been Presidents otherwise so various as Andrew Jackson, John Tyler, Abraham Lincoln, Grover Cleveland and Calvin Coolidge. Washington would seem to have declared—in theory—a complete executive immunity to the investigatory power: "The executive ought to communicate such papers as the public good would permit and ought to refuse those, the disclosure of which would injure the public." Jackson, when Congress wished to look more closely into the working of his Spoils System, replied indignantly: "For myself, I shall repel all such atempts as an invasion of the principles of justice, as well as of the Constitution; and I shall esteem it my sacred duty to the people of the United States to resist them as I would the establishment of a Spanish inquisition." Even Calvin Coolidge denounced with unwonted sharpness the investigatory feelers directed by the Couzens committee at Secretary Andrew Mellon's administration of the Treasury Department.

But if we look more closely at the offered precedents in the pre-Franklin Roosevelt past, we will learn that they have little bearing on the executive practice that has become established since 1933. In the first place, the earlier incidents were exceedingly rare. Attorney General Brownell's memorandum[16] states at the outset that "American history abounds in countless illustrations of the refusal, on occasion, by the President and heads of departments to furnish papers to Congress, or its committees." In fact, however, he cites only twenty-six instances in all, of which fifteen are from the Franklin Roosevelt and Truman administrations.

Moreover, nearly all the pre-1933 instances have certain common characteristics. They almost invariably concern either treaty negotiations or appointments. The papers or information that the executive refuses[17] are the record of confidential, often informal discussions and reports—in which, as a rule, the President has himself been personally involved—that have entered into preliminary stages of treaty negotiations, appointments, or diplomatic missions. Constitutional niceties aside, the Presidents were taking a reasonable and common sense position when they argued that administration of the public business, or of any business, would be impossible if the chief administrator could not have confidential preparatory discussions with his immediate subordinates and agents.

The same message from Washington, quoted above, that claimed an executive privilege to withhold certain material, explicitly recognized that Congress "might call for papers generally." Grover Cleveland had more of a contest on this score than any other pre-1933 President, but in the incident concerning appointments that Mr. Brownell cites from his administration, Cleveland declared in his formal communication to the Senate: "The Senate is invited to the fullest scrutiny of the persons submitted to them for public office. . . . I shall furnish, at the request of the confirming body, all the information I possess touching the fitness of the nominees placed before them for their action." He objected only to the transmittal of "letters and papers of a private and unofficial nature." [18]

This earlier occasional practice—which like so much in the older American tradition commends itself to ordinary common sense—has now been blown up into a polished routine. By an administrative fiction, the "confi-

---

[16] The memorandum is reprinted in *The Federal Bar Journal*, Vol. XIV, No. 1, Jan.-Mar. 1954, pp. 73-86.

[17] Or merely claims the right to refuse. In several cases, including one of the two that Mr. Brownell cites from Washington's administration, the President, having made the claim, supplied the data nevertheless.

[18] Richardson, *Messages & Papers of the Presidents*, Vol. 8, pp. 377, 381-2.

dential" relation between President and subordinates—which in the past meant a literal personal relation between man and man—has been extended to the entire bureaucracy, so that the executive now claims a right to order any official or employee of the bureaucracy to refuse to testify to an investigating committee, or to withhold almost any sort of document or record pertaining to any department or agency.

In explaining Congress' 1958 attempt to restore the traditional interpretation of the 1789 housekeeping act as a mere authorization to preserve public records, Representative John E. Moss of California commented:

> The "housekeeping act" has been twisted and tortured by federal officials seeking to withhold information from the public and from the Congress. . . .
> A few of the recent examples of misuse of the act include the withholding by the Treasury Department of information about imports and exports; the attempt by the Agriculture Department to impose censorship as the price for cooperation in the making of newsreel and television films about agricultural subjects; the withholding of information by the Farmers' Home Administration and the Rural Electrification Administration on loans of public money.

Mr. Moss added a revealing datum: "Each of the ten Cabinet departments opposed this amendment to restore the traditional interpretation." [19]

With the shibboleths of secrecy, security and "classification," the executive has still further darkened the screen constructed out of the claims of constitutional privilege and separation of powers. Whenever the executive (or the bureaucracy) wishes to hide information from congressional scrutiny, it is only necessary to declare it "classified." Sometimes, granted the

conditions of our age, this procedure is justified—as, for example, in the case of advanced military experiments, or the Federal Bureau of Investigation's "raw" (*i.e., unevaluated*) security files on individuals[20]—but the secrecy labels have been extended over a considerable portion of the nation's ordinary business, which thus becomes removed from congressional (and thereby also from public) scrutiny.

The results are sometimes curious, from a traditional point of view. The executive, for example, will call on Congress to vote appropriations for foreign aid, but will decline to furnish the information about what has been, is being and is intended to be done with the foreign aid. On the basis of a special commission study, like the 1957 "Gaither report," the executive will demand certain armament funds; but will not show Congress the report which supplies the motivation. The executive will insist on Senate confirmation of a military treaty, like those establishing the North Atlantic or the Southeast Asia treaty organizations, without disclosing the commitments that the treaty entails. Thus, inevitably, the weakening of the congressional investigatory power leads to a correlated further weakening of the congressional share in the power of the purse, the war power and the treaty power.

It would be wrong to exaggerate the stage that the contest has reached. The investigatory power is bruised and shaken, but it is still vigorous. In fact, it is just because the investigatory power is so vigorous, because it retains more vitality than any other of the

[19] *New York Times*, Aug. 17, 1958.

[20] Common sense would agree that it would be improper to turn over such files to a large and factionally minded congressional committee. But even in this case there are solutions other than total executive immunity: *e.g.,* the British practice of showing the confidential material to a small parliamentary committee of authoritative and trusted members. Something of this sort was done in Washington during the 1953 conflict over the appointment of Charles Bohlen as Ambassador to Moscow.

congressional powers, that it is so sharply under attack. It becomes easier to see why Dr. Ehrmann, reflecting on the experiences of many nations, concluded the study to which we have made reference with the summary judg-ment: "Certainly 'government by investigation is not government,' but government without investigation might easily turn out to be democratic government no longer."

21. The Fight Against the Filibuster*

PAUL H. DOUGLAS

[*Though this piece was published in early 1953, it does present the basic elements of the liberal argument against the filibuster.*]

I AM writing this on the eve of the convening of the 83rd Congress. In the Senate, all bills introduced in the 82nd Congress will have died and if they are to be considered in the 83rd Congress they will have to be reintroduced. All appointments made by the President during the 82nd Congress which were not then confirmed by the Senate will have died. All treaties submitted during the 82nd Congress which were not ratified will have to be dealt with anew. The new Senate will have to elect its officers for the 83rd Congress. It will have to re-form its committees, and with the shift of power many committee changes will be made.

The old Senate will therefore have died with the 82nd Congress. It will be a new Senate which convenes on January 3 as one branch of the 83rd Congress.

We of the bipartisan progressive bloc believe that this is as true in the matter of rules and procedure as it is in legislation, appointments, treaties, officers and committees.

The defenders of the old order, primarily composed of the ruling coalition of Southern Democrats and Middle-western Republicans, contend, how-

* *New Republic* (January 12, 1953), pp. 6-8. Reprinted by permission of the *New Republic*.

ever, that this is not so and that the rules of the Senate are in effect immortal and do not have to be adopted afresh with each Congress.

The issue thus stated may seem to be a barren and arid matter of parliamentary procedure. It involves, however, the whole question as to whether Congress will ever be able to pass civil-rights legislation. The issue is indeed far broader even than that. It is whether the Senate can ever free itself for decision by breaking filibusters conducted by a small minority. The principle of majority rule is the real issue.

A filibuster, it should be needless to say, is prolonged discussion of a measure designed to prevent it from ever coming to a vote. It is not discussion for the purpose of making voting more intelligent. Its purpose is to tie up business so completely that a vote will never occur. It is, therefore, a method of preventing the majority from making its decisions effective. Hence it is a form of minority rule.

We all know how, in recent years, filibusters have been used to prevent civil-rights legislation from being passed. Historically, it has also been used against many other proposed measures as well. This is well shown by Dr. Franklin L. Burdette in his classic book on the subject, *Filibustering in the Senate*. There was absolutely no check upon filibustering in the Senate until after the "willful 11" in March, 1917, and in the closing days of the

64th Congress had talked to death President Wilson's proposal to arm merchantmen to resist German submarine attack. Then, after Sens. Thomas J. Walsh and Robert L. Owen had asserted the right of the new Senate of the 65th Congress to adopt new rules and to curb filibusters, a partial beginning was made. Rule 22 was altered so that a vote to limit debate (or for cloture) could be passed by two-thirds of those present and voting, and after such a cloture motion was passed each Senator could speak for an hour. After this right had been exercised the substantive measure under consideration would then be voted upon.

In practice this provision proved ineffective. This was shown most notably in the filibuster against the Federal Fair Employment Practices bill of 1946. The opponents of that measure were in a minority, but with covert allies they did number more than a third and hence were able to talk the measure to death. Once again they were able to prevent it even from coming to a vote. This led in 1949 to the attempt of the liberal bloc to make it easier to terminate or limit debate.

The dramatic adoption of the Civil-Rights Plank by the Democratic convention in July, 1948, followed by the striking Democratic victory in November, filled us all with the hope that something could be done to remove the road block of the filibuster. We, therefore, introduced an amendment to Rule 22 providing, after a decent initial interval for debate, that further debate could be limited by a majority of the Senate. But the Southerners and most of the Republicans brought their coalition out into the open and then passed an amendment to Rule 22 which gave far greater protection to filibusters than did the 1917 rule.

This was done in two ways: (a) The new rule provided that debate could only be limited upon vote of two-thirds of the Senators "duly chosen and sworn," or by a so-called constitutional two-thirds, or 64 affirmative votes.

Thirty-three Senators voting in the negative or *absenting themselves* from the vote could therefore prevent debate from being limited and permit a filibuster to go on. Since the average vote on cloture proposals had been approximately 82, this in itself greatly raised the barrier by requiring 64 affirmative votes as against a probable average under the old rule of around 56. (b) Even more important was the addition of a third paragraph to Rule 22, namely, that there could be absolutely no limitation of debate upon any motion to bring up a change in the rules. This meant that debate could never be legally ended or limited on any proposal to liberalize the cloture provisions, except by unanimous consent. For, if any proposal to limit debate by majority vote or by some such ratio were introduced and if a motion were made to bring it to the floor of the Senate, then a small group could talk it to death and not even a constitutional two-thirds could stop them. The debate could be terminated only by unanimous consent which in vital matters would be impossible to obtain.

This then was the celebrated so-called Wherry Rule which ties our hands once the Senate is fully organized and is considered to have adopted or carried over its rules of procedure. For under it any later proposal to alter the rules could be filibustered and would never be permitted to come to a vote.

Therefore, if it be permanently decided that the rules of the preceding Senate apply automatically as the new Senate organizes, we may as well say farewell to any chance either for civil-rights legislation or needed changes in Senate procedure.

If, on the other hand, the Senate of a given Congress, such as the 83rd, first proclaims its existing right to adopt rules of procedure as it organizes, the way is then opened before organization is completed for the immediate revision of Rule 22, which would permit debate to be limited upon some variant of a majority vote and also allow us to strike from the books the final and third paragraph of Rule 22. It would then be possible for the Senate to decide and to act. Discussion would become an aid to, but not a preventive of, action.

I should like to emphasize the fact that while civil rights is probably the most notable field which would thus be opened up for legislation, it is by no means the only one. For example, the procedure of the Senate seems to cry aloud for the adoption of the rule of relevance in debate, so that discussion on a bill may not be totally disassociated from the measure under consideration. But such a reform can probably never be put into effect as long as paragraph 3 of Rule 22 remains.

What then are the objections advanced against our proposal that each Senate should adopt its rules afresh?

(1) It is contended that the Senate is a continuing body because only one-third of its members are elected every two years, and two-thirds of the members carry over from one Congress to another. It is argued that this is what differentiates the Senate from the House.

But this argument, as Sen. Thomas J. Walsh pointed out in 1917, confuses the Senate as a body with its members as individuals. Individual Senators serve for three successive Congresses in the Senatorial branch of Congress. But even though a bill may be signed in their offices or homes by each and every one of the 96 Senators, it does not thereby become a law. For this to be done a measure must be passed by the Senate meeting as a body and operating under agreed rules and procedures.

The contention that the Senate as a body is continuous and immortal and cannot in effect change its rules is indeed, upon close examination, seen to be ridiculous. For if one holds to this objection, he must be forced to argue that the Senate which convenes tomorrow is the very same body that first met in 1789 or 164 years ago and that

we must be bound by their rules. Or that the so-called Wherry provisions which were riveted into the rules in 1949 must, as a practical matter, be continued to the end of time, and that even a Senate meeting for organization in the year 2100 would be the same body as today and hence would be bound by the work of the Senate of 1949.

Surely the only sensible conclusion is that each Congress is separate and distinct from its predecessors; that the Senate is only one branch of Congress (a fact that its members sometimes forget); and that hence this separate character is true of each Senate as it is of the House of Representatives.

Despite the hold-over of two-thirds of its members in each new Congress, it is conceded by everyone that the Senate is not a continuing body for the consideration of legislation, executive appointments, treaties, officers or committees. There is no basis for a different conclusion on the matter of rules. Just as the House can adopt or modify its rules prior to the completion of organization (as Rep. John E. Rankin abundantly demonstrated in 1945), so can the Senate.

(2) It is contended that if the rules of the Senate do not apply prior to its organization, there will be no rules to govern procedures during this transitional period and hence there will be parliamentary chaos.

This is sheer nonsense. In the absence of Senatorial rules, the generally established rules of parliamentary procedure will govern. These are well stated in the classic American handbook of Robert's *Rules of Order,* with Jefferson's *Manual* serving as a supplement. Under these rules, the chair can rule initially that a motion proclaiming the right of each Senate to adopt its own rules can be made and if upheld by the Senate will prevail, then before organization is completed another motion can follow that will call for the adoption of all present rules except Rule 22 for which an adequate substitute can be submitted. After the chair has made its rulings, appeals can then be taken to the body of the Senate.

And now this is the point: after a decent interval of debate, and for the very purpose of preventing filibustering, a member under approved parliamentary procedure may move "the previous question" or move to table the appeal. Neither of these motions is debatable, and a vote upon them must be taken immediately. Upon request of one-fifth of those present, under the Constitution (Article I, section 5 (3)) this vote must be by rollcall. A motion to table requires only a majority; for the previous question to be put, a two-thirds vote is required. This would enable the Senate to do what the House can do and what every parliamentary or private body in the world can do.

(3) It is contended that the Supreme Court has ruled in the case of *McGrain* v. *Daugherty, 273 US* 135, that the Senate is a continuing body and that we should therefore abide by the rulings of the Court.

It is truly extraordinary how the very men who object violently to decisions of the Supreme Court when these go against their beliefs and interests, and who then demand that Congress pass acts to reverse the Court's decisions, will predominantly insist that those decisions of which they approve shall be accepted by Congress as final, and shall not even be questioned.

The vast majority of those who want this Congress to reverse three successive opinions of the Supreme Court which gave "paramount rights" to off-shore oil to the federal government, and who want us to give this rich treasure to the states, form the hard core of the group which is now insisting that the Daugherty Case shall be accepted as final.

Upon analysis, however, it will be seen that the Daugherty Case did not really involve the question of whether the Senate is in fact a continuing body. It did not decide that a committee may continue beyond the life of an expired Senate. It merely ruled that such committee could be revived by a succeeding Congress. But if so, it would be by a different body, and hence the issue in the Daugherty Case was very different from the issue which is here raised. Any statements by the Court in that case to the effect that the Senate is a continuing body were therefore *obiter dicta* and in no sense legally binding.

We need to go back to the Constitution itself to get a clearer idea of the powers of the Senate to form its rules. Article I, section 5 (2) states that "each House may determine the Rules of its Proceedings." The House can do so with each new Congress. There is no reason for differentiation in the case of the Senate.

(4) It is contended that even if the Senate once had the right to adopt new rules at the beginning of a new Congress, it has lost that right by failing to exercise it over its historical past. This is what the lawyers call the doctrine of *laches*.

But Senators Walsh and Owen both asserted at the opening of the 65th Congress in March, 1917, that the Senate had the right to adopt rules for its procedure prior to organization. This issue was not finally pushed to a test because, as I have stated, these Senators were later able to change Rule 22 to permit a limited power of cloture. But no ruling was made against the contention of Walsh and Owen, and a preliminary ruling by the Vice-President refusing to allow bills to be submitted to committees until the Senate was organized slanted in their direction.

As a matter of fact, the same argument that the failure of a branch of Congress to adopt rules constitutes an abandonment of that right was made in the House of Representatives in 1890 when the Republican majority sought to change the rules of that body. This objection was, however, overruled and the House then proceeded to adopt its old rules plus changes recommended by Thomas B. Reed and Joseph G.

Cannon. A strict legalist might also contend that the acquiescence by the Senate in the past in the carrying over of old rules constituted a tacit act of passing upon them and was in no sense an abandonment of the right to do so.

It is moreover, a bad principle to hold that one generation or one Congress can give up the rights of future generations or future Congresses by a failure to act. This was well stated by Thomas Jefferson in a letter to John Cartright in 1824:

> Can one generation bind another, and all others, in succession forever? I think not. The Creator has made the earth for the living, not the dead. . . . A generation may bind itself as long as its majority continues in life; when that has disappeared, another

majority is in place, holds all the rights and powers their predecessors once held, and may change their laws and institutions to suit themselves. Nothing, then, is unchangeable but the inherent and unalienable rights of man.—*The Jeffersonian Cyclopedia,* volume vii, pp. 377, 378.

In short, the issue at stake is not merely procedural. The decision upon it is likely to determine much of the political course of the next few years. We of the progressive group feel that right is on our side. We ask that the matter be carefully studied by the general public. Ultimately in a democracy such as ours, the issue will be settled by the people.

22. Attack on Constitutional Balance*

WILLIAM S. WHITE

UNDER cover of demands for seemingly dusty changes in Senate rules, a profound attack on the very constitutional balance in this country is now unfolding.

The ultimate objective is to reduce the power of the smaller, less urbanized States in the only national forum where such power still exists—the United States Senate. The ultimate effect would be the substitution of a Gallup Poll kind of majority rule, based almost wholly upon the wishes of the populous urban centers and States and interests, for the matchless system of checks and balances written into the Constitution nearly two centuries ago.

The end of it would be a new majoritarian rule based upon megalopo-

* *The Washington Evening Star,* April 1, 1963. Reprinted by permission of the United Feature Syndicate. Copyright 1963 by the United Feature Syndicate, Inc.

lis—the super-city, the super-state—which would give little time and less heed to any and every section or interest in the United States which was not allied with the new majoritarianism.

In short, what is finally sought here is the creation of a new political system of totally unchecked majority rule—instant government like instant coffee—in spite of the fact that the whole heart of the Constitution is meant to restrain majorities from running over minorities. Not even a majority of 99 per cent can presently take away the basic rights of minorities, even the irreducible minority of one man, to free speech, free religion, the private enjoyment of private property.

The Last Bastion

Those attempting this fateful amendment of the Constitution by unconstitutional means are naturally centering upon the one place where they have not already won the game—the Senate. They are generally called "liberals" and generally they are Democratic Senators from big urban-controlled States, plus a handful of Republican "liberals" from the same kind of States.

A more exact term for them, however, is majoritarians. Chief among them are such Democratic Senators as Paul Douglas of Illinois, Wayne Morse of Oregon and Joseph Clark of Pennsylvania and such Republican Senators as Jacob Javits of New York and Clifford Case of New Jersey.

Their immediate objective is to end the effective power of any minority to resist by prolonged talking in the Senate through applying a parliamentary gag. Their case is superficially attractive. The filibuster has a bad name because Southern Senators have long used it to retard civil rights legislation. The fact, however, is that what is poison to the majoritarians in other hands is meat in the hands of the majoritarians themselves. The same weapon has been used by them more often than their opponents, to retard legislation sought by conservatives generally.

Civil Rights Only a Vehicle

Civil rights therefore is only the vehicle by which the majoritarians really intend to break not merely Southern resistance to civil rights bills but any and all minority resistance on any and every issue with which minorities may dare to disagree with the majoritarians. For when a minority, however "wrong," can be gagged today, a minority, however "right," can be gagged tomorrow.

There was a time when 26 States were soundly estimated to be in control of the shadowy Ku Klux Klan. These 26 States could have voted a clear majority in the Senate and, under the new debate restrictions now being demanded, undeniably could have halted all debate on any issue whatever.

The great, bottom truth is that the Senate is literally the only place left where political minorities have truly effective rights. The House is a strictly majority-rule-by-one institution. And minorities, including small-populated States, have little to say about either the nomination or election of a President.

All this is specifically why the Constitution gave each State, regardless of size, two votes in the Senate.

Those demanding "changes in the Senate rules" are demanding infinitely more than this. They are demanding, consciously or not, a revolutionary overturn in the basic form of Government toward a monolithic, automatic, foredoomed conformism to whatever megalopolis might decide at any given moment.

Chapter IV

WHAT TO DO ABOUT THE PRESIDENCY?

How decisions are to be made foremost to what decisions are to be made.

Introduction

O NE of the great continuing debates in American politics, as we have noted above, centers around the question of *how* decisions are to be made, rather than *what* decisions should be made. We have also noted that it is never easy, and why it is never easy, to tell whether the participants in this debate are in "good faith." That is, are they *really* interested in the "how," or merely concerned about the "what" and prepared to adopt, with regard to the "how," whatever position seems most likely to get them the *policies* they wish to see adopted. We can see most clearly how this works, perhaps, in the on-going controversy over "states' rights." The "states-righters" are often accused of masking a determination to go slow on, for example, "civil rights" behind loud noises (with principally Southern overtones) about the constitutional issues surrounding federalism, particularly those dealing with the proper spheres of state and national decision-making authority. And the accusation is the more plausible because we readily see why, in the present climate of opinion about the Bill of Rights, equality, etc., anyone opposed to current proposals for expanding "civil rights" and correcting inequalities would be tempted to fight those issues out *indirectly,* on the level of states' rights, rather than *directly,* by openly opposing "civil rights" and equality.

America, we believe, has every reason to be proud of the ever-growing corpus of political theory that emerges from our controversies about the "how." *The Federalist* and John C. Calhoun's *Disquisition on Government* are only the most distinguished examples of how debate in America produces theoretical works that continue to stimulate and instruct long after the immediate issues involved have been decided. Each decade produces its contributions to the corpus, many of which, we may be sure, have yet to receive the attention they deserve. (A well-known American political scientist will publish, a couple of years hence, excerpts from the debate about "separation of powers" during the years 1789-1796, and will argue that they compare favorably, alike in profundity and in literary excellence, with *The Federalist* itself. Indeed, much of the corpus, whose vastness any student will appreciate who takes a look at the admirable bibliography Clinton

213

Rossiter has prepared over the years, remains virtually untouched by American scholarship.)

America is engaged, at the present time, in an ever-mounting controversy concerning the role of the President, and the powers he should exercise, in our system of government. This controversy (as we might expect from the foregoing), can be fully understood only if we bear in mind that it involves, over and above the *overt* issue as to how decisions are to be made, a wide range of *covert* issues of a purely "policy" character; so that the man whose heart *seems* to go pit-a-pat over what we may fairly call "presidential supremacy" would be equally content to get his welfare state, or his cooperative commonwealth of free and equal men, or his rapprochement with the U.S.S.R., from Congress —*if* he thought he had a prayer of doing so. More than most such debates, however, it affords an opportunity for the most searching and comprehensive examination of the fundamental principles upon which the American republic was founded—though with this difference as compared to other debates. The reformers, that is the proponents of an expanded presidency capable of "making the top spin," cannot so easily in this debate (as in others) make it appear that their proposals are a natural development of, or at least wholly consistent with, those of the Framers, so that they, the reformers, have the "tradition" on their side (and are, as we often hear, the "real" conservatives). Here the would-be revolutionizers of the American political system have the tradition *clearly* against them, and must stand forth as the protagonists of something so novel, so remote from the ideas and intentions of the Founding Fathers, as to require a wholly different type of argument from that which they employ in other debates (e.g., that over the Supreme Court). Put otherwise, the reformers in their theorizing about the presidency have had a notably harder row to hoe than elsewhere, and have responded to the challenge by bringing to bear on the problem greater resourcefulness and ingenuity, greater boldness and candor, and a greater theoretical nicety, than has been required of them in other branches of their endeavors. Here we see them accordingly in their most confident mood, because engaged in a fight they think they are sure to win—and to win because they have on their side *not* tradition (with which they never feel much at home) but something far more powerful, namely History, the "imperatives of the age," and—no small matter—the "need" for "efficiency," for "getting on with the job," for "keeping up with the times." And here we find the defenders of the traditional system in their most pessimistic stance—not very sure of themselves, not so ready with the answers, not so prompt to place their bets on the wisdom of the past as they are to defend Congress.

Expansion of Presidential Powers

"Taken by the large," writes Edward S. Corwin, "the history of the presidency is a history of aggrandizement."[1] It is not, to be sure, possible to fix on any one administration or date that marks the beginning of the "aggrandizement" in question. The line of development is, rather, *discontinuous,* with some presidents adding to presidential power, others consolidating newly-gained powers, and still others "retreating." Many competent observers would point, however, to 1933 and the beginning of Franklin Roosevelt's first term as the major turning point. Certainly in Roosevelt's first term the power of the presidency reached a level of potency that earlier presidents would hardly have dared dream of, unless in time of war. And it is there that we must go in order to see most vividly the powers and techniques of the so-called "modern" presidency. Here we will briefly survey some of the important powers of the presidency that have led many close students of American politics to conclude that today the presidency is the predominant institution of our system.

1. As Roosevelt's first 100 days clearly show, the "modern" (or "streamlined," or "jazzed up," as a conservative might put it) President exercises unprecedented "powers" as regards the initiation of legislation—so much so that some writers do not hesitate now to confer upon him the title "Chief Legislator." The President's capacity to "recommend" to Congress for its consideration "such measures as he shall judge necessary and expedient" is, of course, vouchsafed to him by the Constitution itself. But the men who wrote those words certainly did not see in them any promise of the power and responsibility in the domain of legislation that our day is accustomed to; nor, we may confidently assert, did the men who read them over many succeeding decades. The President does now initiate most legislation. That is not only how it is but—what is more important perhaps—how Congress now expects it to be, as it demonstrates by willingly devoting the bulk of its time to consideration of the President's program. Moreover, the "modern" President has means at his disposal that enable him, or at least have enabled him in normal circumstances, to pressure Congress into at least partial acquiescence in at least the major items of his program. During the initial period of his first term, for example, he has jobs to bestow (less jobs, to be sure, than his less powerful prede-

[1] *The President: Office and Powers* (New York University Press, 1957), p. 22.

cessors), and can use them in dealing with important but reluctant congressmen. As the leader of his party throughout the nation, he can appeal for support to party loyalty, especially when his party controls one or both houses of Congress, and on grounds of the need to chalk up accomplishments with an eye to the next election. He has a certain amount of "say" in dispensing "favors," such as defense contracts and public works projects. And he can carry—or, for that is enough, sometimes, threaten to carry—his "case" to the "people," and so stir up public sympathy for his program. Furthermore, congressional power to legislate "on its own hook" has been eroded considerably by increasingly frequent use of the presidential veto. Up to the Civil War there had been only 51 instances of presidential vetoes—a statistic that must be read over against Franklin Roosevelt's astronomical total of 631 vetoes (of which only 9 were "overridden," and 622, therefore, effective) in approximately a twelve-year period. We readily see why the "modern" President's role in the legislative process sends the commentators, both friendly and hostile, to Roget's *Thesaurus* in search of adjectives capable of describing it.[2]

2. Executive powers in the field of foreign policy have grown at a rapid rate since 1933, and this is the more significant because foreign affairs have constituted an ever-larger and ever-more-important share of the public business. With the help of his subordinates in the Department of State, the Department of Defense, and the Central Intelligence Agency, the President "conducts" (as Congress cannot possibly conduct) the day-to-day business of our foreign relations, and in doing so makes, quite independently of any control by Congress, the countless small decisions that in large part determine the broader patterns of foreign policy. The Constitution, to be sure, provides that the Senate shall share in the treaty-making power; but it is of interest to note that since the First World War the Senate has rejected only one treaty of significance, the Treaty of Versailles (1920). Indeed, some observers interpret this as meaning that the Senate has largely abdicated its foreign-policy role, leaving the President an almost completely free hand in this area. But even that, taken by itself, is no true measure of executive authority in the field of foreign affairs. Recent presidents have increasingly embodied their deals with foreign governments in "executive agreements," few of which require approval of any kind by Congress although they have, the Supreme Court has held, the same legal force and effect as treaties. And how far a daring President might go in avoiding the constitutional rule concerning

[2] We should also note the importance of a threatened veto in stifling congressional initiative.

Senate approval we learned at the time the United States had to decide whether or not to go into the United Nations. Some of the President's supporters at that time, fearing that the Senate might say "Nothing doing," urged him to beat the game by adhering to it by executive agreement (which would have needed only majority approval of both houses of Congress).[3]

3. The "modern" presidency has also been able to make good use, by way of expanding its sphere of autonomy, of the constitutional clause that makes the President "commander in chief." While the Constitution reserves to Congress the authority to declare war, everyone knows these days that a President can actually commit the nation to war by independent military démarches that leave Congress, when the chips are finally down, no choice but to declare formally that a state of war exists. This particular aspect of presidential power moreover has assumed increased significance in recent decades because of our many far-reaching treaty commitments, especially those involved in such regional alliances as NATO, ANZUS, and SEATO. Prudence dictates that the President should, if possible, seek "prior" Congressional consent for the commitment of American armed forces under such treaties—as President Eisenhower in fact did on two occasions (the defense of Formosa and the Middle East). Yet the power of the President to act unilaterally and without such prior Congressional consent is still enormous—as witness President Truman's commitment of American forces in Korea without even so much as consulting congressional leaders.

4. Congress has itself speeded presidential "aggrandizement" by "delegating" important functions to the President. Since 1921, for example, the President has been responsible for drafting the budget, which accordingly takes virtually final shape before Congress so much as sees it. Similarly, for another example, the President now exercises great control over the organization of the nation's administrative apparatus, and does so by *legislative* decree—though time was when Congress would not have dreamed of letting such matters pass out of its own sphere of authority. The President, in consequence, can now "reorganize" the administrative branch in any way he sees fit, subject only to the proviso that Congress, by majority vote, may within 60 days disallow the action he has taken. And, for a final example, Con-

---

[3] For this view see Kenneth Colegrove, *The American Senate and World Peace* (New York: 1954).

The President could have committed the United States to the United Nations via executive agreement without congressional approval. However, in order to participate effectively in this organization eventually he would have had to ask for congressional support.

gress has delegated large discretionary authority, difficult to distinguish from the power to legislate, in areas (tariff rates, for instance) over which earlier congresses kept a jealously-guarded monopoly.

With each such renunciation by Congress, effective presidential power clearly grows still further. Nor is it, for our immediate purpose, any answer here to say Congress can withdraw any such power any time it sees fit. The record, up to now at least, would seem to show that the delegation of congressional power is a one-way street. And expanded presidential power in these areas combined with that which the President has traditionally possessed (as Chief Executive, with ample power to appoint and remove his principal subordinates, and as Chief of State, authorized to act as the ceremonial representative of the American people) explains why many commentators, as we were saying a moment ago, today regard the presidency as the foremost branch of our government. To be sure, the "modern" presidency now and then gets its come-uppance from elsewhere in the system (a fact which pro-President folk mourn as intervention on the part of the "dead hand of the past," and pro-Congress folk rub their hands over)—as when the Supreme Court held President Truman's seizure of the steel mills during the Korean War unconstitutional, primarily on the grounds that Congress had provided, in the Taft-Hartley law, an alternative remedy that he might have called into play. Similarly, the 22nd Amendment, which limits the President to two terms of office and so reduces his effectiveness with Congress during his second term, may be regarded as a come-uppance-in-retrospect for F.D.R. and, by inheritance, for all "modern" presidents. But it would be difficult to argue that the come-uppances by any means keep pace with the aggrandizement, or that Congress could resume its traditional role without bringing about changes so drastic that we may fairly speak of them this late in the day as revolutionary.

Views on Expanded Presidential Authority

There are three more or less clearly distinct schools of thought with respect to presidential power: There are, firstly, those who insist, in the teeth of the kind of evidence we have just examined, that Congress, save possibly in the area of foreign policy, remains the predominant branch of our government. There are, secondly, those (probably the majority of contemporary American political scientists) who hold that presidential power has indeed grown but has not grown fast enough to enable us to meet in a positive manner the problems and demands of the present and future. And there are, thirdly, those who predict that presidential power must, unavoidably, continue to expand, and expand precisely at the expense of that of Congress. The end-result, they insist, will be "Caesarism" and the end of free government in America. Let us briefly examine each of these schools of thought.

a. A case can be made out, as we noted in the preceding chapter, for the view that Congress has *not* fallen from its intended position of predominance. We can, perhaps, best illustrate this point as follows: Two institutions, the President and Congress, participate in our policy-making process. Now suppose that first one, then the other, of these two institutions were, by magic, to disappear—or, if you like, that first the one then the other might suddenly begin to have its way without any interference or influence of any kind on the part of the other. Then let us ask ourselves which of the two cases would involve the greater departure from the present state of affairs? Concretely, might we expect a greater change if the President were suddenly given authority to enact any legislation he wanted, or if Congress were suddenly able to carry out its will without interference from the President? Except in foreign affairs, surely, the second situation would, for all the loose talk we hear that would seem to suggest the contrary, be about what we have now, and would result in no great shifts in public policy; while every newspaper reader knows that the first situation, that of the President having immediate and unrestricted access to the statute-book, would promptly usher in policies calculated to change the face of America in a thousand ways. Now, according to the proponents of this view, that means several things:

First, that what political scientists call the "growth" of "presidential power" under the "modern" presidency is, in *the* crucial sense, an optical illusion, reflecting a series of free and in any case readily-reversible decisions, on Congress' part, not to exercise for the moment certain powers that it continues to enjoy and, under our system, cannot really divest itself of.

Second, the apologists for the "modern" presidency continue to worry about Congress and sustain the "attack on Congress" for good reason—namely that Congress, as our little theoretical exercise has just demonstrated, actually could, if it were of a mind to, impose its will on the President. If it does not do so, that—as a matter of strict constitutional law—is because it does not choose *to* do so. The President, by contrast, is evidently about as far from being in position to impose his will on Congress as he was fifty years ago.

Third, the delegation of authority and the other manifestations of "expanded" presidential power of which we have been speaking emerge

on this view in a different light. This we may see by reminding ourselves of the following: The European monarchs of the age of absolutism also delegated authority—to courts of law, to bureaucracies,
sometimes to military commanders, subject merely to the proviso that
they could withdraw it at any time. They did this, as we readily see
in retrospect, because the great power they enjoyed, insofar as they
tried to exercise it single handed, was worthless; no one individual
could know enough, or move around fast enough, to exercise all of it.
The delegations of authority, in other words, had the effect of *increasing* royal power (the capacity of the king to get his way) rather than
that of diminishing it; and who is to say that this is not true of Congress as well? Most discussions of this matter, even James Burnham's,
gratuitously assume that the President exercises his delegated authority
as if it were somehow not delegated authority, and somehow uses it,
as a matter of course, in a fashion that Congress does not intend. All
very well, of course, except that we are left without any explanation
of why Congress does not revoke the delegations. It would appear
simpler, simpler and more in accord with the principle of "Occam's
razor," to assume that Congress delegates in the same way, and for
the same good reason, as the absolute monarchs: to get done the things
that it wants done but does not have the time and skill and energy to
do for and by itself; to, in sober truth, increase its overall control of
public policy, that is, its power *sensu stricto;* and to reserve for itself
those matters that (as one writer has put it) it deems "most important."
In short the "decline" of Congress on this showing has not merely
been enormously exaggerated; it has not occurred at all. What Congress consents to, to paraphrase Rousseau, we must suppose it to
command.

   b. A second school of thought, while acknowledging that presidential powers have increased considerably, argues that they have not
reached the levels that would be necessary in order for us to avoid
"serious lags" in domestic and foreign policy. Only at moments of
severe crisis, this school contends, has the national government been
able to adopt e.g. the social welfare legislation to which some of us
today point so proudly, or to assume the "international responsibilities"
that, because of our size and wealth, some of us deem to be rightfully
ours. Witness, says this school, the sluggishness with which we move
in the areas of civil rights, tax reform, medical care, federal aid to
education, and urban redevelopment. It would be quite otherwise, the
argument runs, if the President enjoyed adequate power, and that is
just what we must get for him. Only increased presidential powers

and leadership, coupled with reform of our political parties, can carry us to our rendezvous with our true destiny as a nation. James Mc-Gregor Burns gives us the following picture of what a President must do to provide the necessary leadership:

> He must gain leadership of a big national party and guide it in seizing and holding majority status. He must publicize his and his party's program and goals with such clarity and conviction that he can help convert latent and amorphous popular attitudes into a powerful public opinion bolstering his cause. He must build structural support in his personal following by merging it with his national party organization or by creating new political units. . . . He must be willing in emergencies to take sweeping action, no matter how controversial, and then appeal to the electorate for a majority . . .[4]

c. A President with such far-reaching power and such lofty status is, in the opinion of a third school, what constitutes the greatest threat to free self-government in America;[5] and the student will find, in the following selections, an eloquent statement of that view of the matter. And such warnings, we must remember, are as old in this country as *The Federalist* itself, whose authors had great fear of the kind of concentrated authority and power advocated today by the "presidential supremacists." "The accumulation of all powers legislative, executive and judiciary in the same hands, whether of one, a few or many, and whether hereditary, self appointed, or elective," wrote Publius, "may justly be pronounced the very definition of tyranny." [6]

Is there any real reason, we may pause to ask, to take so dim a view of concentrated power? Were the Framers' anxieties in fact justified? Might they, in the passage we have just quoted, have been indulging in a little "rhetoric"? And, finally, is it not possible, whatever the Framers thought, that in "modern conditions" such warnings are neither necessary nor relevant? The answers to these and other such questions are as various as variety itself. Some argue, and with no small show of reason, that the probabilities of arbitrary and despotic government certainly do increase with concentration of power and authority. Our present-day decision-making system, they contend, attempts to resolve differences largely through a process of "compromise," the essence of which is that it merely leaves each competing group or

---

[4] *The Deadlock of Democracy* (Englewood Cliffs, New Jersey: Prentice-Hall, Inc., 1963), pp. 337-38.

[5] James Burnham and Amaury de Riencourt are two leading spokesmen of this point of view.

[6] *The Federalist*, Jacob Cooke (ed.), (New York: Meridian Books, 1961), p. 324.

interest as "satisfied" as possible—or, if you like, as little dissatisfied as possible. At worst, however, each group or interest has ample opportunity to "participate," to "air" its point of view, and this provides a guarantee of sorts that the resulting decision will receive willing acquiescence on all sides. With vast powers concentrated in the President, however, that guarantee of sorts might well lapse: some interested parties might find themselves denied the opportunity to "participate" and, worse still, opponents of the President's program might be labeled "obstructionists" or "reactionaries" seeking to thwart the "General Will"—as expressed by the President as "leader" of *all* the people. And we might, before long, be without any recognized countervailing power capable of forcing the President to justify and debate the merits of his programs.

Other political scientists contend that the Framers' reliance upon separation of powers and checks and balances, as guards against the tyranny they feared, was both naive and unsound. They point to the British political system, in which political authority is notoriously centralized, and ask in effect: Are not democracy and individual freedom just as "safe" under it as under our system? Separation of powers and checks and balances, then, are *not* necessary conditions for the prevention of tyranny. The argument, as far as it goes, is convincing, since Britons are indeed not yet slaves. But that of course does not prove that we in America have no further need of the Framers' "barriers." It merely proves that Britons have found another way of remaining free. Opinions might differ, therefore, as to how many Americans are likely to change their minds on this issue as a result of mulling over such a passage as the following:

> The Madisonian argument exaggerates the importance, in preventing tyranny, of specified checks to governmental officials by other specified governmental officials; it underestimates the importance of inherent social checks and balances existing in every pluralistic society. Without these social checks and balances, it is doubtful that the intragovernmental checks on officials would in fact operate to prevent tyranny; with them, it is doubtful that all of the intragovernmental checks of the Madisonian system as it operates in the United States are necessary to prevent tyranny.[7]

The proponents of presidential supremacy do indeed stress the importance of "social" checks and balances. James McGregor Burns, for

[7] Robert Dahl, *A Preface to Democratic Theory* (Chicago: University of Chicago Press, 1956), p. 22.

example, argues that the "diversity" of American society, and the absence within its bosom of deep-seated ideological, religious, and economic conflicts, will always force presidential leaders to adopt a moderate, that is "representative," position on all major issues, since only by doing this can he gain the support he must have for his program. Thus, it is argued, there would be no need to fear tyranny or arbitrary rule even if the bulk of governmental powers were concentrated in the hands of the President.[8]

The presidential supremacists naturally find little in the Madisonian model that is to their liking. They dream dreams of a system in which authority will be unified, and endowed with a capacity to make bold, rapid, and far reaching decisions. The Madisonian system, by contrast, places a high premium on deliberation, delay, compromise, diffusion of authority. Here, as in most areas of controversy surrounding American institutions, the student who wishes to decide where he stands must answer for himself at least the following questions: Do the conditions in our modern world really render obsolete the devices built into our Constitution by the Framers to avoid tyranny? Did the Framers lack knowledge, knowledge that we now possess, as to how best to avoid majority tyranny? Do conditions in the modern world impell us to give the President additional authority? What risks, if any, does this involve for the survival of democratic government? Has the Madisonian model worked as badly as its critics contend? Are we in need of a new system built upon principles more in keeping with the demands of the present world?

The idea of increased presidential power, as it figures in contemporary political discussion, runs up against some objections that are not easy to answer. The question arises, for example, whether the President, even as matters now stand, is able to exercise effective direction and control over the bureaucracy which he formally heads, and whether, if his powers were greatly increased, things would not get entirely out of hand. Professor Rossiter, for example, writes (a little regretfully, perhaps) that one of the chief restraints on presidential powers is "the persons and politics and prejudices of . . . the top twenty thousand civil and military officials of the government of the United States."[9] This kind of point may be pressed, moreover, various ways: The very *size* of the bureaucracy makes effective control extremely difficult—must do so, even if we suppose every last bureaucrat to be loyal and obedient. But in any large human organization there is

---

[8] See *Deadlock of Democracy* for an elaboration of this position.
[9] *The American Presidency* (New York: Harcourt, Brace and Co., 1956), p. 40.

bound to be a problem that arises because every last bureaucrat is *not* a mere creature of the President's will, namely: that of recalcitrance on the part of some subordinates as regards carrying out programs with which they disagree or have little sympathy. The President can, to be sure, pile orders and directives upon orders and directives; but he can never be sure that, somewhere along the chain of command, they are not going to be ignored or "interpreted" in such a way so as to defeat the purpose he intends. Such recalcitrance, or "inertia," is well-known to students of bureaucracy and it raises at least the following critical questions: Are our presidents, in point of fact, "captives" of the bureaucracy? Is the bureaucracy actually making many of the important substantive decisions of governmental policy? Are congressional grants of authority to the President really grants of power to the bureaucracy? Is democratic government endangered by the discretionary powers possessed by the higher ranking members of the bureaucracy? These, like the questions we listed a moment ago, the student must find a way to answer for himself before making up his mind on the proper role of the President in our system of government.

Presidential Power: Liberalism and Conservatism

The student will not, at this point, need to be told again why the liberals, insofar as they are more interested in the "what" than in the "how," tend to look with favor upon "strong" presidents and upon the programs of "reform" that would give the President additional powers —or why the conservative views expanded presidential authority with disfavor. There is one aspect of the two positions on this issue, however, that deserves special attention. For a number of reasons (as we have seen in the introductions to our chapters on the Congress and the Parties), the President is indeed more apt than Congress to promote liberal programs, Congress indeed more apt than the President to leave things pretty much as they are; so that on that level we readily understand the rational of current liberal and conservative stands on the presidency. For a number of reasons also the liberal, insofar as he is interested in the "how" as such, again favors a strong presidency, which is a better vehicle than Congress for the equal-suffrage, majority-mandate system to which his political theory leads him; while the conservative's political theory tends to lead him in the opposite direction. In any case, we must now notice that the two camps appear to have made permanent and well-nigh irreversible commitments on the President-versus-Congress issue—so that one wonders what would happen if and when the future might bring any considerable shift in the power alignment of these institutions. What if, for instance, we elected a series of conservative presidents? What if Congress, through reapportionment, became liberal? Would liberal and conservative spokesmen, schooled as they are to the arguments and rhetoric of their present positions, be able to switch sides? That, we may content ourselves with saying, would now take some doing!

There are, we may notice by way of concluding, strong reasons for thinking that neither of the "imaginery horribles" in question will present itself, at least within the foreseeable future. Certainly this is how the two camps themselves see the matter. The conservative, as we know him, tends to be pessimistic about the political future of the White House—and, given the nature of the appeals that seem necessary for victory in a presidential campaign, he would be foolish not to. Similarly, even the fondest liberal, given the nature of congressional campaigning and politics, knows that he will not see liberal majorities in Congress any time soon. Perhaps, then, there are "built in" or "inherent" characteristics of our institutions that make of the permanent conservative and liberal commitments we have mentioned luxuries that the two camps can, after all, afford.

A. The Modern President

23. The Powers of the Presidency*

CLINTON ROSSITER

SOMETIMES the stranger outside the gates has a clearer vision of an American institution than we who have lived with it all our lives. John Bright, best friend in all England of the embattled Union, paid this tribute to the Presidency in 1861:

I think the whole world offers no finer spectacle than this; it offers no higher dignity; and there is no greater object of ambition on the political stage on which men are permitted to move. You may point, if you will, to hereditary rulers, to crowns coming down through successive generations of the same family, to thrones based on prescription or on conquest, to sceptres wielded over veteran legions and subject realms,—but to my mind there is nothing more worthy of reverence and obedience, and nothing more sacred, than the authority of the freely chosen magistrate of a great and free people; and if there be on earth and amongst men any right divine to govern, surely it rests with a ruler so chosen and so appointed.

My purpose it to confirm Bright's splendid judgment by presenting the American Presidency as what I honestly believe it to be: one of the few truly successful institutions created by men in their endless quest for the blessings

* Chapter 1, *The American Presidency* (New York: Harcourt Brace and Co., 1956), pp. 15-43. Reprinted by permission of Harcourt Brace and Co.

of free government. This great office, like even the greatest men who have filled it, displays its fair share of warts, and I shall try to paint them as large as life. Yet I would be less than candid were I not to make clear at the outset my own feeling of veneration, if not exactly reverence, for the authority and dignity of the Presidency.

This book is very far from a detailed or definitive portrait of this astounding institution. It is at best an impressionistic rendering of the main dimensions, and I beg early forgiveness for all the things I cannot possibly find room to say about it. My hope is simply that those who read these chapters may come to a sharper understanding of the position the Presidency occupies in the annals of our past and the hopes of our future.

*   *   *

This presentation must begin with a careful accounting of those tasks we call upon the President to perform, for if there is any one thing about him that strikes the eye immediately, it is the staggering burden he bears for all of us. Those who cherish Gilbert and Sullivan will remember Pooh-Bah, the "particularly haughty and exclusive person" in *The Mikado* who filled the offices of "First Lord of the Treasury, Lord Chief Justice, Commander-in-Chief, Lord High Admiral, Master of the Buckhounds, Groom of the Back Stairs, Archbishop of Titipu, and Lord

Mayor, both acting and elect." We chuckle at the fictitious Pooh-Bah; we can only wonder at the real one that history has made of the American President. He has at least three jobs for every one of Pooh-Bah's, and they are not performed with the flick of a lacquered fan. At the risk of being perhaps too analytical, let me review the functions of the modern President. These, as I interpret them, are the major roles he plays in the sprawling drama of American government.

First, the President is Chief of State. He remains today, as he has always been, the ceremonial head of the government of the United States, and he must take part with real or apparent enthusiasm in a range of activities that would keep him running and posing from sunrise to bedtime if he were not protected by a cold-blooded staff. Some of these activities are solemn or even priestly in nature; others, through no fault of his own, are flirtations with vulgarity. The long catalogue of public duties that the Queen discharges in England, the President of the Republic in France, and the Governor-General in Canada is the President's responsibility in this country, and the catalogue is even longer because he is not a king, or even the agent of one, and is therefore expected to go through some rather undignified paces by a people who think of him as a combination of scoutmaster, Delphic oracle, hero of the silver screen, and father of the multitudes.

As figurehead rather than working head of our government, he greets distinguished visitors from all parts of the world, lays wreaths on the tomb of the Unknown Soldier and before the statue of Lincoln, makes proclamations of thanksgiving and commemoration, bestows medals on flustered pilots, holds state dinners for the diplomatic corps and the Supreme Court, lights the nation's Christmas tree, buys the first poppy from the Veterans of Foreign Wars, gives the first crisp banknote to the Red Cross, throws out the first ball for the Senators (the harmless ones out at Griffith Stadium), rolls the first egg for the Easter Bunny, and in the course of any month greets a fantastic procession of firemen, athletes, veterans, Boy Scouts, Campfire Girls, boosters, hog callers, exchange students, and heroic school children. The annual United Fund Drive could not possibly get get under way without a five-minute telecast from the White House; Sunday is not Sunday if the President and his lady skip church; a public-works project is not public until the President presses a silver key in Washington and explodes a charge of dynamite in Fort Peck or Hanford or the Tennessee Valley.

The President is not permitted to confine this sort of activity to the White House and the city around it. The people expect him to come to them from time to time, and the presidential grand tour, a precedent set conspicuously by George Washington, is an important aspect of the ceremonial function. Nor is this function, for obvious political and cultural reasons, untainted with commercialism. If it isn't one "Week" for him to proclaim or salute, it's another, and what President, especially in an election year, would turn away the Maid of Cotton or the Railroad Man of the Year or, to keep everybody happy, the Truck Driver of the Year from the White House door?

The President, in short, is the one-man distillation of the American people just as surely as the Queen is of the British people; he is, in President Taft's words, "the personal embodiment and representative of their dignity and majesty." (Mr. Taft, it will be remembered, was uniquely shaped by nature's lavish hand to be a personal embodiment of dignity and majesty.) Or as Attorney General Stanberry argued before the Supreme Court in 1867 in the case of *Mississippi* v. *Johnson:*

Undoubtedly so far as the mere individual man is concerned there is a great difference between the President and a king; but so far as the office is concerned—so far as the great executive office of this government is conerned—I deny that there is a particle less dignity belonging to the office of President than to the office of King of Great Britain or of any other potentate on the face of the earth. He represents the majesty of the law and of the people as fully and as essentially, and with the same dignity, as does any absolute monarch or the head of any independent government in the world.

The role of Chief of State may often seem trivial, yet it cannot be neglected by a President who proposes to stay in favor and, more to the point, in touch with the people, the ultimate source of all his power. It is a conspicuous thief of his precious time, yet more than one President, most notably Harry S Truman, has played it in such a way as to gain genuine release from the routine tasks and hard decisions that filled the rest of his day. And whether or not he enjoys this role, no President can fail to realize that all his powers are invigorated, indeed are given a new dimension of authority, because he is the symbol of our sovereignty, continuity, and grandeur. When he asks a Senator to lunch in order to enlist his support for a pet project, when he thumps his desk and reminds the antagonists in a labor dispute of the larger interests of the American people, when he orders a general to cease caviling or else be removed from his command, the Senator and the disputants and the general are well aware —especially if the scene is laid in the White House—that they are dealing with no ordinary head of government. The framers of the Constitution took a momentous step when they fused the dignity of a king and the power of a prime minister in one elective office. And, if they did nothing else, they gave us a "father image" that should satisfy even the most demanding political Freudians.

*   *   *

The second of the President's roles is that of Chief Executive. He reigns, but he also rules; he symbolizes the people, but he also runs their government. "The true test of a good government is its aptitude and tendency to produce a good administration," Hamilton wrote in *The Federalist,* at the same time making clear that it would be the first duty of the proposed President to produce this "good administration." For reasons that I shall touch upon later, the President (and I mean any President, no matter how happily he may wallow in the details of administration) has more trouble playing this role successfully than he does any of the others. It is, in fact, the one major area of presidential activity in which his powers are simply not equal to his responsibilities. Yet the role is an important one, and we cannot savor the fullness of the President's duties unless we recall that he is held primarily and often exclusively accountable for the ethics, loyalty, efficiency, frugality, and responsiveness to the public's wishes of the two and a third million Americans in the national administration.

Both the Constitution and Congress have recognized his authority to supervise the day-to-day activities of the executive branch, strained and restrained though this supervision may often be in practice. From the Constitution, explicitly or implicitly, he receives the twin powers of appointment and removal, as well as the primary duty, which no law or plan or circumstance can ever take away from him, to "take care that the laws be faithfully executed." He alone may appoint, with the advice and consent of the Senate, the several thousand top officials who run the government; he alone may remove, with varying degrees of abruptness, those who are not executing the laws faithfully—or, in the case of all those Secretaries and generals and attorneys directly under his command, not executing them in a manner consistent with his own policies.

It is the power of removal—the "gun behind the door"—that makes it possible for the President to bend his "team" to his will. More to the point, this power is the symbol and final sanction of his position as Chief Executive, and no official in the administration, not even the most nonpartisan chairman of the most independent regulatory commission, is entirely immune to a fatal attack of presidential displeasure. A member of the Federal Trade Commission or Interstate Commerce Commission is protected by statute and judicial decision against the kind of arbitrary removal the President may visit upon a Secretary of the Army or Director of the Budget, but if he has stepped out of line in a way for all the world to see—if, to take a crude example, he has been drunk on the job for weeks on end—then he cannot hope to stand up to the man who has been commanded by the Constitution to see to the faithful execution of the laws of the United States. His official life would be forfeit; a veiled threat of removal, especially if the threat were fortified by "pressure from the White House," would be enough to force the surrender of even the most thick-skinned wrong-doer. The "voluntary" resignation of Richard A. Mack from the Federal Communications Commission in 1958 is the most recent case in point. The disclosure by a committee of Congress of an apparent conflict of interest between Mack the Commissioner and Mack the Friend of National Airlines, Inc. was enough to set the White House (more precisely, Sherman Adams) in motion, and Mr. Mack gave up his post without a struggle. Occasionally, to be sure, the President must come right out and remove an official—because the official has sinned too greviously to be allowed to resign, or, as is more likely, because he is so proud of his record and convinced of his rectitude that he refuses

to resign. Hard cases, Justice Holmes once said, make bad law, yet I doubt that there has ever been a more forceful vindication of the President's authority "to produce a good administration" than Mr. Roosevelt's cashiering of Dr. A. E. Morgan from the chairmanship of the Tennessee Valley Authority in 1938. Frustrated in his attempts to secure Dr. Morgan's co-operation in clearing up a nasty clash of personalities that had brought the activities of T.V.A.'s governing board to a standstill, the President removed him peremptorily, made a new appointment to the position, and sent T.V.A. about its business. There were screams of anguish and prophecies of dictatorship, but there was no effective challenge to the President's contention that, although he could not construe Morgan's duties for him nor substitute his own judgment for that of a board rendered independent by statute and custom, he could and must act to keep T.V.A. in operation.

From Congress, through such legislative mandates as the Budget and Accounting Act of 1921 and the succession of Reorganization Acts, the President has received further acknowledgment of his administrative leadership. Although independent agencies such as the Interstate Commerce Commission and the National Labor Relations Board operate by design outside his immediate area of responsibility, most of the government's administrative tasks are still carried on within the fuzzy-edged pyramid that has the President at its lonely peak. The laws that are executed daily in his name and under his general supervision are numbered in the hundreds. One task illustrates the scope of the President's administrative responsibility: the preparation and execution of the federal budget. One program attests the power he wields over the public's servants: the loyalty standards instituted by President Truman's Executive Order 9835 of March 21, 1947, and tightened by President Eisenhower's Executive Order 10450 of April 29, 1953. One passage from the *United States Code* makes clear that Congress itself expects much of him:

The President is authorized to prescribe such regulations for the admission of persons into the civil service of the United States as may best promote the efficiency thereof, and ascertain the fitness of each candidate in respect to age, health, character, knowledge, and ability for the branch of service into which he seeks to enter; and for this purpose he may employ suitable persons to conduct such inquiries, and may prescribe their duties, and establish regulations for the conduct of persons who may receive appointment in the civil service.

It might be useful to hear the opinion of the acknowledged experts in this field. I take these paragraphs from the report of the sixth American Assembly, which met at Arden House in October 1954 to consider the "character, prestige, and problems" of the public service:

The President has the responsibility for leadership of the Executive Branch of the Federal Government service. Constitutional principles, the necessities of our national life and the example of successful corporate enterprise all underscore the indispensability of executive responsibility for the personnel policies and the personnel management of the Federal Government.

This leadership must be acknowledged and supported by the heads and employees of executive departments, by the party leaders and by the members of the Congress. This leadership must be accepted and exercised by the President, if the business of the National Government is to be efficiently performed.

Whether it is his letters or his taxes the ordinary citizen wants more effi-ciently collected, he looks first of all to the President as business manager of the administration. There was a time when Presidents could and did pay strict attention to matters such as these, and about a hundred million people still do not seem to realize that the time has long since passed.

* * *

The President's third major function is one he could not escape if he wished, and several Presidents have wished it mightily. The Constitution designates him specifically as "Commander-in-Chief of the Army and Navy of the United States, and of the militia of the several States when called into the actual service of the United States." In peace and war he is the supreme commander of the armed forces, the living guarantee of the American belief in "the supremacy of the civil over military authority."

In time of peace he raises, trains, supervises, and deploys the forces that Congress is willing to maintain, and he has a great deal to say about the size and make-up of these forces. With the aid of the Secretary of Defense, the Secretaries of the three services, the Joint Chiefs of Staff, and the members of the National Security Council —every one of these men his personal choice—he looks constantly to the state of the nation's defenses. He is never for one day allowed to forget that he will be held accountable by people, Congress, and history for the nation's readiness to meet an enemy assault. There is no more striking indication of the present latitude of the President's military power than these matter-of-fact words in the Atomic Energy Act of 1946:

Sec. 6(a) Authority. The *Commission* is authorized to—
(1) conduct experiments and do research and development work in the military application of atomic energy; and
(2) engage in the production of

atomic bombs, atomic bomb parts, or other military weapons utilizing fissionable materials; except that such activities shall be carried on only to the extent that the express consent and direction of the President of the United States has been obtained, which consent and direction shall be obtained at least once each year.

The President from time to time may direct the Commission (1) to deliver such quantities of fissionable materials or weapons to the armed forces for such use as he deems necessary in the interest of the national defense or (2) to authorize the armed forces to manufacture, produce, or acquire any equipment or device utilizing fissionable material or atomic energy as a military weapon.

It should be added that, despite the wounded protests of Senator Bricker, most citizens agreed with Mr. Truman's brisk assertion in 1950 that it was for the President to decide whether the H-bomb should be built. Congress might have refused to grant funds for such an undertaking, but this would not have stopped the President from pushing ahead as best he could with the other resources at his command. And, as the same doughty man demonstrated in 1945, it is for the President to decide in time of war when and where and how the H-bomb or A-bomb or any other bomb should be dropped.

In such time, "when the blast of war blows in our ears," the President's power to command the forces swells out of all proportion to his other powers. All major decisions of strategy, and many of his tactics as well, are his alone to make or to approve. Lincoln and Franklin Roosevelt, each in his own way and time, showed how far the power of military command can be driven by a President anxious to have his generals and admirals get on with the war. No small part of his time, as we know from Lincoln's experience, can be spent searching for the right generals and admirals.

But this, the power of command, is only a fraction of the vast responsibility the modern President draws from the Commander in Chief clause. The framers of the Constitution, to be sure, took a narrow view of the authority they had granted. "It would amount," Hamilton wrote offhandedly in *The Federalist,* "to nothing more than the supreme command and direction of the military and naval forces, as first General and Admiral of the Confederacy." This view of presidential power as something purely military foundered on the hard facts of the first of our modern wars. Faced by an overriding necessity for harsh, even dictatorial action, Lincoln used the Commander in Chief clause, at first gingerly, in the end boldly, to justify an unprecedented series of measures that cut deeply into the accepted liberties of the people and the routine pattern of government. Wilson added another cubit to the stature of the wartime Presidency by demanding that Congress give him those powers over the economy about which there was any constitutional doubt, and Franklin Roosevelt, who had read about Lincoln and lived with Wilson, carried the wartime Presidency to breath-taking heights of authority over the American economy and social order. The creation and staffing of a whole array of emergency boards and offices, the seizure and operation of more than sixty strike-bound or strike-threatened plants and industries, and the forced evacuation of 70,000 American citizens of Japanese descent from the West Coast are three startling and prophetic examples of what a President can do as Commander in Chief to stiffen the home front in support of the fighting forces. It is important to recall that Congress came to Roosevelt's aid in each of these series of actions by passing laws empowering him to do what he had done already or by fixing penalties for violating the orders of his subordinates. Congress, too, likes to win wars, and Congressmen are more likely to needle the President for inactivity and timidity than to accuse him of acting too swiftly and arbitrarily.

Now that total war, which ignores the old line between battlefield and home front, has been compounded by the absolute weapon, which mocks every rule we have ever tried to honor, we may expect the President to be nothing short of a "constitutional dictator" in the event of war. The next wartime President, who may well be our last, will have the right, of which Lincoln spoke with feeling, to take "any measure which may best subdue the enemy," and he alone will be the judge of what is 'best" for the survival of the republic. We have placed a shocking amount of military power in the President's keeping, but where else, we may ask, could it possibly have been placed?

*   *   *

Next, the President is Chief Diplomat. Although authority in the field of foreign relations is shared constitutionally among three organs—President, Congress, and, for two special purposes, the Senate—his position is paramount, if not indeed dominant. In 1799 John Marshall, no particular friend of executive power, spoke of the President as "the sole organ of the nation in its external relations, and its sole representative with foreign nations." In 1936 Justice Sutherland, no particular friend of executive power and even less of Franklin D. Roosevelt, put the Court's stamp of approval on "the very delicate, plenary and exclusive power of the President as the sole organ of the government in the field of international relations."

The primacy of the executive comes under vigorous attack from time to time, chiefly from those who object to a specific policy even more strongly than to a President's pursuit of it, and it is true that he acts more arbitrarily and independently than the framers of the Constitution ever intended him to act. Yet the growth of presidential authority in this area seems to have

been almost inevitable, and hardly the outcome of a shameful conspiracy by the three Democratic Presidents of the twentieth century. Constitution, laws, custom, the practice of other nations, and the logic of history have combined to place the President in a dominant position. Secrecy, dispatch, unity, continuity, and access to information—the ingredients of successful diplomacy—are properties of his office, and Congress, I need hardly add, possesses none of them. It is a body with immense power of its own in the field of foreign relations—a fact perfectly symbolized by the unprecedented conference between Prime Minister Macmillan and the leaders of Congress in March 1959—but the power is essentially negative in character and application. And as if all this were not enough to insure the President's dominance, he is also, as we have just noted, Commander in Chief, the man who controls and directs the armed might of the United States in a world in which force, real or threatened, is the essence of diplomacy.

The field of foreign relations can be conveniently if somewhat inexactly divided into two sectors: the formulation of policy and the conduct of affairs. The first of these is a joint undertaking in which the President proposes, Congress disposes, and the wishes of the people prevail in the end. The President's leadership is usually vindicated. Our most ancient and honored policy is significantly known as the *Monroe* Doctrine; our leading policies of recent years have been the *Truman* Doctrine and the *Eisenhower* Doctrine. From Washington's Proclamation of Neutrality in 1793 to Eisenhower's decision to stand fast in Berlin in 1959, the President has repeatedly committed the nation to decisive attitudes and actions abroad, more than once to war itself. Occasionally Congress has compelled him to abandon a policy already put forward, as it did in the case of Grant's plans for Santo Domingo, or has forced distasteful policies upon him, as it did upon Madison in 1812 and McKinley in 1898. Nevertheless, a stubborn President is hard to budge, a crusading President hard to thwart. The diplomatic lives of the two Roosevelts are proof enough of these assertions. Mr. Truman was not exaggerating much when he told an informal gathering of the Jewish War Veterans in 1948: "I make American foreign policy."

The transaction of business with foreign nations is, as Jefferson once wrote, "executive altogether," and Congress finds it difficult to exercise effective control or to deliver constructive criticism, not that Congress can be accused of lack of trying. The State Department carries on its many activities in the name of the President, and he is or ought to be in command of every procedure through which our foreign relations are carried on from one day to the next: negotiation of treaties and executive agreements, recognition of new governments and nations, selection and supervision of diplomatic personnel, adjustment of tariff barriers within statutory limits, direction of our delegation to the United Nations, and communications with foreign powers. As Commander in Chief he deploys our armed forces abroad and occasionally supports our policies with what is known as "presidential warmaking." The conduct of foreign relations as a short-range proposition is a presidential prerogative, and short-range actions—the recognition of a revolutionary regime in Cuba, the reception of a Burmese prime minister, the raising of the duty on Swiss watches—can have long-range consequences.

In recent years, the role of Chief Diplomat has become the most important and exacting of all those we call upon the President to play. Indeed, when one thinks of the hours of "prayerful consideration" President Eisenhower devoted each week to briefing sessions with the Dulles brothers, conferences with the National Security Council, lunches with Senators Fullbright and Wiley, chats with Nehru or Macmillan or Diefenbaker or whoever else might be in town, explanatory and inspirational speeches to the nation, and lonely wrestling bouts with appointments and reports and messages to Congress—not to mention his correspondence with Khrushchev, Zhukov, and Bulganin—it is a wonder that he had a moment's time for any of his other duties.

* * *

The President's duties are not all purely executive in nature. He is also intimately associated, by Constitution and custom, with the legislative process, and we may therefore consider him to be the Chief Legislator. Congress has a wealth of strong and talented men, but the complexity of the problems they are asked to solve by a people who assume that all problems are solvable has made *external* leadership a requisite of effective operation. The President alone is in a political, constitutional, and practical position to provide such leadership, and he is therefore expected, within the limits of constitutional and political propriety, to guide Congress in much of its lawmaking activity. Indeed, since Congress is no longer organized to guide itself, not even under such toughminded leaders as Senator Johnson and Speaker Rayburn, the refusal or inability of the President to point out the way results in weak or, at best, stalemated government.

Success in the delicate area of executive-legislative relations depends on several variables: the political complexion of President and Congress, the state of the Union and of the world around us, the vigor and tact of the President's leadership, and the mood of Congress, which is generally friendly near the beginning of a President's term and rebellious near the end. Yet even the President whose announced policy is to "restore our hallowed system of the separation of powers" and leave Congress strictly alone (Coolidge is a capital example, one not likely to

be repeated) must exercise his constitutional option to veto or not to veto
about a thousand times each session,
must discourse once a year on the state
of the Union and occasionally recommend "such measures as he shall judge
necessary and expedient," must present
the annual budget, and must make some
effort to realize at least the less controversial promises in his party's platform.
"After all," Mr. Eisenhower told a
press conference in 1959, "the Constitution puts the President right square
into the legislative business." In the
hands of a Wilson or a Roosevelt, even
at times in the hands of an Eisenhower,
the Presidency becomes a sort of prime
ministership or "third House of Congress," and the chief concern of the
President is to push for the enactment
of his own or his party's legislative desires.

Upon many of our most celebrated
laws the presidential imprint is clearly
stamped. Each of these was drafted in
the President's offices, introduced and
supported by his friends, defended in
committee by his aides, voted through
by a party over which every form of
discipline and persuasion was exerted,
and then made law by his signature.
The signature, of course, was affixed
with several dozen fountain pens,
which were then passed out among the
beaming friends and aides. Among
the "ploys and gambits" the President
may have used in the process were the
White House breakfast with his chief
lieutenants, or perhaps with his chief
obstructionists; the fireside chat with
his constituents, some of whom were
also constituents of the obstructionists;
the press conference, in which he proclaimed his astonishment at the way
Congress was dragging its feet; the
dangled patronage or favor, which
brought a wavering or even hostile
Senator to his side; and the threat of
a veto, which he brandished like the
Gorgon's head to frighten the maver-
icks into removing objectionable
amendments to the bill he had first sent
over.

Even the President who lacks a congressional majority must go through
the motions of leadership. The Republicans in the Eightieth Congress always
waited politely for Mr. Truman's proposals on labor, taxes, inflation, civil
rights, and education, however scant
the regard they intended to pay them.
The Democrats, if we may believe the
protests of Speaker Rayburn and Senator Johnson, were impatient to hear
President Eisenhower's proposals and
to feel the lash of his leadership. In
any case, the chief responsibility for
bridging the constitutional gulf between executive and legislature now
rests irrevocably with the President.
His tasks as leader of Congress are difficult and delicate, yet he must bend to
them steadily or be judged a failure.
The President who will not give his
best thoughts to guiding Congress,
more so the President who is tempera-
mentally or politically unfitted to "get
along with Congress," is now rightly
considered a national liability.

Chief of State, Chief Executive,
Commander in Chief, Chief Diplomat,
Chief Legislator—these functions make
up the strictly constitutional burden of
the President. As Mr. Truman himself
allowed in several of his folksy sermons
on the Presidency, they form an aggregate of power that would have made
Caesar or Genghis Khan or Napoleon
bite his nails with envy. Yet even these
are not the whole weight of presidential responsibility. I count at least five
additional functions that have been
piled on top of the original load.

The first of these is the President's
role as Chief of Party, one that he has
played by popular demand and to a
mixed reception ever since the administration of Thomas Jefferson. However
sincere Washington's abhorrence of
"factions" may have been, his own administration and policies spawned our
first two parties, and their arrival upon
the scene altered the character of the
Presidency radically. No matter how
fondly or how often we may long for
a President who is above the heat of

political strife, we must acknowledge resolutely his right and duty to be the leader of his party. He is at once the least political and most political of all heads of government.

The value of this function has been attested by all our first-rate Presidents. Jackson, Lincoln, Wilson, and the two Roosevelts were especially skillful party leaders. By playing the politician with unashamed zest the first of these gave his epic administration a unique sense of cohesion, the second rallied doubting Republican leaders and their followings to the cause of the Union, and the other three achieved genuine triumphs as catalysts of congressional action. That elegant amateur, Dwight D. Eisenhower, played the role with devotion if not exactly zest. It would have astonished George Washington, but it cannot even ruffle us, to learn that the President devoted breakfast and most of the morning of June 20, 1955—a day otherwise given over to solemn celebration of the tenth birthday of the United Nations—to mending a few fences with Republican leaders of California. He was demonstrating only what close observers of the Presidency know well: that its incumbent must devote an hour or two of every working day to the profession of Chief Democrat or Chief Republican. The President dictates the selection of the national chairman and other top party officials, reminds his partisans in Congress that the legislative record must be bright if victory is to crown their joint efforts, delivers "fight talks" to the endless procession of professionals who call upon him, and, through the careful distribution of the loaves and fishes of federal patronage, keeps the party a going concern. The loaves and fishes are not so plentiful as they were in the days of Jackson and Lincoln, but the President is still a wholesale distributor of "jobs for the boys."

It troubles many good people, not entirely without reason, to watch their Chief of State dabbling in politics, smiling on party hacks, and endorsing candidates he knows to be unfit for anything but immediate delivery to the county jail. Yet if he is to persuade Congress, if he is to achieve a loyal and cohesive administration, if he is to be elected in the first place (and reelected in the second), he must put his hand firmly to the plow of politics. The working head of government in a constitutional democracy must be the nation's number-one boss, and most Presidents have had no trouble swallowing this truth.

Yet he is, at the same time if not in the same breath, the Voice of the People, the leading formulator and expounder of public opinion in the United States. While he acts as political leader of some, he serves as moral spokesman for all. Well before Woodrow Wilson had come to the Presidency, but not before he had begun to dream of it, he expressed the essence of this role:

> His is the only national voice in affairs. Let him once win the admiration and confidence of the country, and no other single force can withstand him, no combination of forces will easily overpower him. His position takes the imagination of the country. He is the representative of no constituency, but of the whole people. When he speaks in his true character, he speaks for no special interest. If he rightly interpret the national thought and boldly insist upon it, he is irresistible; and the country never feels the zest for action so much as when its President is of such insight and calibre.

Throughout our history there have been moments of triumph or dedication or frustration or even shame when the will of the people—would it be wrong to call it the General Will?—demanded to be heard clearly and unmistakably. It took the line of Presidents some time to grasp the meaning of this function, but since the day when Andrew Jackson thundered against the Nullifiers of South Carolina no effective President has doubted his prerogative to speak the people's mind on the great issues of his time, to act, again in Wilson's words, as "the spokesman for the real sentiment and purpose of the country."

The coming of the radio, and now of television, has added immeasurably to the range and power of the President's voice, offering the man who occupies this "bully pulpit" (as Theodore Roosevelt described it) an opportunity to preach the gospel of America in every home and, indeed, in almost every land. Neither Steve Allen nor Ed Sullivan, neither Bishop Sheen nor Edward R. Murrow—not even, I would insist, the men of the mythical West who fill every channel with the sound of their guns—can gain access to so many millions of American homes. Indeed, the President must be especially on his guard not to pervert these mighty media that are his to command. It is one thing for a huckster to appeal to the people to buy a mouthwash; it would be quite another for a President to appeal to them to stampede the Senate. I like to think that our sales resistance would be as dogged in the second case as in the first, but there is no denying that, even in defeat, a President could do a great deal of damage to our scheme of representative government.

Sometimes, of course, it is no easy thing, even for the most sensitive and large-minded of Presidents, to know the real sentiment of the people or to be bold enough to state it in defiance of loudly voiced contrary opinion. There are definite limits to presidential free speech, as Mr. Eisenhower learned in 1959 when he was egged into a few plaintive comments on the size and shape of American automobiles. Yet the President who senses the popular mood and spots new tides even before they start to run, who practices shrewd economy in his appearances as spokesman for the nation, who is conscious of his unique power to compel discussion on his own terms, and who talks the language of Christian morality and

the American tradition, can shout down any other voice or chorus of voices in the land. There have been times, to be sure, when we seemed as willing to listen to an antagonist as to the President—to Senator Taft in 1950, General MacArthur in 1951, Clarence Randall of Inland Steel in June 1952—but in the end, we knew, and the antagonist knew, too, that the battle was no Armageddon, that it was a frustrating skirmish fought between grossly ill-matched forces. And if we learned anything from Senator Johnson's speech of January 6, 1958, to his Democratic colleagues, it was that two addresses on the state of the Union are one too many.

The President is the American people's one authentic trumpet, and he has no higher duty than to give a clear and certain sound. "Words at great moments of history are deeds," Clement Attlee said of Winston Churchill on the day the latter stepped down in 1945. The strong and imaginative President can make with his own words the kind of history that Churchill made in 1940 and 1941. When the events of 1933 are all but forgotten, we shall still recall Roosevelt's words, "The only thing we have to fear is fear itself."

*   *   *

In the memorable case of *In re Neagle* (1890), which still makes good reading for those who like a touch of horse opera in their constitutional law, Justice Samuel Miller spoke with feeling of the "peace of the United States" —a happy condition, it would appear, of domestic tranquillity and national prosperity that is often broken by violent men and forces and just as often restored by the President. Perhaps the least known of his functions is the mandate he holds from the Constitution and the laws, but even more positively from the people of the United States, to act as Protector of the Peace. The emergencies that can disturb the peace of the United States seem to grow thicker and more vexing every year, and hardly a week now goes by that the President is not called upon to take forceful steps in behalf of a section or city or group or enterprise that has been hit hard and suddenly by disaster. Generally, it is for state and local authorities to deal with social and natural calamities, but in the face of a riot in Detroit or floods in New England or a tornado in Missouri or a railroad strike in Chicago or a panic in Wall Street, the people turn almost instinctively to the White House and its occupant for aid and comfort.

And he, certainly, is the person to give it. No man or combination of men in the United States can muster so quickly and authoritatively the troops, experts, food, money, loans, equipment, medical supplies, and moral support that may be needed in a disaster. Are thousands of homes flooded in the Missouri and Ohio Valleys?—then the President will order Coast Guardsmen and their boats to be flown to the scene for rescue and patrol work, and he will go himself to bring cheer to the homeless. Are cattle starving on the snow-bound western plains?—then the President will order the Air Force to engage in Operation Haylift. Are the farmers of Rhode Island and Massachusetts facing ruin in the wake of a September hurricane?—then the President will designate these states as disaster areas and order the Secretary of Agriculture to release surplus foods and make emergency loans on easy terms. Is Maine scourged by forest fires? Is Texas parched with drought? Is Kansas invaded by grasshoppers? Is Little Rock soiled with the blood of men and tears of children?—then in every instance the President must take the lead to restore the normal pattern of existence.

Or are we having a March 1933 all over again, and are we caught up in the first dreadful moments of a financial panic?—then the President will issue the necessary orders on the authority of two laws that have been waiting quietly on the books since the first years of the New Deal:

Section 4 of the Emergency Banking Act of 1933:

> In order to provide for the safer and more effective operation of the National Banking System . . . during such emergency period as the President of the United States by proclamation may prescribe, no member bank of the Federal Reserve System shall transact any banking business except to such extent and subject to such regulations, limitations and restrictions as may be prescribed by the Secretary of the Treasury, with the approval of the President.

Section 19 (a) of the Securities Exchange Act of 1934:

> The Commission is authorized . . . if in its opinion the public interest so requires, summarily to suspend trading in any registered security on any national securities exchange for a period not exceeding ten days, or with the approval of the President, summarily to suspend all trading on any national securities exchange for a period not exceeding ninety days.

If I may reduce the meaning of these two laws to simple terms, they empower the President to meet the challenge of any future panic like that of March 1933 by declaring a state of financial martial law. At the same time, he remains constitutionally, we might even say extraconstitutionally, empowered to respond to an atomic attack by declaring straight-out martial law through all the land. This, be it noted for future reference, is exactly what President Eisenhower pretended to do in the simulated hydrogen-bomb attack of June 1955. One of the remarkable events of that three-day test of our readiness for atomic war was the startled discovery by Mr. Eisenhower and his staff that "the inherent powers of the

Presidency," something about which Republicans usually maintain uneasy silence, would be the nation's chief crutch in the aftermath of the ultimate disaster. This fact, and thus his status as Protector of the Peace, had already been recognized by a group of Senators who called on Mr. Eisenhower to "assume personal responsibility" for creating an adequate program of civil defense, something he shortly proceeded to do within the limits of his budget and our expectations.

There is at least one area of American life, the economy, in which the people of this country are no longer content to let disaster fall upon them unopposed. They now expect their government, under the direct leadership of the President, to prevent a depression or panic and not simply to wait until one has developed before putting it to rout. Thus the President has a new function, which is still taking shape, that of Manager of Prosperity.

The origin of this function can be fixed with unusual exactness. The Employment Act of 1946 was the first clear acknowledgement by the federal government of a general responsibility for maintaining a stable and prosperous economy:

Sec. 2. The Congress hereby declares that it is the continuing policy and responsibility of the Federal Government to use all practicable means consistent with its needs and obligations and other essential considerations of national policy, with the assistance and cooperation of industry, agriculture, labor, and State and local governments to coordinate and utilize all its plans, functions, and resources for the purpose of creating and maintaining, in a manner calculated to foster and promote free competitive enterprise and the general welfare, conditions under which there will be afforded useful employment opportunities, including self-employment, for those able, willing, and seeking to work, and to promote maximum employment, production, and purchasing power.

The significant feature of this law from our point of view is the deliberate manner in which, in section after section, the President is singled out as the official who is "to foster and promote free competitive enterprise, to avoid economic fluctuations or to diminish the effects thereof, and to maintain employment, production, and purchasing power." He is granted the handsome gift of the Council of Economic Advisers; he is requested to make the annual Economic Report and such supplementary reports as may be advisable; he is expected to propose "a program for carrying out the policy declared in section 2, together with such recommendations for legislation as he may deem necessary or desirable." There is apparently no doubt in Congress's collective mind that one of the President's prime duties is to watch like a mother hen over all the eggs in all our baskets. As for the American people, it is a notorious fact that we give our President small credit for prosperity and full blame for hard times.

Yet even if the Employment Act had never been passed, he would have this duty and most of the powers that go with it. We have built some remarkable stabilizing devices into our political economy since 1929, and the men who control them—in the Federal Reserve System, the Securities and Exchange Commission, the Federal Security Agency, the countless credit organizations, the Federal Deposit Insurance Corporation—are wide open to suggestions, even directions from the President. There are limits, both strategic and physical, to what can be done in the White House, but certainly the alert President stands always ready to invite the managers of a sick industry or the leading citizens of a city plagued by chronic unemployment to come together and take counsel under his leadership. Of course, it is not his counsel but a well-placed government contract or a hike in the tariff or a dramatic recommendation to Congress for which they have come. Fortunately for the President, his position as overseer of the entire economy is obvious to even the most embittered spokesmen for special interests, and he can take refuge from their pleas for relief by insisting that he must consider the whole picture before deciding on action in their behalf.

The very notion of the President as Manager of Prosperity strikes many people as an economic and political heresy, especially those who still swear allegiance to the tattered doctrine of the self-healing economy. Most of us, however, now accept the idea of a federal government openly engaged in preventing runaway booms and plunging busts. We need only think of Mr. Eisenhower's creditable performance in the slack days of 1954—or, for that matter, of his uninspired performance in the harder days of 1958-1959—to recognize the central position of the Presidency in this new kind of government. Lest there be any doubt how the President himself felt about the new dimension of government responsibility, let me quote from his message to Congress accompanying the Economic Report for 1953:

> The demands of modern life and the unsettled status of the world require a more important role for government than it played in earlier and quieter times. . . .
>
> Government must use its vast power to help maintain employment and purchasing power as well as to maintain reasonably stable prices.
>
> Government must be alert and sensitive to economic developments, including its own myriad activities. It must be prepared to take preventive as well as remedial action; and it must be ready to cope with new situations that may arise. This is not a start-and-stop responsibility, but a continuous one.
>
> The arsenal of weapons at the disposal of Government for maintaining economic stability is formidable. It includes credit controls administered by the Federal Reserve System; the debt-management policies of the Treasury; authority of the President to vary the terms of mortgages carrying Federal insurance; flexibility in administration of the budget; agricultural supports; modification of the tax structure; and public works. We shall not hesitate to use any or all of these weapons as the situation may require.

And this from a Republican President dedicated to the glories of free enterprise! Thus far have we and the Presidency moved in a generation of welfare and warfare.

*   *   *

In order to grasp the full import of the last of the President's roles, we must take him as Chief Diplomat, Commander in Chief, and Chief of State, then thrust him onto a far wider stage, there to perform before a much more numerous and more critical audience. For the modern President is, whether we or our friends abroad like it or not, marked out for duty as a World Leader. The President has a much larger constituency than the American electorate: his words and deeds in behalf of our own survival as a free nation have a direct bearing upon the freedom and stability of at least several score other countries.

The reasons why he, rather than the British Prime Minister or French President or an outstanding figure from one of the smaller countries, should be singled out for supranational leadership are too clear to require extended mention. Not only are we the richest and most powerful member of any coalition we may enter, not only are we the chief target of the enemy and thus the most truculent of the powers arrayed against him, but the Presidency, for the very reasons I have dwelled upon in this chapter, unites power, drama, and prestige as does no other office in the world. Its incumbent sits, wherever he sits, at the head of the table. Winston Churchill, an A-plus student of our system of government, recognized this great truth with unerring eye when he insisted that not he, the elder statesman, but Mr. Eisenhower, the American President, take the chair in the middle at the Big Three conference in Bermuda in 1953. No British Prime Minister would ever be likely to forget that the President with whom he must deal every week of the year is a head of state as well as a head of government, a king and a prime minister rolled into one.

This role is not much more than a decade old, although there was a short rehearsal of it in late 1918 and the first few months of 1919. Whether it will continue to grow in the years of tension ahead depends, of course, on just how high the tension remains. It does seem probable that the President will have no choice but to act consciously for and speak openly to the nations with whom we are associated in defense of freedom —to act as Truman did in the North Korean aggression of June 1950, to speak as Eisenhower did in his proposal for an international atomic-energy pool delivered to the Assembly of the United Nations in December 1953, to act and speak together as Eisenhower did in the Berlin crisis of 1959. If the British Prime Minister often seemed to be the most influential figure in the Atlantic coalition during the first part of that nerve-racking year, this could be ascribed to the reluctance of the President rather than to any decline in the stature of the Presidency. Whoever the incumbent of our first office may be, its stature in the world grows mightier with every passing year. For some time to come the President of the United States will also be the "President of the West."

*   *   *

Having engaged in this piecemeal analysis of the Presidency, I hasten to fit the pieces back together into a seamless unity. For that, after all, is what the Presidency is, and I hope this exercise in political taxonomy has not obscured the paramount fact that it is a single office filled by a single man. I feel something like a professor of nutritional science who has just ticked off the ingredients of a wonderful stew. The members of the audience may be clear in their minds about the items in the pot, but they have not the slightest notion of what the final product looks like or tastes like or will feel like in their stomachs. The Presidency, too, is a wonderful stew whose unique flavor cannot be accounted for simply by making a list of its ingredients. It is a whole greater than and different from the sum of its parts, an office whose power and prestige are something more than the arithmetical total of all its functions. The President is not one kind of official during one part of the day, another kind during another part—administrator in the morning, legislator at lunch, king in the afternoon, commander before dinner, and politician at odd moments that come his weary way. He is all these things all the time, and any one of his functions feeds upon and into all the others. He is a more exalted Chief of State because he is also Voice of the People, a more forceful Chief Diplomat because he commands the armed forces personally, a more effective Chief Legislator because the political system forces him to be Chief of Party, a more artful Manager of Prosperity because he is Chief Executive.

At the same time, several of these functions are plainly in competition, even in conflict, with one another, and not just in terms of their demands on the President's time and energy. The roles of Voice of the People and Chief of Party cannot both be played with equal fervor, as Mr. Truman proved on several occasions that had best be forgotten, while to act as Chief Diplomat but to think as Chief of Party, as he was apparently persuaded to do in the Palestine crisis of 1948, can throw our foreign relations into indelicate confusion. Mr. Eisenhower certainly had his periods in which, despite perfect health, he reigned too much and thus ruled too little, and one can think of several competent Presidents—Cleveland and Taft and Hoover, to name three out of the last hundred years—who tried much too hard to be faithful Chief Executives.

There is no easy formula for solving this problem inherent in the nature of the office. If the Presidency is a chamber orchestra of ten pieces, all played by the leader, he must learn for himself by hard practice how to blend them together, remembering always that perfect harmony is unattainable, remembering, too, with Whitman, to "resist anything better than my own diversity." The only thing he can know for certain before he begins to make presidential music is that there are several parts, notably those of Chief of Party and Chief Executive, that he must not play too long and loud lest he drown out the others.

The burden of these ten functions is monstrous, and the President carries it as well as he does only because a remarkable array of administrative machinery has been invented to help him in his daily tasks, because

Thousands at his bidding speed,
And post o'er land and ocean without rest.

Yet the activities of this train of experts, the Executive Office and the Cabinet and all their offshoots and auxiliaries, must not draw our final attention away from the man all alone at the head. The Presidency, as I shall try to show in Chapter 4, has been converted into an institution during the past quarter-century, and we can never again talk about it sensibly without accounting for "the men around the President." Yet if it has become a thousand-man job in the budget and in the minds of students of public administration, it remains a one-man job in the Constitution and in the minds of the people—a truth of which we were dramatically reminded when the President fell ill in September 1955. Since it is a one-man job, the one man who holds it can never escape making the final decisions in each of the many areas in which the American people and their Constitution hold him responsible.

Mr. Truman, so it is said, used to keep a sign on his desk that read: "The buck stops here." That, in the end, is the essence of the Presidency. It is the one office in all the land whose occupant is forbidden to pass the buck.

24. Coming Caesars in America? *

AMAURY DE RIENCOURT

[In the following selection, Amaury de Riencourt, far from extolling the virtues of the "modern" Presidency, views this institution as a potential

* Excerpts from The Coming Caesars (New York: Coward-McCann, Inc., 1957). Reprinted by permission of Coward-McCann, Inc. Copyright 1957 by Amaury de Riencourt.

source of tyranny. We see here his major reasons for holding this belief.]

"The English, after having cut off the head of one king, and expelled another from his throne, were still wont to address the successors of those princes only upon their knees. On the other hand, when a republic *falls under the sway of one single man, the demeanor of the sovereign remains as simple and unpretending as if his authority was not yet paramount. When the emperors exercised an unlimited control over the fortunes and the lives of their fellow citizens, it was customary to call them Caesar in conversation; and they were in the habit of supping without formality at their friends' houses."*— Alexis de Tocqueville in his famous book, "Democracy in America" (1835).

OUR Western world, America and Europe, is threatened with Caesarism on a scale unknown since the dawn of the Roman Empire. In order to see this threat in its proper perspective, we have to assess the relationship between America and Europe, and define their historical destinies. It is the contention of this book that expanding democracy leads unintentionally to imperialism and that imperialism inevitably ends in destroying the republican institutions of earlier days; further, that the greater the social equality, the dimmer the prospects of liberty, and that as society becomes more equalitarian, it tends increasingly to concentrate absolute power in the hands of one single man.

Caesarism is not dictatorship, not the result of one man's overriding ambition, not a brutal seizure of power through revolution. It is not based on a specific doctrine or philosophy. It is essentially pragmatic and untheoretical. It is a slow, often century-old, unconscious development that ends in a voluntary surrender of a free people escaping from freedom to one autocratic master.

New concentrations of power during the past fifty years of world wars, revolutions, and crises, have made this threat of Caesarism increasingly evident. Political power in the Western world has become increasingly concentrated in the United States of America, and in the office of the President within America.

The power and prestige of the President have grown with the growth of America and of democracy within America, with the multiplication of economic, political, and military emergencies, with the necessity of ruling what is virtually becoming an American empire—the universal state of a Western civilization at bay.

Caesarism is therefore the logical outcome of a double current very much in evidence today: the growth of a world empire that cannot be ruled by republican institutions, and the gradual extension of mass democracy, which ends in the destruction of freedom and in the concentration of supreme power in the hands of one man. This is the ominous prospect facing the Western world on the second half of the twentieth century. But just as Caesarism could arise only in Classical Rome and not in Greece, it will, if left free to develop unchecked, arise in modern America and not in Europe.

It is in Washington and not in London, Paris, or Berlin that the Caesars of the future will arise. It will not be the result of conspiracy, revolution, or personal ambition. It will be the end result of an instinctive evolution in which we are all taking part like somnambulists.

The evidence is all around us today, but to see it in its full magnitude we must step back into history and look at the present from a distance. We shall then have a clear perspective of the road on which we have been traveling for centuries—and a glimpse of the road that lies ahead. We shall then notice that, instead of forever inclining toward the republican left, we are in fact swinging toward the autocratic right and that it is our leftist leaders who, whenever they are in power, are unwittingly taking us in this direction. In fact, they have quite unconsciously been driving us around in a century-wide circle, back to the point from which our ancestors started when they revolted in the name of liberty against the tyranny of absolute monarchs.

Familiarity breeds contempt, dulls perception and understanding. What is familiar has to become unfamiliar and strange before we can truly grasp its full meaning.

We must see in the President of the United States not merely the Chief Executive of one of the Western democracies, but one already endowed with powers of truly Caesarian magnitude.

Today, one man is directly in command, either as peacetime President or wartime Commander in Chief, of more than half the globe's economic and technical power. Along the militarized borders of the Western world he is in full control, as Augustus and the Roman emperors after him were in full control of the *limes* [frontiers].

As an autonomous Executive who is constitutionally free from parliamentary interference, he is all at once Chief of State and head of government in control of all cabinet appointments as well as Commander in Chief of the most powerful armed forces in the world. He is the only statesman in the Western world who can make major decisions alone in an emergency. He is in control of a *de facto* empire into which the scattered fragments of the dissolving British Commonwealth are gradually being merged.

Everywhere on the European continent, in the Western Hemisphere, and in the Far East, he can make the weight of his incalculable power felt with immediate and crushing speed.

Trend to "One-Man Leadership"

Yet, all this is nothing but the reflection of an underlying reality. The prime element in this situation is neither political nor strategic—it is essentially psychological. It is the growing "father complex" that is increasingly evident in America, the willingness to follow in any emergency, economic or military, the leadership of one man. It is the growing distrust of parliaments, congresses, and all other representative assemblies, the growing impatience of Western public opinion at their irresponsibility, lack of foresight, sluggishness, indecisiveness.

This distrust and impatience is evident in America as in Europe. Further, it is the impulsive emotionalism of American public opinion, which swings widely from apathetic isolationism to dynamic internationalism, lacks continuity in its global views, stumbles from one emergency into another, and mistakes temporary lulls for the long-expected millennium. Such was Rome's public opinion in the first century B.C. Each new crisis calls for a strong man and there are always strong men present who are willing to shoulder responsibilities shirked by timid legislatures.

When, at the beginning of 1955, for instance, President Eisenhower went to Congress and requested emergency powers to deal with Formosa's offshore islands, how many Congressmen recoiled in fear and pointed out to him that he already had those powers, implying in effect that they wanted no part of this terrifying responsibility?

Even with the utmost good will, a President who sincerely attempts to build up the sense of responsibility of the legislature cannot halt a secular trend. And this development suits public opinion perfectly well. The public wants to personalize issues and responsibilities and instinctively looks down upon the collective anonymity of assemblies.

Those who doubt that today an American President might be elected for life should remember that no constitutional amendment, such as was voted after World War II, can stand in the way of public opinion if it truly wishes to elect a Caesar for life. In fact, the amendment limiting presidential terms of office is itself proof that many in America saw in Franklin Roosevelt the first pre-Caesarian who was, as it turned out, virtually elected for life.

The purpose of this book is to demonstrate that such concentration of power is no accident due to unexpected emergencies, but the natural outcome of an historical evolution. Those who believe that swift revolutions or accidents can alter the course of history should keep in mind the Roman saying *Historia non facit saltum,* history makes no leaps. What happens today germinated generations ago. Yesterday's seeds are today's blossoms. We must recognize exactly what kind of seeds we are sowing today if we want to know what tomorrow's blossoms are going to be.

*   *   *

So far, all Civilizations have chosen the easy solution of Caesarism. But Caesarism itself, if allowed to develop unchecked, implies organic death for the society that gives itself up to it out of fear of freedom. And whereas in the past a new Culture has always sprung from the ruins of an antecedent Civilization and blossomed forth, the wreck of our own Western Civilization might well mean absolute death for the entire human race.

What was only an episodic drama in the past might be final tragedy tomorrow. Modern man's technological power will no longer allow him to make those grievous mistakes that past Civilizations were free to indulge in—nor can he ignore the lessons of a past that other Civilizations did not possess. Man's technical knowledge makes it possible for him to build heaven on earth or destroy his planet, and his historical knowledge makes it possible, for the first time, to avoid those deadly shoals on which every other Civilization has destroyed itself.

*   *   *

How Jackson Used the Veto

Andrew Jackson—"King Andrew" to his enemies—knew exactly where he stood. He told the Senate that the President alone is "the direct representative of the people, and responsible to them,"

the Senate itself being "a body not directly amenable to the people."

Until then, in forty years of American political life, only nine bills had been vetoed by the Executive. Jackson alone vetoed twelve—and thus started the steady rise of executive pressure on the legislative branch, the transformation of the negative veto into a positive force at the Executive's disposal, until the days when Franklin Roosevelt would veto 631 acts of Congress. The Senate protested vehemently and Henry Clay could rightly point out:

"Really and in practice, the veto power drew after it the power of initiating laws, and in its effects must ultimately amount to conferring on the executive the entire legislative power of the government. With the power to initiate and the power to consummate legislation, to give vitality and vigor to every law, or to strike it dead at his pleasure, the President must ultimately become the ruler of the nation."

And Clay added: "The government will have been transformed into an elective monarchy."

The Senate mourned its diminished stature but the House lost even more power and prestige. The democratic revolution had considerably damaged the practice of representative government, but it was the inevitable counterpart of the changing social and psychological landscape.

*   *   *

The cult of Napoleon was widespread in America and the American thirst for hero worship was already marked in those days. Napoleonism somehow affected American public opinion to such an extent that an early portrait of Jackson, the victorious liberator of New Orleans, pictured him crowned with Napoleon's spit curls rather than his own bushy hair.

There is no doubt that Napoleonism had a real influence in determining the political posture of strong popular leaders in America as in Europe, as Alexander the Great's impact affected not only Hellenistic statesmen but even distant Roman leaders, all the way from the censor Appius Claudius to the democratic leader and conquering general Gaius Flaminius—and the whole political history of the transition from Culture's twilight to Civilization's dawn lies in the transition from romantic Napoleonism to realistic Caesarism.

But Alexis de Tocqueville, who was a contemporary observer, and probably the most penetrating of all, remarked: "It has been imagined that General Jackson is bent on establishing a dictatorship in America, introducing a military spirit, and giving a degree of influence to the central authority that cannot but be dangerous to provincial liberty."

Then de Tocqueville added those ominous words: "But in America the time for similar undertakings and the age for men of this kind, has not yet come."

*   *   *

The Rise of "Big Business"

The Jacksonian revolution consolidated the simultaneous rise of democracy and tribunician-presidential power. Its democratic element was partly abortive, in the sense that it was merely a prelude to the rule of Big Business. It had destroyed the rule of the old gentry, only to let it fall later into the hands of a new and exclusively financial plutocracy. Several generations would have to go by before there was democratic progress in the field of economics.

But Andrew Jackson left a legacy: the notion of a democratic, popular, and powerful Executive who could, if he wanted to, dominate Big Business and overpower economic oligarchy and financial privilege. In his days, the issue was not yet clear cut. The gentry was not wholly done with, Business was still a fledgling and the South was still dominated by its aristocracy. Those obstacles had to be swept away by the Civil War before the naked power of

Big Business came into its own—as it did in Rome after the democratic Hortensian Law and the Second Punic War. But from now on, popular attention focused on the new Presidency as the champion of democracy and social equality.

From 1840 onward, the vast increase in presidential power and prestige was curbed by the only device left at the disposal of oligarchies and vested interests: the election of obscure men who could be manipulated by the political machines. It took wars and economic depressions to break down the systematic endeavor of the politicians to put the lid on the tribune of the people. In normal circumstances, there was no great need for Executive initiative and the isolated United States could afford a minimum of centralization.

But in times of crisis, with the election of military heroes or great personalities, there were next to no limits to the overriding power of the Executive. As Lincoln's Secretary of State said to a British correspondent: "We elect a king for four years, and give him absolute powers within certain limits, which after all he can interpret for himself."

The splendor of Rome was erected on the backs of subjugated people. As long as there remained spoils to be had in the Classical world, Roman business leaders grabbed them—through the ruthless destruction of such commercial rivals as Carthage and Corinth, outrageous taxation and confiscation in the provinces and protectorates. Money and business dominated Rome, demoralized the remains of the aristocracy, corrupted the masses, and virtually destroyed the freeholding farmers.

The same unchallenged domination of money and business was exercised in America between the Civil War and the New Deal. New York's Wall Street erected its gigantic buildings on the backs of southern and western farming populations as well as on those of immigrants and industrial workers.

All this started while the South remained a conquered province at the mercy of Washington and the West was still an expanding territory ruled directly or strongly influenced by the federal government. Big Business could do as it pleased. It was the real winner of the Civil War.

General Grant's election to the White House proved an important point: professional soldiers are not the stuff that Caesars are made of.

There were no professional generals in the Classical world. Caesar himself was a remarkably astute politician and statesman, a businessman and a leader of the democratic party, rather than a conquering general. Neither Washington nor Jackson had been professional soldiers in the full sense of the term. The first was a remarkable statesman, the second an unparalleled leader of men. Both had political flair. Grant had nothing of the kind.

Tactless, blunt, autocratic when he had no cause to be, without psychological insight, Grant was easily maneuvered by the triumphant legislative branch. Unable to rule, Grant virtually handed his presidential prerogatives to a Congress that had become the chaotic battleground of pressure groups and special interests.

* * *

After Slaves Were Freed—

The disaster of Reconstruction was plainly the result of Congressional supremacy. The Executive had abdicated and, once more, Congress irrefutably proved that it was totally unable to frame an intelligent policy and carry it out consistently. Nowhere in the world was emancipation from slavery followed by such misery for the former slaves and such hatred on the part of the former owners. Slavery had been gradually abolished in the West Indies and elsewhere in a just, orderly manner, in striking contrast to the wreckage of the American South at a time of fabulous prosperity and dynamic economic development all over the world.

* * *

Theodore Roosevelt closed the optimistic, dynamic era of American growth with a great flourish. The power of the Executive had increased immeasurably and all eras of transition had been managed by strong Presidents —Jackson's establishment of the rising democracy, his institution of tribunician power in the White House and decent burial of the former ruling gentry; Lincoln's preservation and consolidation of the Union; Theodore Roosevelt's partial establishment of administrative ascendancy over Big Business.

Weak Presidents had permitted the disastrous drift toward the Civil War. Lincoln's towering strength through the war years was followed by renewed presidential weakness and the tragedy of Reconstruction. Historical evidence now pointed to the inevitable trend toward presidential Caesarism as being the natural counterpart of the trend toward democratic equality.

Writing at the turn of the century, James Bryce remarked: "The tendency everywhere in America to concentrate power and responsibility in one man is unmistakable."

And this in a time of peace and world prosperity. Nothing more would be needed than the great era of wars and revolutions and national emergencies of the twentieth century to bring this long-term trend to its natural conclusion. Rome was saved time and time again by her temporary constitutional dictators as America had been by her strong Presidents—until Caesars came along to establish their personal rule on a permanent footing.

* * *

1932: "Major Turning Point"

The election of Franklin Roosevelt in 1932 was a major turning point in the history of America, and indirectly of the world. America elected a new tribune of the people, a tribune who was no longer the captive of business and vested interests but one who felt responsible to the entire nation. He was a Democrat but also the champion of a revolt that had started forty years before under the Populists' leadership and had often cut across party lines.

Conscious of this national rather than merely partisan backing, Franklin Roosevelt was determined to establish a semidictatorial rule, a personal rule, such as none of his strong predecessors would have dared contemplate in their wildest dreams. He had no wish to carry out a revolution and explained quite clearly that no such revolution was necessary: "Our Constitution is so simple and practical that it is possible always to meet extraordinary needs by changes in emphasis and arrangement without loss of essential form. . . ."

During the four months between Roosevelt's election and his inauguration, Hoover's policy-making was utterly paralyzed and the Depression deepened to the extent of becoming a calamity. Respect for constitutional forms resulted in a grinding economic breakdown and illustrated the weakness of an outgoing President who could not come to terms with his successor.

Years before, writing in a more peaceful age, James Bryce reminded his readers of a Classical parallel. Choosing one example among many, he explained that in an emergency the Greeks were quite willing to disregard constitutional forms. And he concluded: "This effort . . . to escape from the consequence of the system could not have occurred in governments like those of Rome, England or the United States, where the 'reign of law' is far stricter than it was in the Greek Republics"—or for that matter than it was in any European country.

Respect for law and Constitution deepened the economic disaster in which America was plunged during the winter of 1932-33. The people wanted an immediate change of rulers but constitutional law stood in the way and it was respected. The tragedy was that there could be no meeting ground between the President and the President-elect, no agreement of any sort. They did not speak the same language and the President-elect would not assume the responsibility of underwriting his predecessor's fumbling decisions.

* * *

Throughout the first year of his rule, Roosevelt concentrated an increasing amount of power in his hands, overriding the reluctance of a disgruntled Congress. Administrative agencies assumed a degree of power and independence that left the legislative branch with very little influence on the dizzy course of events. Final decisions rested with a President who handled his huge power with increasing assurance as time went on. Roosevelt was not carrying out a constitutional revolution, as his enemies asserted, but was merely leading America back to the one and only path along which her history had been proceeding: the path toward growing executive power. It was not a fresh start but the fulfillment of a profound trend whose origin lay deep in the past.

All those who deplored the trend, who lamented the waning of the former "rugged individualism," were belated romanticists who refused to move with the times. The spirit of the Roman *panem et circenses* [bread and circuses] was slowly pervading the atmosphere, without destroying the willingness to work but weakening the former self-reliance of pioneering days.

The mainstay of American freedom —freedom *from* authority—began to give way now that a large majority of the people were willing to barter freedom for security.

* * *

"Fireside Chats": "Mass Hypnotism"

Much has been and will be written about Franklin Roosevelt's exceedingly complex character, his courage and yet his evasiveness, his idealism and his acute realism. Mommsen's succinct summing up of Julius Caesar's character—"the most supple master of intrigue"—is perhaps the most fitting description of Roosevelt. What Roosevelt had to a supreme degree was a charismatic charm that poured out naturally, the irresistible charm of a born leader of men. As soon as he was in office he communicated with the American people through his "fireside chats," a remarkable exercise in mass hypnotism. The fact that he came, in time, to have the major part of the press against him did not make a dent in his popular appeal.

A new device, the radio, had prevailed over the older printed word; and when his magnetic voice purred its way into the ears of millions of his compatriots, he managed to cast an unbreakable spell on America. Logical argumentation could no longer prevail, as it had in the days of the Founding Fathers. Political speeches had already long ago become what rhetoric and diatribe had become in the Classical world when they displaced eloquence: they were used for effect, not for content. They conjured emotions but did not appeal to the intellect; and at this game, Franklin Roosevelt was unrivaled.

The greatest reward of this projection of one man's warm personality on the national consciousness was a remarkable recrudescence of confidence which economic circumstances did not really warrant—and many political opponents were quick to point out the numerous flaws in the Administration's policy. But against Roosevelt's personality, conservatives were as powerless as radical demagogues like Huey Long.

The Caesarian flavor of this highly personal rule was partly masked from his contemporaries by the easygoing familiarity of the man. As a New Dealer remarked: "The New Deal is a laughing revolution. It is purging our institutions in the fires of mockery,

and it is led by a group of men who possess two supreme qualifications for the task: common sense and a sense of humor."

Certainly this leadership was closer to that of popular pre-Caesarian Rome than it was to the Wagnerian tyranny of Germany's Naziism with its terrifying *Götterdämmerung* atmosphere. But its humane and humorous aspect was only a mask, a psychological compensation for the almost absolute power behind it. It was not issued of a brutal revolution as was the fashion in the unstable worlds of the Hellenes and the Europeans; it was the actualization of an old trend and those who lived through it and trembled for the safety of their republican institutions could always attempt to comfort themselves by pointing out its familiar, even traditional features. But the lengthening shadow of growing Caesarism was unmistakably there.

Another source of Roosevelt's power was in his knowledge of how to handle the political world, Congress especially. He was a consummate politician whose leadership within his party could no longer be challenged, who used patronage with considerable effectiveness. Skill in handling Congress and full use of his veto power gave him, in fact, almost unlimited influence on lawmaking, thanks to the fact that he always had the initiative. It was all strictly constitutional and yet the separation of powers so fondly cherished by the Founding Fathers was no more than a ghost by then.

* * *

How Political Machines Work

The rise of democratic political power in Rome took place, as it did in America, through the big political machines. The corrupt rule of ring-and-bossdom in an elective democracy is almost inevitable. Franklin Roosevelt's strength lay in his shrewd manipulation of the big city Democratic machines, not in the national Democratic party as such. National parties, agglomerations of discordant local interests without specific doctrine and philosophy, were and are increasingly dominated by the "indispensable man."

Vitality resides in the local organizations, not in their federal structure. Roosevelt could fight relentlessly against Huey Long's machine in Louisiana and James Curley's machine in Massachusetts. But he could only do so successfully by depending on a majority of the other machines. His alliance with Edward Flynn, boss of the Bronx, was comparable to Caesar's reliance on Clodius' machine against Milo's "Tammany Hall." Clodius' machine was primarily a vote-buying organization that distributed free wheat to its clientele, standing on a platform advocating the emancipation of slaves and freedom for Roman labor to organize itself.

But centralization is greater in America than it was in Rome, in a sense at least. Political power is more concentrated in the one elected tribune instead of being parceled out among many officials of equal rank as was the case in Rome. So it was that Roosevelt was able to dominate most local machines by making the W.P.A. itself into a gigantic, nation-wide super-machine with extensive political ramifications. The vote-buying that characterizes local machines was applied on a federal scale and paid rich dividends to the Roosevelt Administration.

From now on, this federal dwarfing of such petty machines as Tammany Hall became a prime factor in American politics. A great deal of the political credit still granted to local organizations depends on their ability to obtain funds from the federal treasury rather than on their own local resources.

*   *   *

As in America, each new economic depression and financial breakdown in Rome fostered inevitably the growth of state control—all the way from the collapse of Asiatic stocks in 86 B.C. with the freezing of credit, devaluation, and

partial moratorium, to the panic of 63 B.C. with its speculation, flight of gold, and eventual embargo on all gold exports, as well as inflation and cheap credit, to the next panic of 49 B.C. Economic emergencies called for practical and concrete measures, not theoretical plans and ambitious schemes such as appealed to the more intellectual Greeks.

Roman Big Business was curbed under the impact of widening New and Fair Deals as American Big Business was curbed by Franklin Roosevelt and succeeding Democratic administrations. But in neither case were they destroyed as by a revolution. They fell under the domination of Big Government but in the end always managtd to come to terms with it.

In both cases, it was evolution rather than revolution. Roman Big Business still retained its over-all supremacy in the Classical world, with its vast financial resources and know-how, its remarkable organization, the destruction of its last Carthaginian and Corinthian rivals, and the tacit alliance of all the foreign business communities left in the Mediterranean world. The north side of Rome's Forum had become the Classical world's "Wall Street," with its tremendous accumulation of banks, stock exchanges, brokerage houses, and innumerable offies of financial corporations and joint-stock companies.

Rome had become, like London and New York, the clearinghouse and banking center of the civilized world. No Roman New Deal could or wished to alter that fact; and it would be inconceivable that any future administration in Washington would want to cripple America's preponderant position in the world of business and finance.

Under Franklin Roosevelt's New Deal, America took a decisive step toward Caesarism. The remarkable feature of this subtle evolution was that it could take place constitutionally, without any illegal move, simply by stretching the extremely pliable fabric of America's political institutions. Romans had a far greater distrust of concentrated power than the Americans and they had so fragmented political authority that any man who aspired to full executive power had to hold, simultaneously and unconstitutionally, the official positions of Consul, Proconsul, Tribune, Quaestor, Censor and Pontifex Maximus—never forgetting that each of those offices, save the last, was split between several incumbents.

"Hostility of the Supreme Court"

In America, the existence of the Presidency makes the transition far easier and wholly constitutional. Where constitutional obstacles appear insurmountable—the hostility of the Supreme Court, mostly—intimidation can usually be just as effective if it is backed by public opinion. Roosevelt was quick to point this out when he insisted in the autumn of 1937 that the Supreme Court had been "forced" into line after his threatening message in February of the same year.

It is essential to keep in mind that all this is the result of profound historical trends, not of any one man's dictatorial ambitions. Circumstances, not conscious desires, create Caesarism. In the case of America, it is clear that psychological reasons favor this historical evolution. Americans are hero worshipers to a far greater extent than any European people. Concrete-minded and repelled by the abstract, they always tend to personalize issues, and in every walk of life they look up to the "boss." They are led by insensible degrees to foster a Caesarism that historical evolution favors anyway.

A friend of Roosevelt's could write with great perception: "For one who knows the President it is impossible to believe that he is aiming at a future dictatorship; but it is also impossible not to recognize the packing of the Supreme Court as exactly what a dictator would adopt as his first step. The President may not know where he is

going, but he is on his way." [Quoted by E. E. Robinson in his book, "The Roosevelt Leadership."]

European-type dictatorship, like Greek tyranny, is usually the result of brutal revolutions, Caesarism the result of a long secular trend. One is temporary and often short lived, the other as lasting as the secular trend that fosters it. Caesarism is the natural counterpart of the leveling process of democratic equality. We can well trust Franklin Roosevelt's absolute sincerity when he disclaimed any intention of setting up a dictatorship in the United States. The great Roman Tribunes who hacked out the path toward Caesarism had no greater desire to imitate the tyrants of Greek city-states or the Hellenistic autocrats, all of whom had been destroyed or overpowered by the Roman Republic. It was historical destiny that made them the unconscious precursors of the coming Caesars—internal circumstances, to a certain extent, but even more the compelling nature of foreign involvements.

*   *   *

War: Aid to President's Powers

Historical evidence shows that each new war adds to the already tremendous powers of a President, who is simultaneously Chief of State, Prime Minister in charge of all the Executive departments, and Commander in Chief of the armed forces. When Franklin Roosevelt talked about "his" ambassador, referring to an American envoy abroad, he was only stating, over the loud protests of his advisers as well as his Republican opponents, what was a plain fact: one man was already largely in control of the world's greatest power.

*   *   *

What was ominous in this situation was not so much Roosevelt's full use of powers that were of truly Caesarian magnitude. It was the American people's full acceptance of this concentration of immense powers in the hands of one man and their firm belief that it should remain there in spite of traditions against third, fourth, or more terms.

An incident of the 1940 campaign epitomized this popular feeling: "In the Cleveland speech, he made his first and last reference to the third term issue. It was a glancing reference and produced a surprising reaction from the crowd. Roosevelt said that, when the next four years are over 'there will be another President'—at which point the crowd started to shout 'No! No!' Thinking remarkably quickly, Roosevelt thrust his mouth close to the microphone and went on talking so that the shouts which suggested that he might be elected permanently should not be heard over the radio." [Robert E. Sherwood in his book, "Roosevelt and Hopkins."]

The first ghostly contours of Caesarism were appearing and, as always, welling up from the people themselves.

* * *

America was finally propelled into the war by the attack on Pearl Harbor. For all those who search for an understanding of the broad issue of the war, the controversy over the responsibilities for this disaster is unimportant. No one knows exactly what was in Roosevelt's mind, no one knows to what extent he could foresee what was going to happen. What is certain is that he knew by then that American participation in the war had become inevitable—and that, whether he did use it as such or not, he *had* the power to precipitate America into the war by using the fleet in Hawaii as a decoy.

The mere fact that he *could* do it, that he alone could modify American policy in the Far East so as to stand across the path of Japanese imperialism and coordinate all the secret information indicating the imminence of an attack, is enough to prove that he had the power to shape decisively the future of America, and of the world in the process. How he actually used this tremendous power in those obscure days is an academic matter for historians to debate.

* * *

The increasing stature of President Roosevelt as a world leader dimmed the authority of Congress. The recurrent pattern of the President-Congress relationship is suggested by the following incident, as described by Robert E. Sherwood. In 1942, the "President had the power to stabilize prices and wages by Executive order without reference to Congress and some of us believed that he should do just that immediately and not run the risk of hostile action or no action at all on Capitol Hill. There were unquestionably many Congressmen who fervently hoped that he would do it this way and thereby absolve them from all responsibility for decision on such a controversial issue. It was an ironic fact that many of the Congressmen who were loudest in accusing Roosevelt of dictatorial ambitions were the most anxious to have him act like a dictator on all measures which might be unpopular with the people but obviously valuable for the winning of the war."

This fear of responsibility is perennial in all democratic assemblies, and nothing contributes more to the rise of Caesarism than this factual abdication masked by verbal denunciations. It was quite clear that Congress was almost voluntarily relegating itself to an entirely subordinate position since it could not control policy-making and could only envision the fluid situation as it would congeal years later.

With absolute power at home, the President could speak with full authority to other statesmen and extend his leadership to the entire world controlled by the United Nations.

* * *

"Roosevelt's Views Prevailed"

All through the war, this gradual transfer of global power and responsibilities from London to Washington went on ceaselessly, discreetly but irreversibly. It was not always welcome in Washington but Roosevelt's views and will always prevailed. It was even less welcome in London where Churchill was unwilling to accept the dramatic metamorphosis of Britain into a second-rate power, virtually shorn of her worldwide empire.

When Roosevelt decided after the Yalta Conference to go to the Middle East and interview personally the various Oriental potentates, Churchill was "greatly disturbed." The Middle East had long been a British preserve, with a few crumbs left over for the French. Roosevelt's conferences with the tarbooshed King of Egypt, the colorful ruler of Saudi Arabia, and the Ethiopian Emperor, Haile Selassie, could and should have reminded readers of history of similar meetings between the elected representatives of Rome and such old-fashioned Oriental potentates as Massinissa, King of Numidia, or the Ptolemies of Egypt, or any of the numerous Asiatic monarchs who were already if unofficially clients and protégés of the all-powerful Roman Republic. Those were interviews between the pre-Caesarian officials of the globe's most powerful nation and the autocratic relics of a colorful past that was slowly dying out of the modern world.

The Wartime Conferences

Each one of the major international conferences—Casablanca, Washington, Quebec, Moscow, Cairo, Teheran—was dominated by Franklin Roosevelt or Secretary of State Cordell Hull. Roosevelt was the initial sponsor of the "unconditional surrender" doctrine that backfired so dramatically after the war. It was Cato's implacable *"Ceterum censeo delendum esse Carthaginem"* ["Besides, I think that Carthage must be destroyed"] all over again, the "total wars" and total destruction that saw the razing of Carthage and Corinth, saturation bombing, the Morgenthau Plan,

and other extreme measures of the kind, up to and including the atomic bomb.

But it was the President's own policy, not that of Congress or even of his British allies. Of course, he sensed the mood of an emotional and aroused public opinion in a state of exasperation, prepared to countenance any extreme measure against cruel foes. Roosevelt was powerful to the extent that he could interpret public feelings and the storm of protest raised by his handling of the Darlan issue in French North Africa was a reminder that some of these sharp feelings could not be brushed aside for the sake of wise expediency.

Yet, as Judge Samuel Rosenman stated, in all these conferences, "it was he [Roosevelt] who made the final decisions; and it was his leadership which dominated the major decisions which involved international diplomacy or politics." And the fact that early in 1943, the current of war began to flow in a direction that was favorable to the United Nations could only reinforce the authority of the President, for whom Churchill's heroic and lonely battle in 1940 and 1941 seemed to have become merely a holding operation.

Just as in Roosevelt's exceptional power and authority there was a premonition of the Caesarism to come, there was in his conceptions of world organization after the war a faint outline of the global "Roman" order to come. As he saw it, the United Nations Organization would replace the former precarious balance of power whose breakdown had finally shattered the modern "Hellenistic" order. His idealistic views prompted him time and again to advocate the voluntary dissolution of all colonial empires, with some form of international trusteeship to take over in case of need.

Robert E. Sherwood states in his study on Harry Hopkins that Roosevelt "believed in a system of strategic bases—he gave as examples Dakar, the tip of Tunisia and Formosa—which would be under United Nations control." He then goes on to state that Roosevelt also believed "that France and other occupied countries in Europe should not have to bear the economic and physical burden of rearmament after the war—that the burden of ensuing postwar security should be borne by the nations that were of necessity already armed for combat purposes." These, of course, were the English-speaking world and Russia.

Time and again, throughout the war, Roosevelt discussed the organization of the world of the future and always came back to the obvious solution for difficult problems: a United Nations trusteeship. For instance, strong in his belief that Serbs and Croats could never live together in one composite state like Yugoslavia, he advocated placing Croatia under such international trusteeship.

All this was very well. But if the United Nations Organization was to police the world, who would police the United Nations? Then and there, a new problem was born. As usual, those who establish enduring institutions have only a dim perception of the true historical implications of their own doings. Roosevelt, in his idealistic mood, thought that he was laying the basis of world peace through voluntary cooperation of the victorious powers. He was, in fact, laying the basis of a very different world, of a new "Roman" order revolving around a strong American leadership. What was said of him in connection with the Supreme Court "packing" scheme could be repeated now in connection with the establishment of the United Nations: he "may not know where he is going, but he is on his way."

*   *   *

An American historian [E. E. Robinson], criticizing Franklin Roosevelt's personal conferences, his by-passing of representatives of his own administration, his committing the United States beyond possibilities of recall by Congress, stated that "the concentration of power of the enemy was thereby matched, but the game was played according to the enemy's rules."

This situation which also weighed heavily on the Roman statesmen of the first century B.C. is the contagious element that often tends to make adversaries or chance partners increasingly alike. The impulse to imitate the opponent and duplicate his method comes from the fact that enemies have to fight it out on a common ground and with similar weapons. Not only did the American leaders have to match the Nazi concentration of power but, thrown in temporary intimacy with the Russians during the war, they had to listen to Russian sermons on the unchallengeable power of dictatorial machines and take advice as to how to lead the American people.

Americans and "Obedience"

At the Yalta Conference, Andrei Vishinsky, after having claimed that small nations should never be allowed to pass judgment on the behavior of big powers, went on to state categorically that "the American people should learn to obey their leaders."

Such remarks, repeated generation after generation, can never fail to alter the psychological climate and induce the democratic leaders to assume gradually the trappings of Caesarism. Sooner or later, the political coloring of the East begins to come off on the West. The transition from Sulla to Caesar and from Caesar to the absolutism of Vespasian was partly the result of the growing orientalization of Rome and the decline in prestige of elective institutions. In the modern instance, it is clear that "democrat" Roosevelt was not half as much repelled by Stalin's views on strong executive power and absolute supremacy of the great superpowers as "conservative" Churchill was.

The America that emerged from the war was very different from the one that had entered it. The nation moved from uncompromising isolationism to world-wide commitments requiring a large military establishment. Presidential power had experienced renewed growth, a growth now bolstered by full control over nuclear power. "In truth, the office of the President had been altered beyond recognition as Mr. Roosevelt exercised the powers of a dictator," claimed an American historian [E. E. Robinson] a few years later.

But it was not so much Roosevelt's own doing as that of profound and uncontrollable historical forces. The President was no more responsible for the unquestionable decline in self-reliance and autonomy of the average individual, or for the growth of a huge bureaucracy and the Welfare State, than any one man was responsible for the gradual transformation of Rome between the Gracchi and Caesar. Opponents and partisans of Franklin Roosevelt could have been reconciled if they had been willing to see the profound changes in the light of historical necessity rather than as the whimsicalities of one or several individual men.

The U.S. After World War II

The great power of postwar America was due in part to the vast increase in industrial productivity brought about by the war effort, partly to the fact that America was the only great nation untouched by the military devastations that had ravaged France, Britain, Germany, Italy, Central and Eastern Europe, Russia, China, and Japan. The cost in American lives was a fraction of what it had been in Germany or Russia. This tremendous power added to the total collapse of Europe's "Hellenistic" order, the rise of a gigantic Eurasian Marxist empire, and the full-scale revolt of the Orient creates the contemporary setting for the New Roman Age upon which we are entering in the second half of our century.

*　　*　　*

Caesars are preceded by men of vision who instinctively understand the re-

quirements of a new age. A world ruled or influenced by the Roman Senate remained in chaos because Rome did not want to assume responsibilities, and because Rome's executive power was weak.

It took Lucullus' campaigns against Mithridates' revolutionary power to bring the truth home to Roman statesmen. And it was Lucullus who was the first to understand that to put an end to the chaos, Rome had to assume burdens and responsibilities, who also saw that Rome's foreign policy was paralyzed by irrational fears of her inflated enemies, exaggerated reliance on the nonexistent strength of allies, slackness and lack of continuity, misinformation about the real strength alike of friend and foe. Rome had always preferred diplomacy to war, had refused to lay down long-term policies, and had always preferred to solve problems in a pragmatic and piecemeal way that took only the present and not the future into account.

Lucullus had to prove to Rome that the Near East had the shadow but not the substance of power, that a strong policy would always be respected and lead to lasting peace if it was farsighted and generous. Pompey and Caesar were, in this respect, nothing more than his disciples. In a sense, Lucullus was to Rome what Douglas MacArthur was to America—the imperious but capable conqueror who shows the path to a new type of generous imperialism, more conscious of its duties and responsibilities than its prerogatives. "MacArthur warned against exerting American influence 'in an imperialistic manner, or for the sole purpose of commercial advantage'; our influence and our strength, he insisted, must be expressed 'in terms of essential liberalism' if we are to retain the friendship of the Asian peoples." [A. M. Schlesinger, Jr., and R. Rovere in their book, "The General and the President."]

This is no more and no less than the true Caesarian policy in the Classical world, from Lucullus to Julius Caesar himself. "Unlike the merely brisk and efficient commanders of the Lucius Clay type, MacArthur felt that he was performing not one more army assignment but an exalted historical mission. He communicated his sense of high historical significance to the Japanese, swept them up in the great drama and mystery of reconstruction, and gave them a feeling of spiritual purpose in a moment of unsurpassed national disaster." [Schlesinger and Rovere].

Lucullus and MacArthur were both political conservatives who were able to rise above the limitations of their own traditions and put a brake on unchecked capitalism. Lucullus' severe repression of Roman capitalists, taxfarmers, bankers, and usurers was the counterpart of MacArthur's distinctly "New Deal" reconstruction of postwar Japan. MacArthur himself claimed that it was "extraordinarily successful. I don't think that since the Gracchi effort at land reform in the days of the Roman Empire there has been anything quite as successful of that nature."

And yet, both Lucullus and MacArthur were unable to become true Caesarian figures, in spite of their ambitions, because they lacked the popularity with their troops and the democratic masses at home that goes with Caesarian genius. Both were disliked by their men because of their inflexibility and both forfeited to others brilliant political carers.

When MacArthur Was Recalled—

Lucullus' recall in 67 B.C. in semidisgrace and MacArthur in 1951 were comparable events. Lucullus was on the verge of dealing a death blow to Mithridates' revolutionary power when the Senate deprived him of his command and jeopardized Rome's position in the East for generations afterward. President Truman's recall of MacArthur implied America's tacit acceptance of a new and powerful Red empire in the Far East, as well as her reluctance to reclaim her European

heritage in China by forcible means, just as Rome forsook her Hellenistic heritage beyond the Euphrates.

* * *

The new Roman Age, with its defensive frontiers girdling the globe, is the *reality* of our times. The United Nations is the precarious materialization of the idealistic *dream* woven during World War II—a more sophisticated dream than the rather brutal and simple dream of the Classical world— an attempt to reconqued the Communist East peacefully and ideologically.

* * *

The legitimacy of all institutions rests on one factor: *time.* Those that endure over a long period of time are legitimate. Those that happen to seem logical at the immediate moment are not necessarily legitimate. This is the cardinal difference between Caesarism and tyrannies or dictatorships. Legitimacy involves a slow build-up over a period of generations, not a sudden seizure of power. Aristotle had already observed, from Greek experience, that tyrannies are short-lived. Not so Caesarism, which is a slow, organic growth within a society tending toward democratic equality.

Western society today, and especially American society, presents the spectacle of an immense multitude of equal and similar men and women who think alike, work alike, and enjoy the same standardized pleasures. The more uniform the level, the less the inequality and greater the compact emotional power of the multitude of like-minded men. But this power has to be concentrated and personalized by one man who acts as its articulate spokesman. Who can this man be, today, except the incumbent of the most powerful office in the most powerful state in the world—the President of the United States?

The United States Congress has repeatedly expressed its fear, especially since the New Deal and World War

II, that the Constitution and the separation of powers is being steadily undermined—and so it is. Under present conditions, democratic equality ends inevitably in Caesarism. No system of checks and balances can hold out against this profound evolution, a psychological alteration that by-passes specific institutions. The thirst for equality and distrust of any form of hierarchy have even weakened Congress itself through its seniority rule. Dislike for aristocratic distinctions eventually ends by eliminating that most indispensable of all elites—the aristocracy of talent. This is the elite that in Britain, substituting for the former aristocracy of birth and wealth, makes the parliamentary system workable.

Limitations of Congress

Since most of the work of the U.S. Congress is done in committees, there is little occasion for great debates on the floor of either House or Senate comparable with the dramatic debates of European parliaments. The need of Americans to personalize and dramatize all issues can be satisfied only by concentrating attention on the President—thereby giving him increasing power. Because he can now communicate over the head of Congress with the nation, he can always dominate legislative proceedings. He can dramatize, Congress cannot—or if it does, as in the case of Senator Joseph McCarthy, it is largely because of presidential failure or unwillingness to use the immense potentialities vested in the White House.

Long ago, James Bryce discounted the usual fears of Americans and Europeans who thought that some ambitious President might attempt to seize absolute power through a brutal *coup d'etat*. But he added this warning: "If there be any danger, it would seem to lie in another direction.

"The larger a community becomes, the less does it seem to respect an assembly, the more it is attracted by an individual man."

The reason for this is plain: the larger the masses, the more they display *feminine* traits by emphasizing emotional reactions rather than rational judgment. They instinctively tend to look for masculine leadership as a compensation—the leadership they can find in a strong man but never in an assembly, which is after all only a reproduction in miniature of their own faults and weaknesses. Instinct always prevails in the end. The great predominance of women in contemporary America can only bolster this trend.

Alongside this internal evolution, another trend asserts itself unmistakably: the development of imperial expansion, military might, and foreign commitments continues to increase the power of the American Executive. This trend was still concealed a century ago when Alexis de Tocqueville wrote:

"The President of the United States, it is true, is the Commander in Chief of the army, but the army is composed of only six thousand men; he commands the fleet, but the fleet reckons but few sail; he conducts the foreign relations of the Union, but the United States is a nation without neighbors. Separated from the rest of the world by the ocean, and too weak as yet to aim at the dominion of the seas, it has no enemies and its interests rarely come into contact with those of any other nations on the globe."

Now, compare this picture with the present: armies of millions of men, the most powerful fleets in the world, commitments all over the globe, and vast nuclear power.

The President's role as Commander in Chief has now become preponderant in an age of world-wide wars and tensions. His role as director of American foreign policy has grown correspondingly. He can take many steps that are beyond recall or repair. He can start a war according to his own judgment. Singlehanded, he can influence decisively the political situation in scores of foreign nations. President Truman sent American troops into the Korean fray without waiting for Congressional approval, in spite of Senator Taft's vehement protests. But there can be no collective initiative, no collective action, and no collective responsibility.

President Truman's formula "the buck stops here" sums up the immense responsibility of the one man who heads the American government. His cabinet is entirely his own tool because he alone decides on policy and is not bound to consult its members as a prime minister in a parliamentary regime. New emergencies after World War II led to the creation of the National Security Council in 1947, a body independent of both the cabinet and Congress. And to what extent can Congress control the actual working of the Atomic Energy Commission? The President's already considerable veto power has been reinforced by the new possibility of applying it to single items of the appropriation bills. The veto becomes more sensitive and discriminating.

How the President Makes Laws

From being largely negative, the President's legislative power becomes increasingly positive, fulfilling Henry Clay's dire prophecy. His power has been increasingly emphasized in the annual legislative program submitted in the "State of the Union" message, and if he controls his party, through his overriding influence in pushing it through.

In truth, no mental effort is required to understand that the President of the United States is the most powerful single human being in the world today. Future crises will inevitably transform him into a full-fledged Caesar, if we do not beware. Today he wears ten hats—as Head of State, Chief Executive, Minister of Foreign Affairs, Chief Legislator, Head of Party, Tribune of the People, Ultimate Arbitrator of Social Justice, Guardian of Economic Prosperity, and World Leader of Western Civilization. Slowly and unobtrusively, these hats are becoming crowns and this pyramid of hats is slowly metamorphosing itself into a tiara, the tiara of one man's world imperium.

Wars are the main harbingers of Caesarism. The Punic and Macedonian wars proved to Rome that great undertakings in an increasingly equalitarian society can be the responsibility of one man only, never of a democratic assembly. In grave emergencies, leadership can never be collective, and we are now living in an age of permanent emergency. Presidential power in America has grown as American power and expansion have grown, one developing within the other. This fact has not remained unnoticed in America since the passing of Franklin Roosevelt and a great deal of the postwar developments in American politics can be written down as Congressional reaction against the power of the White House.

Although by no means a weak President, Harry Truman did not have the authority of his predecessor and Congress raised its head once more. And when the Republicans came back to power in 1952, a deliberate effort was made by President Eisenhower to restore to Congress that dignity and prestige which had been so damaged during the New Deal and World War II. A similar reaction took place in Rome when Sulla attempted to undo some of the worst features of Marius' New Deal and eliminate all possibility of another such concentration of supreme power in the hands of one man.

"Belated Moves" Against Caesarism

After World War II, the American Congress voted a Constitutional amendment forbidding future Presidents more than two terms of office. But the precedent has been set and in America historical precedents have an overwhelming influence. Such belated moves can no more halt the trend toward Caesarism than those of Sulla limiting all offices to a one-year tenure, specifying that no one could ever be, as

Marius had been, both Commander in Chief and supreme magistrate, and handing back military authority to the Roman Senate.

*   *   *

Growing public indifference to politics was already deplored in Caesar's days, lamented by Augustus, and bitterly resented by Tiberius. But it was too late.

With Caesarism and Civilization, the great struggles between political parties are no longer concerned with principles, programs, and ideologies but with *men*.

Marius, Sulla, Cato, Brutus still fought for principles.

But now, everything became personalized.

Under Augustus, parties still existed, but there were no more *Optimates* or *Populares,* no more conservatives nor democrats.

Men campaigned for or against Tiberius or Drusus or Caius Caesar.

No one believed any more in the efficacy of ideas, political panaceas, doctrines, or systems, just as the Greeks had given up building great philosophic systems generations before.

Abstractions, ideas, and philosophies were rejected to the periphery of their lives and of the empire, to the East where Jews, Gnostics, Christians, and Mithraists attempted to conquer the world of souls and minds while the Caesars ruled their material existence.

*   *   *

The rise of Caesarism in America is considerably eased by a number of American features. In the first place, democratic equality, with its concomitant conformism and psychological socialization, is more fully developed in the United States than it has ever been anywhere, at any time. There are no social barriers, such as existed in Rome's remnants of aristocratic tradition, because Britain's ruling class played that part on behalf of America. Whatever tensions there were within the Roman state are partly transmuted in our modern world into international tensions between Britain and America.

The next most important feature is that Caesarism can come to America constitutionally, without having to alter or break down any existing institution. The White House is already the seat of the most powerful tribunician authority ever known to history. All it needs is amplification and extension. Caesarism in America does not have to challenge the Constitution as in Rome or engage in civil warfare and cross any fateful Rubicon. It can slip in quite naturally, discreetly, through constitutional channels.

The psychological climate is almost ripe. What irked the Romans of the stamp of Brutus was not so much Julius Caesar's effective power as the ostentation with which he displayed it. Republican institutions can long be dead and still survive as a sacred ideal in the minds of men. Most Romans were ready to admit the reality of Caesarism but not the symbol of a hated monarchy. It is not too different today. Ideology, the realities of geography, and insularity have made of the Americans tamers of nature rather than subduers of men.

"Hero Worship" in the U.S.

Americans have always tended to be repelled by open display of authority over men as much as they enjoy power over "things." So far, they have been nonmilitaristic out of circumstances rather than conviction. Individually, they are far from disliking violence. Their nonmilitaristic disposition does not spring from dislike of effective power—hero worship and bossism are marked American features—nor from dislike for military discipline, since they are more disciplined, group-minded, and eager for leadership than most Europeans. It comes simply from their instinct for equality, which makes them dislike the inevitable hierarchy of military organization. They frown on any form of hierarchy whatsoever.

They have no feeling of awe or reverence for other human beings and would, if circumstances warranted it, behave as did the Romans who hurled insults and mocked the victorious generals during their "triumph" in order to deflate their swelling vanity and thus compensate for the supreme honors decreed to them.

Americans have no appreciation for the majestic symbolism that moves Englishmen when they face their powerless Crown. They enjoy calling their President Tom, Dick, or Harry, even though he is probably the most powerful human being in the world.

Americans will accept immense, almost autocratic power over them so long as they do not have to see in it a transcendent authority, and they will always attempt to "humanize" such authority with the help of humor or incongruity. What they will always seek to cut down is not effective power but its awe-inspiring character. Through the gap thus opened between appearance and reality, the coming Caesars will march in if left free to do so. We shall legislate against them and rave against them. But there they will be, towering over us, far above such petty attacks, symbols of a mortal disease within our Western Civilization. And, like a Shakespearean Brutus, all that will be left to us will be to cry in despair:

> "O Julius Caesar, thou art
> mighty yet!
> Thy spirit walks abroad, and
> turns our swords
> in our own proper en-
> trails."

25. The Man on Top*

SIDNEY HYMAN

[*Though this article was written in 1962 when John F. Kennedy was President, it does reflect what would seem to be the dominant attitudes of the intellectual community regarding Congress and the President.*]

WHEN the malaise of an anti-politics gripped the nation in the last years of the Eisenhower Presidency, the search for a cure came to center on the idea of "Presidential leadership." A President who would push, pull, cajole, inspire, threaten—that's what we needed.

This new President would use all the legal power and the political authority of his office to advance the nation's business. When opposed by the Congress, he would do more than make a few phone calls, have some

men in for lunch, or dangle before them a postmastership or two. He would appeal over the head of the Congress to the people. He would be their conscience, their tribune, their prophet and their captain sounding a call for a stand to arms. And they would not fail him. In a mass rally from below, they would help him force the Congress to fall in line.

John F. Kennedy subscribed to this concept of Presidential leadership, and as a candidate helped to popularize it. Yet he had not been in the White House a full year before friendly critics were heard to mutter about the uncomfortable resemblance between the manner and the results of the Kennedy and Eisenhower Presidencies. The critics were not blind to Mr. Kennedy's special problems. They knew that he had to consolidate a post-election ma-

* *New Republic* (June 11, 1962), pp. 15-18. Reprinted by permission of the *New Republic*.

jority that would "legitimize" his presence in the White House as the youngest and as the first Catholic President in American history. They knew that the international troubles he inherited imposed their own priority on what he did first, and at the same time made him wary about doing anything that could divide the nation when it faced so many external dangers. They also respected the argument that the "balance of payments" problem, with its widespread ramifications, set certain limits on the scope of the domestic programs the new President could initiate. Nonetheless, when the critics in question looked at Mr. Kennedy's performance in domestic matters, what they saw resembled the familiar Eisenhower cycle of the Big Build-up followed by the Big Let-down.

There was talk of "let's get America moving again," and not much motion. Scarcely a day passed which did not see a new manifesto of good intentions. But the day afterward, the subject of the manifesto either lost its follow-through predicate, or an accomplishment the size of a gold-fish was made to seem as big as a whale. Meanwhile, there was the tendency to bypass a contest in the public forum, even for long-range educational purposes, and to manage things in a corner. There was the inclination to think that the President's first duty, like the paramount aim of progressive education, was to "integrate himself with the group"—the legislators, the publishers, even the opposition. There was the defensive wish to see in the popularity polls a certificate of political virtue. There was the reluctance to draw on the enormous fund of good will toward the man in the White House and his charming family, to sustain a fight in the nation with the object of winning a fight in the Congressional forum.

The critics who felt these things to be true about Mr. Kennedy's Presidency and were made uncomfortable by them are now witnessing a dramatic reversal in the President's tone and style—a real battle to sell health insurance for the aged.

It does not detract from the effort to say that the battle, if won, would bring America abreast of where Bismarck's Germany stood in its social security program in the 1880's, and the point reached by the greater part of Western Europe around 1910. In this particular fight, Mr. Kennedy is updating the manner of Franklin D. Roosevelt and Harry S. Truman and is using to the hilt all the personal prestige and all the political powers of the Presidency. In preparation for the climactic struggle with the Congress, he has personally mounted and openly led a war to undercut the AMA, to divide the counsel in its inner citadel, and to detach the rank-and-file doctors from the self-perpetuating oligarchy that manages it. More importantly, he has helped to engineer mass rallies of "senior citizens" in support of health insurance, and hopes they will ignite a blaze that sweeps up from the prairies and makes Congressmen jump for safety to the side of the President. "The business of the government is the business of the people," Mr. Kennedy proclaimed to thousands of admiring oldsters who came to Madison Square Garden on a hot May 20 (and to many thousands more who watched on TV). "We ask you. . . . We depend on your help. . . . Give us your help." And the people responded to his appeal with cheers.

Leadership of this vigor and dash conforms so closely to what many people have been urging, that to stand back now and reflect on its limits—from the standpoint of practical results—seems as odd as an announcement from the Vatican that God might be dead. Yet the limits are real where domestic matters are concerned. They operate regardless of who is in the White House, and what he wants to do. What's more, they point up a little appreciated distinction that has come to rule the relationship between the President and the Congress.

Yes Abroad, No at Home

I mean, specifically, that in the last 25 years Presidents Roosevelt, Truman, Eisenhower and Kennedy jointly, have won the support of the Congress for virtually every major foreign policy move on which they placed great store. The "destroyer-for-bases" deal, Selective Service, Lend-Lease, US membership in the UN, the Greek-Turkish aid program, the Marshall Plan, the Berlin airlift, technical assistance for underdeveloped countries, military support for the UN as in the case of the Communist attack on South Korea, the formation of NATO and other mutual security alliances, the stationing of US troops in Europe, "Atoms for Peace," the formation of new international financial institutions, long-range planning of foreign aid, the creation of the Peace Corps, and all other major Presidential initiatives in the field of foreign affairs, have been approved by the Congress. Points of detail could be and often were compromised in the face of Congressional objections. But the heart of what the President of the hour wanted, the Congress approved.

In that same 25-year period, however, regardless of how often or how eloquently the Presidents appealed to the people in matters of domestic policy, the Congress has just as often said no as it has said yes. Since 1938, the Congress has approved various Presidential initiatives affecting social security coverage, wages and hours, housing, roads, urban renewal, and special measures in support of educational programs related to the national defense effort. But it has marked time, has by-passed, or has directly obstructed virtually all Presidential moves to get at the root of the major unfinished business left over from the high-water mark of the New Deal's domestic accomplishments. Banking reform, tax reform, the problems created by automation, the need for a comprehensive program of federal support for education, the problems of the metropolitan areas, and so on, have found the Congressional anvil breaking whatever Presidential hammer was brought into play.

It is too early to say whether, in the specific case of health insurance, the President will in the end have his way. There has been a pronounced increase in the volume of incoming Congressional mail, but beyond this the light of prophecy fails. The President himself at a recent press conference discounted the nature of the mail as an index to popular feeling. . . .

. . . . .

The first great limitation, then, on a President aiming to govern by "public opinion" is the difficulty of ascertaining what that opinion actually is on the specific domestic matter at issue.

The second, related limitation was expressed by Machiavelli when he observed several hundred years ago that before there can be a Moses, there must first be children of Israel who want to get out of Egypt. Thus a President can "go to the people" but the people may not be predisposed to make his case their own. They will ignore him, or even resent his seeming to be too much of a leader.

The third great limitation is the reverse of the foregoing. It is nonsensical to assume that in any controversy the President is right and Congress wrong, and that it is tantamount to a national calamity when the people don't rally to the side of the White House. The President can err. And when there is mobilized behind his error all the power a President has, the people can spare themselves a calamity by *not* falling in step with his wishes. They know that too.

But when all this has been said, we return to the truism that the Presidency represents a national constituency, and Congress does not. In the Senate's case, it represents the states, viewed as sovereign equals. In the case of the House, it's a gerrymandered institution in which the seniority system and fantastically unequal representation enables a small minority, from static rural and "non-issue oriented" urban districts alike, to impose their will on the very districts where Presidential elections are won or lost—where the President has the greatest personal interest in winning public opinion to his side—and where public opinion cannot reach the minority of men in control of the House.

Moreover, the Senate and the House rarely sit as a Committee of the Whole, after the fashion of the House of Commons when a measure is debated. The Congress does its work through a maze of Committees and Subcommittees—some 250 or so by the last count. Confronted by this maze, public opinion, assuming there is one, does not know where to turn to speak its piece. It tends to wander around the political landscape like a displaced person, growing more diffuse in its aim, and more discouraged by its own sense of confusion. Nor is it helped much by the masters of the Committee who are skilled in passing responsibility for what is done from hand to hand, so that no one, except paid lobbyists resident the year round on the Washington scene, can pinpoint the real source of any transaction or the "swing-man" who can decide it.

Do these men on Capitol Hill believe the President speaks for the nation, while they do not? To expect such modesty from legislators would be as contrary to nature as the creation of mountains without valleys. The Congress does not like to think that it is being downgraded in national importance. It suspects that it is not structurally equipped nor does it have the expert knowledge to maintain a position of co-equality with the President in matters of diplomatic or military interest—as it once did. In this area, it suspects that the march of history, intersecting with the President's traditional Constitutional role as chief organ of foreign affairs and as the Commander-in-Chief, has reduced the significance of the Congress. It can revise, refine, review and come to the support of the Executive's initiatives in national security matters, but it can take few initiatives on its own. And its pride is hurt by its encounter with this truth. What, then, is there left for the Congress to do? If it were the House of Commons, it could enjoy being the electoral body that chooses the Executive and makes the Executive depend on its pleasure. But it is denied even that satisfaction. It has no direct role to play in the election of the Executive, and short of an impeachment cannot overthrow him.

What there is left for it to do is to entrench itself as the arbiter of what goes on in America's cities, towns and farms. Here is where the Congress can parade itself as the defender and the only true representative of all local and regional interests against the "centralizing tendencies" of the Presidency. And it is here, in a grim and sometimes passion-ridden defense of its own institutional importance, that the Congress will fight for the right to have the paramount say in what goes on. It will fight for this right in defiance of the President, in defiance of the public opinion he mobilizes, and in defiance of the fact that the sum of all local and regional interests do not necessarily add up these days to the national interest. Above all, it will fight for right of primacy in domestic matters in defiance of the fact that what we do at home, where the Congress regards itself as supreme, often predetermines what the President can do abroad—just as what we must do abroad often defines what we must do at home.

Short of a war or a 1929-style depression, then, we must ask to what extent "Presidential leadership"—a concept to which I myself subscribed for a long time—can change the way Congress goes about disposing of the nation's domestic affairs. The redistricting drive sparked by the Supreme Court's recent decision may provide a measure of relief in the long run. But what may be in store for us meanwhile may prove to be not a crisis of "Presidential leadership" but a bona-fide *constitutional* crisis, in which the Congress—and the House in particular—having taken on itself the willful obstructionist function of the Supreme Court in the early New Deal Days, provokes another clash with the Presidency which does no one any good.

26. White House vs. Congress —Is Power Balance Shifting? *

GORDON ALLOTT

[*In this speech Allott touches upon the problem of controlling the bureaucracy. Note throughout his basic conservative theme.*]

I MEASURE my words when I define this one great issue of American public policy: We must face up to a full-scale, no-quarter assault on the very foundations of the American constitutional system.

We live in a revolutionary era—and revolutionary in the deepest sense, pointing to the overturn of all those systems and structures of ordered liberty that have been both sword and shield against every form of tyranny through all the years of the American national experience.

Who or what is the prime agent of this revolutionary assault? Again I carefully measure my words: The attack comes from the executive establishment—not the President as a man, nor even the President as party leader, but from a bureaucratic behemoth that conspicuously lacks any sense of built-in self-imposed limitation, that treats the whole arena of public policy and of the national interest as its own exclusive playground, and that responds to every challenge to its undivided author-

ity with thinly veiled contempt and, at the end, with sheer fury.

Or, I must add, with cynical manipulation of information and with crude personal blackmail—underscored always with the overwhelming power of government and with pious rationalizations in the name of the popular will.

Who or what is the target of this unrelenting attack? The essential target, I repeat, is the American constitutional system itself and thus the whole fabric of our social and economic order. But, in particular, the target is one political institution which I am proud to represent—the Congress of the United States —and the American system of free and creative enterprise. . . .

That I am not speaking simply of some fantastic "spook," called into being for partisan political purposes, is a fact that can be amply and grimly documented.

Mr. Roger Blough [chairman of the board of U.S. Steel Corporation] can provide some of this documentation— not to mention those newsmen with their hair-raising reports of midnight callers during the appalling April days of the steel-price showdown. General Electric and General Motors and a thousand other firms and corporations can add still more—as they confront an Antitrust Division which now treats bigness as a crime and business success as a mortal sin.

* Excerpts from an address to the directors of the National Association of Manufacturers in Washington, D.C., April 3, 1963.

It is no mere question of antibusiness bias along the New Frontier; it is, infinitely more seriously, an executive establishment whose dream of a new paternalism leaves no room for private initiative or for personal liberties, least of all for the unpredictable and irrepressible choices of free individuals.

And I, as a member of the United States Senate, could pile up an endless catalogue of case histories—all of them with this one factor in common: each one a gross inroad by the executive into the area, traditionally, of *shared* responsibility and of *balanced* power. Let me tick off just a few illustrations of what I mean:

*   *   *

• There was the recent case of a steam power plant to be built in Colorado with REA [Rural Electrification Administration] loan funds. While the question of certification by the State public-utilities commission was under active consideration, the U.S. Secretary of the Interior took it upon himself publicly to accuse private power firms of bad faith and to threaten a shift in federal funds to neighboring States.

• There is the present case of new regulations for power-transmission lines running across federal lands, regulations under the uncontrolled jurisdiction of either the Secretary of the Interior or of Agriculture. Even the Federal Power Commission, a part of the executive branch itself, strongly objected. Its grounds: an invasion of its own statutory responsibilities—responsibilities, that is to say, laid down by Congress in the first instance. But, by executive order, these new regulations, only slightly modified, went into effect just last week.

• There are such cases as the Bureau of Outdoor Recreation and, more blatantly still, of the so-called Domestic Peace Corps. In neither case is there open and avowed statutory authority —in the latter case, public debate has barely even begun—and yet the funds have been scraped together and the

staffs are being hired, with the inevitable promise of yet bigger staffs and of inflated budgets still to come. By executive order, and by executive fiat only, these new bureaucracies of enormous potential power have been spawned. Congressional authorization? Merely an afterthought.

• And there are grabs for future power, without number and without effective limit, in areas of concern running from urban affairs to national water resources, from agricultural commodity-production control to health insurance for the aged. I speak here of requests now under consideration by the Congress—and thus of congressional resistance to executive power still maintained.

But the pressure is relentless. And by its cynical manipulation and its exploitation of special-interest groups, the executive establishment masks these power grabs in the guise of public interest and popular will.

If our counterattack is to succeed— ours in the Congress and yours in the free American business community— we must bring to bear an equal intensity, equal endurance and still greater devotion to the principles of freedom.

In all these cases, I have been saying, the attack is a full-scale revolution against the traditional American constitutional system, a system of ordered liberty and of balanced power.

*   *   *

We can say that this or that Administration, for instance, is probusiness or antibusiness. And such evaluations have validity. But the excesses of the executive which, today for instance, have earned the label of antibusiness can be curbed by Congress. You may ask why they haven't, if that's the case.

Threat to "Free Economic System"

My answer would be that the Congress today, on both sides of the aisle, does in fact represent an active curb against executive excesses which, if given fully free rein, would completely swamp our free economic system in the bow wave of advancing state economic control by economic theoreticians.

We have only to look at the rising bipartisan objection to the President's budget and tax plans to see that the executive party's plans are being subjected to the closest scrutiny by both of the legislative parties.

Still, we often think of elections, of government itself, in terms of the Presidency. When we engage in programs to get out the vote, for instance, we are getting out presidential votes, by and large. When great issues are debated, they often are debated in terms of presidential candidates who espouse or oppose them. The major emphasis, in fact, of most so-called grass-roots movements is presidential in emphasis, whether consciously or not.

We see, also, extensive programs in so-called economic education without any equivalent programs in governmental education.

If there were such programs and emphasis we might hear less criticism of Congress for taking its time in considering legislation and more criticism of those times when, at presidential prodding, it rushes pell-mell into programs it has not studied adequately.

Perhaps even more to the point are programs of direct relationship to the legislative branch.

While great national organizations pour immense resources into their grass-roots programs, to educate the so-called man in the street, what support do these organizations provide for the representatives of the man in the street who, ultimately, must do the work that directs our destiny? There are precious few.

Congress, without the vast research resources available to the executive, must depend upon a comparatively skeletal staff for much of its research. Its members desperately need informational and research assistance, day by day, session by session. It can, of course, call upon expert witnesses during committee hearings. But even then the information may be too little and too late.

If great public organizations, and individual citizens and corporations, could divert even a fraction of their great grass-roots enthusiasms and support toward truly bipartisan efforts to provide research assistance to the legislative branch, a mighty step would have been taken toward restoring the balance between legislative and executive impact. As it is, I can think of only a tiny handful of conscientious research efforts which, without grinding axes, attempt to bolster the Congress directly and effectively.

At election time, of course, the difference in emphasis becomes more painful—from a legislative point of view. We have national organizations aplenty, with millions aplenty, devoted to action during presidential campaigns. At the State level there also are committees and organizations to beat the drum and pass the hat for State officials. Even at the local level, our friends and neighbors get out their precinct books and hiking shoes to work for the sheriff, the councilman, the mayor and so forth.

The Senator often stands in this equation rather like the poor relative of the State ticket. The poor Congressman stands there almost like an orphan. In off-year contests he is lucky to even have his name mentioned amid the other, apparently really important, races, such as that for dog catcher.

Where are the programs, the committees, the resources devoted year-round to the support of good candidates to the most representative and, I think, most crucial house of our entire governmental structure? They are lacking, by and large, because we, all of us, have a diminishing sense of Senate and Congress.

We are beginning to accept the caricaturist's version of the legislator. We are beginning to stare hypnotically at the television-like screen of the executive's awesome power.

The symbol of this great land is becoming a grin, a smile, a hairdo, a painting on the White House wall. It should be the dome of the mightiest edifice of freedom ever constructed: the Capitol of the United States.

Issues with "Crucial Meaning"

For the public at large this requires firm answers to some questions which have taken on new and crucial meaning:

If Congress puts the brakes on executive agreements to disarm this land, or even disarm the whole free world, will you say that Congress is filled by war hawks? The executive will.

If Congress demands that the Soviet satellite to our south be put under the full pressures of the Monroe Doctrine, will you say that Congress is moving to the brink of destruction? The executive has, and will.

If Congress asks that every projected federal expenditure be subjected to careful weighing as to need, cost and result, will you say that Congress is a stumbling block? The executive has, and will.

If Congress asks that our national budget be handled with the good sense of our business and household budgets, will you accuse us of being old-fashioned? The executive will.

If Congress seeks to crack open the walls of secrecy and news management that are arising in Washington, will you say that they are meddling in matters best left to the selected few? The executive will.

If Congress is jealous of your rights in the making of law, if Congress seeks to strengthen the responsibilities of your States and your municipalities, will you say that we are walking an outdated frontier? The executive will.

If Congress seeks answers for our major problems outside the central Government, will you say that we are Stone Age advocates of an individual responsibility that no longer has a place in our life? The executive will.

Or will you, instead, return your support and your attention to your own representatives, giving the executive the deference due the office but not abdicating to it all your powers and your future? A free people will.

27. An Incredible Week*

THE WALL STREET JOURNAL

[*This editorial appeared shortly after John F. Kennedy's "battle" with the major steel companies over price rises. This particular maneuver of J.F.K. raises the routine question of a president exceeding his institutionally given powers.*]

* Editorial, *The Wall Street Journal* (April 16, 1962). Reprinted by permission of *The Wall Street Journal*. Copyright 1962 by *The Wall Street Journal*.

IN a long life not without its share of amazements, we never saw anything like it.

On Tuesday one of the country's steel companies announced it was going to try to get more money for its product. And promptly all hell busted loose.

We wouldn't have been surprised ourselves if some people had shaken their heads in puzzlement at the new price list. Although after 20 years of inflation a price rise in anything is hardly unusual, there was some reason for wondering if the company officials had made the right decision in today's market.

But what happened was no mere head-shaking. The President of the United States went into what can only be described as a tirade. Not only had the company changed its price list without consulting him but it had also set a price which, in his opinion, was "wholly unjustified." With a long preamble in which he rang in the Berlin crisis, the soldiers killed the other day in Vietnam, the wives and mothers separated from their husbands by the reserve call-up—all of which he cast at the feet of these "irresponsible" steel officials—he wound up by crying that these men had shown their "utter contempt" for the welfare of the country.

The response in Washington was instantaneous. The Justice Department, the Federal Trade Commission, the Congressional inquisitors all leaped to arms.

Then came the night riders. At three a.m. Thursday morning a reporter for the Associated Press was awakened by Government agents unable to wait even for regular office hours in their driven haste to find out what testimony he could give about the criminal conduct of these steel officials. At five a.m. it was the turn of our own reporter in Philadelphia. At six-thirty a.m. the scene was repeated in Wilmington, Delaware, for a reporter on the Evening Journal. All this without any warrants, only orders from the Attorney General of the United States.

By mid-Thursday morning the U.S. Steel Corporation had been subpoenaed for all documents bearing on the crime and had learned that a Federal Grand Jury would move swiftly to see what laws had been violated by asking three tenths of a cent a pound more for a piece of steel.

This brought us to Thursday afternoon. Then Mr. Roger Blough, the chairman of this company, felt forced to stand up to an assembly of microphones and television cameras and defend himself before the country for the wickedness of his deeds. And to be treated by the reporters at that gathering as if they were a part of the prosecution and he was, indeed, a malefactor in the dock.

And that leads to what is probably the most amazing thing of all about last week. Across the country—on the radio, in newspapers and at street corners—the necessity of the defenders to "justify" themselves before the righteous accusers was simply accepted as a premise from which the trial should begin. There were few to say otherwise.

In such a climate it was not at all surprising what the mailed fist could do. All day Friday steel company offices were awash with Government agents, while the threats of punishment were mingled with promises of reward for doing the rulers' bidding. It is a technique of government not unknown elsewhere in the world, and it is a combination almost irresistible. So by Friday night Mr. Kennedy had his victory.

Finally the jubilation. The President himself said all the people of the United States should be gratified. Around him there was joy unrestrained at this proof positive of how naked political power, ruthlessly used, could smash any private citizen who got in its way. So far as we could tell, the people did seem relieved that it was all over and that the malefactors had been brought to heel.

Yet what, in all truth, is this "crime" with which these men stood charged by a wrathful President?

It had nothing to do with arguments about whether this particular asking price was economically justified, or fair to the steel stockholders, or somehow responsible for dead soldiers in Vietnam. This last is sheer demagoguery, and the others are questions no man can answer—neither Mr. Blough nor Mr. Kennedy.

What was really at issue here, and still is, is whether the price of steel is to be determined by the constant bargaining in the market place between the makers and buyers of steel; you may be sure that if the makers guessed wrong the market would promptly change their decision. Or whether the price of steel is to be decided and then enforced by the Government. In short, the issue is whether we have a free market system or whether we do not. That, and nothing more.

Thus the true "crime" of this company was that it did not get permission from the Government and that its attempted asking price did not suit the ideas of a tiny handful of men around the White House.

It was for this that last week we saw the President of the United States in a fury, a public pillorying of an industry, threatened reprisals against all business, the spectacle of a private citizen helplessly trying to defend himself against unnamed accusations, the knock of policemen on the midnight door. And there was hardly a voice rising above the clamor to ask what it was all about.

If we had not seen it with our eyes and heard it with our own ears, we would not have been able to believe that in America it actually happened.

B. The Unmodern Electoral College

28. The Case Against Electoral Reform

ANTHONY LEWIS

Of the many might-have-beens that can be constructed about the 1960 election, none is more intriguing than this: If a first-term senator named John F. Kennedy had not, in March of 1956, led the fight against an electoral-reform proposal first made by his Senate predecessor, Henry Cabot Lodge, Jr., the proposal might have become part of the Constitution. And if it had, John F. Kennedy might well not be President-elect today.

The story offers more than a nice bit of historical irony. For the closeness of the 1960 election has brought a flurry of interest in the perennial topic of electoral reform. An urgent cry for change in our method of choosing a President has come from such interesting bedfellows as Senators Mike Mansfield, Sam J. Ervin, Karl Mundt, and Jacob K. Javits, columnist Roscoe Drummond, and the editors of the Washington *Post*.

The suggestion most frequently discussed is known as the Lodge-Gossett amendment because it was first sponsored by Senator Lodge and Representative Ed Gossett, a Texas Democrat. Its basic idea is that the electoral vote of each state, instead of being awarded

as a bloc to the winner of the popular vote in that state, should be divided proportionally according to the popular vote.

This year, for example, Senator Kennedy won 50.1 per cent of the vote in Illinois and got all of its twenty-seven electoral votes. Under the Lodge-Gossett amendment he would have had 13.527 electoral votes from Illinois against Vice-President Nixon's 13.473. (The amendment specified that the apportionment should be carried to three decimal places.)

The pros and cons of this kind of change in our Presidential electoral system can be set out most fairly and completely by referring to what was said in the two great Senate debates on the question, in 1950 and 1956. The most articulate spokesmen on opposite sides—surely an accident of history, but one almost too perfect to believe—were Senators Lodge and Kennedy.

Lodge's Logic

Opening the debate in 1950, Senator Lodge listed what he termed the "defects, unhealthy practices and potential evils" of the unit-rule system of giving all a state's electoral votes to the popular-vote victor. One was the possibility that the winner of the popu-

* *The Reporter* (December 8, 1960), pp. 31-33. Reprinted by permission of the author and *The Reporter*. Copyright 1960 by the Reporter Magazine Co.

lar vote nationally would lose in the Electoral College. A second was the thesis that the hopelessness of upsetting the majority in one-party states discouraged minority voters from bothering to turn out on Election Day; if they knew that every vote would count in the electoral total, it was reasoned, more would care and one-party rule would be threatened. Third was the argument that under the unit rule all votes cast for the losing candidate in a state are "wasted."

But the main attack made by Senator Lodge on the existing unit-rule system was that it "strongly tends to overemphasize the political importance of the large, politically doubtful states." The system, said Mr. Lodge, encourages the selection of Presidential nominees from the large states and encourages the candidates to do most of their campaigning there. Even more important, he said, "It not only permits but actually invites the domination of Presidential campaigns by small, organized, well-disciplined minority or pressure groups within the large so-called pivotal states."

Senator Lodge's logic was apparently persuasive. The only effective opposition during a one-sided debate in 1950 was put up by Senator Robert A. Taft, who was blunt enough to say that his Ohio would not have as much influence in a Presidential election if its electoral vote were divided instead of going as a lump.

The Lodge-Gossett amendment passed the Senate by 64 to 27, more than the necessary two-thirds. The majority included most of the Senate's noted liberals—Douglas of Illinois, Humphrey of Minnesota, Kefauver of Tennessee, Lehman of New York, Morse of Oregon—as well as such right-wing Democrats as McCarran of Nevada and Eastland of Mississippi. Most of the negative votes came from conservative Republicans.

But the amendment died in the House in 1950. It was held in the Rules Committee, then chaired by Adolph Sabath of Illinois, and an effort to bring it to the floor by suspending the rules failed.

As it came to the Senate floor in 1956, the electoral-reform proposal was a hybrid. Attached to the Lodge-Gossett plan, now sponsored in chief by Senator Price Daniel of Texas, was a wholly different alternative bearing the name of Mundt of South Dakota. The Mundt idea was to choose electors in each state by districts—one for each representative and two at large for the senators. The Lodge-Gossett approach would prevail under the combined proposal, unless any state itself chose to vote for President by districts.

The 1956 amendment had what appeared to be overwhelming support. It was introduced jointly by fifty-four senators. The fact that as junior a member as Mr. Kennedy (then in his fourth year as a senator) was floor leader of the opposition indicates how thin the troops were on that side.

All those who think the John F. Kennedy who finished the 1960 Presidential campaign was a wholly new man, one whose mind and style could not have been forecast from past performance, should read the week's debate on the Daniel-Mundt amendment. Senator Kennedy held the floor himself for the better part of two days, and he was there almost continuously with questions for the other side. And through it all flashed the sharpness, the candor, the fascination with the Presidency, the love of history, the taste for quotation that characterized him as a Presidential candidate.

"These are crucial times . . . ," Senator Kennedy said. "Nevertheless, it is proposed to change this system—under which we have, on the whole, obtained able Presidents capable of meeting the increased demands upon our Executive —for an unknown, untried but obviously precarious system which was abandoned in this country long ago, which previous Congresses have rejected and which has been thoroughly discredited in Europe. . . .

"No urgent necessity for immediate change has been proven. . . . It seems to me that Falkland's definition of conservatism is quite appropriate—'When it is not necessary to change, it is necessary not to change.'"

Although he did not refer to his predecessor, Senator Kennedy in time answered each of the Lodge arguments against the existing unit-rule system. To the first, that it may give the election to a loser in the popular vote, Senator Kennedy replied by pointing out that the system had, in effect, done so only once, in the Harrison-Cleveland election of 1888. Moreover, he said, an analysis of past elections indicated that under the Lodge-Gossett arrangement two Democrats would have been elected with fewer popular votes than their opponents: Hancock over Garfield in 1880, Bryan over McKinley in 1896 and 1900.

"In short, what the committee report calls the 'minority President evil' occurs at a rate of once every 175 years— hardly cause for an immediate and drastic change which the proponents admit will not even do away with it."

Senator Kennedy doubted that the amendment would have the effect Senator Lodge forecast of evening up one-party states. (By 1960 they seem to be evening up without the amendment.) He dismissed as semantics the idea that votes for the losing candidate in a state under the unit rule were "wasted." The same can be said of any district system of elections, such as Britain's or Canada's or our Congressional elections or the Mundt proposal for the Presidency. In all these instances only one man can win a district.

Where the Plums Are

But the heart of the Kennedy attack was against the thesis that the present electoral system gives too much power to the large doubtful states and their "minority" and "pressure" groups. He did not deny that the large states gain power from the unit rule. When the prize is forty-five electoral votes, any national party is going to look to New York when it is drafting a platform or nominating a candidate or running a campaign. But Senator Kennedy argued that the urban interests *ought* to have this power—that it has been built into our political system as a compensation for other ways in which these interests are at a disadvantage.

He noted that each state, regardless of size, has two senators: "New York is the largest state in the union. It has only two Senators but it has forty-three Representatives. One of New York's great hopes of recapturing its relative loss of influence in the legislative branch is to have an effective influence on the presidency." And the senatorial distortion is reflected in the fact that even the smallest state has three electoral votes to match its one congressman and two senators.

Moreover, rural and conservative interests have maintained a grip on most of the state legislatures in the country through gerrymandering. The legislatures in turn work their will on Congressional districts, so that even in the House urban areas are sharply under-represented.

The Mundt proposal, Senator Kennedy said, would invite gerrymandering on a grandiose scale, with Republican legislatures choosing the option of election by districts to cut Democratic electoral votes. And the Lodge formula would have its own drastic effect on the influence of urban interests. The point Senator Kennedy made was that Presidential elections are usually so close in the large urban states that neither side could hope for a margin of more than a few electoral votes under the Lodge proposal. The big plums would be in the one-party states.

As a sample, Senator Kennedy supposed that the 1948 election had been held in just seven states: Connecticut, New York, New Jersey, Michigan, Indiana, Pennsylvania, and Georgia. Mr. Dewey won the first six industrial states, getting 138 electoral votes, while losing Georgia's twelve. But his popular-vote margins were so small in the six that under the Lodge plan they would have given him a net electoral-vote edge of only three, while one-party Georgia would have given Mr. Truman a margin of five electoral votes. Georgia, in effect, would have outweighed the other six.

"It is not only the unit vote for the Presidency we are talking about," Senator Kennedy concluded, "but a whole solar system of governmental power. If it is proposed to change the balance of power of one of the elements of the solar system, it is necessary to consider the others."

The impression should not be left that Senator Kennedy was alone in 1956. Since 1950 more and more liberals had come to see that the "small, organized, well-disciplined minority or pressure groups within the large so-called pivotal states," as Mr. Lodge had put it, meant the N.A.A.C.P. and the AFL-CIO, the Negroes and Catholics and Jews. To end their influence in Presidential elections, as Mr. Lodge candidly proposed to do, was to end their political influence altogether.

Senators Lehman and Douglas, notably, recanted their 1950 support of Lodge-Gossett and spoke effectively against the new amendment. In 1950, Senator Douglas said, he had been "somewhat unwary and . . . believed that if the big States made sacrifices it might induce some reciprocal yielding on the part of other States. Since then the Senator from Illinois has become wiser and more acquainted with the realities. He now understands that there are certain sections of the country which will yield nothing, and which are seeking constantly to diminish the power of the large States and of the large cities and to hold them in bondage. The Senator from Illinois is a wiser man now than he was in 1950. His hair is whiter, but his wisdom is greater."

On a test vote the Daniel-Mundt amendment carried by only forty-eight

to thirty-seven, far less than the two-thirds required for Constitutional amendments. Eight sponsors, including Senator Morse, voted against it. Several sponsors, including Senator Kefauver, were not recorded. Neither was Senator Humphrey, although this time he was announced as being against. With that test, the sponsors gave up and agreed to send the proposal back to committee.

A Crystal Ball?

Some future writer of fictional biography will doubtless speculate that Senator Kennedy did what he did in March, 1956, because he had a good idea he was going to be running for President four years later—with Mr. Lodge on the other ticket. If one were to accept that fantasy, certainly Senator Kennedy would get a remarkable score for prescience.

If the Lodge plan for a proportional division of electoral votes had been in effect in 1960, the latest returns indicate that Senator Kennedy would have 268.871 and Vice-President Nixon 265.036 electoral votes. That assumes a division of Mississippi among the three tickets that actually were on the ballot, giving the independent slate there 3.093 electoral votes.

The Kennedy total would be enough to win, since under the final 1956 version of the electoral-reform plan the leading candidate would need only forty-five per cent of the electoral votes instead of an absolute majority as at present. But the tabulation does not reflect the probability that third-party tickets would have been put forward in many Southern states if the Lodge plan had been in effect, and that they would have drawn votes from Senator Kennedy in states other than Mississippi—Alabama, for example, whose six unpledged electors have all been awarded to Senator Kennedy in this tabulation because they ran on the Democratic slate.

Since under the Lodge plan third parties could hope to win at least a small part of a state's electoral vote, they would be encouraged to try, and therefore the results in 1960 would have depended on the strength of a Southern third-party ticket and Kennedy might well have lost; in any case the outcome would have been decided by a few fractional electoral votes—or thrown into the House of Representatives for decision. Incidentally, the intricacies of the computations (as the writer can testify) and the closeness of the result are persuasive practical arguments themselves against proportional division of state electoral votes. The country might drift in torment and indecision for weeks while handfuls of votes were counted and recounted and the electoral vote then recomputed.

By prevailing against the establish-ment of a proportional division of state electoral votes in 1956, Senator Kennedy certainly served his own purposes in 1960 well. But it is clear from reading the debate that Senator Kennedy acted as he did not because he had a crystal ball focused on 1960 but because he was a realist who knew something about history and about political theory. He knew that government is not an abstract entity such as "the popular will." It is a system of power—of conflicting forces that have worked out their balance over a long history. To weaken one element, such as urban influence on the Presidency, without weakening another, such as rural control of the legislatures, is to change the whole system.

All of which might be worth keeping in mind as a new campaign begins for "electoral reform."

Chapter V

WHAT TO DO
ABOUT THE COURT?

Introduction

THE proper role and function of the Supreme Court in our system of government has been, almost since the beginning of the republic, a subject of bitter controversy. Of all the "enduring" issues of American politics, indeed this has probably been the most controversial, and we may safely assume that it will remain so for quite some time. A survey of the leading schools of thought with respect to the proper role and function of the Court would, for that reason, be too large a task for us to attempt here. At most we can identify certain recurring areas of controversy with which the student should be familiar.

First, there is the perennial and unresolved question of whether the Founding Fathers themselves intended the Court to possess the power of judicial review. On the one hand, there are those who assert that if that *had* been their intention, the Framers would have explicitly given this power to the Court in the Philadelphia Constitution. Such critics make much of the fact that in the Constitution, as it stands, there is simply no mention of the power of judicial review. On the other hand, there are those, "supporters" of the Court of course, who point to Federalist No. 78, in which Hamilton not only recognizes the power of the Court to invalidate legislative acts "contrary to the manifest tenor of the Constitution" but also sets forth what we might term a theoretical defense of the practice of judicial review. That defense of judicial review, it should be noted, is repeated to a large extent in Marshall's famed opinion in *Marbury v. Madison,* the first case in which the Court exercised this power.[1]

At still another level, there is the question of whether judicial review is compatible with the system of government devised by the Framers. For example, if the legislature was intended to be the predominant branch of the national government, as some critics believe, the question arises whether judicial review does not actually place the Supreme

[1] On the question of the practice of judicial review in the colonies and the intent of the Framers, the student can profitably consult: Edward S. Corwin's, *The Doctrine of Judicial Review* (Princeton: Princeton University Press, 1914), also, his *Court Over Constitution* (Princeton: Princeton University Press, 1938); Louis Boudin, *Government by Judiciary* (2 Vols.; New York: William Godwin, 1932); and Charles G. Haines, *The American Doctrine of Judicial Supremacy* (Berkeley: University of California Press, 1932).

Court itself in a position of supremacy, and whether that does or does not upset the constitutional applecart. On this question we note that Hamilton in No. 78 contends that the Court, in rendering an authoritative interpretation of the Constitution, is in fact expressing the will of the majority of the people as expressed in the fundamental and binding document he "holds in his hand." Certainly, however, Hamilton's defense of the Court does not answer some of the questions which logically arise. What, for example, if the legislature is acting in a perfectly constitutional manner, yet an "arbitrary" majority of the Court invalidates its actions—under the *pretext* that they are unconstitutional? What then? Is there any appeal from a decision of the Court? To what extent are the people bound to obey decisions of the Court even when such decisions are felt to be clearly "arbitrary," and so *not* in keeping with the will of the people as expressed in the Constitution? What recourse is available to the legislature, to the President, and to the people, in such circumstances?

To ask such questions, moreover, only raises even more difficult ones. How are we to say when the Court is or is not acting in an arbitrary manner? Or, to use Hamilton's terminology, how can we tell when the Court is exercising its "will" and not its "judgment"? Are we to assume that every time the Court renders a decision on the constitutionality of a statute, it is, as a matter of course, *merely* exercising its "judgment"? These questions assume great importance in our present system, since it is generally, though perhaps not universally, acknowledged that the Supreme Court does possess the authority to declare acts of Congress and of the state legislatures unconstitutional.

In this connection, various doctrines have been advanced with regard to the Court's *use* of its power to review statutes of Congress and the state legislatures. Recognizing that the Supreme Court is the court of last resort, and that a majority of the justices could well act, in determining the constitutionality of a statute, on the basis of personal preferences rather than the "manifest tenor" of the Constitution, the school of "judicial self-restraint" urges that the Court use its power of judicial review with the "greatest caution." (We recommend to the student Justice Frankfurter's dissent in *West Virginia v. Barnette,* 319 U.S. 624 (1943) for a classic statement of this position.) At the other extreme there are the "judicial activists," who insist that it is a legitimate function of the Court to protect and advance the ideals and rights that are embodied in the Constitution. A proponent of this school writes:

The powers of the Court are a vital and altogether legitimate part of the American Constitution. They should be used positively and affirmatively to help improve the public law of a free society capable of fulfilling the democratic dream of its Constitution in the second half of the twentieth century. The court should be the proponent and protector of the values which are the premises, goals, needs, and ambitions of our culture, as they have been expressed in its living constitution. The inescapable ethical ideas which determine how the men of any time think and react give ultimate shape to the decisions of the Supreme Court, as they do to the decisions of the judges of other courts. The Justices should discharge their duties with a sense of strategy and purpose, illuminated by their understanding of the constitution as the charter of a nation intended to enjoy liberty.[2]

The "activists," clearly, are far less inclined than members of the "self-restraint" school to enjoin "caution" upon the Court in its exercise of judicial review. For example, there are justices of the activist persuasion who hold what is now called the "preferred position" doctrine, that is, they *presume* legislative restrictions on the First Amendment freedoms unconstitutional unless it can be clearly demonstrated that such legislation is necessary to prevent a substantial evil or wrong. In this they appear to depart from the standard and time-honored judicial rule of presuming the constitutionality of a statute until its *unconstitutionality* is clearly demonstrated.

These controversies over the role which the Court should assume have become more important since the Civil War and the passage of the Fourteenth Amendment. Most students in undergraduate American Government courses go through the tedious process of learning how the Supreme Court has "applied" the "equal protection" and "due process" clauses of the Fourteenth Amendment to the states. In reviewing this process, they are apt to forget the revolutionary significance of the Fourteenth Amendment—as it has been "interpreted" to allow the Court to act as the final arbiter for *state* legislation involving the freedoms vouchsafed in the *national* Bill of Rights—such as freedom of religion, speech, assembly, and the right to certain criminal trial procedures. It is not surprising to find that, as judicial power has grown, criticisms directed at the Court have increased. What is to some extent surprising, however, is that the critics of the Court over

[2] Eugene V. Rostow, *The Sovereign Prerogative: The Supreme Court and the Quest for Law* (New Haven: Yale University Press, 1962), p. xxxiv.

time have not always been of the same political persuasion. To put it otherwise: there have been times when the Supreme Court has been the "darling" of the conservatives and other times, particularly the present, when its staunchest defenders are liberals.

This proposition can easily be documented. Between roughly 1890 and 1937, the Court more or less consistently propounded a laissez-faire position with respect to both national and state regulation of the economy and social welfare legislation.[3] In the famous case of *Lochner v. New York* (198 U.S. 45 [1905]), for example, the Court invalidated a New York state law regulating the hours of bakery workers—on the grounds that such regulation, as the majority opinion put it, infringed "liberty of contract." Again in 1923 (*Adkins v. Children's Hospital*, 261 U.S. 525 [1923]), the Court invalidated a Congressional act intended to provide minimum wages for women and children working in the District of Columbia. The Court, of course, was strongly criticized for these decisions. And, as frequently happens, the strongest criticism came from members of the Supreme Court itself, in the form of dissenting opinions. In the Lochner case Mr. Justice Holmes wrote:

> This case is decided upon an economic theory which a large part of this country does not entertain. . . . But a Constitution is not intended to embody a particular economic theory, whether of paternalism and the organic relation of the citizen to the state or of *laissez faire*. It is made for people of fundamentally differing views, and the accident of our finding certain opinions natural and familiar, or novel, and even shocking, ought not to conclude our judgment upon the question whether statutes embodying them conflict with the Constitution of the United States.

Holmes is clearly arguing for the adoption of the doctrine of "self-restraint" in applying the "due process" clause of the Fourteenth Amendment to economic and social reform legislation of the states. And if the Court had adopted a posture of "self-restraint," the states would presumably have been left a considerably greater area of freedom than, in economic matters at least, they now enjoy.

By 1937 the Court found itself the center of a heated controversy. After several devastating "blows" had been dealt to Roosevelt's New Deal program by the Court, Roosevelt proposed his famous "court-packing" plan that would, in effect, have allowed him to appoint enough justices to assure favorable majority decisions from the Court

---

[3] There were exceptions to this trend. For example, *Muller v. Oregon*, 208 U.S. 412 (1908) and *Bunting v. Oregon*, 243 U.S. 426 (1917).

on the social and economic "reform" measures of his New Deal program. Although the "packing" plan was duly defeated in the Senate, most observers believe that it did achieve its purpose. The Court, in 1937, "switched" and began to uphold New Deal measures. Finally, when vacancies occurred on the Court, Roosevelt was able to appoint justices favorably inclined to his programs. Thus since 1937 the Court's view of economic and social legislation has been decidedly liberal.

At this point it should be mentioned that the Court, during the period 1890 to 1937, was defended first and foremost by conservatives. We do not have to look very hard for the reason for this. By striking down social and economic reform legislation, the Court was successfully resisting liberal movements toward greater equality—at both the state and national level. So long as the Court could serve as an effective barrier to these liberal programs, it could count on the endorsement and support of the conservatives.

But we have not reached the end of the story. Increasingly the Court, since the 1920's, has turned its attention to questions of civil rights.[4] The "due process" and "equal protection" clauses of the Fourteenth Amendment are now used to advance the cause of civil and individual *equality*. Much state legislation that touches, for example, on the so-called "First Amendment freedoms" has, during this period, been invalidated by the Court. This, in itself, has prompted a good deal of conservative criticism, particularly from state authorities. However, there is little question that it is the segregation decision (*Brown v. The Board of Education of Topeka*, 347 U.S. 483 [1954]) that has generated the greatest furor. The charges and counter-charges that have been made with respect to the Court's decision in this case would fill many volumes, yet the fundamental issues in the controversy are not new. Among them we find these: What is the nature of our Constitution? What is the proper role of the Supreme Court *vis-a-vis* the legislature? What is the meaning and scope of federalism? How much should the Supreme Court be bound by its own precedents?

Critics of the Court's present use of the Fourteenth Amendment are quick to point out that the Court is engaging in the same practices for which it was so strongly condemned in the years 1890-1937. That is, the majority of the Court is imposing its will upon the states, and thereby limiting the range of permissible choice available to the state governments in handling their internal affairs. The only difference, present critics maintain, is that instead of prohibiting state interference in the economic sector, the Court now limits state actions in the area

[4] Starting with *Gitlow v. New York*, 268 U.S. 652 (1925).

of civil rights. In either case, it is contended, the Court is acting in
an arbitrary manner by seeking to advance its own will, and so is
undermining the fundamental principles of democratic self-government. But, "civil rights" being involved, the liberals by the same token
can today hardly avoid the role of the Court's foremost defenders and
apologists.

Contemporary controversy is not confined to the Fourteenth Amendment, its scope and its meaning. In the last fifteen years there have
been a number of "communist cases," in which the issue of free speech
has been, either directly or indirectly, prominently "up." The liberal
position has long been that the "anti-communist" legislation of the state
and national governments poses definite threats to the First Amendment freedoms. (We leave to one side the contention, sometimes heard
in the course of the controversy, that restriction of those freedoms is
its "real" purpose.) The conservatives, who tend to believe that the
threat to our national security from internal communist subversion is
far greater than the liberals suppose, have not only supported this new
state and national legislation, but also have demanded stringent application of existing laws. These are the positions that we might well, in
light of our previous discussion of the nature of liberalism and conservatism, expect the two camps to adopt. The liberal is far more inclined to
accept all opinions on the basis of equality, and so to resist government legislation and activity which is predicated on the belief that
certain opinions and activities are not to be accorded equal toleration.

The Court's record in these cases has not, to be sure, been entirely
pleasing to either liberals or conservatives. Yet, on balance, the Court
has more often than not made decisions that are in line with liberal
premises. For this reason, the bulk of criticism recently directed toward
the Court has, here too, come from conservative quarters, while the
liberals have, in general, rallied to the Court's defense—some, indeed,
would say that they have "glorified" it in a way that is quite novel in
our history.[5] The student, if he keeps his eyes focused on the Court's
activity in this area in the years ahead may well witness an interesting
political phenomenon in American politics. If the Court "switches"
to the conservative side on this matter—and this is at least a possibility
—then we can expect, on the basis of past performance, the liberals and
conservatives to "flip-flop" in their attitudes toward the Court's role
and function in this area.

[5] We give it as our opinion that one did not hear in the American past the note liberals
often strike in contemporary discussion—according to which decisions by the Supreme Court
are not only *legally* binding, but *morally* binding as well.

Judicial Review: Liberalism and Conservatism

Judicial review poses theoretical problems for both conservatives and liberals. The liberal position toward the Court best illustrates, we feel, the nature of these difficulties. We can see good reason for the liberal to defend the Supreme Court at the present time. The defense is to a large extent based on *what* the Court has done. Presently the Court tends to give great weight to "civil liberties" and to be very sensitive to "minority rights" (for example, Negro rights, and the rights of atheists and agnostics). The Court, since 1937, has tended in short to promote the general goals of liberalism.

But we have noted in previous sections that the liberal seeks to advance political equality and majority rule in our system of government. He has protested against the House Rules Committee, on the grounds that it allows a few representatives to "block" what the many want; he has consistently opposed the seniority principle as a basis for selecting committee chairmen, on the grounds that this allows certain sections (the South and Midwest with their "one party" politics) to have greater weight in the legislative process than their numbers justify; and, among other things, he has sought to eliminate the filibuster in the Senate, on the grounds that it also allows a small minority to thwart the majority. In a more positive vein, as the next section will indicate, the liberal is inclined to argue for responsible and disciplined political parties, which will serve to translate the will of the popular majority more easily and with less distortion into public policy—on the grounds, precisely, that the majority are more *numerous* than the minority.

However—and here is the difficulty—it is obvious that, of all our institutions, the Supreme Court is that which is structured in a manner most inconsistent with the principles of political equality and majority rule. In fact, the Framers' obvious intent was to *isolate* the Supreme Court from those institutions, principally Congress, which would be most responsive to popular pressures and opinions. The judges serve for life; they can only be removed through the cumbersome process of impeachment; and their pay may not be diminished during their term. Furthermore, there is no direct formal structural linkage, between the justices of the Supreme Court and the people, that would enable the latter to hold the justices responsible for their decisions. It might seem surprising, in this context, that the liberals, who usually seem to be concerned about any and all demonstrable deviations from the majority rule principle, are today defending the role and function of the Supreme Court.

Some of the selections which follow will touch upon this theoretical problem. It should be noted here, however, and before we go further, that the liberal can, in this area, reasonably plead a "higher" consistency than would be involved in his forcing his views on the Supreme Court into the Procrustean bed of majority-rule doctrine. When the liberal today defends the Court, he defends a Court that he sees as engaged in blocking popular majorities that seek to infringe civil rights that are not only guaranteed by the Constitution (largely through the Bill of Rights and the Fourteenth Amendment), but are also, he believes, *necessary* in order for majority-rule to function at all. Thus one important area that needs to be investigated is what the liberal and conservative views are with respect to such rights. To this end, we have included writings that, we hope, will give the student a better picture of how liberals and conservatives tend to look at the major civil rights, such as those of speech, non-self-incrimination, and religious freedom. At this level the student will perceive important differences between the two camps that ultimately *must* lead them to different evaluations of the proper role and function of a Supreme Court in a democratic society.

A. Usurper or Faithful Watchdog?

29. The Supreme Court in the American Constitutional System*

EUGENE V. ROSTOW

TOWARD the end of the war, the German authorities ordered the Vichy government to build an aircraft factory in a cave near a small and remote French village. The French engineers assigned to the job were as painstaking, as meticulous—and as slow—as they dared be. They constructed elaborate ventilating systems, extensive dining rooms, and other arrangements for the welfare and safety of the working force. At length, when they could delay no longer, they began to make aircraft. Each stage of the project was of course known to the local leaders of the Resistance and reported fully by them to Allied Headquarters in London. As the first machines were at last loaded on trucks and started toward their destinations, they were ambushed in a forest and destroyed. In reprisal, the German army commander ordered fifty villagers picked by lot and had them shot.

A few weeks later, in midsummer 1944, as the tide of war turned, the French underground forces of the neighborhood captured the German garrison. Strong voices urged that at least fifty German soldiers be executed in turn. There were plausible arguments of international law for such a course: that the factory and its work violated the armistice agreement and

that the shooting of the villagers breached the laws of war. But one of the leaders of the group was a retired colonel of the regular army. After a long night's debate, his view prevailed. The men of the Maquis, he said, were soldiers of France. And the French Army did not kill its prisoners.

This episode illustrates much of what I propose to say. It is an instance in which the authority of the law, in some recognizable sense, prevailed over the passionate will of an aroused majority. Democracy was revealed as a process more complex than the taking of a single vote. And the law was vindicated, as it must be finally vindicated in a society of consent, not merely as a command—for here the colonel had no power to command—but as an appeal to what every man knew, at the decisive level of his own consciousness, was his own culture's vision of the right.

In this situation, the normal social machinery of order had almost completely broken down. It was being re-established as quickly as the pride and habits of a people long accustomed to government could put it together. But on that heated summer night in the village square, which had witnessed so much over the centuries, under the statue of some marshal or poet or minister of France, the angry men of the Maquis yielded unwillingly to their

* *Notre Dame Lawyer* 573 (1958). Reprinted by permission.

own ideal of law. The spokesman for the law was a man whose opinion had some symbolic meaning for his audience by reason of his status. But a retired colonel in his hunting clothes hardly represented either the dignity of a court or the coercive power of the state.

The subject with which I am concerned is the function of the Supreme Court of the United States in our system of government. We are experiencing another in the long cycle of political attacks on the integrity of the Court —the most serious since the Court-packing proposals of 1937. I believe that these attacks represent a challenge to the very possibility of survival of our constitutional system as an institution for assuring the free government of free men.

In deciding constitutional cases the judges must not only interpret the law and find the law, but make law too, as surely as they make law when they decide cases of tort, contract, or corporations. In a passage often quoted, Holmes once said, "I recognize without hesitation that judges do and must legislate, but they can do so only interstitially; they are confined from molar to molecular motions." [1] And one recalls Jeremiah Smith's pungent remark, after he left the Supreme Court of New Hampshire for the Harvard Law faculty: "Do judges make law? Of course they do. Made some myself." There is no tangible meaning in the charge often advanced that the Supreme Court is not interpreting the Constitution but acting as a super-legislature when it changes its views and reverses old cases. The Court's opinions may be good or bad as constitutional law—good or bad, that is to say, as projections and applications of what the Court conceives to be the purposes and ends of the Constitution. But no valid distinction of kind can

be drawn between the interpretive and the creative aspects of the judicial process in constitutional law or in any other branch of the law. This is not to say that the judges arrogate to themselves functions of the Congress or of the people in their creative reading of the Constitution. Such action on their part is an indistinguishable and inevitable part of their work as judges.

The topic I shall discuss is the propriety of this activity in a community which regards itself as a democracy. How can a society of majority rule condone the exercise of such far-reaching power by judges who are appointed for life? Is it true, as many have said, that the role of the Supreme Court in construing the Constitution makes it an oligarchic or aristocratic excrescence on our Constitution, to be abolished if possible, or at the least restricted to the narrowest possible jurisdiction?

This issue has been a matter of debate throughout our national history, and it is being vehemently debated today. Anxiety on this score has colored the temper in which some of our best judges have approached their work. Many have found in this issue a paradox impossible to reconcile with their faith as democrats.

I do not propose here to review the earlier stages of the controversy, nor to take an apologetic or a defensive position about the Court's power—indeed, its duty—to declare statutes or acts of the executive unconstitutional, where such a declaration is necessary to the decision of a case properly before it.[2] Such a power appears to me to be implicit, at the very least, in the Constitution itself. I am quite content to read the supremacy clause as making the power explicit, both with regard to state statutes and to acts of Congress, which are declared to be the supreme law of the land only when made "in Pursu-

---

[1] Southern Pac. Co. v. Jensen, 244 U.S. 205, 221 (1917) (dissenting opinion).

[2] Other aspects of the subject are treated in *The Democratic Character of Judicial Review*, infra, p. 147.

ance" of the Constitution.[3] This feature of the Court's authority was accepted by many contemporaries and asserted in the *Federalist* papers. It has been exercised by the Court from the beginning, as comparable power had been exercised by colonial courts. And it stands now, whatever the Founding Fathers may in fact have meant, as an integral feature of the living constitution, long since established as a working part of the democratic political life of the nation.

So notable a doubter as Judge Learned Hand has recently come around to the view that the Court's power is legitimate, even in cases under the Bill of Rights, although in his opinion the power exists only by judicial fiat. The judges properly engrafted the practice of judicial review upon the Constitution, he concludes, by applying the maxim that a document must be construed to assure the accomplishment of its clear purposes. The denial of the power, he contends, would have denied the constitutional experiment any chance of success. Without an arbiter to construe the Constitution, the system would have collapsed into endless conflicts over the boundaries of authority, otherwise incapable of resolution. And no branch of government other than the Court, Judge Hand says, could have taken on the task with anything like an equal expectation of preventing failure.[4]

There is no substance in the sup-

posed paradox of having appointed judges interpret the written constitution of a democratic society.

Popular sovereignty is a more subtle idea than the phrase "majority rule" sometimes implies.

The Constitution of the United States is the juridical act of the American people, not that of their Congress. It was, and is, a commitment to what the Founders called the republican form of government. Manhood suffrage was not universal in 1789 and equal manhood suffrage is not universal today. Equal manhood suffrage is, however, the ideal of the present stage of our constitutional theory as the ultimate source of sovereign authority in the American political system: the true base of what we should now identify as the republican form of government.

But universal manhood suffrage does not imply, in theory or in fact, that policy can properly be determined in a democracy only through universal popular elections, or that universal popular elections have or should have the capacity to make any and all decisions of democratic government without limits or delays of any kind. Representative government is, after all, a legitimate form of democracy, through which the people delegate to their elected representatives in legislatures, or in executive offices, some but not necessarily all of their powers, for a period of years. Neither the town meeting nor the Swiss referendum is an indispensable feature of democratic decision-making.

The object of the men who established the American Constitution, like the object of democratic theorists in all countries, and at all times, was not omnicompetent popular government, but the freedom of man as an individual being within a free society whose policies are based ultimately upon his consenting will. The Constitution did not give Congress the full powers of the British Parliament. If that had been the Founders' idea, no written

---

[3] U.S. Const., Art. VI, cl. 2. In Art. III, § 2, the judicial power is established as extending "to all Cases, in Law and Equity, arising under this Constitution, the Laws of the United States, and Treaties made, or which shall be made, under their authority." Hart and Wechsler go much further and consider the power to be clear beyond possibility of doubt, in terms both of the language and the legislative history of the document, *The Federal Courts and the Federal System* 14-19 (1953). The contrary view is most fully presented in Haines, *The Role of the Supreme Court in American Government and Politics, 1789-1935*, at 16-26, 227-45 (1944).

[4] Hand, *The Bill of Rights* 14-30 (1958).

constitution would have been necessary. On the contrary, the Constitution provided for a federal system of divided and delegated powers. Not only the courts, but the desirable friction of contending authority—the President versus the Congress, the states versus the nation—were relied upon to help preserve an equilibrium and thus to enforce the grand design of the Constitution.

For the highest aim of our Constitution is that it seeks to protect the freedom and dignity of man by imposing severe and enforceable limitations upon the freedom of the state. Americans thought then, and their wisdom is confirmed by all our subsequent experience, that man can be free, that political processes can in truth be democratic only when, and only because, the state is not free.

Every plan for democratic government, and every democratic constitution, contains vital elements beyond its ultimate derivation from the will of a majority. The Constitution provides a significant self-limitation upon the amendatory powers of the people—that no constitutional amendment can deny a state its equal suffrage in the Senate without its consent.[5] Every democracy divides issues of policy into several categories, to be settled by different means. Some decisions are made, without violating the principle of ultimate popular sovereignty, by appointed officials to whom important powers are delegated; e.g., to the boards which license doctors and lawyers, innkeepers and chiropodists; to the Federal Reserve Board or the Tariff Commission, the armed forces and the Department of Agriculture. The President has wide authority in the conduct of foreign relations. Other classes of decisions in all systems of democracy are remitted to legislative or judicial bodies, or are reserved for decision to regular or special elections, or to constituent assemblies. Still others, in most democratic societies, are set

apart and protected against the risk of hasty decision—issues of policy which are regarded as essential in assuring the division of functions among the branches of government, and the democratic character, over the long run, of the decision-making process itself. Even a classic Vermont town meeting knows limits on its jurisdiction. The town meeting can fix the tax rate, embark on a school lunch program, or decide to buy a fire engine or a snow plow. But it cannot abolish the town meeting, nor delegate its powers to the selectmen. It cannot deny a resident citizen his right to vote, nor confiscate the land of a Democrat, nor impose a sentence of exile, nor try a law suit over boundaries or the habits of cattle. Any change in the basic procedures through which policy is made requires a longer and more carefully considered series of votes.

This pattern for decision-making is characteristic of all democratic communities, whatever devices they may use for accomplishing the goal. And it is a pattern entirely consistent with their democratic character. Laws fixing different procedures for different kinds of elections do not deny the people their ultimate power. The reason for practices of this kind is a fundamental one. For democracy is more, much more, than a commitment to popular sovereignty. It is also, and equally, a commitment to popular sovereignty under law. Sometimes the precautionary devices to assure the legality of particular classes of decisions by particular elections are declared in a written constitution. Sometimes they are enforced only by the pattern of custom, the weight of tradition, or the influence and the residual powers of institutions of special prestige, like the crown in Great Britain and Sweden, or the presidency in France, Germany, and other countries.

Under our practice, limitations of this character determine the contours of the Constitution.

We often fall back, as Mr. Justice

---

[5] U.S. Const., Art. V.

Frankfurter has recently and eloquently done, upon Chief Justice Marshall's pregnant dictum: "It is a constitution we are expounding." [6] Marshall's comment is usually read, and properly read, to stress the need for flexibility in constitutional interpretation. In this perspective, emphasis is put on the fact that the Constitution provides a plan for government designed to last for centuries. Such an arrangement must bend, we are reminded, if it is not to break. It must give all the elected branches of government wide-ranging areas of discretion so that society may, by its own democratic decisions, adapt itself to circumstances and stresses vastly different from those of the isolated agricultural communities which put down their roots along the Atlantic coast during the seventeenth and eighteenth centuries.

All this is true enough. But Chief Justice Marshall's dictum cuts the other way with equal force. It is indeed a constitution we are expounding, a document to assure continuity as well as flexibility, boundaries of power as well as freedom of choice. Congress and the President must have enough authority under the Constitution to govern effectively, and they must be able to exercise their own political judgment in selecting among the alternative means available for dealing with the emergent problems of each new age. But it has never been supposed that elected officials had untrammeled discretion. The Constitution sets limits on their ambit of choice, and some of its limits can be enforced by the courts. For until the people change it, the Constitution is a document intended to assure them that their representatives function within the borders of their offices, and do not roam at will among the pastures of power; that certain essential values in our public life be preserved, not ignored; and, in government's choice among the instruments of action, that

those be selected which advance the cause of human freedom and those eschewed which threaten it. The idea was expressed by Bryce in these terms:

> The Supreme Court is the living voice of the Constitution—that is, of the will of the people expressed in the fundamental law they have enacted. It is, therefore, as some one has said, the conscience of the people, who have resolved to restrain themselves from hasty or unjust action by placing their representatives under the restriction of a permanent law. It is the guarantee of the minority, who, when threatened by the impatient vehemence of a majority, can appeal to this permanent law, finding the interpreter and enforcer thereof in a Court set high above the assaults of faction.[7]

We are not so naïve as to suppose that the ideas of the eighteenth century survive unchanged and by their own force fix both the limits of governmental power and the definition of men's political and social rights, privileges, and immunities in relation to government. We have all long since agreed that judges are men, not automatons—if indeed there ever was much doubt about it. Most judges are men who have had a lifetime of experience, or of study, in the world of the constitutional process. They come to their posts from the Senate or the courts, from the bar, or politics, or the law schools, with a considerable exposure to the role of the Constitution as a guiding force in American public life. Inevitably they bring different views to the Court—not differing personal and idiosyncratic views of what the Constitution might have been, but differing views, as constitutional lawyers, as to what the Constitution is, and what it ought to become, in terms of its own animating premises.

---

[6] "John Marshall and the Judicial Function," in *Government under Law* 6, 8 (A. E. Sutherland ed. 1956).

[7] *The American Commonwealth* 273 (1913). I am indebted to Dean Joseph O'Meara of the Notre Dame Law School for recalling this passage to my attention.

The nub of the present conflict over the Supreme Court concerns certain parts of the Constitution intended to have continuity—its definition of the ends to be sought by government through flexibly adapted means. There are two broad categories of issues in this realm: those of federalism and the division of powers on the one hand, and those dealing with the civil and political rights of persons on the other. While recent years have produced important cases dealing with the first of these two classes of problems, the stress in the current debate is certainly on the second—on the meaning, that is to say, which the Court has given to the constitutional guarantees of due process and of the equal protection of the laws in the relationships between the individual and the state. During the balance of this presentation, my attention will mainly be directed to such problems of civil rights under the Constitution.

It has occasionally been suggested that the reason for the extraordinarily rich and significant development of constitutional doctrine recently in the civil rights area is that wilful judges have been appointed to the Court, bent on legislating their personal opinions into the corpus of the law. The charge is unfair and untrue. By and large, the Supreme Court has not gone past the frontier of its power, nor taken on issues beyond its duty to decide, in its recent cycle of constitutional cases.

Why then, have there been so many civil rights cases recently, and why have they been so strongly libertarian?

Several basic factors lie behind the current flood of civil rights litigation. Along with the element of chance in the process of appointment to the bench, these factors also account for the character and quality of the trend of doctrine.

The first is that since the 1930s, and more acutely since World War II, the United States has been seeking to deal with novel and difficult problems of totalitarian aggression. Fifth column activity was an experience which stimu-

lated anxiety. The massive and uncompromising threat of communism is a reality beyond debate. It has caused, and will rightly continue to cause, grave anxiety as we seek to protect our national security against the challenging growth of communism as a force in world politics. Some of the numerous means selected to deal with problems of internal security have raised serious questions of constitutional right. It was inevitable and proper that these regulations, directly affecting the status and reputation of thousands of citizens, should be tested in the courts and ultimately presented for adjudication to the Supreme Court. There is nothing abnormal in this sequence, any more than it should have been considered abnormal for the Court after the Civil War to have faced the problems of *Ex parte Milligan*[8] and *Ex parte Garland*.[9] In addition, a variety of problems affecting the personal rights of citizens have naturally arisen out of the conduct of the war—like that of the *Korematsu* case[10]—and the presence abroad of American troops and their families. It was to be expected that many cases concerning the relation of military and civil authority should emerge in a period when we have more men under arms than ever before in peacetime.

The second general reason for the recent concentration of cases under the Bill of Rights on the docket of the Court is the process of social development in the United States, and especially the changing status of the Negro. The circumstances of world politics have given an important special accent to that development and have forcibly reminded us that we have been remiss in making good the pledge of equality for the Negro which we made

---

[8] 71 U.S. (4 Wall.) 2 (1866). See infra, pp. 249-57, for further discussion of this case.
[9] 71 U.S. (4 Wall.) 333 (1867).
[10] Korematsu v. United States, 323 U.S. 214 (1944). See infra, p. 193, for further discussion of this case.

in the Thirteenth, Fourteenth and Fifteenth Amendments to the Constitution. But this cycle of change would have proceeded of its own momentum, even without the stimulus of Soviet propaganda and the emergence all over the world of new and proud nations composed largely of colored peoples. The advance of the American Negro, since the end of slavery less than one hundred years ago, is a story of progress as well as of passivity; of blind resistance, but of inspiring efforts, too, carried on against the pressure of real and deep-seated psychological difficulty. Now the pace of development has quickened. More and more Negroes are receiving educational opportunities, and a larger proportion of the Negro group is being educated. In steadily increasing numbers, Negroes are succeeding in the occupations and professions of the middle class. They are gaining and keeping better employment opportunities throughout the nation, helped by periodic shortages of labor, the influence of legislation, and the spread of principle. The experience of the war posed the moral dilemma of the Negro's position with a clarity which has impressed many anew. And Negroes have become a political force in many elections. Changes of this order inevitably carry with them an intensification of the Negro's rightful demand that he be treated as a citizen of equal dignity in the public life of the United States. There is no brooking, and no blinking, the reality of this tide.

The third general reason for the current importance of civil rights problems in our constitutional law has been the growth of the law itself, and the character of public opinion, public fears, and public attitudes at this point in American history. The simple sentences of the Bill of Rights take on new meaning as they are used, case after case, court after court, Congress after Congress, in what is after all the biological process of life itself. These are not dead words on a piece of paper, but the seeds of living plants. And at this moment, the soil strongly favors vigorous growth for the tree of liberty.

The quickened zeal of the American people for the protection of their civil rights is hardly a surprising response to the circumstances of life in this century. Two brutal wars have had their impact. In many areas of the world, fascist and communist tyrannies of great power and influence have ruthlessly destroyed the rights of man and have degraded and humiliated man himself. The development of huge organizations of business, labor, and government has been accelerated by the circumstances of the Cold War, which requires apparently perpetual semi-mobilization. The fear that man as an individual will be submerged, coordinated, organized, and brainwashed into a social robot has been added to the other fears of the time. A mass egalitarian culture carries its own threat, at best. Against this background, it is healthy and natural that our powerful and continuous libertarian tradition has been so strongly reasserted. The spirit of the country has been not only to resist the conformity of a garrison society, but to counterattack where possible. In that process of thesis and antithesis, the Supreme Court has played a leading part. The great opinions of Chief Justice Hughes, of Justice Sutherland in the *Scottsboro* case,[11] of Justices Brandeis, Holmes, Stone, and Cardozo, are yielding now their intended fruit. In our common law approach to the problem of constitutional construction, one case leads to another as lawyers see new vistas opening and develop new possibilities for their clients within the ambit of evolving doctrine. And the Court has thus been an educational force, along with many others, in helping to mold a state of opinion far more sensitive to civil liberties than that which prevailed in the United States thirty or fifty years ago.

Timid men see danger in this de-

---

[11] Powell v. Alabama, 287 U.S. 45 (1932).

velopment. They fear that by striking down the decisions of powerful legislators, the courts will weaken their authority and expose the judicial institution itself to attacks which may sweep it away. From time to time, indeed, such attacks have developed, and one is now being mounted. So far, happily, all such threats to the power of the Court have been defeated, on sober reflection, by the historic confidence of the American people in the Supreme Court as a detached agency of the Constitution itself, one remove at least from what Judge Learned Hand recently called "the pressure of public hysteria, public panic and public greed." [12]

The question remains, however, whether the Court, in its own wisdom, as one among the instruments of democratic American government, should continue on its present course or retreat prudently from the field, leaving the constitutional guarantees of personal and political freedom largely to the discretion of legislatures and presidents.

The beloved and respected Judge Learned Hand expressed himself again to this general effect in his Holmes Lectures at the Harvard Law School.[13] These lectures modify in important ways the views he had previously advanced on the subject. A few years ago, he seemed to be urging that the broad, general commandments of the Bill of Rights should not be enforced at all by the courts, but should be left as moral admonitions to the conscience of legislators and other public officials.[14] In his Holmes Lectures, he takes a long step forward. In the realm of the Bill of Rights, as in other realms, he says, the courts should annul statutes or other acts of government which are

outside the grant of power to the grantee, and should not include a

review of how the power has been exercised. This distinction in the case of legislation demands an analysis of its component factors. These are an estimate of the relevant existing facts and a forecast of the changes that the proposed measure will bring about. In addition it involves an appraisal of the values that the change will produce, as to which there are no postulates specific enough to serve as guides on concrete occasions. In the end all that can be asked on review by a court is that the appraisals and the choice shall be impartial. The statute may be far from the best solution of the conflicts with which it deals; but if it is the result of an honest effort to embody that compromise or adjustment that will secure the widest acceptance and most avoid resentment, it is "Due Process of Law" and conforms to the First Amendment. In theory any statute is always open to challenge upon the ground that it was not in truth the result of an impartial effort, but from the outset it was seen that any such inquiry was almost always practically impossible, and moreover it would be to the last degree "political." [15]

I am at a loss to understand the Judge's argument. Any breach of his rule, he says, moves the judges across the subtle boundary between the judicial and the legislative function. By seeking to apply the vague and general ideas of the Bill of Rights to concrete

[12] Hand, *The Bill of Rights* 68 (1958).

[13] *The Bill of Rights* (1958).

[14] Hand, "The Contribution of an Independent Judiciary to Civilization," in *The Spirit of Liberty* 155-65 (Dilliard ed. 1952).

[15] *The Bill of Rights* 66-67 (1958). My colleague Alexander M. Bickel does not read *The Bill of Rights* as modifying in any substantial sense the views which Judge Learned Hand expressed in his earlier essay, referred to in note 14. I freely admit that there is difficulty in construing the judge's eloquent and elegant, but sometimes impressionistic nonjudicial prose. It is, as always, a delight to read; but in this case it is hard to parse. Mr. Bickel may well be right, that what Judge Hand seems to concede on certain pages, he takes away on others. But the note of concession is there. See, especially, pp. 30, 33, 56, 64.

situations, and especially by taking one step beyond what he seems to regard as the easy issue of ultra vires, the Court would in effect exercise the suspensive veto of the House of Lords. In the face of such conduct, he says, we should lose the bracing privilege of self-government and submit to the overlordship of judges as a bevy of Platonic Guardians, a state of affairs he finds irksome and repugnant to his staunch democratic principles.[16]

Judge Hand would be the first to recognize that in applying a statute or a clause of the Constitution the judges must often make the law while they interpret it. Yet the heart of his argument seems to rest on a deceptively simple distinction between the judicial and the legislative functions. He defines "A" as not being "B." Legislators make certain decisions after weighing and balancing a series of conflicting interests, including their own interpretation of the constitutional limitations on their authority. The judicial function, by his definition, should be non-legislative in character. The crucial leap in his syllogism is the passage from this proposition to the thought that the judges must rigidly exclude from their minds consideration of the factors which influenced the legislative decision. The only exception he admits is that the courts may review the legislative decision on the constitutional question whether the legislature had the power to act at all in a given realm, and may go further, along a path whose implications I for one do not pretend to understand, and enquire whether the legislative decision was honest and impartial.

The distinction does not correspond to the realities of either the judicial or the legislative process. The Court's function is recognizably different from that of the legislature or of the executive, even when it must weigh the same considerations in the scales. The forum is different. The time is different, so that the pressure of contending interests appears in a different perspective. And the constitutional issues are not peripheral, as often must be the case in legislative or executive decisions, but central to the problem before the Court. The judges may be foolhardy or prudent, in error or in doubt, grasping for power or circumspect in the exercise of their duty. Yet the Court, as a Court, must consider many of the problems previously evaluated by the institutions of action. Judge Hand's attempt to draw a line which would neatly exclude from the Court's view all the issues passed upon by the legislature or the executive fails, as all such attempts have failed in the past. Even in determining whether a given set of circumstances sufficiently affects the national economy to justify the invocation of the commerce power—a function which Judge Hand concedes is proper —the judges cannot escape reviewing some aspects of the substance of Congress' prior decision. They may call that decision "arbitrary," or the connection "insubstantial," or go further, according to Judge Hand, and find it not "impartial." These various verbal formulas are all unconvincing in identifying what the courts must in fact do in exercising the limited, Handian power of judicial review. That function cannot be distinguished, as a function, from what the judges do in interpreting statutes, some of which are as general as constitutional prescriptions, or in deciding common law cases in the light of what they conceive to be the ultimate social purposes of the received tradition.

The judges do not, of course, have complete freedom to make the Constitution what they say it is, despite the breadth of its language. But they cannot escape this part of their judicial function—their work as lawmakers in applying the words and history of the Constitution to new situations, often unknown in the eighteenth century, in the interest of preserving and protecting the social values the Constitution

[16] Id. at 67-73.

was designed to assure. In doing this part of their job, Judge Hand says, they should be concerned only with the existence of the legislative or executive power, not with substituting their judgment for that of the legislature or the executive as to whether the power has been rightly used. This is true, but the distinction is not very useful, however often repeated. The trouble with Judge Hand's test is that it fails to deal with the problem the judges in fact face, and denounces them instead for various crimes they could not well commit. It is rare, indeed impossible, to catch a judge openly "substituting" his legislative judgment for that of the Congress. His problems are in another realm. Many of them arise as slippery verbal issues of qualification or classification. In terms of the record, have the defendants practiced coercion or persuasion? Did Congress punish for a crime, or merely regulate foreign affairs? Collisions between the exercise of two conceded powers, or a clash between two clauses of the Constitution which must be reconciled in a given situation, raise most of the remaining difficulty.

Let me propose an example, in the interest of testing Judge Hand's thesis by the classic maneuver of the case method. The Securities Act of 1933 makes it unlawful for those who issue, underwrite, or deal in securities to use any means of communication in interstate commerce, or of the mails, to sell certain kinds of securities unless a registration statement meeting the requirements of the Act is in effect, and unless they duly deliver a formal and approved prospectus to their potential customers.[17] Comparable restrictions on freedom of speech can be found in the Labor Management Relations Act,[18]

dealing with what employers can say to their employees in the context of a dispute about union recognition, and in certain other statutes dealing with the distribution of securities, proxy fights, and reorganizations. Congress has power to regulate interstate commerce, a rubric which includes a large part of securities transactions and labor relations. And it is under the flat injunction of the First Amendment: Congress shall make no law abridging the freedom of speech. Extended investigations, committee reports, and legislative debates preceded the passage both of the Securities Act and of the basic federal labor legislation. Presumably Congress weighed the rival claims of freedom and of order in these realms and took into account the prohibition of the First Amendment.

Suppose the issue came before the Supreme Court. The Court is bound by its history to enforce the First Amendment. Judge Hand says that the case for wide judicial review is strongest where freedom of speech is threatened, although he disapproves of much, perhaps all, that has been done by the courts in this area in the name of judicial review.[19] In such a case, the Court would face an apparent conflict between the policies of the First Amendment and that of congressional action based on the commerce power.

Of what help is Judge Hand's rule in such a case? Can the Court stop by saying that its role is to determine the boundaries of power, and that it will not consider in any way whether the exercise of power is justifiable—whether, that is, the situation calling for legislation was serious, whether the regulation in question was necessary or only incidental, whether the legitimate goal of the legislation could have been achieved without the restriction on freedom of speech, etc.? It could hardly evade the question by saying that the restraint on freedom of speech is not in fact an "abridgement" of that freedom, or that the First Amendment

[17] 48 Stat. 77 (1933), 15 U.S.C. §§ 77(d), (e) (1951). Subsequent amendments have not altered the character of the conflict presented. 15 U.S.C.A. § 77(e) (1957).

[18] 49 Stat. 452, § 8 (1935), as amended, 61 Stat. 142, § 8(c) (1947), 29 U.S.C. § 158 (1956). Mr. Justice Douglas discusses the problem briefly in *The Right of the People* 56 (1958).

[19] Hand, *op. cit.,* supra note 13, at 69.

deals only with political speech, not commercial speech. No such loopholes are available. What meaning is there in the charge that the Court would be taking over the "legislative" function and going beyond its role as "judicial" arbiter of the Constitution, if in this case it did what has to be done—to weigh and balance the relative importance of the two considerations equally involved, Congress' judgment that the protection of commerce made it desirable to impose a "prior" restraint on speech, and the apparent absolutism of the First Amendment?

Or, alternatively, should we read Judge Hand's approach—although it is not posed in such terms—as implying a special rule for the judicial review of the Bill of Rights, on the ground that in this area the constitutional phrases are so vague that they give the judges no footing sufficiently assured to permit a rational exercise of the judicial method? Is the language of the Bill of Rights so different from that of other clauses in the Constitution, or from the broad language of many statutes, as to make the judicial function here utterly indistinguishable from that of a legislature? The difficulties which the Courts have encountered in construing many, many clauses of the Constitution—those dealing, for example, with treason, with the privileges and immunities of citizenship, the commerce clause, or the taxing powers—cast doubt upon the thought that there is a tenable distinction of kind or of degree to be drawn between the Bill of Rights and the rest of the Constitution on this ground. And of course the weight of history stands heavily against so easy an escape from the burden of duty.

I submit that Judge Hand's formula would not permit the most restrained judge to escape the reality of the Court's task in passing on the constitutionality of the Securities Act and a thousand comparable cases. Nor, equally, would it help him to see, describe, and understand the problem he does face. To take Marshall's dictum in still another sense, it *is* a Constitution the Court is expounding, a single document whose various parts must often be interpreted together, like those of other legal instruments, to give effect to the purpose of the Constitution as a whole. I, for one, can see no way on the Court's part to evade the necessity for such an evaluation in a case of this kind—not as a third chamber, but as the Court charged with responsibility to the people for interpreting their Constitution. The Court may say that one interest or the other prevails. It may be right or wrong in the eyes of law professors, the Congress, or the people. Its decision may be reversed by a later Court, altered by Congress, or overturned by constitutional amendment. But it does not advance clarity or exactness of thought to say that the Court's construction of the Constitution is not a judicial, but a legislative act.

Mr. Justice Douglas put the issue faced by the Court in cases of this order more realistically in his recent lectures at Franklin and Marshall College.[20] In his chapter on freedom of expression, for example, he contrasts the opposing claims the Court must weigh in several groups of cases. Even the seeming absolutism of the First Amendment occasionally yields, in his survey, despite the weight he gives to the value it represents, in favor of civil order itself. Thus he would permit official restraint of speech where a sensational newspaper threatened the possibility of a fair trial; where picketing was an integral part of a breach of the peace or an antitrust violation; or where an employer's words addressed to his employees sought not merely to persuade but to coerce.[21] The results advocated in his survey are not as important, for present purposes, as the method he uses. For he does analyze, as Judge Hand does not, the issues

[20] *The Right of the People* (1958).
[21] *Ibid.*, Lecture 1.

which the Court must determine in situations of this kind: the classification of factual situations with respect to constitutional categories; the delineation of the boundaries of power; and the resolution of conflicts between interests and powers of seemingly equal dignity, in the light of a theory of the Constitution as a whole.

It is on this phase of the problem that Judge Hand's critique of the present Court is most vulnerable. For he would subordinate the Bill of Rights as an effective working part of the constitutional universe. The language of the Bill of Rights, he says, is vague and general. Its application to highly charged situations of conflict is almost always full of political dynamite. Therefore he urges that the Bill be confined to the narrowest possible scope. In the case of freedom of speech, freedom of religion, and the due process clause, review should be limited to one issue: legislation should be upheld if it comes within a granted power, unless the Court is satisfied that the statute or regulation was not the product of an effort "impartially to balance the conflicting values." [22] As to the other provisions of the first eight amendments, Judge Hand says,

except perhaps the last [they] are all addressed to specific occasions and have no such scope as those I have mentioned. Many of them embody political victories of the seventeenth century over the Crown, and carry their own nimbus of precedent. So far as they do, any extension beyond their historical meaning seems to me unwarranted, though that limitation is not always observed. It is true that at times they may present issues not unlike those that arise under the First Amendment and the "Due

[22] Hand, *op. cit.* supra note 12, at 61. See also pp. 37-55. I have never before heard it suggested that the decisions of a political and partisan body like the Congress of the United States could be impeached if a court concludes that the Congressmen were not "impartial."

Process Clause," and in such cases I cannot see why courts should intervene, unless it appears that the statutes are not honest choices between values and sacrifices honestly appraised.[23]

These prescriptions seem to me to be utterly wrong as maxims of construction for a Constitution designed to help preserve an essential continuity in our legal tradition through long periods of time. They derive, as Judge Hand frankly admits, from his qualified, but still strongly held, conviction that the exercise of the power of judicial review is undemocratic in character, and is therefore to be confined as severely by judicial self-restraint as strong-willed men find it possible to do.

The contrary view seems to me by far the stronger, both in theory and as an interpretation of our history. The dominance of the popular will through the mechanisms of our system of government is achieved in large part by having the courts enforce limitations on the power of elected officials, in the name of constitutional provisions which only the people can alter by amendment. Those limitations are of peculiar importance where the individual is being protected against the pervasive influence of the modern state. If the individual is to have a considerable scope for personal freedom in the American society of the future, he will have to continue to rely on the courts to see to it that people are treated by the state in ways which conform to constitutional standards of democratic propriety. The weight of history is evidence that the people do expect the courts to interpret, declare, adapt, and apply these constitutional provisions, as one of their main protections against the possibility of abuse by Presidents and legislatures. The history leaves no room, it seems to me, for a thesis like Judge Hand's, that the courts should refuse to exercise their constitutional

[23] Id. at 65-66.

powers, especially in the area of civil rights.

The Chief Justice's recent answer, somber and simple, perhaps even simplistic, reverts to the position of Hamilton in No. 78 of *The Federalist:*

we are mindful of the gravity of the issue inevitably raised whenever the constitutionality of an Act of the National Legislature is challenged. No member of the Court believes that in this case the statute before us can be construed to avoid the issue of constitutionality. That issue confronts us, and the task of resolving it is inescapably ours. This task requires the exercise of judgment, not the reliance upon personal preferences. Courts must not consider the wisdom of statutes but neither can they sanction as being merely unwise that which the Constitution forbids.

We are oath-bound to defend the Constitution. This obligation requires that congressional enactments be judged by the standards of the Constitution. The Judiciary has the duty of implementing the constitutional safeguards that protect individual rights. When the Government acts to take away the fundamental right of citizenship, the safeguards of the Constitution should be examined with special diligence.

The provisions of the Constitution are not timeworn adages or hollow shibboleths. They are vital, living principles that authorize and limit governmental powers in our nation. They are the rules of government. When the constitutionality of an Act of Congress is challenged in this Court, we must apply those rules. If we do not, the words of the Constitution become little more than good advice.

When it appears that an Act of Congress conflicts with one of these provisions, we have no choice but to enforce the paramount commands of the Constitution. We are sworn to do no less. We cannot push back the limits of the Constitution merely to accommodate challenged legislation. We must apply those limits as the Constitution prescribes them, bearing in mind both the broad scope of legislative discretion and the ultimate responsibility of constitutional adjudication. We do well to approach this task cautiously, as all our predecessors have counseled. But the ordeal of judgment cannot be shirked. In some 81 instances since this Court was established it has determined that congressional action exceeded the bounds of the Constitution. It is so in this case.[24]

Thus I should conclude that there can be no justification for treating the essential canons of the Bill of Rights as more static, more narrowly confined to their eighteenth-century meaning, than other clauses of the Constitution—the commerce clause or the war power, for example. On the contrary, these aspects of the Constitution are the very soul of the document. As my colleague Charles L. Black, Jr., has recently said:

There is an even deeper reason for the creative and broad construction of the civil liberties guarantees in the Constitution. Consider the place of these phrases—"equal protection," "freedom of speech," and the rest—in the moral life of our nation. They state our highest aspirations. They are our political reason for being; they are the things we talk about when we would persuade ourselves or others that our country deserves well of history, deserves to be rallied to in its present struggle with a system in which "freedom of speech" is freedom to say what is welcome to authority, and "equal protection" is the equality of the cemetery. Surely such words, standing where they do and serving such a function, are to be construed with the utmost

[24] Trop v. Dulles, 356 U.S. 86, 103-04 (1958).

breadth. The proper office of legal acumen is to give them new scope and life, rather than to prune them down to whatever may currently be regarded as harmlessness. Yet, we must not forget that, if they are to be construed broadly, the Court has no choice but to apply them broadly, even against legislation, and if the Court applies them narrowly, its only justification must be that their scope is narrow.[25]

There is another reason for having the Court approach its problems under the Bill of Rights in the spirit of the common law judges, elaborating certain simple ideas, in response to the pressure of changing fact situations, into the splendor of their full potential. The ideas of the Constitution about the relation of man to the state are positive, as well as negative. There is more to the Constitution than a set of limitations and prohibitions. These rules are not meant merely to confine governmental agencies, but strongly to influence the development of society and of men's ideas.

As the men of the eighteenth century knew well, following Locke and Montesquieu, the law is a continuing force in the process of public life. It has consequences, as well as causes. The changing dispositions of law respond to changing conditions in society itself. But in turn they profoundly influence the character of men and of their society. The law is not a mere artifact, reflecting the pressure of events. It is and should be a vital element in the movement of society toward its ultimate goals. In this perspective, the constitutional decisions of the Court are more than a factor of continuity in protecting the democratic character of our political arrangements and in protecting the individual against arbitrary action by the state. They are also among the significant forces influencing the evolution of our constitutional

[25] "Old and New Ways in Judicial Review," *Bowdoin College Bulletin* 11 (1957).

ideal itself. Montesquieu defined the ideal of law for each culture as the spirit of its laws—the cultural norm toward which each society aspires in the day-to-day processes of its lawmaking. But, he pointed out, that spirit was not fixed and immutable even for a given culture. It could and did evolve through time, for better or for worse, toward tyranny or toward the ideal of responsible freedom. And the principal function of law, in his view, is to serve as one of the educational and formative influences of the culture, not merely in bringing the law in action up to the standard of the existing goal of law, but in perfecting the goal of the law. Thus, in construing and enforcing the basic purposes of the Bill of Rights, the Court is a leading participant in the endless striving of our culture to approach the values of dignity and freedom for the individual whose grandeur dominates our Constitution. To preserve, to enrich, to further these ideas of the highest good in the experience of our people is one of the first aims of the Constitution.

It will not do to say that in construing these provisions of the Constitution the Court should be limited to the meaning the terms had when they were written. The broad general purposes of the Founding Fathers abide, as aspirations, as guidelines to the interpreters of the future. But the circumstances to which their words refer are gone. The context is changed. The old perspective cannot be recaptured, because it no longer exists. The scope and meaning of the provisions of the Bill of Rights evolve, like the meaning of other constitutional terms and other terms in law. They are stages in the organic process by which ideas flourish or languish as new generations find for themselves new and valid meanings for the old words. Our constitutional doctrines do not grow quite as freely as do those of Great Britain, for the written constitution has its own powerful limiting influence. But they grow in the same soil of history. As the Court said in 1914, "the provisions of the Constitution are not mathematical formulas having their essence in their form. . . . Their significance is vital, not formal; it is to be gathered not simply by taking the words and a dictionary, but by considering their origin and the line of their growth." [26] These words, Justice Frankfurter has well said, are "purposely left to gather meaning from experience." [27] Each Justice of the Court meets his highest challenge in seeking to interpret these words in ways which contribute to the advancement of the rule of law, and to the advancement of the law itself. Thus can the Court help in the education of opinion and play its part in the colloquium through which the ideas of the community about law and justice are formed.

For the people, and not the courts, are the final interpreters of the Constitution. The Supreme Court and the Constitution it expounds cannot survive unless the people are willing, by and large, to live under it. And this is the ultimate issue to consider, as we review the relationship between the work of the Court and the state of public opinion. For in a political system resting on popular sovereignty, obedience to the law is not a sufficient rule.

The nature of the problem is most starkly presented by the present reaction of some of our fellow citizens in the South to the opinions of the federal courts in the cases holding racial segregation in various forms a violation of the Fourteenth Amendment. They find these decisions disturbing, contrary to their customs, and threatening in many acute ways. They believe the decisions represent a usurpation of power by the judges. They realize that these cases could not possibly be reversed by a constitutional amendment. Yet many are resolved to disobey the law of the Constitution as declared by the Court. The potentialities of this conflict are far more serious than those presented by the Jenner Bill and the Butler amendments to it. Law can retain its vitality even though it is not instantly or completely obeyed. But it cannot survive if it is openly and generally defied. In handling the first great public manifestation of civil disobedience, in Little Rock, President Eisenhower put his action squarely and exclusively on the issue of law enforcement: the undoubted obligation of the executive to see to it that court orders are obeyed.

This proposition, however weighty, calls up some disturbing and fundamental echoes in a democratic society, where citizen responsibility goes beyond that implicit in the electoral process itself. A hundred years ago, in the decade before the Civil War, the problem of civil disobedience was debated throughout the land. Thoreau had helped stir up the issue with his writings and his dramatic refusal to pay taxes to a government which tolerated human slavery. Emerson and others joined in widely supported movements to deny enforcement to the Fugitive Slave Law. And there was a great debate in Boston between Benjamin R. Curtis, later a Justice of the Supreme Court, and other leaders of the time about the citizen's duty as juror to vote for conviction in Fugitive Slave Law Cases.[28] The question whether there may be public duties that transcend the duty to obey the law has arisen in other settings: President Eisenhower, as a commanding general, signed an appeal in 1942 to the French officers in North Africa to disobey the orders of the Vichy government, which we recognized as having authority over them. In some cases before our courts of military justice, superior orders are not necessarily a justification for brutal and inhuman acts on the part of soldiers. Above all, of course, the problem

[26] Gompers v. United States, 233 U.S. 604, 610 (1914).

[27] National Mut. Ins. Co. v. Tidewater Transfer Co., 337 U.S. 582, 646 (1949) (dissenting opinion).

[28] 1 Curtis, *A Memoir of Benjamin Robbins Curtis, LL.D.* 112-36 (1879).

is posed by the Nuremberg trials themselves.

This series of experiences raises an ultimate issue in the moral life of a democracy: the freedom of the citizen to disobey the law when his conscience is deeply engaged. I do not assert that such a *right* exists. But there are times in the history of law when the most law-abiding citizen must acknowledge that a *conflict* exists, and a serious one: when, that is, the positive law seems to be inconsistent with the mores, the purposes, even the objective will of the community. We acknowledge the reality of the problem by exempting conscientious objectors from the military service—an act of grace and civilization with far-reaching implications. Many have claimed that the ultimate difference between democracies and totalitarian systems is that a democracy recognizes the citizen's ultimate responsibility for the moral content of the law, and for his own moral ratification and acceptance of the law.

The problem can be put in another form: the relative importance of force and consent in law. Is law, as Holmes once remarked, merely what is at the end of the policeman's stick? Is such apparent positivism an adequate explanation of law? Or must there be acceptance by the community of the rightness of law, as well as the rightness of the procedures by which law is made?

We must start our consideration of the constitutional crisis precipitated by the segregation cases by sympathetically facing the fact that many of our fellow citizens in the South are deeply troubled, and that they believe these decisions are wrong.

I myself should claim that the demands of order against chaos require every government to enforce the law as the judges make it. This is true, at least, in states generally ordered by the procedures of law. But I suggest also that in a democratic society, dealing with a problem like this one, enforcement is not enough. The law must be an educational force as well as a force, and a moral force too. Official enforcement efforts do not meet the full obligation of the executive to the law unless they include something more than the use of the policeman's stick. They must assert with equal power what in this case I believe to be true—that our developing constitutional law of equality for all is right; that it expresses the strongest force in American life, our commitment to the corpus of ideals represented by the Declaration of Independence and the Constitution; and that at some level of consciousness or unconsciousness, silently or openly, all our people, including our brothers of the South, know this, believe it, and will in the end accept it.[29]

It is a test of our capacity for self-government to resolve this conflict without sacrificing the ultimate dignity of man. Does freedom in a free society ever permit, or require, a citizen to disobey the positive law? At what point might the appeal of conscience be justified against the obligation to obey? In this realm—the conflict of individual freedom and order—we must beware lest action in the name of order lose the power which in this case it so clearly has—of being action also in the highest interests of freedom.

Those who believe that the Supreme Court is right in its course must wrestle with the minds and hearts of those who believe it is wrong, until a national consensus emerges and prevails. Lawyers, who are officers of the law, and government officials charged with enforcement responsibility cannot leave the task of persuasion exclusively to the federal judges, who have so firmly led the way. Each should accept his share in the process of education which is indispensable if the law is to be vindicated, in the end, by our people's willing acceptance of its rightness, not merely by their sullen acquiescence in the principle of order alone.

[29] Black, "Paths to Desegregation," *New Republic* 10-15 (Oct. 21, 1957).

30. Frontiers of Judicial Power*

CHARLES S. HYNEMAN

THIS book comes to an end with a brief discussion of some problems that, in my judgment, are certain to confront the judges if they push further into the realm of affairs traditionally thought the special domain of the elected branches of government. I select for attention three possible avenues of aggrandizement which the Supreme Court might pursue. They are worthy of consideration because each is earnestly recommended to the Supreme Court today and because certain acts of the Court in recent years indicate that some of the judges may be ready to move in the directions proposed. The three recommendations for more aggressive judicial activity are (1) that the Supreme Court rescue the nation from major failures by the elected branches, (2) that the Supreme Court assume a special responsibility to make the democratic process secure, and (3) that the Court be bolder in identifying ideals and setting public officials in pursuit of those ideals.

1. For the Correction of Political Failures

This proposal at its extreme has come to me in conversation. I have been told that the Supreme Court has a mandate from the Constitution to order termination of segregation in the schools and other places of assembly, but also that, even if the Constitution contained no such mandate, it would still have been the duty of the Supreme Court to order termination of

segregation in 1954. This would have been its duty because segregation was the key to incipient revolution; another year or two without hope of relief from segregation, and there would have been bloodshed and burnings extensive enough to be called revolution. When the price of failure to act is so high, all departments of government have an obligation to do the act which avoids the failure and averts the danger. If I interpret the argument correctly, Congress having failed to act, the president had as great an obligation to order the termination of segregation as did the Supreme Court.

The taproot that feeds this new growth of constitutional doctrine is the belief that the Constitution does more than grant authority to exercise governmental power; it requires the lawmaking authority to exploit the power granted to it. We encountered this position earlier in the proposition that the equal-protection clause requires state governments to protect the weaker part of the population from discriminatory treatment at the hands of the stronger.

If this new constitutional doctrine, as yet hardly noticed in the literature, persists, whole books will be necessary for its explication. I shall here limit myself to two very general comments.

A. *The doctrine of political obligation and judicial intervention in policy-making implies a deep devotion to the democratic ideal and a lack of confidence in the political process as a way of realizing that ideal.* The most aggressive judicial intervention may be justified on the ground that the political departments, by failure to enact and enforce law, are thwarting the expectations and preferences of the pop-

* Chapter 20, *The Supreme Court on Trial* (New York: Atherton Press, 1963), pp. 261-275. Reprinted by permission of Atherton Press. Copyright 1963 by Prentice-Hall, Inc., Atherton Press, 70 Fifth Avenue, New York.

ulation. The judicial branch thus becomes a backstop for the legislature and Executive. When the latter fail to read the public mind correctly, the judges are authorized to come in with a correct reading. When the political departments read correctly but fail to respond to the instructions they read, the judges may order those departments to act, or may even formulate and announce the policies which they suspect they can never force from the elected officials.

The new doctrine does not necessarily imply a rejection of the basic political structure and main political processes of the United States. One may contend that the American electoral-representative system is more responsive to public expectations and preferences than any other yet constructed, but at the same time insist that all political systems suffer failures. To argue that the Supreme Court must take up where Congress and the president leave off is only to argue that the elective and nonelective branches of the government complement or supplement one another; it is not to argue that either should withdraw from the field of action or that the nation would be wise to give the whole of policy-making to the one institution and process which may be most trusted by most people.

B. *Adherents to the new doctrine must face the question: When is there a political failure?* We may differentiate four sets of circumstances that might account for the failure of the political departments to act when the judges think they should have done so.

First, there may be a lack of sensitiveness to, or a reluctance to respond to, popular expectations and preferences. Can we assume that judicial knowledge, pleadings, and the evidence and argument presented in the course of a trial will provide a better reading of the public mind than the lawmakers can obtain from their unrestrained contacts with their constituents and the forceful demands for

attention put on them by people who favor and people who oppose any contemplated action? Can we assume that the appointed judges, when convinced that they know what the people want, will feel greater compulsion to respond to popular demands than an assembly made up of elected men who must soon win re-election or terminate their service?

Second, there may be a need for action when there is little public support for it. The statesman has a vision of public need that reaches far beyond that of the average man; otherwise he is no statesman. Statesmanship may lie in judges as surely as in elected officials. If they see no clear instruction in the Constitution and hear no clamor from an agitated population, how are the judges to explain their invasion of the policy-making area? Or is this an irrelevant question? It may be that the proponents of the new doctrine of positive obligation and judicial intervention do not recommend judicial action when there is no discernible will of the people.

Third, elected officials may fail to act when they are agreed that action is required. They fail to act because they cannot agree on the appropriate solution for the problem confronting them. This predicament raises all the questions discussed above in connection with scheduling solutions and adapting corrective measures. And it challenges one to review his confidence in the time-honored supposition that an assembly of men popularly elected and representative of all parts of the population is the best assurance that social problems will be dealt with when the emotional state of the nation is favorable to effective solution. If one undertakes a careful and thorough justification of judicial intervention to escape the political impasse, his inquiry will have much more to say about the distribution of popular expectations and demands and about experience with electoral-representative instruments th..n it will about the promise that judges will find solutions that bring tranquility to the population and free the society to realize its common ideals.

Fourth, elected officials may pursue policies which some people think tyrannical. This dilemma arises for any man when he concludes that the policy-makers are doing what most of the people want done, but he is at the same time certain that the majority of the people are demanding a wrong thing. How is one to know when the demands of any part of the population are tyrannous? The literature we call political theory has not developed tests on which scholars have agreed. If there are any trusted tests of tyranny in American law, they must be the tests which an earlier Court applied in due-process cases and which the present Court applies in cases arising under the First Amendment. I think the evidence shows that, in the application of these tests, differences of position among the judges are as great as the difference between a majority of the judges and the lawmakers who enacted the law.

Perhaps it is a doubt that suitable tests of political failure can be found that induces some contemporary judicial activists to propose a different primary objective for an aggressive judicial review. If one believes that judgments about political failure are too much an expression of undisciplined opinion, he may nevertheless be convinced that there are objective tests for deciding whether laws are the product of a healthy, functioning, efficacious democratic system. Such a belief is behind the second of the three recommendations cited at the beginning of this chapter.

2. To Secure a Democratic Process

The most pointed and positive proposal for the judiciary to undertake a general policing of the democratic process appears in an article by the same law school dean who supplied the figure of judges in endless conversation with the nation.

The freedom of the legislatures to act within wide limits of constitutional construction is the wise rule of judicial policy only if the processes through which they act are reasonably democratic.

One of the central responsibilities of the judiciary in exercising its constitutional power is to help keep the other arms of government democratic in their precedures. The Constitution should guarantee the democratic legitimacy of political decisions by establishing essential rules for the political process. It provides that each state should have a republican form of government. And it gives each citizen the political as well as the personal protection of the Bill of Rights and other fundamental constitutional guarantees. The enforcement of these rights would assure Americans that legislative and executive policy would be formed out of free debate, democratic suffrage, untrammeled political effort, and full inquiry.[1]

Rostow does not say whether he thinks all or nearly all the main tests of democratic character were written into the Constitution or whether the absence of some important ones will require the Supreme Court judges to identify a set of ideal institutions and behaviors and imbed them in the Constitution at points where its language most yields to impression—for instance, by making the Constitution's references to "republican form of government," "privileges and immunities of citizens," and "due process of law" requirements for the establishment of arrangements and practices that meet the judges' conceptions of a healthy democracy. The history of controversy over judicial power to date leaves no

[1] Eugene V. Rostow, "The Democratic Character of Judicial Review," *Harvard Law Review,* 66 (1952), 202, 210.

room to doubt that, for a great many people, the decision to accept or reject Rostow's proposal will turn on the answer to that question—whether the judges are to make effective the plain meaning of plain words in the Constitution or whether they are to impose idealizations which they are able to construct by drawing on our vast literature and experience.

If the judges, following the advice of contemporary judicial activists, strike boldly to realize Rostow's vision, they will have to construct an imposing body of constitutional law. They will have to adopt policy on points of great significance for which there is little guidance in law and little more in the literature of government and politics. The Supreme Court's contributions will of necessity be exploratory and creative in two sectors of democratic theory. The judges will have to go beyond the present reach of law and thoughtful literature in fixing the outer limits of mind and action thought relevant to the democratic process; and they will find sharp differences of position, at least in the general literature, if not in the law, relating to institutions and practices admitted to be at the center of the democratic way in government.

A. *The bounds of relevance.* Democratic government is more than formal organization and legal provision for an array of procedures. It is critically conditioned by the readiness and determination of the people to participate in their own government, to scrutinize what their officials do, to make clear their satisfactions and dissatisfactions with specific policies and the general character of public policy. Agreement is so nearly universal on this that argument would be superfluous.

The Constitution contains two provisions that are recognized to protect the democratic process at its outer bounds: the prohibition of laws abridging freedom of speech and press and the right to peaceably assemble and to petition the government for redress of grievances. The language chosen for the right to assemble was clearly not intended to cover all of the organization and interaction among men and women which James Madison deplored as a "dangerous vice" but which we today regard as essential to government by the people. Recent research creates a strong presumption that the men who adopted the free-speech and free-press guarantee did not intend that it should clear the way for that self-aggrandizing, irrational, and violent criticism of public policy and attack on public officials which today is generally defended as essential to popular self-government.[2] But forget these two facts. Assume that the nation will support the Supreme Court in pushing these two guarantees, free expression and free assembly, as far as the judges want to go. Still we are not at the bounds of relevance for the democratic process. Consider the distribution of wealth and the vigor of the nation's free-enterprise economy.

No thoughtful man will argue that freedom to speak, to write, to assemble, and to organize guarantees that adult citizens will be nearly equal in ability to influence the political process at the points of impact listed at the beginning of Chapter XVIII. The "untrammeled political effort" which Rostow appears to favor promises victory to those who move with greatest dispatch and the greatest array of force. The Constitution gives no assurance that every man shall have the resources necessary for influence or that resources shall be distributed in a fashion that gives all men an even break. Should we suppose that courageous judges, committed to an activist policy and having equality and majority rule as their ideals, will demand a further trammeling of political effort than we have put on the statute books of most of the states? Can we anticipate that idealizations of equality and majority rule

[2] See Leonard W. Levy, *Legacy of Suppression* (Cambridge: Harvard University Press, 1960).

will always be adapted to the wealth structure that happens to exist at any time? Or must we allow for activist judges, bent on the high judicial vigilance and fortified by the unembarrassed courage which Professor Black envisages (see Section 3, Chapter XVII), insisting on provision for a minimum income which allows a little surplus for investment in the outcome of elections?

I shall not press a question about ownership and control of the main channels of communication. When the ideals of equality and majority rule are wedded to the Constitution's provision for a state of freedom in speech and press, attention is inevitably directed to the policies that fix the content and presentation of news and opinion that are distributed by great news services, radio networks, organizations that control television productions, and newspapers that escape the discipline of competition in a nation spotted with one-newspaper towns. The agenda of an activist Supreme Court might well include an inquiry as to whether America meets the specifications for a market place of ideas in which truth stands a fair chance to conquer error.

The nation's economic structure is related to the security of its democratic government in another and very different way. The point of contact is the prospect of a *coup d'état*. What do you do when the men who come to power in government make up their minds to use all the authority of office to keep themselves in power? The methods confirmed by success in other countries include: hold fast to the office after the term of office has expired; enact the new laws that make the usurpation appear lawful; revise the laws specifying who may vote; take over the machinery that administers the balloting, counts the votes, and announces the winners.

An assertion that we have a system that precludes the coup will not satisfy the thoughtful man. He asks: What is it in our system that discourages the

bid for unrestrained power and makes failure certain if the bid is made? The answer seems to be that our security lies at two points. *First,* in the evidences that the population generally has a deep attachment to the elective principle, will not readily join the group that proposes a forcible takeover, and will stubbornly resist the effort when it is made. *Second,* in a social structure that maintains organizations which can collectively overpower the men who have a monopoly on public offices. Every viable organization is a nexus of loyalties, a structure of leadership, and a repository of resources. The society that evolved in this country raises economic organizations to primacy—the great industrial empire, the trade association, the labor union, the association of men sharing a common profession. Undoubtedly religious denominations combine loyalties, leadership, and resources. But I suppose most readers of this book would bet on the economic structure of the American people to furnish the first and main resistance to a political coup.

If my reasoning is approved, one must conclude that an activist Supreme Court committed to custody of the democratic process will be attentive to charges that the nation is being stripped of the muscle that might deliver it from those who reject the democratic way. If the Court again happens to be dominated by judges who believe that a competitive free-enterprise system is essential to a secure democratic government—it is a tenable thesis, honored in political theory—they may see steps toward a welfare state as steps away from the ideal they are pledged to realize and make secure. What they might do about it would depend on how fully they adopt the activists' recommendations for aggressive judicial review.

B. *The core of democratic method.* Difficulties encountered in fixing the outer limits of the democratic process are matched by problems relating to the main foundations. Any careful listing of points at which popular government may break down will give a high place to each of these: definition of the electorate; administration of voting, including the counting and reporting of results; assignment of seats in the legislature and district-making; procedure in lawmaking assemblies. These are only a few of many essential features of government by the people; they call up problems enough for our purposes here.

The men who compose the legislature at any time and the man who occupies the chair of the chief executive have a deep personal interest in each of these four matters. All stand to gain or lose by manipulation of the first three. These three items constitute a system which brought these men to their high places in government. Many of them have a vested interest in retaining the arrangements by which they were lifted up. Some, who fear they may go out by the same route they came in, will see personal advantages in changing the system. The fourth item, legislative procedure, may present less evidence of vested personal interest, but certainly one legislator gains in influence and another loses as the rules of the chamber are fitted to their respective statuses, roles, and policy objectives.

Perhaps no one can be trusted more than the elected law-makers themselves to fix the rules that govern their deliberations and actions. An external group could possibly draw up rules that offer greatest promise of fulfilling an ideal of careful study, illuminating debate, above-board compromise, and an open outlet for every legislator's talents. Even if that be the case, the legislators will determine the actual effects of the rules by the way they respond to them, and, if enough of them refuse to comply, they will effectively nullify any code that others impose on them. This suggests the possibility that there is no way by which a legislative body may be policed while it is engaged in the business of making laws. Such a conclusion would, presumably, discourage intervention by even the boldest of judges, no matter how certain they might be that the filibuster or gag rule are major subversions of the democratic way.

The prospect for successful judicial intervention is quite different in the case of admission to the polls and conduct of elections. Legislatures and elected chief executives cannot control these matters by their personal acts in the way that legislators can determine the procedures of a legislative chamber. They can only make the rules by which these things are done, establish machinery and supervise its operation, fix penalties for violating the rules and obstructing the machinery, and appropriate the money that enables the machinery to work. Judges who are committed to an aggressive role, if convinced that the rules and their administration fall too far short of the democratic ideal, may believe that it lies within judicial power to improve them.

Allocating legislative positions among the population and fixing boundaries of the districts that choose them have always been frustrating experiences. The legislator is uniquely interested in the definition of his district. He faces no problem of altering boundaries if his district is frozen to the political map, as is the case for the United States senator. But, if the district is a special creation, made solely for the choice of one or more legislators, then the legislator will always be conscious that a change in boundaries will work to his gain or loss when he seeks re-election. The reluctance of American state legislators to reapportion their own seats is notorious.

The Supreme Court ruled in March, 1962 (*Baker* v. *Carr,* 369 U.S. 186), that a federal court may adjudicate a claim that the allocation of seats in a state legislature denies equal protection of the laws to citizens in certain parts of the state or deprives them of life, liberty, or property without due process of law. Frankfurter, speaking also for Harlan, protested. He thought federal judges were being catapulted into a mathematical quagmire. In this area of social conflict, he said, judges "do not have accepted legal standards or even reliable analogies to draw upon for making judicial judgments." He arrayed an impressive amount of evidence from American and British experience to buttress his argument that this is the case.

I am obliged to say that the judges will not find in the literature we call political theory any surer guide than Frankfurter was able to find in Anglo-American practice. No doubt this literature reveals a high agreement that legislative seats *ought* to be distributed in keeping with a constant ratio of constituent population to legislative member. This is the declaration of an ideal, not an assertion of what experience proves to be socially achievable, socially preferred, or socially acceptable. This literature does not refute Frankfurter's declaration that "representation proportioned to the geographic spread of population . . . has never been generally practiced, today or in the past."

Pleas for acceptance of the ideal—the rule of equal numbers—have not been supported by analysis worthy of the complicated lawmaking structure we have developed in this country. A statute is the product of three centers of authority—two legislative chambers and a chief executive. Surely our prime concern is to achieve an ideal representation in the combination of offices that makes the major public policies. If experience proves, in a given state, that the governor is traditionally especially responsive to an identifiable sector of the population, one might reasonably argue that the remaining parts of the population ought to be given a compensating advantage when seats in one or both of the legislative chambers are apportioned. This is only one of many unexplored or little-explored complications besetting the policy-making ma-

chinery of our national and state governments. Until they have received far more penetrating scrutiny than they have yet had, the literature of political science will offer little to the judge seeking a thoughtful presentation of realizable democratic ideals.

3. *Judges, Ideals, and Conflicting Moralities*

All contemporary recommendations for aggressive judicial review that I have seen confront the Supreme Court with two challenges. They urge the Court to identify and honor ideals— to go beyond the words of the Constitution in search of more fundamental purposes that lie behind the express language. And they urge the Court to grasp new means for making ideals effective in the day-to-day conduct of government.

Consider, *first,* the point about new means for achieving the judges' ends. Throughout this chapter, in discussing possible judicial strategies, I have talked as if judges possessed lawmaking power. One may protest that judges, including Supreme Court judges, do not do things like this, that I have created a giant straw man for some hoped-for advantage in tearing him down. The fact is that contemporary writers about constitutional law are urging changes in judicial conduct in language which implies, if it does not expressly state, that judges should boldly order compliance with new standards of conduct. And, more significant, at least two recent experiences in judicial action suggest that the Supreme Court may be ready for some bold new ventures in policy formation.

I have said why I believe that the desegregation orders of 1955 were an innovation in display of authority by the Supreme Court. The more recent decisions relating to apportionment of state legislatures are a second demonstration of willingness to devise and order significant changes in public policy. In the first apportionment case,

Baker v. *Carr,* the Supreme Court instructed a federal district court to hear a complaint that certain residents of Tennessee were denied equal protection of the laws because of improper allocation of seats in the Tennessee legislature. The leading opinion, written by Brennan, asserted that "we have no cause at this stage to doubt the District Court will be able to fashion relief if violations of constitutional rights are found." Clark, concurring, made clear that he thought it proper for the lower court to devise a more equitable assignment of legislative seats and put the judge-made apportionment into effect by order of the court. Orders since issued by a number of federal courts make it clear that federal judges are both ready to correct inequities in representation and ingenious in devising remedies.

These recent developments in use of judicial power cause me to think it is not premature to ponder the social consequences likely to follow upon judicial acceptance of the recommendations for more aggressive action outlined in this chapter.

The *second* challenge thrust on the Supreme Court by the recommended strategies for more aggressive judicial review urges the judges to strive for a finer vision of the good life.

The appeal for this finer vision, to which I have attached the terms "grander purpose" and "ideal," is advanced, characteristically, in language suffering from want of precision. Some of these appeals may have been credited with too refined an intent when I cited them as proposed strategies or recommendations for judicial action. It may be, in the case of most of these writings, that the thought supporting the appeal has advanced little beyond a sentiment that the country could stand a round of uplift. One may wonder, for instance, which of the rules worked out over time to regulate the activity that produces public policy would have to go down in order to establish the life of the forum that Ros-

tow has in mind when he endorses "untrammeled political effort."

Want of precision is quickly corrected when serious students conclude that they are not understood as they wish to be. A more serious deficiency in contemporary appeals for a finer judicial vision, it seems to me, is failure to identify the several levels of a nation's morality and differentially relate the judicial role to them. A quick reminder of the tension between two of these levels should make my point clear.

We readily acknowledge that most white men in the United States have two moral positions vis-à-vis the Negro. I may call one position that of distant contemplation; the other, that of immediate confrontation.

Contemplating relations between the races as a problem enduring over time, as a challenge to one's sense of justice or commitment to Christian ideals, as a source of indignity and pain in places far away—contemplating racial discrimination in such a frame of mind, no doubt most white American citizens come out against it. They would feel better if it did not exist. They experience again the bitter taste of guilt, and they would like to be absolved. This is the morality of distant contemplation.

The responses are different when the facts are those of immediate confrontation. The man who is strong for justice at a distance may be among the first to resist Negro invasion of his residential area, among the first to shore up against admission of Negroes to his own employment status. It is possible for a man to say on Sunday that the Negro cannot rise esthetically, intellectually, or morally unless he be accepted in fellowship by those who have attained the higher levels; it is possible for him on Monday to send his own children to a private academy so that they need not pay the price of giving the Negro what was so readily promised on Sunday.

These significantly different levels of

morality are a reality in the United States today. I see no reason to doubt that they have at all times been a fact of life among all peoples. They are not to be wished away. They are to be lived with and accommodated to. But they are not to be segregated in our thinking. Too sharply segregated, today's distant contemplation would have no ameliorating effect when immediate confrontation occurs tomorrow. Surely, the long view ought to bring lessons to the short view. But, equally, the hard look at what is at hand ought to instruct the speculative image of what might be the best achievable.

Surely, also, organization for government should in some way respond to the different levels of morality. Recent writing by political scientists makes much of the fact that this is accomplished in the government of the United States. The long-run view of the general welfare gets differing receptions in local government, at the state house, and in Washington, D.C. The American people elect their congressmen with one set of values uppermost in mind; they respond to a significantly different array of values when they choose a president.

In the national government, it is Congress that hears most about the sacrifices necessary for achievement, least about the delights of vision and the rewards of magnanimity. The political roots of the congressmen are in the soil of immediate confrontation. The congressmen may say that they traffic in ideals marked with a high price, for they suffer when they commit the people to more than their constituents will tolerate.

The congressmen may say that the Supreme Court traffics in low-priced ideals. The judges are not confronted by the people who make the sacrifices necessary for achieving ideals. Peckham was not visited by a delegation of bakers demanding relief after ten hours in front of an oven. Sutherland was not taken on a tour of the rooming houses for women in the District of Columbia. Warren and his colleagues were not given a preview by the men who rioted in Little Rock, by the women who picketed in New Orleans, or by the state officials and state police who stood off federal marshals in Oxford, Mississippi.

One reason for having an independent judiciary, no doubt, is to free one part of the great complex called government for response to ideals not always likely to be honored by officials who are more readily accountable to the population. The practice of judicial review gives the members of the United States Supreme Court unusual opportunities to impress their visions, individual and collective, on public policy. Surely, all thoughtful men who look with favor on a principle of separation of powers would wish the judges to be imaginative in conceiving ideals and courageous in expressing them.

But such a commitment does not force the thoughtful man to conclude that the nation's highest judges should feel free, or be freed, to impose their noblest visions on the life of the people. He may think that the judge should learn something from the experience of the clergyman. It is a national belief, I suppose, that the minister of the gospel typically speaks for the highest ethical conceptions of the population. It is also a national commitment that the ministers, associated in religious organizations, should have no power but that of persuasion to induce the people to live by the ethics which the ministers recommend.

The judicial branch of government is not a religious organization, and the wall that separates church from state is not matched by a wall between the judges and the elected officials. But there is a lesson in the analogy. There is a place for persuasion and there is a place for force in the progress of a people to higher ethical levels. The judicial office was constructed for the coercive act, not for argument, pleading, exhortation. The traffic of judges in ethical standards must be confined to standards that can be made effective in conduct by orders for compliance.

The norms of conduct which I have called the morality of immediate confrontation set inescapable conditions for advance to a higher morality. The realities of current conduct and the persisting expectations as to probable conduct determine what changes must come first in order that more significant changes may come later. They dictate the compensations which are exacted as the price for each crucial concession. The strategy of advance to a more praiseworthy reality must be constructed with fine appreciation of these restraining conditions.

Those conscious acts which, in the judgment of time, contribute significantly to progress are a product of statesmanship. It is a task of scholarship to assist the act of statesmanship —to identify immediate and long-range goals, to clarify the problems of choice when choice among goals must be made, to calculate feasibilities and make recommendations on means to ends. It is most improbable that schol-arship will adequately prepare the way for statesmanship; indeed, it is likely that most scholarly effort will be spent on explication of what statesmen have already done.

There is a better prospect that scholarship may prepare the nation for a wise location of authority to deal with the problems that present the greatest demands for statesmanship. Scholarly writing which examines the judicial process and evaluates the practice of judicial review has made only a marginal attack on the central question of how power is most wisely distributed in a system of government. This is, indeed, the central question for the student who directs his attention to the judges and their activities, as it is for the student who starts his inquiry with the elected officials and what they do. We will appreciate what our judges have in fact been doing and we will be prepared for judgments about a proper use of judicial power in the future only when we understand how judges, elected officials, and appointed bureaucracies are knitted together in a compact governmental structure.

31. Decision-Making in a Democracy: The Supreme Court as a National Policy-Maker*

ROBERT A. DAHL

To consider the Supreme Court of the United States strictly as a legal institution is to underestimate its significance in the American political system. For it is also a political institution, an institution, that is to say, for arriving at decisions on controversial questions of

* 6 *Journal of Public Law* 279 (1957). Reprinted by permission.

national policy. As a political institution, the Court is highly unusual, not least because Americans are not quite willing to accept the fact that it *is* a political institution and not quite capable of denying it; so that frequently we take both positions at once. This is confusing to foreigners, amusing to logicians, and rewarding to ordinary

Americans who thus manage to retain the best of both worlds.

I

A policy decision might be defined as an effective choice among alternatives about which there is, at least initially, some uncertainty. This uncertainty may arise because of inadequate information as to (a) the alternatives that are thought to be "open"; (b) the consequences that will probably ensue from choosing a given alternative; (c) the level of probability that these consequences will actually ensue; and (d) the relative value of the different alternatives, that is, an ordering of the alternatives from most preferable to least preferable, given the expected consequences and the expected probability of the consequences actually occurring. An *effective* choice is a selection of the most preferable alternative accompanied by measures to insure that the alternative selected will be acted upon.

No one, I imagine, will quarrel with the proposition that the Supreme Court, or indeed any court, must make and does make policy decisions in this sense. But such a proposition is not really useful to the question before us. What is critical is the extent to which a court can and does make policy decisions by going outside established "legal" criteria found in precedent, statute, and constitution. Now in this respect the Supreme Court occupies a most peculiar position, for it is an essential characteristic of the institution that from time to time its members decide cases where legal criteria are not in any realistic sense adequate to the task. A distinguished associate justice of the present Court has recently described the business of the Supreme Court in these words:

It is essentially accurate to say that the Court's preoccupation today is with the application of rather fundamental aspirations and what Judge Learned Hand calls "moods," em-

bodied in provisions like the due process clauses, which were designed not to be precise and positive directions for rules of action. The judicial process in applying them involves a judgment . . . that is, on the views of the direct representatives of the people in meeting the needs of society, on the views of Presidents and Governors, and by their construction of the will of legislatures the Court breathes life, feeble or strong, into the inert pages of the Constitution and the statute books.[1]

Very often, then, the cases before the Court involve alternatives about which there is severe disagreement in the society, as in the case of segregation or economic regulation; that is, the setting of the case is "political." Moreover, they are usually cases where competent students of constitutional law, including the learned justices of the Supreme Court themselves, disagree; where the words of the Constitution are general, vague, ambiguous, or not clearly applicable; where precedent may be found on both sides; and where experts differ in predicting the consequences of the various alternatives or the degree of probability that the possible consequences will actually ensue. Typically, in other words, although there may be considerable agreement as to the alternatives thought to be open [(a)], there is very serious disagreement as to questions of fact bearing on consequences and probabilities [(b) and (c)], and as to questions of value, or the way in which different alternatives are to be ordered according to criteria establishing relative preferability [(d)].

If the Court were assumed to be a "political" institution, no particular problems would arise, for it would be taken for granted that the members of the Court would resolve questions of fact and value by introducing assumptions derived from their own predispo-

[1] Frankfurter, The Supreme Court in the Mirror of Justices, 105 U. of Pa. L. Rev. 781, 793 (1957).

sitions or those of influential clienteles and constituents. But, since much of the legitimacy of the Court's decisions rests upon the fiction that it is not a political institution but exclusively a legal one, to accept the Court as a political institution would solve one set of problems at the price of creating another. Nonetheless, if it is true that the nature of the cases arriving before the Court is sometimes of the kind I have described, then the Court cannot act strictly as a legal institution. It must, that is to say, choose among controversial alternatives of public policy by appealing to at least some criteria of acceptability on questions of fact and value that cannot be found in or deduced from precedent, statute, and Constitution. It is in this sense that the Court is a national policy-maker, and it is this role that gives rise to the problem of the Court's existence in a political system ordinarily held to be democratic.

Now I take it that except for differences in emphasis and presentation, what I have said so far is today widely accepted by almost all American political scientists and by most lawyers. To anyone who believes that the Court is not, in at least some of its activities, a policy-making institution, the discussion that follows may seem irrelevant. But to anyone who holds that at least one role of the Court is as a policy-making institution in cases where strictly legal criteria are inadequate, then a serious and much debated question arises, to wit: Who gets what and why? Or in less elegant language: What groups are benefited or handicapped by the Court and how does the allocation by the Court of these rewards and penalties fit into our presumably democratic political system?

II

In determining and appraising the role of the Court, two different and conflicting criteria are sometimes employed. These are the majority criterion and the criterion of Right or Justice.

Every policy dispute can be tested, at least in principle, by the majority criterion, because (again: in principle) the dispute can be analyzed according to the numbers of people for and against the various alternatives at issue, and therefore according to the proportions of the citizens or eligible members who are for and against the alternatives. Logically speaking, except for a trivial case, every conflict within a given society must be a dispute between a majority of those eligible to participate and a minority or minorities; or else it must be a dispute between or among minorities only.[2] Within certain limits, both possibilities are independent of the number of policy alternatives at issue, and since the argument is not significantly affected by the number of alternatives, it is convenient to assume that each policy dispute represents only two alternatives.[3]

---

[2] Provided that the total membership of the society is an even number, it is technically possible for a dispute to occur that divides the membership into two equal parts, neither of which can be said to be either a majority or minority of the total membership. But even in the instances where the number of members is even (which should occur on the average only half the time), the probability of an exactly even split, in any group of more than a few thousand people, is so small that it may be ignored.

[3] Suppose the number of citizens, or members eligible to participate in collective decisions, is n. Let each member indicate his "most preferred alternative." Then it is obvious that the maximum number of most preferred alternatives is n. It is equally obvious that if the number of most preferred alternatives is more than or equal to $n/2$, then no majority is possible. But for all practical purposes those formal limitations can be ignored, for we are dealing with a large society where the number of alternatives at issue before the Supreme Court is invariably quite small. If the number of alternatives is greater than two, it is theoretically possible for preferences to be distributed so that no outcome is consistent with the majority criterion, even

If everyone prefers one of two alternatives, then no significant problem arises. But a case will hardly come before the Supreme Court unless at least one person prefers an alternative that is opposed by another person. Strictly speaking, then, no matter how the Court acts in determining the legality or constitutionality of one alternative or the other, the outcome of the Court's decision must either (1) accord with the preferences of a minority of citizens and run counter to the preferences of a majority; (2) accord with the preferences of a majority and run counter to the preferences of a minority; or (3) accord with the preferences of one minority and run counter to the preferences of another minority, the rest being indifferent.

In a democratic system with a more or less representative legislature, it is unnecessary to maintain a special court to secure the second class of outcomes. A case might be made out that the Court protects the rights of national majorities against local interests in federal questions, but so far as I am aware, the role of the Court as a policy-maker is not usually defended in this fashion; in what follows, therefore, I propose to pass over the ticklish question of federalism and deal only with "national" majorities and minorities. The third kind of outcome, although relevant according to other criteria, is hardly relevant to the majority criterion, and may also be passed over for the moment.

One influential view of the Court, however, is that it stands in some special way as a protection of minorities against tyranny by majorities. In the course of its 167 years, in seventy-eight cases, the Court has struck down eighty-six different provisions of fed-

where all members can rank all the alternatives and where there is perfect information as to their preferences; but this difficulty does not bear on the subsequent discussion, and it is disregarded. For an examination of this problem, consult Arrow, Social Choice and Individual Values (1951).

eral law as unconstitutional,[4] and by interpretation it has modified a good many more. It might be argued, then, that in all or in a very large number of these cases the Court was, in fact, defending the rights of some minority against a "tyrannical" majority. There are, however, some exceedingly serious difficulties with this interpretation of the Court's activities.

III

One problem, which is essentially ideological in character, is the difficulty of reconciling such an interpretation with the existence of a democratic polity, for it is not at all difficult to show by appeals to authorities as various and imposing as Aristotle, Locke, Rousseau, Jefferson, and Lincoln that the term democracy means, among other things, that the power to rule resides in popular majorities and their representatives. Moreover, from en-

[4] Actually, the matter is somewhat ambiguous. There appear to have been seventy-eight cases in which the Court has held provisions of federal law unconstitutional. Sixty-four different acts in the technical sense have been construed, and eighty-six different provisions in law have been in some respects invalidated. I rely here on the figures and the table given in Library of Congress, Legislative Reference Service, Provisions of Federal Law Held Unconstitutional By the Supreme Court of the United States 95, 141-47 (1936), to which I have added United States v. Lovett, 328 U.S. 303 (1946), and United States ex rel. Toth v. Quarles, 350 U.S. 11 (1955). There are some minor discrepancies in totals (not attributable to the differences in publication dates) between this volume and Acts of Congress Held Unconstitutional in Whole or in Part by the Supreme Court of the United States, in Library of Congress, Legislative Reference Service, The Constitution of the United States of America, Analysis and Interpretation (Corwin ed., 1953). The difference is a result of classification. The latter document lists seventy-three acts held unconstitutional (to which Toth v. Quarles, supra, should be added) but different sections of the same act are sometimes counted separately.

tirely reasonable and traditional definitions of popular sovereignty and political equality, the principle of majority
rule can be shown to follow by logical
necessity.[5] Thus to affirm that the
Court supports minority preferences
against majorities is to deny that popular sovereignty and political equality,
at least in the traditional sense, exist in
the United States; and to affirm that
the Court *ought* to act in this way is to
deny that popular sovereignty and political equality *ought* to prevail in this
country. In a country that glories in
its democratic tradition, this is not a
happy state of affairs for the Court's
defenders; and it is no wonder that a
great deal of effort has gone into the
enterprise of proving that, even if the
Court consistently defends minorities
against majorities, nonetheless it is a
thoroughly "democratic" institution.
But no amount of tampering with democratic theory can conceal the fact that
a system in which the policy preferences of minorities prevail over majorities is at odds with the traditional
criteria for distinguishing a democracy
from other political systems.[6]

Fortunately, however, we do not
need to traverse this well-worn ground;
for the view of the Court as a protector of the liberties of minorities
against the tyranny of majorities is beset with other difficulties that are not
so much ideological as matters of fact
and logic. If one wishes to be at all
rigorous about the question, it is probably impossible to demonstrate that any
particular Court decisions have or have
not been at odds with the preferences
of a "national majority." It is clear
that unless one makes *some* assumptions as to the kind of evidence one
will require for the existence of a set
of minority and majority preferences
in the general population, the view under consideration is incapable of being
proved at all. In any strict sense, no

[5] Dahl, A Preface to Democratic Theory,
c. 2 (1956).
[6] Compare Commager, Majority Rule and
Minority Rights (1943).

adequate evidence exists, for scientific
opinion polls are of relatively recent
origin, and national elections are little
more than an indication of the first
preferences of a number of citizens—
in the United States the number ranges
between about forty and sixty per cent
of the adult population—for certain
candidates for public office. I do not
mean to say that there is no relation
between preferences among candidates
and preferences among alternative public policies, but the connection is a
highly tenuous one, and on the basis
of an election it is almost never possible
to adduce whether a majority does or
does not support one of two or more
policy alternatives about which members of the political elite are divided.
For the greater part of the Court's history, then, there is simply no way of
establishing with any high degree of
confidence whether a given alternative
was or was not supported by a majority
or a minority of adults or even of
voters.

In the absence of relatively direct information, we are thrown back on indirect tests. The eighty-six provisions
of federal law that have been declared
unconstitutional were, of course, initially passed by majorities of those voting in the Senate and in the House.
They also had the president's formal
approval. We could, therefore, speak
of a majority of those voting in the
House and Senate, together with the
president, as a "lawmaking majority."
It is not easy to determine whether any
such constellation of forces within the
political elites actually coincides with
the preferences of a majority of American adults or even with the preferences of a majority of that half of the
adult population which, on the average,
votes in congressional elections. Such
evidence as we have from opinion polls
suggests that Congress is not markedly
out of line with public opinion, or at
any rate with such public opinion as
there is after one discards the answers
of people who fall into the category,
often large, labelled "no response" or

"don't know." If we may, on these somewhat uncertain grounds, take a "lawmaking majority" as equivalent to a "national majority," then it is possible to test the hypothesis that the Supreme Court is shield and buckler for minorities against national majorities.

Under any reasonable assumptions about the nature of the political process, it would appear to be somewhat naive to assume that the Supreme Court either would or could play the role of Galahad. Over the whole history of the Court, on the average one new justice has been appointed every twenty-two months. Thus a president can expect to appoint about two new justices during one term of office; and if this were not enough to tip the balance on a normally divided Court, he is almost certain to succeed in two terms. Thus, Hoover had three appointments; Roosevelt, nine; Truman, four; and Eisenhower, so far, has had four. Presidents are not famous for appointing justices hostile to their own views on public policy nor could they expect to secure confirmation of a man whose stance on key questions was flagrantly at odds with that of the dominant majority in the Senate. Justices are typically men who, prior to appointment, have engaged in public life and have committed themselves publicly on the great questions of the day. As Mr. Justice Frankfurter has recently reminded us, a surprisingly large proportion of the justices, particularly of the great justices who have left their stamp upon the decisions of the Court, have had little or no prior judicial experience.[7] Nor have the justices—certainly not the great justices—been timid men with a passion for anonymity. Indeed, it is not too much to say that is justices were appointed primarily for their "judicial" qualities without regard to their basic attitudes on fundamental questions of public policy, the Court could not play the influential role

[7] Frankfurter, op. cit. supra note 1, at 782-84.

in the American political system that it does in reality play.

The fact is, then, that the policy views dominant on the Court are never for long out of line with the policy views dominant among the lawmaking majorities of the United States. Consequently it would be most unrealistic to suppose that the Court would, for more than a few years at most, stand against any major alternatives sought by a lawmaking majority. The judicial agonies of the New Deal will, of course, quickly come to mind; but Mr. Roosevelt's difficulties with the Court were truly exceptional. Generalizing over the whole history of the Court, the chances are about one out of five that a president will make one appointment to the Court in less than a

TABLE I

The Interval Between Appointments to the Supreme Court.

Interval in Years	Per Cent of Total Appointments	Cumulative Per Cent
Less than 1	21	21
1	34	55
2	18	73
3	9	82
4	8	90
5	7	97
6	2	99
—	—	—
12	1	100
Total	100	100

Note: The table excludes the six appointments made in 1789. Except for the four most recent appointments, it is based on data in the Encyclopedia of American History 461-62 (Morris ed., 1953). It may be slightly inaccurate because the source shows only the year of appointment, not the month. The twelve-year interval was from 1811 to 1823.

year, better than one out of two that
he will make one within two years,
and three out of four that he will make
one within three years. Mr. Roosevelt
had unusually bad luck: he had to
wait four years for his first appointment; the odds against this long an
interval are four to one. With average
luck, the battle with the Court would
never have occurred; even as it was,
although the "court-packing" proposal
did formally fail, by the end of his second term Mr. Roosevelt had appointed
five new justices and by 1941 Mr. Justice Roberts was the only remaining
holdover from the Hoover era.

It is to be expected, then, that the
Court is least likely to be successful in
blocking a determined and persistent
lawmaking majority on a major policy
and most likely to succeed against a
"weak" majority; e.g., a dead one, a
transient one, a fragile one, or one
weakly united upon a policy of subordinate importance.

IV

An examination of the cases in
which the Court has held federal legislation unconstitutional confirms, on the
whole, our expectations. Over the
whole history of the Court, about half
the decisions have been rendered more
than four years after the legislation was
passed.

Of the twenty-four laws held unconstitutional within two years, eleven
were measures enacted in the early
years of the New Deal. Indeed, New
Deal measures comprise nearly a third
of all the legislation that has ever been
declared unconstitutional within four
years after enactment.

It is illuminating to examine the
cases where the Court has acted on legislation within four years after enactment—where the presumption is, that
is to say, that the lawmaking majority
is not necessarily a dead one. Of the
twelve New Deal cases, two were, from
a policy point of view, trivial; and two,
although perhaps not trivial, were of

TABLE 2

Percentage of Cases Held Unconstitutional Arranged by Time Intervals
Between Legislation and Decision.

Number of Years	New Deal Legis- lation %	Other %	All Legis- lation %
2 or Less	92	19	30
3- 4	8	19	18
5- 8	0	28	24
9-12	0	13	11
13-16	0	8	6
17-20	0	1	1
21 or More	0	12	10
Total	100	100	100

minor importance to the New Deal
program. A fifth involved the NRA,
which was to expire within three weeks
of the decision. Insofar as the unconstitutional provisions allowed "codes of
fair competition" to be established by
industrial groups, it is fair to say that
President Roosevelt and his advisers
were relieved by the Court's decision
of a policy they had come to find increasingly embarrassing. In view of the
tenacity with which Mr. Roosevelt held
to his major program, there can hardly
be any doubt that had he wanted to
pursue the major policy objective involved in the NRA codes, as he did,
for example, with the labor provisions,
he would not have been stopped by the
Court's special theory of the Constitution. As to the seven other cases, it is
entirely correct to say, I think, that
whatever some of the eminent justices
might have thought during their fleet-
ing moments of glory, they did not succeed in interposing a barrier to the
achievement of the objectives of the
legislation; and in a few years most of
the constitutional interpretation on
which the decisions rested had been
unceremoniously swept under the rug.

The remainder of the thirty-eight

TABLE 3

Cases Holding Legislation Unconstitutional Within Four Years
After Enactment.

Interval in Years	New Deal		Other		Total	
	No.	%	No.	%	No.	%
2 or Less	11	29	13	34	24	63
3 to 4	1	3	13	34	14	37
Total	12	32	26	68	38	100

cases where the Court has declared legislation unconstitutional within four years of enactment tend to fall into two rather distinct groups: those involving legislation that could reasonably be regarded as important *from the point of view of the lawmaking majority* and those involving minor legislation. Although the one category merges into the other, so that some legislation must be classified rather arbitrarily, probably there will be little disagreement with classifying the specific legislative provisions involved in eleven cases as essentially minor from the point of view of the lawmaking majority (however important they may have been as constitutional interpretations). The specific legislative provisions involved in the remaining fifteen cases are by no means of uniform importance, but with one or two possible exceptions it seems reasonable to classify them as major policy issues from the point of view of the lawmaking majority. We would expect that cases involving major legislative policy would be propelled to the Court much more rapidly than cases involving minor policy, and, as the table below [4] shows, this is in fact what happens.

Thus a lawmaking majority with major policy objectives in mind usually has an opportunity to seek for ways of overcoming the Court's veto. It is an interesting and highly significant fact that Congress and the president do generally succeed in overcoming a hostile Court on major policy issues.

It is particularly instructive to examine the cases involving major policy. In two cases involving punitive legislation enacted by Radical Republican Congresses against supporters of the Confederacy during the Civil War, the Court faced a rapidly crumbling majority whose death knell as an effective national force was sounded with the election of 1876. Three cases are difficult to classify and I have labelled them "unclear." Of these, two were decisions made in 1921 involving a 1919 amendment to the Lever Act to control prices. The legislation was important, and the provision in question was clearly struck down, but the Lever Act terminated three days after the decision and Congress did not return to the subject of price control until World War II, when it experienced no constitutional difficulties arising from these cases (which were primarily concerned with

TABLE 4

Number of Cases Involving Legislative Policy Other than Those Arising Under New Deal Legislation Holding Legislation Unconstitutional Within Four Years After Enactment.

Interval in Years	Major Policy	Minor Policy	Total
2 or Less	11	2	13
3 to 4	4	9	13
Total	15	11	26

TABLE 5

Type of Congressional Action Following Supreme Court Decisions Holding Legislation Unconstitutional Within Four Years After Enactment (Other than New Deal Legislation).

Congressional Action	Major Policy	Minor Policy	Total
Reverses Court's Policy	10	2	12
Changes Own Policy	2	0	2
None	0	8	8
Unclear	3	1	4
Total	15	11	26

the lack of an ascertainable standard of guilt). The third case in this category successfully eliminated stock dividends from the scope of the Sixteenth Amendment, although a year later Congress enacted legislation taxing the actual income from such stock.

The remaining ten cases were ultimately followed by a reversal of the actual policy results of the Court's action, although not necessarily of the specific constitutional interpretation. In four cases, the policy consequences of the Court's decision were overcome in less than a year. The other six required a long struggle. Workmen's compensation for longshoremen and harbor workers was invalidated by the Court in 1920; in 1922 Congress passed a new law which was, in its turn, knocked down by the Court in 1924; in 1927 Congress passed a third law, which was finally upheld in 1932. The notorious income tax cases of 1895 were first somewhat narrowed by the Court itself; the Sixteenth Amendment was recommended by President Taft in 1909 and was ratified in 1913, some eighteen years after the Court's decisions. The two child labor cases represent the most effective battle ever waged by the Court against legislative policy-makers. The original legislation outlawing child labor, based on the commerce clause, was passed in 1916 as a part of Wilson's New Freedom.

Like Roosevelt later, Wilson was somewhat unlucky in his Supreme Court appointments; he made only three appointments during his eight years, and one of these was wasted, from a policy point of view, on McReynolds. Had McReynolds voted "right," the subsequent struggle over the problem of child labor need not have occurred, for the decision in 1918 was by a Court divided five to four, McReynolds voting with the majority. Congress moved at once to circumvent the decision by means of the tax power, but in 1922 the Court blocked that approach. In 1924 Congress returned to the engagement with a constitutional amendment that was rapidly endorsed by a number of state legislatures before it began to meet so much resistance in the states remaining that the enterprise miscarried. In 1938, under a second reformist president, new legislation was passed, twenty-two years after the first; this a chastened Court accepted in 1941, and thereby brought to an end a battle that had lasted a full quarter-century.

The entire record of the duel between the Court and the lawmaking majority, in cases where the Court has held legislation unconstitutional within four years after enactment, is summarized in Table 6.

Thus the application of the majority criterion seems to show the following: First, if the Court did in fact uphold

TABLE 6

Type of Congressional Action After Supreme Court Decisions Holding Legislation Unconstitutional Within Four Years After Enactment (Including New Deal Legislation).

Congressional Action	Major Policy	Minor Policy	Total
Reverses Court's Policy	17	2	19
None	0	12	12
Other	6*	1	7
Total	23	15	38

* In addition to the actions in Table 5 under "Changes Own Policy" and "Unclear," this figure includes the NRA legislation affected by the *Schechter Poultry* case.

minorities against national majorities, as both its supporters and critics often seem to believe, it would be an extremely anomalous institution from a democratic point of view. Second, the elaborate "democratic" rationalizations of the Court's defenders and the hostility of its "democratic" critics are largely irrelevant, for lawmaking majorities generally have had their way. Third, although the Court seems never to have succeeded in holding out indefinitely, in a very small number of important cases it has delayed the application of policy up to as much as twenty-five years.

V

How can we appraise decisions of the third kind just mentioned? Earlier I referred to the criterion of Right or Justice as a norm sometimes invoked to describe the role of the Court. In accordance with this norm, it might be argued that the most important policy function of the Court is to protect rights that are in some sense basic or fundamental. Thus (the argument might run) in a country where basic rights are, on the whole, respected, one should not expect more than a small number of cases where the Court has had to plant itself firmly against a law-making majority. But majorities may, on rare occasions, become "tyrannical"; and when they do, the Court intervenes; and although the constitutional issue may, strictly speaking, be technically open, the Constitution assumes an underlying fundamental body of rights and liberties which the Court guarantees by its decisions.

Here again, however, even without examining the actual cases, it would appear, on political grounds, somewhat unrealistic to suppose that a Court whose members are recruited in the fashion of Supreme Court justices would long hold to norms of Right or Justice substantially at odds with the rest of the political elite. Moreover, in an earlier day it was perhaps easier to believe that certain rights are so natural and self-evident that their fundamental validity is as much a matter of definite knowledge, at least to all reasonable creatures, as the color of a ripe apple. To say that this view is unlikely to find many articulate defenders today is, of course, not to disprove it; it is rather to suggest that we do not need to elaborate the case against it in this essay.

In any event the best rebuttal to the view of the Court suggested above will be found in the record of the Court's decisions. Surely the six cases referred to a moment ago, where the policy consequences of the Court's decisions were overcome only after long battles, will not appeal to many contemporary minds as evidence for the proposition under examination. A natural right to employ child labor in mills and mines? To be free of income taxes by the federal government? To employ longshoremen and harbor workers without the proctection of workmen's compensation? The Court itself did not rely upon such arguments in these cases, and it would be no credit to their opinions to reconstruct them along such lines.

So far, however, our evidence has been drawn from cases in which the Court has held legislation unconstitutional within four years after enactment. What of the other forty cases? Do we have evidence in these that the Court has protected fundamental or natural rights and liberties against the dead hand of some past tyranny by the lawmakers? The evidence is not impressive. In the entire history of the Court there is not one case arising under the First Amendment in which the Court has held federal legislation unconstitutional. If we turn from these fundamental liberties of religion, speech, press and assembly, we do find a handful of cases—something less than ten—arising under Amendments Four to Seven in which the Court has declared acts unconstitutional that might properly be regarded as involving rather basic liberties. An inspection of these cases leaves the impression that, in all of them, the lawmakers and the Court were not very far apart; moreover, it is doubtful that the fundamental conditions of liberty in this country have been altered by more than a hair's breadth as a result of these decisions. However, let us give the Court its due; it is little enough.

Over against these decisions we must put the fifteen or so cases in which the Court used the protections of the Fifth, Thirteenth, Fourteenth and Fifteenth Amendments to preserve the rights and liberties of a relatively privileged group at the expense of the rights and liberties of a submerged group: chiefly slaveholders at the expense of slaves, white people at the expense of colored people, and property holders at the expense of wage earners and other groups. These cases, unlike the relatively innocuous ones of the preceding set, all involved liberties of genuinely fundamental importance, where an opposite policy would have meant thoroughly basic shifts in the distribution of rights, liberties, and opportunities in the United States—where, moreover, the policies sustained by the Court's action have since been repudiated in every civilized nation of the Western world, including our own. Yet, if our earlier argument is correct, it is futile— precisely because the basic distribution of privilege *was* at issue—to suppose that the Court could have possibly acted much differently in these areas of policy from the way in which it did in fact act.

VI

Thus the role of the Court as a policy-making institution is not simple; and it is an error to suppose that its functions can be either described or appraised by means of simple concepts drawn from democratic or moral theory. It is possible, nonetheless, to derive a few general conclusions about the Court's role as a policy-making institution.

National politics in the United States, as in other stable democracies, is dominated by relatively cohesive alliances that endure for long periods of time. One recalls the Jeffersonian alliance, the Jacksonian, the extraordinarily long-lived Republican dominance of the post-Civil War years, and the New Deal alliance shaped by Franklin Roosevelt. Each is marked by a break with past policies, a period of intense struggle, followed by consolidation, and finally decay and distintegration of the alliance.

Except for short-lived transitional

periods when the old alliance is disintegrating and the new one is struggling to take control of political institutions, the Supreme Court is inevitably a part of the dominant national alliance. As an element in the political leadership of the dominant alliance, the Court of course supports the major policies of the alliance. By itself, the Court is almost powerless to affect the course of national policy. In the absence of substantial agreement within the alliance, an attempt by the Court to make national policy is likely to lead to disaster, as the *Dred Scott* decision and the early New Deal cases demonstrate. Conceivably, the cases of the last three decades involving the freedom of Negroes, culminating in the now famous decision on school integration, are exceptions to this generalization; I shall have more to say about them in a moment.

The Supreme Court is not, however, simply an *agent* of the alliance. It is an essential part of the political leadership and possesses some bases of power of its own, the most important of which is the unique legitimacy attributed to its interpretations of the Constitution. This legitimacy the Court jeopardizes if it flagrantly opposes the major policies of the dominant alliance; such a course of action, as we have seen, is one in which the Court will not normally be tempted to engage.

It follows that within the somewhat narrow limits set by the basic policy goals of the dominant alliance, the Court *can* make national policy. Its discretion, then, is not unlike that of a powerful committee chairman in Congress who cannot, generally speaking, nullify the basic policies substantially agreed on by the rest of the dominant leadership, but who can, within these limits, often determine important questions of timing, effectiveness, and subordinate policy. Thus the Court is least effective against a current lawmaking majority—and evidently least inclined to act. It is most effective when it sets the bounds of policy for

officials, agencies, state governments or even regions, a task that has come to occupy a very large part of the Court's business.

Few of the Court's policy decisions can be interpreted sensibly in terms of a "majority" versus a "minority." In this respect the Court is no different from the rest of the political leadership. Generally speaking, policy at the national level is the outcome of conflict, bargaining, and agreement among minorities; the process is neither minority rule nor majority rule but what might better be called *minorities* rule, where one aggregation of minorities achieves policies opposed by another aggregation.

The main objective of presidential leadership is to build a stable and dominant aggregation of minorities with a high probability of winning the presidency and one or both houses of Congress. The main task of the Court is to confer legitimacy on the fundamental policies of the successful coalition. There are times when the coalition is unstable with respect to certain key policies; at very great risk to its legitimacy powers, the Court can intervene in such cases and may even succeed in establishing policy. Probably in such cases it can succeed only if its action conforms to and reinforces a widespread set of explicit or implicit norms held by the political leadership; norms which are not strong enough or are not distributed in such a way as to insure the existence of an effective lawmaking majority but are, nonetheless, sufficiently powerful to prevent any successful attack on the legitimacy powers of the Court. This is probably the explanation for the relatively successful work of the Court in enlarging the freedom of Negroes to vote during the past three decades and in its famous school integration decisions.

Yet the Court is more than this. Considered as a political system, democracy is a set of basic procedures for arriving at decisions. The operation of these procedures presupposes the existence of certain rights, obligations, liberties and restraints; in short, certain patterns of behavior. The existence of these patterns of behavior in turn presupposes widespread agreement (particularly among the politically active and influential segments of the population) on the validity and propriety of the behavior. Although its record is by no means lacking in serious blemishes, at its best the Court operates to confer legitimacy, not simply on the particular and parochial policies of the dominant political alliance, but upon the basic patterns of behavior required for the operation of a democracy.

B. Free Speech: Absolutely
Yes or Not Absolutely?

32. Justice Black and First Amendment
"Absolutes": A Public Interview*

The Introduction

EDMOND CAHN: I have the function of revealing the secret of the greatness of this great jurist and American, and that is the theme of the remarks I am about to give you. Probably no word in the English language has been cheapened so much by indiscriminate use as the word "great." For this reason, I usually dole it out with a caution approaching miserliness. When, therefore, I tell you unreservedly that Hugo Black is a great judge, you may be certain that I intend to employ a full superlative and am prepared to give particulars.

There are two respects in which he ranks clearly among the foremost and best in our judicial annals. I refer, on the one hand, to his sense of injustice and deep concern for the oppressed and, on the other hand, to his professional skill and technical acumen. In each of these he is not surpassed by anyone. But I do not think it is they that make him unique.

What does make Hugo Black one of the few authentically great judges in the history of the American bench? I believe I have found the answer. He is great because he belongs to a certain select company of heroes who, at various

* 37 New York University Law Review 549 (June, 1962). Reprinted by permission.

crises in the destiny of our land, have created, nurtured, and preserved the essence of the American ideal. It is interesting to look back on our history and see the same phenomenon appearing time and time again. As a crisis approaches, some man, who might otherwise remain relatively unimportant and obscure, discovers a word, a phrase, a sentence in a basic text that history and legal tradition have placed in his hands. He reads, kindles, ignites, and bursts into flames of zeal and resolution. The torch of his spirit leads first a few, then the vast majority of his countrymen—like a pillar of cloud by day and a pillar of fire by night—toward freedom, equality, and social justice.

This is what happened at the very birth of our country. Our founding fathers and revolutionary heroes examined the charters that had been granted to the colonies by the Crown of England. There they read the King's solemn promise that they were to possess and enjoy the "rights of free-born Englishmen." This became their fundamental text. Beginning in the 1760's, their insistence on this promise inflamed them to rebellion, revolution, and national independence.

It was the same kind of inspiration that later gave us our national Bill of Rights. As you know, the original Constitution, drafted at the Philadelphia Convention, contained no bill of rights. The Federalists contended that though bills of rights might be necessary against emperors and kings, they were needless in a republican form of government. They argued that the people ought to repose trust in popularly chosen representatives. But Thomas Jefferson indignantly referred them to the words of the Declaration of Independence which announced that governments derived their just powers from the consent of the governed: words to be taken literally, absolutely, and without exception. He declared, "A bill of rights is what the people are entitled to against every government on earth." His demand succeeded, and a Bill of Rights was added to the Constitution. The Bill of Rights protects us today because Jefferson stood firm on the inspired text.

Then there is the next momentous episode, the series of court decisions in which Chief Justice John Marshall held that acts of legislation that violated the Constitution of the United States were null and void. What was the clause on which Marshall relied in asserting this awesome power for the Supreme Court? It was the provision, to which all Americans had pledged themselves, that the Constitution of the United States must be "the supreme law of the land."

President Lincoln also drew guidance and inspiration from a single basic text. He opposed the institution of slavery because, as he said, the country was dedicated to the proposition that "all men are created equal." Our own epoch has again demonstrated the explosive validity of that proposition.

What does one see happening in each of these historic instances? The majority of people, at least at the beginning, are wont to say that though the basic text may embody a fine ideal, it cannot work in practical application. They say it is utopian, visionary, unrealistic. They remark condescendingly that any experienced person would know better than to take it literally or absolutely.

Accepting the words at face value would be naive, if not simple-minded. In 1776 Worldly Wisemen of this kind said that while the colonists might be entitled to the rights of Englishmen, they ought to put their trust in the King and Parliament and submit to a few convenient adjustments in the interest of imperial security. In 1788 they said that while a bill of rights might be desirable in theory, the people must learn to show confidence in their rulers. Why not leave it all to a majority, whether in Congress or in the Supreme Court? In every generation, the lesser minds, the half-hearted, the timorous, the trimmers talked this way, and so they always will. Ours would be a poor, undernourished, scorbutic freedom indeed if the great men of our history had not shown determination and valor, declaring, "Here are the words of our fundamental text. Here are the principles to which we are dedicated. Let us hold ourselves erect and walk in their light."

It is to this rare company of inspired leaders that Hugo Black belongs. He has been inflamed by the political and ethical ideals that Jefferson, Madison, and other libertarians of the 18th century prized the highest. Child of the 18th century Enlightenment and champion of the 20th century Enlightenment (that is how I think of him), he draws his highest inspiration from the First Amendment in the Bill of Rights, which forbids the Government to abridge our freedom of speech, freedom of press, freedom of religion, and freedom of association. Since his appointment to the bench in 1937, he has incessantly called on the state and federal governments to respect these freedoms literally, completely, and without exception. They are, to him, the meaning and inner purpose of the American saga.

Justice Black's major premise and point of departure is the text of the Constitution, which he emphasizes in all his decisions. He believes that the main purpose of the Founders, in drafting and adopting a written constitution, was to preserve their civil liberties and keep them intact. On their own behalf and on ours, they were not satisfied with a fragment or fraction of the basic freedoms; they wanted us to have the whole of them.

Some people display a curious set of values. If government employees were to come into their homes and start slicing off parts of the chairs, the tables and the television set, they would have no doubt that what was happening was absolutely wrong. Not relatively or debatably, but absolutely wrong. But when the same Government slices their civil liberties, slashes their basic freedoms or saws away at their elementary rights, these people can only comment that the case is too complicated for a doctrinaire judgment, that much can be said on both sides of the matter, and that in times like these the experts on sedition, subversion, and national security know what they are doing. (Sometimes I wonder whether it is quite fair to assume that the experts know what they are doing; perhaps it would be more charitable to assume that they do not know.)

Justice Black's uncompromising zeal for freedom of speech, press, religion, and association might not have seemed so urgently necessary in previous periods of our history. In Lincoln's day, men naturally felt more excited about emancipation from slavery; in Franklin D. Roosevelt's day, more excited about food, employment, and social welfare. But today, when democracy stands here and on every continent presenting its case at the bar of destiny, our supreme need is to share Hugo Black's devotion to the First Amendment and his intrepid defense of the people's rights.

The American covenant was solemnly inscribed in the hearts of our ancestors and on the doorposts of our political history. It is a covenant of freedom, justice, and human dignity. Through keeping it in a quarter-century of judicial decisions, he has proved himself a great jurist. Through keeping it in all

the transactions of our public life, we can prove ourselves a great and enlightened nation.

The Interview

CAHN: Let me start by explaining the purpose of this interview. Two years ago, when you delivered your James Madison Lecture[1] at New York University, you declared your basic attitude toward our Bill of Rights. This was the positive side of your constitutional philosophy. Tonight I propose we bring out the other side, that is your answers to the people who disagree with and criticize your principles. The questions I will ask, most of them at least, will be based on the criticisms. As you know, I consider your answers so convincing that I want the public to have them.

Suppose we start with one of the key sentences in your James Madison Lecture where you said, "It is my belief that there *are* 'absolutes' in our Bill of Rights, and that they were put there on purpose by men who knew what words meant and meant their prohibitions to be 'absolutes.' " Will you please explain your reasons for this.

JUSTICE BLACK: My first reason is that I believe the words do mean what they say. I have no reason to challenge the intelligence, integrity or honesty of the men who wrote the First Amendment. Among those I call the great men of the world are Thomas Jefferson, James Madison, and various others who participated in formulating the ideas behind the First Amendment for this country and in writing it.

I learned a long time ago that there are affirmative and negative words. The beginning of the First Amendment[2]

[1] The lecture, entitled "The Bill of Rights," was delivered at the New York University School of Law on February 17, 1960. It is published in 35 N.Y.U.L. Rev. 865 (1960).

[2] The First Amendment reads as follows: "Congress shall make no law respecting an establishment of religion, or prohibiting the free exercise thereof; or abridging the freedom of speech, or of the press; or the right of the

is that "Congress shall make no law." I understand that it is rather old-fashioned and shows a slight naivete to say that "no law" means no law. It is one of the most amazing things about the ingeniousness of the times that strong arguments are made, which *almost* convince me, that it is very foolish of me to think "no law" means no law. But what it *says* is "Congress shall make no law respecting an establishment of religion," and so on.

I have to be honest about it. I confess not only that I think the Amendment means what it says but also that I may be slightly influenced by the fact that I do not think Congress *should* make any law with respect to these subjects. That has become a rather bad confession to make in these days, the confession that one is actually for something because he believes in it.

Then we move on, and it says "or prohibiting the free exercise thereof." I have not always exercised myself in regard to religion as much as I should, or perhaps as much as all of you have. Nevertheless, I want to be able to do it when I want to do it. I do not want anybody who is my servant, who is my agent, elected by me and others like me, to tell me that I can or cannot do it. Of course, some will remark that that is too simple on my part. To them, all this discussion of mine is too simple, because I come back to saying that these few plain words actually mean what they say, and I know of no college professor or law school professor, outside of my friend, Professor Cahn here, and a few others, who could not write one hundred pages to show that the Amendment does not mean what it says.

Then I move on to the words "abridging the freedom of speech or of the press." It *says* Congress shall make no law doing that. What it *means*—according to a current philosophy that I do not share—is that Congress shall be able to make just such a law unless we judges object too strongly. One of the statements of that philosophy is that if it shocks us too much, then they cannot do it. But when I get down to the really basic reason why I believe that "no law" means no law, I presume it could come to this, that I took an obligation to support and defend the Constitution as I understand it. And being a rather backward country fellow, I understand it to mean what the words say. Gesticulations apart, I know of no way in the world to communicate ideas except by words. And if I were to talk at great length on the subject, I would still be saying—although I understand that some people say that I just say it and do not believe it—that I believe when our Founding Fathers, with their wisdom and patriotism, wrote this Amendment, they knew what they were talking about. They knew what history was behind them and they wanted to ordain in this country that Congress, elected by the people, should not tell the people what religion they should have or what they should believe or say or publish, and that is about it. It says "no law," and that is what I believe it means.

CAHN: Some of your colleagues would say that it is better to interpret the Bill of Rights so as to permit Congress to take what it considers reasonable steps to preserve the security of the nation even at some sacrifice of freedom of speech and association. Otherwise what will happen to the nation and the Bill of Rights as well? What is your view of this?

JUSTICE BLACK: I fully agree with them that the country should protect itself. It should protect itself in peace and in war. It should do whatever is necessary to preserve itself. But the question is: preserve what? And how?

It is not very much trouble for a dictator to know how it is best to preserve his government. He wants to stay in power, and the best way to stay in power is to have plenty of force behind him. He cannot stay in power

people peaceably to assemble, and to petition the Government for a redress of grievances."

without force. He is afraid of too much talk; it is dangerous for him. And he should be afraid, because dictators do not have a way of contributing very greatly to the happiness, joy, contentment, and prosperity of the plain, everyday citizen. Their business is to protect themselves. Therefore, they need an army; they need to be able to stop people from talking; they need to have one religion, and that is the religion they promulgate. Frequently in the past it has been the worship of the dictator himself. To preserve a dictatorship, you must be able to stifle thought, imprison the human mind and intellect.

I want this Government to protect itself. If there is any man in the United States who owes a great deal to this Government, I am that man. Seventy years ago, when I was a boy, perhaps no one who knew me thought I would ever get beyond the confines of the small country county in which I was born. There was no reason for them to suspect that I would. But we had a free country and the way was open for me. The Government and the people of the United States have been good to me. Of course, I want this country to do what will preserve it. I want it to be preserved as the kind of Government it was intended to be. I would not desire to live at any place where my thoughts were under the suspicion of government and where my words could be censored by government, and where worship, whatever it was or wasn't, had to be determined by an officer of the government. That is not the kind of government I want preserved.

I agree with those who wrote our Constitution, that too much power in the hands of officials is a dangerous thing. What was government created for except to serve the people? Why was a Constitution written for the first time in this country except to limit the power of government and those who were selected to exercise it at the moment?

My answer to the statement that this Government should preserve itself is:

yes. The method I would adopt is different, however, from that of some other people. I think it can be preserved only by leaving people with the utmost freedom to think and to hope and to talk and to dream if they want to dream. I do not think this Government must look to force, stifling the minds and aspirations of the people. Yes, I believe in self-preservation, but I would preserve it as the founders said, by leaving people free. I think here, as in another time, it cannot live half slave and half free.

CAHN: I do not suppose that since the days of Socrates a questioner ever got answers that were so co-operative.

In order to preserve the guaranteed freedom of the press, are you willing to allow sensational newspaper reports about a crime and about police investigation of the crime to go so far that they prejudice and inflame a whole state and thus deprive the accused of his right to a fair jury?

JUSTICE BLACK: The question assumes in the first place that a whole state can be inflamed so that a fair trial is not possible. On most of these assumptions that are made with reference to the dangers of the spread of information, I perhaps diverge at a point from many of those who disagree with my views. I have again a kind of an old-fashioned trust in human beings. I learned it as a boy and have never wholly lost that faith.

I believe in trial by jury. Here again perhaps I am a literalist. I do not think that trial by jury is a perfect way of determining facts, of adjudicating guilt, or of adjudicating controversies. But I do not know of a better way. That is where I stand on that.

I do not think myself that anyone can say that there can be enough poblicity completely to destroy the ideas of fairness in the minds of people, including the judges. One of the great things about trials by jury in criminal cases that have developed in this country— I refer to criminal cases because there is where most of the persecutions are found in connection with bringing charges against unpopular people or people in unpopular causes—we should not forget that if the jury happens to go wrong, the judge has a solemn duty in a criminal case not to let an unfair verdict stand. Also, in this country, an appellate court can hear the case.

I realize that we do not have cases now like they had when William Penn was tried for preaching on the streets of London. The jury which was called in to send him off quicky to jail refused to do so, and suffered punishment from the judge because they would not convict a man for preaching on the streets. But that is a part of history, and it is but one of thousands of cases of the kind. Those people had publicity; that is why they would not convict William Penn. They knew, because the people had been talking, despite the fact that there was so much censorship then, that William Penn was being prosecuted largely because he was a dissenter from the orthodox views. So they stood up like men and would not convict. They lost their property, some of them their liberty. But they stood up like men.

I do not myself think that it is necessary to stifle the press in order to reach fair verdicts. Of course, we do not want juries to be influenced wrongfully. But with our system of education we should be in better condition than they were in those days in England, when they found that the jury was one of [the] greatest steps on their way to freedom. As a matter of fact, Madison placed trial by jury along with freedom of the press and freedom of conscience as the three most highly cherished liberties of the American people in his time.

I do not withdraw my loyalty to the First Amendment or say that the press should be censored on the theory that in order to preserve fair trials it is necessary to try the people of the press in summary contempt proceedings and send them to jail for what they have published. I want both fair trials and freedom of the press. I grant that you cannot get everything you want perfectly, and you never will. But you won't do any good in this country, which aspires to freedom, by saying just give the courts a little more power, just a little more power to suppress the people and the press, and things will be all right. You just take a little chunk off here and a little bit there. I would not take it off anywhere. I believe that they meant what they said about freedom of the press just as they meant what they said about establishment of religion, and I would answer this question as I have answered the other one.

CAHN: Do you make an exception in freedom of speech and press for the law of defamation? That is, are you willing to allow people to sue for damages when they are subjected to libel or slander?

JUSTICE BLACK: My view of the First Amendment, as originally ratified, is that it said Congress should pass none of these kinds of laws. As written at that time, the Amendment applied only to Congress. I have no doubt myself that the provision, as written and adopted, intended that there should be no libel or defamation law in the United States under the United States Government, just absolutely none so far as I am concerned.

That is, no federal law. At that time —I will have to state this in order to let you know what I think about libel and defamation—people were afraid of the new Federal Government. I hope that they have not wholly lost that fear up to this time because, while government is a wonderful and an essential thing in order to have any kind of liberty, order or peace, it has such power that people must always remember to check them here and balance them there and limit them here in order to see that you do not lose too much liberty in exchange for government. So I have no doubt about what the Amendment intended. As a matter of fact, shortly after the Constitution was written, a man named St. George Tucker, a great friend of Madison's, who served as one of the commissioners at the Annapolis Convention of 1786 which first attempted to fill the need for a national constitution, put out a revised edition of Blackstone. In it he explained what our Constitution meant with reference to freedom of speech and press. He said there was no doubt in his mind, as one of the earliest participants in the development of the Constitution, that it was intended that there should be no libel under the laws of the United States. Lawyers might profit from consulting Tucker's edition of Blackstone on that subject.

As far as public libel is concerned, or seditious libel, I have been very much disturbed sometimes to see that there is present an idea that because we have had the practice of suing individuals for libel, seditious libel still remains for the use of government in this country. Seditious libel, as it has been put into practice throughout the centuries, is nothing in the world except the prosecution of people who are on the wrong side politically; they have said something and their group has lost and they are prosecuted. Those of you who read the newspaper see that this is happening all over the world now, every week somewhere. Somebody gets out, somebody else gets in, they call a military court or a special commission, and they try him. When he gets through sometimes he is not living.

My belief is that the First Amendment was made applicable to the states by the Fourteenth. I do not hesitate, so far as my own view is concerned, as to what should be and what I hope will sometime be the constitutional doctrine that just as it was not intended to authorize damage suits for mere words as distinguished from conduct as far as the Federal Government is concerned, the same rule should apply to the states.

I realize that sometimes you have a libel suit that accomplishes some good. I practiced law twenty years. I was a pretty active trial lawyer. The biggest judgment I ever got for a libel was $300. I never took a case for political libel because I found out that Alabama juries, at least, do not believe in political libel suits and they just do not give verdicts. I knew of one verdict given against a big newspaper down there for $25,000, and the Supreme Court of Alabama reversed it. So even that one did not pan out very well.

I believe with Jefferson that it is time enough for government to step in to regulate people when they *do* something, not when they *say* something, and I do not believe myself that there is *any* halfway ground if you enforce the protections of the First Amendment.

CAHN: Would it be constitutional to prosecute someone who falsely shouted "fire" in a theater?

JUSTICE BLACK: I went to a theater last night with you. I have an idea if you and I had gotten up and marched around that theater, whether we said anything or not, we would have been arrested. Nobody has ever said that the First Amendment gives people a right to go anywhere in the world they want to go or say anything in the world they want to say. Buying the theater tickets did not buy the opportunity to make a speech there. We have a system of property in this country which is also protected by the Constitution. We have a system of property, which means that a man does not have a right to do anything he wants anywhere he wants to do it. For instance, I would feel a little badly if somebody were to try to come into my house and tell me that he had a constitutional right to come in there because he wanted to make a speech against the Supreme Court. I realize the freedom of people to make a speech against the Supreme Court, but I do not want him to make it in my house.

That is a wonderful aphorism about shouting "fire" in a crowded theater. But you do not have to shout "fire" to get arrested. If a person creates a disorder in a theater, they would get him there not because of *what* he hollered but because he *hollered*. They would get him not because of any views he had but because they thought he did not have any views that they wanted to hear there. That is the way I would answer: not because of what he shouted but because he shouted.

CAHN: Is there any kind of obscene material, whether defined as hard-core pornography or otherwise, the distribution and sale of which can be constitutionally restricted in any manner whatever, in your opinion?

JUSTICE BLACK: I will say it can in this country, because the courts have held that it can.

CAHN: Yes, but you won't get off so easily. I want to know what you think.

JUSTICE BLACK: My view is, without deviation, without exception, without any ifs, buts, or whereases, that freedom of speech means that you shall not do something to people either for the views they have or the views they express or the words they speak or write.

There is strong argument for the position taken by a man whom I admire very greatly, Dr. Meiklejohn, that the First Amendment really was intended to protect *political* speech, and I do think that was the basic purpose; that plus the fact that they wanted to protect *religious* speech. Those were the two main things they had in mind.

It is the law that there can be an arrest made for obscenity. It was the law in Rome that they could arrest people for obscenity after Augustus became Caesar. Tacitus says that then it became obscene to criticize the Emperor. It is not any trouble to establish a classification so that whatever it is that you do not want said is within that classification. So far as I am concerned, I do not believe there is any halfway ground for protecting freedom of speech and press. If you say it is half free, you can rest assured that it will not remain as much as half free. Madison explained that in his great Remonstrance when he said in effect, "If you make laws to force people to speak the words of Christianity, it

won't be long until the same power will narrow the sole religion to the most powerful sect in it." I realize that there are dangers in freedom of speech, but I do not believe there are any halfway marks.

CAHN: Do you subscribe to the idea involved in the clear and present danger rule?

JUSTICE BLACK: I do not.

CAHN: By way of conclusion, Justice Black, would you kindly summarize what you consider the judge's role in cases arising under the First Amendment and the Bill of Rights?

JUSTICE BLACK: The Bill of Rights to me constitutes the difference between this country and many others. I will not attempt to say most others or nearly all others or all others. But I will say it constitutes the difference to me between a free country and a country that is not free.

My idea of the whole thing is this: There has been a lot of trouble in the world between people and government. The people were afraid of government; they had a right to be afraid. All over the world men had been destroyed—and when I say "government" I mean the individuals who actually happened to be in control of it at the moment, whether they were elected, whether they were appointed, whether they got there with the sword, however they got there—the people always had a lot of trouble because power is a heady thing, a dangerous thing. There have been very few individuals in the history of the world who could be trusted with complete, unadulterated, omnipotent power over their fellowmen.

Millions of people have died throughout the world because of the evils of their governments. Those days had not wholly passed when the Pilgrims came over to this country. Many of them had suffered personally. Some of them had their ears cut off. Many of them had been mutilated. Many of their ancestors had. Some of your ancestors came here to get away from persecution. Certainly, mine did.

There had been struggles throughout the ages to curb the dangerous power governors. Rome had a sound government at one time. Those who study it carefully will find that, except for the slave class, they had, so far as most of the people were concerned, a good form of government. But it turned, and then they had Augustus and the other Caesars, and the Neros and Caligulas and Tiberiuses.

One of the interesting things about Tiberius is that in all the history I have read he is about the only man of great prominence who ever defended informers. He made the statement that the informers were the guardians of Rome. Recently I have heard that said here once or twice.

When our ancestors came over here and started this country, they had some more persecutions of their own. It was not limited to any one religion. A lot of my Baptist brethren got into trouble; a lot of the Methodist brethren got in trouble; a lot of the Episcopal Church got in trouble, the Congregational Church—each of them in turn. A lot of the Catholics got in trouble. Whichever sect was in control in a state for a time, they would say that the others could not hold office, which is an easy way of getting rid of your adversaries if you can put it over. Even for half a century after the Constitution was adopted, some of the states barred the members of certain faiths from holding office.

Throughout all of this—as the Jewish people know as well as any people on earth—persecutions were abroad everywhere in the world. A man never knew, when he got home, whether his family would be there, and the family at home never knew whether the head of the family would get back. There was nothing strange about that when Hitler did it. It was simply a repetition of the course of history when people get too much power.

I like what the Jewish people did when they took what amounted to a written constitution. Some of the states did it before the time of the Federal Constitution; they adopted written constitutions. Why? Because they wanted to mark boundaries beyond which government could not go, stripping people of their liberty to think, to talk, to write, to work, to be happy.

So we have a written Constitution. What good is it? What good is it if, as some judges say, all it means is: "Government, you can still do this unless it is so bad that it shocks the conscience of the judges." It does not say that to me. We have certain provisions in the Constitution which say "Thou shalt not." They do not say, "You can do this unless it offends the sense of decency of the English-speaking world." They do not say that. They do not say, "You can go ahead and do this unless it is offensive to the universal sense of decency." If they did, they would say virtually nothing. There would be no definite, binding place, no specific prohibition, if that were all it said.

I believe with Locke in the system of checks and balances. I do not think that the Constitution leaves any one department of government free without there being a check on it somewhere. Of course, things are different in England; they do have unchecked powers, and they also have a very impressive history. But it was *not* the kind of history that suited the people that formed our Constitution. Madison said that explicitly when he offered the Bill of Rights to the Congress. Jefferson repeated it time and time again. Why was it not? Because it left Parliament with power to pass such laws as it saw fit to pass. It was not the kind of government they wanted. So we have a Bill of Rights. It is intended to see that a man cannot be jerked by the back of the neck by any government official; he cannot have his home invaded; he cannot be picked up legally and carried away because his views are not satisfactory to the majority, even if they are terrible views, however bad they may be. Our system of justice is based on the assumption that men can best work out their own opinions, and that they are not under the control of government. Of course, this is particularly true in the field of religion, because a man's religion is between himself and his Creator, not between himself and his government.

I am not going to say any more except this: I was asked a question about preserving this country. I confess I am a complete chauvinist. I think it is the greatest country in the world. I think it is the greatest because it has a Bill of Rights. I think it could be the worst if it did not have one. It does not take a nation long to degenerate. We saw, only a short time ago, a neighboring country where people were walking the streets in reasonable peace one day and within a month we saw them marched to the back of a wall to meet a firing squad without a trial.

I am a chauvinist because this country offers the greatest opportunities of any country in the world to people of every kind, of every type, of every race, of every origin, of every religion —without regard to wealth, without regard to poverty. It offers an opportunity to the child born today to be reared among his people by his people, to worship his God, whatever his God may be, or to refuse to worship anybody's God if that is his wish. It is a free country; it will remain free only, however, if we recognize that the boundaries of freedom are not so flexible; they are not made of mush. They say "Thou shalt not," and I think that is what they mean.

Now, I have read that every sophisticated person knows that you cannot have any absolute "thou shalt nots." But you know when I drive my car against a red light, I do not expect them to turn me loose if I can prove that though I was going across

that red light, it was not offensive to the so-called "universal sense of decency." I have an idea there are some absolutes. I do not think I am far in that respect from the Holy Scriptures.

The Jewish people have had a glorious history. It is wonderful to think about the contributions that were made to the world from a small, remote area in the East. I have to admit that most of my ideas stem basically from there.

It is largely because of these same contributions that I am here tonight as a member of what I consider the greatest Court in the world. It is great because it is independent. If it were not independent, it would not be great. If all nine of those men came out each Monday morning like a phonograph speaking one voice, you could rest assured it would not be independent. But it does not come that way. I want to assure you that the fact that it does not come that way does not mean that there is not a good, sound, wholesome respect on the part of every justice for every other justice.

I do hope that this occasion may cause you to think a little more and study a little more about the Constitution, which is the source of your liberty; no, not the source—I will take that back—but a protection of your liberty. Yesterday a man sent me a copy of a recent speech entitled "Is the First Amendment Obsolete?" The conclusion of the writer, who is a distinguished law school dean, was that the Amendment no longer fits the times and that it needs to be modified to get away from its rigidity. The author contends that the thing to do is to take the term "due process of law" and measure everything by that standard, "due process of law" meaning that unless a law is so bad that it shocks the conscience of the Court, it cannot be unconstitutional. I do not wish to have to pass on the laws of this country according to the degree of shock I receive! Some people get shocked more readily than others at certain things. I get shocked pretty quickly, I confess, when I see—and this I say with trepidation because it is considered bad to admit it—but I do get shocked now and then when I see some gross injustice has been done, although I am solemnly informed that we do not sit to administer justice, we sit to administer law in the abstract.

I am for the First Amendment from the first word to the last. I believe it means what it says, and it says to me, "Government shall keep its hands off religion. Government shall not attempt to control the ideas a man has. Government shall not attempt to establish a religion of any kind. Government shall not abridge freedom of the press or speech. It shall let anybody talk in this country." I have never been shaken in the faith that the American people are the kind of people and have the kind of loyalty to their government that we need not fear the talk of Communists or of anybody else. Let them talk! In the American way, we will answer them.

33. Lord Monboddo and the Supreme Court*

SIDNEY HOOK

"The most important thing about a judge," Professor Paul Freund has wisely observed, "is his philosophy; and if it be dangerous for him to have one, it is at all events less dangerous than the self-deception of not having one."

No one can read this collection of Justice Hugo Black's opinions without becoming aware of the overriding importance of his philosophy. It is more in evidence than judicial reasoning based on legal principle and precedent. For most judges it is only when the texts and resources of the law, the rules of evidence, and the facts in the case are insufficient to point clearly to a decision that what Holmes called "can't helps," and Freund "ultimate convictions or values," show themselves—and even then by indirection. In Justice Black's opinions, however, his "can't helps" lie on the surface. His opinions follow from them almost automatically.

Fortunately, the editor has opened and closed the collection with two statements of Black's views. The first is a lecture on the Bill of Rights. The second is the verbatim text of his answers to questions put to him by an admiring interlocutor in a public interview. They are forceful expressions of Justice Black's basic philosophy, and are highly commendable for their frankness.

Since Black insists upon his words being taken in the same literal sense with which he believes he interprets the words of the Constitution, readers whose minds have not been drugged by rhetoric will find his views startling both for their intellectual simplicity and practical extremism. Indeed, the implications of Black's articulated philosophy are so terrifying that if it were to prevail, the entire structure of human freedom would be more seriously undermined than if the legislative measures he deplores were multiplied a thousand times over. For Justice Black would strip American citizens of any legal protection against every form of

* *The New Leader* (May 13, 1963), pp. 11-15. Reprinted by permission of the author.

slander, libel and defamation, no matter how grave and irreparable the consequent damage to life, limb, property and reputation. The very foundations of civil society—and not merely of democratic society, whose viability depends more than any other on certain standards of public virtue—would collapse if speech which falsely charged citizens with murder, theft, rape, arson and treason was regarded as public discussion and hence privileged under the law.

It may be instructive to examine the assumptions from which Justice Black derives his position. Most jurists are very sensitive to the charge of absolutism, for an absolutist, like a fanatic, is one who refuses to test his principles in the light of reason and experience, and explore alternatives to what may be no more than arbitrary prejudices tricked out as self-evident axioms or convictions. Justice Black, however, is proud of his absolutism with respect to the Bill of Rights. The starting point of his public colloquy is the emphatic reassertion that "there are 'absolutes' in our Bill of Rights and that they were put there on purpose by men who knew what words meant and meant their prohibitions to be 'absolutes.' "

Now there are obvious and elementary difficulties with the notion of rights being so absolute that they can never be legitimately abridged. The first difficulty is that it makes intellectually incoherent the acceptance of certain laws whose justice is acknowledged even by alleged believers in absolute rights. For example, the First Amendment forbids the making of any law "prohibiting the free exercise" of religion. As everyone knows, some religions involve morally objectionable practices ranging from polygamy to human sacrifice, all of which are forbidden by law. Simple consistency would require absolutists to deny to Congress or any other legislative body the right to proscribe the exercise of such religions. But as

far as I know all absolutists, on the bench or off, approve of these laws.

The difficulty in the absolutists' position, although formidable, is not insuperable. For theoretically the absolutist of religious freedom can always abandon his rejection of inhuman or morally objectionable religious practices and in principle declare for the toleration of any religious practice. Cicero somewhere asserts that there is no absurdity to which some human beings will not resort to defend another absurdity. Those who make an absolute of the free exercise of religion or any other right will not necessarily be brought up short by the realization of the absurdity of their position if they are prepared to swallow all its consequences.

The second elementary difficulty with the doctrine of absolute rights, however, *is* insuperable. One of the commonest experiences in life is the conflict of rights. But if rights are absolute how can there be more than one of them? In this respect, rights are like the obligation to keep a promise. If promises conflict, how can we believe that *all* promises must be kept? Suppose the right to speak interferes, as it very well might, with the free exercise of someone else's religion —which one must be abridged? Or suppose, to relate the discussion to Justice Black's own text, that freedom of speech or press conflicts with a man's right to a fair trial?

Justice Black explicitly states that he wants "both fair trials and freedom of the press." He agrees with Madison that "trial by jury along with freedom of the press and freedom of conscience [are] the three most highly cherished liberties of the American people." Very well. What happens when a newspaper publishes, or a station broadcasts, so highly inflammatory an account of a crime and of an arrested suspect that it prejudices the latter's right to a fair trial by a jury? Black's reply to the question is that this *never* occurs. He does not believe it possible for a state to be so inflamed by press or radio as to prejudice a man's right to a fair trial. I think his reply is irrelevant because it avoids giving a direct answer to the hypothetical question. Even if we did not know of a situation in which a conflict like this has arisen, we could easily conceive of one. Which right should yield?

But we do not have to conceive of such a situation as if it were merely a fancied possibility. Very often motions for a change of venue are granted, among other reasons, on the ground that press reports have been prejudicial to the defendant. A newspaper often has state-wide circulation, and a radio station frequently reaches an audience in every village and hamlet in a state. Black's reply seems blithe as well as irrelevant because it substitutes his subjective impression for an entire encyclopedia of authenticated facts in legal history.

"I do not think myself," he says, "that anyone can say there can be enough publicity completely to destroy the ideas of fairness in the minds of people, including judges." Note the use of the word "completely." What can be established "completely" in law or life? If only one man remains unprejudiced by an incendiary editorial urging that a defendant be legally lynched, does that mean that a fair trial is possible? One or more persons may be unprejudiced and yet every person on the jury as well as the judge may have been profoundly influenced by tendentious press or radio reports.

A trial is unfair even if only some member or members of a jury have been prejudiced by what they have read. The wisdom of the law has no place for complete or final or absolute proof in matters of this sort. It recognizes that even when a man's very life is at stake we cannot forego reaching a verdict merely because the conclusion is less than certain. It is sufficient to reach conclusions that are beyond reasonable doubt. There are many cases in which there can be no reasonable doubt that the press treatment of a crime and of a suspect has prejudiced the defendant's right to a fair trial. When that happens, which of the two freedoms in conflict should be abridged?

An idea becomes a dogma when it blinds one to the facts of experience. The more important the recognition of these facts is to the intelligent defense of human liberty, the more dangerous these dogmas become. Were Black's position to become the dominant view of the United States Supreme Court, its effects on the already irresponsible practices of the sensationalist press in reporting criminal cases would be fearful to contemplate. The English public is far freer from racial, religious and sectional prejudice than the American public. Yet everyone knows how jealously the rights of a defendant in a criminal case are safeguarded in England. Neither the press nor the radio feels muzzled because its freedom to comment on a criminal case before the verdict is rendered is not absolute.

Justice Black refuses to admit the possibility that freedom of speech may conflict with the right to a fair trial. Nonetheless, his altogether unconvincing attempt to explain away the conflict reveals that despite what he says, he does *not* believe in the absolute right to a fair trial. In cases of actual conflict he would rule, apparently on purely *a priori* grounds, that the right to speech or press must be upheld whatever its consequences for other rights, especially the right of an individual not to be prejudged by his judges.

This creates another difficulty for him even more obvious and formidable than the ones we have considered. In developing their doctrine of "clear and present danger" as a rule which governs limitations on speech and press, Justices Holmes and Brandeis were wont to use some specific illustrations which have until now seemed very plausible to common sense. Black has no use for the doctrine of "clear and present danger," but he recognizes one of Holmes' illustrations as a challenge to his position. In his famous opinion in *Schenck* v. *U.S.,* Holmes wrote: "The most stringent protection of free speech would not protect a man in falsely shouting 'fire' in a theatre, and causing a panic." The illustration has become a paradigm case of the kind of speech which is not legally protected and morally should not be.

Justice Black's friendly questioner, Professor Edmond Cahn, with this paradigm case in mind, asked him: "Would it be constitutional to prosecute someone who falsely shouted 'fire' in a theatre?" To which Justice Black replied affirmatively but *not* for the reasons Holmes gives. Such a man would be prosecuted, he asserts, "not because of what he shouted but because he shouted." Black explains:

"Nobody has ever said that the First Amendment gives people a right to go anywhere in the world they want to go or say anything in the world they want to say. Buying theatre tickets did not buy the opportunity to make a speech there. We have a system of property in this country which is also protected by the Constitution . . .

"That is a wonderful aphorism about shouting 'fire' in a crowded theatre. But you do not have to shout 'fire' to get arrested. If a person creates a disorder in a theatre, they would get him there not because of *what* he hollered but because he *hollered*." (Italics in original.)

This is a permanent contribution to the humor of the law! Suppose someone falsely shouted "fire," not in a theater but in a church or school or a public place where there is no question of the right of property. Would the shout then be privileged? And if *what* a person hollers is irrelevant but the mere *fact* that he hollered justifies prosecution, suppose

he hollers "fire" in a crowded theater, and it is true. There *is* a fire! Would Black hold that he should be arrested for creating a disturbance, that *what* he shouted was irrelevant?

The law would be an ass if it failed to take account of *what* a person shouted. For in that case it could not distinguish between the man who shouted "fire" falsely and one who shouted "fire" when there really was one. The effects of the shout depend almost entirely upon the meaning of the words shouted.

The law would be doubly asinine if it treated shouts of "fire" merely as forms of disorderly conduct whether or not there was a fire, and independently of the intent of the shouter. But it does no such thing. If panic and death resulted from a knowingly false shout of "fire," say in order to facilitate pickpocketing or to get "kicks" out of watching the frenzied rush to safety, the malefactor might be subject to a charge of manslaughter. On the other hand, a truthful shout of "fire," even if it were unwise, would not be actionable.

One can, of course, knowingly shout many things in a theater that are false without incurring the penalties which would follow on the normal consequences of falsely shouting something that would cause a riot. No one is arrested for disorderly conduct for shouting barefaced lies about the great talent or beauty of the performers. If we disregard the meaning and intent of what a man hollers, none of these distinctions can be drawn.

Despite the absurdity of Justice Black's attempt to square his position with the judgments of common sense, he seems unaware of the fact that he has breached the absoluteness of the right to speak when its exercise interferes with the right to property which, as he reminds us, is also protected by the Constitution. Holmes' rule limits freedom of speech when it incites to illegal violence or when it threatens life, as does the false cry of "fire" in the theater. Justice Black apparently would limit freedom of speech only when its expression is a trespass on private property. It is a fair inference from his dissenting opinion in *Yates vs. United States* that he would not penalize speech about a public issue which incites to an illegal action like lynching. ("I believe," he wrote, "that the First Amendment forbids Congress to punish people for talking about public affairs, whether or not such discussion incites to action legal or illegal.") But is not the right to life more precious than the right to property and the right to speech?

One would imagine that with these remarks Black has reached the limits of doctrinaire extremism. Yet he has another surprise in store for us. Not only does he hold—by a remarkably original feat of constitutional reinterpretation—that the First Amendment forbids all libel or defamation laws, but he asserts that since the First Amendment was made applicable to the states by the Fourteenth, this should be the general rule valid everywhere:

"I have no doubt that the provision [the First Amendment] as written and adopted, intended that there should be no libel or defamation law in the United States under the United States Government, just absolutely none so far as I am concerned . . .

"My belief is that the First Amendment was made applicable to the states by the Fourteenth. I do not hesitate, so far as my view is concerned, as to what should be and what I hope will sometimes be the constitutional doctrine that just as it was not intended to authorize damage suits for mere words as distinguished from conduct as far as the Federal Government is concerned, the same rule should apply to the states."

This means that if one falsely charges a person in a position of trust with being an embezzler, or charges a scholar with plagiarism, or a teacher with perverse abuse of his students or an official with handing over secret documents to enemy agents, or a nurse with poisoning a patient (to mention only a few notorious cases in recent years), and that as a consequence of these false and malicious charges the innocent person's professional life has been ruined, the victim can have no redress from the calumniator. It is only a matter of words, not of actions, says Justice Black.

This means, also, that if one falsely charges that the butcher or grocer is using dishonest scales or selling deceptively packaged meat and foodstuffs which have been officially condemned as unfit for human consumption, and that in consequence an honest merchant suffers irreparable damage, he cannot sue the architect of his ruin. Here again it is only a matter of words, not of actions. One wonders what has happened to the right of property previously recognized by Black.

This means, finally, that if a racist and anti-Semite not merely accused Jews as a group of ritual blood murder but accuses a specific Jew of the ritual blood murder of a missing non-Jewish child, or a specific Negro of a specific unsolved crime against a white, and the Jew or Negro suffers acutely in consequence, there can be no redress at law against this criminal and wicked libel. It, too, is only a matter of words, not of actions.

All of this goes four-square against the grain of Anglo-American law, which permits not only a civil suit for damages if a man has been libelled but sometimes also a criminal prosecution. It runs counter to the humane legal tradition which allows truth to be a legitimate defense in a civil action for damages, but refuses to accept even the truth as a legitimate defense in an action for criminal libel if it can be shown that the charge was made with a malicious intent which served no good public end. It outrages the moral sensibility of those who believe that their good name or honor "is the immediate jewel of their souls," more precious to them than the size of their purse.

It does not seem to have occurred to Justice Black that words, as distinct from unspoken thoughts, are a class of actions, and that under some circumstances the consequences of words on the structure of our freedoms may be equally as fateful as other types of action. The most charitable interpretation of Black's own words is that he does not understand their meaning. He is like Lord Monboddo rather than like Rousseau. In contrasting the kinds of nonsense both of them talked, Samuel Johnson once remarked to Boswell: "Why, Sir, a man [Rousseau] who talks nonsense so well, must know that he is talking nonsense. But I am *afraid* Monboddo does *not* know that he is talking nonsense."

Justice Black is under the illusion that his doctrinaire extremism is a bulwark of our freedom, especially of the strategic freedoms of the Bill of Rights.

The truth is that if his views became the law of the land, and the citizens of our republic could libel and slander each other with complete impunity, democratic self-government would be impossible and the entire structure of our freedoms would go down in dust and turmoil.

If views such as these were held by a judge of an inferior court, they could be dismissed as a quaint peccadillo. When they are held with passionate conviction by a distingushed and influential Justice of the highest court in the land, a Supreme Court which often functions as a third legislative body, they should be a cause of grave concern to all who cherish the ideals of multiple freedoms under law. They should give especial pause to those who believe it is possible to make absolutes out of any particular freedom, or, in other words, who wish to be liberal without being intelligent.

C. Out, Out Brief Prayer?

34. School Prayers and the Founding Fathers*

LEONARD W. LEVY

[*When these articles by Professors Levy and Berns (immediately following) were written, the "prayer issue" and the Supreme Court's interpretation of the religious clauses of the First Amendment were among the most controversial subjects on the American political scene. These two articles reflect different attitudes toward the prudence of the Supreme Court's recent "prayer decisions."*]

WHAT was the original intention of the First Amendment's injunction against laws "respecting an establishment of religion"? That question is being asked once again in the wake of the recent Supreme Court decision against the nonsectarian prayer prescribed by the New York State Board of Regents for daily recitation in the schools. The hostile reaction to the decision reveals how little the establishment clause is understood, how welcome to certain groups are the many breaches in the "wall of separation" between religion and government. These breaches are the more easily justified if the Court, as its critics insist, has really misread, indeed perverted, the intentions of the framers of the First Amendment. But the critics are wrong, their history faulty.

No one, of course, would really per-

mit his judgment of a contemporary church-state issue to be determined by an antiquarian examination of the original meaning of the clause against establishments of religion. There is, to be sure, a comforting assurance in having the authority of the past coincide with present legislative preferences, and it is an old American custom to invoke the names of the framers to buttress an argument. However, it is also an old American custom to dismiss the framers when it becomes clear that they cannot be conscripted into service. After all, one can always argue that what passed for wisdom in their era may very well by now have passed out of date. Even so, few would openly reject the principles on which the Constitution was based.

The principle that government and religion be kept separate is not directly, at least not yet, under attack by the critics of the Court's recent decision. Their tactic is to argue that the purpose of separation was merely to prevent government *preference* of one religious group over another, so as to insure religious liberty for all.

The stakes in the current controversy are large: the question of federal and state aid (as well as tax-supported bus rides) to sectarian schools accounts for much of the Catholics' bitterness against the Court. The school-prayer decision was quickly condemned, for

* *Commentary* (September, 1962), pp. 225-230. Reprinted by permission of the author.

example, by the national Catholic weekly *America,* as a "stupid decision . . . a decision that spits in the face of our history." And William Buckley, Jr., prominent Catholic layman and the editor of the *National Review,* states in his nationally syndicated column, "The First Amendment to the Constitution was not designed to secularize American life, merely to guard against an institutionalized preeminence of a single religion over others on a national scale."

The implied outlawing of Bible-reading, Christmas plays, and religious songs in the public schools, public crèches, and released-time programs, has also united many Protestant spokesmen in similar criticism of the decision, despite their usually outspoken declarations in favor of separation of church and state and against public aid to sectarian schools. Thus, Reinhold Niebuhr, the distinguished Protestant theologian and political liberal, protested that the Court did not follow "what the First Amendment intended." California's Bishop James A. Pike has used even stronger language, charging that the Court's decision "has just deconsecrated the nation." He urged that the decision be overridden by a constitutional amendment which would insert in place of "establishment of religion" in the First Amendment, the phrase ". . . the establishment of any denomination, sect, or other organized religious association. . . ." The First Amendment, according to Pike, "merely meant to prevent the establishment of a particular religion or the suppression of a particular religion."

This narrow view of the meaning of the establishment clause has also been supported by one of our leading constitutional scholars, Professor Edward S. Corwin, who concluded a sketchy survey of the historical sources by affirming that the Court's interpretation of the First Amendment as making government aid to religion in general unconstitutional is "untrue historically." "In a word," Professor Cor-

win added, "what the 'establishment of religion' clause of the First Amendment does, and all that it does, is to forbid Congress to give any religious faith, sect, or denomination preferred status. . . . The historical record shows beyond peradventure that the core idea of 'an establishment of religion' comprises the idea of preference; and that any act of public authority favorable to religion in general cannot, without manifest falsification of history, be brought under the ban of that phrase." Justice Potter Stewart, the only dissenter in the school-prayer case, indicated his agreement with this interpretation when he pointed out that the Court was not confronted by "the establishment of a state church" or an "official religion."

In defense of the Court, and out of respect for history, the erroneous nature of the narrow interpretation of the establishment clause should be exposed. According to that interpretation—as we have seen from the above quotations— the wall of separation was not meant to enjoin the government from fostering religion generally or from helping all such religious groups as are willing to accept government support or aid, whether in the form of tax benefits, promotional activities, or direct subsidy. Now, it is true that the framers did not speak loudly, clearly, and in a single voice on behalf of the broad interpretation adopted by the Court in the school-prayer case. But the preponderance of the evidence certainly supports the broad interpretation as historically more accurate.

Justice Black, the Court's spokesman in the school-prayer case, advanced the broad interpretation in its most authoritative form in the school-bus case of 1947. He then declared:

The "establishment of religion" clause of the First Amendment means at least this: Neither a state nor the Federal government can set up a church. Neither can pass laws which aid one religion, aid all religions, or prefer one religion over another. Neither can force nor influence a person to go to or to remain away from church against his will or force him to profess a belief or disbelief in any religion. No person can be punished for entertaining or professing religious beliefs or disbeliefs, for church attendance or non-attendance. No tax in any amount, large or small, can be levied to support any religious activities or institutions, whatever they may be called, or whatever form they may adopt to teach or practice religion. Neither a state nor the Federal government can, openly or secretly, participate in the affairs of any religious organizations or groups and vice versa. In the words of Jefferson, the clause against establishment of religion by law was intended to erect "a wall of separation between Church and State."

The dissenting justices in the school-bus case, while disagreeing with the majority on the question of whether the "wall of separation" had in fact been breached by the practice at issue, nevertheless concurred with the majority view of the intentions of the framers. Justice Rutledge's opinion, which was endorsed by all the dissenting justices, declared:

The Amendment's purpose was not to strike merely at the official establishment of a single sect, creed or religion, outlawing only a formal relation such as had prevailed in England and some of the colonies. Necessarily it was to uproot all such relationships. But the object was broader than separating church and state in this narrow sense. It was to create a complete and permanent separation of the spheres of religious activity and civil authority by comprehensively forbidding every form of public aid or support for religion.

In other words, according to the broad interpretation, even government aid that is impartially and equitably ad-ministered to all religious groups is barred by the First Amendment.

The debate in the First Congress, which drafted the Bill of Rights, provides support neither for the broad nor the narrow interpretation. Yet the drafting history of the clause, in contrast to the debate, is revealing. In the House, the prohibitory phrase was aimed against laws "establishing religion." In the Senate, three motions, each of which clearly expressed a narrow intent, were introduced and defeated. All were explicitly directed against laws preferring one religious "sect" or "denomination" above others. Although their defeat would seem to show that the Senate intended something broader than merely a ban on preference to one sect, it finally did adopt a narrow prohibition: "Congress shall make no law establishing articles of faith or a mode of worship. . . ." But the Senate's wording provoked the House to clarify its intent; for the House rejected the Senate's article on religion. To resolve the disagreement between the two branches, the House proposed a joint conference committee. The six-man committee—four of whom had been influential members of the constitutional convention—included James Madison as chairman of the House conferees, and Oliver Ellsworth (later Chief Justice) as chairman of the Senate conferees. The House members flatly refused to accept the Senate's version of the amendment on religion, indicating that the House would not be satisfied with merely a ban against the preference of one sect or religion over others. The Senate conferees then abandoned the Senate version, and the amendment was re-drafted to give it the phraseology which has come down to us: "Congress shall make no law respecting an establishment of religion, or prohibiting the free exercise thereof. . . ."

The one fact which stands out from this review of the drafting of the amendment is that Congress very carefully considered and rejected the phraseology which spells out the narrow interpretation. At bottom the amendment was an expression of the intention of the framers of the Constitution to prevent Congress from acting in the field of religion. The "great object" of the Bill of Rights, as Madison explicitly said when introducing his draft of amendments to the House, was to "limit and qualify the powers of Government" for the purpose of making certain that none of the powers granted could be exercised in forbidden fields. And one such forbidden field was religion.

The history of the drafting of the no-establishment clause does not provide a clear understanding of what was meant by the phrase "an establishment of religion." To argue, however, as proponents of the narrow interpretation do, that the amendment permits government aid and support to religion in general or to all churches without discrimination, leads to the impossible conclusion that the First Amendment *added* to Congress's powers. There is nothing to support this notion. Every bit of evidence we have goes to prove that the First Amendment, like the others, was intended to *restrict* Congress to its enumerated powers. Since Congress was given no power by the Constitutional Convention to legislate on matters concerning religion, and therefore could not support all religious groups nonpreferentially, Congress would have had no such power even in the absence of the First Amendment. It is therefore unreasonable to suppose that an express prohibition of power —"Congress shall make no law respecting an establishment of religion"—vests or creates the power, previously nonexistent, of supporting religion by aid to one or all religious groups. The Bill of Rights, as Madison said, was not framed "to imply powers not meant to be included in the enumeration."

Madison and his colleagues were not merely logicians or hair-splitting lawyers. Nor were they abstract theoreticians. If they did not carefully define what they meant by an establishment of religion, the reason is simply that they knew from common experience what they were talking about. At the time of the framing of the First Amendment, six states maintained or authorized establishments of religion. By that amendment, Congress was denied the power to do what those states were doing—and since the adoption of the Fourteenth Amendment, the states have been included in the ban. "An establishment of religion" meant to the framers what it meant in those states. Thus, reference to the American *experience* with establishments of religion at the time of the framing of the Bill of Rights is essential for any understanding of what the framers intended.

The American experience was in many respects unique, for it did not always follow the pattern of European precedents. Persons unaware of this fact have arbitrarily assigned to the phrase, "an establishment of religion," its European meaning only. James M. O'Neill, for example, whose *Religion and Education under the Constitution* presents the best argument on behalf of the narrow interpretation of the establishment clause, ignored the American establishments and therefore concluded, in capital letters, that "an establishment of religion" has always and everywhere meant what he found it meant in Europe and in the *Encyclopaedia Britannica*:

A SINGLE CHURCH OR RELIGION ENJOYING FORMAL, LEGAL, OFFICIAL, MONOPOLISTIC PRIVILEGE THROUGH A UNION WITH THE GOVERNMENT OF THE STATE. . . . The phrase has been used this way for centuries in speaking of the established Protestant churches of England, Scotland, Germany, and other countries, and of the established Catholic Church in Italy, Spain, and elsewhere. There is not an item of dependable evidence . . . which shows that the term means, or ever has meant, anything else.

The encyclopedia and the European precedents notwithstanding, there is abundant evidence that the European form of an establishment was not the American form, and that the European meaning of establishment was not the American meaning. The American Revolution triggered a pent-up movement for the separation of church and state. Four states had never experienced establishments of religion. Of the remaining states, three completely abolished their establishments during the Revolution, and the other six—Massachusetts, New Hampshire, Connecticut, Maryland, South Carolina, and Georgia—converted to comprehensive or multiple establishments. Significantly, *every one of the six states explicitly provided that no sect or denomination should be subordinated to any other;* all denominations enjoyed equal status before the law on a wholly nonpreferential basis. It is true that in no state was there an establishment which took in every religion without exception. Neither Judaism, Buddhism, Mohammedanism, nor any religion but a Christian one was ever established in America. In half of the six multiple establishments existing in 1789, Christianity was the established religion; Protestantism was specified in the other half.

In each of the six states where plural establishments existed, they included the churches of *every* denomination and sect with a sufficient number of adherents to form a church. There were probably a few isolated towns or counties in each of the states where the letter of the law was not followed, particularly where a congregation of some sect like the Quakers conscientiously opposed compulsory tax support even of their own church; but such cases were comparatively rare. In general, where Protestantism was established, it was synonymous with religion; there were either no Jews or Catholics, or too few of them to make a difference; and where Christianity was established, as in Maryland which had many Catholics, Jews were scarcely known. It

would be a misleading half-truth, therefore, to argue that exclusive establishments of one religion existed in each of the six states; it would miss the novel equalitarianism of the American establishments.

The provisions of these six states show beyond doubt that to understand the American meaning of "an establishment of religion," one cannot arbitrarily adopt a definition based on European experience. In every European precedent of an establishment, the religion established was that of a single church. It never happened in any European nation that many different churches, or the religion held in common by all of them—i.e., Christianity or Protestantism—were simultaneously established. Establishments in America, on the other hand, both in the colonial and early state periods, were not limited in nature or in meaning to state support of one church. An establishment of religion in America at the time of the framing of the Bill of Rights meant government recognition, aid, or sponsorship of religion, principally through impartial or nonpreferential tax support to the churches. The framers of the First Amendment understood "an establishment of religion" to mean what their experience showed them it meant.

Madison, for example, who is known justifiably as the "father of the Constitution and of the Bill of Rights," explicitly characterized as an establishment of religion Virginia's proposed "General Assessment Bill" of 1784, which would have underwritten all the existing churches by the taxes of their adherents. He opposed the bill in principle, not because it did not also provide for the establishment of religious groups that did not then exist in Virginia. Madison's constitutional scruples were so refined on the question of establishments of religion that he regarded as unconstitutional such legal recognition of financial aids as Presidential proclamations of Thanksgiving, tax exemptions for religious societies, chaplains for Congress and the armed services if paid from government funds, incorporation of churches by the federal government in the District of Columbia, and nonpreferential land grants for the support of religion generally. Jefferson shared the same views. As Rector of the University of Virginia, a state-supported institution, he refused to permit Sunday religious services to be performed on university property. And it is not without current interest that as President, Jefferson refused even to designate or recommend a day of thanksgiving or prayer, on the theory that even so innocuous and interdenominational an act violated the establishment clause.

These early Presidents were deeply religious men, but they opposed any government aid, however beneficent and equitable, to religion. They reasoned that religion should remain a voluntary and private matter, the exclusive concern of the individual and his Creator. Any "alliance or coalition between Government and Religion," advised the aged Madison, "cannot be too carefully guarded against." He argued for a *"perfect separation,"* believing that "religion and Government will exist in greater purity, without than with the aid of Government."

Thus the legislative evolution of the establishment clause, the experience with establishments at the time of its drafting, and the opinions of Madison and Jefferson (as well as of other framers) demonstrate the validity of the Supreme Court's interpretation of the original intention of the framers.

The policy of the First Amendment embodies the wisdom gathered from American colonial and European experience. Since that policy, like a vaccine, is preventive in character, and since that wisdom is subtle, the majority, who benefit from it most, often fail to credit the source of their good fortune. Impatiently they dismiss the ancient warnings that the time to take alarm is at the first experiment with their liberties. In the school-prayer case, the Court was quite sensitive to the

dangers of such experimentation, but this has unfortunately not always been true of its decisions. From the time that it enunciated the broad interpretation in the school-bus case and yet found no constitutional breach in the wall—provoking Justice Jackson to note that the majority opinion reminded him of Byron's Julia who "whispering, 'I will ne'er consent,'—consented"—the Court has been extremely inconsistent, even erratic, in its interpretation of the establishment clause.

The public, which has little patience with legal distinctions, has a right to be appalled at the contradictory results of the Court's various decisions on the establishment clause: New York's released-time program of religious education for public school children, New Jersey's subsidized bus-rides for parochial school children, and Massachusetts' Sunday closing or blue laws are not, the Court has ruled, violations of the establishment clause. Yet New York's brief, non-denominational school prayer—"Almighty God, we acknowledge our dependence upon Thee, and we beg Thy blessings upon us, our parents, our teachers, and our country"—the Court has declared unconstitutional. That Justice Black, the author of the school-bus decision (constitutional) is also the author of the school-prayer decision (unconstitutional) only adds to the public's confusion.

Even more confusing is Justice Douglas's record. In his opinion for the Court in the released-time case, he spoke of America as a religious nation "whose institutions presuppose a Supreme Being," called approving attention to the many trivial breaches in the wall of separation, and remarked, with seeming sarcasm, that a "fastidious atheist or agnostic could even object to the supplication with which the Court opens each session: "God save the United States and this Honorable Court." Now, in his well-publicized concurring opinion in the school-prayer case, Justice Douglas clearly indicates his belief that that supplication, like the New York

Board of Regents prayer, is unconstitutional.

The Court has reaped the scorn of a confused and aroused public because it has been inconsistent; moreover, its past compromises failed to prepare the public for a principled decision. The school-prayer decision, however impolitic, is sound, constitutionally and historically, and has the effect of reinforcing the framers' original injunction against any form of an establishment of religion. One may hope that the Court, having now decided rightly, will shun a policy of appeasement, and that this decision will serve not merely as another incident in a history of vacillation, but as a strong reconnection with the principles and intentions of the framers.

35. School Prayers and Religious Warfare*

WALTER BERNS

LAST year the Supreme Court of the United States held that New York could not encourage recitation of the Regents' Prayer in its schools. The decision was greeted by a great public outcry and was followed by the introduction of more than fifty proposals to amend the Constitution. These, in turn, inspired a statement in favor of the prayer decision submitted to the Senate Judiciary Committee by 132 deans and professors of law and political science, a statement that concluded with these words: "The intrusion of religion upon the public school system both threatens the separation of church and state and challenges the traditional integrity of the public schools. That intrusion, if permitted, will greatly endanger the institutions which have preserved religious and political freedom in the United States and have prevented religious warfare in this nation. The decision of the Supreme Court in the Regents' Prayer case has warded off that threat."

If we may be permitted to indulge, for the moment, in the same hyperbole, we would say that the decision is more likely to promote religious warfare. At a minimum, it will thrust religion into the political arena, and whether the resulting discord will be serious depends on what the Court does in the cases spawned by the prayer decision; for, by ruling against the ill-advised religious enthusiasts in New York, the Court has inspired the ill-advised anti-religious enthusiasts around the country to mount one legal assault after another on whatever elements of religious establishment they can find, and there are many.

The decision against the New York prayer will surely not in itself be detrimental to religion in this country: any prayer adopted in the schools of a heterogeneous state like New York is likely to be innocuous, if not profane, and the Regents' Prayer was denounced by some leading churchmen on this ground; whereas the schools with a religiously homogeneous student body may very well ignore the decision, just as most of the 2,200 schools with released-time programs for religious instruction apparently ignored the 1948 decision of the Court invalidating the program in Champaign, Illinois. (There is reason to believe that federal marshals will not be ordered to swoop down upon the nation's schoolrooms and arrest teachers leading their children in daily prayer.) It could never be omitted officially, but this wide-

* *National Review* (April 23, 1963), pp. 315-318. Reprinted by permission.

spread public rejection of the decision undoubtedly contributed to the upholding of New York City's released-time program four years later, when the Court tempered its logic with a greater concern for the "public sentiment" that Lincoln said makes "statutes and decisions possible or impossible to be executed."

This term the Court has agreed to decide whether Maryland and Pennsylvania may permit or require the reading of Bible verses in their schools. Looming up in the future are cases involving the recitation of the Lord's Prayer, and others, such as one decided in the Florida courts last June, involving hymn-singing, observance of religious holidays, the showing of films with religious themes or content, and even the conducting of baccalaureate services tinged (or, to the Unitarian petitioner, tainted) with religious elements. And surely it will not be long before a group of devout Ethical Culturalists will take Justice Douglas at his word, expressed in his concurring opinion in the New York prayer case, and seek to enjoin the use of the Bible in the administration of oaths and of the slogan, "In God we trust," on the coin of the realm.

Facing the Future

Still further in the future, but logically very present, are cases involving the decoration of public buildings during religious seasons, such as the blue cross that, for a couple of weeks each year, adorns the Olin Library at Cornell, a university with state-supported colleges within it. (A crisis was averted this year by the suggestion that the library display a blue shield alongside the blue cross, thus permitting each student who insists upon it an alternative significance.) And surely the courts will soon be asked to enjoin the Post Office from cancelling letter stamps with the religious admonition, "Pray for Peace."

It is always hazardous to predict what the Court will do, but it is reasonably certain that decisions against the religious ceremonies and symbols involved in these cases will provoke a storm greater and more sustained than the one that greeted the New York prayer decision. A doctrinairism of one extreme is certain to provoke a doctrinairism at the other, and one can only shudder at the prospect of the reaction—even in this country in the mid-twentieth century—to a Douglas-inspired decision requiring the armed forces to get rid of their chaplains, the mint to issue new coins, the schools to refrain from singing the national songs unless certain lines, such as "God shed His grace on thee," are deleted, or perhaps merely hummed; and requiring both Congress and the states to amend their tax laws so as to deprive the churches of the extensive tax benefits they now enjoy—and probably need.

The policy of separating church and state represented the hope that religious passions, which had been responsible in the past for the most terrible wars and civil discord, would not in this country be transformed into political passions. Surely we should know that such a transformation can be the consequence not only of the attempt to end the separation by requiring adherence to a particular creed—such an attempt, and the New York prayer was not one, is not likely to be made in our time—or by the "intrusion of religion upon the public school system," as the 132 deans and professors put it (as if prayers in public schools were some sort of an innovation). We should also know that it can be the consequence of the attempt to create an absolute separation by removing every official acknowledgment of God, which is what Justice Douglas would have us do, and every prudent statesman would have us avoid. The adoption of the prayer was a mistake on the part of the Regents, surely; but the suit to enjoin it was a mistake on the part of the anti-religious zealots of New Hyde Park, New York (who but an anti-religious zealot would find the Regents' Prayer sufficiently offensive to justify the hiring of counsel and the expenditure of a great deal of time, money and energy needed to fight the case through the various levels of the judicial system?); but the biggest mistake, and the one most readily avoided, was the Court's decision declaring the prayer unconstitutional.

To say that the Court made a mistake is not to say that there is validity in some of the harsh things said about the decision by the Court's most vocal critics. The standard of validity of any decision, the standard against which the work of the Court is to be measured, is not so readily ascertained as some of the critics would have it. Not much is gained by saying that this standard can be found in the words of the Constitution. If the process of constitutional interpretation were that simple, anyone with a dictionary could be a judge and, what is more to the point, there would be little criticism of the Court. Who, for example, would be disposed to attack the Court were it to invalidate, say, a Texas statute granting General Walker a letter of "marque and reprisal" entitling him to fit out a privateer and seize Cuban commerce on the high seas? But no state is likely to do such a thing, at least, not in so many words. What disinterested person would be disposed to attack the Court were it to declare unconstitutional a joint resolution of Congress declaring some impatient member of the Kennedy family not yet thirty years old eligible to serve in the Senate? Congress is certainly not about to pass such a resolution; but if it were to do so, only a blindly partisan person would abuse the Court for striking it down, for such a resolution would be clearly prohibited by the Constitution.

Nation and States

Nor is the standard of a valid constitutional decision always to be found through an examination of historical records to learn the intent of the men who wrote and accepted the words of the relevant clause. There is no doubt that the words, "Congress shall make no law respecting an establishment of religion," were not intended to prevent a state from encouraging recitation of an official prayer in its public schools, or even from establishing an official church. But much has happened to alter the constitutional relation of nation and states since those words were written, and when, to cite only a few examples of religious establishment, the Congregationalists controlled Connecticut, Massachusetts required its towns to provide, at their own expense, "for the institution of the public worship of God," and the North Carolina constitution provided that no one except a Protestant was eligible to hold public office in the state. The most important event was the ratification of the Fourteenth Amendment after the Civil War. The principal source of constitutional limitations on state power, its most relevant clause forbids states to deprive anyone of liberty without due process of law. What this means in all its manifestations is one of the most hotly disputed points dividing constitutional scholars, but one thing can be said with certainty: the Court has long since held that the religious liberties of the First Amendment are part of the "liberty" that the states are forbidden to deprive any person of. Thus, in our time, *neither* Congress *nor* the states may make a law respecting an establishment of religion or prohibiting the free exercise thereof. This "incorporation" of the First by the Fourteenth Amendment is so familiar a part of our constitutional law now that Justice Black in his opinion for the Court in the Regents' Prayer case made no more than a casual reference to it. Is the Court to be criticized for doing this? Anyone disposed to do so is required to ponder the desirability in this day of the alternative: states would still be free to disfranchise men and women because of their religious beliefs, or to require persons to subscribe to specific articles of faith as a condition of incorporating a religious body, or to do some of the other things they were doing during the first years under the Constitution.

But New York did not banish recusants from its polity; it did not demand taxes for the support of an official church; it merely encouraged its school children to say, "Almighty God, we acknowledge our dependence upon Thee, and we beg Thy blessings upon us, our parents, our teachers and our country." True enough, said Justice Black, but, he added in the familiar words of Madison, " 'It is proper to take alarm at the first experiment on our liberties.' " The reply to this is that there are times when it is prudent to hold one's logic on a short leash, and for its failure to do this the Court deserves to be criticized. One successful suit leads to another (the truly zealous Unitarian will not rest content with a victory in the New York skirmish), and somewhere along the line— whether at the Bible-reading, the Lord's Prayer, the tax exemptions, the chaplains, the coins, the prayers at the opening of a session of Congress, or the Bible at the inauguration of a President —Justice Black and his zealous colleagues are going to have to call a halt to their logic, or the people and the Congress will surely do it for them. Where the Court made its mistake was in agreeing to apply its logic at all— that is, in agreeing to decide the case on its merits. What is more, if it had followed precedent, the precedent of a wiser past, it would have refused to decide it.

The Question of Standing

It so happens, and not by chance, that the Court has in its judicial armory a device that permits it to exercise a great deal of discretion as to the cases it will hear and decide. The term for this is "standing," or standing to litigate. When ten years ago the parents

of some New Jersey school children protested the reading of Bible verses in the public schools of that state, the Court dismissed the case by denying standing to the parents. This is done, or used to be done, when a petitioner cannot show that he has been injured, either as a taxpayer or in a more subtle manner, by the practice complained of. Justice Brandeis, whose credentials as a great judge are accepted by all Liberals, once wrote as follows: "The Court developed, for its own governance in the cases confessedly within its jurisdiction, a series of rules under which it has avoided passing upon a large part of all the constitutional questions pressed upon it for decision." One of these rules, he went on, is the one that the Court "will not pass upon the validity of a statute upon complaint of one who fails to show that he is injured by its operation." There is nothing reprehensible about this; in part it rests on the sound proposition that not everyone who dislikes some law should be able to go to court and ask it to be declared unconstitutional. The Court in the New Jersey Bible-reading case was only quoting from one of its earlier decisions when it said: " 'The party who invokes the power [of the federal courts] must be able to show, not only that the statute is invalid, but that he has sustained or is immediately in danger of sustaining some direct injury as a result of its enforcement, and not merely that he suffers in some indefinite way in common with people generally.' "

What injury was sustained by the parents or their children as a result of the recitation of the Regents' Prayer? The parents could not show that recitation of these 22 words every morning added to their annual school taxes; the children were not coerced—they could have left the room, arrived late, sat down, turned their backs, or crossed their fingers, and no one would have commented on it. Were they humiliated in some fashion? Neither Black in his opinion for the Court nor Douglas in his concurring opinion rests his opposition to the prayer on that ground, and this is not by chance, for the record is barren of any evidence that the children themselves had protested the prayer recitation. Were the parents injured in the sense of being deprived of the freedom to raise their children to be irreligious—that is, was there some danger that the children would be converted? The Court did not base its decision on this ground, which was prudent, because only ten years earlier Justice Douglas had said in another religious case that "we are a religious people whose institutions presuppose a Supreme Being," from which it follows, logically if not for Douglas, that to convert the irreligious to religion would be good for the polity. Not only did the Court refuse to follow precedent and dismiss the case without ruling on the merits, but the opinion of the Court contains *not one word* on the question of standing. One wonders why.

Principle vs. Desirability

If neither the parents nor the children were required to show that they had sustained, or were in immediate danger of sustaining, some direct injury as a result of the prayer, does this mean that anyone can now get standing in a federal court to protest some law that in his opinion violates the Constitution? For example, for all that appears in the opinion of the Court, a person who had no children in the schools, and whose interest in the recitation of the prayer was "undifferentiated from the mass of his fellow citizens," might have brought the suit to enjoin its recitation. It is doubtful that the Court meant to go so far, although many persons, including the Unitarians who have protested chapel services at the Naval Academy, and other such practices, have assumed that it ought to do so. (This, too, may prove ill-advised on their part, for what is sauce for the goose can turn out to be sauce for the gander. What is needed

as the first step is for someone with the same litigious proclivities to ask the courts to enjoin the states from granting charters of incorporation, with all the considerable advantages of that legal status, to Unitarian churches.) And if anyone can get standing in a federal court to protest state practices of or aid to religion, does this mean that someone may now sue to enjoin federal aid to religion? Specifically (and one wonders if it was not this that the Court had in mind when it ignored precedent and granted standing to the New York parents in order to strike down that innocuous prayer), is the way now open for someone to sue to enjoin an appropriation to parochial schools? The proposed financial aid to church schools is by no means innocuous—to judge from the heat of the debate it has inspired so far—and many persons have claimed it to be a clear violation of the First Amendment. Prior to the school prayer decision, however, there was no way for anyone to challenge its constitutionality in the courts. Has the Supreme Court now provided a way of doing this?

Although a ruling on the constitutionality of an issue can sometimes moderate political strife by transforming what had been a question of principle into a question of mere desirability, the example of the *Dred Scott* decision, which the Court could have avoided by holding that Scott, because he was not a citizen of Missouri, had no right to bring his suit in a federal court, is sufficient to show that the Court cannot settle every intense political issue dividing the nation. The justices are sometimes criticized for using the standing device as a dodge enabling them to avoid issues, but issues like that involved in the *Dred Scott* case should be avoided by the Court, and the Court acts in its best tradition when it sometimes refuses standing to the party who insists on a proclamation of principle. This is also true when it resorts to the standing device to avoid exacerbating differences, which is what it did not do in the school prayer case; and because it did not, because it was not prudent, it has opened the way to those private groups that are not prudent, and perhaps not even tolerant. One might have thought the 22-word prayer a small price for the general freedom of opinion that prevails in this country, or for the benefits of American life generally; and certainly one can avoid seeing it as an "experiment on our liberties" or as posing a threat of "religious warfare."

Readers of today's sophisticated books will know that some words appear in these books only in inverted commas ("justice," "good," "bad," etc.) to indicate that they cannot be used seriously in a scientific and rigorous vocabulary. If, by its decision in the school prayer case, the Court intended to clear the way for every anti-religious zealot who is offended by every public mention or acknowledgment of God, then, to adopt the only supplication permitted, "God" save this Honorable Court.

D. Out of His Own Mouth?

36. The Fifth Amendment
—A Great Landmark*

ERWIN S. GRISWOLD

I WOULD like to venture the suggestion that the privilege against self-incrimination is one of the great landmarks in man's struggle to make himself civilized. As I have already pointed out, the establishment of the privilege is closely linked historically with the abolition of torture. Now we look upon torture with abhorrence. But torture was once used by honest and conscientious public servants as a means of obtaining information about crimes which could not otherwise be disclosed. We want none of that today, I am sure. For a very similar reason, we do not make even the most hardened criminal sign his own death warrant, or dig his own grave, or pull the lever that springs the trap on which he stands. We have through the course of history developed a considerable feeling of the dignity and intrinsic importance of the individual man. Even the evil man is a human being.

If a man has done wrong, he should be punished. But the evidence against him should be produced, and evaluated by a proper court in a fair trial. Neither torture nor an oath nor the threat of punishment such as imprisonment for contempt should be used to compel him to provide the evidence to

accuse or to convict himself. If his crime is a serious one, careful and often laborious police work may be required to prove it by other evidence. Sometimes no other evidence can be found. But for about three centuries in the Anglo-American legal system we have accepted the standard that even then we do not compel the accused to provide that evidence. I believe that is a good standard, and that it is an expression of one of the fundamental decencies in the relation we have developed between government and man.

As that old tartar Mr. Justice Stephen J. Field said, "The essential and inherent cruelty of compelling a man to expose his own guilt is obvious to every one, and needs no illustration." And in words which he approved, the privilege is the "result of the long struggle between the opposing forces of the spirit of individual liberty on the one hand and the collective power of the State on the other." *Brown v. Walker,* 161 U.S. 591, 637 (1896).

Where matters of a man's belief or opinions or political views are essential elements in the charge, it may be most difficult to get evidence from sources other than the suspected or accused person himself. Hence, the significance of the privilege over the years has perhaps been greatest in connection with resistance to prosecution for such offenses as heresy or political crimes. In these areas the privilege against self-

* The Fifth Amendment Today (Cambridge, Harvard University Press, 1955), pp. 7-24. Reprinted by permission of the publishers from Erwin S. Griswold. Copyright 1955 by the President and Fellows of Harvard College.

incrimination has been a protection for freedom of thought and a hindrance to any government which might wish to prosecute for thoughts and opinions alone.

But the privilege is broader than that. It is applicable to any sort of crime, even the most sordid. Don't we go too far in giving this protection to criminals? Isn't the claim of the privilege the clearest sort of proof that the person who claims it is guilty of a crime? This has been asserted by high authority, but I do not believe it is true.

Apart from its expression of our view of civilized governmental conduct, another purpose of the Fifth Amendment is to protect the innocent. But how can a man claim the privilege if he is innocent? How can a man fear he will incriminate himself if he knows he has committed no crime? This may happen in several ways. A simple illustration will show the possibility.

Consider, for example, the case of the man who has killed another in self-defense, or by accident, without design or fault. He has committed no crime, yet his answer to the question whether he killed the man may well incriminate him. At the very least it will in effect shift the burden of proof to him so that he will have to prove his own innocence. Indeed, the privilege against self-incrimination may well be thought of as a companion of our established rule that a man is innocent until he has been proved guilty.

In this connection let me quote from a Supreme Court decision written long before our present troubles. In *Burdick v. United States*, 236 U.S. 79 (1915), Mr. Justice McKenna wrote, "If it be objected that the sensitiveness of Burdick was extreme because his refusal to answer was itself an implication of crime, we answer, not necessarily in fact, not at all in theory of law."

*　　*　　*

Now let us turn to an area which is closer to that which has recently been of concern. I am going to ask you to assume two sets of facts. You may think that both of the sets of facts are unlikely, and that they do not correspond with any case you have ever heard of. All I ask is that you assume the facts. I am simply putting a hypothetical case; and the facts are not the facts of any specific case.

Here is Case 1. A man is a college teacher. He is an idealist and perhaps slow to recognize realities, as idealists sometimes are. He has a great urge for what he regards as social reform. He is native born, went to American schools, and loves his country despite what he regards as its imperfections. You may not agree with his ideas but you would respect his honesty and sincerity. He believes himself thoroughly attached to the country and the Constitution, and he abhors anything involving force and violence. He is a good teacher and works hard on his subjects. He has always believed that as a good citizen he should be interested in politics. Neither of the established political parties provided what he wanted. In the relatively calm period of the past middle 1930's, on the solicitation of a friend, he went to a communist meeting and soon joined the Communist Party. At that time the Communist Party was perfectly legal, and regularly appeared on our ballot. He thought he was simply joining a political party. One of the reasons that led him to join was that he regarded fascism as highly immoral and a great danger to the world, and he felt that the communists were fighting fascism in Spain at this time. His interest was not merely in protecting Spain, but, because the danger which many men then feared most was that of the spread of fascism, he thought that fighting fascism in Spain was an important means of guarding against such a danger here.

Now you may say that this is all very unlikely. To this I reply that I am, for the moment, only assuming a hypothetical case, and I should be able to assume any hypothetical case I want,

So these are the facts I put before you. You may feel that such a man must have been very naive or lacking in intelligence. To that I would make two replies: First, that conclusion rests on a large amount of hindsight. A man's actions at any time should be evaluated on the basis of the facts then available to him, and the state of his own mind —on the basis of what he actually knew, and not by facts we learn later that were not known to him. And my second reply would be that the man may have been naive or obtuse. I would say that he was at least misguided and unwise. But I would point out that being obtuse or naive is a very different thing from being a traitor or a spy.

Let me add a few more facts, assumed by me as before. Our teacher was in a communist cell, with other teachers. The communists had great plans for this group. They wanted to use it to infiltrate American education. However, the communist command was canny. They knew that many or all of the members of this cell of teachers were politically innocent, and that they would recoil quickly from any proposals for sabotage or the use of force and violence. So they treated this group with great care. The group was never subjected to the rigors of communist discipline. It was a study group, and its discussions were kept on a high intellectual plane. The more sordid features of the communist doctrine were kept thoroughly in the background. Our teacher never engaged in espionage or sabotage or anything like that, and never saw or heard of any such activities by any member of his group. He would have been horrified by any such actions.

Nevertheless, there were things from time to time which he did not like. He rationalized them in various ways: nothing can be perfect; the thing to do is to stay inside and work against excesses; and so on. Besides, he was a stubborn fellow. Once having started out on something he thought was

good, he did not lightly give it up. But he became troubled; and after the war he slowly drifted away from the group. He never formally resigned. He just turned away. By the time of the Korean invasion in 1950, he was thoroughly disgusted and saw that he had been used as a dupe. But he was also convinced in his own heart of the rectitude of his actions, if not of their wisdom; and he did not doubt that many of the people who had been associated with him in the venture were just as innocent of wrongdoing as he was sure he was.

Remember, I am doing the assuming. You may feel that these facts do not fit in actual case: But I am not trying to state an actual case. I am just assuming a hypothetical case, which is one of the ancient rights of any law teacher.

Now let me turn to Case 2. This man is also a college teacher. He never joined the Communist Party. He never thought of joining the Communist Party. He knew a good deal about the realities of communism, and he was thoroughly opposed to it. He was, however, a man who was interested in causes. His father had been a minister, who had dedicated his life to helping people. He himself had a great urge to participate in activities which he felt would help to alleviate suffering or contribute to social progress. In fact he was a sucker for almost any kind of an appeal. He contributed modest amounts to China Relief. He had always had a warm feeling for the Chinese. Sometimes he found himself on some of the letterheads of some of these organizations as a sponsor. He was not sure that he remembered giving permission to use his name this way; but the cause, as indicated by the attractive name of the organization, was one that appealed to him, and he did not bother himself much about it. After a while he heard some rumblings that there might be some communist influence in these organizations, but he was slow to believe that that could be true. In some of the organizations, he had been on committees with thoroughly respectable fellow citizens. He did not want to pull out, because he felt that this would let his friends down. Eventually he heard that some of these organizations had been ruled to be subversive by the Attorney General. But he, too, was a stubborn fellow. He believed in the stated objectives of these organizations. He was also a freeborn American, proud of his country's great traditions, and he allowed his name to be used by some of these organizations, as has been said in a recent article, "as a gesture of opposition to the procedure of proscribing organizations without giving them the right to be heard."

*   *   *

Well, that is the end of my assuming. Let us see what happens to these two individuals. Remember that both of these individuals feel that they are innocent of any wrongdoing. Each one is pure in heart, and perhaps a little too certain of his own rectitude. Each one may now regret some of the things he did, but he does not think that they were wrong. Each one is certain that he is morally innocent of any crime.

We can consider Case 1 first. He is the man who was a member of the Communist Party. He is summoned to appear before a Congressional Committee, and is asked whether he is a communist. He answers truthfully: "No." Then he is asked whether he ever was a communist. He is now surely subjected to a substantial risk, even though he honestly believes that he has committed no crime. He knows that a number of communists have been convicted under the Smith Act of 1940, and more have been indicted. Our teacher perhaps magnifies his own predicament. He sees the jail doors opening up if he himself gives the evidence that he was once a communist. Interestingly enough, Section 4(f) of the Internal Security Act of 1950 (commonly known as the McCarran Act)

provides specifically that "neither the holding of office nor membership in any communist organization by any person shall constitute per se a violation of . . . this section or of any other criminal statute." But this was enacted after his period of Party membership. It has been declared to be a crime to be a communist in Massachusetts since 1951, but there may be some possible room to question the effectiveness of this statute in view of the provision of the federal Act.

After much internal torment, the witness finally decides to claim the privilege of the Fifth Amendment with respect to the question of his past membership in the Communist Party. Putting aside the question of his wisdom in doing this, can there be any doubt that the claim is legally proper? Past membership in the Communist Party is not a crime in itself; but admitting such membership may well be a link in a chain of proof of a criminal charge against him. Persons have been prosecuted under the Smith Act for membership in the Communist Party plus something else. If he supplies the proof of his own membership in the Party, he does not know what other evidence may then be brought against him to show that he has committed a crime. Thus, an answer to the question will definitely incriminate him, that is, provide evidence which could be used in a prosecution against him. Yet, remember that he thoroughly believes that he is not guilty of any crime; and on the facts I have given he is not guilty of a crime.

There are other factors that influence his conclusion. His own experience is an ordeal. He does not want his friends to be subjected to it. He believes in their innocence of any crime. If he thought that they had committed crimes, he would promptly tell the proper officers of the government. By claiming the privilege against self-incrimination, he can refrain from naming any of his associates. He feels a strong sense of loyalty to them. He feels a strong sense of loyalty to his country, too; but since he is convinced that neither he nor his associates have in fact done anything wrong, his desire to protect them from having to experience his own predicament seems to him to have prevailing weight in the actual circumstances.

He claims the privilege. He cannot be prosecuted on the basis of any evidence he has provided. There can be no doubt, I believe, that his claim of privilege is legally justified. Yet, note that on the facts I have assumed he is not guilty of any crime. Of course his claim of privilege as to his membership in the Communist Party means that he must also claim the privilege as to all other questions which relate in any way to what he did, or to his associates in the activity. For if he answers any of those questions, it will clearly connote his own communist activity.

There is one small point which might be brought in here. It is sometimes said that the privilege may only be rightly claimed if the answer to the incriminating question would be "Yes." I do not believe that is true. Our man in Case 1 has testified that he is not now a communist. He claims the privilege as to a question which asks him if he ever was a member of the Communist Party. He is then asked: "When did you cease to be a member?" He must claim the privilege as to this, or else his answer will disclose that he once was a member, as to which he has legitimately claimed the privilege. Then the examiner starts a new line. He says: "Were you a member of the Communist Party yesterday?" Now the answer is "No." But the witness who has taken this line cannot answer that question. For if he does, the questions will be continued: "Were you a member of the Party last year?—two years ago?—three years ago?" If he answers any of these accurately with a "No," he will come to the place where he must claim the privilege if he is to maintain his basic position. In this way, the date of his withdrawal could be pinpointed, thus giving valuable information for a possible prosecution. Moreover, he may not be sure just when he withdrew; it was a gradual process. And he may have legitimate fears that an honest answer he might give to a question relating to the transitional period might get him involved in a prosecution for perjury. At any rate, it seems clear that questions of this sort are an illustration of a type of question as to which the privilege may be legitimately claimed, as far as the law is concerned, even though the answer to the question would be "No."

*   *   *

Let us turn to Case 2, which we can dispose of briefly. You will remember that was the man who had lent his name to causes, and had contributed money; and the causes have now turned out to be communist fronts, although they were attractively named, and many good Americans were, at one time or another, associated with them. But he was never a member of the Communist Party.

This man likewise is summoned before a Congressional Investigating Committee. The mere fact that he is summoned shows that he is suspected of something rather serious, and he is badly worried. He is asked whether he is now a member of the Communist Party; and he answers "No." Then he is asked whether he ever was in the past. The answer is in fact "No," as we have seen. But he is now in great fear. If he says: "No," then he may be subjecting himself to a real risk of a prosecution for perjury. He may rightly fear that proof of the fact of his joining and contributing to so many agencies which have turned out to be front organizations might lead a jury to believe that he actually was a communist.

Now it is probably true that fear of a prosecution for perjury for an answer given to a question is not a proper basis for a claim of the privilege. If it was, almost any witness could claim the privilege as to any question. But our man is in a somewhat different situation. If he says "No" to the question of communist membership, then in his own interest he may have to undertake to state and explain his membership and activities in the various front organizations. The net result may be that he will have to give much evidence which could be used against him in an attempt to prove that he was a member of the communist conspiracy. It would appear, therefore, that he can properly claim the privilege even though his answer to the question as to Communist Party membership at any time would honestly and rightly be "No."

In both of the cases I have put, the privilege may be claimed although the individual was guilty of no crime. In the second case it may be claimed although the person was never a member of the Communist Party. In each case, there may be a "natural" inference from the claim of the privilege, and in each case that inference would in fact be unwaranted. The claim of the privilege is surely a serious business, but it is equally surely not the equivalent of an admission of criminal conduct.

There are other reasons why a person may claim the privilege in a particular case. He might get bad advice; but I do not want to press that, as I think that in many of these cases the individual's troubles are caused in part by the fact that he chooses to make his own decisions and does not accept sound advice. But we should not forget that a person on the witness stand may be badly frightened, even though he is wholly innocent. For example, the Supreme Court of the United States has said, in *Wilson v. United States,* 149 U.S. 60, 66 (1893):

"It is not every one who can safely venture on the witness stand though entirely innocent of the charge against him. Excessive timidity, nervousness when facing others and attempting to explain transactions of a suspicious character, and offences charged against

him, will often confuse and embarrass him to such a degree as to increase rather than remove prejudices against him. It is not every one, however honest, who would, therefore, willingly be placed on the witness stand."

A witness lost in fear and confusion might turn to the privilege as a means of sanctuary from a situation which he feels himself incompetent to handle. Consider also how much the chance of a witness losing his calm and collected demeanor is enhanced by such things as television, radio microphones, movie cameras, flashing flash bulbs, and procedures which may not seem to him to be based upon the finest spirit of fairness. In connection with this I might mention the recent decision of the United States Court of Appeals for the Sixth Circuit in *Aiuppa v. United States,* 201 F.2d 287, 300 (1952), where we find the following language in the opinion:

"But, in concluding, we think it may not be amiss to say that, notwithstanding the pronouncements of the committee chairman as to intended fairness, the courts of the United States could not emulate the committee's example and maintain even a semblance of fair and dispassionate conduct of trials in criminal cases.

"Despite the enjoyment by millions of spectators and auditors of the exhibition by television of the confusion and writhings of widely known malefactors and criminals, when sharply questioned as to their nefarious activities, we are unable to give judicial sanction, in the teeth of the Fifth Amendment, to the employment by a committee of the United States Senate of methods of examination of witnesses constituting a triple threat: answer truly and you have given evidence leading to your conviction for a violation of federal law; answer falsely and you will be convicted of perjury; refuse to answer and you will be found guilty of criminal contempt and punished by fine and imprisonment. In our humble judgment, to place a person not even on trial for a specified crime in such predicament is not only not a manifestation of fair play, but is in direct violation of the Fifth Amendment to our national Constitution."

Ordinarily when the privilege of the Fifth Amendment is exercised, it is in a criminal trial. There a specific charge has been made, and the prosecution has by evidence established a prima facie case of guilt of the particular crime charged in the complaint or indictment. Under such circumstances there is much more than the mere claim of the privilege on which to rest an inference of guilt.

In investigations, however, there are no carefully formulated charges. Evidence to support such charges has not been introduced and made known to the witness before he is called upon to answer. He has no opportunity for cross-examination of other witnesses, and often little or no opportunity to make explanations which might have a material bearing on the whole situation. In the setting of an investigation, therefore, the basis for the inference from a claim of privilege against self-incrimination is much less than it is when the privilege is exercised in an ordinary criminal trial.

*   *   *

There are two more matters to which I should like to make brief reference. The first of these is the rather technical legal doctrine known as waiver of the privilege. A clear instance of waiver occurs when a defendant in a criminal case voluntarily takes the stand. He then becomes subject to cross-examination, and must answer relevant questions. So far as witnesses at investigations are concerned, our current learning on this is based largely on the Supreme Court's decision in *Rogers v. United States,* 340 U.S. 367 (1951). In that case, a witness testified that she had been treasurer of a local communist party, had had possession of the records, and had turned them over to another person. She then declined to name the person to whom she had given them, claiming the privilege under the Fifth Amendment. The Supreme Court held that by giving the testimony she did she had waived the privilege, and that she was guilty of contempt for refusing to answer the further questions. There was a dissenting opinion by Justices Black, Frankfurter, and Douglas.

My own view is that this decision was not soundly reasoned, and that it has led to unfortunate results. To me the analogy of an adversary proceeding is not apt when applied to an investigation. As a consequence of this case, witnesses who have legitimate fears of prosecution, but who might be willing to cooperate as far as they could, are induced (if not actually compelled) to refuse to answer any questions at all. For if they do answer a single question, it may be contended that they have waived the privilege so that thereafter they may be compelled to testify against themselves. This threat of waiver is not an imaginary matter. It may be found frequently in the transcripts of the proceedings of Congressional committees.

My guess as to the law is that the *Rogers* case applies only where the witness has given an incriminating answer to a prior question. I do not think it would apply if a witness was asked if he had been a member of the Communist Party in 1945, and he said "No." By the latter answer he has not opened up anything which he refuses to explain. Nevertheless, it will take a Supreme Court decision to provide this clarification of the *Rogers* case; and counsel advising a client may well hesitate to make his client bear the risk and expense of taking a case all the way to the Supreme Court. With the *Rogers* case on the books, the only safe advice may be to claim the privilege at the earliest possible moment, so as to be sure to avoid a charge of waiver.

This doctrine of waiver is, I believe, the true explanation of the refusal of some witnesses to answer such questions as "Have you ever taught communist doctrine in your classroom?" or "Have you ever solicited students to join the Communist Party?" These refusals have been deeply disturbing to the public. Yet, the answer to these questions may be "No"; but the witness nevertheless fears that he cannot give that answer without its being said that he has waived the privilege as to questions about other sorts of communist activity. Here again we have a situation where the obvious inference from the refusal to answer the question may be completely unwarranted.

37. Logic and the Fifth Amendment*

SIDNEY HOOK

SOMETHING may be said in support of one of the dogmas of the school of new criticism, that a poem, drama, or any other work of literature can be understood in its own terms without reference to ideas and events that fall outside its self-contained structure. Nothing can be said in support of such a view in the reading and understanding of legal documents. No one who reads the Fifth Amendment to the Constitution without reference to the decisions of the U.S. Supreme Court could possibly understand the meaning and scope of the provision which states: "No person shall be compelled in any criminal case to be a witness against himself."

At first glance this seems definite enough. It does not carry with it the aura of indefiniteness and ambiguity which attends some of the other provisions of the Fifth Amendment like "No person shall be . . . deprived of life, liberty, or property, without due process of law." The phrase "due process" begs for interpretation. The phrase "criminal case" in ordinary parlance suggests a criminal court proceeding. The actual meaning of the phrase, however, as interpreted by the U.S. Supreme Court extends not only to crim-

* Common Sense and the Fifth Amendment (New York: Criterion Books, 1957), pp. 20-45. Reprinted by permission of the author.

inal court cases but, with certain narrow exceptions covered under Federal Rules of Civil Procedure, to non-criminal court proceedings. In other words, the term "criminal" might just as well be dropped. Further, it turns out that the normal presumption that this privilege is one enjoyed by the defendants is mistaken. It covers *all* witnesses whether defendants or not. Even more striking, the privilege may be invoked not only in court proceedings but in any kind of legislative proceeding, particularly in Congressional hearings.

The ordinary connotation of the phrase "to be a witness against himself" suggests that the defendant may not be asked questions the truthful answers to which would tend to support a conviction under a criminal statute. The extent of the privilege, however, as interpreted by the Supreme Court goes much further. A witness in any proceeding need not answer any question a truthful answer to which might furnish "a link in the chain of evidence" required for prosecution under some criminal statute (*Blau* v. *United States,* 340 U.S. 159). This takes in a tremendous amount of ground, even aside from the difficulty of telling whether the witness' answer (a) *might* furnish a link in the chain of evidence, (b) *would* furnish a link, or (c) whether his *belief* that it would or might justifies him in invoking the privilege although in actual fact his truthful response would do no such thing. The courts have held that no witness is required to state the ground on which he believes his answer might be self-incriminating since he could not state the ground without running the risk of incriminating himself. In strict logic—and fortunately the law is not bound by strict logic—this would give the witness the right to invoke the privilege with reference to any question, including his name and address.

We are not yet through. In any case a witness is privileged to invoke the Fifth Amendment in the event that a truthful answer to a question would or might furnish "a link in the chain of evidence" required to prosecute him. His privilege goes beyond this. It also extends to questions in which by common agreement his answer could not possibly incriminate him—provided those questions are in a field or are about a subject that might give rise to questions, answers to which *would* be self-incriminating. In actual court cases, a defendant or any witness who voluntarily takes the stand waives his privilege against giving self-incriminatory answers with respect to any relevant aspect of his testimony. The Supreme Court has extended this doctrine of waiver to witnesses before Congressional committees (*Rogers* v. *United States,* 340 U.S. 367). If a witness answers a question without fear of incriminating himself in a certain field, say, as to whether he ever joined the Communist Party, he cannot thereafter invoke the privilege with respect to whether he joined recently because his answer to the first question opened up the field of inquiry. To avoid answering the second question with impunity, he must invoke the privilege with respect to the first. Consequently if a witness is asked whether he joined the Communist Party or a Communist espionage ring *in a year before he was born,* he could invoke the privilege

against self-incrimination because he fears that if he answers it, he would have to answer a question about his memberships in recent years.

It should be obvious by now that a reading of "the plain text" of the Constitution would never enable us to tell that the meaning of the self-incriminatory clause of the Fifth Amendment is so comprehensive. It will be more comprehensive or less depending upon how the justices of the Supreme Court in the future interpret it. And since some of the opinions which have extended its meaning have been five to four decisions, it may very well be only one man who will fix its meaning in a given period. There is no guarantee that he will be another Justice Holmes or Brandeis or Cardozo; and even they were not always wise.

The historical development of the meaning of the privilege against self-incrimination indicates that there is an initial implausibility in the view that we must accept it in an "all or nothing" spirit. It is entirely conceivable that a good case could be made for retaining the privilege for actual criminal proceedings in the court room and restricting it before Congressional committees, or circumscribing it so that the privilege may be legitimately invoked in answer to all criminal charges except those involving kidnaping, murder, and treason, or preserving its almost unlimited legal latitude but bringing to bear in certain areas immunity statutes which trade immunity from prosecution for relevant information.

The more basic question, however, must be faced. Why a privilege against answering relevant questions on the ground that a truthful answer would tend to be self-incriminating? Is it self-evidently wrong to require a defendant or witness to give *truthful* testimony? After all, it is self-evidently wrong for a defendant or witness to give *false* testimony, for every system of law frowns on perjury. We must, therefore, rephrase our question: Is it self-evidently wrong to require a defendant or witness to give testimony at all? Notice that Anglo-American law does not recognize an unqualified right to be silent. Refusal to testify to a relevant question before an appropriately authorized tribunal may incur a sentence of contempt unless the ground given is that one's answer would tend to be self-incriminating. Our question, then, is: Is it self-evidently right to absolve a defendant or witness from answering a relevant question by a legally authorized body on the ground that a truthful answer would tend to be self-incriminating?

It may be right, but it is certainly far from being self-evidently right. The concept of self-evidence is epistemologically troublesome, but the point I am making does not depend upon it. It is sufficient to say that the wisdom and justice of the privilege against giving self-incriminatory testimony are far less evident than most of the rights and privileges of the Bill of Rights (in the American Constitution). If one compares the privilege against self-incrimination with the other provisions enumerated in the Fifth Amendment, it is apparent at a glance that the rights not to be placed in double jeopardy for the same offense, not to be put on trial for one's life without a presentment or indictment of a Grand Jury, and not to be expropriated of one's property without just compensation are much more easily defensible.

Further the privilege against self-incrimination is not found in Roman law, in canon law, in Magna Charta, the English Bill of Rights or the Petition of Right, the Declaration of Independence, or the French Declaration of the Rights of Man. In Continental law the situation is complicated by the fact that the defendant is not sworn to tell the truth. With respect to the privileges of *witnesses,* not defendants, in withholding testimony, the provisions of the Italian Criminal Code, if not typical, seem general. Section 348 expressly provides that witnesses cannot be excused from truthfully testify-

ing except in special cases indicated in Sections 350-352. These special cases cover close relatives, privileges of confessional and professional secrecy, and the exercise of the responsibility of a government post. Aside from these limitations, a witness is not excused from testifying on grounds of self-incrimination. To the extent that, and in places where, this is true, it seems warranted to assert that the relevant provisions of American law enable a witness legitimately to refuse to answer many more questions about *himself* than he would be free to refuse to answer on the Continent.

There is an obvious need for a defense of the privilege against self-incrimination in view of the fact that outstanding thinkers like Jeremy Bentham have held not only that there is no justification for it but that it is a positive mischief and an obstacle to justice. We should be all the more indebted to Dean Griswold for his small but enormously influential book, *The Fifth Amendment Today,* for it contains not only a comprehensive discussion of the legal aspects of the Fifth Amendment but a forthright and eloquent defense of the provision. The book gives a sympathetic account of some *hypothetical* cases of individuals who have invoked the privilege and for whom Dean Griswold pleads warmly as decent, if somewhat confused, people. The reader is wooed to make an emotional transfer to actual cases although no evidence is offered that any actual case coincides with the hypothetical ones. Not unrelated to the particular emphasis Dean Griswold gives his discussion are his observations about the nature of communism and anti-communism, the history of the Fifth Amendment, and its moral significance.

Dean Griswold recognizes that there is something curiously unsatisfactory in the character of the justifications previously offered in behalf of the privilege against self-incrimination. "A good many efforts have been made to rationalize the privilege, to explain why it is a desirable or essential part of our basic law. None of the explanations is wholly satisfactory" (p. 9). He then adds boldly and bravely: "I am going to offer my own attempt to express the reason for the Fifth Amendment, and why I think it is a sound provision of our basic laws, both federal and state." This is, indeed, very promising, for if he is successful in doing this he will have succeeded in achieving something which even the great Wigmore did not altogether bring off. Although obviously impressed by Bentham's criticism of the privilege as involving the sacrifice of truth and justice on the altar of sentimentalism, John Henry Wigmore, in his classic *Treatise on Evidence* (secs. 2250 ff.), concluded that, on the whole, the retention of the privilege would do less harm than its abolition. But he left no doubt that he thought it was being grossly abused and that the prime duty of the citizen in a legal proceeding, subject to certain special circumstances, is "to give what evidence one is capable of giving." In referring to the fact that previous explanations of the desirability of the privilege as part of our basic law were not wholly satisfactory, Dean Griswold must have had Wigmore in mind—and rightly so.

Our expectations are raised to an even greater pitch by Dean Griswold's declaration that the privilege—which is a procedural rule—is "a symbol of our moral striving." For although there have been defenders of the privilege as a legal safeguard, no one hitherto has assumed—at least no great jurist or philosopher of law—that there is any moral grandeur involved either in its invocation or in its retention as a procedural principle.

Dean Griswold offers two main reasons, and one peripheral reason, almost by way of an aside, in justification of the privilege. The first reason is that it is cruel to require a man to provide evidence of his guilt. The second reason is that it constitutes a protection for the innocent. That is all. He adduces no other *basic reasons*. (The peripheral reason is that it protects the citizen, guilty or innocent, against the government.)

One rubs one's eyes. New reasons? Sound reasons? The first reason was already considered by Bentham who calls it "the old woman's reason." The second reason is referred to by Wigmore and is far from conclusive until we know to what extent the innocent need it and to what extent the guilty profit by it.

It is hard upon a man to be obliged to incriminate himself. True, replies Bentham, "What is no less hard upon him is that he should be punished! But did it ever yet occur to a man to propose a general abolition of all punishment, with this hardship for a reason for it?" (*Rationale of Judicial Evidence* [London, 1827], V, 230.) Further, this view is inconsistent with the acceptance of other lines of evidence which may be just as self-incriminatory as oral discourse, e.g., a man's letters and diaries. It is inconsistent with other procedures. A gently put question to a witness concerning the whereabouts of a document needed to do justice in a case is ruled out because of the agony it might cause him to tell the truth, but armed with a search warrant we can violently break into his home in the dead of night and seize the document by force. Bentham would have made much of certain current practices like compelling a defendant by force, if necessary, to surrender his fingerprints which may be gravely self-incriminating. To Bentham, Dean Griswold's reason is the veriest sentimentality.

> Nor yet is all this plea of tenderness, this double distilled and treble-refined sentimentality, anything better than a pretence. From his own mouth you will not receive the evidence of the culprit against him; but in his own hand, or from the mouth of another, you receive it without scruple; so that at bottom all this

sentimentality resolves itself into neither more nor less than a predilection, a confirmed and most extensive
predilection for bad evidence. . . .
—*loc. cit.*

This is of coure a drastic oversimplifi-
cation, but it raises a genuine question
about the sufficiency of this reason to
justify the privilege against self-incrimination. It would be hazardous to
charge Bentham, the man who played
such an heroic role in humanizing and
liberalizing the laws of England, with
sadism or insensitiveness to human
suffering.

Dean Griswold quotes Justice Field
about "the essential and inherent cruelty of compelling a man to expose his
own guilt." Now if a man is compelled to expose his own guilt by torture or threat of torture, this is certainly
cruel and should not be countenanced
in civilized society. But as Bentham
points out, a question is not a thumb-
screw. Today many laws prevent the
use of torture. If a man charged with
murder, kidnaping, or treason refuses
to affirm or deny his guilt, wherein
does the cruelty lie in insisting that as
a citizen of the community, enjoying
the protection of its laws, "he has a
duty to respond to orderly inquiry,"
and in making a derogatory inference
from his continued refusal? The fact
that torture was *once* used to wring a
confession from a man about his guilt
seems sufficient to Dean Griswold to
disapprove of requiring the defendant
to answer questions today even if he
is safeguarded not only from torture
but from bullying and intimidation by
watchful counsel and judge. After all,
torture was also used in the past to
wring an accusation from a man
against *others*. Should we therefore
relieve a witness from the obligation of
answering a question today if his answer would tend to incriminate *others*?
Were we to do so, our whole system
of law would collapse.

Needless cruelty is one of the worst
moral offenses. And with respect to
punishment, after guilt is established,
that punishment is morally bad whose
ends, rehabilitation, deterrence, and
justice, can be achieved by a lighter or
lesser degree of punishment. But there
is not only cruelty to the defendant to
be considered but cruelty to the victim
and to a whole class of possible future
victims.

Dean Griswold assumes that even
if a person charged with a crime were
actually guilty it would still be cruel
to require him to answer relevant
questions that would tend to incriminate him, and this in the absence of
torture or intimidation. But the alternative of not requiring him to answer
relevant questions might in the end
have consequences of greater cruelty.
In cases where the invocation of the
privilege enables a guilty person
charged with a crime to escape conviction, the possible cruelty to the victims,
actual and potential, may offset whatever cruelty there is in requiring the
person charged to make a material response. In a certain class of cases this
is hardly contestable. Think of the
agony and heartbreak involved in kidnaping cases where even the payment
of ransom money is no assurance that
the victim will be restored alive. If an
individual had kidnaped a child, which
alternative would be more cruel: to
require him to answer questions in an
orderly inquiry to establish the truth,
which might lead to the apprehension
of his confederates or the recovery of
the victim, or to permit him to get off
scot free if his truthful testimony could
with impunity be withheld? After all,
the punishment for refusal to answer a
question is much milder than the punishment for the crime of which he is
presumably guilty. And it is hard to
understand why it is more cruel for a
man to be required to answer questions
that would tend to incriminate him, a
measure condemned by Dean Griswold, than for a man to be required to
answer questions that would tend to
incriminate close friends, or even father, sister, mother, and child, a prac-

tice permitted in Anglo-American legal procedure and *not* condemned by Dean Griswold or others who accept the reasons he gives in justification of the privilege against self-incrimination.

Now the situation is that we do not know whether the individual charged with a crime is actually guilty or innocent. Bentham, following the lead of common sense, points out that there is a general psychological connection between innocence and truthfulness, and between guilt and delinquency, in giving honest and candid answers to relevant questions. An innocent man normally protests his innocence. He normally does not refuse to answer, and if he does refuse to answer, he normally does not refuse to answer on the ground that a truthful answer would tend to incriminate him but on some other ground. That is why the invocation of the privilege always gives rise to some legitimate presumption, weak or strong depending upon the attendant circumstances and evidence, but nonetheless a presumption of guilt, with respect either to the specific question or to the class of related questions to which answers are refused. The reader will note that the operating phrase in the previous sentence is "some legitimate presumption," not "conclusive presumption."

This is denied by Dean Griswold, by Professor Zechariah Chafee, Jr., Mr. Telford Taylor, and, more unfortunately, by some Supreme Court justices. It is of the highest importance to examine carefully the logic of their argument since it constitutes the nub of their position.

Dean Griswold devotes many pages to prove that a perfectly innocent man might legitimately claim the privilege, as if this disproved the assertion that a legitimate inference of probable guilt could be drawn whenever the privilege is invoked. His procedure is very instructive. He asks us to *postulate* or *hypothesize* the case of an individual who joined the Communist Party but who is entirely innocent of any kind

of misconduct, professional, political, or criminal. The individual in question denies present membership but in reply to questions about past membership invokes the Fifth Amendment. He is then asked all sorts of questions about actions in which some Communists have engaged, the very thought of which would make decent men blanch. With respect to all of them, he invokes the privilege. He is legally justified, says Dean Griswold. Agreed. Dean Griswold then adds that from the fact of his invocation nothing derogatory, except possibly his foolishness, can be inferred *because by hypothesis* he is innocent of any wrongdoing.

The second case is of a college teacher who *by hypothesis* never was a member of the Communist Party, who, despite the fact that he joined n-teen Communist front organizations, is absolutely pure of heart, also by hypothesis. He is asked whether he is a member of the Communist Party. If he makes a truthful answer and denies membership, he might have to explain his Communist front activities. Such explanations might embarrass him and others. Therefore he invokes the privilege with respect to the question about membership in the Communist Party. Since by *hypothesis* he does not belong to the Communist Party and has not been guilty of any of the monstrous actions he has refused to answer questions about, on the ground that a truthful answer would be self-incriminating, any natural inference on our part that he is a member of the Communist Party and/or has something compromising to hide is illegitimate and mistaken. One could elaborate these cases with details as one pleased, which would suggest that either one or both of the men are dangerous malefactors and perjurors to boot. Still the derogatory inferences about them would be mistaken, for by Dean Griswold's *hypothesis,* although they might be undiscriminating to the point of stupidity in their idealism, they are absolutely innocent of the activities about which they have been questioned, and in the second case even of membership in the Communist Party.

To see what is wrong with Dean Griswold's logical procedure, let us examine another case. Assume that X, charged with the worst crime imaginable, is innocent by *hypothesis*. Every piece of direct and circumstantial evidence points to his guilt. Twenty witnesses swear that they saw him commit the crime. He confesses, or is prepared to do so, in open court. Motive and opportunity have been proved. What follows? That the jury has no right to conclude he is guilty? Absurd! Even though by *hypothesis* he is innocent, the obvious fact is that the jury does not know this any more than we know the hypothetical innocence of the individuals described by Dean Griswold. The jury must go by the evidence. It has a logical, legal, and moral right to conclude that the man is guilty (even though *by hypothesis,* he is innocent) because the class of inferences in cases of this kind leads to true results in the overwhelming majority of situations which arise. At the very least there is a presumption of guilt. If any other procedure were followed, the guilty could never be properly convicted.

All that Dean Griswold has established is that there is no *strictly logical* contradiction between being innocent of membership in the Communist Party and of involvement in its activities and invoking the privilege against self-incrimination, just as there is no strictly *logical* contradiction between being innocent and being involved in a state of affairs in which by every principle of evidence, direct and circumstantial, the verdict of guilty is warranted. Men have been convicted—even hanged—on the best of evidence for crimes which subsequently it turned out they did not commit. What then? Should we abandon all the rules of evidence because they give us only a probability, only a conclusion beyond reasonable doubt? It is very odd that

those who properly warn us against the quest for absolute security and certainty should suddenly invoke the logical commonplace that no strict equivalence or relation of entailment can be drawn between a fact and the empirical evidence for it. The question, I repeat, is not whether as a purely *logical* possibility (or even on a bare chance) an innocent person can invoke the Fifth Amendment. The question is: *Not knowing whether a person is innocent or guilty, what can reasonably or naturally be inferred from a refusal to answer a pertinent question, put by someone authorized to ask the question, on the ground that a truthful answer would tend to be incriminating?* Specifically, not knowing the hypothetical assumptions about Dean Griswold's two individuals, is the natural inference justified from the answers of the first that there is a good presumption he was a member of the Communist Party, and from the answers of the second that he is a member? Common sense answers: "Yes." Dean Griswold answers: "No." More specifically, he answers: "In each case, there may be a 'natural' inference from the claim of privilege, and in each case that inference would in fact be unwarranted" (*op. cit.,* p. 19). Common sense asserts there *is* a natural inference, not there *may* be; it recognizes the inference as natural, it does not impugn it as "natural."

I am not asserting that the invocation of the privilege against self-incrimination establishes beyond a reasonable doubt the guilt of the person who invokes it. Sometimes it does, sometimes it doesn't, depending upon circumstances. What I am asserting is this: if the fact that inference of guilt, when the privilege is taken, falls short of certainty constitutes a sufficient reason for not allowing the inference of guilt to be drawn, then even the rule concerning "guilt beyond a reasonable doubt" would have to be abandoned as well as other justified principles of evidence.

The methodological error involved here has betrayed not only Dean Griswold but many others. For example, Professor Chafee refers to "the *possibility* . . . that the witness is an innocent man, who claims the privilege because he has got into a situation where he is apparently guilty of a crime he did not commit" (*The Blessings of Liberty,* p. 186, my italics), as if this invalidates the justifications of an inference about the probable guilt of one who exercises his legal right to the privilege. He, too, hypothecates the case of Smith questioned before a grand jury about the murder of Jones committed by means of a pistol found near Jones' body. Motive, opportunity, and bad character are established. To all questions like: "Do you know anything about the gun?" or "Did you fire the gun which killed Jones?" Smith invokes the privilege against self-incrimination. But if anyone concludes that Smith is guilty, he would be completely wrong because by hypothesis "he had nothing whatever to do with the murder of Jones" (*loc. cit.*). And suppose we did *not* know that Smith had nothing to do with the murder of Jones, which approaches the situations in real life? If he refuses to tell us whether or not he fired the gun that killed Jones, not on the ground that it is none of our business, but on the ground that a truthful answer would tend to incriminate him, which conclusion would be more likely, granted that no conclusion is certain: (a) that Smith had something to do with Jones' murder or (b) that Smith had nothing to do with it? I find it very difficult from the foregoing why Professor Chafee does not see that Smith's answer establishes some presumption of his involvement, irrespective of whether the inference is given weight as legal evidence or not.

The presumption that may legitimately be drawn from the invocation of the Fifth Amendment is not necessarily *sufficient* or *conclusive* evidence of guilt or involvement with respect to the issue under inquiry. To assess its weight it must be taken into account in relation to all other pieces of relevant evidence, including the bearing and mien of the person who makes answer. And even when we have fairly determined its weight, it may not be legally admissible because of traditional rules of evidence. A signature attested to by a saint may be overwhelmingly satisfactory evidence to us of its genuineness, more so than if it were attested to by a regiment of publicans, but it may not have any probative value if the rules of evidence require two witnesses to a document. All these questions must be distinguished. The question which concerns us at the moment is whether or not there is a justification in common sense and scientific inference for a derogatory conclusion concerning the person who invokes the privilege against self-incrimination. In the form in which it has most frequently come up, the question is whether if a person refuses to answer a legitimate query concerning his membership in the Communist Party or his activities as a Communist on the ground that a truthful answer would tend to incriminate him, can we legitimately infer that he is or was a member, that he is or was active in Communist work? That we may be mistaken in our inference is granted, but since we will be much more frequently mistaken in denying the inference than in affirming it, the inference is legitimate. The law cannot make that inference logically illegitimate; it can only rule out its legal relevance or, more strictly, try to rule it out where men of common sense hear testimony.

But if it is true that once a witness replies positively or negatively to a question, q, about a subject, he loses his privilege not to reply to any subsequent questions (r, s, t, etc.) about that subject and to avoid doing this, therefore, invokes his privilege with respect to question q, can we still draw a legitimate inference from his invocation of the privilege with respect to the entire *series* of questions: q, r, s, t?

My answer would be affirmative; if I understand Dean Griswold, he would deny it.

This brings us to the case of the two Harvard twins which Dean Griswold uses to illustrate his position (1955-6 *Marquette Law Review* 148). Asked whether they held Communist meetings or collected Communist dues in their rooms at Harvard Law School, they invoked the Fifth Amendment. (Surprisingly enough, not allowing for the vagaries of students, Dean Griswold asserts that if they had done these things, their connection with the school would have been terminated, thus depriving Harvard of an opportunity of re-educating them.) These students knew that if they answered the question truthfully in the negative concerning Harvard, they would have to answer the question concerning their membership and activity at Cornell, on which testimony involving them had been given. In order to avoid answering the latter question, they avoided answering the former question by invoking the Fifth Amendment. The purpose of the inquiry was to uncover the pattern of Communist penetration in educational institutions. Whether we approve of the inquiry is not here relevant. It was lawful, even though it may have been unnecessary or unwise. What could be inferred from the testimony of the Harvard twins? This: that the probability that they conducted Communist activity at "Harvard or Cornell" is *at least* as great as the probability that they conducted such activities at Cornell or that they conducted such activities at Harvard. It is this inference which is relevant to the purposes of the inquiry. Dean Griswold adds that subsequent investigation led to the conclusion that they had not engaged in Communist activities at Harvard. In other words, additional evidence refuted the presumption with respect to Harvard but *not Cornell*. What Dean Griswold leaves unexplained, on the hypothesis that *nothing* could be legitimately inferred about the twins' activity from

their invocation of the privilege, is not only his wish to investigate their careers at Harvard Law School but *his common sense assumption that they answered as they did when asked about Harvard because they wished to conceal the nature of their Communist activities at Cornell.* If there had been no Communist activities at Cornell or at Harvard, it is extremely unlikely, although not absolutely impossible, that the famous twins would have invoked the privilege or that they would have had valid legal grounds if they did.

Mr. C. Dickerman Williams in his searching and learned essay "Problems of the Fifth Amendment" (24 *Fordham Law Review* 38) calls our attention to a host of circumstances in law, not only in civil cases but also in criminal cases, in which silence or any reluctance to face a situation with candor —e.g., flight, interference with witnesses, signs pointing to consciousness of guilt—gives rise to a prima-facie adverse inference. Common sense recognizes that evidence against a man acquires a greater force when it is not denied, particularly when a man is in a position to deny or refute the evidence. *Whose* common sense? the reader may inquire. Literally the common sense of the moral tradition of at least the Western world, including the common sense of those who believe that the invocation of the privilege does not warrant an adverse inference. For outside a legal context, they think just like everyone else on the matter. Suppose stolen property is found in the possession of X. Is it not more likely that he is a thief than that some indeterminate Y, picked at random, who does not possess the property, is a thief? Suppose X is asked to explain his possession of the stolen property and he refuses to speak. Suppose now that X is innocent; he has found the property or it has been planted on him or he never saw it before. Is it not wildly improbable that he will remain silent in the face of the danger from the law, the censure of society, the heartbreak of friends and family? As one judge put it who must have read Bentham to some purpose:

> Instant impulse, spontaneous anxiety and deep yearning to repel charges thus impugning his honor would be expected from an innocent man. Refusal to testify himself or to call available witnesses in his own behalf under such circumstances warrants inferences unfavorable to the respondent. It is conduct in the nature of an admission. It is evidence against him. This principle of law has long been established and constantly applied. The reason is that it is an attribute of human nature to resent such imputations. In the face of such accusations, men commonly do not remain mute but voice their denial with earnestness, if they can do so with honesty. Culpability alone seals their lips.—*Attorney General* v. *Pelletier,* 240 Mass. 264, 316, 134 N.E. 407, 423 (1922).

The learned judge has read Bentham too well and imbibed some of Bentham's extremism. It is false that culpability *alone* seals their lips. He should have written culpability *usually* or *commonly* seals their lips. It is theoretically conceivable that love and not culpability may seal the lips of a person accused of a heinous crime, and Dean Griswold could easily *hypothecate* such situations. But we are dealing with common-sense inferences in situations where a grave charge is made, the witness silent, and no evidence present that the witness is sacrificing himself for someone else.

To return to X. His silence constitutes, as a rule, a more weighty ground for doubting his innocence than his lack of candor; his outright and persistent refusal to answer counts more heavily against him than his mere initial silence; and in this scale of weights, a refusal anchored to the admission that a truthful answer would tend to be self-incriminating is the heaviest obstacle of all to belief in his innocence.

Natural or reasonable inference in law as in life is guided not by pure logic or abstract mathematical possibilities but by reliable generalizations concerning human beings, their psychology and customary behavior. A man may be merely drinking tea in a woman's hotel bedroom at 2 A.M. even though both are registered under false names. In a divorce action this evidence gives rise to a presumption that drinking tea wasn't the only purpose for which he was there. The presumption, of course, may be rebutted. But the question is: Is it a legitimate assumption? If we take Dean Griswold's illustrations as a paradigm of his discussion of such questions, then having started from an assumption or hypothesis about the man's innocence, the answer is clearly no. Dean Griswold is absolved even from making any inquiry, for no matter what the results of such an inquiry, he knows *in advance* that they cannot affect the original postulation of innocence. In ordinary life, however, we cannot determine legal guilt or innocence by postulate or assumption.

How stands it then with the assertions that a valid reason for the privilege against self-incrimination is that it is a good shield for the innocent as well as a shelter for the guilty? Or that it is a good safeguard for the accused? Or that it is an aid to establishing the truth and doing justice? We shall know better how to answer these questions if we can answer two prior ones: Is there a legitimate *presumption* that an individual who invokes the privilege against self-incrimination has something to conceal? Is there a legitimate *presumption* that a person who invokes the privilege is guilty of what he is being questioned about—whether the matter of inquiry be venial or venal? We grant that affirmative answers to these questions are compatible with the logical possibility of innocence. We hold, however, that whether the answers be affirmative or negative, they cannot be reached by logic alone but by psychology, and by knowledge of the relevant social and political facts.

We shall continue the discussion of these psychological questions in the second chapter. Before doing so it is necessary to examine another observation of Dean Griswold which might be taken as a strong reason for the privilege against self-incrimination. He asserts that the privilege against self-incrimination can be "thought of as a companion of our established rule [in Anglo-American law] that a man is innocent until he has been proved guilty" (p. 9). And this seems to suggest that if it is a good and desirable principle that "a man is innocent until he has been proved guilty," it is a good and desirable principle that a man enjoy the privilege of not giving testimony that would tend to incriminate him.

It is, of course, true that the first principle can be "thought of" as a "companion" of the second. But we must first know what the force of the word "companion" is before we can judge whether the comparison is *well* thought of. Obviously it is not a logical companion in the sense that the first strictly entails the second or the second the first. Grant that a man is innocent until he is proved guilty. But cannot his invocation of the privilege against self-incrimination, sometimes at least, be legitimately considered as *part* of the evidence of his guilt? How is it with our own thinking in ordinary affairs? If a child left alone with the cat refuses to reply to the question whether he locked it in the refrigerator, the refusal certainly has *some* evidential weight that he did. How much more so if he were to say, "I refuse to tell you because if I answered your question truthfully it would tend to show me guilty"? In any case it is not likely that in the future we would leave him alone with a cat and a refrigerator. Or suppose we heard a cry and a splash and then found the drowned body of a man who was known to have gone fishing with a companion. What would we think if when asked whether he pushed him into the water, his companion, who is "innocent until he has been proved guilty," refused to reply and grounded his refusal with the statement "truthfully my answer would tend to show me guilty of a crime"? Would we not assume that taken together with the conjunction of all the known circumstances this was *some* evidence of culpability? And if so, the privilege against self-incrimination cannot be reasonably considered a companion of the rule "a man is innocent until he has been proved guilty."

The maxim "a man is innocent until he has been proved guilty" has several different meanings, depending upon context. Not one of them has any relevant logical bearing on the privilege against self-incrimination.

Taken strictly, the maxim means a man is *legally* innocent (or not *legally* guilty) until he has been *proved* legally guilty. The accent must fall on the word "proved" to prevent this from being a tautology. The situation is somewhat different where questions of *moral* guilt or *moral* innocence or blamelessness are involved. In such cases, it is surely false to say that we hold, or should hold, a man morally innocent or blameless until he is proved legally guilty. Who proved Hitler legally guilty? Or Stalin? And did we need the legal farce of the Nuremberg trials, in which the murderers of Katyn sat in judgment on the murderers of Ausschwitz and Belsen, to prove that Göring was a moral monster? Nor in our dealings with human beings in ordinary affairs do we *necessarily* hold a man morally innocent or blameless when he has been declared legally innocent. How many times have gangsters been legally acquitted because witnesses against them disappear and then turn up as corpses? Does Shacht's "legal" exoneration at Nuremberg absolve him of the moral guilt of cooperating with Nazi cruelty and infamy? Nor do we hold a man *necessarily* morally guilty when he is proved legally guilty. The law in question may be unjust. Or his motives for violating a just law may be loyalty too high, if not supreme, moral values as in some instances of mercy killing. Outside the context of legal procedure, the most comprehensive meaning of the expression "a man is innocent until proved guilty" is that a man should be considered morally innocent until warranted evidence or good reasons exist to believe otherwise. It presses upon us, to adapt Erskine's well-known phrase, the moral obligation to judge intelligently. And a refusal to answer on grounds of possible self-incrimination constitutes on its very face, *in all moral* situations, relevant evidence of the involvement of the individual questioned. It constitutes a presumption of greater or lesser strength, depending upon attendant circumstances, but nonetheless some presumption, of guilt.

Nor does the maxim "a man is innocent until he has been proved guilty" mean even *in law* that "a man *should be regarded* as innocent until proved guilty." For in that case what in the world would he be doing in the courtroom? If everyone *should be regarded* as innocent until proved guilty, on what possible moral or legal grounds should anyone be indicted or arrested? Every arrest would be arbitrary. Everyone would be an actual or potential suspect. In other words, in a decent or civilized system of law there must in justice be *some* ground for doubting a person's innocence or regarding him guilty *before* he is tried in order to determine his legal guilt. There must be sufficient grounds to indict before there are sufficient grounds to convict, otherwise a defendant is being victimized. This contradicts the view according to which a man must always be regarded as innocent until he is proved legally guilty.

The unwary reader may easily misunderstand this, or interpret it as empty word play. But I am uttering commonplaces which appear paradoxically only because I am counterposing them to absurdities. A man *is* legally innocent until he is proved legally guilty. A man

is still legally innocent even when there exists *some* ground for doubting his innocence or believing his guilt. Indeed, the point is important enough to stress. Unless there existed *some* grounds for regarding a man legally guilty, it would be morally monstrous to bring a charge against him, indict and jail him, and compel him to undergo the ordeal and disgrace of a trial. The trial which establishes legal guilt is the process by which we go from a warranted *suspicion* of guilt to the warranted assertion, warranted under the rules of evidence, of legal innocence or legal guilt.

Finally, the maxim or rule "a man is innocent until proved guilty" may mean only that the burden of proof must rest with the prosecution in criminal cases and with the plaintiff in civil cases. This is its sole operational significance. But why does it follow that if we are making a case against the defendant, we cannot in the interest of truth and justice question him, under appropriate safeguards against bullying and intimidation, ask for a truthful answer, and drawn an adverse inference, prejudicial to him, if he refuses to reply on grounds that a truthful answer would tend to be self-incriminating? This is by no means shifting the burden of proof to the defendant so that *he* will have to prove his innocence. He is simply being requested to make a truthful answer to a relevant question in the plaintiff's case against him. The plaintiff builds up a case by knowing which questions to ask that are material to the issue. The defendant is asked not to prove his innocence but only not to conceal evidence necessary to establish the truth and a just outcome. It is perfectly possible, therefore, to still continue to hold that the burden of proof *always* rests with the prosecutor or plaintiff and still permit him to draw adverse inferences from the refusal of the defendant to testify on grounds of self-incrimination.

To say that the burden of proof rests with the prosecutor or plaintiff does not mean that he cannot use information and admission in the testimony of the defendant. Normally he does. And he is also permitted to call attention to awkward phases of the situation or aspects of compromising testimony which the defendant makes no attempt to explain. What the defendant *fails* to say sometimes counts as evidence in law. Why should it be different, once he is questioned, with his *refusal* to say? Indeed his refusal to say always counts as evidence against him no matter what his motives are for refusing, with one exception. That exception is when a truthful answer would tend to incriminate him. The exception cannot be justified by the logic of inquiry since in affairs of war or peace, science or business, medicine or psychiatry, refusals of this kind constitute excellent evidence.

For purpose of summary, and to guard against misinterpretation, I should like to stress that this analysis of "the presumption of innocence" does not subvert anything which is valid or precious in the humane traditions of our legal experience. It tries to clarify the *meaning* of the presumption by reference to the practices that have been justified in its name. The upshot is an interpretation of the *meaning* of the presumption of innocence, in the words of Wigmore, as "a rule about the duty of producing evidence," a rule which makes it always incumbent upon the prosecution in criminal cases and the plaintiff in civil cases to accept the burden of proof. The point is that there is no logical incompatibility between accepting this rule and still permitting adverse inference to be drawn from refusal to reply to relevant questions. As a matter of fact, Great Britain as well as Ohio, California, New Jersey, and a few other states allow the inference in criminal cases; and almost all jurisdictions allow the inference in civil cases in which plaintiff charges conduct which is criminal, and in which the defendant is silent through the claim of privilege or otherwise. If this analysis is sound, it follows that the privilege against self-incrimination cannot be justified as a logical consequence of the justification of the presumption of innocence—or of the rule of proof beyond a reasonable doubt. It needs some other justification.

E. What Rights for Communists?

38. Communism and the Court*

AMERICAN BAR ASSOCIATION COMMITTEE ON COMMUNIST TACTICS, STRATEGY, AND OBJECTIVES

[*While the issue of what rights communists should enjoy is nowhere nearly as controversial today as it was in the early 1950's, it is still very much with us. We certainly can expect this to be a continuing issue in American politics. The following articles clearly reflect two states of mind about how communists should be treated.*]

MODERN history is filled with the wrecks of republics which were destroyed from within by conspiracies masquerading as political parties. The nine justices of the Supreme Tribunal of Germany refused to see that the Nazis were a conspiracy against the very existence of the German Republic. The Kerensky Government of Russia thought it could tolerate and coexist with the Communist conspirators. The Communists responded to this toleration by disbanding the Constituent Assembly at bayonet point and destroying the newborn republic of Russia. The republics of Czechoslovakia, Poland and China tried valiantly to coexist with the Communist Party in their midst, but were unable to do so.

We are spending more to equip and defend ourselves and our allies from Communist aggression than we ever

* Excerpts from a report made to the 80th annual meeting of the American Bar Association on July 25, 1957 by former Senator Herbert R. O'Conor, chairman of the Association's Committee on Communist Tactics, Strategy and Objectives.

spent to stop Japanese aggression. The Japanese found it difficult to purloin our military secrets, but the Communists have stolen many of our military secrets, including vital details of the atomic and hydrogen bombs which were known to the traitors Dr. Klaus Fuchs and Dr. Bruno Pontecorvo.

The cynical cruelty with which the Kremlin crushed the Hungarian patriots and executed their leaders is proof by deeds that "the spirit of Geneva" was always a tactic and a sham. Likewise, the admission of Mao Tse-tung in his recently published Peiping speech of February, 1956, that the Chinese Communists completed the "liquidation" of 800,000 persons between October, 1949, and January, 1954, and the report published June 15, 1957, by the Senate Internal Security Subcommittee that, in fact, more than 15 million persons have been executed in Red China since 1951 prove the fatuity of those who argue that Red China should be admitted into the family of nations and recognized by our Government.

The Communists have conquered large areas of the world according to a carefully enunciated plan. In 1903, Lenin established Communism with 17 supporters. In 1917, the Communists conquered Russia with 40,000. In 1957, the Communists are in iron control of 900 million people. Their advance since the end of World War II has been especially tragic.

The Korean war proved that aggression does pay because it was followed by Communist aggression in Tibet, Indo-China and Hungary. After Soviet tanks rolled into Hungary, the Communists succeeded by clever propaganda in electing their first government by forms of democratic processes—in the state of Kerala, in India. To the Communists "peaceful co-existence" means Communist conquest without war.

The greatest asset the Communists have at the present time is not the hydrogen bomb, certainly not Soviet satellites, but world ignorance of their tactics, strategy and objectives. The biggest need today is for the free peoples to develop an awareness of the menace of Communism and the ability to isolate the Communist line so that it can be detected no matter who utters it. One speech from the mouth of an important American innocent can be worth a truckload of "Daily Workers" in advancing the international Communist conspiracy. The current Communist line includes the following:

1. Repeal or weaken the anti-Communist legislation on the books, especially the Smith Act, the Internal Security Act, and the Subversive Activities Control Act.

2. Discredit and hamper the Senate Internal Security Subcommittee, the House Un-American Activities Committee, and State officials investigating Communism.

3. Weaken the effectiveness of the FBI and reveal its sources of information.

4. Destroy the federal security system.

5. Recognize Red China and admit her to the United Nations.

6. Oppose the possibility of the United States' breaking off diplomatic relations with Soviet Russia.

7. Enlarge East-West trade, especially in items in short supply behind the Iron Curtain.

8. Revive the idea that the Communist Party is just another political party.

9. Use the recent shake-up in the Kremlin as a guise to revive the Communist peace offensive, just as a previous shake-up in the Kremlin brought about the "spirit of Geneva."

Decisions in 15 Cases—

In the last 15 months the United States Supreme Court has decided 15 cases which directly affect the right of the United States of America to protect itself from Communist subversion:

1. *Communist Party v. Subversive Activities Control Board*
The Court refused to uphold or pass on the constitutionality of the Subversive Activities Control Act of 1950, and delayed the effectiveness of the Act.

2. *Pennsylvania v. Steve Nelson*
The Court held that it was unlawful for Pennsylvania to prosecute a Pennsylvania Communist Party leader under the Pennsylvania Sedition Act, and indicated that the antisedition laws of 42 States and of Alaska and Hawaii cannot be enforced.

3. *Fourteen California Communists v. United States*
The Court reversed two federal courts and ruled that teaching and advocating forcible overthrow of our Government, even "with evil intent," was not punishable under the Smith Act as long as it was "divorced from any effort to instigate action to that end," and ordered five Communist Party leaders freed and new trials for another nine.

4. *Cole v. Young*
The Court reversed two federal courts and held that, although the Summary Suspension Act of 1950 gave the Federal Government the right to dismiss employes "in the interest of the national security of the United States," it was not in the interest of the national security to dismiss an employe who contributed funds and services to a not-disputed subversive organization, un-

less that employe was in a "sensitive position."

5. *Service v. Dulles*

The Court reversed two federal courts which had refused to set aside the discharge of [John Stewart] Service by the State Department. The FBI had a recording of a conversation between Service and an editor of the pro-Communist magazine "Amerasia," in the latter's hotel room in which Service spoke of military plans which were "very secret." Earlier the FBI had found large numbers of secret and confidential State Department documents in the "Amerasia" office. The lower courts had followed the McCarran amendment which gave the Secretary of State "absolute discretion" to discharge any employe "in the interests of the United States."

6. *Slochower v. Board of Education of New York*

The Court reversed the decisions of three New York courts and held it was unconstitutional to automatically discharge a teacher, in accordance with New York law, because he took the Fifth Amendment when asked about Communist activities. On petition for rehearing, the Court admitted that its opinion was in error in stating that Slochower was not aware that his claim of the Fifth Amendment would *ipso facto* result in his discharge; however, the Court denied rehearing.

7. *Sweezy v. New Hampshire*

The Court reversed the New Hampshire Supreme Court and held that the Attorney General of New Hampshire was without authority to question Professor Sweezy, a lecturer at the State University, concerning a lecture and other suspected subversive activities. Questions which the Court said that Sweezy properly refused to answer included: "Did you advocate Marxism at that time?" and "Do you believe in Communism?"

8. *United States v. Witkovich*

The Court decided that, under the Immigration and Nationality Act of 1952, which provides that any alien against whom there is a final order of deportation shall "give information under oath as to his nationality, circumstances, habits, associations and activities and such other information, whether unrelated to the foregoing, as the Attorney General may deem fit and proper," the Attorney General did not have the right to ask Witkovich: "Since the order of deportation was entered in your case on June 25, 1953, have you attended any meetings of the Communist Party of the U.S.A.?"

9. *Schware v. Board of Bar Examiners of New Mexico*

The Court reversed the decisions of the New Mexico Board of Bar Examiners and of the New Mexico Supreme Court, which had said:

"We believe one who has knowingly given his loyalties to the Communist Party for six to seven years during a period of responsible adulthood is a person of questionable character."

The Supreme Court substituted its judgment for that of New Mexico and ruled that "membership in the Communist Party during the 1930s cannot be said to raise substantial doubts about his present good moral character."

10. *Konigsberg v. State Bar of California*

The Court reversed the decisions of the California Committee of Bar Examiners and of the California Supreme Court and held that it was unconstitutional to deny a license to practice law to an applicant who refused to answer this question put by the Bar Committee: "Mr. Konigsberg, are you a Communist?" and a series of similar questions.

Opening "Confidential Files"

11. *Jencks v. United States*

The Court reversed two federal courts and held that Jencks, who was convicted of filing a false non-Communist affidavit, must be given the contents of all confidential FBI reports which were made by any Government witness in the case even though Jencks "restricted his motions to a request for production of the reports to the trial judge for the judge's inspection and determination whether and to what extent the reports should be made available."

12. *Watkins v. United States*

The Court reversed the Federal District Court and six judges of the Court of Appeals of the District of Columbia, and held that the House Un-American Activities Committee should not require a witness who admitted, "I freely co-operated with the Communist Party" to name his Communist associates, even though the witness did not invoke the Fifth Amendment. The Court said: "We remain unenlightened as to the subject to which the questions asked petitioner were pertinent."

13. *Raley, Stern and Brown v. Ohio*

The Court reversed the Ohio Supreme Court and lower courts and set aside the conviction of three men who had refused to answer questions about Communist activities put to them by the Ohio Un-American Activities Commission.

14. *Flaxner v. United States*

The Court reversed two federal courts and set aside the conviction of Flaxner of contempt for refusing to produce records of alleged Communist activities subpoenaed by the Senate Internal Security Subcommittee.

15. *Sacher v. United States*

The Court reversed two federal courts and set aside the conviction of Sacher of contempt for refusing to tell the Senate Permanent Investigations Subcommittee whether he was or ever had been a Communist.

The Communist "Daily Worker" described the effect of these decisions as follows:

"The Court delivered a triple-barreled attack on (1) the Department of Justice and its Smith Act trials; (2) the freewheeling congressional inquisitions; and (3) the hateful loyalty-security program of the Executive. Monday, June 17, is already a historic land-mark. . . . The curtain is closing on one of our worst periods."

The Watkins case decided that it is not "pertinent" for a congressional committee, established for the investigation of un-American activities, to ask a witness to give information concerning persons known to him to have been members of the Communist Party.

How Questioning Is Limited

The courts have repeatedly said: "The power to legislate carries with it by necessary implication ample authority to obtain information needed in the rightful exercise of that power, and to employ compulsory process for that purpose."

Although many people consider the congressional investigations into Communism by the House Un-American Activities Committee [which was a particular target of the Watkins opinion] and the Senate Internal Security Subcommittee [which was ruled against in the subsequent decision of *Flaxner v. U.S.*] may be considered as primarily the information type of inquiry, they have resulted in a considerable quantity of important legislation. This includes the Smith Act, the Subversive Activities Control Act of 1950, the Internal Security Act of 1950, the Summary Suspension Act of 1950, certain sections of the McCarran-Walter Immigration Act, the Immunity Act of 1954, the Communist Control Act of 1954 and considerable State legislation such as the United States Supreme Court-approved New York Feinberg and Maryland Ober laws. . . .

The repeal or the weakening of these anti-Communist laws and committees is in the forefront of the program of the Communist Party of the United States.

Until the Watkins case, the Court had never interfered with the work of the House Un-American Activities Committee, and had on four occasions specifically refused to set aside contempt convictions imposed on witnesses who balked at testifying before this Committee.

Until the Watkins case, the Court had upheld the information function of legislative committees, and had always refused to interfere with the work of congressional committees investigating Communism. In a unanimous decision which was considered for more than two years before its pronouncement, the Supreme Court said:

*   *   *

"A legislative body cannot legislate wisely or effectively in the absence of information respecting the conditions which the legislation is intended to effect or change: and where the legislative body does not itself possess the requisite information—which not infrequently is true—recourse must be had to others who do possess it."

In defending the congressional power to investigate the Teapot Dome scandals, Mr. Justice Felix Frankfurter (then a professor) wrote:

"The question is not whether people's feelings here and there may be hurt, or names 'dragged through the mud' as it is called. The real issue is whether . . . the grave risks of fettering free congressional inquiry are to be incurred by artificial and technical limitations upon inquiry . . . the abuses of the printing press are not sought to be corrected by legal restrictions or censorship in advance because the remedy is worse than the disease. For the same reason, congressional inquiry ought not to be fettered by advance rigidities because, in the light of experience, there can be no reasonable doubt that such curtailment would make effective investigations almost impossible . . . the power of investigation should be left untrammeled."

In defending the congressional power to investigate the abuses of business, Mr. Justice Hugo L. Black (then a Senator) wrote:

*   *   *

"Witnesses have declined to answer questions from time to time. The chief reason advanced has been that the testimony related to purely private affairs. In each instance with which I am familiar the House and Senate have steadfastly adhered to their right to compel reply, and the witness has either answered or been imprisoned. . . .

"Public investigating committees . . . have always been opposed by groups that seek or have special privileges. That is because special privilege thrives in secrecy and darkness and is destroyed by the rays of pitiless publicity."

*   *   *

In refusing to enjoin Senator Black's lobby-inquiry committee from what was widely charged to be improper use of the congressional power of exposure, the Court said: "It is legislative discretion which is exercised, and that discretion, whether rightfully or wrongfully exercised, is not subject to interference by the judiciary."

If it is proper for congressional committees to investigate businessmen, it is surely proper to investigate Communists. If congressional inquiry into dishonesty "ought not to be fettered by advance rigidities," neither should congressional inquiries into disloyalty.

The Watkins opinion points to the Royal Commissions of Inquiry as something to be imitated by congressional committees because of the commissions' "success in fulfilling their fact-finding missions without resort to coercive tactics."

Canadian Law and Communists

The report of the Canadian Royal Commission on Espionage, which was created on Feb. 5, 1946, to investigate the charges of Igor Gouzenko, and which is the Royal Commission most nearly comparable in purpose to the House Un-American Activities Committee, reveals the following differences between the methods used by a Royal Commission investigating subversion, and the methods used by a congressional committee investigating subversion:

1. A Royal Commission can arrest and jail witnesses. A congressional committee has no such power.

2. A Royal Commission can hold witnesses without bail and incommunicado for many days and until after they are questioned. A congressional committee has no such power.

3. A Royal Commission can compel witnesses to testify and impose sanctions for refusing to testify. It does not recognize a "fifth amendment" or privilege against self incrimination, as do our congressional committees.

4. A Royal Commission can have its police agents search witnesses' homes and seize their papers. A congressional committee has no such power.

5. A Royal Commission may forbid a witness to have his lawyer present at the hearing. Congressional committees permit a witness to have his lawyer present and even to consult with him before answering each specific question.

6. A Royal Commission can require all concerned in the inquiry, including witnesses, to take an oath of secrecy. The questioning by the Commission can be secret and, since only selected excerpts from the testimony are then made public, it is impossible to know whether a fair selection was made. Most congressional committee hearings are public and open to the press.

7. A Royal Commission is not subject to or under the control of the courts, Parliament or the Cabinet, and a Commission "is the sole judge of its own procedure." Congressional committees are completely subject to Congress, and they need the assistance of the courts in dealing with contemptuous witnesses.

We do not approve, or urge, all of the foregoing practices, but cite them to show what other freedom-loving nations do to protect their security.

What Legislation Is Necessary

Our Committee deems the bill introduced to overcome the effect of the Steve Nelson decision to be in the public interests. Serious consideration must be given to legislation which will:

1. Safeguard the confidential nature of the FBI files;

2. Give to congressional committees the same freedom to investigate Communists and pro-Communists that these committees have always had to investigate businessmen and labor leaders;

3. Sanction the right of the Federal Government to discharge security risks even though they occupy so-called nonsensitive positions;

4. Vest in the Department of Justice the right to question aliens awaiting deportation about any subversive associations and contacts;

5. Correct the notion that the Smith Act was not intended to prohibit advocacy and teaching of forcible overthrow as an abstract principle;

6. Permit schools, universities, bar associations and other organizations to set standards of membership high enough to exclude those who refuse to testify frankly and fully about their past activities in furtherance of Communist plans to conquer the free world by subversion.

In recent weeks the New York "Daily Worker" has been replete with articles and editorials proclaiming that the usefulness of FBI informants in future prosecutions has been destroyed; that the Smith Act is now ineffective and for all practical purposes invalidated; that the effectiveness of congressional inquiries into subversive activities has been curtailed and that the Government loyalty-security program is under serious attack. In reporting on its current fund drive the "Daily Worker" has stated it has experienced an enlivening of contributions which is attributed to renewed hope by its supporters for its future.

The reaction of the Communist Party to the recent Supreme Court decisions clearly depicts the resilience of the organization and the speed with which its leadership recognizes an advantage and presses to capitalize to the fullest extent on circumstances conducive to the growth of the organization.

Some Americans may wonder whether an organization the size of the Communist Party, U.S.A., with a consistent decline in membership in recent years, represents a danger to the security of this country. It must be remembered that numbers alone do not mean everything. The party has never boasted of a large membership but rather has continually endeavored to confine its membership to hard-core members who have adhered to Communist discipline down through the years and who can be relied upon to carry out the party's orders without question.

Our Committee believes that special mention should be made of the June 3, 1957, decision of the United States Supreme Court in *Jencks v. United States* and legislation subsequently introduced in Congress to define the scope of the rule announced by the Court in that case.

In the Jencks case the Court held that one accused by the United States of a criminal offense is entitled to inspect, for purposes of impeachment, prior statements and reports which the prosecution witnesses had previously made to the Government and which touch upon the subject of their testimony at the trial. Further, the defense need not first lay a foundation of inconsistent testimony in order to obtain production of these documents.

We are in firm agreement with the Court's view that the accused's right to make up adequate defense must not be jeopardized by an arbitrary withholding of pertinent documents by the prosecution.

We are equally strong in our belief, however, that the rules by which these documents are produced should be defined with sufficient restriction that one accused of subversion against this nation and its people will not be allowed to rummage at will through Government documents containing confidential information important to the national security and of no relevance whatever to the defense of the accused. There is danger of such a result.

"Grave Emergency" from Ruling

The Attorney General himself testified before the Congress only recently, declaring that a grave emergency resulted from the Supreme Court decision in the Jencks case. He asserted that some trial courts have interpreted the Jencks decision to require that the Government submit to the defense not only those reports and statements specified by the Supreme Court, but also the investigative report of the case, much of which is neither relevant nor material to the defense of the accused.

We believe the effect of such interpretations is to weaken immeasurably the proper and necessary defenses of society, without granting to the accused any additional information which he rightfully needs to make his defense. We also point out that the investigative reports sometimes contain the names of third persons who originally were linked to the case in a manner subsequently found to be innocent. To release the names of these innocent people from the bond of Government secrecy would not promote the interests of justice. On the contrary, it would be injustice of the rankest sort.

Accordingly we believe that a firm stand should be taken in support of legislation, already introduced in the Congress, which would recognize the rights of the accused as defined by the Supreme Court in the Jencks decision, but at the same time prohibit those rights from being used by criminals and subversives as a lever to pry out of the Government files information to which they are not entitled and the release of which can serve no purpose but to jeopardize the rights of innocent persons and the public at large.

Your Committee calls attention to the report to the Congress which was recently made by the Commission on Government Security, of which Loyd Wright, past president of the American Bar Association, is chairman. This report points out the critical situation with respect to national security. We urge the careful study and consideration of this report by the lawyers of our country and, further, that the efforts to strengthen our internal-security defenses have wholehearted support and co-operation.

Efforts to "Achieve Security"

Chairman Wright, his fellow members of the Commission on Government Security, the advisory group and staff of the Commission are entitled to the commendation and gratitude of the citizenry for their monumental undertaking, which has been so efficiently and painstakingly performed. It is heartening to note the unselfish efforts exerted by Chairman Wright and his colleagues to achieve the desired goal of Government security, at the same time safeguarding the legitimate interests of everyone involved in the considerations of Government security.

This committee again commends President George Meany of the AFL-CIO for his prompt detection of the current Communist line and his warnings to his fellow Americans of the folly of trying to do business with a government which has violated every agreement that it ever signed.

We also commend Mr. Albert Hayes, of the International Association of Machinists, for promptly dismissing three organizers who took the Fifth Amendment when asked by the Senate Internal Security Subcommittee about their Communist activities. It is hoped that leaders in other fields of American life will react with equal courage to current Communist tactics.

We desire to record emphatically our approval of the organization and functioning of the two congressional committees, which have given special attention to the problem of subversive activities, namely: the Senate Internal Security Committee and the House Un-American Activities Committee. It is our considered opinion, for close observation of the work of these two groups, that they have rendered immeasurable service to the American people and that their operations have been of inestimable value in the defense of our country against those who would undermine our basic institutions.

It is also our privilege to comment upon the painstaking and intelligent efforts of the Federal Bureau of Investigation. Under the able leadership of Director J. Edgar Hoover, this devoted group has become a tower of strength in the all-out effort to detect and to apprehend subversion, among their other important undertakings. We praise their work and urge the American people to give continuous aid and provisions to uphold and support the operation of this protective agency.

*   *   *

Lawyers, by training and tradition, know and appreciate the vital importance of an independent judiciary. Wherever we find it, we respect it. Where the independence is exercised with courage and soundness, we revere it—for then we have justice under law. Our training has also given us, and we must impart the benefit of it to the American people, a tolerance and an understanding of difference of viewpoint.

The judicial branch is one of the three cornerstones of our constitutional government—and the ultimate determinant of our individual rights but, as we said in our brief to the Supreme Court in the Communist Party case, "There can be no individual rights or freedoms without national security."

For the reason that our Committee has been charged with the duty of studying the problems caused by international Communism and we have observed the Communist tactics and realized the danger to American life and to the free world, we must urge an unremitting effort to maintain a judicial system which will ever function as impartial, resolute and vigilant. There must ever be one standard of justice under law for both high and low, for those who are accused of serious offenses as well as for lesser crimes.

There must never be different and varying standards for determination of rights or duties or violations applicable to cases involving Communist problems as compared to other issues.

It must be remembered that it is one of the cardinal policies of the Communist movement not to be concerned with actions, proceedings, charges or indictments so much as their ultimate determination and consequences. For that reason, the strategy of delay is employed by them in every case and at every stage.

It should not happen that sound and established concepts of law and standards are disregarded and different standards employed simply because the problem involved Communist activity. To conjure hypothetical fears not involved in a case submitted for determination is neither sound judicial administration nor good government. Again, to quote from our brief in the Communist Party case, may we repeat, "Where no constitutional or statutory provision is violated, the Courts are no more immune from the duty to safeguard the nation than is the Congress or the President."

The criterion of justice must in this country be high—but it must be human —and cannot be perfect. We believe and shall always strive for the same high standard of justice for any Communist or Communist organization as for any loyal American citizen or any legal entity, but likewise, we will deplore special and extraordinary treatment for Communists or Communist organizations.

The momentous and dangerous times in which we live present serious problems to every branch of Government and entail sacred responsibilities. It is imperative that our bench and bar must be sound as well as courageous, realistic as well as idealistic.

The desire to preserve liberty, in all its forms and the absolute necessity of protecting our countries and our families from international Communism pose a problem that is admittedly very difficult. On the one hand, England and the United States have for centuries cherished the ideal that uniformity of opinion among the citizens is neither desirable nor obtainable; on the other hand, we are not so blind as to think that Communism is merely another shade of political opinion.

The dilemma that confronts our two countries is monumental.

Needed: "Proper Balance"

The duty of the bar to play an important part in finding a solution to the dilemma is self-evident. We must strive to find the proper degree of balance between liberty and authority.

It is traditional and right that our courts are zealous in protecting individual rights. It is equally necessary that the executive and legislative branches take effective action to gird our country in defense against Communist infiltration and aggression.

If the courts lean too far backward in the maintenance of theoretical individual rights, it may be that we have tied the hands of our country and have rendered it incapable of carrying out the first law of mankind—the right of self-preservation.

39. New Critics of the Court*

DAVID RIESMAN

I HAVE been spending the Fourth of July, 1957, reading the great Supreme Court decisions of June 17—the best news the friends of freedom in this country have had for a long time. And I have also been trying to get a sense of public response to the decisions, and this I find disturbing. I want in this article to comment on the negative climate of response in terms of some concepts of contemporary social science, as well as to indicate some of the sources for support of the Court and of civil liberties.

In a book published a few years ago, a group of scholars at the University of California developed a significant distinction between genuine conservatives and those whom they termed "pseudo-conservatives": people of conventional exterior opinion, superficially deferential to constituted authority, but who unconsciously were filled with destructiveness and rebellion.[1] Fundamentally cynical, and fearing above all else to be weak and gullible, such people tended to attach themselves to power, and to such symbols of power as the nation-state, though resenting it. They could not come to terms with their own ambivalence toward authority, among other things because they could not tolerate ambiguity: they perceived both the world and themselves in grossly oversimplified fashion, in black and white. The Berkeley authors saw fascism and fascistic attitudes as drawing support from the inner dynamics

of these types; and while explanations of social events in terms of psychological syndromes must of course be handled with care, it seems to me that a good deal of the recent criticism of the Supreme Court by people who claim to be conservatives reveals that they are, in fact, such pseudo-conservatives. They care, not for America's heritage, but for its power; and when the Court reminds them that the heritage is at least as important as the power, their hidden nihilism turns against the Court.

They would not dare do this if the Court were unequivocally powerful and aggressive. But the Court, though theoretically a coordinate branch of the government, has minuscule powers of implementation; it depends entirely on its prestige (the Pope, too, is short on divisions, but he does have Orders, like that of the Jesuits, to spread his views). Moreover, there may be times when the Court is not only weak politically, because unpopular, but also divided: in the great decisions of June 17, it spoke with more than one voice and, unlike the desegregation cases, the eloquent Chief Justice wrote (notably in the *Sweezy* case) for less than a majority; moreover, Mr. Justice Clark, who joined the unanimous bench in the desegregation cases and wrote for the Court in the *Slochower* case, spoke in the recent civil liberties cases with the forceful and unambiguous simplicities of the pseudo-conservative. In civil liberties cases, principles alone are not enough, for they often contradict each other; the Court must choose among competing goods, as well as among the competing precedents which enshrine its previous choices among those goods.

In this perspective, the recent decisions are more courageous even than

* *New Republic* (July 29, 1957), pp. 9-13. Reprinted by permission of the *New Republic*.
[1] See T. W. Adorno, Else Frenkel-Brunswik, D. J. Levinson, and R. Nevitt Sanford, *The Authoritarian Personality* (Harper's, 1950); see, also, Daniel Bell, ed., *The New American Right* (Criterion, 1955).

the admirable school desegregation cases (especially coming as they do in the wake of the fury stirred up by the latter). For racial bigotry is now largely "impossible" in educated circles in America, outside the Black Belt counties of the South where the white colonists huddle together like Boers in an alien veldt. Markedly since World War II, racial bigotry has lost the biological and other rationalizations which once served to subdue what Gunnar Myrdal referred to as an American dilemma (a dilemma primarily for the college-educated upper-middle-class American and not for the naïvely and unselfconsciously bigoted of lesser education). In contrast, there are easy rationalizations for violations of civil liberties—the Soviet Union, Red China, their satellite parties, and their fellow-travelers provide them every day. Thus, it is not surprising that the vocal reactionaries in and out of Congress have launched an attack on the Court as itself "subversive."

It is possible, especially for the uneducated, to believe in good faith that domestic subversion remains at least a potential threat; and for the sophisticated in slightly less good faith to believe that taking the spotlight off the investigating committees may jeopardize national defense indirectly, on the ground that Americans only vote appropriations for defense and foreign aid under pressure of fear and misinformation. So, too, the question of the constitutionality and good sense of the Smith Act can be argued either way. Nonetheless, I believe that most of the attacks on the Court come from people who should know better, and who often do. In a battle between Court and Congress, the immediate rhetorical advantages lie with the latter: the individual Congressman can speak in slogans which make ambiguity seem unAmerican *per se,* while the court in civil liberties cases has a task of inherent intricacy which it must seek to explain to its own new recruits, to lower federal and state courts and dis-

trict attorneys, as well as to prideful if not spiteful Congressmen, the practicing and criticizing bar, and the literate public.

Because this is so complex a task in the face of millions who distrust complexity—who "don't get it"—Mr. Eisenhower's comments on the decisions at his press conference were unsatisfactory. Unwilling to take the risk of bringing the Court under his protection, he failed to respond with enthusiasm to the Court's renewed role as monitor of national sanity. Rather, he repeated his frequent adage about the separation of powers: in effect, "they do their job and I do mine." And he added that, like anyone else, he was entitled to his own strong views on this or that decision—leaving the pretty clear implication that these views were negative. Yet, being not simply a pseudo-conservative, but a genuine one, too, he was troubled when reminded by a newspaperman that the Court could not defend itself; he responded that the Court could in fact defend itself, and did so by writing opinions for all to read.

To be sure, those who do read are much more likely to value civil liberties than those who do not; they have, if not a vested interest in freedom, at least some exposure to it. But the constituency of civil liberties in this country has always been quite small. The public-opinion data in Professor Samuel Stouffer's *Communism, Conformity and Civil Liberties* show that college education and middle-class circumstances tend to make people less xenophobic, less suspicious, more interested in and less frightened of new currents of thought; thus, even DAR chapter presidents who have been to college are in these respects more enlightened than union members who have not. But the pseudo-conservative exists, being a characterological rather than a political type, among the college educated as well as in the lower-middle class: Stouffer shows that there still is a substantial minority of college-educated people who would fire professors who are socialists or atheists—as would the vast majority of the non-college educated; and his data indicate that this outlook goes together with some of the motivational patterns delineated by the authors of *The Authoritarian Personality*. Thus, if we look simply at the distribution of attitudes in the population at large, it becomes clear that civil liberties depend more on the apathy of some than on the sympathy of others; moreover, the "average" American does not distinguish between Communists, socialists, atheists, or the scientists who would tamper with "God's water" by fluoridation (they are less hostile to those who tamper with "God's air" by hydrogen bombs).[2]

As I have indicated, the defense of civil liberties is weak not only because the issues involved are rhetorically complex, but also because, outside the Court itself, few organized interests lobby for liberty (while, of course, the greatly augmented security forces in and out of government, not to mention certain individual politicians and Congressmen, now have a vested interest directly opposed to civil liberties as the Court interprets them). The press, to be sure, has supported the First Amendment, though presently with disquieting moderation; book publishers have often been valiant, and movie-makers understandably only on occasion. The brokerage function of the city boss and of the party system, on which ethnic minorities can rely for some protection—as well as gangsters and other outlawed groups for "protection"—cannot be invoked to assist freedom of speech and

association.[3] While the NAACP and the Urban League, by fighting for Negro civil rights, can help mobilize liberal and Christian white sentiment, and while, moreover, racial tolerance is part of the code of conduct of many educated young people today—part of the ethic of their behavior in private life—there are no similar points of mobilization for civil liberties issues. Indeed, the dismaying withdrawal of the Fund for the Republic from concern with emergency problems of civil liberties to concern with perhaps more remote and probably less tendentious issues (see *NR*, June 24, 1957, p. 5) deprives the ACLU and the handful of disinterested supporters of civil liberties of one of their few modest props. Furthermore, free speech and association cannot by their nature become part of the code of tolerance in private life which the young have adopted: to defend free speech, or to put civilized limits on loyalty investigations, they would have to organize and become political. And while the producers of ideas—writers and professors—have some rudimentary organization, as in the American Association of University Professors, the consumers of ideas, including students, are about as badly off as other unorganized consumer groups.

The professors, moreover, and other intellectual groups have achieved only a modicum of solidarity on many current civil liberties issues. The rightist press and politicians, without their brain trust of ex-Communists, ex-fellow-travelers, and pseudo-conservatives,

[2] This generalization must be qualified by the fact that historically the Democratic Party has linked welfare goals with civil liberty trimmings, and, through its leadership and that of such union leaders as the Reuthers, has periodically been brought into the defense of civil liberties. Professor S. M. Lipset develops this point, and applies it to the mass parties of the Left in Europe, in his paper before the Congress for Cultural Freedom at Milan.

[3] I have heard it said that the drive for respectability of book and magazine distributors (I am speaking of paperbound books) makes them vulnerable to organizations which seek to censor "indecent" literature: they are insufficiently callous and profit-motivated to defend free enterprise in printed matter. This social mobility of a once-fringe trade makes the Supreme Court's decision in the obscenity cases all the more serious and regrettable. Cf. the excellent issue on "Obscenity and the Arts" in *Law and Contemporary Problems*, Vol. 20, Duke University Press, 1955, p. 531.

would have been unable to conduct most of their investigations and onslaughts: they could hardly have hit even the barn door of Communist espionage and infiltration, let alone added anything to the FBI's watchfulness. Uncompromisingly opposed to the investigations and all security measures were some brave pacifists and Socialists, as well as those we might term "pseudo-liberals," a small handful of men witlessly or disingenuously blind to Communism, or applying a double standard to it (and supporters of the Court only when it was useful and not when its decisions, as during the New Deal, impeded desirable legislative reforms). In the middle have been most liberal professors and serious intellectuals, myself included, who have been awake to the conspiratorial nature of the Communist Party—and all too aware of the near impossibility of publicly defending the rights of Communist professors and civil servants even in nonsensitive jobs. We have tended to range ourselves along a continuum of reasons and rationalizations, some of them provided by the forensic skill of Sidney Hook; a few among us have remained unreconciled to the whole security and investigative apparatus, while the rest of us have come to reluctant terms, as in signing loyalty oaths for teachers, with the less unequivocally indefensible parts of the civic and academic legacy of the Cold and the Korean Wars. It is salutary for us to be reminded by the opinions of the Chief and of Justice Frankfurter in the *Sweezy* case how far-fetched have been some of the arguments advanced to justify the investigations into alleged subversion.

No small handful are the pseudo-conservatives among the educated and the semi-educated who must combat a very different internal dilemma: they must reconcile their self-image as conventional, as believers in the tried and true, with their actual contempt and hostility toward the Supreme Court. Some have done this in recent weeks by attacking the Court for "changing

its mind," for wavering; but this won't quite do, for such change is part of the Court's tradition; and so they often add that the Court is led by a conspiracy, if not gulled by Communists. If they can brand the Court as vacillating and unpatriotic, they can rob it of the aura of soundness and stability to which they lay claim.

To be sure, the audience for this argument among the general population is not very large. Even at the height of McCarthy's power, as poll data show, there were many Americans who had never heard of him; and millions who were "for" him, in my judgment, found emotional gratification in his vindictiveness and toughness—as they might from other mass-media figures of equal aggression—but were only marginally his partisans in terms of specific and sustained political support. Many Americans, avid readers of *Confidential, Whisper, Hush,* and the other magazines which have, for a large population, replaced the idolatrous fan magazines with savage (rather than simply sexy) exposure, will no doubt be glad to be told that the Justices of the Supreme Court, like other celebrities, are traitors and connivers.[4] A few years ago a poll of the comparative prestige of occupations, conducted by the National Opinion Research Center, showed that the Justices were ranked at the very top (higher even than physicians)—all the more reason, then, for delight in the debunking of them. But these "anti-fans," as one might term them, are not a lobby or a party, being inactive save in occasional

[4] The pseudo-conservatives, as I have remarked, fear above all to be thought gullible, and prefer to jump to cynical conclusions; they can dismiss the Court's lessons in civic decency by shouting "It's all politics"—they are, of course, "above" politics (and often, also, as self-styled independents, "above" party). That Mr. Eisenhower, too, is considered to be above politics helps explain the fact that he remains, for the great majority even of pseudo-conservatives, undebunked; moreover, he claims no eminence, no cleverness, no complexity: if above party, he is not above people.

elections; they are too fundamentally unpolitical to constitute a serious danger to the Court (outside the South).

It is important to realize this, lest the Court itself conceivably be intimidated by the current wave of attack to the point of failing to carry further the implications of its recent decisions, or even to stick by them unequivocally in the face of attempts by Congress and state legislatures to get around them.[5] Some of the more thoughtful members of the present Court are historically minded: they know the Court has often acted prematurely, as in the *Dred Scott* case, or the income tax case of the 1890s, or the Liberty League decisions of the 1935-36 term. Justice Frankfurter, for instance, is preternaturally aware that the Court has been wrong before, and could be wrong again, a view which leads him to want to postpone judgment on critical constitutional issues or to decide them on peripheral points. Having seen it abused, such Justices fear to make extensive use of the countervailing power of the Court —no doubt, they also fear nullification if they go "too far" too often.[6] In

[5] Quite apart from his personal views, the President, who hates to quarrel with Congress, may defer to the Court's critics in future appointments to the Federal Bench—not realizing that his appointment of Chief Justice Warren may turn out to be his most creative contribution to domestic policy. Likewise, the humiliating inquisition by the Judiciary Committee of the Senate before Mr. Justice Brennan was allowed to take his seat was not encouraging as to Congressional respect for freedom of opinion on that Bench: Mr. Justice Brennan answered questions not markedly dissimilar in tone to those asked Mr. Sweezy by Attorney-General Louis Wyman of New Hampshire.

[6] As law clerk to Mr. Justice Brandeis in the 1935-36 term of the Court, I was well indoctrinated in this outlook, as well as sharing Brandeis' disapproval of the Roosevelt court-packing scheme the following year. Constitutional government, of course, requires respect for both legislative and judicial decisions one detests—just as the Bill of Rights, in my opinion, requires permitting pornography and even *Confidential* to circulate.

earlier days, before public-opinion polls and the massification of the media, the educated were only periodically made aware of the fact that the underprivileged did not share their outlook: a fact they might regard as socially depressing but not personally relevant. Today, in contrast, the educated are more aware, sometimes more tolerant of the intolerant, and in any event less arrogant. For better and worse, it is harder for them to assume that all "right-thinking people" react as they do.

Those who react otherwise have, of course, extremely vocal spokesmen in Congress and in the state legislatures: bodies that reflect what Professor W. Lloyd Warner refers to as the "middle majority"; the great lower-middle-class and middle-middle-class levels of American life.[7] The upper strata are, of course, far from voiceless in this representative body: that is what lobbyists, much of the press and other media, and occasional Senators are for; but they can protect their money and corporate power somewhat less badly than they can protect what are, for them, only peripheral preoccupations with civil liberties.

Nevertheless, it is from these strata that much of the politically influential support for civil liberties has come. The trustees of leading private colleges and universities, when properly led by the institution's officials, have frequently been true conservatives and, as such, indispensable supports for academic freedom. (Very likely, had Paul Sweezy lectured at Sarah Lawrence, Harvard, MIT, Chicago, Stanford, or the University of Wisconsin, he would have had more protection than the hard-pressed officials of the University of

[7] In its committees, and occasionally under brave leadership outside them, Congress can rise higher than its own origins and constituencies; it might rise higher still if Congressmen and their staffs were not forced to live in a city less of a company town than it was in earlier generations, but still only marginally civilized.

New Hampshire dared provide.) It is noteworthy that, as shown in Professor Stouffer's study, leadership groups are more supportive of civil liberties even than educated groups in general; among them, the most staunch for civil liberties are the local newspaper publishers and the presidents of local bar associations.

Indeed, outside of academic and intellectual circles, it is only among newspapermen and lawyers that there is much of a tradition, and much training, in handling complex and dialectical problems—or in hearing and stating differentiated positions. Tocqueville saw the press as an indispensable support for freedom in America, but the number of papers which take this responsibility seriously, when it comes to explicating serious problems, remains small. Tocqueville also thought when he visited America that the lawyers might become a new aristocracy, but I suspect that the views of the profession (even outside the ranks of lawyer-Congressmen) are becoming steadily "democratized." In fact, many eminent, conservative lawyers have been hesitant to defend men accused of disloyalty, fearing their own and even more their firms' guilt by association with such clients; in this way, the bar has given signs of losing its previously jealously guarded independence as a vested interest of its own.[8]

To be sure, had there not been a few lawyers, non-Communists of vigor and principle who had faith in the eventual vindication of civil decency and freedom, these cases of the last few weeks would not have reached the Supreme Court or would have done so without the illumination the briefs ably gave the Court amid the conflicting precedents. But on the whole it seems fair to say that the bar has been silent during the whole build-up of the pseudo-conservative climate of thought, as if the security nightmare and McCarthyism generally were none of its particular business. In theory, practicing lawyers are "officers of the court"; historically, the bar has expounded and developed constitutional government, frequently with a proud aloofness toward interests other than those of property. Today, the issues which divide Americans seldom concern property; they concern ideas and the protection of intangible interests. The Supreme Court needs "officers" and friends—professional *amici* and lay brethren alike—to explain its recent judgments as an aspect of the never-ending task of subduing the raging chauvinisms of our day to judicial scrutiny and limitation.

---

[8] This is one reason, I believe, why the defense of some men accused before investigating committees has gravitated to counsel under Communist control who encouraged their clients to plead the Fifth Amendment (rather than the First, when asked about former associates no longer actively disloyal), thus obfuscating the issue to the advantage both of the committees and of the Communist Party.

Chapter VI

WHAT TO DO ABOUT THE PARTIES?

Introduction

THOSE who seek to establish just governments, based on the consent of the governed, run up against two major problems: (a) how to prevent one portion of the people from tyrannizing over another through the agencies of government, and (b) how to prevent the government itself from tyrannizing over the people. The Framers, as *The Federalist* shows, thought they had devised for us a system that would guard against both these dangers. The key characteristics of their system are the *diffusion of power* and *built-in delay* in its exercise.

Alike the diffusion and the delay have a carefully-thought-out rationale: The Framers sought to provide a decision-making system in which there would be genuine and assured *deliberation*. The majority, they were convinced, if given enough time and motive to deliberate on a given issue, would *not* act in a tyrannical manner toward minorities. Thus, if we examine our system in detail (it is more and more frequently being called the "Madisonian model"), we can find any number of devices intended to provide for delay in the decision-making process and for diffusion of authority among decision-makers, and to assure deliberation in law- and policy-making. The delay obliges the participants to take time to explain themselves to each other, and so to themselves; the diffusion so situates them that they can be effective only through explaining themselves. And in explaining themselves, they *deliberate*.

First, and perhaps most important, we find division or separation of powers, and federalism. To quote Publius: "In the compound republic of America, the power surrendered by the people is first divided between two distinct governments, and then the portion allotted to each subdivided among distinct and separate departments. Hence, a double security arises to the rights of the people. The different governments will control each other at the same time that each will be controlled by itself." [1]

Second, the very extensiveness of the republic helps to insure that unjust or factious majorities will not be able to form at all, which is

[1] *The Federalist,* Jacob E. Cooke (Ed.), (New York: Meridian Books, 1961), No. 51, p. 351. All citations to *The Federalist* are from this edition.

the most certain method, surely, to prevent such majorities from carrying out their will. Again to quote Publius:

> Extend the sphere (of the republic), and you take in a greater variety of parties and interests; you make it less probable that a majority of the whole will have a common motive to invade the rights of other citizens; or if such a common motive exists, it will be more difficult for all who feel it to discover their own strength, and to act in unison with each other. Besides other impediments, it may be remarked that where there is a consciousness of unjust or dishonorable purposes, communication is always checked by distrust in proportion to the number whose concurrence is necessary.[2]

Third, the legislature, which is to be the most powerful and hence is to be feared the most, is divided into two bodies which will check each other, thus minimizing the danger of legislative encroachment on the other branches of government or the rights of the people. The Senate, according to Publius, "doubles the security to the people, by requiring the concurrence of two distinct bodies in schemes of usurpation or perfidy, where the ambition or corruption of one would otherwise be sufficient." Reasons Publius:

> The cool and deliberate sense of the community ought in all governments, and actually will in all free governments, ultimately prevail over the views of its rulers; so there are particular moments in public affairs, when the people stimulated by some irregular passion, or some illicit advantage, or misled by the artful misrepresentations of interested men, may call for measures which they themselves will afterwards be the most ready to lament and condemn. In these critical moments, how salutary will be the interference of some temperate and respectable body of citizens, in order to check the misguided career, and to suspend the blow meditated by the people against themselves, until reason, justice and truth can regain their authority over the public mind?[3]

Fourth, we find a system of *representation,* intended "to refine and enlarge the public views, by passing them through the medium of a chosen body of citizens, whose wisdom may best discern the true interest of their country, and whose patriotism, and love of justice, will be least likely to sacrifice it to temporary or partial considerations."[4]

[2] *Op. cit.,* No. 10, p. 64.
[3] *Op. cit.,* No. 63, p. 425.
[4] *Op. cit.,* No. 10, p. 62.

The Framers' Constitution includes other structural devices designed to provide for diffusion and delay: staggered elections, which make it likely that an unjust majority would have to wait as much as four years before it would be in a position to enact its will; different modes of election, which make it unlikely that a single factious group can control both houses of the legislature and the Presidency; and certain "weapons," which each of the branches can use against the others (e.g., the veto, the capacity of Congress, because the President cannot "dissolve" it, to remain in session when it chooses to do so, etc.).

Even now, our list does not exhaust the devices by which the Framers sought to provide for diffusion of function and authority and for delay and deliberation. Yet this much should be clear: those who would prefer a *plebiscitary* system, one that would respond to the will of the majority with a minimum of delay and distortion, tend, for fairly obvious reasons, to be unhappy with the Madisonian system. And, as if to make matters worse from the viewpoint of those who desire such a plebiscitary system, subsequent institutional developments in the American political system have, as if by preordination, followed Madisonian principles. The development of the committee system in Congress, for example, serves to diffuse authority and power within that body still further. Of even greater importance, however, is the fact that our political parties have developed along lines thoroughly consistent with the Madisonian model. One authority, after surveying the organization of American political parties, concludes:

> Viewed over the entire nation, the party organization constitutes no disciplined army. It consists rather of many state and local points of power, each with its own local following and each comparatively independent of external control.[5]

Thus we find even in our party system, *extra*-constitutional institutional development that the Framers could not have anticipated, our old friends diffusion of authority and power on the one hand, and built-in delay on the other.

There are those who contend that it is no accident that our political parties have developed along these lines rather than some other (for example, British) lines. On the contrary, they assert: this development, though extra-constitutional and though it occurred long after the Framers had been gathered to their fathers, was the unavoidable result of the political system devised for us at Philadelphia. On this matter

[5] V. O. Key, Jr., *Politics, Parties and Pressure Groups,* 4th Ed. (New York: Crowell, 1958), p. 361.

James McGregor Burns, long an advocate of centralized and disciplined political parties, writes:

> . . . the implications of Madison's insight are clear today. Around every position established under the new Constitution—around 'the interest of the man,' whether President, legislator, or even judge or bureaucrat—a circle of sub-leaders and followers would also grow, the size of the circle depending on the importance of the office and the appeal and skills of the leader. Other factions would grow around politicians outside government, trying to get in. And of course the Constitution left intact a proliferation of offices in the states, counties, and localities, which in turn were the centers of the thousands of other little circles of political action and influence.[6]

Which is to say: given the basic "Madisonian" scheme, the parties could not have "happened" otherwise, could not have been very different from what they are. To which we may add: no one much in America seems ever to have wished them to happen otherwise; it is as if the American people had *sought* a party-system congenial to Madisonian principles, and done so because they cherished those principles.

Those who think the majority entitled to direct and immediate impact on our law- and policy-making institutions, we repeat, unavoidably find themselves frustrated by the Madisonian model. This is true for a number of reasons, which emerge clearly from the following contentions that they have put forward:

1. Fragmentation of powers means that on any given issue the majority will probably not control all critical points in the decision-making process. Thus, at some point in this process, the majority-will is likely to be blocked and set completely at naught.

2. Not all of the institutions which participate in making public policy (Senate, House, President, and Judiciary) respond rapidly to the wishes of the majority as expressed in elections, and this produces delays that are indefensible from the standpoint of democracy.

3. The system is designed to encourage "log-rolling," so that significant interests, both functional and geographic, are forced to compromise and "bargain" with one another because each of them controls some crucial point in the decision-making process. This usually means, it is contended, that majority demands are significantly modified as they pass through the decision-making system.

4. Some of our institutions are actually so structured that they will

---

[6] James McGregor Burns, *The Deadlock of Democracy* (Englewood Cliffs, New Jersey: Prentice Hall, 1963), p. 22.

never accurately reflect the views of the majority. Here the Senate has usually been singled out for special notice. Of late, however, special attention has been directed to the "gerrymandering" activities of state legislatures. This, the "plebiscitarians" contend, has resulted in "over-representation" of rural areas in the House of Representatives.

Some Historical Background

The doctrine of responsible and disciplined parties, which we may fairly call the prevailing doctrine in the United States today, was not born overnight. Rather it is the product of a number of seemingly distinct tendencies that have presented themselves, over the decades, within the American political tradition and the literature about it. And it represents, as such, the most comprehensive, consistent, and workable theory we have for overcoming the diffusion and delay built into our system by the Founding Fathers. We may profitably note here certain lines of argument that contributed, from an early moment, to the form and substance of the present doctrine.

Concern about the extent to which the majority is unable to make its demands felt on government is not by any means of recent origin. Rather, those who today are most critical of our system on these grounds are strongly bound, ideologically, to both Jefferson and Jackson, both of whom stressed the principle of direct majority rule. Jefferson, for example, could argue:

> . . . let it be agreed that a government is republican in proportion as every member composing it has his equal voice in the direction of its concerns (not indeed in person, which would be impracticable beyond the limits of a city or small township, but by representatives chosen by himself and responsible to him at short periods), and let us bring to the test of the canon every branch of our constitution.[7]

Much the same kind of thinking is reflected in Jacksonian theory:

> We are opposed to all self-styled "wholesome restraints" on the free action of the popular opinion and will, other than those which have for their sole object the prevention of precipitate legislation. This latter object is to be attained by the expedient of the division of power, and by causing all legislation to pass through the ordeal of successive forms, [and] to be sifted through the discussion of coordinate legislative branches with mutual suspensive veto powers.

---

[7] The Political Writings of Thomas Jefferson, Edward Dumbauld (Ed.) (New York: Liberal Arts Press, 1955), p. 114.

Yet all should be dependent with equal directness and promptness on the influence of public opinion; the popular will should be equally the animating and moving spirit of them all, and ought never to find in any of its own creatures a self-imposed power, capable, when misused either by corrupt ambition or honest error, or resisting itself and defeating its own determined object. We cannot, therefore, look with an eye of favor on any such forms of representation as, by length of tenure of delegated power, tend to weaken that universal and unrelaxing responsibility to the vigilance of public opinion which is the true conservative principle of our institutions.[8]

The Jeffersonian and Jacksonian theories had, it is easy to demonstrate, a very definite impact on the practices and structure of state governments. Between, roughly, the year 1830 and the year 1855, the election of governors was increasingly vested in the people rather than legislatures, judges in several states came to be directly elected for short terms, and state constitutions had to be submitted to the people for ratification before going into effect. These early theories, then, clearly sought to maximize majority control over all the institutions of government, which is also one of the chief ends of the modern doctrine of responsible and disciplined parties. But they were not sufficiently comprehensive in scope to overcome certain other obstacles to the fulfillment of the purpose in question. Jefferson, for example, sought majority control always within the context of separated powers; he believed, along with the Federalists, that the accumulation of all powers in the same hands was the very definition of tyranny. Jacksonian theory also operates in a context of separation of powers, and never really kicks over the traces.

Any such commitment to separation of powers, however, runs up against certain theoretical and practical difficulties, as was clearly illustrated during Jackson's administration. Jackson could assert, as he in fact did, that he was, as President, the voice of the people, and as truly "representative" of the majority-will as Congress. Most commentators had of course assumed, prior to the time of Jackson, that Congress, and especially the House of Representatives, was the voice of the majority-will of the American people.

What happens, on Jackson's showing, when Congress and the President differ over matters of public policy? Logically, no such situation should arise, since if both are responsive to the majority on

[8] From the "Introduction" to *The United States Magazine and Democratic Review* (October, 1837) reprinted in *Social Theories of Jacksonian Democracy*, Joseph L. Blau (Ed.) (New York: Liberal Arts Press, 1954), pp. 22-23.

a specific issue they should, in theory at least, adopt precisely the same posture on the issue in question. In practice, however, conflict between the President and Congress did in due course occur, and has tended to increase with the passing decades. This, of course, leads to the further question: Which of the two institutions, Congress or the President, *more* accurately reflects the will of the people? For, if there is conflict between these institutions although both are presumed to reflect the majority-will then it follows, logically, that one or the other is not accurately reflecting this majority-will. And, as the "bank controversy" during Jackson's administration shows, the Madisonian model had by that time "taken roots"; that is, the individuals who occupied the principal positions in the system had indeed developed "rival and opposite" interests. Thus, for example, we find the Senate censuring Jackson for what it considered to be his unconstitutional usurpation of powers in removing federal government funds from the national bank. And we find Jackson, in his turn, strongly questioning the constitutional authority of the Senate to pass any such resolution of censure. The incident, in any case, points up a new dimension of the problem of securing unified and coordinate governmental response within a system of divided powers.

Nor is that all: Both Jefferson and Jackson wanted a viable federal system, in which the states would retain a large degree of sovereignty. Yet any such attachment to the federal principle must create still further difficulties as regards attaining direct response to the majority-will. For one thing, what we find is that on certain questions a national majority simply does not have the rightful authority to rule, so that geographical majorities located in the states are left free to follow policies and practices at variance with those that the national majority would like to adopt. Commitment to federalism, then, limits the power of the national majority; that is, it sets up a barrier to the powers of the national majority. In a "going" federal system, therefore, a number of extremely difficult questions arise, and have to be answered: When and on what types of issues should the national majority be able to prevail over the geographic majorities? Who is to determine the rightful boundaries of the national and state powers when there is disagreement?

An even more serious difficulty, perhaps, is this: It would seem that so long as we have a federal system in the United States, the locus of political power will remain at the state and local levels. And for just so long there will be a decentralization of political authority and power that makes the achievement of unified action at the national level a difficult task—far more difficult than if control were exercised by some centralized national agency. Similarly, because of the diversity of interests to be found in the localities across the United States, the feat of securing concerted action, when the representatives of these localities gather to make decisions at the national level, is often appallingly difficult. In sum: a viable federal system involves fragmentation of power and effective representation of diverse geographical and even functional interests. And, in doing so, it immensely complicates the task of translating the will of the numerical majority of the people into public policy.

It would seem, for these reasons, that any program designed to transform our system into a plebiscitary democracy must "overcome" separation of powers and federalism. One of the first individuals to perceive this was Woodrow Wilson, who to a very considerable extent became the "founding father" of the modern disciplined and responsible two-party doctrine. And we must now notice certain elements of Wilson's thinking that merit special attention.[9]

First, Wilson stressed the diffusion and lack of responsibility in the American political system. He did not say that the national government did not possess a center of power or that national authority had not become predominant over that of the states. On this point, Wilson was quite emphatic. There was, he held, no question but that Congress was the predominant institution of our governmental system. As he wrote in his *Congressional Government,* completed in 1884:

> The leading inquiry in the examination of any system of government must, of course, concern primarily the real depositaries and the essential machinery of power. There is always a centre of power: where in this system is that centre? In whose hands is self-sufficient authority lodged and through what agencies does that authority speak and act? . . . It is said that there is no single or central force in our federal scheme; and so there is not in the federal *scheme,* but only a balance of powers and a nice adjustment of interactive checks, as all the books say. How is it, however, in the practical conduct of federal government? In that, unquestionably, the predominant and controlling force, the centre and source of all motive and of all regulative power, is Congress.[10]

[9] For an excellent survey of the growth and development of the responsible and disciplined two-party doctrine see Austin Ranney, *The Doctrine of Responsible Party Government,* Illinois Studies in the Social Sciences, Vol. 34, No. 3 (Urbana: University of Illinois Press, 1954).

[10] Woodrow Wilson, *Congressional Government* (New York: Meridian Books, 1956), pp. 30-31.

Congress as a body, then, exercised according to Wilson the predominant role and was the center of power. But when he looked *inside* Congress, at its internal organization, he found that its power was diffused among the chairmen of the standing committees. Wilson went so far as to observe that it is " 'no great departure from the fact' to describe ours as a government of Standing Committees of Congress." [11] And the chairmen of these committees, who possessed almost complete control over them, "do not," observed Wilson, "constitute a cooperative body like a ministry." Rather "each Committee goes its own way at its own pace." [12] Since there were 47 standing committees in the House and 29 in the Senate at the time Wilson wrote, there can be little wonder that he concluded that Congress lacked unity, and was incapable of concerted action. For, like many commentators who have followed in his footsteps, Wilson refused to consider the possibility that Congress was unified, was acting concertedly, on behalf of the principle of diffusion and the principle of delay.

Second, then, Wilson deplored the diffusion of authority that presented itself to his eyes. It was, he contended, contrary to the tenets both of good government and democratic control. Observed Wilson:

Public opinion has no *easy* vehicle for its judgements, no *quick* channel for its action. Nothing about the system is *direct* and *simple*. Authority is perplexingly subdivided and distributed, and responsibility has to be hunted down in out-of-the-way corners. So that the sum of the whole matter is that the means of working for the fruits of good government are not readily to be found. The average citizen may be excused for esteeming government at best but a haphazard affair, upon which his vote and all of his influence can have but little effect.[13]

Third, Wilson was ready enough with "answers" when it came to the question of how to overcome this fragmentation and diffusion of power. Here there are three major emphases in Wilson's thinking: (a) we must provide an institutional structure that will provide genuine concentration of authority within the governmental system; (b) we must achieve coordination between this structure and the other branches of government; and (c) we must provide a link between the

[11] *Ibid.*, pp. 55-56.
[12] *Ibid.*, p. 59
[13] *Ibid.*, p. 214. (Italics added. Note that the words italicized have a quite different significance when transferred to the universe of Madisonian thought.)

structure which exercises centralized authority within the government
and the people, and so insure responsibility and accountability.

In his early writings, Wilson advocated a British-style cabinet system for America—was, indeed, still an undergraduate at Princeton
when he published his article entitled "Cabinet Government in the
United States." He was, to be sure, never very precise about how this
cabinet government was to operate, but he did want key Congressional
leaders, chosen however by the President, to comprise the cabinet.
Further, the cabinet was to serve as the focal point of power in the
system since, among other things, it was to initiate legislation.

It is not surprising that at first Wilson should have advocated a
cabinet system, and a cabinet system of just that kind. Seeing power
centered in Congress, he assumed, not surprisingly, that a workable
reform of the existing system would have to revolve around the more
powerful members of Congress. But since he also believed that no
existing branch of government provided or could provide centralized
direction and control, he had to go further and propose the creation of
a hitherto nonexistent *ad hoc* agency for this purpose, and so came
unavoidably to the idea of a new institution calculated to "bridge the
gap" between Congress and the Presidency. His cabinet system would
weld the two key branches together (note that the last thing on Wilson's mind was the Supreme Court), and thus modify to a great extent
the separation intended by the Framers. Wilson certainly intended such
a modification. He believed separation of powers to be one of the
greatest obstacles to responsible and responsive government, and precisely because it distributed rather than centralized authority. He had,
then, made a clean break with Madisonian political thought.

*   *   *

In his later writings, however, Wilson pretty well abandoned his
notion of a cabinet system,[14] and looked rather to the Presidency
itself as the means of providing unity, responsibility and direction in
our political system. Many have speculated that his views changed
because he saw a new and greater potential in the office of the Presidency during the administrations of Cleveland and Roosevelt—two
"strong" Presidents, at least when compared with their predecessors.
It should be noted, however, that from the standpoint of "theory" this
change in Wilson's thinking was entirely logical. First, a cabinet

---

[14] For example, in his *Constitutional Government in the United States*.

system, though it would provide for greater unity than the traditional United States Congress could provide, clearly could not provide the kind and degree of unity that could be expected from a single individual—if only that individual were President and were in position to get his way. Second, the Presidency is a "national" office, or so Wilson now decided, one which has a *national* constituency. Under the cabinet system he had originally pled for, by contrast, the chief cabinet officers, whether collectively or individually, would not themselves have been directly responsible to a national majority. Third, a "Presidential system" would simplify the task of providing unity and responsibility (which, one is tempted to say, begin to take on the status, in Wilson's mind, of ends in themselves). Moreover, no sweeping or drastic changes (of a kind that could only be achieved by Constitutional amendment) would be needed for this new "solution" that Wilson finally ideated.

*   *   *

Yet two major problems would remain, whether under the cabinet system or the Presidential system as Wilson conceived them, namely: (a) how to make sure that the desired unity and concerted action would actually be forthcoming, and (b) how to make the unity and concerted action "accountable" to and "responsible" to the people. One might say that Wilson's proposals, up to this point, would at most have made these goals *possible,* but could not *guarantee* them. And this is where Wilson ran up against the critical role that political parties must play in any adequate theoretical solution to the problem he had posed. Not parties as the United States had hitherto known them, not American political parties as "given" by History, but something new and different, in the way of parties, that would be called *"disciplined"* political parties. Such parties, Wilson claimed, would really "bridge the gap" between the President and Congress—and so would insure unified, responsible and concerted action on the part of the two major branches of government. More: let there be disciplined parties, and let them be genuinely responsible to the electorate, Wilson held, and other great goods would emerge as by-products: citizen interest in political questions would increase, and there would be greater popular understanding of the alternatives available on any given issue of public policy. Still more: with clear-cut party programs, the people would be able to hold their elected leaders "responsible" and "accountable." Because of their promise of performing all these functions, disciplined parties became a central and critical element in Wilson's entire program of reform.

Finally, Wilson seems to have believed that once concentration of authority and disciplined parties had become a reality, the locus of *party* power would naturally gravitate to the national level. The party leadership, once given the institutional means of making binding decisions, would be able to overcome the "divisive" influence of localism.

The Party System: Liberalism and Conservatism

The present-day advocates of a disciplined two-party system share most of Wilson's fundamental beliefs. And, like Wilson, they stress the urgent need for reform. In their view, our present system moves in "fits and starts," failing to meet existing and anticipated social problems with consistent, "rational," long-range planning. Moreover, they contend, the present system, when finally it does act, allows various "partial" interests to have great impact upon the formulation of public policy. And the result is that the transcendent national interest is frequently compromised, or completely lost sight of.

Contemporary theories of party discipline and responsibility represent, we repeat, the most comprehensive and systematic possible assault upon the Madisonian system. As we have suggested above, however, most of the criticisms of our system that emanate from this school, are far from novel. They are also far from lacking support from other quarters. Rather, they are echoed far and wide by commentators who are not proponents of disciplined parties, or at least do not take the need for such parties as their point of departure. The advocates of a "strong" President, or of greater coordination between Congress and the President, all plead for measures that would in fact serve to advance the ends of the disciplined party theory. Similarly, most suggested reforms of procedure and of organizational structure in the Senate and the House of Representatives advance those same ends, inasmuch as they seek to unify leadership in these assemblies and to give it the authority it would need in order to direct and control their activities. Indeed, the attractiveness of the disciplined two-party theory appears to stem from its ability to catch up within itself a wide range of criticisms that have been leveled at the American system, and to formulate the broad ends and goals that reforms of the system would allegedly forward. In short, the theory offers a neat theoretical "package," all complete with fairly definite objectives that can serve variously as guides for determining in detail what reforms are to be carried out, or as added benefits that can be promised by commentators attracted to these reforms for their own sakes.[15]

This theory is, even conservatives must concede, highly ingenious. In the first place, it concentrates on the one institution, political parties, that does provide a kind of unifying thread in our diffuse institutional fabric. Once the parties have been reformed, its advocates can reasonably argue, we can still have the outward form of separation of powers, while by concentrating power in the party structure with, most probably, the President as the dominant figure, we shall sidestep the disadvantages that have allegedly accompanied separation in our rather benighted past. We shall not, then, need to eliminate the institutions which only *seem* to distort or thwart majority rule—such as, for example, the Senate, which could probably rally much popular support any time it is attacked. Armed with the theory before us, then, the proponents of change can work for the most part outside the realm of our formal institutions, and yet hope to obtain the selfsame results that others have wished to seek through remaking the system inside-out. The conservatives are sure to answer, if they have their wits about them, that—and the student should always bear this in mind—the "reform" of our parties would nevertheless bring about a "revolutionary" change in our political system, the more "dangerous" because it could be accomplished with great economy of effort—without, above all, having recourse to the amendment process (which conservatives cherish, and liberals decry). In short: the Madisonian system is brought low with as little recourse as possible to actual changes in our basic law.

Although the student is no doubt aware of this fact by now, it should be emphasized that the disciplined and responsible two-party doctrine is widely defended in terms of what it would do to advance *liberal* goals and values. The doctrine, some commentators have been tempted to conclude, must have been born out of a sense of frustration with a system that seemingly allows minorities to block and frustrate all proposals for the drastic reform of American society and the American economic system. The principal objective of the responsible party advocates is, beyond doubt, to remove all obstacles in our insti-

---

[15] Much of the criticism that has been directed against certain amendment proposals now "making the rounds" of the state legislatures (that, for example, looking to a super-Supreme-Court made up of the justices of the state supreme courts, and that which would forbid the Supreme Court to intervene in the apportionment of legislative seats) seems, from a conservative point of view, to call into question the right of the American people to amend their Constitution in accordance with the procedures laid down in Article V. A great newspaper has referred to one of the proposals as, *mirabile dictu,* "subversive."

tutional structure that appear to stand in the way of majority rule. They would prefer a system under which the majority of the electorate could and would make binding decisions, directly, at election-time, by endorsing one or the other of the political parties. Their values and goals stem, it appears, from a strong initial commitment to a highly formal conception of *political equality,* so understood as to demand a plebiscitary system that will assure each individual that he will count for one and that none shall count for more than one. In the area of *political* liberalism (that is, the area that concerns itself with *how* decisions are made rather than *what* decisions should be made), the responsible party doctrine represents the extreme liberal program for institutional and procedural reform.

Because the doctrine of responsible and disciplined parties is, on this showing, "revolutionary" in character, the student should examine the arguments both for and against it with the greatest care. Despite all the criticisms of the Madisonian model with its subsequent developments, it has, if its conservative defenders are to be believed, at least one great virtue, namely: it has worked. Judgments, of course, may well vary on how well it has worked; perhaps one can go so far as to say that this is the ultimate issue on which the student of these matters must make up his mind.

How well *has* it worked? To what extent have the American people achieved, under the Madisonian system, the goals they set themselves in the Preamble to their Constitution—a more perfect union, the blessings of liberty, justice? Are we, as conservatives tend to claim, the most prosperous people in the world and, into the bargain, the freest, and are we those things because of our inherited political system? What grounds are there for believing that the goals could have been achieved more fully had our political system been fundamentally altered, somewhere along the way? Are there cogent reasons for thinking that our circumstances have so changed that our inherited system will be less fruitful of benefits in the future? These are the questions the student should answer for himself before either adopting the cause of the disciplined party system, which fundamentally alters the "Madisonian" system, or that of its opponents, who would perpetuate the "Madisonian" system through an indefinite future.

40. The Need for Greater Party Responsibility*

COMMITTEE ON POLITICAL PARTIES, A.P.S.A.

1. The Role of the Political Parties

1. *The Parties and Public Policy.* Throughout this report political parties are treated as indispensable instruments of government. That is to say, we proceed on the proposition that *popular government in a nation of more than 150 million people requires political parties which provide the electorate with a proper range of choice between alternatives of action.* The party system thus serves as the main device for bringing into continuing relationship those ideas about liberty, majority rule and leadership which Americans are largely taking for granted.

For the great majority of Americans, the most valuable opportunity to influence the course of public affairs is the choice they are able to make between the parties in the principal elections. While in an election the party alternative necessarily takes the form of a choice between candidates, putting a particular candidate into office is not an end in itself. The concern of the parties with candidates, elections and appointments is misunderstood if it is assumed that parties can afford to bring forth aspirants for office without regard to the views of those so selected. Actually, the party struggle is concerned with the direction of public affairs. Party nominations are no more than a means to this end. In short,

party politics inevitably involves public policy in one way or another. *In order to keep the parties apart, one must consider the relations between each and public policy.*

This is not to ignore that in the past the American two-party system has shown little propensity for evolving original or creative ideas about public policy; that it has even been rather sluggish in responding to such ideas in the public interest; that it reflects in an enlarged way those differences throughout the country which are expressed in the operation of the federal structure of government; and that in all political organizations a considerable measure of irrationality manifests itself.

Giving due weight to each of these factors, we are nevertheless led to conclude that the choices provided by the two-party system are valuable to the American people in proportion to their definition in terms of public policy. *The reasons for the growing emphasis on public policy in party politics are to be found, above all, in the very operations of modern government.* With the extraordinary growth of the responsibilities of government, the discussion of public affairs for the most part makes sense only in terms of public policy.

2. *The New Importance of Program.* One of the most pressing requirements of contemporary politics is for the party in power to furnish a general kind of direction over the government as a whole. *The crux of public affairs lies in the necessity for more effective formulation of general policies and programs and for better integration of all of the far-flung activities of modern government.*

* Part I, "Towards a More Responsible Two-Party System," by the Committee on Political Parties of the American Political Science Association. *American Political Science Review* (September, 1950), Supplement, pp. 15-36. Reprinted by permission.

Only large-scale and representative political organizations possess the qualifications needed for these tasks. The ascendancy of national issues in an industrial society, the impact of the widening concern of government with problems of the general welfare, the entrance into the realm of politics of millions of new voters—all of these factors have tended to broaden the base of the parties as the largest political organizations in the country. *It is in terms of party programs that political leaders can attempt to consolidate public attitudes toward the work plans of government.*

Modern public policy, therefore, accentuates the importance of the parties, not as mere brokers between different groups and interests, but as agencies of the electorate. Because it affects unprecedented numbers of people and because it depends for its execution on extensive and widespread public support, modern public policy requires a broad political base. That base can be provided only by the parties, which reach people touched by no other political organization.

3. *The Potentialities of the Party System. The potentialities of the two-party system are suggested, on the one hand, by the fact that for all practical purposes the major parties monopolize elections; and, on the other, by the fact that both parties have in the past managed to adapt themselves to the demands made upon them by external necessities.*

Moreover, in contrast with any other political organization today in existence, the major parties even now are forced to consider public policy at least broadly enough to make it likely for them to win elections. If public esteem of the parties is much less high than it might be, the depressed state of their reputation has resulted in the main from their past indifference to broadly conceived public policy. This indifference has fixed in the popular mind the idea of spoils, patronage and plunder. It is hence not astonishing when one hears a chosen representative assert for the public ear that in his state "people put principles above party." Much of the agitation for nonpartisanship—despite the impossibility of nonpartisan organization on a national level—is rooted in the same attitudes.

Bad reputations die hard, but things are no longer what they used to be. Certainly success in presidential campaigns today is based on broad national appeals to the widest possible constituencies. To a much greater extent than in the past, elections are won by influences and trends that are felt throughout the country. *It is therefore good practical politics to reconsider party organization in the light of the changing conditions of politics.*

It appeared desirable in this report to relate the potentialities of the party system to both the conditions that confront the nation and the expected role of the parties. *Happily such an effort entails an application of ideas about the party system that are no longer unfamiliar.*

Consideration of ways and means of producing a more responsible party system leads into the hazards of political invention. This is a challenge that has usually been accepted with misgivings by political scientists, who are trained to describe what is and feel less well qualified to fashion innovations. We hope that our own effort will stimulate both other political scientists and participants in practical politics to attempt similar undertakings on their own account. Only by a continuous process of invention and adjustment can the party system be adapted to meet the needs of our day.

2. What Kind of Party System Is Needed?

There is little point to talking about the American party system in terms of its deficiencies and potentialities except against a picture of what the parties ought to be. Our report would be lacking in exactness without an indication of the sort of model we have in mind.

Americans are reasonably well agreed about the purposes served by the two major parties as long as the matter is discussed in generalities. When specific questions are raised, however, agreement is much more limited. We cannot assume, therefore, a commonly shared view about the essential characteristics of the party system. But we can and must state our own view.

In brief, our view is this: *The party system that is needed must be democratic, responsible and effective*—a system that is accountable to the public, respects and expresses differences of opinion, and is able to cope with the great problems of modern government. Some of the implications warrant special statement, which is the purpose of this section.

I. A STRONGER TWO-PARTY SYSTEM

1. *The Need for an Effective Party System.* In an era beset with problems of unprecedented magnitude at home and abroad, it is dangerous to drift without a party system that helps the nation to set a general course of policy for the government as a whole. In a two-party system, when both parties are weakened or confused by internal divisions or ineffective organization it is the nation that suffers. When the parties are unable to reach and pursue responsible decisions, difficulties accumulate and cynicism about all democratic institutions grows.

An effective party system requires, first, that the parties are able to bring forth programs to which they commit themselves and, second, that the parties possess sufficient internal cohesion to carry out these programs. In such a system, the party program becomes the work program of the party, so recognized by the party leaders in and out of the government, by the party body as a whole, and by the public. This condition is unattainable unless party institutions have been created through which agreement can be reached about the general position of the party.

Clearly *such a degree of unity within the parties cannot be brought about without party procedures that give a large body of people an opportunity to share in the development of the party program.* One great function of the party system is to bring about the widest possible consent in relation to defined political goals, which provides the majority party with the essential means of building public support for the policies of the government. Democratic procedures in the internal affairs of the parties are best suited to the development of agreement within each party.

2. *The Need for an Effective Opposition Party.* The argument for a stronger party system cannot be divorced from measures designed to make the parties more fully accountable to the public. *The fundamental requirement of such accountability is a two-party system in which the opposition party acts as the critic of the party in power, developing, defining and presenting the policy alternatives which are necessary for a true choice in reaching public decisions.*

Beyond that, the case for the American two-party system need not be restated here. The two-party system is so strongly rooted in the political traditions of this country and public preference for it is so well established that consideration of other possibilities seems entirely academic. When we speak of the parties without further qualification, we mean throughout our report the two major parties. The inference is not that we consider third or minor parties undesirable or ineffectual within their limited orbit. Rather, we feel that the minor parties in the longer run have failed to leave a lasting imprint upon both the two-party system and the basic processes of American government.

In spite of the fact that the two-party system is part of the American political tradition, it cannot be said that the role of the opposition party is well understood. This is unfortunate because democratic government is greatly influenced by the character of the opposition party. The measures proposed elsewhere in our report to help the party in power to clarify its policies are equally applicable to the opposition.

The opposition most conducive to responsible government is an organized party opposition, produced by the organic operation of the two-party system. When there are two parties identifiable by the kinds of action they propose, the voters have an actual choice. On the other hand, the sort of opposition presented by a coalition that cuts across party lines, as a regular thing, tends to deprive the public of a meaningful alternative. When such coalitions are formed after the elections are over, the public usually finds it difficult to understand the new situation and to reconcile it with the purpose of the ballot. Moreover, on that basis it is next to impossible to hold either party responsible for its political record. This is a serious source of public discontent.

II. BETTER INTEGRATED PARTIES

1. *The Need for a Party System with Greater Resistance to Pressure.* As a consciously defined and consistently followed line of action keeps individuals from losing themselves in irresponsible ventures, so a program-conscious party develops greater resistance against the inroads of pressure groups.

The value of special-interest groups in a diversified society made up of countless groupings and specializations should be obvious. But organized interest groups cannot do the job of the parties. Indeed, it is only when a working formula of the public interest in its *general* character is made manifest by the parties in terms of coherent programs that the claims of interest groups can be adjusted on the basis of political responsibility. Such adjustment, once again, calls for the party's ability to honor its word.

There is little to suggest that the phenomenal growth of interest organiza- *tions in recent decades has come to its end.* Organization along such lines is a characteristic feature of our civilization. To some extent these interest groups have replaced or absorbed into themselves older local institutions in that they make it possible for the government and substantial segments of the nation to maintain contact with each other. It must be obvious, however, that *the whole development makes necessary a reinforced party system that can cope with the multiplied organized pressures.* The alternative would be a scheme perhaps best described as government by pressure groups intent upon using the parties to deflect political attention from themselves.

By themselves, the interest groups cannot attempt to define public policy democratically. Coherent public policies do not emerge as the mathematical result of the claims of all of the pressure groups. The integration of the interest groups into the political system is a function of the parties. Any tendency in the direction of a strengthened party system encourages the interest groups to align themselves with one or the other of the major parties. Such a tendency is already at work. One of the noteworthy features of contemporary American politics is the fact that not a few interest groups have found it impossible to remain neutral toward both parties. To illustrate, the entry of organized labor upon the political scene has in turn impelled antagonistic special interests to coalesce in closer political alignments.

In one respect the growth of the modern interest groups is exerting a direct effect upon the internal distribution of power within the parties. They counteract and offset local interests; they are a nationalizing influence. Indeed, the proliferation of interest groups has been one of the factors in the rise of national issues because these groups tend to organize and define their objectives on a national scale.

Parties whose political commitments

count are of particular significance to interest organizations with large membership such as exist among industrial workers and farmers, but to a lesser extent also among businessmen. Unlike the great majority of pressure groups, these organizations through their membership—and in proportion to their voting strength—are able to play a measurable role in elections. Interest groups of this kind are the equivalent of organizations of voters. For reasons of mutual interest, the relationship between them and the parties tends to become explicit and continuing.

A stronger party system is less likely to give cause for the deterioration and confusion of purposes which sometimes passes for compromise but is really an unjustifiable surrender to narrow interests. *Compromise among interests is compatible with the aims of a free society only when the terms of reference reflect an openly acknowledged concept of the public interest.* There is every reason to insist that the parties be held accountable to the public for the compromises they accept.

2. *The Need for a Party System with Sufficient Party Loyalty.* It is here not suggested, of course, that the parties should disagree about everything. Parties do not, and need not, take a position on all questions that allow for controversy. The proper function of the parties is to develop and define policy alternatives on matters likely to be of interest to the whole country, on issues related to the responsibility of the parties for the conduct of either the government or the opposition.

Needed clarification of party policy in itself *will not cause the parties to differ more fundamentally or more sharply than they have in the past.* The contrary is much more likely to be the case. The clarification of party policy may be expected to produce a more reasonable discussion of public affairs, more closely related to the political performance of the parties in their actions rather than their words. *Nor is it to be assumed that increasing concern with*

their programs will cause the parties to erect between themselves an ideological wall. There is no real ideological division in the American electorate, and hence programs of action presented by responsible parties for the voter's support could hardly be expected to reflect or strive toward such division.

It is true at the same time that ultimately any political party must establish some conditions for membership and place some obligations on its representatives in government. Without so defining its identity the party is in danger of ceasing to be a party. To make party policy effective the *parties have the right and the duty to announce the terms to govern participation in the common enterprise.* This basic proposition is rarely denied, nor are precedents lacking. But there are practical difficulties in the way of applying restraints upon those who disregard the stated terms.

It is obvious that an effective party cannot be based merely or primarily on the expulsion of the disloyal. To impose discipline in any voluntary association is possible only as a last resort and only when a wide consensus is present within the association. Discipline and consensus are simply the front and rear sides of the same coin. *The emphasis in all consideration of party discipline must be,* therefore, *on positive measures to create a strong and general agreement on policies.* Thereafter, the problem of discipline is secondary and marginal.

When the membership of the party has become well aware of party policy and stands behind it, assumptions about teamwork within the party are likely to pervade the whole organization. Ultimately it is the electorate itself which will determine how firmly it wants the lines of party allegiance to be drawn. Yet even a small shift of emphasis toward party cohesion is likely to produce changes not only in the structure of the parties but also in the degree to which members identify themselves with their party.

Party unity is always a relative matter. It may be fostered, but the whole weight of tradition in American politics is against very rigid party discipline. As a general rule, the parties have a basis for expecting adherence to the party program when their position is reasonably explicit. Thus it is evident that the disciplinary difficulties of the parties do not result primarily from a reluctance to impose restraints but from the neglect of positive measures to give meaning to party programs.

As for party cohesion in Congress, the parties have done little to build up the kind of unity within the congressional party that is now so widely desired. Traditionally congressional candidates are treated as if they were the orphans of the political system, with no truly adequate party mechanism available for the conduct of their campaigns. Enjoying remarkably little national or local party support, congressional candidates have mostly been left to cope with the political hazards of their occupation on their own account. *A basis for party cohesion in Congress will be established as soon as the parties interest themselves sufficiently in their congressional candidates to set up strong and active campaign organizations in the constituencies.* Discipline is less a matter of what the parties do *to* their congressional candidates than what the parties do *for* them.

III. MORE RESPONSIBLE PARTIES

1. *The Need for Parties Responsible to the Public. Party responsibility means the responsibility of both parties to the general public, as enforced in elections.* Responsibility of the party in power centers on the conduct of the government, usually in terms of policies. The party in power has a responsibility, broadly defined, for the general management of the government, for its manner of getting results, for the results achieved, for the consequences of inaction as well as action, for the in-

tended and unintended outcome of its conduct of public affairs, for all that it plans to do, for all that it might have foreseen, for the leadership it provides, for the acts of all of its agents, and for what it says as well as for what it does.

Party responsibility includes the responsibility of the opposition party, also broadly defined, for the conduct of its opposition, for the management of public discussion, for the development of alternative policies and programs, for the bipartisan policies which it supports, for its failures and successes in developing the issues of public policy, and for its leadership of public opinion. The opposition is as responsible for its record in Congress as is the party in power. It is important that the opposition party be effective but it is equally important that it be responsible, for an irresponsible opposition is dangerous to the whole political system.

Party responsibility to the public, enforced in elections, implies that there be more than one party, for the public can hold a party responsible only if it has a choice. Again, unless the parties identify themselves with programs, the public is unable to make an intelligent choice between them. The public can understand the general management of the government only in terms of policies. When the parties lack the capacity to define their actions in terms of policies, they turn irresponsible because the electoral choice between the parties becomes devoid of meaning.

As a means of achieving responsibility, the clarification of party policy also tends to keep public debate on a more realistic level, restraining the inclination of party spokesmen to make unsubstantiated statements and charges. When party policy is made clear, the result to be expected is a more reasonable and profitable discussion, tied more closely to the record of party action. When there is no clear basis for rating party performance, when party policies cannot be defined in terms of a concrete program, party debate tears itself loose from the facts. Then wild fictions are used to excite the imagination of the public.

2. *The Need for Parties Responsible to Their Members.* *Party responsibility includes also the responsibility of party leaders to the party membership, as enforced in primaries, caucuses and conventions.* To this end the internal processes of the parties must be democratic, the party members must have an opportunity to participate in intraparty business, and the leaders must be accountable to the party. Responsibility demands that the parties concern themselves with the development of good relations between the leaders and the members. Only thus can the parties act as intermediaries between the government and the people. Strengthening the parties involves, therefore, the improvement of the internal democratic processes by which the leaders of the party are kept in contact with the members.

The external and the internal kinds of party responsibility need not conflict. Responsibility of party leaders to party members promotes the clarification of party policy when it means that the leaders find it necessary to explain the policy to the membership. Certainly the lack of unity within the membership cannot be overcome by the fiat of an irresponsible party leadership. A democratic internal procedure can be used not merely to test the strength of the various factions within a party but also to resolve the conflicts. The motives for enlarging the areas of agreement within the parties are persuasive because unity is the condition of success.

Intraparty conflict will be minimized if it is generally recognized that national, state and local party leaders have a common responsibility to the party membership. Intraparty conflict is invited and exaggerated by dogmas that assign to local party leaders an exclusive right to appeal to the party membership in their area.

Occasions may arise in which the parties will find it necessary to apply sanctions against a state or local party organization, especially when that organization is in open rebellion against policies established for the whole party. There are a variety of ways in which recognition may be withdrawn. It is possible to refuse to seat delegates to the National Convention; to drop from the National Committee members representing the dissident state organization; to deny legislative committee assignments to members of Congress sponsored by the disloyal organization; and to appeal directly to the party membership in the state or locality, perhaps even promoting a rival organization. The power to take strong measures is there.

It would be unfortunate, however, if the problem of party unity were thought of as primarily a matter of punishment. Nothing prevents the parties from explaining themselves to their own members. The party members have power to insist that local and state party organizations and leaders cooperate with the party as a whole; all the members need is a better opportunity to find out what party politics is about. The need for sanctions is relatively small when state and local organizations are not treated as the restricted preserve of their immediate leaders. National party leaders ought to have access to party members everywhere as a normal and regular procedure because they share with local party leaders responsibility to the same party membership. It would always be proper for the national party leaders to discuss all party matters with the membership of any state or local party organization. Considering their great prestige, wise and able national party leaders will need very little more than this opportunity.

The political developments of our time place a heavy emphasis on national issues as the basis of party programs. As a result, the party membership is coming to look to the national party leaders for a larger role in intraparty affairs. There is some evidence of growing general agreement within the membership of each party, strong enough to form a basis of party unity, provided the parties maintain close contact with their own supporters.

In particular, *national party leaders have a legitimate interest in the nomination of congressional candidates,* though normally they try hard to avoid the appearance of any intervention. Depending on the circumstances, this interest can be expressed quite sufficiently by seeking a chance to discuss the nomination with the party membership in the congressional district. On the other hand, it should not be assumed that state and local party leaders usually have an interest in congressional nominations antagonistic to the interest of the national leaders in maintaining the general party policy. As a matter of fact, congressional nominations are not considered great prizes by the local party organization as generally as one might think. It is neglect of congressional nominations and elections more than any other factor that weakens party unity in Congress. It should be added, however, that what is said here about intraparty relations with respect to congressional nominations applies also to other party nominations.

3. *The Inadequacy of the Existing Party System*

The existing party system is inadequately prepared to meet the demands now being made upon it chiefly because its central institutions are not well organized to deal with national questions. The sort of party organization needed today is indirectly suggested by the origin of the traditional party structure. This structure developed in a period in which local interests were dominant and positive governmental action at the national level did not play the role it assumed later.

I. BEGINNING TRANSITION

1. *Change and Self-examination.* Having outlined the kind of party system we accept as our basic model, we are now able to list briefly some of the principal deficiencies of the existing national party institutions. At the same time we can identify some of the conspicuous failings that show up in the operations of the two parties, in particular their failure to bring about adequate popular participation in politics and to develop satisfactory relations between the central and the local party organizations.

Marked changes have occurred *in the structure and processes of American society* during the twentieth century. Their general effect upon the political scene will be indicated in the following section. Here it will be enough to point out that most of these changes *have necessarily affected the party system.* In many respects the party system is today far from what it was fifty years ago, even though there has not been as yet a conscious and planned adjustment. When a party system is undergoing such a slow transformation, it is difficult to describe its operation accurately or to enumerate its deficiencies precisely as they now exist. The Democratic party is today almost a new creation, produced since 1932. Some of its leaders have given much thought to its present-day characteristics. On the opposite side, the Republican party has been the subject of extensive and repeated self-examination for nearly two decades. It is *the prevailing climate of self-examination as well as the current tendencies toward change in the party system* that *give point to inquiries like that represented by our report.*

2. *Burden of the Past.* Despite these tendencies toward change, however, *formal party organization in its main features is still substantially what it was before the Civil War.* Aside from the adoption of the direct primary, organizational forms have not been overhauled for nearly a century. The result is that the parties are now probably the most archaic institutions in the United States.

Under these circumstances, it is not surprising that *the main trends of*

American politics, especially the emphasis on effective national action, *have tended to outflank the party system.* Until rather recently neither of the two parties has found it necessary to concern itself seriously with the question of adequate party organization at the national level. The familiar description of the parties as loose confederations of state and local machines has too long remained reasonably accurate.

II. SOME BASIC PROBLEMS

Party institutions and their operations cannot be divorced from the general conditions that govern the nature of the party system. Before we focus specifically on the deficiencies of existing party institutions, we must account for some of the more important factors that impress themselves upon both major parties.

What are the general features of party organization that have cast up continuing problems?

1. *The Federal Basis. The two parties are organized on a federal basis,* probably as a natural result of our federal type of government. In Charles E. Merriam's words, "The American party system has its roots in the states. Its regulation and control is conducted almost wholly, although not entirely, by the states acting separately."[1] This means that *the national and state party organizations are largely independent of one another,* each operating within its own sphere, *without appreciable common approach to problems of party policy and strategy.*

Such independence has led to frequent and sharp differences between state and national organizations. Antagonisms are illustrated by such terms as national Republicans and Wisconsin Republicans, national Democrats and Dixiecrats. Moreover, state party organizations too often define their interests quite narrowly. This does not merely mean substantial disregard of national needs or matters of national interest, but it also means piecemeal as well as one-sided use of state power and state resources. As John M. Gaus has put it, "In many states—probably in almost all—the party systems are inadequate as instruments for reflecting the needs of our citizens for carefully thought-out, alternative programs of public housekeeping."[2]

It is not being argued here that the party system should be cut free from its federal basis. Federalism is not a negative influence in itself; it is equally capable of positive accomplishments in the public interest. Whether it works in the one or the other direction depends in large part on how well the balance of forces within a federal organization accords with the needs of society. In the case of the American party system, *the real issue is not over the federal form of organization but over the right balance of forces within this type of organization.*

On that score, the party system is weighted much more heavily toward the state-local side than is true today of the federal system of government in the United States. The gap produces serious disabilities in government. It needs to be closed, even though obviously our traditions of localism, states rights and sectionalism will inevitably affect the pace of progress that can be expected.

A corollary of the kind of federalism now expressed in the party system is an excessive measure of internal separatism. The congressional party organization is independent of the national organization, and the House and Senate organizations of the same party are independent of each other. As a result, cooperation between these parts of the national party structure has not been easy to secure.

2. *The Location of Leadership.* In

[1] Charles E. Merriam, "State Government at Mid-Century," *State Government,* Vol. 23, p. 118 (June, 1950).

[2] John M. Gaus, "The States Are in the Middle," *ibid.,* p. 140.

part because of the centrifugal drives that run through the party system, *party organization does not vest leadership of the party as a whole in either a single person or a committee.* The President, by virtue of his conspicuous position and his real as well as symbolic role in public opinion, is commonly considered the leader of his party. If he has a vigorous personality and the disposition to press his views on party policy and strategy, he may become the actual leader during his presidential term. But even the President has no official position within the party organization, and his leadership is often resented and opposed. The presidential nominee of the defeated party is generally recognized as the "titular leader" of his party, yet the very title implies a lack of authority.

The National Chairman is most nearly in the top position, but if he tries to exercise initiative and leadership in matters other than the presidential campaign, his authority is almost certain to be challenged. Ill feeling, rather than harmony of policy and action, is likely to result. In sum, *there is at present no central figure or organ which could claim authority to take up party problems, policies and strategy.*

3. *The Ambiguity of Membership.* The vagueness of formal leadership that prevails at the top has its counterpart in the vagueness of formal membership at the bottom. *No understandings or rules or criteria exist with respect to membership in a party.* The general situation was well put by Senator Borah in a statement made in 1923:

Any man who can carry a Republican primary is a Republican. He might believe in free trade, in unconditional membership in the League of Nations, in states' rights, and in every policy that the Democratic party ever advocated; yet, if he carried his Republican primary, he would be a Republican. He might go to the other extreme and believe in the communistic state, in the dic-

tatorship of the proletariat, in the abolition of private property, and in the extermination of the bourgeoisie; yet, if he carried his Republican primary, he would still be a Republican.

It is obviously difficult, if not impossible, to secure anything like harmony of policy and action within political parties so loosely organized as this. On the other hand, it is easy to see that the voter's political choice when confined to candidates without a common bond in terms of program amounts to no more than taking a chance with an individual candidate. *Those who suggest that elections should deal with personalities but not with programs suggest at the same time that party membership should mean nothing at all.*

III. SPECIFIC DEFICIENCIES

So much for the most conspicuous consequences that stem from the general features of existing party organization. Now let us consider some more specific aspects pertinent to a reorganization of the national party structure.

1. *National Party Organs. The National Convention, as at present constituted and operated, is an unwieldy, unrepresentative and less than responsible body.* In 1948 the Republican convention was composed of 1,094 delegates, and the Democratic convention of 1,234, with an equal additional number of alternates in each case. Both conventions are expected to be still larger in 1952.

The unrepresentative character of the convention has been recognized in both parties by changes in the apportionment of delegates. Yet no one would maintain in either case that the party's rank-and-file strength in the several states is truly represented. The apportionment of delegates to the Democratic National Convention is based, not on number of Democratic voters in the various states, but on the apportionment of presidential electors. Theoretically, therefore, the delegates represent simply population— Republican voters and nonvoters as well as Democratic voters. Because the rural population is greatly overrepresented in Congress, the urban centers, though virtually the party's backbone, are strongly discriminated against. The following table illustrates the extent of this distortion in eleven states.

Democratic National Convention, 1948

State	Democratic votors per delegate
Maine	11,191
Vermont	7,443
Connecticut	21,164
New York	28,960
Pennsylvania	26,955
Illinois	33,245
Wyoming	8,725
Nevada	3,129
Texas	15,014
South Carolina	1,721
Louisiana	5,680

In spite of a number of attempts to reduce the overrepresentation of southern Republicans in the Republican National Convention it is clear from the next table that much remains to be done.

Republican National Convention, 1948

State	Republican voters per delegate
New York	29,290
Pennsylvania	19,021
Ohio	27,277
Kansas	24,884
South Carolina	894
Georgia	5,478
Alabama	2,923
Mississippi	630
Louisiana	5,589

This lack of balance in representation, together with the peculiar atmosphere within which the Convention operates, makes it very hard for such a body to act in a deliberative and responsible manner. The moral authority of the National Convention to act in the name of the whole party would be greatly strengthened if more care were used to make the convention really representative of the party as a whole.

It can be said equally well of other institutions at the national level that they are not very well suited to carry today's burdens of an effective party system. *The National Committee is seldom a generally influential body and much less a working body.* Indeed, it rarely meets at all.

In *House and Senate,* the *campaign committee* of each party is concerned with aiding in the reelection of members of its chamber. These *committees do not always have a good working relationship with the National Committee.* They do not plan joint election strategy for both chambers and traditionally accept little responsibility for party leadership. Only in the past generation have the parties shown signs of developing a continuous working organization at the national level. *Although their interest in questions of party policy has grown, the national party organs are not so constituted nor so coordinated as to make it simple for them to pay enough attention to these questions.*

2. *Party Platforms.* The growing importance of national issues in American politics puts weight into the formulation of general statements of party policy. Of course, no single statement of party policy can express the whole program of the party in all of its particulars, including questions of timing. But it is obvious that a serious attempt to define the propositions on which the parties intend to seek the voter's support would serve both party unity and party responsibility.

One of the reasons for the widespread lack of respect for party platforms is that they have seldom been used by the parties to get a mandate from the people. By and large, *alternatives between the parties are defined so badly that it is often difficult to determine what the election has decided even in broadest terms.* Yet unused resources are available to the parties in the democratic process itself if they learn to use a statement of policy as the basis for the election campaign. Platforms acquire authority when they are so used.

The prevailing procedure for the writing and adoption of national party platforms is too hurried and too remote from the process by which actual decisions are made to command the respect of the whole party and the electorate. The drafting of a platform ought to be the work of months, not of a day or two; it ought to be linked closely with the formulation of party policy as a continuing activity. Party policy—in its bricks and straws—is made, applied, explored and tested in congressional and presidential decisions, in the executive departments, in the work of research staffs, in committee hearings, and in congressional debates. No party convention can pull a party program out of the air. *The platform should be the end product of a long search for a working agreement within the party.*

3. *Intraparty Democracy.* One of the principal functions of the parties—in terms of the concept of party we elaborated in the preceding section—is to extend to the fullest the citizen's participation in public affairs. Measured by this standard, the existing parties are painfully deficient. Direct primary legislation offers opportunities for the creation of a broad base on which to build the party structure, but these opportunities have rarely been fully utilized.

Too little consideration has been given to ways and means of bringing about a constructive relationship between the party and its members. Indeed, any organization really concerned about this relationship does a multitude of things that American parties generally do not do to maintain close contact with the membership. Party membership ought to become a year-round matter, both with constructive activities by the members and with mechanisms by which the party organizations can absorb the benefits of wider political participation.

If we take the total vote cast in elections as a crude measure of the effectiveness of the parties *in making the most of popular participation, the performance of American parties is very unsatisfactory.* In the 1948 presidential election, approximately 47,000,000 citizens of voting age did not vote. In the congressional election of 1946 only a little more than one-third of the potential vote was cast. This is evidence of low-grade performance, compared with the record of the parties in other democratic countries.

4. *Party Research.* An unimaginative attitude is shown by party organizations in their reluctance to develop party research to the full level of its potentialities. In view of the complexity and difficulty of the problems with which the parties must deal, it can hardly be denied that *a party stands as much in need of research as does business enterprise or the government itself.*

It is a remarkable indication of small party interest, for instance, that politically useful research by government agencies is being carried on to a very limited extent. Thus the United States Census Bureau does not collect and publish comprehensive election statistics, and much of the raw statistical data for party research is not produced by government. Relatively little use has been made by the parties of social survey techniques as a basis for political campaigns. Nor have the parties shown much interest in the study of the social, economic and psychological factors that influence the results of the election contests. At a time when the discussion of public policy is necessarily becoming the focus of party business, the parties have not yet established research staffs adequately equipped to provide party leaders with technical data and findings grounded in scientific analysis.

4. New Demands Upon Party Leadership

I. THE NATURE OF MODERN PUBLIC POLICY

1. *Broad Range of Policy. The expanding responsibilities of modern government have brought about so extensive an interlacing of governmental action with the country's economic and social life that the need for coordinated and coherent programs, legislative as well as administrative, has become paramount.* Formulating and executing such general programs involves more than technical knowledge. *In a democracy no general program can be adopted and carried out without wide political support.* Support must be strong enough and stable enough to guard the program as far as possible against such drives as come forth constantly from a multitude of special interests seeking their own ends. This kind of political support can be mobilized on a continuing basis only by stronger parties.

Broad governmental programs need to be built on a foundation of political commitments as written into the programs of adequately organized parties. This is true today also of governmental programs erected on bipartisan backing. In that respect the political requirements to sustain American diplomacy are very different from those of the period before World War I, for example. As Walter Lippmann has recently written of the requirements of bipartisan foreign policy, "It takes two organized parties, each with its recognized leaders in the field of foreign affairs. Today neither party is organized. Neither party has leaders in the field of foreign affairs. In this chaos no Secretary of State can function successfully." [3]

[3] *New York Herald Tribune,* March 27, 1950.

2. *Impact on the Public.* What is said here about the need for an adequate political base for foreign policy applies equally to such other large sectors of public concern as national defense and economic policy. In each area, the problems are so interrelated that the activities of the government must be integrated over a very wide front. *In a predominantly industrial society, public policy tends to be widely inclusive, involving in its objectives and effects very large segments of the public or even the whole country.*

This is true of a great many fields, such as labor relations, credit regulation, social security, housing, price support, aid to veterans, and even revenue administration. To quote the Bureau of Internal Revenue, ". . . the Bureau . . . reaches into every town and hamlet throughout the United States and directly affects the finances of some 65 million people in the form of one or more levies." [4] Mark Sullivan has described the activities of the United States Department of Agriculture in language strikingly similar, if with a bit of poetic license: "It enters every home in the country, stands beside every citizen as he eats his meals, and every member of his family. It determines or conclusively influences the price of nearly every form of food. In doing this the department goes a second time into the homes of a large class of citizens, the farmers. To them it in many cases pays large amounts of money to buy large quantities of their crops and keep them off the market, in order to support the price." [5]

3. *Governmental Program Machinery. On the side of government, in the administrative and the legislative spheres, the twin needs for program formulation and for program machinery have long been recognized.* A series of laws has aimed in this direction.

[4] *The Budget for the Fiscal Year 1951,* p. 1033.
[5] *New York Herald Tribune,* March 24, 1950.

The Budget and Accounting Act of 1921, with its emphasis on the government's financial program and thus on the government's work plan in its entirety, including the legislative program of the President; the Employment Act of 1946, in its concern with a program to sustain high-level production and employment; the Legislative Reorganization Act of the same year, giving added strength to Congress in the exercise of its function of review of programs proposed by the executive branch; the National Security Act of 1947, creating the National Security Council as policy coordinator for national defense—these acts illustrate the trend.

The governmental advance toward program formulation needs now to be paralleled in the political sphere proper —above all in the party system. Without mobilization of political support the best-conceived programs of modern government come to naught.

II. RISE OF NATION-WIDE POLICY ISSUES

1. *An Historic Trend.* Even if the international scene did not look as it does, *the changes in the nature and scope of public policy* here indicated would press upon the political process. For they *are the result of changes in the social structure and the economy of the United States.* The long-range transformations expressed in industrialization and urbanization and the revolution in transportation and communication were bound to create a truly national economy and to affect significantly the bases of American politics.

After the experience of the great depression in the thirties, the public has become particularly conscious of the need for economic stability. It is now regarded as obvious by large groups of voters that only the national government has the span of jurisdiction and resources adequate to cope with this problem. On the same grounds many of the other anxieties which people feel living in the uncertain conditions of the modern world stimulate demands on the national government.

2. *Past and Present Factors.* It is much the same thing to say that *there has been in recent decades a continuing decline of sectionalism,* first noted by Arthur N. Holcombe nearly twenty years ago. Statistical evidence such as is available for the last generation shows that the most significant political trends in the country have been national, not sectional or local. This is not to say that sectionalism is likely to drop to insignificance as a factor in American politics. Here as elsewhere in the political system, change is a matter of degree. The relative decline of the strength of sectional alignments is nevertheless a matter of great consequence. Elections are increasingly won and lost by influences felt throughout the land.

The measurable shift from sectional to national politics cannot fail to have a corresponding effect on party organization and the locus of power within the parties. *Party organization designed to deal with the increasing volume of national issues must give wider range to the national party leadership.* With sectionalism in steady if slow decline, a change of the rules of politics is taking place. Long-range political success is likely to come to those leaders and that party quickest to go by the new rules.

As long as sectional alignments were dominant in American politics, strong party organization was not needed. As a matter of fact, sectionalism has long been the great enemy of true party organization. In its extreme form, sectionalism tends to eliminate the opposition party altogether. In the one-party areas so often linked to sectional alignments, the opposition party is a mere shadow.

Without effective party opposition, strong organization becomes very difficult to attain even for the dominant party. Illustrative of this condition has been the Solid South, where as a rule neither of the parties has produced strong state and local organizations, but only rather informal groupings built around individual leaders.

On the other hand, a stronger national party organization tends to play down sectional differences. The transition from predominantly sectional to primarily national politics generates a trend toward appropriate reorganization of the parties. It is in the main this trend that forms the practical base for the revision of party structure and procedures contemplated in our report.

3. *New Interest Groups in Politics.* *The economic and social factors that have reduced the weight of sectionalism have also resulted in the development of a new type of interest groups, built upon large membership.* These new interest groups, found principally in the areas of industrial labor and agriculture, are pursuing a novel political strategy. *To a much greater extent than in the past, they operate as if they were auxiliary organizations of one or the other party.* The growing conversion of most of the labor movement to party action is a case in point. Labor organizations now participate energetically in election contests. They register voters, take part in the nominating process, raise campaign funds, issue campaign literature and perform other functions once on the whole reserved for the parties.

Thus the old local monopolies of the regular party organizations have been broken by new large-membership groups. To a very considerable extent the regular party organizations are now so yoked into a partnership with the newcomers that they have lost much of their old freedom of action. The successful political leader in the future is likely to be one who is skillful in maintaining a good working alliance between the older and the newer types of political organization. This applies partly even to conditions today.

The emphasis of the new large-membership organizations is on national rather than sectional issues. What is no less significant, the interests of the membership are not identified with any single product or commodity. Farmers, for instance, cannot hope to prosper in an ailing economy. Workers must measure their pay against the level of prices as well as the value of social security. Hence the large-membership groups are inevitably pushed into consideration of all of the factors that affect the national well-being. How parties stand on programs designed to bring about stability and healthy expansion in the economy as a whole is therefore of great concern to most of the new groups in American politics.

5. The Question of Constitutional Amendment

1. *A Cabinet System?* It is altogether clear that party responsibility cannot be legislated into being. Not a few Americans have argued, however, that something like the British system of responsible cabinet government would have to be grafted to ours before an effective party system could come about in the United States. Usually this idea takes the form of proposals to amend the Constitution to give the President the right to dissolve Congress and to call a new election at any time, besides certain other changes in the Constitution.

A responsible cabinet system makes the leaders of the majority party in the legislature the heads of the executive departments, *collectively accountable* to their own legislative majority *for the conduct of the government.* Such a relationship prompts close cooperation between the executive and legislative branches. The legislative majority of the cabinet forms a party team which as such can readily be held responsible for its policies. This governmental system is built around the parties, which play the key role in it.

2. *Strong Parties as a Condition.* We do not here need to take a position on the abstract merits of the cabinet system. On the question whether it could

be successfully fitted into the American scheme of congressional-presidential government, opinions are widely divided. Even if it were conceded to be desirable *to amend the Constitution in order to create a responsible cabinet system,* it should be plain that this *is not a practicable way of getting more effective parties.* Such an amendment, if it offered likelihood of being adopted at all, would make sense only when the parties have actually demonstrated the strength they now lack. When they show that strength, a constitutional amendment to achieve this end would be unnecessary.

On the other hand, the experience of foreign countries suggests that adoption of the cabinet system does not automatically result in an effective party system. Cabinet systems differ in their results and affect the party system in different ways. Moreover, it is easy to overestimate not only the expected benefits of a constitutional amendment but also the rigidity of the existing constitutional

arrangements in the United States. Certainly the roles of the President and Congress are defined by the Constitution in terms that leave both free to cooperate and to rely on the concept of party responsibility.

3. *Adaptation within the Constitution. The parties can do much to adapt the usages under the Constitution to their purposes.* When strong enough, the parties obviously can furnish the President and Congress a political basis of cooperation within the Constitution as it stands today.

Actually the parties have not carefully explored the opportunities they have for more responsible operation under existing constitutional arrangements. It is logical first to find out what can be done under present conditions to invigorate the parties before accepting the conclusion that action has to begin with changing a constitutional system that did not contemplate the growing need for party responsibility when it was set up.

41. The American Party System and Majority Rule*

AUSTIN RANNEY AND WILLMOORE KENDALL

Extreme Majoritarian Criticism of the Constitution. . . . We have spoken of the so-called "anti-majoritarian" features of our formal-governmental system, and of the extent to which they reflect the avowed intentions of the Founding Fathers. There is, as we noted, an impressive array of them—so impressive that it has led at least some partisans of majoritarian democracy to conclude that the majority of the American people (by which these critics seem

* *Democracy and the American Party System* (New York: Harcourt, Brace and Company, 1956), pp. 519-533. Reprinted by permission of Harcourt, Brace and Company.

to mean the low-income strata of American society) are, in terms of both governmental procedures and public policy, permanently at the mercy of a small minority (by which they seem to mean the rich and prosperous), and that it will continue so until steps are taken to revise the system from top to bottom. The best-known of these critics is J. Allen Smith, whose work *The Spirit of American Government* (1907) has profoundly influenced a number of commentators on our Constitution writing since his time.

What Smith appears to have wanted (he wrote as an unabashed majoritarian) was a series of constitutional reforms that would make the American constitutional system as much as possible like the British system. A large number of writers on American government after Smith have followed his lead in attacking particular anti-majoritarian features of our system—particularly the seniority principle in legislative committees, and the electoral college; but, curiously enough, few writers on American government after Smith have attacked (as Smith did) the *whole* array of anti-majoritarian features, or put themselves forward as out-and-out majoritarians. Smith's view as to the *facts* of the matter, on the other hand, has become the prevailing view among most present-day writers on American politics, who tend to assume that our system puts insurmountable barriers in the way of popular majorities. Thus no one in recent decades has reopened the *factual* question Smith raised, either to ask whether he was right about the situation as of fifty years ago, or to ask whether the situation has perhaps changed somewhat in the interim.

Considerations of space in the present chapter forbid an exhaustive inquiry into this problem, but there is reason to believe that Smith overstated his case, that the case has grown weaker as the years have passed, and that recognition of its weaknesses is essential to a correct understanding of our constitutional and political system. Let us, therefore, fix attention briefly on those weaknesses, and state what the present facts of the matter appear to be.

In order to do so, however, we must distinguish sharply between two aspects of the problem that have been confused over the years during which it has been neglected, namely, the position of popular majorities vis-à-vis the Constitution itself, and their position vis-à-vis the federal statute book.

Popular Majorities and the Amending Process. Those majoritarians who have adopted Smith's position direct their harshest criticisms at the arrangements the Founding Fathers provided for amending the Constitution. What the framers set out to do, they argue, was to make the Constitution impossible to amend save in response to overwhelming nationwide sentiment in favor of a proposed change, and yet keep it from having the look of an attempt on their part to subject the nation indefinitely to the dead hand of the past. Concretely, they point out, the arrangements the framers wrote into their draft gave to one-third-plus-one of the members of *either* house of Congress the power to prevent any proposal for constitutional change from even being initiated, and gave one-fourth-plus-one of the states the power to block ratification of any proposed amendment. Like Smith, they draw attention to two types of data: first, data regarding the number of proposed amendments that have been defeated, and second, data calculated to show how, because of alleged over-representation of certain states in Congress, and because of the veto power in one-fourth-plus-one of the states, it is logically possible for such-and-such a combination of thinly populated states, accounting for such-and-such a shockingly small percentage of the nation's population, to force its preferences about the Constitution upon the remainder. In both cases the arithmetic is scrupulously careful and sufficiently elaborate to distract attention from the following considerations: First, in order to prove that the Constitution is impossible or even very difficult to amend, it is necessary to show, not that a great many proposed amendments have failed, but that one or more amendments have failed despite such-and-such evidence that they enjoyed at least majority support. (The fact that Mary has turned down 1,873 suitors for her hand does *not* prove that Mary is unmarriageable, but merely that none of the 1,873 has met her requirements.) Second, the power of such-and-such combinations of states to prevent constitutional change against the wishes of a popular majority is just as great as, and no greater

reform the amendment process

than, the realistic chances of the combination's actually being formed.

In short, the case against the amending process, which enables these critics to deny to the anti-majoritarian aspects of the legislative process the presumptive justification that they must be desired by the majority else they would have been set aside by amendments, not only fails; it is not, in view of the lack of attention to data relevant to the issue, even plausible. Or, to put it a little differently, it does not meet at any point this objection: Any bare numerical majority of the nation's citizens, *if fairly evenly distributed over the country,* ought to be able to account for two-thirds-plus-one of the members of the two houses, and ought to be able to put through ratification in three-quarters of the states. In order to prove their point, the critics must show that there is some good reason to expect bare numerical majorities *not* to be evenly distributed geographically. The framers, to be sure, put their bets, as far as the amending process was concerned, on the likelihood that proposed constitutional amendments would necessarily pit geographical section against geographical section, and that popular majorities on such issues could not be evenly distributed. But even by Smith's time this notion had, with the blurring of sectional differences, lost most of what plausibility it had ever had; and in our time the presumption against it appears overwhelming.

The present writers' view is that there is little reason to expect future issues concerning the Constitution to divide the nation regionally in such a way as to give a smallish minority the kind of veto the framers intended it to have and the majoritarian critics believe that it does have. The amending process is therefore always at the disposal of any movement that can rally a numerical majority behind its proposal for constitutional change, and the anti-majoritarian features of our legislative process therefore do have the presumptive approval of at least a majority of the electorate.

Popular Majorities and the Legislative Process. The writers whose criticisms we are summarizing are also indignant about constitutional barriers which they think stand in the way of majority access to the statute book. Suppose, they say in effect, a majority out over the country wants such-and-such a new law passed, and organizes so as to get control of one-half-plus-one of the seats in both houses of Congress (which means keeping itself in being for two years, and so getting around the "barrier" of staggered election of senators). One barrier it may run up against at once is federalism: the power to make laws on the topic in hand may be one of the powers reserved to the states (in which case, on these writers' showing, the representatives must launch themselves upon the impossible venture of amending the Constitution). Another barrier is the seniority rule in congressional committees, which may enable a hostile committee chairman to bottle the bill up in committee for a long period. Still another is the veto power of the president, who may well have been elected before the majority came into being, or, because of the electoral college, may have become president against the wishes of the majority. Even if the majority hurdles all these barriers, however, it may find itself up against a judicial veto by having the Supreme Court declare its new law unconstitutional. Here again, then, what these critics see in our constitutional system is an unbeatable set of arrangements for frustrating majorities and placing in the hands of minorities an unlimited power to block legislative action they deem distasteful.

The first thing to notice about this argument is that it proves that the majority cannot control the statute book only if we accept two premises: first (and one that is entirely unrelated to the constitutional system itself), that a popular majority cannot be kept in being for the four years it would need to exist in order to surmount all the barriers save that of judicial review; and second, that there is nothing a determined congressional majority backed up by a friendly president can do about a judicial veto. The latter premise is clearly false: Congress and the president can increase the size of the Supreme Court and pack it with appointees congenial to their point of view; or Congress can use its constitutional power over the appellate jurisdiction of the Court to see to it that no further case involving the statute comes before it. And once the majority has Congress, the president, *and* the Court on its side, the Constitution is no longer a barrier to whatever it desires. As Dean McBain put it:

> There is no limitation imposed upon the national government which Congress, the President, and the Supreme Court, acting in consecutive agreement, may not legally override. In this sense the government as a whole is clearly a government of unlimited powers; for by interpretation it stakes out its own boundaries.

As for the barriers other than judicial review, Smith and his followers have undoubtedly overestimated them. A numerical majority of the population, more or less evenly spread over the entire nation, would overnight find itself in control not of a mere majority of the House, but very probably of the two-thirds majority required for overriding a presidential veto. Within two years it would have similar strength in the Senate. And once it had a two-thirds majority of both houses, the extent to which the president would dare frustrate the majority's wishes by vetoing its legislation would depend, for the most part, on the extent to which the majority was willing to use the separation-of-powers weapons that the Constitution clearly places in Congress's hands. It would have the power, for example, to bring the whole machinery of government to a standstill by withholding appropriations and refusing confirmation of presidential appointments.

It therefore appears that there is nothing in our *formal* constitutional machinery to prevent a movement that can mobilize a majority of the nation's citizens from either amending the Constitution or passing a law without amending the Constitution. At most one can say that our constitutional machinery prevents action by *temporary* majorities (that is, majorities that, by definition, cannot keep themselves in being for the two to four years that may be needed in order to get full control of Congress and the presidency). What prevents legislative action by longer-lived majorities is *not* our formal constitutional machinery, but the whole complex of the people's attitudes and the character that those attitudes impose on our policies. In other words, the *main* barrier that any movement bidding for majority support runs against is the sheer *unmobilizability* of average Americans for political purposes. This unmobilizability, the present writers believe, is largely a matter of that fundamental unwillingness to use the unlimited power of the majority in an unlimited way that . . . we [call] *forbearance* on the part of the majority. In practical politics, that forbearance appears to work in the following fashion. The first hundred thousand supporters for a constitutional amendment calling for, say, the abolition of the states, or a statute providing for, say, the legalization of bullfights, may be easy to get; but the second hundred thousand will be more difficult than the first, the third still more difficult—and so it continues to at least that degree necessary for bringing political mobilization in America under the operation of what economists call the "law of diminishing returns,"

In short, relatively persistent national popular majorities do have unlimited power under our present Constitution despite what the framers intended; and that unlimited power is always present as a necessary part of the context our politico-governmental system requires for its normal working. Such majorities arise relatively infrequently, to be sure; but the reason for that lies in the nature of the American community and its belief system, not in any insurmountable barriers set up by the formal constitutional system.

The Major Parties and Majority Rule. As we [have] noted, the typical popular majority in American politics—that is, one which votes a president into office, or switches control of Congress from one party to the other—is a "bundle of compromises," composed of a number of variegated interest groups, each of which holds many beliefs and values in common with the groups in the minority *and* many conflicting beliefs and values as among its own members and as between itself and the other groups who are temporarily co-operating with it to make up the majority. Its program is the product of pluralistic bargaining and compromise among its constituent groups, and is not, therefore, a clear, logically precise, and internally consistent body of doctrine to which all the individual persons making up the majority are deeply committed. But let us be quite clear as to the reason for this: *political majorities in America tend to be cross sections, not segments, of the community.*

. . . The party system more than any other American institution sustains and perpetuates the pluralistic politico-governmental system that produces the kind of popular majorities just described. By doing so it enables the American people to have their governmental cake and eat it too—that is, it enables them to reconcile their logically self-contradictory beliefs in "majority rule *and* minority rights" and in "popular sovereignty *and* checks and balances" in the following manner. On the one hand, by organizing elections, organizing government, and staffing the bureaucracy, the party system is the principal agency in the American system that enables popular majorities of *whatever* nature and composition to make known their desires and to induce the government to act upon them despite such formal anti-majoritarian features of the constitutional system as federalism, separation of powers, and judicial review. On the other hand, the party system also does much to ensure that the actual popular majorities that arise *shall* be "bundles of compromises," and, accordingly, will seek such modest and limited goals that no minority is likely to regard them as intolerable.

The Party System and Democracy: A Summary

The American party system, when measured against the conception of popular consultation . . . gets very high marks indeed. By sustaining and refreshing the consensus on which our society and governmental system are based, it makes possible our characteristic brand of pluralistic bargaining-compromising discussion of public issues, which is probably about as close to the model of creative democratic discussion in the nation-state as a community like the United States can hope to get. Moreover, the party system usually produces clear popular mandates on the issue of *who* shall rule, although, like every other traditional institution for popular consultation except perhaps the town meeting, it rarely produces clear popular mandates on the issue of *what* the government shall do on this or that matter of public policy. Finally, the parties, more than any other aspect of our governing system, do see to it that law-making and law-enforcing go forward under a loose sort of majority control, the essence of which we do not understand unless we think of the relevant majority as usually cutting across party lines, and in such a way as to create no irreconcilable minorities that will divide the nation into warring camps.

For these reasons, therefore, few

persons today would argue that American government would be more democratic with *no* party system at all than with the one it has; and few would quarrel with the proposition that the party system is one of the most powerful forces, if not *the* most powerful, operating to "democratize" our formal-governmental system, which, be it remembered, was not intended to be democratic and which, if permitted to operate in its "pure" form, would probably provide a far less democratic system of popular consultation and majority rule than that which we actually have.

In pondering the role and appraising the value of the present system, accordingly, the fruitful question is not whether it is more democratic than *no* party system at all, but where some *other* kind of party system would be more democratic than our present one. A number of eminent and thoughtful commentators, including Woodrow Wilson, Henry Jones Ford, Frank J. Goodnow, E. E. Schattschneider, James M. Burns, and the members of the Committee on Political Parties of the American Political Science Association, have answered the latter question in the affirmative by arguing that a more "responsible" party system would be more "democratic" than our present one. And other writers, including Pendleton Herring, Herbert Agar, Ernest S. Griffith, and the authors of this book, take the contrary position that a more "responsible" party system would probably be *less* "democratic" than our present system, given the nature of the American community.

We cannot hope to settle this controversy once and for all. We can, however, conclude our appraisal of the American party system by summarizing in some detail the position of each group of writers, so that the areas of agreement and disagreement between them can be clearly understood by the reader as a basis for making up his own mind as to what kind of party system he wants. That task we propose to undertake in the following section.

Would a More "Responsible" Party System Be More "Democratic"?

THE DOCTRINE OF RESPONSIBLE PARTY GOVERNMENT

The Need for Improved Governmental Action. The advocates of responsible party government argue that the government of the United States today faces domestic and foreign problems of such magnitude that they can be solved only by comprehensive, internally consistent, and expertly designed programs of public policy that are consistently supported both by a majority of federal officeholders and by a majority of the people throughout the nation. Anything less than such programs risks national disaster. We do not, however, want such programs *any* way we can get them; rather we want them to be developed, adopted, and executed *democratically*. In other words, we want not *action* alone, but *democratic* action as well.

The Crucial Role of the Parties. The national political parties, according to these writers, are the only agencies that can conceivably provide us with the kind of governmental action just described. They are comprehensive and representative in their membership and leadership, while their only possible rivals, the pressure groups, are limited and narrow in both respects. The parties are concerned with the *national* interest, while each pressure group is concerned only with its particular *special* interest. The parties operate in the open and deal directly with the voters, while the pressure groups operate largely in secret and deal for the most part only with governmental officials. If we are to have democratic and comprehensive programs for the national interest, then, only the national parties can provide them.

The Inadequacy of Our Present Party System. The responsible-party-government writers are convinced that our present national parties are incapable of furnishing the nation with the kind of governmental action described above. The argument runs as follows. The parties' lack of cohesion both inside and outside the government makes it impossible for them to draw up or execute sense-making programs of public policy. And this same lack of cohesion also prevents the voters from holding *either* party "responsible" in any meaningful sense for whatever the government does or does not do. Our present system of decentralized and loose parties and the pluralistic "concurrent-majority" kind of policy-making process they foster makes for *inaction* rather than action; and it therefore simply cannot handle such problems as resisting Communist aggression without bringing on thermonuclear war, or stabilizing the economy without stagnating it—problems that by their very nature demand vigorous, coherent, and *national* action. Consequently, the present party system breaks down in time of crisis and in the face of such problems, and policy is made by "presidential dictatorship." We therefore cannot escape the conclusion that the present parties are incapable of sustaining democratic government at such times.

Necessary Party Reforms. In order to get the kind of governmental action we need, these writers contend, we must make our party system more "responsible." In particular, they advocate at least the following types of party reforms.

CENTRALIZATION. The control of the parties must be taken out of the hands of the congeries of state and local leaders and organizations where it now resides, and put into the hands of the *national* leaders and organizations. The Committee on Political Parties has made the most specific proposal for accomplishing this reform. They propose that each major party create a party council of fifty members, composed of representatives from the national committee, the congressional party organizations, the state committees, the party's governors, organizations like the Young Republicans and Young Democrats, members-at-large chosen by the national convention, the presidential and vice-presidential incumbents and nominees, and the highest national party officials. The council should meet regularly and often, and propose a preliminary draft of the platform to the national convention, interpret the platform during the campaign and after, and generally act as the party's authoritative spokesman on policy matters.

DISCIPLINE. The national party leaders must have the power to keep the party's members in public office in line behind the party's program. Although exactly *how* this power is to be exercised is not made clear, the implication seems to be that our national party leaders should, like their counterparts in the British parties, have the power to control local party nominations and thus to grant or refuse permission for a congressional candidate to run for office under the party's label.

INTRAPARTY DEMOCRACY? The Committee on Political Parties argues that "intraparty democracy" (i.e., "the responsibility of the party leaders to the party members, as enforced in primaries, caucuses, and conventions") must be maximized, since it is a good thing in itself and since it will induce party members to argue themselves into agreement and thus supplement discipline as a device for getting party cohesion. On the other hand, Schattschneider . . . argues that such notions, if acted upon, are likely to keep the parties loose and decentralized and therefore "irresponsible." Democracy, he insists, can result only from a certain kind of relation *between* the parties, never from any kind of situation *within* the parties. This, however, is the only major issue on which the advocates of more "responsible" parties are seriously divided among themselves.

The Prospects for Action. . . . The advocates of more centralized and disciplined parties argue that the American people can have such parties any time they want them. Admittedly, the people have not as yet set up any great clamor for a reformed party system; but, as Schattschneider argues,

The revolution in communications, the dissolution of nationality blocs, the impact of the labor movement, urbanization, the revolution in public policy, the expansion of the practicing electorate in recent years, and the new world position of the United States are only a few of the influences likely to give an impetus to political reorganization in the present generation. It is obvious that the *purposes* of political organization are not what they once were. There was a time when it might have been said that the *purpose* of the party system, or of large parts of it, was *obstruction.* In an era of perpetual crisis political organization is reasonably certain to reflect the anxieties that now dominate all public life.

THE DEFENSE OF THE
PRESENT PARTY SYSTEM

The case against making our parties more centralized and disciplined may be briefly summarized as follows.

Questions About the British Model. The advocates of more "responsible" parties regard the British party system —or rather an idealized version of it —as a working model of the kind of party system they want to see the United States adopt. British parties, they feel, actually do put forth internally consistent, sense-making, *and* clearly distinguishable programs arrived at in each party by a process of intraparty discussion and decision. Accordingly, British parties present the voters with a clear choice at each election. Moreover, the high party cohesion and discipline that result from the national party leaders' power to approve or disapprove local candidates for Parliament mean that the majority party is always clearly and unequivocally responsible for how the government is run. Hence, if someone objects, "But the kind of party system you advocate simply cannot work," these writers can (and often do) reply, "Of course it can: look at the British system!"

Some writers, however, have raised questions about the British model and its applicability to American conditions. For one thing, they, the British party system does not in fact operate as its idealizers believe. And they have received impressive support for this argument from a recent article by David Butler, Fellow of Nuffield College, Oxford, and one of the leading British writers on the British party system, in which he explodes two "American myths about British parties." The first of these "myths" is that British parties offer the voters distinct and sharply differentiated programs. The fact is, says Butler, that the Conservative and Labor parties have clearly disagreed with each other on only one issue since 1945, that of the nationalization of certain industries; and even that issue has become very minor, since Labor now makes few demands for more nationalization and the Tories are willing to accept what nationalization now exists. The main differences between the parties now are merely those between "ins" and the "outs." Butler even argues that "the fate of Britain ten years hence will be far less affected by whether the Conservatives or the Labour Party win the next election, than the fate of the United States will be affected by the decision it will have to take in 1956 between a Republican and a Democrat [for president]." The second "myth" is that party policy is made by the rank and file via "intraparty democracy." Here, Butler says, Americans should not mistake the form for the reality; for the fact is that the parliamentary leadership of each party makes the party's policy, though with due regard for the forms and for the sensibilities of the rank and file, and sees that it gets adopted. For example, despite the fact that the Labor rank and file in many of the constituency organizations are enthusiastic followers of Aneurin Bevan, the party itself is unquestionably controlled by Bevan's right-wing opponents—so that in a considerable number of instances Bevanite constituency organizations have to accept and campaign for *anti*-Bevanite Labor candidates. Butler concludes: "Much may be wrong with American parties, but those who have looked to the British system for remedies have surely erred in their analysis of its excellencies."

The "excellency" of the British system most admired by American advocates of more "responsible" American parties, however, is the high cohesion and strong discipline of the British parliamentary parties; and Butler does not deny that these phenomena exist. But British parties are cohesive and disciplined, according to our second group of writers, because of the special nature of the British community and its belief system, which, in certain crucial respects, differs sharply from the American community and *its* belief system. Concretely, the leaders of both British parties are for the most part drawn from the public-school–Oxford–Cambridge "ruling class"; and the parties operate within a highly centralized culture, in which most Britons read London newspapers, listen to the B.B.C., and have no commitment to anything resembling the American traditions of "federalism" and "states' rights." Until we develop American equivalents for the British traditions of the "gentleman in politics" and unitarism, argue these writers, we are not likely either to want or to be able to get British-type parties.

Great Britain, moreover, pays a price for having the kind of parties it has. In Ernest Griffith's words, when the investigator goes behind the

scenes in England, he finds such things as these:

A bureaucracy maturing almost all legislation and increasing by leaps and bounds; the two parties outbidding each other with promises of governmental largesse, so as to attract marginal groups; a division of the nation along class lines; the sacrifice of independence of thought and action on the part of the individual member; the pressing home of such a drastic measure as the nationalization of steel, though a majority of the voters supported candidates opposed to it at the last election.

The British party system, furthermore, breaks down in a crisis every bit as much as does the American system. As Professor Arthur N. Holcombe points out, of the fourteen ministries that have held office since the Parliament Act of 1911, only six, holding office only about a third of the time, have been composed solely of representatives of a single party approved by a majority of all the voters. Of the others, which together have held office about two-thirds of the time, five have been coalition or "national" ministries composed of representatives from several parties, and three have been formed by a single party having less than a majority in the House of Commons and in the nation, and have held office only by the temporary sufferance of the other parties. In the British party system, therefore, the "national" or "all-party" ministry is the equivalent of "presidential dictatorship" in the American system—that is, what the governing system turns to when, in time of crisis, the party system ceases to function "normally." And the incidence of such deviations from the party-system "norm" are certainly at least as frequent in Great Britain as in the United States.

The Probable Price of Centralized and Disciplined Parties. In order to determine whether we want centralized and disciplined parties, say our second group of writers, Americans must understand the probable price of such parties and decide whether the probable benefits are worth it. The major items in the bill such parties would present the nation are as follows.

THE BREAKDOWN OF FEDERALISM. The primary purpose of centralizing and disciplining our parties is to enable them to formulate and execute *national* programs without regard to the demands of state and local interests and organizations. The technique for accomplishing it is to vest control of the state and local parties—and, through them, the state and local governments —in the hands of the national party leaders, so that state and local interference with national programs will be reduced to an absolute minimum. It may well be, therefore, that if such a party system were developed in the United States, it would mean the end of the reality if not of the form of federalism, and the states would become little more than administrative subdivisions of the national government. Perhaps the American people desire—or ought to desire—the demise of federalism and the installation of unitarism; but at least they should recognize that such a development would likely be a part of the price for centralized and disciplined national parties.

A MULTIPLE-PARTY SYSTEM. The advocates of more "responsible" national parties seem to assume that the new party alignments would pit a party made up of all the nation's "liberals" against another made up of all its "conservatives," thus retaining at least the two-party feature of our present national party system. But political conflict in the United States is enormously more multifarious and complicated than a simple division between pro-New Dealers and anti-New Dealers; and a great many groups could find their home in neither party. Suppose, for example, that the "conservative" party firmly and unmistakably

pledged itself to oppose any federal civil-rights legislation, to end or greatly reduce farm price-supports, to end or greatly reduce our economic and military commitments abroad, and to prevent any further federal development of electric power and water resources. Could such a party hope to carry the South, the rural and urban areas of the East and Middle West, and the Northwest? By the same token, could a "liberal" party taking the opposite stand on each of these issues hope to carry all those sections? If the "liberals," for instance, pledged themselves to a national civil-rights program and meant business about it, the conservatives could hardly do less unless they were resigned to being a permanent minority. In such a situation, what would the South do? Form a third party? Or, as now, simply defy the national platform of whatever party it operated within? In the former case, we would get a multiple-party system; in the latter, there would be no essential change from our present system.

It has often been remarked that the congeries of bipartisan and intraparty "blocs" in Congress is, in effect, a multiple-party system masquerading under the labels and formalities of a two-party system. To the extent that this is an accurate description of our present national party system, it results, not from any mere organizational deficiency in our national party machinery, but rather from the diversity and multiplicity of our interest groups and the heterogeneity and complexity of the political conflict they express. So long as the basic nature of the American community remains the same, therefore, centralizing and disciplining our national parties would very likely result in a multiple-party rather than a two-party system.

But perhaps the new parties could change the nature of the community itself. What would be the likely result of that?

THE BREAKDOWN OF CONSENSUS. If

each of our national parties were centralized and disciplined, it would have to mobilize electoral support in a considerably different manner from that employed by our present parties. It would have to make specific promises to certain groups, and, accordingly, reject with equal specificity the demands of certain other groups. Moreover, the winning party would have to fulfill its promises pretty much to the limit, since the groups supporting it might well regard the party's failure to keep its promises as even worse than not making them at all or making them in vague and loose terms. The most likely result of such a situation would be the near-complete identification of particular groups with particular parties—labor and the lower-income groups with the "liberals," business and the higher-income groups with the "conservatives." And this, in turn, would clearly and unmistakably pit one class against another class in such a way that conflicts between them would become cumulative rather than, as at present, blurred and dispersed.

Take, for example, the present bitter controversy over racial segregation in the southern public schools. On the one hand we have a group, spoken for by the NAACP, which regards the ending of all such segregation immediately as a matter of the most sacred rights of man and the most urgent necessity. On the other hand we have opposed to them another group, spoken for by the "Dixiecrat" element of the Democratic party, which regards the continuation of such segregation as absolutely essential to the whole southern way of life and its most cherished values. Clearly there is a high "civil-war potential" in this explosive situation. Our present politico-governmental system, . . . is handling it as it handles all such matters: both major parties make vague platform declarations in favor of "equal rights for all races," but neither pledges itself to the federal enforcement of desegregation of southern schools come

what may. The Supreme Court greatly pleases the anti-segregation group by declaring segregation unconstitutional —but federal troops are not ordered into South Carolina and Mississippi to make sure the Court's decision is carried out; and if the anti-segregationists were to make any such proposal, the southern senators would certainly filibuster it to death. The situation, however, is not entirely static: in Washington, D.C., and in the border states, segregation is being ended completely in some schools and modified in others. Thus the anti-segregationists and the pro-segregationists each get part—but not all—of what they want; no interracial or intersectional civil war breaks out; and a situation is preserved in which the gradual erosion of southern-white attitudes toward the Negroes that has been taking place during the past quarter-century or more—and in which, in the present writers' opinion, lies the best hope for the ultimate solution of this difficult problem— can continue its work. Certainly this is not the "swift, purposive, and vigorous" national governmental action demanded by the advocates of more "responsible" parties; but it *is* a kind of action which, whatever else can be said about it, preserves our consensus and yet does not permanently fix the status of Negro schoolchildren at its present level.

Suppose, however, we had centralized and disciplined parties. Both the Negroes and the southern whites are large and significant blocs of voters, and it seems unlikely that either would be content with parties which took clear positions on all other issues and acted upon them when in power but remained silent or vague on this particular issue. Either each group would form a third party, or one of the major parties would take up its cause. Suppose, again, that the "liberal" party pledged itself to end segregation and the "conservative" party to defend it. If, as now seems likely, the "liberals" won an election on this issue, they would either have to redeem their pledge, probably by sending federal troops into the South to enforce desegregation, or welsh on it in an "irresponsible" manner. Neither line of action would satisfy *both* groups to the extent that they are being satisfied under our present party system; and the consequences of the former for the American community are too obvious to be described, and should be taken into account in any attempt to calculate the social costs of centralized, disciplined, and programmatically precise national political parties in the United States.

Conclusion

As the reader should be well aware, the present writers, like the second group of commentators whose views we have just summarized, feel that the American party system as it now exists performs a role of great usefuless in our national politics and government; that, judged by the criterion of our conception of democracy, that role is of great value and deserving of high praise; and that the price America would probably have to pay for more centralized and disciplined national parties is, from the standpoint of democracy and in the light of the present nature of the American community, too high. We are, however, aware that other students of these matters have come to quite different conclusions. Our purpose, therefore, has been, not to persuade the reader to adopt our point of view and to accept uncritically our particular conclusions, but rather to help him understand the issues involved as they affect the prospects for realizing *his*—not our—values. And our hope is that, in this at least, we have had some success.

42. Two-Party Stalemate: The Crisis in Our Politics*

JAMES MAC GREGOR BURNS

[*For a further elaboration on the central thesis of this article, the student should read Burns'* Deadlock of Democracy.]

A CENTURY ago, pressures in the Democratic Party were nearing the bursting point. "We are for principles—damn the party!" proclaimed a Mississippi delegate to the Democratic National Convention in the soft Charleston spring of 1860. A Northern delegate, spurning a Southern demand

* *Atlantic Monthly* (February, 1960), pp. 37-41. Reprinted by permission of author and the *Atlantic Monthly.* Copyright 1960 by the Atlantic Monthly Co.

for a proslavery platform, declared, "Gentlemen of the South, you mistake us, you mistake us—we will not do it." The pressure mounted; soon the party burst into pieces. Waiting to pick some of them up was a young, virile party that would capture the presidency behind Abraham Lincoln and hold it, with few interruptions, for seven decades.

A hundred years later, new pressures are coming to a head in our politics and parties. There are clear signs that the 1960s, like the 1860s, will see major transformations in our political life. We need not fear the bloodshed of civil war; still, the American political scene may change as much by the 1970s as it did during the decade of Lincoln and Johnson.

Three things cause the stream of events to cut new channels across the political landscape: 1) intensifying economic and social changes; 2) the new ideas and expectations accompanying those changes; 3) the sensitivity of political leaders to what is happening.

Consider first the population explosion. Barring depression or war, our population will increase by 30 million in the next ten years. Our birth rate has accelerated the process of urbanization. Almost two out of every three Americans now live in urban or near-urban areas. Urbanization will bring profound political changes here, as it did in Britain. Many more Americans will be facing city problems that can be met only through government action. As people move to the outer suburbs, they will find city problems following them.

Inevitably the South must fall into step: the mighty changes there are making it more like the rest of the nation. Negroes are migrating from Southern farms to Southern cities; many of them are moving out of the South and heading North and West. The school desegregation issue may slow down this whole process, but only for a time.

Bigness is on the increase: it appears to be an irresistible tendency in our national economy. The trend toward business centralization is continuing, and perhaps intensifying. The merger of the two great wings of national labor has been followed by union consolidation at the state and local levels. In agriculture we see the supremacy of the big mechanized farm with its hundreds of hired hands. The Organization Man is not confined to corporations alone; he is staffing the bureaucracies of bigness everywhere. Even churches are holding unity talks at the summit.

Finally, observe the impact of the mass media in nationalizing our political attitudes. The magazines manufactured in New York and Chicago that pour into tens of millions of homes across the country; the role of a single journal, the New York *Times,* that has become virtually a national daily; the editorials and features canned in some word factory and gulped down straight by once proudly independent local newspapers; syndicated national columnists, political or gossip or both—these and other forces are having a pervasive influence on American opinion.

All of this tends to nationalize American politics. As sectionalism declines, as religious and nationality groups are blended into the whole of American life, as the new melting pot of suburbia expands, we are being subjected to enormous homogenizing forces. Many of us will show little enthusiasm for this drift toward national Togetherness; we fear a gray, drab society that rejects not only the unadjusted man but the unadjusted group as well. But for good or for ill, these trends exist, and they will have their influence in the world of the 1960s.

The trend toward "a mass society living in congested urban agglomerations," as Walter Lippmann has called it, is nothing new. Why, then, should we expect precipitate political changes in the new decade? One answer is that of Arthur Schlesinger, Jr. In a memorandum privately circulated last summer, Mr. Schlesinger contended that two decades of depression, reform, and wars hot and cold had left the American people, by 1950, morally and emotionally exhausted; that the Eisenhower Administration had been an expression of this ennui; that ferment and unrest were now growing, "batteries are being recharged," to be soon followed by a "breakthrough into a new political epoch." To confirm this probability, Schlesinger quoted the cyclical theories of his father, who had found that liberal and conservative periods succeeded one another in our national life without demonstrable correlations with economic or any other particular circumstances. "If past rhythms hold," Arthur Schlesinger, Jr., concluded, "the conservative period should run its course by about 1961-1962."

Unhappily, an inspection of the cycles worked out by the elder Schlesinger reveals that, while the average length of the periods (defined in terms of the effective tendency in government) was about sixteen years, the actual lengths of the periods varied widely; one liberal period (1861-1869) was only eight years long, and one conservative period (1869-1901) lasted thirty-two years. Can it be that the cycle of Eisenhower normalcy and quietism will last another decade or more before the pendulum swings back?

My answer is "No," partly because Mr. Schlesinger, Jr., is correct, I think, in discerning discontent and unrest all around us today, but mainly because of a series of challenges from without. That series was heralded by Sputnik two and a half years ago. It was dramatized by Khrushchev's warning that the United States might be enjoying the "last years of its greatness" and by his less subtle boast about digging the grave of capitalism. It has consisted of solid, dramatic accomplishments by the Soviets in space exploration, education, transportation, resource development, and other public services.

These events have served to make liberalism acceptable. The expansion of our government commitments has become less a partisan issue, more a nationally recognized need. Each new revelation of Soviet power has been followed in America by a frenzy of soul-searching, scapegoat-seeking, and renewed calls to action. Almost weekly now, businessmen, politicians, educators, and others return from Russia with ominous reports of Soviet advances in resource development, ma-

chine tools, basic research. Some of these reports are doubtless exaggerated; some perhaps are special pleading. But they are having a pronounced effect on what Americans now expect from their government.

It is rather a pity that many of these changes could not be accepted for their own sake rather than as merely a counter to Soviet advances. Are not foreign aid, economic growth at home, basic research, better resource development good in themselves? So they are—but not necessarily to most Americans. What is important is that politicians, who like to raise issues that unite people in their support, have found that liberalism has become, for many voters, good Americanism. Proposals that formerly could not be sold on their own merits can now be packaged as "Beat the Russians."

We are, then, entering the 1960s with growing concern over the drift and inertia in government and the severe lag in our public services as compared with the enormous extent of private spending. There is widespread agreement, cutting across party lines, about our specific failings. The most serious lag is in education; Secretary of Health, Education, and Welfare Arthur Flemming reports a shortage of at least 130,000 public school classrooms, and one that at the present rate of building would take thirteen years to eliminate. Educational opportunity is still uneven; New York spends three times more on education per child than Mississippi. Public health and medical services are lagging; 65 million Americans have no coverage under prepayment types of hospital care. Segments of our transportation system are in a state of chronic, and mounting, crisis. Urban blight—congested streets, air pollution, deteriorating housing—has struck deep into the core of cities and infects suburbia itself. The condition of rural slums has hardly been touched. The problem of dire poverty is by no means solved; in our

Affluent Society, 35 million people still live on family incomes of less than $2000 a year. We have fallen behind in the conservation and wise development of water, soil, and other resources.

In foreign policy, despite the growing economic effort of the Russians in underdeveloped countries, we have formulated nothing in recent years to match the breadth and vision of Roosevelt's lend-lease program in 1941, the Marshall Plan in 1947, or Point Four in 1949. Militarily, the lag in basic research and weapons development means a dangerous gap between Soviet and American missile power during at least the early 1960s. To make matters worse, government itself—most notably the federal regulatory boards and taxing and regulatory power in many of the states—seems to be increasingly purposeless or frustrated.

And, above all, there are the towering problems of school integration and civil rights. The Supreme Court ruled that its decision be enforced with "all deliberate speed." In the deep South, the possibility of speed has long been abandoned; it is apparent now, almost six years after the decision that action will not even be deliberate. Only in a few fringe areas of the outer South has there been even marginal action.

It is easy to compile lists of urgent tasks to be undertaken, but why should we expect that anyone besides the usual minority of perpetual worriers will be listening? And yet, evidently a lot of people *are* listening. The breadth and intensity of popular concern today can be measured by a document, "Decisions for a Better America," produced last fall by forty prominent Americans. This 42,000-word report showed a firm grasp of the threat posed by a "resourceful Communist leadership" abroad, of the wide sweep of foreign and domestic problems facing the country, and of the speed of all the changes and their effect on "social relationships." Although the report made the customary obeisance to individual enterprise and partnership be-

tween private groups and government, it laid heavy stress on the role of government—especially the federal government. "The Federal Government must do its part"; "the Federal Government must never allow"; "government must aid": the report is studded with such phrases, and many of its nods toward partnership programs simply cloak a call for leadership and money from the federal government.

The most arresting aspect of the report, however, was not its content but its sponsorship—the Republican Party. The report was commissioned a year ago by Meade Alcorn, chairman of the Republican National Committee, and was accepted last fall by his successor, Senator Thruston B. Morton, as marking a "new and vigorous phase in our Party's history." It was drawn up by four Republican task forces, made up of businessmen, politicians, and members of the Republican Party intelligentsia, headed by Charles H. Percy, president of the respectable Bell & Howell Company, and including White House speech writer Malcolm Moos.

No doubt it was coincidence that, about the time Senator Morton made public the report, the Conservatives in Britain won, for the first time in this century, their third victory in a row. The Conservatives were demonstrating in the arena of practical politics that "progressive conservatism," alert to the needs of a highly industrialized and urbanized nation, pays off in the politician's soundest currency—votes. Modern Republicans had the heady feeling that Meade Alcorn's task forces were charting a political program that could help them hold the presidency for years.

What about the Democrats? Ever since their second trouncing by Eisenhower they have been speaking out nationally through the Democratic Advisory Council. Boycotted by Sam Rayburn and Lyndon Johnson, dismissed by many as one of Paul Butler's aberrations, the council got off to a slow start. But it has grown steadily in prestige and influence, partly because Democrats of the stature of Eleanor Roosevelt, Harry Truman, and Adlai Stevenson are among its members, partly because people seem hungry for more clear-cut party doctrine than a vague convention platform can supply. Today the Democratic Advisory Council speaks squarely in the liberal, internationalist tradition of the Wilson-Roosevelt-Truman party.

The leading presidential candidates in both parties are conspicuously working the liberal side of the street. Senators John F. Kennedy, Hubert H. Humphrey, and Stuart Symington have established perfect voting records according to the criteria of Americans for Democratic Action. Kennedy and Symington recently joined their party's advisory council. And what about Richard Nixon, the Republican Party's front-runner now that Nelson Rockefeller has withdrawn from the presidential race? The Vice President has a way of confounding those who assign him to some intellectual or political pigeonhole, but he has been behaving like a "modern Republican" and seems to want more vigorous statecraft in Washington than the President has been supplying.

This much seems clear amid all the uncertainties of an election year: both national parties will speak with a strong liberal, internationalist voice during 1960. Alarmed by Soviet competition abroad and economic and social lags at home, Americans will respond to leaders who promise forceful national action. The presidential candidates, sensitive to the demands for leadership, will focus on the tough national and world problems besetting the country. The victor will enter the White House next January with a heavy burden of promises to keep. Will he be able to deliver?

The answer is "Yes" for the short run and "Probably not" for the longer run. The new President will be carried for a time by the momentum of this fall's electoral mandate. But only for a time. Soon the mandate psychology will wear off; new problems and new political alignments will rise; and all the old forces of check, delay, and defeat, sanctioned by Constitution and custom, will come into play. In moments of sharp crisis the President can wield vast powers, but in normal times he lacks the steady, assured power necessary for his day-to-day mobilization of the nation's strength.

The crisis of our parties lies here: our political leaders in Washington cannot lead, over the long run, because they have no solid political organization to help summon their forces and sustain their power. What is lacking in America is the crucial link between the nation's leaders and the voters—namely, a party system that offers people a choice between two intelligible sets of alternatives; mobilizes opinion and votes and candidates behind those sets of alternatives; and, in the case of the winning party, both holds the President accountable for enacting party doctrine and helps him to enact it.

We simply do not have parties in this sense. There is a "conventional wisdom," to use Galbraith's phrase, in politics as well as economics, and from this wisdom we have learned that, while our parties nationally may be rather feeble, they are strong at the state, county, and local levels. But this is not the case in present-day America. Except in a few states, such as Connecticut, and a few cities, such as Albany, our parties, as organizations, are futile, flimsy things, shunted aside by the politicians who understand political power. For some years political scientists have insisted that at *no* level of government do we have a two-party system, for we have neither parties nor a system; but nobody has been listening. At best our parties are mere jousting grounds for warring politicians. At worst they do not exist at all, as in the case of Republican organizations in the South or Demo-

neither parties nor a system

cratic committees in many rural areas of the North. The more powerful party machines, on closer examination, turn out to be the personal organizations of local officeholders.

Is this too bleak a picture of party organization? If the reader thinks so, he can try a few simple tests. Is he a "card-carrying" Democrat or Republican, paying regular dues? Does he take part in the affairs of his local party, as he does in the affairs of his church or nonpartisan civic group? Does he contribute money to his party? Does he work for the party at election time, or just for individual candidates? Does he even know the name of his local, county, or state party chairman?

All but a small percentage of Americans—even of civic-minded Americans—would answer "No" to most of these questions. And they would do so without apology. They would contend—quite rightly in most cases—that *their* state or local party is run by hacks, job holders, and even crooks, that the party pros are cool to outsiders anyway, and that at best the party nominates so many candidates of such varying quality for so many offices, high and low, that no good citizen could work in the party organization. There is no point in lecturing to these people from the Conventional Wisdom of politics, of preaching the old sermon "Be active in your party." They see no party to be active in. Far better, they feel, to work directly for some candidate they admire or to join some nonpartisan organization like the League of Women Voters. Even if they could get control of a party, ofttimes it would be like grabbing a handful of water.

This is not to say that parties symbolically are unimportant. Our two major parties do help keep alive two great sets of fuzzy but significant traditions, goals, and policies. Nor do I assert that winning a major-party nomination is worthless; it is worth a great deal, but not as a result of party or-

ganization. Our political parties could play a far more notable part than they do, but throughout most of the country they are decrepit and disorganized.

Who, then, does run American politics? Not party leaders, but officeholders and office seekers who achieve power through their personal followings rather than through their party power. These followings are organized around their chief, inside, outside, and across party lines. They are far more dedicated to their leader than to their party, for they will advance as their leader advances, even though the party as a whole declines. Anyone doubting the power of personal organization can try another simple test: during an election campaign he should stop in at the headquarters of some candidate, and then look in on the headquarters of the local party. In most states, the chances are strong that the candidate's headquarters will be filled with scores of enthusiasts in a setting of wild but productive disarray, while the party headquarters will be the hangout of a few oldtimers grumbling over the lack of money, posters, and help. Or note sometime, in a report on campaign finance, the tremendous amount of money donated to candidates compared with the pittances given the party.

The impotence of party is the main cause of our most serious political malaise: as a nation, we lack control of our politics. For example:

1. As a nation we lack the most elementary control of all—the power to determine who may vote in national elections. This power is left in the hands of the state legislatures, most of them gerrymandered. One result is that we are unable to extend to millions of Southern Negroes the right to vote even for national offices, such as President and Senator.

2. We cannot exercise another elementary right—control of the nation's electoral arrangements. Countless congressional districts are unfairly drawn, but only the state legislatures can do

anything about this, and most of them do not want to. For decades we have deplored our antiquated electoral college system and have done nothing about it.

3. We have lost control of political finance. To most politicians, our laws regulating contributions and spending are a joke or a nuisance. Despite efforts at grass-roots financing, the big political money still comes from the fat cats.

4. Our opposition parties do not oppose; they duck or fade away. This is perhaps least true at the national level, but even the Democrats have done a poor job of opposing the Administration. As a party, the Democrats have not known whether to be more liberal than the President or more conservative, more internationalist or more isolationist. So the party has split into factions, each taking a different line of opposition. Individual Democrats, of course, have been effective critics, but that is no credit to the opposition party. At state and lower levels, the opposition party is usually even feebler, and in one-party states, of course, it does not exist at all.

5. The parties have lost control of the nomination process, especially at the state and local levels. The party primary method of nominating candidates, adopted to democratize the system, allows the responsible party leadership and membership little control over the nominees who will carry the party banner in battle, and hence impairs party responsibility. Men and women who in national politics proudly call themselves Democrats or Republicans often cannot stomach the office seekers who win their party's nomination for state jobs.

6. We lack popular control of the policy-making process. Our splintered parties set up barriers between the people and their governments rather than simplifying the alternatives, clarifying competing party doctrines, and allowing the victorious majority to govern.

7. Teamwork is lacking in government, or, where it exists, it produces only the integration of drift, as is so often the case with the Eisenhower Administration. Ideally, the winning party under a two-party system pulls together the executive and legislative branches in order to deliver on the party's promises to the people, as in Britain. But a fragmented party system cannot do this, because the party factions are at war among themselves.

It is supremely ironic that, just as France under De Gaulle has junked its multiparty system, at least superficially and temporarily, America is entering a most demanding decade with a chaotic, multiparty system of its own. For the bigger personal organizations are virtually parties in themselves, with their own leadership, organization, money, doctrine, and political goals. Can we meet the stiff demands of the 1960s with a splintered, disorganized party system? What leader of this decade will see the possibility of strengthening not only his own power but also his party's power? Could this be done by anyone besides the new President? The answers to these questions will illuminate the problems and the possibilities of the new decade.

43. A Key to American Politics: Calhoun's Pluralism*

PETER F. DRUCKER

[*This article is considered by most to be one of the classics in the political science literature. Here Drucker seeks to explain in theoretical terms just how and on what principles the American political system operates. The student should not be disturbed by the fact that many of Drucker's examples seem "out-dated." The critical questions are these: How well and to what extent has Drucker explained the processes of the American political system? Is Drucker's thesis still "sound"?*]

THE American party system has been under attack almost continuously since it took definite form in the time of Andrew Jackson. The criticism has always been directed at the same point: America's political pluralism, the distinctively American organization of government by compromise of interests, pressure groups and sections. And the aim of the critics from Thaddeus Stevens to Henry Wallace has always been to substitute for this "unprincipled" pluralism a government based as in Europe on "ideologies" and "principles." But never before—at least not since the Civil War years—has the crisis been as acute as in this last decade; for the political problems which dominate our national life today: foreign policy and industrial policy, are precisely the problems which interest and pressure-group compromise is least equipped to handle. And while the crisis symptoms: a left-wing Third

Party and the threatened split-off of the Southern Wing, are more alarming in the Democratic Party, the Republicans are hardly much better off. The 1940 boom for the "idealist" Willkie and the continued inability to attract a substantial portion of the labor vote, are definite signs that the Republican Party too is under severe *ideological* pressure.

* * *

Yet, there is almost no understanding of the problem—precisely because there is so little understanding of the basic principles of American pluralism. Of course, every politician in this country must be able instinctively to work in terms of sectional and interest compromise; and the voter takes it for granted. But there is practically no awareness of the fact that organization on the basis of sectional and interest compromise is both the distinctly American form of political organization and the cornerstone of practically all major political institutions of the modern U.S.A. As acute an observer as Winston Churchill apparently does not understand that Congress works on a basis entirely different from that of Britain's Parliament; neither do nine out of ten Americans and 999 out of a 1000 teachers of those courses in "Civics." There is even less understanding that sectional and interest-group pluralism is not just the venal expediency of that stock-villain of American folklore, the "politician," but that it in itself is a basic ideology, a basic principle—and the one which is

* *The Review of Politics* (October, 1948), pp. 412-426. Reprinted by permission.

the very foundation of our free society and government.[1]

I

To find an adequate analysis of the principle of government by sectional and interest compromise we have to go back almost a hundred years to John C. Calhoun and to his two political treatises[2] published after his death in 1852. Absurd, you will say, for it is practically an axiom of American history that Calhoun's political theories, subtle, even profound though they may have been, were reduced to absurdity and irrelevance by the Civil War. Yet, this "axiom" is nothing but a partisan vote of the Reconstruction Period. Of course, the specific occasion for which Calhoun formulated his theories, the Slavery issue, has been decided; and for the constitutional veto power of the states over national legislation, by means of which Calhoun proposed to formalize the principle of sectional and interest compromise, was substituted in actual practice the much more powerful and much more elastic but extra-constitutional and extra-legal veto power of sections, interests and pressure groups in Congress and within the parties.[3] But *his basic principle itself: that every major interest in the country, whether regional,*

[1] A perfect illustration was the outraged amazement with which most book reviewers greeted Edward J. Flynn's *You're the Boss*—a simple and straight recital of facts every American should really have known and understood all along.

[2] *A Disquisition on Government*; and *A Discourse on the Constitution and Government of the United States.*

[3] Calhoun's extreme legalism, his belief that everything had to be spelled out in the written Constitution—a belief he shared with his generation—is one of the major reasons why the importance of his thesis has not been generally recognized. Indeed it is of the very essence of the concept of "concurrent majority" that it cannot be made official and legal in an effective government—the express veto such as the UN Charter gives to the Great Powers makes government impossible.

economic or religious, is to possess a veto power on political decisions directly affecting it, the principle which Calhoun called—rather obscurely— "the rule of concurrent majority," has become the organizing principle of American politics. And it is precisely this principle that is under fire today.

What makes Calhoun so important as the major key to the understanding of American politics, is not just that he saw the importance in American political life of sectional and interest pluralism; other major analysts of our government, Tocqueville, for instance, or Bryce or Wilson, saw that too. But Calhoun, perhaps alone, saw in it more than a rule of expediency, imposed by the country's size and justifiable by results, if at all. He saw in it a basic principle of free government.

Without this (*the rule of concurrent majority based on interests rather than on principles*) there can be . . . no constitution. The assertion is true in reference to all constitutional governments, be their forms what they may: It is, indeed, the negative power which makes the constitution,—and the positive which makes the government. The one is the power of acting;—and the other the power of preventing or arresting action. The two, combined, make constitutional government.

. . . it follows, necessarily, that where the numerical majority has the sole control of the government, there can be no constitution . . . and hence, the numerical, unmixed with the concurrent majority, necessarily forms, in all cases, absolute government.

. . . The principle by which they (governments) are upheld and preserved . . . in constitutional governments is *compromise*;—and in absolute governments is *force*. . . .[4]

[4] Quotations from *A Disquisition on Government*, (Columbia, S.C., 1852), pp. 35 to 37.

And however much the American people may complain in words about the "unprincipled" nature of their political system, by their actions they have always shown that they too believe that without sectional and interest compromises there can be no constitutional government. If this is not grasped, American government and politics must appear not only as cheap to the point of venality, they must appear as utterly irrational and unpredictable.

II

Sectional and interest pluralism has molded all American political institutions. It is the method—entirely unofficial and extra-constitutional—through which the organs of government are made to function, through which leaders are selected, policies developed, men and groups organized for the conquest and management of political power. In particular it is the explanation for the most distinctive features of the American political system: the way in which the Congress operates, the way in which major government departments are set up and run, the qualifications for "eligibility" as a candidate for elective office, and the American party structure.

To all foreign observers of Congress two things have always remained mysterious: the distinction between the official party label and the "blocs" which cut across party lines; and the power and function of the Congressional Committees. And most Americans though less amazed by the phenomena are equally baffled.

The "blocs"—the "Farm Bloc" the "Friends of Labor in the Senate," the "Business Groups," etc.—are simply the expression of the basic tenet of sectional and interest pluralism that major interests have a veto power on legislation directly affecting them. For this reason they must cut across party lines —that is, lines expressing the numerical rather than the "concurrent" majority. And because these blocs have (a) only a negative veto, and (b) only on measures directly affecting them, they cannot in themselves be permanent groupings replacing the parties. They must be loosely organized; and one and the same member of Congress must at different times vote with different blocs. The strength of the "blocs" does not rest on their numbers but on the basic mores of American politics which grant every major interest group a limited self-determination—as expressed graphically in the near-sanctity of a senatorial "filibuster." The power of the "Farm Bloc" for instance, does not rest on the numerical strength of the rural vote—a minority vote even in the Senate with its disproportionate representation of the thinly populated agricultural states —but on its "strategic" strength, that is on its being the spokesman for a recognized major interest.

Subordination of a major interest is possible; but only in a "temporary emergency." Most of the New Deal measures were, palpably, neither temporary nor emergency measures; yet their sponsors had to present them, and convincingly, as "temporary emergency measures" because they could be enacted only by over-riding the extra-constitutional veto of the business interests.

Once the excuse of the "temporary emergency" had fully lost its plausibility, that major interest could no longer be voted down; and the policy collapsed. By 1946, for instance, labor troubles could be resolved only on a basis acceptable to both labor and employer: higher wages *and* higher prices. (Even if a numerical majority had been available to legislate against either party—and the business group could probably still have been voted down two and half years ago—the solution had to be acceptable to both parties.)

The principle of sectional and interest compromise leads directly to the congressional committee system—a system to which there is no parallel anywhere in the world. Congress, especially the House, has largely abdicated to its committees because only in the quiet and secrecy of a committee room can sectional compromise be worked out. The discussion on the floor as well as the recorded vote is far too public and therefore largely for the folks back home. But a committee's business is to arrive at an agreement between all major sectional interests affected; which explains the importance of getting a bill before the "right" committee. In any but an American legislature the position of each member, once a bill is introduced, is fixed by the stand of his party which, in turn, is decided on grounds that have little to do with the measure itself but are rather dictated by the balance of power within the government and by party programs. Hence it makes usually little difference which committee discusses a bill or whether it goes before a committee at all. In the United States, however, a bill's assignment to a specific committee decides which interest groups are to be recognized as affected by the measure and therefore entitled to a part in writing it ("who is to have standing before the committee"), for each committee represents a specific constellation of interests. In many cases this first decision therefore decides the fate of a proposed measure, especially as the compromise worked out by the committee is generally accepted once it reaches the floor, especially in the House.

It is not only Congress but every individual member of Congress himself who is expected to operate according to the "rule of concurrent majority." He is considered both a representative of the American people and responsible to the national interest and a delegate of his constituents and responsible to their particular interests. Wherever the immediate interests of his constituents are not in question, he is to be a statesman; wherever their conscience or their pocketbooks are affected, he is to be a business agent.

This is in sharp contrast to the theory on which any parliamentary government is based—a theory developed almost two hundred years ago in Edmund Burke's famous speech to the voters at Bristol—according to which a member of Parliament represents the commonweal rather than his constituents. Hence in all parliamentary countries, the representative can be a stranger to his constituency—in the extreme, as it was practiced in Weimar Germany, there is one long national list of candidates who run in all constituencies—whereas the Congressman in this country must be a resident of his constituency. And while an American Senator considers it a compliment and an assest to be called "Cotton Ed Smith," the Speaker of the House of Commons not so long ago severely reprimanded a member for calling another member—an official of the miners' union—a "representative of the coal miners."

The principle of sectional and interest pluralism also explains why this is the only nation where Cabinet members are charged by law with the representation of special interests—labor, agriculture, commerce. In every other country an agency of the government —any agency of the government—is solemnly sworn to guard the public interests against "the interests." In this country the concept of a government department as the representative of a special interest group is carried down to smaller agencies and even to divisions and branches of a department. This was particularly noticeable during the war in such fights as that between OPA—representing the consumer— and the War Production Board representing the producer, or, within WPB between the Procurement branches speaking for the war industries and the Civilian Requirements Branch speaking for the industries producing for the "home front."

The mystery of "eligibility"—the criteria which decides who will make a promising candidate for public of-

fice—which has baffled so many foreign and American observers, Bryce
for instance—also traces back to the
"rule of the concurrent majority."
Eligibility simply means that a candidate must not be unacceptable to any
major interest, religious or regional
group within the electorate; it is primarily a negative qualification. Eligibility operates on all levels and applies
to all elective offices. It has been brilliantly analyzed in "Boss" Flynn's
You're the Boss. His classical example
is the selection of Harry Truman as
Democratic vice-presidential candidate
in 1944. Truman was "eligible" rather
than Wallace, Byrnes or Douglas precisely because he was unknown; because he was neither Easterner nor
Westerner nor Southerner, because he
was neither New Deal nor Conservative, etc., in short because he had no
one trait strong enough to offend anybody anywhere.

But the central institution based on
sectional pluralism is the American
party. Completely extra-constitutional,
the wonder and the despair of every
foreign observer who cannot fit it into
any of his concepts of political life, the
American party (rather than the
states) has become the instrument to
realize Calhoun's "rule of the concurrent majority."

In stark contrast to the parties of
Europe, the American party has no
program and no purpose except to organize divergent groups for the common pursuit and conquest of power.
Its unity is one of action, not of beliefs.
Its only rule is to attract—or at least
not to repel—the largest possible number of groups. It must, by definition,
be acceptable equally to the right and
the left, the rich and the poor, the
farmer and the worker, the Protestant and the Catholic, the native and
the foreign-born. It must be able to
rally Mr. Rankin of Mississippi and
Mr. Marcantonio of New York—or
Senator Flanders and Colonel McCor-
mick—behind the same presidential
candidate and the same "platform."

As soon as it cannot appeal at least
to a minority in every major group (as
soon, in other words, as it provokes
the veto of one section, interest or
class) a party is in danger of disintegration. Whenever a party loses its
ability to fuse sectional pressures and
class interests into one national policy
—both parties just before the Civil
War, the Republican Party before its
reorganization by Mark Hanna, both
parties again today—the party system
(and with it the American political
system altogether) is in crisis.

It is, consequently, not that Calhoun was repudiated by the Civil War
which is the key to the understanding
of American politics but that he has
become triumphant since.

The apparent victors, the "Radical
Republicans," Thaddeus Stevens, Sew-
ard, Chief Justice Chase, were out to
destroy not only slavery and states
rights but the "rule of the concurrent
majority" itself. And the early Republican Party—before the Civil War and
in the Reconstruction Period—was indeed determined to substitute principle for interest as the lodestar of
American political life. But in the end
it was the political thought of convinced pluralists such as Abraham
Lincoln and Andrew Johnson rather
than the ideologies of the Free Soilers
and Abolitionists which molded the
Republican Party. And ever since, the
major development of American politics have been based on Calhoun's
principle. To this the United States
owes the strength as well as the weaknesses of its political system.

III

The weaknesses of sectional and interest compromise are far more obvious than its virtues; they have been
hammered home for a hundred years.
Francis Lieber, who brought the dominant German political theories of the
early nineteenth century to this country, attacked pluralism in Calhoun's
own state of South Carolina a century

ago. Twenty years later Walter Bagehot contrasted, impressively, General Grant's impotent administration with those of Gladstone and Disraeli to show the superiority of ideological party organization. The most thorough and most uncompromising criticism came from Woodrow Wilson; and every single one of the Professor's points was amply borne out by his later experience as President. Time has not made these weaknesses any less dangerous.

There is, first of all, the inability of a political system based on the "rule of the concurrent majority" to resolve conflicts of principles. All a pluralist system can do is to deny that "ideological" conflicts (as they are called nowadays) do exist. Those conflicts, a pluralist must assert are fundamentally either struggles for naked power or friction between interest groups which could be solved if only the quarreling parties sat down around a conference table. Perhaps, the most perfect, because most naive, expression of this belief remains the late General Patton's remark that the Nazis were, after all, not so very different from Republicans or Democrats. (Calhoun, while less naive, was just unable to understand the reality of "ideological" conflict in and around the slavery problem.)

In nine cases out of ten the refusal to acknowledge the existence of ideological conflict is beneficial. It prevents fights for power, or clashes of interests, from flaring into religious wars where irreconcilable principles collide (a catastrophe against which Europe's ideological politics have almost no defense). It promotes compromise where compromise is possible. But in a genuine clash of principles—and, whatever the pluralists say, there *are* such clashes—the "rule of concurrent majority" breaks down; it did, in Calhoun's generation, before the profound reality of the slavery issue. A legitimate ideological conflict is actually aggravated by the pluralists' refusal to accept its reality:

the compromisers who thought the slavery issue could be settled by the meeting of good intentions, or by the payment of money, may have done more than the Abolitionists to make the Civil War inevitable.

A weakness of sectional and interest pluralism just as serious is that it amounts to a principle of inaction. The popular assertion "it's better to make the wrong decision than to do nothing at all," is, of course, fallacious; but no nation, however unlimited its resources, can have a very effective policy if its government is based on a principle that orders it to do nothing important except unanimously. Moreover, pluralism increases exorbitantly the weight of well organized small interest groups, especially when they lobby *against* a decision. Congress can far too easily be high-pressured into emasculating a bill by the expedient of omitting its pertinent provisions; only with much greater difficulty can Congress be moved to positive action. This explains, to a large extent, the eclipse of Congress during the last hundred years, both in popular respect and in its actual momentum as policy-making organ of government. Congress, which the Founding Fathers had intended to be the central organ of government—a role which it fulfilled up to Andrew Jackson—became the compound representative of sections and interests and, consequently, progressively incapable of national leadership.

Pluralism gives full weight—more than full weight—to sections and interests; but who is to represent the national welfare? Ever since the days of Calhoun, the advocates of pluralism have tried to dodge this question by contending that the national interest is equal to the sum of all particular interests, and that it therefore does not need a special organ of representation. But this most specious argument is contradicted by the most elementary observation. In practice, pluralism tends to resolve sectional and class conflicts at the expense of the national interest which is represented by nobody in particular, by no section and no organization.

These weaknesses had already become painfully obvious while Calhoun was alive and active—during the decade after Andrew Jackson, the first President of pluralism. Within a few years after Calhoun's death, the inability of the new system to comprehend and to resolve an ideological conflict— ultimately its inability to represent and to guard the national interest—had brought catastrophe. For a hundred years and more, American political thought has therefore resolved around attempts to counteract if not to overcome these weaknesses. Three major developments of American constitutional life were the result: the growth of the functions and powers of the President and his emergence as a "leader" rather than as the executive agent of the Congress; the rise of the Supreme Court, with its "rule of law," to the position of arbiter of policy; the development of a unifying ideology—the "American Creed."

Of these the most important—and the least noticed—is the "American Creed." In fact I know of no writer of major importance since Tocqueville who has given much attention to it. Yet even the term "un-American" cannot be translated successfully into any other language, least of all into "English" English. In no other country could the identity of the nation with a certain set of ideas be assumed—at least not under a free government. This unique cohesion on principles shows, for instance, in the refusal of the American voter to accept Socialists and Communists as "normal" parties, simply because both groups refuse to accept the assumption of a common American ideology. It shows, for another example, in the indigenous structure of the American labor movement with its emphasis on interest pressure rather than on a political philosophy. And this is also the only country in which "Civics" could be taught in schools—

the only democratic country which believes that a correct social philosophy could or should be part of public education.

In Europe, a universal creed would be considered incompatible with a free society. Before the advent of totalitarianism, no European country had ever known anything comparable to the flag salute of the American school child.[5] For in Europe all political activity is based on ideological factions; consequently, to introduce a uniform ideology in a European country is to stamp out *all* opposition. In the United States ideological homogeneity is the very basis of political diversity. It makes possible the almost unlimited freedom of interest groups, religious groups, pressure groups, etc.; and in this way it is the very fundament of free government. (It also explains why the preservation of civil liberties has been so much more important a problem in this country—as compared to England or France, for instance.) The assumption of ideological unity gives the United States the minimum of cohesion without which its political system simply could not have worked.

IV

But is even the "American dream" enough to make a system based on the "rule of the concurrent majority" work today? Can pluralism handle the two major problems of American politics— the formulation of a foreign policy, and the political organization of an industrial society—any more successfully than it could handle the slavery issue? Or is the American political system as much in crisis as it was in the last years of Calhoun's life—and for pretty much the same reasons?

A foreign policy can never be evolved

---

[5] The perhaps most profound discussion of the American ideological cohesion can be found in the two decisions of the Supreme Court on the compulsory flag salute, and in the two dissents therefrom, which deserve high rating among American state papers.

by adding particular interests—regional, economic or racial—or by compromising among them; it must supersede them. If Calhoun's contention that the national interest will automatically be served by serving the interests of the parts is wrong anywhere, it is probably wrong in the field of foreign affairs.

A foreign policy and a party system seem to be compatible only if the parties are organized on programmatic grounds, that is on principles. For if not based on general principles, a foreign policy will become a series of improvisations without rhyme or reason. In a free society, in which parties compete for votes and power, the formulation of a foreign policy may thus force the parties into ideological attitudes which will sooner or later be reflected in their domestic policies too.

This was clearly realized in the early years of the Republic when foreign policy was vital to a new nation, clinging precariously to a long seaboard without hinterland, engaged in a radical experiment with new political institutions, surrounded by the Great Powers of that time, England, France and Spain, all of them actually or potentially hostile. This awareness of foreign policy largely explains why the party system of the Founding Fathers —especially of Hamilton—was an ideological one; it also explains why the one positive foreign-policy concept this country developed during the entire nineteenth century—the Monroe Doctrine—was formulated by the last two politically active survivors of the founding generation, Monroe and John Quincy Adams. No matter how little Calhoun himself realized it, his doctrine would have been impossible without the French Revolution and the Napoleonic Wars which, during the most critical period of American integration, kept its potential European enemies busy. By 1820, the country had become too strong, had taken in too much territory, to be easily attacked; and it was still not strong enough, and far too much absorbed in the develop-

ment of its own interior, to play a part in international affairs. Hence Calhoun, and all America with him, could push foreign policy out of their minds—so much so that this is the only country in which it is possible to write a comprehensive work on an important historical period without as much as a mention of foreign affairs, as Arthur M. Schlesinger, Jr. managed to do in his *The Age of Jackson.*

But today foreign policy is again as vital for the survival of the nation as it ever was during the administrations of Washington and Jefferson. And it has to be a foreign *policy,* that is, a making of decisions; hence neither "isolationism" nor "internationalism" will do. (For "internationalism"—the search for formulae which will provide automatic decisions, even in advance —is also a refusal to have a foreign policy; it may well have done this country, and the world, as much harm as "isolationism"—perhaps more.) To survive as the strongest of the Great Powers, the United States might even have to accept permanently the supremacy of foreign policies over domestic affairs, however much this may go against basic American convictions, and indeed against the American grain. But no foreign policy can be evolved by the compromise of sectional interests or economic pressures; yet neither party, as today constituted, could develop a foreign policy based on definite principles.

The other great national need is to resolve the political problems of an industrial society. An industrial society is by nature ultrapluralistic, because it develops class and interest groups that are far stronger, and far more tightly organized, than any interest group in a pre-industrial age. A few big corporations, a few big unions, may be the actually decisive forces in an industrial society. And these groups can put decisive pressure on society: they can throttle social and economic life.

The problem does not lie in "asocial behavior" of this or that group but in the nature of industrial society which bears much closer resemblance to feudalism than to the trading nineteenth century. Its political problems are very similar to those which feudalism had to solve—and failed to solve. It is in perpetual danger of disintegration into virtually autonomous fiefs, principalities, "free cities," "robber baronies" and "exempt bishoprics"—the authority and the interest of the nation trampled underfoot, autonomous groups uniting to control the central power in their own interest or disregarding government in fighting each other in the civil conflict of class warfare. And the alternative to such a collapse into anarchy or civil war—the suppression of classes and interest groups by an all-powerful government—is hardly more attractive.

An industrial society cannot function without an organ able to superimpose the national interest on economic or class interests. More than a mere arbiter is needed. The establishment of the "rules of civilized industrial warfare," as was done by both the Wagner Act and the Taft-Hartley Act, tries to avoid the need for policies by equalizing the strength of the conflicting sections; but that can lead only to deadlock, to collusion against the national interest or, worse still, to the attempt to make the national authority serve the interest of one side against the other. In other words, an industrial society cannot fully accept Calhoun's assumption that the national good will evolve from the satisfaction of particular interests. An industrial society without national policy will become both anarchic and despotic.

Small wonder that there has been increasing demand for a radical change which would substitute ideological parties and programmatic policies for the pluralist parties and the "rule of the concurrent majority" of the American tradition. Henry Wallace's Third-Party Movement, while the most publicized, may well be the least significant development; for third parties are, after all, nothing new in our political history.

But for the first time in a hundred years there is a flood of books—and by serious students of American government—advocating radical constitutional reform. However much Senator Fulbright, Henry Hazlitt and Thomas Fineletter disagree on details, they are one in demanding the elimination—or at least the limitation—of the "rule of the concurrent majority," and its replacement by an ideological system functioning along parliamentary lines. More significant even may be Walter Reuther's new unionism with its blend of traditional pressure tactics and working-class, that is ideological, programs and aims.

V

Yet all these critics and reformers not only fail to ask themselves whether an ideological system of politics would really be any better equipped to cope with the great problems of today—and neither the foreign nor the industrial policy of England, that most successful of all ideologically organized countries, look any too successful right now; the critics also never stop to consider the unique strength of our traditional system.

Our traditional system makes sure that there is always a legitimate government in the country; and to provide such a government is the first job of any political system—a duty which a great many of the political systems known to man have never discharged.

It minimizes conflicts by utilizing, rather than suppressing conflicting forces. It makes it almost impossible for the major parties to become entirely irresponsible: neither party can afford to draw strength from the kind of demagogic opposition, without governmental responsibility, which perpetually nurtures fascist and communist parties abroad. Hence, while the two national parties are willing to embrace any movement or any group within the country that commands sufficient following, they in turn force every group to bring its demands and programs into agreement with the beliefs, traditions and prejudices of the people.

Above all, our system of sectional and interest compromise is one of the only two ways known to man in which a free government and a free society can survive—and the only one at all adapted to the conditions of American life and acceptable to the American people.

The central problem in a free government is that of factions, as we have known since Plato and Aristotle. Logically, a free government and factions are incompatible. But whatever the cause—vanity and pride, lust for power, virtue or wickedness, greed or the desire to help others—factionalism is inherent in human nature and in human society. For 2000 years the best minds in politics have tried to devise a factionless society—through education (Plato), through elimination of property (Thomas More), through concentration on the life of the spirit outside of worldly ambition (the political tradition of Lutheranism). The last great attempt to save freedom by abolishing faction was Rousseau's. But to create the factionless free society is as hopeless as to set up perpetual motion. From Plato to Rousseau, political thought has ended up by demanding that factions be suppressed, that is, that freedom, to be preserved, be abolished.

The Anglo-American political tradition alone has succeeded in breaking out of this vicious circle. Going back to Hooker and Locke, building on the rich tradition of free government in the cities of the late middle ages, Anglo-American political realism discovered: that if factions cannot be suppressed, they must be utilized to make a free government both freer and stronger. This one basic concept distinguishes Anglo-American political theory and practice from continental European politics, and accounts for the singular success of free and popular governments in both countries. Elsewhere in the western world the choice has always been between extreme factionalism which makes government impotent if not impossible and inevitably leads to civil war, and autocracy which justifies the suppression of liberty with the need for effective and orderly government. Nineteenth-century France with its six revolutions, or near revolutions, stands for one, the totalitarian governments of our time for the other alternative of continental politics.

But—and this is the real discovery on which the Anglo-American achievement rests—factions can be used constructively only if they are encompassed within a frame of unity. A free government on the basis of sectional interest groups is possible only when there is no ideological split within the country. This is the American solution. Another conceivable solution is to channel the driving forces, the vectors of society, into ideological factions which obtain their cohesion from a program for the whole of society, and from a creed. But that presupposes an unquestioned ruling class with a common outlook on life, with uniform mores and a traditional, if not inherent, economic security. Given that sort of ruling class, the antagonist in an ideological system can be expected to be a "loyal opposition," that is, to accept the rules of the game and to see himself as a partner rather than as a potential challenger to civil war. But a ruling class accepted by the people as a whole, and feeling itself responsible to the people as a whole, cannot be created by fiat or overnight. In antiquity only Rome, in modern times only England, achieved it. On the Continent, all attempts to create a genuine ruling class have failed dismally.

In this country, the ruling-class solution was envisaged by Alexander Hamilton and seemed close to realization under the presidents of the "Virginia Dynasty." Hamilton arrived at his concept with inescapable consistency; for he was absorbed by the search for a foreign policy and for the proper organization of an industrial society—precisely the two problems which, as we have seen, pluralism is least equipped to resolve. But even if Hamilton had not made the fatal mistake of identifying wealth with rulership, the American people could not have accepted his thesis. A ruling class was incompatible with mass immigration and with the explosive territorial expansion of nineteenth-century America. It was even more incompatible with the American concept of equality. And there is no reason to believe that contemporary America is any more willing to accept Hamilton's concept, Mr. James Burnham's idea of the managerial elite notwithstanding. This country as a free country has no alternative, it seems, to the "rule of the concurrent majority," no alternative to sectional pluralism as the device through which factions can be made politically effective.

It will be very difficult, indeed, to resolve the problems of foreign and of industrial policy on the pluralist basis and within the interest-group system, though not provably more difficult than these problems would be on another, ideological, basis. It will be all the harder as the two problems are closely inter-related; for the effectiveness of any American foreign policy depends, in the last analysis, on our ability to show the world a successful and working model of an industrial society. But if we succeed at all, it will be with the traditional system, horse-trading, log-rolling and politicking all included. An old saying has it that this country lives simultaneously in a world of Jeffersonian beliefs and in one of Hamiltonian realities. Out of these two, Calhoun's concept of "the rule of the concurrent majority" alone can make one viable whole. The need for a formulated foreign policy and for a national policy of industrial order is real—but not more so than the need for a real understanding of this fundamental American fact: the pluralism of sectional and interest compromise is the warp of America's political fabric—it cannot be plucked out without unravelling the whole.